Foreign Ownership and the Consequences of Direct Investment in the United States

Foreign Ownership and the Consequences of Direct Investment in the United States

Beyond Us and Them

Edited by
DOUGLAS WOODWARD
DOUGLAS NIGH

QUORUM BOOKS
Westport, Connecticut • London

Library of Congress Cataloging-in-Publication Data

Foreign ownership and the consequences of direct investment in the
United States : beyond us and them / edited by Douglas Woodward,
Douglas Nigh
      p.   cm.
    Includes bibliographical references and index.
    ISBN 1–56720–113–X (alk. paper)
    1. Investments, Foreign—United States.   2. Corporations, Foreign—
United States.   I. Woodward, Douglas P.   II. Nigh, Douglas
William.
HG4910.F67   1998
332.6′73′0973—dc21   97–23658

British Library Cataloguing in Publication Data is available.

Library of Congress Catalog Card Number: 97–23658
ISBN: 1–56720–113–X

First published in 1998

Quorum Books, 88 Post Road West, Westport, CT 06881
An imprint of Greenwood Publishing Group, Inc.

Printed in the United States of America

The paper used in this book complies with the
Permanent Paper Standard issued by the National
Information Standards Organization (Z39.48–1984).

10 9 8 7 6 5 4 3 2 1

Copyright Acknowledgments

The editors and the publisher gratefully acknowledge permission for use of the following material:

"Competition Pays," figure 15.1 of this volume, reprinted with permission from PA Consulting. Copyright remains vested in Cynthia A. Beltz.

For Norman J. Glickman,
advisor and friend
D.P.W.

In memory of Richard Farmer
and Barry Richman
D.N.

Contents

Part III: R&D and High-Technology Effects

Part IV: Corporate Behavior: Political, Social, and Managerial

Part V: Policy Implications

Preface

This book is a multidisciplinary collaboration. It started when we discovered a common interest in exploring the effects of foreign direct investment on the United States. We also shared some dissatisfaction with the quality of the debate over direct investment and its effects on host countries. We saw the need for improved conceptual development and more sophisticated empirical research. We also saw the need to go beyond the economic effects of foreign direct investment to include political and social dimensions.

While important new research was being carried out during the 1990s, it was dispersed across various institutions and conducted by researchers trained in academic disciplines that too rarely communicate with each other: economics, political science, management, and international business. Thus, we saw an opportunity for a collaborative effort that would advance our understanding of foreign direct investment's effects on recipient countries. Consequently, we designed a conference that would pull together leading research.

In September 1995, twenty researchers met for two days at Georgetown University in Washington, D.C. to present and discuss papers addressing various aspects of direct investment in the United States and the appropriate public policy responses. The conference was designed to present research using newly available, more disaggregated economic data to examine a range of effects (economic, political and social), and to consider the public policy implications of rising foreign ownership in the 1990s. This book includes revised versions of the papers presented at the conference, along with our own assessment of the extent to which the foreign ownership of business enterprises matters for a country.

The contributions of many people were crucial to producing this book. First, we thank The Darla Moore School of Business of the University of South Carolina, Center for International Business Education and Research (CIBER) and its director, Randy Folks, for financial and administrative support throughout the whole project. A special note of thanks goes to Michael Shealy, CIBER Managing Director, for a superb job in organizing the logistics of the Washington conference. Our sincere appreciation also goes to Georgetown University and John Kline of the Landegger

Program in International Business Diplomacy at Georgetown University for providing a splendid site for the conference meetings. Such support contributed greatly to the success of the conference, the discussion that went on there, and the quality of the revised papers.

Moving from conference papers to the book in hand requires the talents and hard work of many people. In particular, we want to recognize the tremendous contribution of the University of South Carolina's Division of Research. Sandra Teel, associate director of the Division, edited and prepared the book for publication, contributing to the overall design and layout of the book, copy editing the manuscripts, working with the contributing authors, and working with the publisher. Sara Coffman and Cissy George of the Division staff maintained communication with the many contributors to the book and generally handled many of the tasks associated with publishing. In addition, we acknowledge the efforts of Eric Valentine and his staff at Quorum Books and thank them for their continuing support in the publication and distribution of this book. While we greatly appreciate the work of all those involved in the production of the book, we reserve for ourselves all responsibility for any remaining errors.

Finally, we want to thank the contributing authors to this book for their willingness to share their research with scholars from a variety of disciplines. Foreign direct investment remains a contentious issue and some authors may still disagree on some points stressed in chapters that follow. Yet dialogue and debate, as reflected in this volume, is the only way to advance our understanding of foreign direct investment's effects on recipient countries. We invite the reader to examine the results of our collaboration.

Introduction: Is National Ownership Relevant?

Douglas P. Woodward and Douglas Nigh

INTRODUCTION

The late twentieth century has seen an unparalleled expansion of international capital. After years of competing blocs and capital restrictions, the floodgates have broken, and private investment has poured across political borders as never before. As a result, private corporations have greatly extended their reach into foreign countries. From tin mining to telecommunications, once sheltered sectors of national economies are increasingly subject to foreign competition on their home terrain.

Driving this globalization process is foreign direct investment (FDI), which reached historic peaks during the 1990s. Early in the decade, recessions in most developed countries led to a significant decline in FDI flows. The growth rate picked up, however, with the revitalized world economy of the mid-1990s. In 1993, foreign-owned firms invested $195 billion in their overseas affiliates—up 14 percent over the previous year, but below the peak at the end of the 1980s expansion (United Nations 1994). By 1996, world FDI flows vaulted to $350 billion, surpassing the previous decade's record by over 40 percent. The estimated FDI stock totaled $3.2 trillion, encompassing 45,000 parent firms and 280,000 affiliates (United Nations 1997).

Both developed and developing countries participated in the direct investment upsurge of the mid-1990s. The growth in emerging markets and developing countries is often regarded as a major thrust of the FDI expansion. According to the latest available figures, foreign firms placed $129 billion in the developing world in 1996 (United Nations 1997). Even so, the majority of FDI remained in developed countries; that is, the triad of Europe, North America, and Japan. Notwithstanding increased flows to other regions, developed countries still received about the same overall share of inward investment (63 percent) as they did in the early 1980s. At the same time, direct investment emanated overwhelmingly from multinational enterprises (MNEs) with headquarters in the developed world—85 percent of the world FDI flow in 1996.

In several important respects, the direct investment surge of the 1990s differed from the 1980s. In the mid-to-late 1980s, for example, Japan emerged as a major source of global investment. The United States was the primary recipient of this new FDI, precipitating the most heated debate on the subject in over 50 years. In the 1990s expansion, on the other hand, the sources were broader, and the country sites for new investment projects spread. Emerging market economies of Central and Eastern Europe participated in the competition for direct investment for the first time in decades. Yet, it was the absolute flow of investment to China that stood out. By 1996, China emerged as the second largest recipient of direct investment. (In 1990, China was not even in the top ten.) China and the United States absorbed one third of world FDI inflows during the year.

One constant has remained in the FDI expansion during the late twentieth century: The United States has received far more investment than any other country. In 1996, companies affiliated with foreign-owned enterprises (mostly from the United Kingdom, continental Europe, Japan, and Canada) placed $85 billion in the United States, twice as much inward direct investment as China (United Nations 1997).[1] The primary motivation for investment in the 1990s appears to be the same as it was in the 1980s: greater access to the large, prosperous, diverse U.S. market. Currency fluctuations also continue to figure into the decision to invest. At the microeconomic level, direct investment has risen as overseas firms have achieved competitive advantages over U.S.-based rivals. These competitive advantages enable foreign firms to enter the U.S. market with onsite production, compensating for the distance costs and other disadvantages of foreign status (Caves 1996; Glickman and Woodward 1990; McCulloch 1993).

This book brings together a set of important papers exploring the significance of foreign direct investment in the United States (FDIUS). Remarkably, the direct investment boom of the 1990s has been almost inconspicuous, with far fewer cover stories or congressional hearings than during the Reagan-Bush era. Ten years earlier, rising foreign ownership was a major rallying point for critics of waning U.S. competitiveness. The clarion call to action was reminiscent of *le défi américain* ("the American challenge") in Europe during the 1960s (Servan-Schreiber 1968). Books warned about takeovers of key industries, about deleterious effects on U.S. productive capacity and technological capabilities, and about grave threats to national security (Frantz and Collins 1989; Tolchin and Tolchin 1988). Others decried the growing foreign corporate influence in the political process (Choate 1990). Bills were proposed in Congress to register, screen, and in some cases restrict foreign operations in the United States. In 1988, the Exon-Florio amendment to the Omnibus Trade Bill called for greater scrutiny of defense-related foreign acquisitions. The legislation authorized the president to block foreign takeovers if there were perceived threats to the U.S. defense industrial base.

Essentially, these concerns about FDI center on foreign *control*. By definition, both direct investment and the multinational enterprise, or MNE,[2] imply managerial control over domestic resources by foreign "persons," usually corporations. This type of capital flow differs from passive, portfolio investment where managerial control is rarely, if ever, exerted— foreign holdings of U.S. government securities, for example. Portfolio investment carries risks of sudden "hot money" movements, leading to rapid currency depreciations and a destabilized national economy. Direct investment implies long-term stakes in the host economy that generally are not subject to erratic capital movements. During the 1990s, the rapid outflow of portfolio capital leading to financial crises in Mexico, Thailand, Malaysia, Indonesia, the Czech Republic, and elsewhere served to elevate the benefits of direct investment in the eyes of many host countries. While most governments now recognize that FDI helps build a country's productive base, it is often difficult to trace exactly how portfolio capital contributes to economic growth. Compared with portfolio investment, however, the greater foreign corporate control implied by FDI raises habitual concerns about the long-run impact on the economy, politics, national defense, and society at large.

In the United States, the legacy of FDIUS over the past two decades has been greater foreign participation in a growing list of sectors—chemicals, publishing, and automobiles, to name a few well-known cases. Less well known is that the share of U.S. high-technology sales accounted for by U.S. affiliates of foreign companies doubled from the mid-1980s to the mid-1990s, reaching 23 percent.[3]

To detractors, foreign-based multinational companies conceal sinister motives in their desire to manage and control domestic resources. During the 1980s, the economic nationalist banner inveighed against foreign takeovers of real estate "trophies," Hollywood film studios, and other icons of U.S. capitalism. The economic nationalist mood mellowed during the recession of the early 1990s and subsequent setbacks in Japanese investment. In the ensuing expansion, foreign ownership, although rising again, was yesterday's news. Despite deep suspicions about foreign corporate participation in U.S. politics and continual apprehension about rising ownership of defense-related companies, the latest wave of FDIUS has generated little outright xenophobia. Ironically, some of the visible symbols of foreign corporate success— Rockefeller Center, Universal Studios—have become textbook cases of multinational blunders in the 1990s.

With the anxiety about FDIUS at least temporarily allayed, this is perhaps an appropriate time to reassess foreign ownership. The effects of rising foreign owner-ship raise fundamental questions for international business research that seem to endure through each successive investment wave.

- Can greater foreign ownership have any real consequences for a nation-state? If so, in what areas of the economy, politics, and society at large?
- Are differences between "us" and "them" diminishing? Or do source country differences in FDI persist?
- Does the continual expansion of direct investment mean that national origin will be irrelevant in the near future?
- Why should anyone care about the nationality of business enterprise in a country?

These questions continue to stimulate international business research. There have been many perspectives, but earlier studies tended to find that not all FDI is the same. Even after the investment waves of the 1980s and 1990s, there remain discernible country differences in FDIUS. The differences may carry positive or negative implications for the host country. For example, Japanese MNEs tend to build new plants (greenfield investment) rather than engage in acquisitions or mergers like European and Canadian investors (Glickman and Woodward 1990). In the process of transplanting production in the United States, the Japanese have clearly revitalized segments of the domestic industry (Kenney and Florida 1991). At the same time, Japanese branch plants tend to exhibit lower productivity and greater import propensities than similar foreign- or U.S.-owned plants (Graham and Krugman 1989; Doms and Jensen 1995).

Some prominent international economists hold that nationality of ownership counts for little anymore. Vernon (1993, 57) wrote that "explanations of the behavior of multinational enterprise which draw on the national origins of the enterprise as a major explanatory variable are rapidly losing their value." Not all analysts agree, however. Responding to Vernon's assertion, Feenstra (1993) countered that Asian direct investment patterns in the United States would not necessarily be "harmonized" with that of Western business. In countries with long histories of the Japanese and Western FDI, like Australia, differences among sources of FDI appeared to persist (Kreinin 1988). Lee Kuan Yew, the architect of the Asian development model and former prime minister of Singapore, observed, "There is much more transfer of skills, management, and technology with American multinationals than with the Japanese."[4] The enduring distinctions between Asian and Western MNE behavior were a prominent theme of U.S. studies during the early 1990s (Office of Technology Assessment 1993). But, how fundamental is this asymmetry among MNEs? In a developed economy like the United States, to what degree is the foreign origin of an enterprise still relevant as a determinant of its overseas behavior and its effects on the host country?

These questions are more than academic. They prompt vigorous debate in international business conferences and among the world's political and business elite, as witnessed at the Davos, Switzerland, World Economic Forum in 1997.[5] The effects of national ownership and FDI have deep implications for trade, technology, and national security policy (Burton, Bloch, and Mahaney 1994).

With detailed information sets available in the 1990s, FDIUS can be explored in greater depth than ever before. This book's aim is to provide a comprehensive investigation of foreign ownership based on the latest and most reliable data.

It should be stressed that the contributors to this book looked at more than just the economic effects of greater foreign ownership. The people of a country are not just consumers and producers; they are also citizens of a nation-state and members of various social groups in their home country. They care not only about the economic effects of businesses in their country but also about the political and social effects. Does the nationality of a business' owner matter when it comes to corporate political behavior and corporate social performance in a particular country? To what extent, if any, is the behavior of foreign-owned companies different from that of domestic U.S. companies in such areas as corporate political action, corporate community involvement, and managerial retention?

THE STRUCTURE OF THE BOOK

To form the basis for the volume, papers were solicited and first presented at a September 1995 conference organized around the theme of corporate nationality and the consequences of FDIUS. The meetings, held at Georgetown University in

Washington, D.C., were sponsored by the Center for International Business Education and Research (CIBER) of The Darla Moore School of Business at the University of South Carolina.

The objective of the Washington meetings was to assemble leading authorities on FDI and debate the basic questions of national ownership. The participants included scholars spanning several academic disciplines—primarily in economics, management, and public policy. Other participants held leading positions at major research institutions. This cross-fertilization of perspectives enlivened and enlightened the conference debate.

The papers that emerged from the meetings offer significant findings on FDI and national competitiveness. Reflecting the authors' disparate backgrounds, the papers cover a spectrum of issues. The common thread is their probe of the extent to which U.S.-based and foreign-based corporations act in ways that distinctly affect the host economy. The papers are presented in four sections that reflect different implications of foreign ownership: economics, technology, corporate behavior, and policy.

Part I explores the implications of foreign ownership for the U.S. economy. In this section new evidence is presented on the relationship between FDI and nationality in the following areas:

- productivity;
- wages;
- greenfield (new plant) construction versus acquisitions;
- regional and state distributions; and
- international trade.

Part II takes an in-depth look at foreign firm activity and the technology base of the United States. Empirical findings cover:

- research and development (R&D) facilities in the United States by source country;
- foreign strategies for R&D; and
- FDI penetration in high-technology sectors of the U.S. economy.

In Part III, the authors address the relationship between nationality and corporate behavior, highlighting:

- lobbying and political participation;
- corporate citizenship; and
- management turnover.

Finally, Part IV examines government policy and regulations concerning FDI. The chapters evaluate:

- whether prevailing FDI policy and regulations make sense in the 1990s;
- the question of national treatment in the telecommunications industry; and
- the implications of foreign ownership for national security and defense policy.

DEBATE OVER FOREIGN OWNERSHIP: BOLD ASSERTIONS, WEAK DATA

A major motivation for the Georgetown conference was to move the debate over national ownership beyond its status in the early 1990s. Discussions about ownership and national identity were rekindled by Harvard's Robert Reich, following a series of articles and a popular book, *The Work of Nations* (Reich 1990; 1991a; 1991b; 1991c).[6] In his many writings, Reich maintained that MNEs operate in a postnational economic climate in which the interests of the corporation and the nation-state diverge. This was contrasted with the prevailing view of the 1950s, when the identity of interests of the nation and the corporations based in that nation was considered axiomatic.[7] By the early 1990s, however, Reich insisted that the identity had been broken by cross-border investment flows. Accordingly, the corporation of the late twentieth century "flies many flags" (Reich 1990). Other global business analysts echoed this sentiment (Ohmae 1990).

No doubt, some global business is becoming increasingly "stateless," making it more difficult to distinguish between the behavior of foreign-owned and domestic-owned capital. Like foreign firms, U.S. MNEs supply the home market from offshore production sites, with no direct benefit to the U.S. economy. Moreover, U.S. corporations now depend more on markets overseas for growth. The competitiveness of a *country* (what happens inside its borders) must be distinguished from the competitiveness of its *companies*. For instance, if one looks at the global trade balance of U.S.-owned companies rather than the territorial trade balance of the United States, which includes activities of foreign firms, then the U.S. trade deficit often turns to a surplus.[8] Over time, a country's competitiveness, the relative status of a country's position in the world economy, seems to have less to do with the national origin of firms.[9]

One hypothesis is that over time foreign MNEs will mirror domestic firms, with any remaining peculiarities of MNE behavior related to "vintage" effects that will disappear. These differences can be dismissed as "outliers" in an otherwise converging pattern of domestic and foreign firm behavior. Everything from domestic content to political participation is expected to mirror that of domestic-owned firms as production is localized in the United States. Such convergence notions have been posited in previous studies of direct investment. Summarizing a diverse set of papers that explored Japanese FDI in Europe, Encarnation and Mason (1994, 441) stated, "In the end, we conclude that ownership can—and does—matter." Still, the differences may be the "vestigial remnants reflecting an earlier stage in a multinational's evolution" (Encarnation and Mason 1994, 441).

Accepting the convergence hypothesis of corporate behavior, the role of culture or national bias in economic decision making may be dismissed. In this vein, Ohmae (1990, 90) advanced the notion that the "global corporation today is fundamentally different from the colonial-style multinationals of the 1960s and 1970s." He alleged that the modern corporation has a value system that is "universal, not dominated by home-country dogma, and it applies everywhere."[10] Likewise, Reich (1991a, 80) argued that the old multinational corporation is "disappearing, a reminder of the 1960s and 1970s."[11]

Sometimes these sweeping statements lead to strong policy positions. Conclusions are derived from particular ironic illustrations, rather than in-depth analysis. Reich (1990), for example, used trade between the United States and Japan in cellular telephones to emphasize that bilateral trade policy does not necessarily promote the interests of U.S. citizens when it sides with the interests of U.S. companies. In the

1980s, U.S. trade negotiators helped open access to the Japanese market for Motorola's cellular phones. The irony, Reich argued, is that Motorola designed and produced the phones in Malaysia. He held that the U.S. citizens who benefitted from this trade initiative would be those working for Japanese-owned companies that export cellular phones from the United States. Thus, Reich posed the question, "Who is us?" The American company that produces cellular phones in Kuala Lumpur or the Japanese company that makes the phones in America? Yet one critic of Reich countered that Motorola produced the cellular phones for export at its Illinois plants, not in Kuala Lumpur (Heimlich 1990, 198). Thus, the trade negotiators who helped open the Japanese market supported the expansion of U.S. employment, the opposite of Reich's allegation.

In any case, to contend that *some* companies increasingly appear to have transcended national identity does not prove we are now moving toward a world of stateless corporations without national loyalties. In a critique of the "stateless corporation" concept, Hu (1992) asserted that there remain "special links" between the home nation and the corporation. Taking the polar view from Reich and others, he claimed there are still only national companies with international operations. The basis for the argument, however, was similar to Reich's. It was primarily anecdotal, with little empirical evidence.

In direct response to the "Who is us?" question, Tyson (1991) took Reich to task for failing to check the basic numbers.[12] Using the annual survey data compiled by Bureau of Economic Analysis (BEA), Tyson (1991, 38) concluded, "We are us." She argued that U.S. MNEs have most of their assets, sales, and employment in the United States and suggested that U.S. MNEs have a higher level of economic commitment than foreign firms.[13] According to her account, the home operations of U.S. MNEs amounted to 78 percent of their total assets, 70 percent of total sales, and 74 percent of total employment. These levels of commitment to the home country were apparently getting *higher* over time. The data, however, were highly aggregated, giving little detail. Over time, the debate became increasingly stale. The popular writing on the subject subsided during the mid-1990s as the principal authors went to serve in high-level U.S. policy positions—Reich as Secretary of Labor under the Clinton administration, Tyson as the Clinton's chief economist.

Meanwhile, scholarly research has dug deeper into the questions raised by nationality and MNE behavior. Until the mid-1990s, most empirical research into FDIUS, at least in economics, was based on limited data sets published by the Bureau of Economic Analysis. The best known work is in this vein is Graham and Krugman (1989), who provided evidence for both sides of the "Who is us?" debate. While foreign firms' behavior appears similar to domestic firms in most respects, it differs in significant ways (as previously mentioned, import propensities and productivity stand out). Graham and Krugman's important work came out just before the Foreign Direct Investment and International Financial Data Improvements Act of 1990, which eventually resulted in an important new information source on foreign and domestic firm behavior in the United States.

The ability to delve deeper into empirical research during the 1990s is the result of earlier frustration with FDIUS data. When called before Congress to explain the implications of foreign ownership, analysts often testified that important questions could not be answered adequately because of data limitations,[14] an oft-mentioned problem being industry classification. The published government data were consolidated at the enterprise level; that is, all operations were classified in the principal industry for the whole enterprise, even when establishments spanned several industries. This proved to be a special problem in understanding Japanese FDIUS, which had automotive manufacturing classified under the "wholesale trade" category because that was the origin of most activity for the enterprise.

More detailed and accurate data on foreign firm activity has been available since 1992, an outcome of the earlier congressional hearings. Following the Foreign Direct Investment and International Financial Data Improvements Act, new information emerged from the combined records of the U.S. Census Bureau, the Bureau of Labor Statistics (BLS), and the Bureau of Economic Analysis (BEA). For the first time, the BEA-BLS-Census link provided researchers with direct comparisons of foreign-owned and domestic establishment activity, including employment and payroll, data that were not previously available. The Census Bureau has detailed establishment (plant-level) data that can be distinguished by national ownership when combined with BEA records compiled by enterprise (company-level). Now, it is possible to analyze foreign and domestic ownership in much greater detail and with greater accuracy. It is safe to say that this database is the most complete record ever assembled concerning foreign firm activity in the United States or perhaps anywhere.[15]

The empirical contributions found in this volume are based on this new information, combined with other original sources that have never been as extensively explored. Some differences in behavior between foreign-owned and domestic enterprises should be expected in empirical research. Business behavior is significantly shaped by the economic, political, and social systems of the home country in which the firm first develops. French firms reflect the environment of France; Japanese firms, Japan; and U.S. firms, the United States. When a foreign firm extends the boundary of its organization across national borders, it brings many patterns of behavior developed in the home country. These are likely to be adapted, perhaps some even replaced, but a significant measure of the home country is likely to remain. Again, it is important to stress that the international investments of concern here are not passive portfolio investments; rather, with FDI, the investor retains the capacity for continuing managerial control of the investment.

Not only does the home society influence foreign-owned firm behavior, but also the host society, particularly the attitudes of local nationals toward foreigners. These attitudes are reflected not only in how individuals choose to interact with foreign-owned firms in their country but also in the political and social institutions that they have collectively created in the home country. Thus, even if a foreign-owned firm wanted to adapt its behavior in the host country to match that of domestic firms, it may not be able to do so because of barriers emanating from the host society. It thus seems likely that behavioral differences do exist between foreign-owned firms and domestic firms in the United States in economics, in public policy processes, in public opinion arenas, in communities, and in civil society in general.

Hence, this volume not only presents new empirical work but also investigates dimensions of FDIUS that have received less attention than the economic effects.

Earlier research on noneconomic effects of FDIUS include Rosenzweig (1994) and Logan (1994). Rosenzweig's study found that the practices of foreign-owned firms in the United States were more like those of domestic U.S. firms, rather than home country firms, in the areas of manufacturing, marketing, and human resource management. In contrast, with regard to financial control practices, these firms were more like the parent in the home country than domestic firms. In concluding that foreign-owned firms are much like domestic firms, Rosenzweig noted one exception: Japanese-owned companies in the United States use home country nationals more extensively, particularly in top management positions.

Logan (1994) surveyed foreign-owned companies concerning their community involvement in the United States. He found that the corporate giving levels of foreign-owned companies were approximately equal to the levels of domestic companies. Further, their giving patterns were quite similar to domestic companies. The extent of community involvement for these foreign-owned firms in the United States represents quite an adaptation to the U.S. environment. In adopting such programs as federated giving, employee volunteering, and matched giving, these foreign-owned companies are taking on activities generally unknown in their home countries. Building on these prior studies, this volume branches out beyond the usual economic concerns that inform the debate over "us" and "them."

SUMMARY OF THE BOOK'S FINDINGS

All the chapters in this book present important research that had not yet circulated on FDIUS—new research that could advance our understanding and enliven the debate over the questions posed earlier. The book also serves as a guide to crucial international policy issues. This section summarizes the authors' principal points and significant findings.

Overview of the Issues

Part I begins with a chapter by John H. Dunning, whose pioneering FDI research began in the United Kingdom during the 1950s (Dunning 1958). Dunning's earlier studies of American investment in the United Kingdom anticipated many of the research questions raised at the Georgetown conference. Dunning found U.S. firms in the United Kingdom paid higher wages, exhibited greater productivity, and had more product innovation. Since then, his prodigious output has earned him a special status in international business research. His eclectic theory of FDI is well known to international business scholars throughout the world. Dunning synthesized three aspects of FDI into one theoretical framework: ownership advantages, location advantages, and internalization.

In this volume, Dunning turns his scholarship to the question: Does ownership matter in a globalizing economy? Dunning argues that the unrelenting rise of FDI (along with market liberalization and the dramatic decrease in transport and communication costs) has led to a realignment of firm interests away from their home countries and toward "the pattern of their internationalization." Dunning draws a sharp distinction between "foreignness" and multinationality. A foreign firm is part of an international network of affiliates as well as part of a home country. Essentially, Dunning argues, *globalization reduces "foreignness."* It is the geographic profile of assets that matters, not nationality. Dunning also cautions that researchers should draw a distinction between the characteristics of multinational enterprise (e.g., ownership advantages) and its consequences (e.g. higher capital intensity). As for consequences, this chapter advances the hypothesis that affiliates of extensive global networks are likely to perform better in host countries like the United States, or at least that is what research has consistently shown since the 1950s. Governments have not always recognized the force of this evidence. Even in the late twentieth century, many governments remain reluctant to afford multinational enterprise the principle of national treatment; that is, non-discrimination between domestic firms and firms with ownership based outside the host country. Yet Dunning's chapter concludes by suggesting that the relationship between governments and multinational companies is more congenial than it was in the 1950s. This is largely because governments are coming to recognize that multinational enterprise offers host countries access to a global network of "created assets" that is critical to advancing country competitiveness. It is no wonder that most governments, including U.S. states, actively court foreign investors: they need the assets of the world's most advanced corporations to remain competitive.

The next chapter in Part I is Edward M. Graham's retrospective on *Foreign Investment in the United States* (Graham and Krugman 1989, 1995), a standard reference on FDIUS throughout the 1990s. After Dunning's chapter, one might wonder how an economic analysis of direct investment could have stirred the public antipathy that Graham alludes to early in this chapter. *Foreign Investment in the United States* was written as dispassionate prose; yet, the book nevertheless drew Graham, a senior research fellow at the Institute for International Economics, into the public spotlight and impassioned debates over FDIUS. This chapter suggests that *Foreign Investment in the United States* has withstood early ad hominem criticism and, more importantly, the test of time. Among other points, the Graham and Krugman book showed that affiliates of foreign firms pay higher wages and exhibit higher productivity than domestic firms. Fresh analyses presented in this book extend this line of research. The essential point of Graham and Krugman's work was that the Cassandras of the 1980s got it wrong: Rising FDI posed no grave threat to the nation's economy or to its defense-industrial base.

Consequences for the Economy

The introductory chapters by Dunning and Graham cover the major concerns that reappear throughout the rest of the book. The empirical chapters begin in Part II. The fruits of efforts to generate reliable microeconomic data for FDIUS emerge in chapter 3, by J. Bradford Jensen and Mark E. Doms, economists at Carnegie Mellon and the Federal Reserve Board, respectively. In many respects, the Doms and Jensen chapter represents a seminal piece of research on the consequences of multinational enterprise (recalling Dunning's distinction between characteristics and consequences). In the mid-1990s, the two economists, then working at the U.S. Census in Maryland, bored into the BEA-BLS-Census data link and tested many important hypotheses about FDIUS. Their analysis is part of a new breed of empirical research using large-scale microeconomic data, much of it being done by the Census Bureau's Center for Economic Studies. Here they present one of the few published works subjecting the government's data link to real scrutiny.[16]

Doms and Jensen first note that there remain major empirical questions about foreign-owned establishments when compared with domestic establishments. In debates during the late 1980s, it was often alleged that foreign firms keep a dispropor-tionate amount of their high value-added, high skilled operations in their home countries. U.S. affiliates of foreign companies were sometimes alleged to comprise relatively low productivity, low value-added, low-skilled assembly operations. Graham and Krugman (1989) countered this charge, but their data were highly aggregated, and subject to varying interpretations.

The problem with allegations about low-performance MNEs is simply that they have no theoretical basis, nor clear microfoundation, let alone an empirical one. The standard industrial organization theory of FDI suggests that foreign firms are able to invest overseas only when they possess specific ownership advantages. In the industrial organization theory of direct investment (Dunning 1988; Buckley and Casson 1976; Caves 1996), a *necessary* condition for the investment is having distinct rent-yielding advantages.[17] The industrial organization (eclectic) theory of FDI suggests that the foreign firms able to invest in advanced economy such as the United States are likely to be efficient. Specific advantages, like operating efficiency, enable firms to overcome barriers to overseas investment. Consequently, it is expected that foreign companies would be likely to pay higher wages, have more highly skilled workers, and have higher productivity than many domestic-owned plants. Most economic analysts would accept that, in general, there are strong reasons to presume that FDI contributes to domestic growth and is more productive than domestic investment (Borensztein, De Gregorio, and Lee 1995). Similar arguments apply to U.S.-based multinationals. The productivity and R&D investment of U.S. MNEs are likely to be higher than those of other domestic firms, all else the same.

The rich detail of the data set used by Doms and Jensen allows for precise empirical tests. Access to plant level data (approximately 115,000 establishments) enabled the researchers to control for industry, size, age, and location. With these factors held constant, they test for differences in establishments by ownership, for example between, U.S.-owned and foreign-owned establishments. They provide regression results with detailed comparisons by source country investment as well. In addition, they separately analyze plants run by U.S. multinationals operating in the United States. They examine whether U.S. multinationals have more skilled and higher wage employment compared with other U.S. firms or the establishments of foreign-based multinationals operating in the U.S. domestic market.

The results of Doms and Jensen's research are striking, confirming much of what would be expected given the theory of the multinational firm. Wages are higher (about 3.8 percent) for foreign-owned establishments when compared with domesti-cally owned plants. Yet U.S. MNEs operating in the United States pay more than similar foreign establishments, a result that does not follow directly from FDI theory.

Arguably the most important contribution of the Doms and Jensen chapter is an original analysis of multinationality. As stated in chapter 1, Dunning's multinationality argument is that as firms become more multinational, their original competitive (ownership) advantages are augmented by advantages derived from a network of assets held overseas. In Doms and Jensen's chapter, the empirical question becomes: Do multinational networks affect plant-level productivity or wages?

To probe the multinationality question, Doms and Jensen test how wages and other characteristics of U.S. MNEs vary depending on the extent of foreign assets held by the parent company. Examining the differences among U.S. MNEs according to this measure, the authors find that U.S. multinationals with more than 20 percent of their assets in foreign countries are the most productive, biggest, most capital intensive, and pay the highest wages. On the other hand, U.S. multinationals with less than 20 percent of their assets in foreign countries appear to be similar to foreign multinationals in pay and productivity. Establishments belonging to an enterprise with no foreign assets pay lower wages and have lower productivity.

Overall, Doms and Jensen's research suggests that multinationals, whether foreign- or domestic-owned, operate the most productive, most capital-intensive, and highest-paying plants. Previous research based on broad comparisons of foreign-owned plants and domestically owned plants without controls for industry, size and other factors compared apples and oranges. Doms and Jensen's work shows that plants owned by MNEs tend to be much larger, on average, in the United States and have characteristics that are associated with size. The evidence supports previous research indicating that foreign-owned plants have desirable consequences for U.S. workers (wages) and industrial competitiveness (productivity). However, relative to plants owned by U.S. MNEs, foreign-owned plants do not compare as favorably.

This volume's second contribution to the empirical literature on the economics of foreign ownership comes from Edward J. Ray, an economics professor at Ohio State University. Ray's prior work contains valuable insights into the determinants of FDIUS (Ray 1989; 1995). In this volume (chapter 4), Ray's research branches out in new directions. It provides an exhaustive record of FDIUS during the 1980s—a period of tremendous expansion in foreign firm activity. The analysis is based on industry and regional data from the International Trade Administration, which separates new plant (greenfield) investment from acquisitions (takeovers). The chapter analyzes FDIUS by source country and includes new evidence on why Japanese MNEs demonstrate a greater propensity to build new plants compared with European and Canadian MNEs.

Ray's chapter also provides an assessment of the concentration of FDIUS by industry and location for different source countries. Industry, state, and macroeconomic factors are used in regression analyses to explain takeovers and new capital investments (greenfield and expansions) by the source countries. Ray found that Japanese new plant investment in U.S. manufacturing has been affected by both existing trade restrictions and the threat of new protectionist measures in the United States. New plant investment also appears to be driven by the need to introduce technology into U.S. manufacturing plants. In contrast, foreign acquisitions are identified with management-intensive industries in which rents associated with administrative expertise are likely to be greatest. Labor force factors, but not tax and business incentive programs, apparently influence the location of greenfield (and expansion) direct investment at the state level.

A critical point of Ray's chapter that deserves further investigation concerns the modeling of FDI by source country. His results suggest that Japanese entry was in many respects easier to model than FDI from other sources; for example, it responded to trade restrictions. During the surge of the 1980s, however, Japanese investment involved more greenfield investment (or transplants) than other sources. It is apparently more difficult to account for acquisitions (or takeovers).

A detailed empirical analysis of the regional dimensions of FDIUS follows in chapter 5, written by Cletus C. Coughlin, an economist and St. Louis Federal Reserve vice president. While a substantial body of literature has been developed in this area, little is known about the locational patterns of FDIUS from different countries.

Coughlin's chapter is an exhaustive attempt to identify differences in the location of foreign-owned manufacturers. Like other researchers in this volume, Coughlin is guided by the eclectic theory of FDI, according to which MNEs tend to develop in industries where firms possess special ownership advantages. The exploitation of these advantages entails production of goods and services in various locations. The attractiveness of a region depends on the characteristics of that location relative to others. If multinational firms from different countries tend to generate different types of firm-specific advantages, Coughlin argues that the sites for foreign production would differ because of different evaluations of the locational characteristics.

Coughlin's chapter includes detailed country comparisons of FDIUS by region. His statistical analysis tests for differences in locational patterns and spatial clustering by source country. Locational patterns differ significantly for the British and the Japanese. Spatial clustering can also be found, especially for German FDI. Over time these differences apparently diminish. Future research should examine how these regional convergence patterns held up in the 1990s and beyond.

Chapter 6, the final chapter in the economics section, is by Simon Reich of the University of Pittsburgh. The chapter involves a lengthy review of an economic aspect of FDIUS that is not well understood: international trade effects. A decade earlier, the work of Graham and Krugman (1989), Glickman and Woodward (1990) and others raised the issue of peculiar differences in trade effects from FDIUS by source country, where the Japanese affiliates appeared to exhibit starkly higher import propensities. Reich looks at the relationship between trade and FDI from a fresh perspective. The chapter begins with a discussion of product cycle theory, which predicts there will be substitution of direct investment and trade. Reich contrasts an alternative view that posits a complementary relationship between trade and investment. From this perspective, wholesaling is a major activity of FDI; it is not only primary extraction and manufacturing. Within manufacturing, final assembly plants may be more prevalent than full production facilities. This suggests that exports may increase from the home country as FDI increases.

Reich offers a counterpoint to the received wisdom about trade and investment. He argues that conventional approaches like the product cycle fail to recognize the strategic relationship between trade and investment implied by intrafirm trade. The thrust of the chapter is to use trade-creating FDI to explain the resilience of the U.S. trade deficit with Japan. But is the trade-creating theory of direct investment verifiable? Reich marshals considerable time series evidence to suggest that it is. He concludes that trade and investment patterns in the United States by Japanese MNEs are not explained by the trade-investment substitution principle of product cycle theory. Rather, there appears to be a persistent pattern of growing intrafirm trade through investment in wholesale facilities. It remains to be seen, Reich argues, whether this trade-creating investment will persist over time. Moreover, Reich does not tie the peculiarities in intrafirm trade patterns to national characteristics; rather, he asserts that they follow from strategic firm behavior. Use of such anomalies to bolster arguments against national treatment for foreign investors may miss the crucial point: firms from any source country can engage in the strategic behavior Reich associates most closely with Japanese MNEs.

Considering all the chapters in Section II, one can safely conclude that national ownership distinctions persist. Doms and Jensen show that there are differences in economic performance measures like wages and productivity by source country. Ray's chapter shows source countries differ in their motives for entering the United States through new plant investment or acquisitions. Also, there are sharp distinctions in locational patterns among different source countries, although Coughlin's chapter finds convergence over time. The intrafirm trade differences found by Reich remain the most pronounced of all source country effects.

For the most part, however, the chapters on economic effects find only small differences between foreign-owned and domestic companies. In particular, careful empirical studies like that of Doms and Jensen conclude that FDIUS has had a positive impact on the U.S. economy, supporting the earlier but less detailed work of Graham and Krugman (1989). Compared to U.S.-owned firms, U.S. affiliates of foreign firms in manufacturing industries are more capital intensive, pay higher wages, employ more highly skilled workers, and have higher productivity.

A promising direction for future research would be to extend beyond differences between foreign and domestic enterprise, or between "us" and "them." Already, as the chapters in Part I intimate, research is also beginning to move beyond distinctions among foreign source countries, or among "them." There are interesting differences to be explored among "us." What may be most intriguing in the future is not foreign ownership per se but, as Dunning suggests, the effects of multinational enterprise networks. The seeds for empirical research in this area may be found in this volume: Doms and Jensen's chapter suggests that the greater the extent of the MNE network, the stronger the economic effects on the home country economy.

R&D and High-Technology Effects

The nature and extent of foreign firm technological commitments in the United States, a controversial consequence of FDIUS, are explored in Part III. Critics of rising FDIUS have alleged that foreign-owned firms would use their control to keep R&D activities in the home country, along with high-wage, high-value added employment (Tolchin and Tolchin, 1988; Prestowitz, 1988). On this point Graham and Krugman stated:

> Such concerns are not absurd in the light of theoretical analysis. Multinational firms are created for a reason; they are more than the sum of their parts, and their subsidiaries therefore ought to behave differently from purely domestic firms. It is not implausible that this difference in behavior might include hiving off some

> high-level activities to the parent firm. On the other hand, it is not certain either. . . .
> Available empirical evidence does not confirm the critics' fears. (Graham and
> Krugman, 1993, 32)

Chapter 7 provides a comprehensive empirical analysis of foreign firm R&D activities in the United States, written by Manuel G. Serapio, Jr., a management professor at the University of Colorado at Denver, and Donald H. Dalton, an economist in the Economics and Statistics Administration of the U.S. Department of Commerce. During the late 1980s and 1990s, R&D spending by foreign-owned firms in the United States increased more rapidly than total R&D expenditures within the United States by U.S. firms. The authors contend that foreign-owned R&D expenditure is now significant enough to have an influence on the overall growth rate of total private U.S. R&D. For example, in the high-technology sector, foreign companies' R&D comprises about one-fifth of total corporate R&D in the United States. By and large, the growth in R&D spending by foreign companies in the United States comes from the U.S. affiliates of six countries: Switzerland, Japan, United Kingdom, Germany, France, and Canada.

Dalton and Serapio find that foreign R&D in the United States has in part compensated for R&D curtailment by U.S. firms and federal funding. Their R&D data, including original survey research, reveals more industry differences than country differences. Dalton and Serapio show that different countries' R&D facilities tend to be more spatially concentrated, not spread as geographically, as Coughlin found for FDIUS in the previous chapter.

The second chapter on in this section focuses on FDI in high-technology industries. In the early 1990s, there were major concerns raised in Washington about the greater involvement of foreign firms in technology-intensive industries.[18] But few observers knew the true extent of penetration by U.S. affiliates. As in much of the debate, there were abundant anecdotes, but little hard data. This chapter, by Sumiye Okubo, an economist at the Economics and Statistics Administration of the U.S. Department of Commerce, looks at the most recent and reliable figures available. Chapter 9 examines the concentration of investment and market shares of U.S. affiliates in U.S. high-technology industries for evidence that foreign firms may have pursued strategies to acquire U.S. technologies. Drawing on a variety of sources, including the BEA–Census and BEA–BLS linkage data, Okubo profiles R&D spending and other R&D activities in the United States and evaluates their possible impact on U.S. technology development. The chapter includes information on royalties and license fees, showing the extent to which U.S. affiliates of foreign firms are shipping technology to foreign parents or are receiving technology from them.

Okubo finds that the sales of U.S. affiliates of foreign firms are more concentrated in high-technology industries compared with those of U.S.-owned firms. Foreign firms in high-technology manufacturing industries account for three-quarters of R&D expenditures by all foreign-owned affiliates. Okubo then examines total U.S. high-technology manufacturing sales. The most remarkable finding is a doubling of the share of high-technology sales accounted for by U.S. affiliates of foreign companies between 1987 and 1994. With 22 percent of high-technology sales, foreign-owned firms held a significant market share by the mid-1990s, with 22 percent of high-technology sales. Okubo also discovered that U.S. affiliates of foreign firms tend to import technology from their foreign parents, as their payments of royalties and licensing fees substantially outstrip their receipts.

The final chapter in Part III is written by Lois S. Peters, a member of Rensselaer Polytechnic Institute's management faculty. The aim of this chapter is to advance our understanding of U.S. affiliates of foreign companies through case studies of R&D strategies from companies based in different countries. This chapter provides a useful complement to Okubo's and Dalton and Serapio's broad empirical assessments. Peters' essay also goes to the crux of concerns about the motives for FDIUS in the U.S. technology base. The chapter describes different foreign firms' modes of entry into the U.S. R&D system. Peters then compares and contrasts the specific strategies of foreign-based MNEs' R&D activity. She interviewed managers at the U.S. laboratory sites of ABB, Philips, Matsushita, Thomson, and Bayer. The evidence suggests that the internationalization of R&D is derived from both information cost reduction and technology generation. According to Peters, investment in R&D is increasingly required in some industries to assimilate technology as well as to garner information about markets and government policy.

In summarizing this section, there are three points worth mentioning. First, the chapters point to many positive contributions to the U.S. economy from FDIUS in the nation's technology base. Again, the results are expected, given the received theory of FDI. Second, the motives for R&D appear to be understood best from a firm perspective (Peters) or an industry perspective, rather than strictly from a source country perspective, such as Japanese firms versus European firms. As Dalton and Serapio note, there are clearly more industry differences than country differences. Finally, given the significant presence of FDIUS in high technology, there may be reasons to be concerned about growing foreign firm activity in the U.S. technology base and its relationship to national defense, an issue taken up by Kudrle and Bobrow (chapter 14) in the policy section of this book.

Corporate Behavior: Political, Social, and Managerial

In Part IV, the book's focus shifts to the political, social, and managerial behavior of foreign firms operating in the United States. Each of its three chapters investigates a particular dimension of issues raised in earlier parts. Chapter 10, the first chapter in Part IV is by Kathleen A. Getz, a management professor at American University. Getz asks, In what ways is the political behavior of foreign-owned firms in the United States different from that of domestic firms? Her answer takes her through an extensive theoretical development drawing on the following social science theories: Resource dependency, collective action, transaction cost, agency, and institutions. From this review come fourteen propositions concerning the likely political behavior of foreign-owned firms in the United States.

Getz argues that what drives the differences in the political behavior of a foreign-owned firm is its lower level of legitimacy in the host society. As a consequence, Getz expects that the foreign-owned firm will use collective, rather than individual, political tactics more than domestic firms. Further, in its collective political activity, she predicts that the foreign-owned firm will be *less* likely *(i)* to initiate coalitions (to keep visibility to society lower) and *(ii)* to participate in multiple-issue collectives (due to lower overlap with interests of potential partners).

Of particular interest, given the concern with campaign finance reform, is Getz's proposition that foreign-owned firms are more likely to use tactics dependent on economic resources (such as, PAC contributions and advocacy advertising) than are domestic firms. Through such expenditures, the foreign-owned firm can obtain the formal institutional political resources that domestic firms have already developed to a greater extent.

Although Getz presents no empirical testing of the hypotheses derived from her theoretical work in this chapter, we do gain a good understanding of the likely differences in the political behavior of foreign-owned firms in the United States. She concludes by noting that the differences between foreign-owned and domestic firms in their corporate behavior are likely to be small and perhaps diminishing over time. Differences in nationality of ownership are overshadowed by similarities as businesses participating in the political process. Both are "elephants among the chickens." The big difference in participation in the political process, Getz argues, is between business and nonbusiness interests.

We now turn from corporate political behavior to corporate social performance, the focus of chapter 11 in Part IV. Tammie S. Pinkston, an analyst at Andersen Consulting, explores the differences between foreign-owned and domestic corporations in various aspects of their corporate citizenship behavior. Do foreign-owned and domestic firms in the United States differ in the priority placed on economic, legal, ethical, and philanthropic responsibilities to the host society? Do they differ in the importance accorded stakeholders such as employees, government, consumers, owners, and communities? Do they differ in the importance they place on various corporate citizenship issues, such as environmental protection, employee health and safety, regulatory compliance, community outreach programming, and minority development?

In her study of the firms in the chemical industry in the United States, Pinkston finds that foreign-owned firms and domestic firms are overall quite similar in their corporate citizenship behavior. The priority placed on the four different areas of responsibility results in the same ranking: Top rank to the economic area, second rank to legal, third rank to ethical, and fourth rank to philanthropic. The three stakeholder groups considered most important are the same: employees, owners, and customers. The three corporate citizenship issues considered most important are the same: employee health and safety, environmental protection, and regulatory compliance.

Yet some differences exist for foreign-owned versus domestic firms. Foreign-owned firms, as a group, place a somewhat higher importance on employees as stakeholders and somewhat lower importance on owners as stakeholders. Foreign-owned firms place somewhat lower importance on such issues as representation of minorities and minority development.

When foreign firms are examined on a country-by-country basis, other noteworthy findings are revealed. German-owned and Swedish-owned firms place the highest priority on legal responsibilities as opposed to economic. German-owned and Japanese-owned firms place a higher priority on philanthropic responsibilities than do American or other foreign firms. Japanese-owned and Swedish-owned firms, in particular, value employees most highly as stakeholders—a finding quite consistent with the home country treatment of employees. Swedish-owned and British-owned firms, in particular, place a lower importance on minority representation and development, again perhaps reflecting the influence of the home country environment. Given the small size of the individual country samples, the country-by-country comparisons should be weighed carefully. Yet these results indicate the potential benefits of disaggregating foreign-owned firms by country of origin for a more fine-grained analysis of their behavior in the United States.

One implication of the Pinkston study is that of significant adaptation to the U.S. business environment by foreign-owned firms in their corporate citizenship behavior. A case in point is the development of Japanese corporate philanthropy in the United States—a practice expected in the U.S. environment, but much rarer in Japan. In this behavior is seen significant adaptation toward the host country expectations. We can still see, however, the influence of the home country in the case of Japan on the issue of job security. Pinkston finds that Japanese-owned firms in the United States place a much higher importance on job security than do U.S. firms or firms from other foreign countries.

The final chapter in Part IV is by Jeffrey A. Krug, management professor at the University of Memphis, and Douglas Nigh of the University of South Carolina's international business faculty. Krug and Nigh examine the fate of top managers of U.S. companies that have been acquired. Does it matter if the acquiring company is foreign-owned or domestic? Are there differences in the retention rates of top executives of these acquired companies for foreign-owned versus domestic acquirers? What happens to the top managers of U.S. corporations is important to understand since they have such a major influence on various strategic decisions, which affect the competitiveness of both companies and countries. Top managers are the ones who, in the end, decide which plant in which location gets to invest in expanded capacity, which workers in which location get advanced training, which location gets the new R&D laboratory, and which plant in which location gets closed down.

Examining the magnitude and timing of executive turnover in acquisitions of U.S. firms, Krug and Nigh find significant differences for foreign-owned versus domestic acquisitions. Foreign acquisitions have a higher rate of top management turnover than do domestic acquisitions, and it takes foreign acquisitions longer (six years) to exhibit the full turnover effects of the acquisition than it takes domestic acquisitions (three years).

Although these differences are significant, they are small compared with the differences in top management turnover rates in acquisitions versus non-acquired firms. Acquisitions, either by foreign-owned or domestic firms, have a much higher turnover of top executives than firms that are not acquired by other firms.

When we review the conclusions of the three studies concerning the differences between foreign-owned versus domestic firms in their corporate political behavior, corporate citizenship, and managerial retention after acquisition, we are struck by the similarity of results. The theoretical and empirical work points to small differences between foreign-owned and domestic firms—differences overshadowed by other, larger differences. For Getz, the big difference is between business and nonbusiness participation in the political process. For Krug and Nigh, the big difference is between managerial retention in acquired versus non-acquired firms. Foreign ownership of a business in the United States matters, just not nearly so much as some other factors.

Policy

Part V of this book tackles the policy implications of foreign ownership. The four chapters evaluate the long-standing principle in the United States of national treatment, or nondiscrimination, for foreign firms. This issue has been at the forefront of the policy agenda of the developed world in the 1990s, particularly with the deregulation and globalization of industries like telecommunications.

The first chapter in this part is by John M. Kline, professor and director of the Landegger Program in International Business Diplomacy at Georgetown University. This chapter illuminates corporate nationality concerns. Kline identifies major policy and program areas where nations employ corporate nationality distinctions and examines both the motivation and the implementation. Kline also analyzes how corporate nationality definitions function in governmental programs that seek competitive national advantage. Next, he investigates the role of corporate nationality in reciprocal investment policies. Finally, chapter 13 attempts to elucidate policy choices and possible trade-offs, especially where the crusade for national advantage may counter international economic principles and multilateral cooperation.

Kline contends that "motivation matters" in understanding discriminatory policies against foreign investors such as those proposed during the late 1980s and early 1990s. Some of the proposed policies and programs that departed from the national treatment standard were spurred on by an attempt to achieve national "competitive advantage." National treatment came under attack by those who would use the notion of "reciprocity" to justify countering discriminatory policies overseas. Kline's major point is unequivocal: Neither "competitiveness" nor "reciprocity" offers a convincing case for discriminating against foreign investors. This is especially true when "us" versus "them" distinctions are made using vague corporate nationality definitions based on ownership or control. This essay sets the tone for the chapters that follow. Kline's policy positions fall in line with investment liberalization efforts by the Organisation for Economic Co-operation and Development and point toward strengthening the negotiations over the Multilateral Agreement on Investment (MAI). The MAI mantle is taken up again by Steven J. Canner in the last chapter.

What about the thorny issue of national defense and FDIUS? Chapter 14 should not be overlooked by anyone interested in international economic policy and national security. The chapter is coauthored by Robert T. Kudrle, professor and director of the Freeman Center for International Economic Policy at the University of Minnesota, and Davis B. Bobrow, professor of International Affairs at the University of Pittsburgh. It is essentially a critique of proposals regarding foreign acquisitions of U.S. defense-related firms, a hotly debated issue that arose during the 1980s FDI surge that persists in the late 1990s.

In an era of rising FDI, successive administrations in Washington have struggled to provide the United States with a sound national defense at sensible cost, while avoiding the risks of foreign dependency in the defense industrial base. If the United States maintains its open-door FDI policy, as generally advocated throughout Part V, it remains open to foreign products flowing into the defense industrial base through foreign-owned or controlled affiliates. In 1988 Congress passed the Exon-Florio amendment to add "teeth" to the chief foreign acquisition monitoring body, the Committee on Foreign Investment in the United States (CFIUS). CFIUS is an inter-agency creation, the chief U.S. review board for foreign investment. CFIUS has the authority to recommend blocking FDI if it would lead to monopolistic or oligopolistic control over a defense-related industry.

In military-related technology, CFIUS may impose selected performance requirements on firms that would exercise potential market domination. Unfortunately, the legislation gave the committee broad authority without specifying what constitutes U.S. security interests. Is market concentration brought on by a foreign acquisition the critical criterion for national security evaluation by CFIUS? Kudrle and Bobrow argue that concentration is *not* the analytical "bullet" needed by CFIUS. Rather, the analysis of defense acquisitions should be based both on the best available empirical evidence and on microeconomic theory. As they show, market concentration is a slippery notion and exceedingly difficult to estimate. In the U.S. economy, almost any level of concentration, and perhaps foreign ownership as well, may serve the national interest. According to Kudrle and Bobrow, it is critical to consider the special characteristics of defense markets and the history of the acquiring firm in the host country.

In the next chapter Cynthia A. Beltz, an economist at the American Enterprise Institute, traces efforts to thwart the long-standing U.S. policy of national treatment. Through a study of recent federal legislation, she inveighs against conditional national treatment (CNT) as misguided and disingenuous. Chapter 15 argues that the CNT proposition advocated to protect U.S. interests is dubious if it seeks to enhance U.S. economic welfare. In contrast, Beltz argues that an open-door policy, based on the national treatment principle, remains the rational rule for practice as we enter the next century.

To focus the CNT debate, Beltz's chapter presents a case study of foreign ownership restrictions in the telecommunications industry. The case examines whether restrictions on FDIUS are needed to force foreign markets into competition. She questions whether foreign governments will respond to U.S. regulatory pressure by opening their markets. The chapter concludes that, in opposition to the CNT proposition, markets worldwide are on a course toward increased competition, regardless of the U.S. posture on FDI restrictions or reciprocity. Given the technology and market forces released by telecommunications deregulation and the changes in the regulation of U.S. trading partners, the CNT proposition makes increasingly less sense. Thus, Beltz soundly rejects reciprocity measures and conditional national treatment, that is, holding foreign companies responsible for home country policies. Reciprocity and conditional national treatment notions militate against domestic goals to promote technology, economic growth, and open-door investment rules that protect the rights of all MNEs no matter where the headquarters is located.

The final chapter by Stephen J. Canner, vice president of International Policy at the U.S. Council of International Business, reviews recent initiatives in the global liberalization of FDI. Actually, the liberalization theme is raised throughout the book. Dunning stresses that the adversarial relations between governments and multinational enterprise may be diminishing in the 1990s. However, as the Beltz chapter emphasizes, we still live in a world where there are substantial violations of national treatment. As Canner points out, after successful rounds of trade liberalization culminating in the World Trade Organization, the free trade forces aligned to bring direct investment and national treatment to the forefront of the debate over globalization in the mid-1990s. Representatives of the 29 advanced countries belonging to the Organisation for Economic Co-operation and Development (OECD) took the lead in negotiating this major new global investment initiative, dubbed the Multilateral Agreement on Investment (MAI). Once the OECD pact was ratified (the original target year was 1999), non-OECD countries would be invited to join. The significance of such a treaty is that it would provide explicit investment rules for the global economy. The draft circulating in the late 1990s disallowed governments the ability to discriminate between foreign investors based on the country of origin. It also contained a section that called for a ban on performance requirements (domestic content legislation, for example).

Essentially, the MAI is designed to reduce restrictions on direct investment. Canner asserts that the MAI will benefit firms competing the twenty-first century and bring mutual benefits to home country and host country economies. Yet critics, many of them in environmental and labor organizations still bruising from battles to thwart trade liberalization, regrouped to defeat the OECD initiative. They argued the pact would prevent governments from imposing sanctions against countries that abuse human rights or spoil the environment. Some concerns were also voiced about the potential for corporations, facing investment restrictions, to bypass the courts of sovereign countries and take their complaints to international tribunals. The original form of the pact did allow exemptions for national security, however.

Is the world ready for a major liberalization of FDI? The MAI initiative began to falter in 1998 and its prospects for passage began to dim, even in the United States. Canner's article presents a strong case for supporting the pact, but the political difficulties in reaching an agreement among developed countries would be no doubt compounded once non-OECD members were brought into the negotiations. Canner's chapter, while emphatically expressing the case for liberalization, will certainly not be the last word on the subject.

To summarize the policy chapters of Part V, it is important to note that the United States still ranks among the countries most open to FDI and remains the champion of liberalization in global negotiations. All the chapters here support the underlying national treatment position of the United States and suggest areas where it may be advanced and improved in the interest of expanding capital movements across national borders. In both developed and developing countries FDI continues to grow, even without an agreement to liberalize investment flows. Economic nationalism and violations of national treatment have apparently diminished over the course of the decade—at least that appears to be true in the United States.

A case in point is Sematech, the U.S. consortium of semiconductor that remains one of the lasting expressions of economic nationalism spawned during the 1980s. As Kline's chapter makes clear, crusades to promote U.S. competitiveness that violate national treatment run counter to the U.S. efforts to foment multilateral cooperation. Sematech was conceived in the late 1980s as public-private partnership to restore U.S. technological leadership in computer chips. The U.S. blocked foreign participation (thus discriminating against foreign companies and breaching national treatment), although all companies had considerable investment overseas. However, by the late 1990s the consortium members recognized that a global approach to many semiconductor issues is essential. For example, advanced lithography for silicon wafers has become so complex that involvement from all of the world's device makers was deemed necessary if the U.S.-based firms were to remain on the cutting edge of technology. Consequently, Sematech embarked on an international expansion, inviting foreign chip makers into a new series of programs. Thus, as Kudrle and Bobrow's analysis suggests, foreign ownership and participation in critical U.S. industries may serve the national interest. One can only conclude that globalization has made "us" and "them" distinctions increasingly futile.

CONCLUSION

The flow of direct investment in the United States accelerated with economic growth in the mid-1990s. Yet, as foreign ownership has continued to swell, there has been a notable change in the debate: Less rhetoric and more research. The heated debate over FDIUS has cooled considerably. Meanwhile, a substantial amount of research has probed the implications of foreign ownership and control.

The research underlying this volume addresses whether nationality of ownership matters for a nation-state. In the past, the available data suffered from problems of aggregation and masked important differences within industries. Based on the evidence herein, ownership differences in FDI apparently exist but for the most part are small. Japanese MNEs do stand out as exceptions (but not necessarily in a negative sense), particularly with reference to new plant investment, trade, and corporate citizenship behavior. Still, the burden of proof resides with those who stress that these differences are strong or will not wither over time. The overarching spirit of this book is to be cautious about using any asymmetries in FDI as "red meat" for those opposed to the principle of national treatment. An open-door policy consensus prevailed at the conference and is reflected in this volume.

The chapters that follow this introduction are designed to advance our understanding of how "foreign" is foreign direct investment. While there remain discernible peculiarities in source country patterns, Dunning is probably right—in the end, globalization reduces "foreignness." Through growing multinationality, firms transfer their competitiveness to the host country. The home country may matter much less in the future than the extent of globalization. In the final analysis, research has only begun to investigate the impact of multinational networks on both home and host countries.

NOTES

1. The United States continues to lead all other countries in outward direct investment as well. In 1996, U.S.companies were responsible for $85 billion in overseas direct investment (United Nations, 1997).

2. Caves (1996, 1) suggests the usage of multinational enterprise (MNE) rather than multinational corporation (MNC) "to direct attention to the top level of coordination in the hierarchy of business decisions." A company "may be the controlled subsidiary of another firm."

3. See Okubo's chapter in this volume.

4. Quoted in *Business Week*, "An Elder Statesman Surveys Asia's Future," November 29, 1993, p. 108.

5. Dobrzynski, Judith H., "A Quick Guide to Big Ideas, if You Didn't Get to Davos," *New York Times*, February 9, 1997.

6. Reich's *Work of Nations* (1991c) served as a guide for major international and national policy initiatives in the first Clinton administration.

7. This view is expressed in the well-known statement by General Motors president Charles Wilson: "What was good for America was good for General Motors, and vice versa." See Robert B. Reich, "Corporation and Nation," *Atlantic Monthly*, May 1988, pp. 76-81.

8. This point was found in Lipsey and Kravis (1986). For an interesting approach to rethinking the notion of national trade balances, see Julius (1990).

9. We recognize that "competitiveness" is vague, although we hope that it may be used without inciting merciless ridicule (cf. Krugman 1996).

10. Actually, Ohmae repeated an argument dating back at least seventy-five years (see Angell 1915).

11. Reich's statements about the 1960s-style multinational corporation recall the rhetoric of that age as much as the reality. In fact, writings on multinational enterprises during the 1960s and early 1970s are replete with references to the coming age of globalism. In one popular book from the mid-1970s, Barnet and Müller (1974, 18) wrote, "What makes the global corporation unique is that unlike corporations of even a few years ago it no longer views overseas factories and markets as adjuncts to home operations." The authors quoted numerous executives, including one who charged that the nation-state is "a very old-fashioned idea and badly adapted to our present complex world." Long before the borderless world entered our vocabulary, the executive declared that the nation-state was "obsolete . . . it will in any meaningful sense be dead—and so will the corporation that remains essentially national" (Barnet and Müller 1974, 21). It is worth noting that the sequel to Barnet and Müller (1974), published twenty years later, was more circumspect than the executive quoted in the text: "The national origin of a global business corporation matters less than it once did, but in a world of nation-states it still matters" (Barnet and Cavanagh 1994, 282).

12. Notwithstanding the debate in the early 1990s, Tyson would join Secretary of Labor Reich in the Clinton administration as chair of the Council of Economic Advisors in 1993.

13. In response, Reich claimed that "this fact is entirely tautological. Firms are *defined* as U.S. multinationals precisely *because* they have most of their assets, sales, and employment in the United States" (Reich 1991b). In this assertion, Reich is wrong. U.S. multinationals are defined by where they are incorporated, at least for the BEA data Tyson cited.

14. See, for example, Douglas P. Woodward, "Foreign Direct Investment in the United States," testimony before the Hearing on Foreign Direct Investment in the United States, The Joint Economic Committee, Congress of the United States, Washington, D.C., September 20, 1991; and Douglas P. Woodward, "Closing the Data Gap: In Support of the 1990 Foreign Investment Policy Improvements Act," testimony before the U.S. House of Representatives, Subcommittee on Commerce, Consumer Protection, and Competitiveness, Committee on Energy and Commerce, Washington, D.C., June 13, 1990.

15. The first data series in this linkage project were published for 1987 establishment data and soon after for the early 1990s (Department of Commerce 1993).

16. See also Howenstine and Shannon, 1996.

17. For a comprehensive review of research (recent and past) on multinational enterprises and FDI, see Caves (1996).

18. An example is an analysis of selected foreign acquisitions of U.S. high-technology companies by the Economic Strategy Institute. See Linda Spencer, *Foreign Investment in the United States: Unencumbered Access* (Washington, D.C.: Economic Strategy Institute, May 1991).

REFERENCES

Angell, Norman. 1915. *America and the New World-State*. New York: G. P. Putnam.

Barnet, Richard J., and John Cavanagh. 1994. *Global Dreams: Imperial Corporations and the New World Order*. New York: Simon and Schuster.

Barnet, Richard J., and Ronald E. Müller. 1974. *Global Reach: The Power of the Multinational Corporations*. New York: Simon and Schuster.

Borensztein, Eduardo, Jose De Gregorio, and Jong-Wha Lee. 1995. "How Does Foreign Direct Investment Affect Economic Growth?" *NBER Working Paper* No. 5057, Cambridge, Mass., March.

Buckley, Peter J., and Mark C. Casson. 1976. *The Future of the Multinational Enterprise*. London: The MacMillan Press.

Burton, Daniel F., Erich Bloch, and Mark S. Mahaney. 1994. "Multinationals: The 'Who Is Us' Debate," *Challenge*, September-October, pp. 33-37.

Caves, Richard E. 1996. *Multinational Enterprise and Economic Analysis*. Second edition. Cambridge, U.K: Cambridge University Press.

Choate, Pat. 1990. *Agents of Influence: How Japan's Lobbyists in the United States Manipulate America's Political and Economic System*. New York: A.A. Knopf.

Department of Commerce. 1992. "Gross Product of U.S. Affiliates of Foreign Direct Investors, 1987-90," *Survey of Current Business*, November, pp. 47-51.

———. 1993. *Foreign Direct Investment in the United States: Establishment Data for Manufacturing, 1990*. Bureau of Economic Analysis and Bureau of the Census, August. Washington, D.C.: GPO.

Doms, Mark E., and J. Bradford Jensen. 1995. "A Comparison between Operating Characteristics of Domestic and Foreign Owned Manufacturing Establishments in the United States." Paper prepared for the Conference on Research in Income and Wealth, Geography and Ownership as Bases for Economic Accounting, May.

Dunning, John H. 1958. *American Investment in British Manufacturing Industry*. London: George Allen and Unwin (reprinted by Arno Press, New York, 1976).

———. 1988. "The Eclectic Paradigm of International Production: A Restatement and Some Possible Extensions," *Journal of International Business Studies* 19(1):1-31.

———. 1994. "Re-evaluating the Benefits of Foreign Direct Investment," *Transnational Corporations* 3(1):23-50.

Encarnation, Dennis, and Mark Mason. 1994. "Does Ownership Matter? Answers and Implications for Europe and America," in *Does Ownership Matter? Japanese Multinationals in Europe*, edited by Mark Mason and Dennis Encarnation. Oxford: Clarendon Press, pp. 441-448.

Feenstra, Robert. 1993. "Discussion Summary," in *Foreign Direct Investment*, edited by Kenneth Froot. Chicago: University of Chicago Press, pp. 83-84.

Frantz, Douglas, and Catherine Collins. 1989. *Selling Out: How We Are Letting Japan Buy Our Land, Our Industries, Our Financial Institutions, and Our Future*. Chicago: Contemporary Books.

Froot, Kenneth, ed. 1993. *Foreign Direct Investment*. Chicago: University of Chicago Press.

Glickman, Norman J., and Douglas P. Woodward. 1990. *The New Competitors: How Foreign Investors Are Changing the U.S. Economy*. New York: Basic Books.

Graham, Edward M., and Paul R. Krugman. 1989. *Foreign Direct Investment in the United States*. Washington, D.C.: Institute for International Economics.

———. 1993. "The Surge in Foreign Direct Investment in the 1980s," in *Foreign Direct Investment*, edited by Kenneth Froot. Chicago: University of Chicago Press, pp. 13-33.

———. 1995. *Foreign Direct Investment in the United States*. Third edition. Washington, D.C.: Institute for International Economics.

Heimlich, Richard W. 1990. "Calling into Question 'Who Is Us,'" *Harvard Business Review*, May-June.

Howenstine, Ned G., and Dale P. Shannon. 1996. "Differences in Foreign-Owned U.S. Manufacturing Establishments by Country of Owner," *Survey of Current Business* 76(March): 43-60.

Hu, Yao-Su. 1992. "Global or Stateless Corporations Are National Firms with International Operations," *California Management Review*, Winter, pp. 106-137.

Julius, DeAnne. 1990. *Global Companies and Public Policy: The Growing Challenge of Foreign Direct Investment*. New York: Council on Foreign Relations.

Kenney, Martin, and Richard L. Florida. 1991. "How Japanese Industry Is Rebuilding the Rust Belt," *Technology Review* 94(Feb-Mar):24-33.

Kreinin, Mordechai E. 1988. "How Closed Is the Japanese Market: Additional Evidence," *The World Economy* 11(4):529-542.

Krugman, Paul. 1996. *Pop Internationalism*. Cambridge, Mass.: MIT Press.

Kwan, Ronald. 1991. "Footloose and Country Free," *Dollars and Sense*, March, pp. 6-9, 21.

Lipsey, Robert E., and Irving B. Kravis. 1986. "The Competitiveness and Comparative Advantage of U.S. Multinationals, 1957-1983," *NBER Working Paper No. 2051*, October.

Logan, David. 1994. *Community Involvement of Foreign-Owned Companies*, Report Number 1089-94-RR. New York: The Conference Board.

Mason, Mark, and Dennis J. Encarnation, eds. 1994. *Does Ownership Matter? Japanese Multinationals in Europe*. Oxford: Oxford University Press.

McCulloch, Rachel. 1993. "New Perspectives on Foreign Direct Investment," in *Foreign Direct Investment*, edited by Kenneth A. Froot. Chicago: University of Chicago Press, pp. 37-53.

Nigh, Douglas. 1997. "Who's on First? Nation-States, National Identity, and Multinational Corporations," in *International Business: An Emerging Vision*, edited by Brian Toyne and Douglas Nigh. Columbia, S.C.: University of South Carolina Press.

Office of Technology Assessment (OTA). 1993. *Multinationals and the National Interest: Playing By Different Rules*, OTA-ITE-569. Washington, D.C.: GPO.

Ohmae, Kenichi. 1990. *The Borderless World: Power and Strategy in the Interlinked Economy*. New York: Harper Business.

Porter, Michael E. 1990. *The Competitive Advantage of Nations*. New York: Free Press (MacMillan, Inc).

Prestowitz, Clyde V., Jr. 1988. *Trading Places: How We Allowed the Japanese to Take the Lead*. New York: Basic Books.

Ray, Edward J. 1989. "The Determinants of Foreign Direct Investment in the United States: 1979-1985," in *Trade Policies for International Competitiveness*, edited by Robert Feenstra. Chicago: University of Chicago Press, pp. 53-77.

————.1995. "Old Myths and New Realities in Foreign Direct Investment in the United States," *International Trade Journal* 9(2):225-246.

Reich, Robert B. 1990. "Who Is Us?" *Harvard Business Review* 68(January-February):53-64.

————. 1991a. "Who Is Them?" *Harvard Business Review*, March-April, pp. 77-88.

————. 1991b. "Who Do We Think They Are?" *The American Prospect*, Winter: 49.

————. 1991c. *The Work of Nations*. New York: Alfred A. Knopf.

Rosenzweig, Philip M. 1994. "Management Practices in U.S. Affiliates of Foreign-Owned Firms: Are 'They' Just Like 'Us'?" *International Executive* 36 (4):393-410.

Servan-Schreiber, J. J. 1968. *The American Challenge*. New York: Atheneum.

Tolchin, Martin, and Susan Tolchin. 1988. *Buying into America: How Foreign Money Is Changing the Face of Our Nation*. New York: Times Books.

Tyson, Laura D'Andrea. 1991. "They Are Not Us: Why American Ownership Still Matters," *The American Prospect*, Winter: 37-49.

Vernon, Raymond. 1993. "Where are the Multinationals Headed?" in *Foreign Direct Investment*, edited by Kenneth A. Froot. Chicago: University of Chicago Press, pp. 57-79.

United Nations. 1994. *World Investment Report 1994: Transnational Corporations, Employment and the Workplace*. New York: United Nations, Conference on Trade and Development, Division on Transnational Corporations (UNCTAD).

————. 1997. *The World Investment Report, 1997: Transnational Corporations, Market Structure and Competition Policy*. New York: United Nations, Conference on Trade and Development (UNCTAD), Division on Transnationals and Investment.

Part I

FDI in a Globalizing Economy

1

Does Ownership Really Matter in a Globalizing Economy?

John H. Dunning

INTRODUCTION

This chapter discusses ownership, multinationality, and related issues facing international business research as global corporate alliances become increasingly more complex. At the outset, it may be useful to make three semantic points. First, on the question of ownership per se, this chapter will be concerned principally with the nationality of a multinational enterprise (MNE), which is usually identified as the home country of the firm, that is, the country in which the firm is incorporated and has its head office.[1] But, as foreign direct investment (FDI), the modality by which firms extend their value-added activities outside their national borders, becomes directed toward more countries, the nationality of a firm (except, perhaps, in the strict legal sense) becomes more porous, and its distinctive characteristics stem increasingly from the extent, depth, and form of its multinationality rather than from its "foreignness."

Second, although de jure the boundaries of a firm may be demarcated by its ownership, increasingly and especially over the past decade other forms of cross-border activities that affect the firm's performance and spheres of influence have become more important. Notably among these are non-equity strategic alliances and interfirm networks. While the propensity to engage in such nonhierarchical relationships may vary with a firm's nationality of ownership,[2] the main consequence of this phenomenon is, like the growth of multinationality per se, a shift of scholarly interest away from the issue of the "foreignness" of the ownership to the ways in which the firm's conduct and competitiveness are influenced by its interaction with foreign firms, and whether these are by way of FDI or some kind of non-equity collaborative agreements. We shall return to this point later.

Third, it is important to distinguish between the differences ownership and control may make to a firm's performance and the impact on the economic and social welfare of the countries in which it operates, as well as the implications of such differences for government policies. This is particularly important for those firms of countries that are hosts to the affiliates of foreign enterprises. Does the word "matter" mean "In what sense does nationality of ownership affect economic performance?" or, given its effect on economic performance, "To what extent should action be taken to discriminate for and against firms according to ownership?"

In short, then, our focus of interest needs to be clear. Is the interest in ownership in the strictly legal sense or in the sense that it permits control or influence on economic activity? If the latter, then this brief becomes wider and more interesting. Similarly, can we afford to neglect issues of multinationality, cf. "foreignness," in discussing the consequences of globalization on the performance of firms? We think not. And, third, surely we must consider both interpretations of the term "matters," if we are to offer any sensible guidance to policy makers regarding the behavior of foreign affiliates compared to domestic-owned firms and multinational[3] enterprises.

PREVIOUS RESEARCH ON (FOREIGN) OWNERSHIP ISSUES

The title of this chapter was chosen primarily because events now occurring in the world economy, most of which are leading toward the deeper structural economic independence of countries, require a reconsideration of the answers previously given by economists and other analysts to the question, "Does ownership matter?" These date back at least to the last quarter of the nineteenth century, when U.S. interests were becoming increasingly concerned about the economic impact of the surge of U.K. FDI in several parts of the United States (notably in the midwest and far west) and in some key sectors (notably railroads, nonferrous mining, brewing, cattle ranching and meat packing, and insurance)[4]; while at the same time, the no less rapid penetration by U.S.-owned firms into the U.K. electrical equipment, tobacco, boot and shoe machinery, and drug industries was regarded by some commentators (McKenzie 1902) as an "invasion" of the United Kingdom by U.S. commercial interests. It was, perhaps, in this era that the initial rumblings of xenophobia began to be heard, although it was not until much later that the first attempts to theorize about and test empirically the specific attributes and effects of "foreignness" were made.

Following some earlier work by Frank Southard (1931), many scholarly studies have confirmed that foreign-owned affiliates do perform differently—and on the whole better—than domestic-owned firms in at least certain sectors.[5] Initially, this superiority of performance was largely attributed to the country-specific or ownership-specific (O) competitive advantages of the parent companies, that is, the investing companies, which were then transferred to the affiliates. However, increasingly over the years, attention has switched to those O advantages of MNEs, which reflect not so much their country of origin as the extent and form of their multinationality and the organization and coordination of their foreign value-added activities. Bruce Kogut (1983) has referred to these as sequential FDI advantages, while the internalization scholars prefer to think of them as transaction-related advantages. The competitive advantages of an enterprise that arise from its privileged possession of a particular asset or group of assets (Oa advantages) are distinguished from those that arise from the way it coordinates these advantages with others (both at home and abroad). These latter (Ot) advantages include those associated with economies of common governance and reduced forms of cross-border risk. While the former are likely to be (home) country specific, the latter arise from the extent and form of the firm's multinationality and the way it organizes its portfolio of domestic and foreign assets. By contrast, strategic asset-acquiring FDI is primarily intended to augment a firm's O specific advantages with those of another firm— usually, but not exclusively, one located in an advanced industrial country. More recently, economists have focused on the role FDI plays in augmenting home-based O advantages (Dunning 1995).

The weight of empirical research has also concluded that the effects of both "foreignness" and multinationality tend to be activity or industry specific. There is some suggestion that contemporary technological and organizational developments favor MNE activity in sectors in which, until quite recently, there was little FDI[6] or alliance-related activity. Other studies have concluded that, when normalized at a three-digit Standard Industrial Classification (SIC) level, the differences in productivity and profitability of foreign, compared to domestic, firms are less pronounced than suggested by some commentators (Solomon and Ingham 1977). There is also some evidence that, over time, the performance gap between the two groups of firms has tended to narrow (Dunning 1985), as has the gap that can be traced specifically to their nationality of ownership (Davies and Lyons 1991). This reflects, in part, the competitive-stimulating knowledge transfer and learning-inducing effects that FDI has on indigenous firms, and, in part, the fact that these indigenous firms have themselves upgraded their O advantages by becoming multinational or by increasing their degrees of multinationality.

One further finding of scholarly research is also worth mentioning. The performance of both foreign-owned affiliates and MNEs, taken as a whole, varies according to nationality; this difference is sector specific and dependent on the country-specific O advantages of the firms in question. For example, in most European countries, in Canada, and in Australia, the performance of U.S.-controlled firms consistently outstripped their other foreign-owned competitors, particularly in technology intensive sectors, until the major upsurge in Japanese FDI in the late 1980s (OECD 1994). In only a few technology-intensive manufacturing industries, in mining, and in trade-related activities did foreign affiliates (of any nationality) do better than their indigenous competitors in the United States. This suggests that the O specific advantages of U.S. firms tend to be different from those of their non-U.S. competitors (Graham and Krugman 1991).[7] In Europe, Japanese affiliates tend to do relatively better than their U.S. counterparts in sectors in which the former record the most pronounced comparative trading advantages, such as the auto and consumer electronics sectors (Dunning 1994). Again, however, it would appear that the nationality of ownership is becoming a less important determinant of productivity, particularly in sectors that are mostly globalized in their activities.

Thus, while all performance measures of firms (be they of the global activities of firms or of particular foreign affiliates) should be treated with a great deal of caution (Dunning 1993, chapter 16), empirical data on the comparative productivity, growth, and profitability of such enterprises[8] suggest that *(i)* these are supportive of the earlier industrial organizational theories of FDI (Hymer 1960; Caves 1971, 1974) and *(ii)* as FDI has become increasingly sequential rather than first-time,[9] the Oa assets of firms of different nationalities have tended to converge, while the Ot assets of firms have rested more on the capabilities to organize a multicountry portfolio of resources and capabilities than on the nationality of ownership per se. The reasons for this second interpretation of the data are now discussed in more detail.

GLOBALIZATION AND ITS IMPLICATIONS FOR FDI

That the unique feature of the globalizing economy[10] is the increasing structural integration of national economies has already been suggested. Further, this is being accomplished primarily through FDI and transnational interfirm agreements, rather than through the arm's-length trade of goods and assets.

Firms and the Globalizing Economy

At a microeconomic level, firms differ considerably in the extent to which they integrate their cross-border value-added activities. Moreover, inside any particular MNE, some functions are likely to be more integrated than others. But, there is little doubt that there is a trend away from *stand alone* FDIs (or the multidomestic MNE[11]) and toward a *network of inter-related foreign affiliates*, each engaging in value-added activities, and pursuing a strategy consistent with the global product and production strategies of their parent enterprises, even though, numerically, most MNEs, particularly those from developing countries, practice simple resource or market-seeking strategies.

This trend, which is likely to continue for the foreseeable future—albeit at a different pace, according to the size, foreign experience, and country of origin of the MNE and the raison d'être for its FDI—is fundamentally a product of a number of major happenings in the global economy. Four of these may be especially highlighted.

1. Advances in informatics and telecommunications have dramatically increased the capacity to process and communicate information over space, while reducing the costs of doing so. These advances, by lowering the transactional and coordination costs of value-added activity, have increased the opportunities for firms to take advantage of the cross-border economies of scale and scope and have pushed back the spatial boundaries of their value-adding activities.

2. There has been a renaissance of the market economy (particularly in the erstwhile Communist countries, China and India) and the privatization or liberalization of many product markets (noticeably in communications and financial services) in many Western economies. In particular, the removal or reduction of trade barriers has enabled firms to rationalize product and process structures within spatially integrated areas and to achieve economies of governance not possible in segmented markets. The restructuring of value-added activities, by both European and non-European MNEs, has been particularly noticeable in the European Community (EC) (now the European Union [EU]) over the past three-and-one-half decades. Prior to 1958, most FDI in Europe was of an import-substituting variety, and the ownership advantages of the investing firms were mainly those which they possessed *prior to* the establishment of European affiliates. Since that date (especially since the Internal Market program was initiated in 1985), most inbound MNE activity directed to individual member states has been geared to supplying

the EC market in toto and to capturing the benefits of an integrated product, production, and marketing strategy[12] sequential to the initial FDI.

3. Partly as a result of "1" and "2" and partly because of the rapid industrialization of emerging economies (especially in East Asia), established Western enterprises and particularly MNEs have been subjected to increasing competitive pressures. These pressures, coupled with the accelerating pace and rising costs of technological change and the value placed by consumers on the innovation and upgrading of products, have compelled firms to restructure their resources, capabilities, and location portfolios, and to seek ever-widening markets. The twin features of much of this restructuring, which is being undertaken at a time when the Fordist paradigm of mass production is being replaced with the Toyota paradigm of flexible production,[13] are that *(a)* firms are tending to increasingly specialize in those activities that, relative to their competitors, they perceive they are best equipped to undertake, and *(b)* rather than completely to disinternalize the remaining activities[14] (particularly those the efficiency and upgrading of which would significantly affect the value of their core assets), firms are concluding a plurality of collaborative arrangements (with their competitors, suppliers, or customers) to ensure that their own competitive positions are best advanced.

Elsewhere, we have referred to the latter feature of economic restructuring as "alliance" or "cooperative" capitalism[15] (Dunning 1995). As its name implies, to be effective, such capitalism requires an organizational structure that balances the advantages of cooperation and competition. At a more microeconomic level, it suggests that, to be successful, firms must not only create and sustain a range of core competencies[16] but also organize these in conjunction with those of other firms and the location-specific endowments and markets of countries in the best possible way. (Foreign) ownership then matters insofar as firms of one nationality are better able than others to achieve this task. And, there is, indeed, some suggestion that, over the last two decades, Japanese-owned firms have demonstrated qualities of both intra- and interfirm collaboration that are superior to those of their European and U.S. counterparts (Mason and Encarnation 1994). While the unique Japanese Oa and Ot advantages leading to the recent internalization of Japanese MNEs may be difficult to establish, relative to those of U.S. MNEs in the 1950s and 1960s, the Ot component was (and is) higher (Dunning 1994). However, the extent to which these advantages can be transferred to a foreign location or will remain Japanese specific in the future remains to be seen.[17]

4. The movement toward complex integration by MNEs and away from the significance of "foreignness" as a competitive variable is being aided by some convergence of consumer tastes across national boundaries and by an increasing pressure from consumers, especially in advanced industrial countries, for a continual improvement in product performance and quality. Illustrative of the growing uniformity of tastes are Nike sports shoes, jeans, electronic goods, cameras, and recorded music; and of innovation-led demand are better and more efficient computers, drugs, autos, and telecommunication equipment. Both facets of demand are making for more concentrated marketing strategies by MNEs. Although there are few examples of truly global goods, there can surely be little doubt, except in the case of goods with substantial (natural) resource content, that the differences in product composition and characteristics of goods and services that can be specifically attributed to the nationality of an enterprise are much less marked than they were fifty or even thirty years ago.[18]

It is our contention that each of these features of the global economy, together with the growing harmonization of technical standards and of environmental regulations across countries—and particularly among advanced industrial countries—is changing (and for the most part reducing) the significance of the "foreignness" of ownership as a factor influencing the performance of firms. Further, in its place, the geographic profile of a firm's assets and the way it organizes these assets in conjunction with those of other institutions are becoming the more distinctive attributes of ownership.

There is, however, an important caveat to our general argument, which has been put forward by some analysts. This concerns the *kind* of value-added activities of firms by different nationalities of ownership. For example, a well-documented fact is that the high value activities of MNEs—including those of globally integrated MNEs—are much more strongly concentrated in their home country than elsewhere. In 1992, for example, only 12.4 percent of the global research and development (R&D) expenditure of U.S. nonbank MNEs was undertaken outside the United States, compared with 32.0 percent of the total sales of these companies (Mataloni 1994). Despite the growth of regional offices, some administrative functions have been decentralized, particularly those related to manufacturing or service activities that also have been decentralized,[19] and more heterarchical organizational structures—for example, by MNEs such as Asea Brown Boveri (ABB)—have evolved. The majority of high-value, office-related, and critical decision-making activities continue to be concentrated in the home countries of MNEs.

Notwithstanding the trend toward a structurally integrated world economy, the different emphases given to the critical decision-making functions and asset-creating activities between foreign affiliates and their indigenous competitors suggest that ownership *does* matter. Indeed, one of the scenarios most feared by many policy makers in both developing and developed countries (which will be addressed in more detail in the following section) is that inbound FDI, far from upgrading the quality of indigenous resources, will lock the host country into a division of labor, in which the higher value activities are undertaken by the investing companies in the home country and the lower value activities undertaken by "satellite" affiliates in host countries. This concern has been frequently expressed with respect to the possible effects of the Japanese on Europe (Strange 1993).[20]

How far can the differences just described be attributed to the "foreignness" of the investing company? Most surely, part of the difference in the product or process structure of a foreign affiliate, compared with that of its indigenous competition, arises simply because the former is a branch plant of an enterprise whose headquarters are in a different location. Two U.S.–owned pharmaceutical firms producing in, say, Ohio (one a branch of a New Jersey corporation and the other a major U.S. MNE with its higher value-added activities centralized in Ohio) might reveal differences similar to those demonstrated between a Swiss-owned branch plant and the same major U.S. MNE. To isolate the foreign ownership from the branch plant effect is not easy, although, for reasons stated earlier, hypothetically, the former is becoming less important as the larger MNEs become less easily identifiable with their home countries. On the one hand, normalizing for industrial activity, there appears to be some convergence in the degree of multinationalization of the investing companies in the kinds of value-added activities carried out in home and foreign countries by MNEs of different nationalities. On the other hand, once one gets down to a four- or five-digit SIC level, it is possible to discriminate among the competitive advantages of firms—particularly with respect to their innovating capabilities—of different countries.[21]

Countries and the Globalizing Economy

Clearly, the location-bound characteristics of countries or regions (such as size, stage of development, portfolio of physical assets, and the policies pursued by their governments) will critically influence both the amount of FDI (attracted and generated) and the kind and quality of that investment. In other words, from a *macro-economic* perspective, the unique characteristics of foreign-owned, compared to indigenously owned, firms are partly determined by economic and other factors exogenous to the firms themselves but endogenous to the environment in which they operate.

Until the later 1980s, there were substantial differences in both the macro-economic and macro-organizational strategies of governments across the world. At one extreme, inbound FDI either was not permitted at all or was restricted in amount or sectoral distribution; at the other extreme, FDI was freely permitted. Between these two extremes, governments offered a wide mixture of incentives and disincentives, which, in one way or another, affected not just the flow of FDI but also its distinctive qualities and its impact on the local economy. In general and ceteris paribus, the more regulatory the policies adopted toward FDI, the more obvious were the operating differences between foreign-owned affiliates and domestic firms. By contrast, in the case of countries pursuing more liberal policies and especially those advanced countries that generated their own MNEs, the "foreignness" of FDI was less evident. Such countries, unlike the former group, attracted rationalized and efficiency-seeking investment, the principal purpose of which was to exploit the benefits of multinationality per se for the investing companies.[22]

During the 1990s, there has been a remarkable convergence in the attitudes and policies of governments throughout the world to both inbound and outbound FDI (Dunning 1993; OECD 1989; United Nations 1995). Most noticeably, many policy instruments by governments, which had discriminated for or against foreign investors, have been scrapped, while restrictions on outbound MNE activity have been dramatically reduced. As the principle of national treatment toward foreign-owned companies has become more widely accepted, so at least some aspects of FDI, which responded to earlier discrimination in favor of or against FDI, have disappeared. In other words, if there is no difference in the treatment of firms according to their nationality, the national characteristics of their conduct are likely to be less distinct. This, coupled with the convergence in the economic structure of at least the larger industrial economies (Narula 1996) and the removal of many intraregional barriers to trade and investment, is bringing about a convergence of national economic environments and, because of this, the behavior of governments toward FDI.

There is, however, one important exception to this general hypothesis. One of the paradoxes of the contemporary global economy is that, on the one hand, the liberalization and deregulation of markets is reducing the direct interventionist role of national governments; on the other hand, governments have an increasing role to support created assets like transportation and communications infrastructure and human resource development.[23] Several recent research studies have shown that FDI, particularly that in globally integrated sectors, is increasingly searching for a location that offers a portfolio of immobile assets which might best complement the distinctive core competencies of the investing firms. In a real sense, governments both of countries and of regions within countries (such as states in the United States) compete with each other to attract FDI, in the belief that its special qualities (including the access it provides to an international network of suppliers, customers, and competitors) will help the upgrading of their domestic capabilities. Thus, governments believe not only that ownership and multinationality matter but also that governmental actions may affect the extent to which and exactly how they matter.

THE EFFECTS OF FOREIGN OWNERSHIP AND GLOBALIZATION

So far in this chapter, we have concentrated on the differential competitive or O specific *characteristics* of MNEs and their foreign affiliates.[24] But globalization is no less affecting the distinctive *consequences* of foreign ownership. For example, a great deal of literature compares the extent to which foreign affiliates engage in more or less capital- or knowledge-intensive production methods or are likely to invest more or less in skill and human resource development or learning experiences than their indigenous competitors (Dunning 1993, chapter 11). The consensus among scholars is that, in import-substituting sectors of highly regulated economies, foreign-owned (and particularly American) firms tend to utilize more capital-intensive and less labor-intensive techniques than their local counterparts; in more open economies (most noticeably in advanced industrial economies), this is not the case. Moreover, as economies have become more integrated and an increasing number of companies are engaging in FDI,[25] best practice techniques are becoming increasingly similar among firms of similar size and degrees of multinationality.[26]

Similarly, in the 1990s, there are only a few areas in which nationality of ownership is an important variable affecting human resource development among the larger MNEs. Even those emanating from different cultures tend to adapt their work practices and industrial relations to local conditions. Apart from some Japanese-owned companies, training procedures are more likely to be based on "global" best practice than on that implemented by the parent company. This was not the case in the early postwar period, when, in Europe for example, the employment and human resource development strategies of U.S. subsidiaries strongly influenced those of their home countries, and in consequence were different from those of their European competitors (Dunning 1958).

Although these illustrations are from just two operating areas of a firm's activities, the conclusions are no less applicable to other areas, such as sourcing, marketing, and logistical decision making. In each case, while the country of origin of a particular firm continues to be of some relevance, the consequences of the multinationality of its activities are becoming the more significant discriminatory factor among firms.[27] However, as already stated, there are exceptions to the general principle, where (home) country-specific characteristics continue to be of foremost significance. These are particularly noticeable in the case of first time investors and in a variety of intrafirm relationships. For example, the management recruitment and training and financial control techniques of even the most globally integrated Japanese MNEs are different from those of their European counterparts; differences in country-specific business cultures continue to exercise considerable sway in the content and significance of interfirm transactions and agreements.

In short, then, the globalizing economy is increasing the awareness of governments of the benefits of both outward and inward FDI, particularly toward the upgrading of the competitiveness of indigenous resources and capabilities. However, many of the benefits sought arise less from the nationality of the investing firms and more from the extent to which they can draw upon and efficiently organize a complex portfolio of geographically dispersed mobile and immobile assets, and link the wealth-creating institutions in the countries in which they operate to an international network of suppliers and customers and factor markets.

DOES OWNERSHIP MATTER? THE POLICY DIMENSION

Previous sections have argued that nationality of ownership continues to affect the core competencies of firms and the ways in which these are combined with the location-bound assets of the countries in which they operate. At the same time, we have suggested that the precise significance of the "foreignness" as compared with the "branch plant," "degree of multinationality," and other attributes of foreign affiliates, compared to domestic firms, is likely to be country, industry, and firm specific and to be critically dependent on the raison d'etre and quality of the FDI.

But, assuming ownership does make a difference to the prosperity of both firms and countries (whether a positive or negative difference), what, if anything, should policy makers do about it? Does ownership matter in the sense that foreign-owned firms should be treated any differently from domestic-owned firms? Should national governments modify their macroeconomic policies, given the growing interdependence of these policies with those of countries with which they compete for mobile created assets? Does the deepening of cross-border trading and FDI relationships and the globalization or regionalization of economic activity impinge on these policies and, if so, in what way?

While a complete answer to these questions would require a separate chapter, one general observation is that, as an economy opens its borders to international commerce, this will affect not only the welfare of its firms and citizens but also the options open to governments to influence the extent and consequences of that "openness." The overwhelming consensus of economic analysis, however, suggests that governments should only consider intervening (on economic grounds) in the restructuring of production and markets brought about by trade and investment in two instances. The first is where the cross-border markets for the products and assets exchanged are distorted by the behavior of one or another of the participants in the market. The second is where some kind of endemic market failure exists, such as that which reflects uncertainty over future demand or supply conditions, the (social) costs of structural adjustment change, the extent and pattern of externalities, the unique character of the market or of the goods or services traded, and the inability of producers to supply a cost-effective level of output without affecting the price elasticity of demand.[28]

Of course, the fact that structural or endemic market failure exists does not necessarily mean that governments *should* intervene to lower the transaction and coordinating costs of economic activity; for it may well be the case that the costs of nonmarket (such as government) failure exceed those of the market and hierarchies. It does, however, open up the possibility that, by themselves, market forces may be insufficient to cope, in a socially optimum way, with such failures.

Two questions now arise. The first is, Does globalization, by affecting the parameters of decision making by firms of different nationalities of ownership, lead to more or fewer market imperfections and hence require a reappraisal of government policy? Assuming the answer is "yes," the second question is, What should be the appropriate response of governments?

The consensus of scholarly research is that while the events of the last twenty or more years have reduced the structural imperfections in cross-border markets, including the distorting effects of nonmarket intervention, these same events have probably increased the likelihood of endemic market failure, which would suggest that governments might react more positively to FDI-related activities. The kind of government intervention (intervention is perhaps an unfortunate word) that endemic market failure requires, however, is rather different from that required by structural market failure. Again, the distinction between FDI and the multinationality of a firm's operations is an important one. In the 1960s and 1970s, for example, host governments intervened in the market for the kind of assets supplied by MNEs in the belief that it was structurally distorted (such as by unacceptable monopolistic or oligopolistic practices of the MNEs) or because the behavior or activities of foreign affiliates were perceived to be "inappropriate" to the needs of the indigenous population. Regulations on the amount and kind of FDI and the imposition of performance requirements were typical responses to this situation, although frequently, like some of the import substitution policies that led to the FDI in the first place, these reduced rather than improved economic welfare.

In the 1990s, the main criterion for evaluating inbound FDI is its contribution to the long-term and stable growth of the domestic economy and to the dynamic comparative advantage of its location-bound natural and created assets. Government action toward FDI is, then, increasingly centered on eliminating or reducing those elements of endemic market failure that inhibit this contribution. Such failure tends to be most pronounced in regionally or globally integrated industrial sectors because it is in those sectors that the geographical diversification of FDI and of a network of interfirm alliances is most pronounced. We have also seen, in the previous section of this chapter, that government policies can play a critical role in influencing the kind of FDI attracted to host countries and that, as intergovernment competition for FDI increases, the kind of policies most likely to be welfare enhancing are those that work with, rather than against, market forces. Exceptions may include the strategic countering of structurally distorting policies of other governments, and situations where it is difficult to achieve international acceptance on a level playing field for trade and FDI-related activities.

While, then, not denying there still may be occasions when governments need to take specific action to reduce structurally distorting strategies of foreign affiliates (which may be attributed to their "foreignness" per se), the globalizing economy is challenging governments to reappraise their *general* macroeconomic and macro-organizational policies (that is, those which do not discriminate among firms of different ownership). This is because of the increasing ease with which firms can move their O specific advantages across national boundaries and conclude non-equity R&D, production, and marketing agreements with foreign suppliers, customers, and competitors. The net result of these trends is that while governments in the 1990s acknowledge the distinctiveness of FDI, they need to recognize that the nature of that distinction has changed and, with it, the kind of policies that they need to implement if the net benefits of that investment (and similar cross-border transactions) are to be maximized.

SUMMARY AND CONCLUSION

The main purpose of this chapter is to clarify some issues about the importance of the nationality of ownership of firms in a globalizing economy. In its initial stages, FDI may be made possible by the distinctive O specific advantages of investing firms, which primarily arise from their internalizing the location-specific advantages of their home countries. As firms become more multinational, these competitive advantages are augmented, often increasingly so, by those derived from access to a portfolio of differentiated (often location-specific) assets in other countries.

The growing multinationalization of firms over the last two or more decades has gone hand-in-hand with the liberalization of cross-border markets and a dramatic reduction in transport and communication costs. This has led to a reconfiguration of the characteristics of the ownership of firms, away from their home countries and toward the extent and pattern of their internationalization. However, in some sectors and for some MNEs (particularly those venturing abroad for the first time) the "foreignness" of a company may still be an important determinant of its behavior, although, even in these cases, it is important to distinguish between the differences in the conduct and performance of foreign affiliates that reflect their branch plant and those that reflect their ownership status.

This chapter suggests that globalization is narrowing the functional differences (such as in the areas of innovation, human resource development, and production systems) among firms (especially MNEs) of different nationalities. The more significant differentiating variable may now be the portfolio of foreign assets that firms own or to which they have privileged access.[29]

Finally, we discuss the question, Does the nationality of firms engaging in value-adding activities within a country affect the economic policies of the government of that country? The discussion begins with an analysis of the rationale for any kind of government intervention and how such intervention might be affected by opening an economy first to arm's-length trade in goods, services, and assets and then to deeper forms of cross-border integration (such as FDI and interfirm alliances). A distinction is made between government intervention to ameliorate structural market imperfections and intervention to reduce endemic market failure. This chapter argues that recent economic events and, in particular, the regionalization or globalization of markets are tending to reduce the structural distorting effects of FDI (and hence the distinctive characteristics of foreign ownership associated with these effects) and to increase the transaction and coordination costs of more complex, specialized, interdependent market transactions.

In the globalizing economy of the 1990s, the relationship between governments and MNEs is less adversarial and more cooperative than it was two or three decades ago, chiefly because the access to an international network of created assets that the modern MNE offers host countries is often critical to advancing country competitiveness. At the same time, to be globally competitive, MNEs need to establish a value-added presence in the major markets of the world. This leads to a synergy of interests between MNEs and governments and a recognition by the latter that only by facilitating efficient markets and aiding the protection and upgrading of the quality of the countries' physical and human resources to attract the unique qualities of FDI can their long term goals be reached. Similarly, with respect to outbound FDI, home governments are increasingly recognizing the contributions of such investment to domestic economic welfare and are framing their general macroeconomic and macro-organizational policies to ensure that their own MNEs are not disadvantaged relative to those of foreign competitors.

NOTES

1. There are, of course, other criteria for identifying and delineating corporate nationality. These include the place of control and decision making of a corporation. Such criteria are currently adopted by several Organisation for Economic Co-operation and Development (OECD) countries in bilateral or multilateral investment treaties. Most definitions of a direct investment enterprise accept that its de facto control or influence may extend to companies in which it has an equity stake as low as 10 percent (Organisation for Economic Co-operation and Development 1993; 1995).

2. For example, in the past, Japanese firms have been more prone to engage in non-equity relationships with foreign firms than with U.S. firms.

3. While the shares of most multinational enterprises (MNEs) are owned by institutions and individuals in many countries, there are relatively few MNEs with headquarters in more than one country or which are multinationally controlled.

4. This is described in detail by Wilkins (1989).

5. These studies are summarized in Chapter 16 of Dunning (1993) and OECD (1994). For a more recent analysis, see a selection of papers presented at an NBER Conference on "Geography and Ownership as Bases for Economic Accounting," held in Washington, D.C., on May 19-20, 1995.

6. Recent examples include public infrastructure development and public utilities, textiles and clothing, and iron and steel especially in developing countries (United Nations 1996). Partly, at least, this new wave of FDI (and also of non-equity collaborative arrangements) reflects the desire to capture Ot advantages rather than exploit Oa advantages by the investing companies.

7. In a more recent study of the operating characteristics of manufacturing plants in the United States, Doms and Jensen (1995) found that plants owned by U.S. MNEs pay higher wages and are the most capital intensive and the most productive, followed by foreign-owned plants owned by large domestic-oriented firms and plants of small domestic size. The authors conclude that "MNEs possess firm specific advantages allowing them to overcome the costs of FDI." This research has been augmented in chapter 3 of this volume.

8. This includes that of MNEs from the Third World, the industrial distribution of whose FDI is different from that of their developed country counterparts.

9. This is evident even though the number of first-time FDIs, particularly from developing countries, has continued to rise. But, over the ten-year period 1982-1992, at least three-quarters of the increase in FDI stock has been through the modality of reinvested profits and mergers and acquisitions by established MNEs.

10. We prefer the expression "globalizing" to "globalized," as the former expresses a movement toward a particular spatial dimension of economic activity rather than an event that has already occurred.

11. Michael Porter (1990) distinguishes between multidomestic MNEs, which own a group of largely autonomous foreign affiliates who largely supply the market of the countries in which they operate, and integrated MNEs, which treat their foreign affiliates as part and parcel of a globally integrated strategy. In their various publications, UNCTAD-DTCI (United Nations 1993; 1994; 1996) categorize MNEs (or transnational corporations) into three groups: *(i)* those which own or control standalone affiliates that operate largely as independent firms within the host country and that are truncated versions of the parent firm; *(ii)* those which operate a strategy of *simple integration*, such as the out-sourcing of clothing production by the large retail stores and of athletic shoes by Nike; and *(iii)* those which practice a *complex integration* strategy, by which a large number of the functional areas (such as research and development, procurement, and manufacturing) of a MNE are, to some extent, integrated across national boundaries, with most affiliates specializing in a relatively narrow range of value-added activities rather than replicating those of their parent companies.

12. For examples of how the distinctive characteristics of ownership have become more related to degrees of multinationality rather than to the nationality of the investing firms, see Mason and Encarnation (1994) and UNCTAD-DTCI (United Nations 1993).

13. This paradigmatic shift in manufacturing techniques is described in several monographs and papers, notably Best (1990) and Womack, Jones, and Roos (1991).

14. By which we mean, substitute a hierarchical for an arm's length market transaction.

15. Sometimes called "relational" or the "new" capitalism.

16. This is the central tenet of the resource-based theory of the firm.

17. While Kogut (1993) has suggested organizational competencies may take longer to transfer across national boundaries than do hard technologies, there is some suggestion that such competencies have been assimilated—sometimes with modification—by firms of other nationalities. For example, the productivity gap between U.S. and Japanese owned automobile producers has considerably narrowed since the mid-1980s, while there has been some convergence in the subcontracting practices of Japanese auto affiliates in the United States and their domestic competitors (Banjerjii and Sambharya 1996).

18. The classic example is the automobile. Compare, for example, U.S. and Japanese vehicles in the 1960s with their counterparts today. Casual observation would suggest this is no less the case for many other products.

19. What Michael Porter, in his various writings, is now referring to as multiple home bases.

20. Bearing in mind that the great bulk of Japanese FDI is less than fifteen years old, it is fair to say there is yet little evidence of this occurring.

21. As is revealed, for example, by patent statistics. In the 1980s, U.S. firms had a marked comparative patenting advantage in telecommunications, microelectronics, software, and biotechnology; Japanese firms in office machinery, photographic equipment, and robotics; British firms in pharmaceuticals; and Italian firms in design footwear and clothing (Cantwell and Hodson 1991).

22. This should not be taken to mean that foreign affiliates and domestic firms respond similarly to policy changes. Indeed, over the years, several studies have shown that the former, often because of their wider options, are more responsive to fiscal and other incentives and disincentives than are their indigenous counterparts (United Nations 1995).

23. For a discussion of the changing role of governments in a globalizing economy, see various chapters in Dunning (1997).

24. The reader may have observed that we have not discussed the advantages of *domestic*, compared to *foreign*-owned, firms, such as knowledge of local supply capabilities and markets, which were first identified by Hymer (1960).

25. Latest data from UNCTAD-DTCI suggest that, by the mid-1990s, there were around 40,000 MNEs with 270,000 foreign affiliates. Of these, just over 4,000 MNEs with more than 100,000 foreign affiliates were from developing countries (United Nations 1996).

26. This is particularly so in the internationally oriented sector, such as autos, pharmaceuticals, semiconductors, computers, and the like.

27. This is particularly well demonstrated in a survey of competitive advantages of some of the larger MNEs. By far the most important determinant of the extent to which the senior executives of the respondent firms perceived they derived their competitive advantages from their overseas operations was the degree of their multinationality, not their country of ownership or the type of activity in which they were engaged (Dunning 1996).

28. These are all well-known market failures, which have been copiously described and analyzed in the literature. For a recent and particularly incisive discussion of both market and government failures, see Chang (1994).

29. Although we would accept that such a portfolio cannot be completely divorced from the firm's nationality of ownership.

REFERENCES

Banjerjii, K., and R. B. Sambharya. 1996. "Vertical Keiretsu and International Market Entry," *Journal of International Business Studies* 27(1):89-113.

Best, Michael H. 1990. *The New Competition: Institutions of Industrial Restructuring*. Cambridge, Mass.: Harvard University Press.

Cantwell, John A., and C. Hodson. 1991. "Global R&D and British Competitiveness," in *Global Research Strategy and International Competitiveness*, edited by Mark C. Casson. Oxford: B. Blackwell, pp. 133-182.

Caves, Richard E. 1971. "International Corporations: The Industrial Economics of Foreign Investment," *Economica* 38(149):1-27.

———.1974. "Causes of Direct Investment: Foreign Firms' Shares in Canadian and United Kingdom Manufacturing Industries," *Review of Economics and Statistics* 56(August):272-293.

Chang, Ha-Joon. 1994. *The Political Economy of Industrial Policy*. New York: St. Martin's Press.

Davies, Stephen W., and B. R. Lyons. 1991. *Characterizing Relative Performance: The Productivity Advantages of Foreign Owned Firms in the U.K*. Norwich: University of East Anglia, mimeo.

Doms, Mark E., and J. Bradford Jensen. 1995. "A Comparison between Operating Characteristics of Domestic and Foreign Owned Manufacturing Establishments in the United States," paper prepared for the Conference on Research in Income and Wealth, Geography and Ownership as Bases for Economic Accounting, May.

Dunning, John H. 1958. *American Investment in British Manufacturing Industry*. London: George Allen and Unwin (reprinted by Arno Press, New York, 1976).

———. 1981. *International Production and the Multinational Enterprise*. London: George Allen and Unwin.

———. 1985. "The United Kingdom," in *Multinational Enterprises, Economic Structure, and International Competitiveness*, edited by John H. Dunning. Chichester: Wiley.

————. 1993. *Multinational Enterprises and the Global Economy*. Wokingham: Eddison-Wesley.

————. 1994. "The Strategy of Japanese and U.S. Manufacturing Investment in Europe," in *Does Ownership Matter? Japanese Multinationals in Europe*, edited by Mark Mason and Dennis J. Encarnation. Oxford: Clarendon Press, pp. 59-96.

————. 1995. "Reappraising the Eclectic Paradigm in the Age of Alliance Capitalism," *Journal of International Business Studies* 26(3):461-491.

————. 1996. "The Geographical Sources of Competitive Advantages of Firms." *Transnational Corporations* 5(3):1-31.

————, ed. 1997. *Governments, Globalization and International Business*. Oxford: Oxford University Press.

Florida, Richard L., and Martin Kenney. 1994. "The Globalization of Japanese R&D: The Economic Geography of Japanese R&D Investment in the United States," *Economic Geography* 70:344-369.

Graham, Edward M., and Paul R. Krugman. 1991. *Foreign Direct Investment in the United States*. Second edition. Washington, D.C.: Institute for International Economics.

Hymer, Stephen H. 1960. "The International Operations of National Firms: A Study of Direct Foreign Investment," doctoral dissertation, Massachusetts Institute of Technology (published by Cambridge, Mass.:M.I.T. Press, 1976).

Kogut, Bruce. 1983. "Foreign Direct Investment as a Sequential Process" in *The Multinational Corporation in the 1980s*, edited by Charles P. Kindleberger and David B. Audretsch. Cambridge, Mass.: MIT Press, pp. 38-56.

————, ed. 1993. *Country Competitiveness: Technology and the Organization of Work*. New York: Oxford University Press.

Mason, Mark, and Dennis J. Encarnation, eds. 1994. *Does Ownership Matter? Japanese Multinationals in Europe*. Oxford: Oxford University Press.

Mataloni, Raymond J., Jr. 1994. "U.S. Multinational Companies: Operations in 1992," *Survey of Current Business* 77(June):42-62.

McKenzie, F. A. 1902. *The American Invasion*. London: G. Richards.

Narula, Rajneesh. 1996. *Multinational Investment and Economic Structure: Globalisation and Competitiveness*. London: Routledge.

Organisation for Economic Co-operation and Development (OECD). 1989. *International Investment and Multinational Enterprises: Investment Incentives and Disincentives: Effects on International Direct Investment*. Paris: OECD.

————. 1993. *Globalization and Corporate Nationality*. Paris: OECD, Mimeo.

————. 1994. *The Performance of Foreign Affiliates in OECD Countries*. Paris: OECD.

————. 1995. *International Direct Investment Statistics Yearbook 1995*. Paris: OECD.

Porter, Michael E. 1990. *The Competitive Advantage of Nations*. New York: Free Press (MacMillan, Inc).

Solomon, R. F., and K. P. D. Ingham. 1977. "Discriminating between MNC Subsidiaries and Indigenous Companies: A Comparative Analysis of the British Mechanical Engineering Industry," *Oxford Bulletin of Economics and Statistics* 39(May):127-138.

Southard, Frank A., Jr. 1931. *American Industry in Europe*. Boston: Houghton Mifflin.

Strange, Roger. 1993. *Japanese Manufacturing Investment in Europe: Its Impact on the UK Economy*. London: Routledge.

Transnational Corporations and Management Division. 1993. *From the Common Market to EC 1992: Regional Economic Integration in the European Community and Transnational Corporations*. New York: United Nations.

United Nations Conference on Trade and Development (UNCTAD). 1993. *World Investment Report 1993: Transnational Corporations and Integrated International Production*, Division on Transnational Corporations and Investment. New York: United Nations.

————. 1994. *World Investment Report 1994: Transnational Corporations, Employment and the Workplace*, Division on Transnational Corporations and Investment. New York: United Nations.

————. 1995. "Incentives and Foreign Direct Investment," Division on Transnational Corporations and Investment, Geneva (TO/B/1TNC/MISC1), March, mimeo.

————. 1996. *World Investment Report 1996: Transnational Corporations, Trade and Foreign Direct Investment*. Department for Economic and Social Development, Transnational Corporations and Management Division. New York: United Nations.

Wilkins, Mira. 1989. *The History of Foreign Investment In the United States to 1914*. Cambridge, Mass.: Harvard University Press.

Womack, James P., Daniel T. Jones, and Davies Roos. 1991. *The Machine That Changed the World: Based on the Massachusetts Institute of Technology 5-Million Dollar 5-Year Study on the Future of the Automobile*. New York: Rawson Associates.

2

A Retrospective on FDIUS

Edward M. Graham

Foreign Direct Investment in the United States (Graham and Krugman 1989) was published in a time of high anxiety. It was an attempt to provide a straightforward and sober economic analysis of rising foreign ownership. In the late 1980s, the book drew considerable press attention and made the authors famous (some would say "infamous") for a brief period of time. Paul Krugman, who was already well known, has become more so during the 1990s, while Edward Graham has fallen back into relative obscurity. This is not entirely a bad thing, if for no other reason than that this brief excursion into fame brought with it, among other things, hate mail.

For a time, letters poured in from across America to chastise the authors for a lack of patriotism or things worse and unmentionable. The tone of most of the mail was anti-Japanese. Few of the senders would have understood, or perhaps even cared, that most of the direct investment flowing into the United States originated in Europe or Canada. To this day, the racist tone of certain letters sends a chill through this author.

What precipitated this brief but intense encounter with public angst in late 1989? Of all things, the book attempted to examine rationally the economic, political, and national security implications of foreign direct investment in the United States (FDIUS). At almost any other time in recent U.S. history, save perhaps the years between the two oil crises, such a book would have been met largely with yawns by most of the public. Economists and policy analysts, of course, would have been the exception. Some may have met the book with derision. But, whatever the case, the book was not an advocacy piece, as many took it. Rather, it was an analytical piece that, on the basis of analysis, concluded that there was little discernible harm and much discernible benefit from FDIUS.

But, 1989 was a special year. It was the fourth year running of a spectacular surge in direct investment in the United States. Fears were running high that "America was selling out to foreign interests" and, in particular, to Japanese interests (Tolchin and Tolchin 1988; Frantz and Collins 1989). People, by and large, do not like change, and the face of the U.S. economy appeared to be changing. The tone of the public on this issue therefore, at times, approached hysteria. The hysteria was fed in part by books that likened FDIUS to an aggressively malignant cancer. Never mind that, for decades, the U.S. government had been actively attempting to persuade other nations to accept U.S. direct investment with equanimity, if not joy: U.S. direct investment, after all, would spur productivity and modernization of foreign economies, and thus it was a good thing for everyone.

But when it came to direct investment into the United States in the late 1980s and early 1990s, U.S. citizens were not so sure. Michael Crichton even enhanced his own already quite substantial fortune by writing a best-seller on the subject entitled *Rising Sun* (1992), which mixed foreign direct investment (FDI) and technology transfer with sex and violence. This novel was perhaps the first work of fiction to include a recommended reading guide to nonfiction works on the Japanese economic ascendancy. Unfortunately, the best antidote to Crichton's *Rising Sun*, Bill Emmott's *The Sun Also Sets* (1989), was not included in the guide.

The Graham and Krugman (1989) book was neither as fast-paced nor as salacious as *Rising Sun* but, perhaps rather immodestly, *Foreign Direct Investment in the United States* more accurately framed and analyzed the issues and drew more pertinent conclusions. Most importantly, the book's major findings pass the test of time. This chapter will review some of the main points made in the book and attempt to assess how well its putative words of wisdom have, or have not, held up.

First, the spectacular surge of FDIUS of the latter half of the 1980s was predicted not to last in the early 1990s. Of course, this was a fairly safe prediction, because the surge would have eventually ended even if every last asset in the United States had been acquired by foreigners. However, the latter point is not what was predicted. Manufacturing assets under foreign control were predicted to not exceed 15 percent to 20 percent of all U.S. manufacturing assets. This proved completely correct; the surge of FDI ended in 1991, and this percentage leveled off at about 15 percent. On what basis were the authors able to make such a precisely accurate prediction? This author admits it was dead reckoning. There was no rational basis whatsoever for claiming 15 percent to 20 percent as a ceiling, other than the observation that in other advanced countries that had experienced previous surges of inward direct investment, this figure never seemed to be over 20 percent. But assertions proved right—or at least they have into the mid-1990s.

Also, on the inherently unknowable side of the ledger, FDIUS was predicted to bring positive externalities to the U.S. economy. Now, positive (and negative) externalities have many of the same characteristics as benign (and malign) spirits. One cannot, under normal circumstances, see them, nor can one measure them with any certitude. Indeed, some externalities can be seen only by an economist, just as some spirits can be seen only by a master of the occult. John Dunning, in his 1958 masterpiece *American Investment in British Manufacturing Industry*, actually found tangible evidence of positive externalities in Britain that emanated from U.S. direct investment in that nation. But, Krugman and I had neither the time nor the patience to attempt to replicate Dunning's detailed measurements in the United States. Our suspicion nonetheless was that positive externalities would come, inter alia, in the form of increased competition, which would shake up indigenous firms so that they would become more efficient. Today, almost everyone, when speaking of the renaissance of the Detroit-based auto producers, cites the challenge of the Japanese transplants in prodding Detroit to develop a better automobile (Florida and Kenney 1993). In at least this instance the evidence, albeit anecdotal in nature, supports the assertion that these externalities would result. And, further, the lot of the average U.S. citizen is the better for it.

Likewise, gains to the U.S. economy from increased integration into the world economy as a result of FDI were predicted. These gains are really an extension of the standard gains from trade. Like externalities, there is little tangible evidence that they have occurred, but this author is nonetheless confident that the gains are there.

What about employment? According to our reasoning in 1987, none of the above gains is correlated with net increases or decreases in employment opportunities in the United States. Unlike the prediction of virtually any other author, the net effect on employment of FDIUS is concluded in our book to be exactly zero. Again, it is hard to measure the net employment effects of trade or FDI; not a whit of evidence exists that would indicate they are other than zero. This assertion was neither popular nor well understood, because every governor of every state in the nation who had succeeded in attracting a foreign investor to locate a plant in his or her state wanted to claim net positive job creation, while most members of Congress who wanted to pass new laws to regulate FDI (and who represented the same states) claimed some sort of job loss. Sometimes the truth hurts the bearer of the truth, and such was the case with us. Our line of clear reason yielded few friends but generated enmity from, as it were, both sides of the debate.

The authors did claim, however, on the basis of an appeal to theory and empirical evidence, that FDI should affect the quality of the jobs in the United States and in a positive direction. The theoretical reason, related to John Dunning's eclectic theory, is related to the notion that firms engaging in FDI possess firm-specific assets (such as technologies or managerial prowess not possessed by local rivals) and are able to internalize these assets to create relatively more efficient operations. On this issue, at first blush, the data have borne us out. At the levels of disaggregation for which data could be obtained in the late 1980s (which were not at all disaggregated), foreign-controlled firms seemed both to generate more value added per worker and to pay higher wages than domestic-controlled firms in the same industries.

In later years, when much more disaggregated data from the U.S. Government's Data Link Project became available (a project that we could take some credit for enabling), this finding had to be nuanced. Foreign-controlled firms in most industries did compensate workers on average as well as or better than domestic-controlled ones, but there proved to be exceptions (as in the auto industry). The exceptions can be well explained by locational and demographic factors (for example, the Japanese transplants are concentrated in relatively low wage regions, and plants operated by the Detroit "Big 3" employ workers of lower average age than the former); but other factors might also be important (such as whether the workers are represented by a union). More analysis can and should be done using the disaggregated data, as Doms and Jensen have done later in this volume (chapter 3). Alas, budget cutting fever on Capitol Hill in the late 1990s could force termination of the Data Link Project, which would preclude future longitudinal analysis based on the new data series created by this project. Were this to happen, it would be unfortunate and devastating to future research on FDIUS.

Trade effects of FDI represent another area explored in Graham and Krugman (1989). Detractors of FDI have claimed that U.S. subsidiaries of foreign firms have been instrumental in creating the U.S. trade deficit. By any decent economic reasoning, the authors disagree, and by and large the empirical evidence bears out the theory once again. In terms of imports and exports per worker employed, foreign-controlled firms in the United States were found to perform not much differently from U.S.-based multinationals. A major exception was the typical subsidiary of a Japanese firm, which did (and, according to the data, continues to) import much more per worker than any other category of firm we could identify. Still, these subsidiaries should not be held responsible for the U.S. trade deficit, and such claims as "If you could wipe out the bilateral United States–Japan deficit in auto parts, most of the trade deficit would disappear" are utterly fallacious. Such claims suffer, as most need not be told, from a serious fallacy of composition. However, one cannot deny that U.S. subsidiaries of Japanese manufacturing firms have a high propensity to import. This could be, as noted in our book, the result of vintage effects. But to test this, longitudinal studies are needed. Later in this volume, Doms and Jensen (chapter 3) and Reich (chapter 6) take a closer look at this issue.

One of the most controversial findings of *Foreign Direct Investment in the United States* had to do with research and development (R&D) performed by U.S. subsidiaries of foreign firms. On the basis of R&D per worker employed, foreign-owned firms do as much R&D in the United States in the manufacturing sector as do domestic-owned firms. Of course, aggregate expenditures by foreign-controlled firms on R&D are much lower than those by domestic-controlled ones; all that was found is that, controlling for size of operation, the amount of R&D done by each class of firm is about the same. Most multinational firms concentrate the majority of their R&D activities in their home nations. This is as true for foreign firms with FDIUS as it is for U.S.-based firms with substantial direct investment abroad. Nevertheless, FDIUS seems exceptionally R&D intensive.

An enormous debate over R&D has emerged around these stylized facts. Questions that are raised include all of the following. Does it matter if a small but significant portion of the U.S. R&D base is under foreign control? Do foreign-controlled R&D operations exist largely as "spying" operations, with a mission to seek out new U.S.-developed technology and ship it back home rather than to develop new technology on site? Do these operations exist to suit specific requirements of the American market or to make minor design modifications on products that are largely engineered at home? Are U.S. R&D operations conducted such that whatever technology is developed requires that other technologies kept outside the United States be utilized? Does foreign-controlled R&D displace or complement domestic-controlled R&D?

The answer to almost all of these questions would appear to depend upon which foreign-controlled R&D operation you are talking about. Foreign-controlled R&D operations run the gamut from basic research centers to product-styling shops. (But, it needs to be said, so do domestic-controlled operations.) Almost all R&D labs, whether under domestic or foreign control, constantly seek to learn from the experience of other labs (in other words, they all spy on one another). Graham and Krugman (1989) argue that, by and large, the more R&D done, the better; and the United States should be thankful that foreign firms do as much of it here as is done. One reason, but by no means the only one, is that R&D tends to generate externalities whose capture is largely confined to the community in which the R&D takes place. But other, reasonable people do not share this generally optimistic assessment of U.S. R&D under foreign control, and this debate will not likely be over soon. For those interested in the empirical dimensions of the issue, Part III of this volume updates and extends our assessment from a decade ago.

Much of Graham and Krugman (1989) is concerned with the national security implications of FDIUS, and those critics who believed there was bias in favor of foreign investors apparently did not read those sections of the book dealing with national security issues. Upon rereading these sections, the book seems to reflect the heightened concerns prevalent in the last years of the cold war. In fact, quite strict measures were advocated, to be applied to foreign investors where national security was at stake, including requirements for inward transfer of technologies and mandatory local production of some items. Graham and Krugman were not soft on national security.

Was our rather tough line warranted? Probably so. But along with tough policies toward FDI in product categories with national security implications, a quite narrow and strict definition of national security was advocated. In other words, calls for the equation of "national security" with "economic security" were rejected. What these calls seemed to imply was that production of almost anything, and certainly anything that was remotely "high-tech," should fall into the domain of security sensitive products. The authors believed, in some contrast, that production of advanced jet fighters clearly was in this domain, whereas production of commodity memory chips was not (unless, perhaps, this production was under the control of a cartel or monopoly). The authors acknowledged their lack of the specialized knowledge necessary to determine exactly what items should be regarded as security sensitive. But, the authors were quite convinced that national security could be misused as a reason to regulate a far wider range of activities than a cool-headed assessment by military experts would identify. A superb, post-cold war analysis of foreign acquisitions of defense-related firms is advanced by Kudrle and Bobrow later in chapter 14.

Looking back, much of the furor over FDIUS in the late 1980s and early 1990s was a "tempest in a teapot." Nonetheless, some of the issues raised during this period were real. By and large, essential points of Graham and Krugman (1989) hold up. When a third edition was produced in 1994, the book needed a lot of updating of data, but few of the major conclusions from the first edition had to be changed. Some small satisfaction is taken from this. But then, in the end, all the authors really did was to apply a modicum of analysis and reason to a situation where hysteria was rising. Usually in such a situation, brilliance is not required to discover where the truth lies, merely a cool head and modest analytical capabilities. The trick is to keep oneself from being lynched before the hysteria subsides. This we succeeded in doing; but, in retrospect, there were quite a few people out there who were prepared to give the mob a coil of rope.

REFERENCES

Crichton, Michael. 1992. *Rising Sun*. New York: Knopf.

Dunning, John H. 1958. *American Investment in British Manufacturing Industry*. London: George Allen and Unwin (reprinted by Arno Press, New York, 1976).

Emmott, Bill. 1989. *The Sun Also Sets: The Limits to Japan's Economic Power*. New York: Times Books.

Florida, Richard L., and Martin Kenney. 1993. *Beyond Mass Production: The Japanese System and Its Transfer to the U.S.* New York: Oxford University Press.

Frantz, Douglas, and Catherine Collins. 1989. *Selling Out: How We Are Letting Japan Buy Our Land, Our Industries, Our Financial Institutions, and Our Future*. Chicago: Contemporary Books.

Graham, Edward M., and Paul R. Krugman. 1989. *Foreign Direct Investment in the United States*. Washington, D.C.: Institute for International Economics.

Tolchin, Martin, and Susan Tolchin. 1988. *Buying into America: How Foreign Money is Changing the Face of Our Nation*. New York: Times Books.

Part II

Consequences for the Economy

3

Productivity, Skill, and Wage Effects of Multinational Corporations in the United States

Mark E. Doms and J. Bradford Jensen

INTRODUCTION

As rising foreign ownership of U.S. assets has raised concerns in the popular media, it has also prompted a number of important studies about its economic characteristics and consequences. As stressed in the last chapter, foreign ownership of U.S. assets sometimes generates heated debate (Graham and Krugman 1989; Froot and Stein 1991; McCulloch 1993). Following Graham and Krugman (1989), research on foreign direct investment (FDI) has compared foreign-owned establishments to domestic establishments in terms of wages, types of jobs provided, and productivity. On the one hand, it is possible that foreign firms keep a disproportionate amount of their high-value-added, high-skilled operations in their home countries, especially when it comes to highly skilled nonproduction workers. In this case, the U.S.-based operations of foreign multinationals may consist primarily of relatively low-value-added, low-skilled assembly operations that may not be very productive. On the other hand, foreign firms able to invest abroad, especially firms that invest in a highly productive and skilled country like the United States, are likely to be firms that possess specific advantages, such as superior product design, greater production efficiency, knowledge of advanced technologies, and advanced marketing skill. These foreign companies might then pay higher wages, have more highly skilled workers, and have higher productivity than many domestic-owned plants.

When thinking about foreign multinational firms investing in the United States, one must remember there are symmetric arguments pertaining to U.S.-based multinationals. Do U.S. multinationals have higher-skilled and higher-paying employment than U.S. firms that focus entirely on the domestic market? How do the wages and productivity of U.S. multinationals compare with those establishments of foreign-based multinationals? Like many debates in economics, differences of opinion arise because data and facts are lacking. Fortunately, better data on foreign direct investment in the United States (FDIUS) are now available, as explained in the introduction to this book.

In related work, Doms and Jensen (1998) compare the operating characteristics of foreign-owned and domestic-owned plants, using detailed data from over 115,000 U.S. manufacturing plants.[1] The authors present evidence comparing foreign-owned plants to domestic-owned plants in terms of employment, wages, productivity, capital intensity, and technology. Even controlling for four-digit industry, state, plant age, and plant size, their results suggest foreign-owned plants are more productive, rely more on capital than labor, and pay higher wages than domestic-owned plants. Thus, foreign-owned plants compare favorably to the average domestic-owned plant. Yet, when foreign-owned plants are compared to plants owned by U.S. firms with foreign assets (U.S. multinationals), the *plants of U.S. multinationals* are the most productive, most capital intensive, and pay the highest wages.

In this chapter, similar plant-level data for 1987 (approximately 115,000 observations) are used to control for industry, size, age, and location and to test more rigorously for differences in the operating characteristics between foreign- and domestic-owned plants than has been done in previous research. In this chapter, the differences between foreign-owned plants and plants of U.S. multinational corporations (MNCs), in particular across industries, are examined. Also examined in greater detail is the effect of foreign assets on the variance of operating characteristics among U.S. MNCs. The result is that, even at the two-digit SIC level, previous results are fairly robust. Further, in terms of differences among U.S. MNCs affected by the extent of foreign assets, U.S. multinationals with more assets in foreign countries are more productive, larger, more capital intensive, and pay higher wages. The foreign multinationals appear similar to U.S. multinationals with fewer assets in foreign countries in terms of pay and productivity. Establishments belonging to firms with no foreign assets pay the lowest wages and have the lowest productivity.

These results suggest that MNCs, whether foreign- or domestic-owned, are the most productive, most capital intensive, and the highest paying plants. Thus, comparing foreign-owned plants to all domestic-owned plants is, in some ways, comparing apples and oranges. Plants owned by multinationals tend to be much bigger than the average plant in the United States and have characteristics associated with plant size. Thus, it is true that foreign-owned plants have desirable characteristics relative to the whole of U.S. manufacturing. However, when compared to plants owned by U.S. multinationals, foreign-owned plants do not compare as favorably. These findings about the extent of foreign assets are pertinent to Dunning's discussion of multinationality versus foreignness given in chapter 1. Further, the results are consistent with the theory that firm-specific advantages, like productivity, enable firms, whether U.S. or foreign, to overcome the barriers to direct foreign investment.

The rest of the chapter is organized as follows. The next section describes the nature of the data and the classification of establishments used in the analysis. The third section of the chapter focuses on regression results comparing foreign- and domestic-owned establishments for basic operating characteristics like wages, worker skill mix, and productivity. The fourth section extends the analysis of the third section by segregating domestic firms into more refined categories based on the extent of their foreign assets. Subsequent sections examine the differences by country of ownership and the issue of whether foreign-owned plants use a greater array of advanced manufacturing technologies than U.S. establishments. The last section concludes the chapter.

DATA DESCRIPTION

This section describes the data used in the subsequent analysis. The data set is a combination of several establishment-level data sets: the 1987 Census of Manufacturers (CM), 1987 Central Administrative Offices and Auxiliary Establishment Survey (Central-Auxiliary), 1988 Survey of Manufacturing Technology (SMT), and the 1987 Bureau of Economic Analysis Foreign Direct Investment Survey (BEA data). Jointly, the BEA and the Census Bureau linked the 1987 BEA data to the 1987 Standard Statistical Establishment List, of which the 1987 CM, 1988 SMT, and Auxiliary reports are subsets.[2] The CM provides information on shipments, value added, capital, production workers, nonproduction workers, wages, and other types of production information. The CM has these data for approximately 200,000 establishments. The SMT provides information on the usage of seventeen advanced manufacturing technologies for a sample of approximately 10,000 manufacturing establishments.

In this chapter, differences in labor productivity, in the mix of production workers to nonproduction workers, and in the wages of production and nonproduction workers are examined across domestic-owned or foreign-owned establishments. Some variables require accurate measures of nonproduction workers. A problem that arises is that nonproduction workers involved in production may not be physically located at manufacturing establishments. Instead, some nonproduction workers may be located at auxiliary manufacturing establishments. Manufacturing auxiliaries are those establishments that do not manufacture goods but house R&D laboratories, headquarters, and data-processing centers. The measurement problem that arises is that these auxiliary functions are performed at manufacturing sites for some firms and at auxiliary establishments for others. If the nonproduction workers located at auxiliaries are excluded, then labor productivity will be biased upward, and nonproduction worker wages will most likely be biased downward since auxiliaries tend to pay above average wages. One reason the issue of nonproduction workers is of particular interest is that this is the only indicator of worker skill in the current data set; the variance in the skill mix of workers by country of ownership is a focus of the research.

Results with and without adjustments for auxiliary employment are presented. Auxiliary adjustments are made using data from the 1987 Central-Auxiliary survey. First, the total number of nonproduction workers located in manufacturing auxiliaries (each firm may have more than one manufacturing auxiliary) and their salaries are calculated for each firm. Second, these auxiliary workers and their wages are distributed across all manufacturing establishments of the firm. The proportion of auxiliary workers (and auxiliary wage bill) allocated to an establishment depends on the share of nonproduction workers that establishment has for the firm. For instance, if an establishment (plant) has 30 percent of the nonproduction workers of all nonproduction workers in all manufacturing establishments of a firm, the plant is allocated 30 percent of the firm's auxiliary workers.

The BEA data provide the country of ultimate beneficial ownership for the enterprise to which each establishment belongs. In the BEA data, "A U.S. affiliate is a U.S. business enterprise that is owned 10 percent or more, directly or indirectly, by a foreign person." Unfortunately, *degree* of foreign ownership is not available. Therefore, in the analysis that follows, all foreign-owned establishments are treated equally.

In this analysis, sample attrition in terms of the number of establishments is significant but has a much smaller impact on manufacturing employment. The 1987 population of manufacturing establishments in the United States was approximately 350,000. About 200,000 of these establishments were mailed a 1987 Census of Manufacturers form to request information on shipments, labor, wages, and capital. Because the production data for the other 150,000 records, known as administrative records,[3] are imputed, they could not be used in our analysis. The next largest source of attrition is the loss of records with an impute flag, which is set if any of the four variables (employment, salaries and wages, materials, and total value of shipments) was not reported by the establishment. All records with an impute flag were dropped.[4] Table 3.1 reports the number of establishments, employment, average employment, and average earnings for the 1987 CM and some basic statistics for the final sample.

Table 3.1
Basic Sample Statistics: Comparison between Samples and Populations

	Number of Establish- ments	Total Employ- ment	Average Employment/ Establishment	Average Annual Earnings ($000s/Employee)
1987 Census of Manufactures:				
Manufacturing				
Population	358,941	17,716,649	49.4	19.1
Total Sample	115,139	12,420,340	107.9	21.4
Foreign				
Population	7,077	1,180,686	166.8	26.6
Foreign Sample	4,463	853,338	191.2	25.0
Domestic				
Population	351,864	16,535,963	47.0	18.9
Domestic Sample	110,681	11,570,660	104.5	21.3

Finally, the 1987 Large Company Survey (ES9100), mailed to all firms with more than 500 employees, provides information used to identify the characteristics of the firm to which U.S. establishments belong. The ES9100 identifies to what extent domestic-owned firms have foreign assets. Firms are asked to report "All assets in foreign countries, and U.S. possessions, regardless of type." The ratio of foreign assets to total assets is computed for each of firm, and the firms with more than 500 employees are classed into five groups based on the value of this ratio:

1. plants owned by U.S. firms with more than 500 employees and no foreign assets,
2. plants owned by U.S. firms with more than 500 employees and foreign assets comprising up to 5 percent of total assets,

3.   plants owned by U.S. firms with more than 500 employees and foreign assets comprising between 5 and 10 percent of total assets,
4.   plants owned by U.S. firms with more than 500 employees and foreign assets comprising between 10 and 20 percent of total assets, and
5.   plants owned by U.S. firms with more than 500 employees and foreign assets comprising over 20 percent of total assets.

Therefore, a total of seven groups comprise the data set: Five groups for establishments belonging to firms with more than 500 employees, one group for foreign-owned plants, and one group for plants belonging to firms with less than 500 employees. Table 3.2 presents summary statistics for the six types of U.S. establishments. Establishments (plants) belonging to firms with more than 500 employees and having more than 20 percent of their assets in other countries have much higher average wages. These plants are also larger.

Table 3.2
Breakdown of Domestic Sample

	Number of Establish-ments	Total Employ-ment	Average Employment/ Establishment	Average Annual Earnings ($000s/Employee)
Small Domestic	87,030	3,902,625	44.8	20.8
Large Domestic	8,398	1,933,084	230.2	21.7
U.S. MNCs*				
0-5 percent	4,006	1,261,043	314.8	23.3
5-10 percent	3,521	1,038,532	295.0	23.1
10-20 percent	3,900	1,192,381	305.7	24.8
20+ percent	3,826	2,242,995	586.3	27.0
Total Domestic	110,681	11,570,660	104.5	21.3

*The categories within U.S. multinationals refer to the percentage of total assets that are foreign.

U.S.-OWNED COMPARED TO FOREIGN-OWNED ESTABLISHMENTS

To begin, the plant characteristics of U.S.-owned establishments are compared with those of foreign-owned establishments (Doms and Jensen 1998). Discussion of foreign ownership of manufacturing facilities has typically focused on employment opportunities. Some suggest foreign-owned plants undertake a set of activities different from that of domestic plants and therefore use a different class of workers, pay lower wages, and are less productive than domestic-owned plants. Other theories of FDI suggest foreign-owned plants belong to firms with specific advantages to enable them to invest in new markets. These advantages include such assets as superior product design, greater production efficiency, and advanced marketing skill. These claims are investigated by comparing measures of average annual wages, skill mix, capital-to-labor ratios, and productivity for foreign-owned and domestic-owned establishments. Table 3.3 provides precise definitions of the operating characteristics used in the comparisons.

A review of the data in table 3.1 reveals that foreign-owned plants are larger than domestic-owned plants. In a more detailed comparison, table 3.4 shows plant means and standard deviations for the operating characteristics of each class of plant. Here, foreign-owned plants differ from domestic-owned plants. Foreign-owned plants pay higher wages to both production workers and nonproduction workers. Foreign-owned plants are also more capital intensive and more productive than domestic-owned plants.

Howenstine and Zeile (1992) find that FDI is most prominent in industries characterized by high capital intensity and high worker skill level. Thus, the findings reported in table 3.1 may result from the composition of the plants in the domestic- and foreign-owned categories. The possibility of composition effects influencing the results is examined by controlling for industry, plant size, plant age, and location.

Table 3.5 presents regression coefficients with dummy variables for foreign ownership of the establishment. The first column (no controls) in table 3.5 is estimated:

$$Y_i = \alpha + \beta \text{ Foreign-Owned}_i + \epsilon_i \tag{1}$$

where Y_i is the dependent variable and Foreign-Owned is a dummy variable equal to one if the establishment is foreign-owned, zero otherwise. The first column in table 3.5 reports the beta estimates and associated standard errors for equation (1). The second column in table 3.5 comes from the following model.

$$Y_i = \alpha + \beta \text{ Foreign-Owned}_i + \Gamma X_i + \epsilon_i \tag{2}$$

where X_i is a matrix of dummy variables for plant size, plant age, state, and industry. Table 3.6 provides definitions for X. The second column of table 3.5 reports the beta estimates from equation (2). Industry and state results are suppressed to conserve space and to avoid disclosure issues.

Table 3.5 also presents some results from a slightly different model, one similar to Globerman, Ries, and Vertinsky (1994). This specification controls for the capital intensity of the plant. The third column of table 3.5 (with controls and capital-to-labor) contains results from the following model.

$$Y_i = \alpha + \beta \text{ Foreign-owned}_i + \delta \text{Capital/Labor}_i + \Gamma X_i + \epsilon_i \tag{3}$$

where X_i is the same as equation (2) (see table 3.6).

The first column of results in table 3.5 tells the same story as told by table 3.4. Foreign-owned plants are significantly more capital intensive, more productive, and pay higher wages, but this may be due to composition effects. When controls for plant size, industry (4-digit SIC), plant age, and plant location (state) are included, the observed differences between foreign-owned and domestic-owned plants decrease, but persist. The results in table 3.5 confirm that not all of the differences in table 3.4 are due to omitted variable bias. Foreign-owned plants are more capital intensive, more productive, and pay higher wages than domestic-owned plants, even after controlling for a host of other variables.

Table 3.3
Dependent Variable Definitions

Variable Name	Definition
Production Worker Wages	Annual salaries ($000s) for production workers/number of production workers
Nonproduction Worker Wages (1)	Annual salaries ($000s) for nonproduction workers/ number of nonproduction workers
Nonproduction Worker Wages (2)	Same as Nonproduction Worker Wages (1) except with an adjustment made for employment and payroll in auxiliaries.
Production Workers/Total Employment (1)	Number of production workers/total employment
Production Workers/Total Employment (2)	Number of production workers/total employment, where total employment is adjusted for auxiliary employment
Capital/ Employment (1)	Book value of machinery and building assets ($000s)/ total employment
Capital/ Employment (2)	Book value of machinery and building assets ($000s)/ total employment, where total employment is adjusted for auxiliary employment
Value Added/ Employment (1)	Value added ($000s)/total employment
Value Added/ Employment (2)	Value added ($000s)/total employment, where total employment is adjusted for auxiliary employment
Total Factor Productivity-Residual	Natural logarithm of total factor productivity calculated from using the residual of a value-added Cobb Douglas production function.*
Total Factor Productivity-Factor Share	Natural logarithm of total factor productivity calculated using a factor share method.**

*The residual measure is calculated using a Cobb-Douglas specification with capital, labor, and materials (including parts, fuels, and services) included as inputs. The regression coefficients are from 4-digit SIC industry regressions.

**The factor share method is calculated using the median factor shares of capital, labor, and materials (including parts, fuels, and services) from the 4-digit SIC industry. This method is similar to that used in Baily, Hulten, and Campbell (1992).

Table 3.4
Variable Means by Foreign and Domestic Ownership*

Variable	Domestic	Foreign
Production Worker Wages ($000s)	18.76	22.29
	(8.13)	(8.57)
Nonproduction Worker Wages (1) ($000s)	30.37	32.10
	(15.74)	(12.44)
Nonproduction Worker Wages (2) ($000s)	32.49	32.94
	(11.06)	(10.58)
Production Workers/ Total Employment (1)	0.73	0.68
	(0.19)	(0.21)
Production Workers/ Total Employment (2)	0.72	0.63
	(0.20)	(0.22)
Capital/Employment (1) ($000s)	39.34	103.10
	(91.1)	(218.40)
Capital/Employment (2) ($000s)	36.84	91.83
	(75.9)	(193.49)
Value Added/Employment (1) ($000s)	56.50	109.48
	(77.9)	(160.35)
Value Added/Employment (2) ($000s)	53.75	96.55
	(66.73)	(137.77)
Total Factor Productivity-Residual	.02	.06
	(.29)	(.28)
Total Factor Prouctivity-Factor Share	.04	.06
	(.36)	(.36)

*See table 3.3 for variable definitions. Standard deviations in parentheses.

The equations controlling for size, age, industry, and location show that foreign-owned plants pay about 7 percent more to production workers and 1-2 percent more to nonproduction workers. Foreign-owned plants of the same age and size, in the same location and industry, are about 30 percent more capital intensive and have about 20 percent higher labor productivity. In terms of total factor productivity (TFP), foreign-owned plants are about 2-4 percent more productive. Further, foreign-owned plants use fewer production workers than domestic-owned plants use.

Following Globerman, Ries, and Vertinsky (1994), the capital-to-labor ratio is included as a control variable. Globerman, Ries, and Vertinsky find that when size, capital intensity, and percentage of males in the plant are included, the observable labor productivity difference between Canadian and foreign-owned plants is not statistically significant. The results of including capital intensity in the controls are shown in the last column of table 3.5. The differences are reduced, but the differential for productivity is still positive and statistically significant. Including the capital-to-labor ratio also reduces the observed wage premium to production workers, but it is still positive at the 5 percent level and statistically significant.

Table 3.5
Differences between Domestic- and Foreign-Owned Establishments*

Dependent Variable	Foreign-Owned No Controls	Foreign-Owned with Controls	Foreign-Owned Controls + K/L
Log (Production Worker Wages)	.190 (.007)	.073 (.006)	.038 (.006)
Log (Nonproduction Worker Wages (1))	.104 (.008)	.012 (.008)	-.020 (.008)
Log (Nonproduction Worker Wages (2))	.130 (.008)	.026 (.008)	-.005 (.008)
Production Workers/ Total Employment (1)	-.052 (.003)	-.020 (.003)	-.018 (.003)
Production Workers/ Total Employment (2)	-.084 (.003)	-.031 (.003)	-.029 (.003)
Log (Capital/ Employment (1))	.941 (.018)	.332 (.015)	-
Log (Capital/ Employment (2))	.877 (.017)	.308 (.014)	-
Log (Value Added/ Employment (1))	.537 (.010)	.211 (.009)	.134 (.008)
Log (Value Added/ Employment (2))	.473 (.010)	.186 (.009)	.118 (.008)
Total Factor Productivity- Residual	.041 (.004)	.037 (.005)	-
Total Factor Prouctivity- Factor Share	.024 (.006)	.023 (.006)	-

*The numbers are regression coefficients from linear models that do and do not control for establishment size, four-digit industry, plant age, and state (standard errors in parentheses). The omitted group is domestic-owned establishments. Number of observations ≈ 115,000.

These results suggest the differences between foreign- and domestic-owned plants are partially the result of industry, size, age, and location effects. Including controls for these effects reduces the observed differences between domestic- and foreign-owned plants. However, the differences do not disappear. Even after controlling for these effects, foreign-owned plants still have superior operating characteristics relative to domestic plants, suggesting that some of the fears expressed about FDI are unwarranted. Foreign-owned plants are more capital intensive, more productive, pay higher wages, and use a higher proportion of nonproduction workers than the average U.S.-owned plant. While these results are suggestive of the impact of foreign-owned plants on the domestic economy, the results do not speak to the potential sources of the different operating characteristics. In the next section, U.S.-owned plants are further decomposed by ownership to investigate potential sources of the differences in operating characteristics.

Table 3.6
Independent Variable Definitions

Variable Name	Definition
Plant Size	Categorical variable based on total plant employment (TE): Size Class 1: $1 \leq TE < 50$ Size Class 2: $50 \leq TE < 100$ Size Class 3: $100 \leq TE < 250$ Size Class 4: $250 \leq TE < 500$ Size Class 5: $500 \leq TE < 1000$ Size Class 6: $1000 \leq TE < 2500$ Size Class 7: $2500 \leq TE$ (omitted category)
Plant Age	Categorical variable based on year of first Census of Manufactures appearance: Age Class 63: First Appearance in Census is 1963 Age Class 67: First Appearance in Census is 1967 Age Class 72: First Appearance in Census is 1972 Age Class 77: First Appearance in Census is 1977 Age Class 82: First Appearance in Census is 1982 Age Class 87: First Appearance in Census is 1987 (omitted category)
Plant Industry	Dummy variables representing 4-digit SIC Industry
Plant Location	Dummy variable representing state in which plant is located

FOREIGN-OWNED VERSUS U.S. MULTINATIONAL ESTABLISHMENTS

The previous section compared foreign-owned plants to all domestic-owned plants, an interesting comparison for some purposes. That comparison had the limitation that all U.S. establishments were lumped into one category. An analysis using a more detailed description of U.S. establishments might be fruitful. Multinational investment theory suggests that firms engaging in FDI have firm-specific advantages that allow them to overcome the hurdles of FDI. Thus, one may expect plants owned by foreign MNCs to be more productive than the average domestic-owned plant. There is also a symmetric argument pertaining to establishments owned by U.S. MNCs. If MNCs in general have superior operating characteristics to firms that participate only in their domestic markets, then one would expect to find plants owned by U.S. MNCs to have these superior characteristics also. To investigate this, the sample was divided; plants owned by U.S. MNCs were compared to the foreign-owned plants.

Foreign-Owned Relative to U.S. MNCs by Industry

In Doms and Jensen (1998), the authors found that when domestic establishments are classed as plants owned by small domestic firms (Small Domestic), by large firms with little or no foreign assets (Large Domestic), and by large firms with significant foreign assets (U.S. MNCs), plants owned by U.S. MNCs are the most productive, most capital intensive, most nonproduction worker intensive, and pay the highest wages. These results are summarized in column 3 of table 3.7. The coefficients reported in column 3 of table 3.7 come from the following model.

$$Y_i = \alpha + \beta \text{ Foreign-Owned}_i + \delta \text{ Small Domestic}_i + \eta \text{ Large Domestic}_i + \Gamma X_i + \epsilon_i$$

$$(4)$$

where X_i is a matrix of categorical and dummy variables for plant size, plant age, state, and industry, and U.S. MNCs are the excluded category. Table 3.6 provides definitions for the categorical and dummy variables. The third column of table 3.7 reports the beta estimates from equation (4).

Table 3.7
Summary Statistics for Two-Digit Industry Regressions
Foreign-Owned Plants Relative to Plants of U.S. MNCs with More Than 500 Employees and Foreign Assets > 10% of Total Assets

Dependent Variable	Number of Industries with Positive Coefficients*	Number of Industries with Negative Coefficients*	Foreign-Owned Coefficients** (Std. Errors)
Log (Production Worker Wages)	3 (1)	16 (6)	-.029 (.007)
Log (Nonproduction Worker Wages (1))	8 (1)	11 (2)	-.004 (.010)
Log (Nonproduction Worker Wages (2))	5 (1)	14 (4)	-.039 (.010)
Production Workers/ Total Employment (1)	3 (1)	16 (9)	-.021 (.003)
Production Workers/ Total Employment (2)	14 (4)	5 (2)	.009 (.003)
Log (Capital/ Employment (1))	7 (1)	12 (4)	-.062 (.017)
Log (Capital/ Employment (2))	10 (5)	9 (2)	-.006 (.017)
Log (Value Added/ Employment (1))	3 (0)	16 (11)	-.082 (.010)
Log (Value Added/ Employment (2))	6 (2)	13 (6)	-.026 (.010)
Total Factor Productivity-Residual	0 (-)	19 (7)	-.036 (.006)
Total Factor Prouctivity-Factor Share	6 (0)	13 (5)	-.024 (.007)

*Number of coefficients statistically significant at the 95% level.

**This coefficient is from the pooled, all manufacturing industry regression.

Although the results presented in this section control for four-digit industry, the regressions assume that the coefficients of the establishment ownership variables are constant across industries. To relax the assumption of the relative ownership effects being constant across industries, equation (4) is estimated by interacting two-digit industry dummy variables with four establishment ownership variables: foreign-owned, owned by a U.S. multinational with more than 10 percent of its assets in foreign countries (U.S. MNCs), owned by a U.S. firm with more than 500 employees and less than 10 percent of its assets in foreign countries (Large Domestic), and owned by a U.S. firm with less than 500 employees (Small Domestic). Establishments owned by a U.S. firm with more than 500 employees and more than 10 percent of its assets in foreign countries is the omitted group. The appendix to this chapter presents a summary of the foreign-owned coefficients across two digit industries in addition to the coefficient and standard error for foreign-owned establishments when constrained to be constant across all industries.

The results in the appendix show considerable variation across two-digit industries, although the aggregate coefficients that are statistically significant at high levels tend to be the result of a majority of industries having coefficients with the same sign. For instance, foreign-owned establishments paid lower production worker wages than U.S. MNCs in sixteen of the nineteen industries examined, although only six of these estimates were statistically significant at the 95 percent level. Although the reasons behind these across-industry results are beyond the scope of this chapter, they are an area for future work.

U.S. MNCs by Extent of Foreign Assets

In chapter 1 of this volume, Dunning hypothesized that an important distinction among firms is not "foreignness," but the extent of "multinationality." The extent of multinationality can be gauged by the firm's foreign assets. In this section, U.S. plants are divided into six categories: (1) plants owned by U.S. firms with fewer than 500 employees, (2) plants owned by U.S. firms with more than 500 employees and no foreign assets, (3) plants owned by U.S. firms with more than 500 employees and foreign assets comprising up to 5 percent of total assets, (4) plants owned by U.S. firms with more than 500 employees and foreign assets comprising between 5 and 10 percent of total assets, (5) plants owned by U.S. firms with more than 500 employees and foreign assets comprising between 10 and 20 percent of total assets, and (6) plants owned by U.S. firms with more than 500 employees and foreign assets comprising over 20 percent of total assets. For ease of exposition, the first group is labeled small U.S. firm plants, and the second group large domestic firm plants. Plants belonging to U.S. firms that have some foreign assets, groups 3-6, are U.S. MNCs.

Table 3.8 presents regression results comparing the plant characteristics for the seven plant types: foreign establishments plus the six U.S. categories. The regression results in table 3.8 are based on equation (4) (page 59), where a set of dummy variables for the six U.S. firm types is added. Plants owned by U.S. firms with more than 500 employees and foreign assets comprising over 20 percent of total assets is the omitted category. Table 3.8 shows substantial differences between U.S.

Table 3.8
Differences between Foreign-Owned Establishments and Domestic Establishments Where Domestic Establishments Are Segregated into Six Types of Firms*

Dependent Variable	U.S.-owned, Firm <500 Employees	U.S.-owned, Firm >500 Employees, No Foreign Assets	Foreign-owned	U.S. MNCs, Percentage of Total Assets That Are Foreign		
				0-5%	5-10%	10-20%
Log (Production Worker Wages)	-.184 (.007)	-.123 (.007)	-.061 (.008)	-.070 (.008)	-.084 (.009)	-.060 (.008)
Log (Nonproduction Worker Wages (1))	-.035 (.009)	.056 (.010)	-.019 (.011)	-.019 (.012)	-.028 (.012)	-.028 (.012)
Log (Nonproduction Worker Wages (2))	-.125 (.009)	-.107 (.010)	-.068 (.011)	-.049 (.011)	-.053 (.012)	-.055 (.011)
Production Workers/ Total Employment (1)	-.005 (.003)	.010 (.003)	-.020 (.004)	.002 (.004)	.020 (.004)	.004 (.004)
Production Workers/ Total Employment (2)	.078 (.003)	.067 (.004)	.031 (.004)	.042 (.004)	.054 (.004)	.042 (.004)
Log (Capital/ Employment (1))	-.721 (.017)	-.413 (.018)	-.173 (.020)	-.222 (.021)	-.235 (.022)	-.213 (.021)
Log (Capital/ Employment (2))	-.559 (.017)	-.295 (.018)	-.073 (.020)	-.137 (.021)	-.159 (.022)	-.130 (.021)
Log (Value Added/ Employment (1))	-.534 (.010)	-.300 (.011)	-.167 (.012)	-.201 (.012)	-.199 (.013)	-.165 (.012)
Log (Value Added/ Employment (2))	-.372 (.010)	-.183 (.011)	-.068 (.012)	-.116 (.012)	-.123 (.013)	-.081 (.012)
Total Factor Productivity-Residual	-.136 (.005)	-.078 (.006)	-.059 (.006)	-.051 (.007)	-.052 (.007)	-.045 (.007)
Total Factor Prouctivity-Factor Share	-.087 (.007)	-.040 (.007)	-.038 (.008)	-.033 (.008)	-.039 (.009)	-.028 (.008)

*All numbers are regression coefficients from linear models that control for establishment size, four-digit industry, plant age, and state (standard errors in parentheses). Number of observations ≈ 115,000. Omitted firm type is U.S.-owned firms with more than 500 employees and foreign assets > 20 percent of total assets.

establishments belonging to U.S. MNCs and U.S. establishments belonging to small U.S. firms or large U.S. firms with no foreign assets. Starting from the bottom, small U.S. firm plants pay the lowest wages and have the lowest capital-to-labor ratios, labor productivity, and total-factor productivity. For instance, small U.S. firm plants have 60-72 percent less capital per employee, 37-53 percent lower labor productivity, and 18 percent lower production worker wages than plants belonging to U.S. firms with more than 500 employees and foreign assets comprising over 20 percent of total assets. The next group is large domestic firm plants. Although generally much better than small U.S. firm plants, large domestic firm plants still generally lag far behind U.S. MNCs. For instance, large U.S. firm plants have 30-41 percent less capital per employee, 18-30 percent lower labor productivity, and 12 percent lower production worker wages than plants belonging to U.S. firms with more than 500 employees and foreign assets comprising over 20 percent of total assets. A similar pattern generally holds for the skill mix of workers and nonproduction worker wages, especially when these variables are adjusted for employment in auxiliary establishments.

The story that emerges from the comparison between the U.S. multinational plant groups and foreign establishments is less clear. In Doms and Jensen (1998), a comparison between foreign-owned establishments and establishments that belong to U.S. MNCs showed that U.S. MNCs dominated foreign-owned firms in terms of wages (for both production and nonproduction workers), productivity (labor and total factor), skill mix, and capital-to-labor ratios. The results in table 3.8 differ from Doms and Jensen (1998) in that U.S. MNCs are grouped into four different categories. Table 3.8 addresses not only whether a firm is a multinational but also whether the proportion of its assets outside the United States is systematically related to the characteristics of domestic establishments. In terms of production worker wages, U.S. firms with more than 500 employees and foreign assets comprising over 20 percent of total assets paid their production workers significantly more than foreign-owned establishments and other U.S. MNCs, with the wage premium ranging from 6.0 to 8.4 percent. The results for nonproduction worker wages are more complex. When no correction is made for auxiliary employment, the wage premium paid to nonproduction workers in U.S. firms with more than 500 employees and foreign assets comprising over 20 percent of total assets ranges only from 1.9 to 2.8 percent and is not always statistically significant at the 95 percent level. But when adjustments are made for auxiliary employment, the nonproduction worker wage premium jumps to 4.9 to 6.8 percent, all of which are statistically significant. Consistent with the results for nonproduction worker wages are the results for the skill mix of workers. After adjusting for auxiliary employment, U.S. firms with more than 500 employees and foreign assets comprising over 20 percent of total assets have a lower production worker to total employment ratio than foreign-owned establishments and other U.S. MNCs.

U.S. firms with more than 500 employees and foreign assets comprising over 20 percent of total assets are also deeper in capital than other U.S. multinationals and foreign-owned establishments. The results for the capital-to-labor ratio range from 7.3 to 23.5 percent depending on specification. Therefore, similar results for labor productivity are not surprising: The results range from 6.8 to 20.1 percent, again depending on specification. Finally, U.S. firms with more than 500 employees and foreign assets comprising over 20 percent of total assets also enjoy higher total factor productivity, ranging from 2.8 to 5.9 percent, all statistically significant at high levels.

These results and the results of the previous section suggest that, while foreign-owned plants do indeed have different and, in many ways, superior characteristics compared to the average U.S.-owned plant, there is considerable heterogeneity within U.S.-owned plants, some of which is related to corporate ownership. Plants of U.S. MNCs compare favorably with foreign-owned plants, especially plants belonging to U.S. MNCs with significant foreign assets. Further, the results suggest that the plants of MNCs, whether U.S. or foreign, are the most alike and possess superior operating characteristics. These results suggest that plants of MNCs are the most productive, most capital intensive, and pay the highest wages. This finding is consistent with the notion that MNCs possess firm-specific advantages, whether superior product design, greater production efficiency, or advanced marketing skill, enabling them to overcome the barriers to foreign direct investment.

COMPARING PLANT CHARACTERISTICS BY COUNTRY OF OWNERSHIP

In this section, the information on country of ownership is exploited for foreign-owned establishments.[5] Vernon (1993) suggests that researchers have found it useful to distinguish multinational enterprises by their national base. He further suggests that this dimension will become less useful in the future. This point was elaborated by Dunning in chapter 1, where he asserted that "foreignness" may matter less over time. Differences in the operating characteristics of foreign-owned plants are here examined by country of ownership, with the results presented in table 3.9.[6] Perhaps the most interesting feature of the results in table 3.9 is that no country compares favorably with plants owned by U.S. multinationals. Moreover, table 3.9 highlights significant differences by country of ownership. Note the substantial variation in the estimates. Plants owned by Japanese firms do not seem to perform as well as might be expected in other respects, based on popular perceptions. Plants owned by Japanese firms have the lowest labor productivity of foreign-owned plants and the lowest and second-lowest measured TFP.[7] However, these data are from 1987. Much of the Japanese investment in the United States was done in the early 1980s. Age effects may not be captured by the plant age control. Thus, the low productivity numbers for Japan may be the result of start-up costs. In terms of labor market characteristics, Japanese MNCs are relatively poor performers. For example, Japanese-based MNCs paid 5.8 percent lower production wages than large, U.S.-based MNCs, while German-based MNCs paid 1.1 percent more. Australian MNCs pay their production workers even less than other Japanese-owned plants. While plants owned by companies from these countries exhibit lower productivity and production worker wages relative to plants owned by other multinationals, they compare favorably to domestic-owned plants belonging to firms without foreign assets.

Table 3.9
Cross-Country Comparisons
All Coefficients Are Relative to U.S. Firms with More Than 500 Employees, and Foreign Assets More Than 10 Percent of Total Assets*

Establishment Ownership Type	Log Production Worker Wages	Log Nonproduction Worker Wages (1)	(2)	PW/TE** (1)	(2)	Log Capital/ Labor (1)	(2)	Log Value Added/ Employee (1)	(2)	TFP*** R	FS
Australia	-.157	.094	.007	-.029	.013	.077	.164	-.192	-106	-.068	-.095
	(.038)	(.053)	(.052)	(.018)	(.018)	(.095)	(.094)	(.056)	(.056)	(.030)	(.038)
Canada	-.036	-.025	-.067	-.027	.008	-.036	.033	-.059	.010	-.013	-.017
	(.015)	(.021)	(.020)	(.007)	(.007)	(.038)	(.037)	(.022)	(.022)	(.012)	(.015)
France	-.054	-.001	-.081	-.022	.020	-.219	-.136	-.121	-.037	-.015	.021
	(.020)	(.030)	(.029)	(.010)	(.010)	(.051)	(.051)	(.030)	(.030)	(.016)	(.020)
Germany	.011	.046	.006	-.026	-.004	.130	.173	-.015	.029	-.032	-.035
	(.018)	(.025)	(.025)	(.009)	(.009)	(.046)	(.046)	(.027)	(.027)	(.015)	(.018)
Japan	-.058	-.028	-.039	.018	.059	-.001	.080	-.207	-.127	-.102	-.078
	(.019)	(.027)	(.026)	(.009)	(.009)	(.047)	(.047)	(.028)	(.028)	(.015)	(.019)
Netherlands	-.047	-.027	.032	.016	.002	.077	.051	.049	.024	-.020	-.019
	(.024)	(.033)	(.032)	(.011)	(.011)	(.059)	(.059)	(.035)	(.035)	(.019)	(.023)
Other	.016	.049	-.009	-.006	.035	-.056	.021	-.101	-.025	-.041	-.042
	(.015)	(.022)	(.021)	(.007)	(.007)	(.039)	(.039)	(.023)	(.023)	(.012)	(.015)
Sweden	.041	-.008	-.039	-.055	-.020	-.117	-.048	-.154	-.084	-.025	-.027
	(.030)	(.043)	(.042)	(.014)	(.015)	(.076)	(.076)	(.045)	(.045)	(.024)	(.030)
Switzerland	-.028	.003	.004	-.006	-.005	.058	.031	.064	.038	-.004	.016
	(.024)	(.033)	(.032)	(.011)	(.011)	(.059)	(.059)	(.035)	(.035)	(.019)	(.023)
UK	-.042	-.032	-.071	-.042	-.007	-.172	-.114	-.097	-.038	-.039	-.013
	(.011)	(.016)	(.015)	(.005)	(.005)	(.027)	(.027)	(.016)	(.016)	(.009)	(.011)
U.S., <500 employees	-.151	-.020	-.095	-.007	.056	-.607	-.489	-.447	-.329	-.112	-.073
	(.005)	(.007)	(.007)	(.002)	(.002)	(.012)	(.012)	(.007)	(.007)	(.004)	(.005)
U.S., >500 Employees, Foreign Assets <10% of Total	-.069	-.025	-.051	.008	.036	-.214	-.157	-.167	-.110	-.042	-.024
	(.005)	(.007)	(.007)	(.002)	(.002)	(.013)	(.013)	(.008)	(.008)	(.004)	(.005)

*All numbers are regression coefficients from linear models that control for establishment size, four-digit industry, plant age, and state (standard errors in parentheses). Number of observations ≈ 115,000.

** PW/TE = Production Workers/Total Employment.

***TFP = Total Factor Productivity; R = residual; FS = factor share.

TECHNOLOGY USAGE AT FOREIGN AND DOMESTIC-OWNED PLANTS

A potential advantage of FDI is technology transfer. If foreign plants are more technologically advanced than domestic plants, these plants might produce technological spillovers. In this section, the use of advanced technologies at foreign-owned and domestic-owned plants is examined.[8] Data from the SMT are used to examine technology use in domestic- and foreign-owned plants. The SMT provides information on the use of seventeen advanced manufacturing technologies for a sample of approximately 10,000 manufacturing plants in 1988.[9] The number of technologies reported as present in the manufacturing plant is used as a measure of the technology intensity at the plant.

Table 3.10 presents results for regressions with the number of technologies as the dependent variable comparing domestic-owned and foreign-owned establishments. On average, foreign plants do use more technologies than domestic plants. Yet, when controlling for industry, location, plant size, and plant age, the difference is reduced and marginally significant. When controlling for the capital-to-labor ratio at the plant, the difference is negligible. Table 3.11 presents results for the comparison of plants owned by U.S. MNCs. Here, plants owned by U.S. MNCs are the most technology-intensive plants. Foreign-owned plants use fewer technologies than plants owned by U.S. MNCs. Plants owned by large domestic firms also use fewer technologies than plants of U.S. MNCs, and plants of small U.S. firms use even fewer technologies.

Table 3.10
Technology Differences between Domestic- and Foreign-Owned Establishments with and without Controls*

Variable	Foreign-Owned No Controls	Foreign-Owned with Controls	Foreign-Owned Controls + K/L
Number of Technologies	.930	.268	.055
	(.189)	(.152)	(.149)

*The numbers are regression coefficients from linear models that do and do not control for establishment size, four-digit industry, plant age, and state (standard errors in parentheses). The omitted group is domestic-owned establishments. Number of observations ≈ 6,800.

These results suggest foreign-owned plants are more technology intensive than the average domestic-owned plant and, thereby, offer the possibility of more technology transfer than the average U.S. plant. The results are consistent with the notion that MNCs, whether foreign or domestic, use the most technology-intensive means of production.

CONCLUSION

The results presented in this chapter show that foreign-owned manufacturing plants in the United States in 1987 have superior operating characteristics relative to the average U.S.-owned plant. Foreign-owned plants pay higher wages, are more

Table 3.11
Technology Differences between Foreign-Owned Establishments and Domestic Establishments Where Domestic Establishments Are Segregated into Three Types of Firms*

	Firm Type		
Dependent Variable	Foreign-Owned	U.S.-owned, Firm > 500 Employees, Foreign Assets < 10% of Total Assets	U.S.-owned, Firm < 500 Employees
Number of Technologies	-.229	-.309	-1.03
	(.165)	(.106)	(.109)

*All numbers are regression coefficients from linear models that control for establishment size, four-digit industry, plant age, and state (standard errors in parentheses). Number of observations ≈ 6,800. Omitted firm type is U.S.-owned firms with more than 500 employees and foreign assets > 10% of total assets.

capital intensive, are more technology intensive, and are more productive than the average U.S. plant. These results suggest foreign direct investment in the United States may not have a detrimental effect on the nature of employment opportunities or the prospects for productivity growth in the U.S. domestic economy. On the contrary, foreign-owned plants seem to offer higher paying employment prospects and more promise of higher productivity than the average U.S.-owned plant. Further, large differences in the foreign-owned plants based on the country of ownership are not apparent.

This being said, the results also suggest foreign ownership of plants is not the important determining factor of plant-operating characteristics; instead, ownership by MNCs is important. Plants owned by U.S. MNCs exhibit the best operating characteristics, with plants of foreign MNCs exhibiting the next best operating characteristics. The combined class of MNCs significantly outperforms both plants owned by large domestic-oriented U.S. firms and plants owned by small U.S. firms. These results are consistent with the concept that MNCs possess firm-specific advantages enabling them to overcome the barriers of FDI.

NOTES

The authors thank the Bureau of Economic Analysis, especially Betty Barker, for access to their Foreign Direct Investment Survey. Doms's research was conducted while he was an employee of the Bureau of the Census. The views expressed in this chapter are the authors' and do not necessarily reflect those of the Bureau of the Census or of the Federal Reserve System.

1. Other research that uses plant- and industry-level data to investigate differences between domestic- and foreign-owned manufacturing plants includes Howenstine and Zeile (1994); Globerman, Ries, and Vertinsky (1994); and Howenstine and Zeile (1992).

2. For more information on the Data Link Project, see Department of Commerce (1992).

3. Administrative records almost always have less than five employees.

4. These records tend to be below average in terms of size.

5. This material is contained in Doms and Jensen (1998).

6. In this section and the next, U.S. multinationals are classed as firms with more than 10 percent of their assets being foreign. If the definition of U.S. multinational is made more strict by increasing the foreign asset share to 20 percent or more, then these results become even stronger, which is not surprising, given the results in table 3.9.

7. The plant's first appearance in the Census of Manufactures is used as a proxy for the age of the plant (going back to 1963). A problem that arises with this definition is that it pertains to new facilities, commonly referred to as "greenfield" plants. But, this definition does not measure how long a facility has been operated by a particular firm or owner. Further, how long each plant has been owned by a foreign company is not known.

8. This material is contained in Doms and Jensen (1998).

9. For more information on the design and coverage of the SMT, see Dunne and Schmitz (1992).

REFERENCES

Baily, Martin N., Charles Hulten, and David Campbell. 1992. "Productivity Dynamics in Manufacturing Plants," *Brookings Papers on Economic Activity*, '92 Microeconomics, pp. 187-267.

Davis, Steve J., and John Haltiwanger. 1991. "Wage Dispersion between and within U.S. Manufacturing Plants, 1963-86," *Brookings Papers on Economic Activity*, '91 Microeconomics, pp. 115-200.

Department of Commerce. 1992. *Foreign Direct Investment in the United States: Establishment Data for 1987*, Bureau of Economic Analysis and Bureau of the Census, June. Washington, D.C.: GPO.

Doms, Mark E., and J. Bradford Jensen. 1998. "Comparing Wages, Skills, and Productivity Between Domestic and Foreign Owned Manufacturing Establishments in the United States," *Geography vs. Ownership in Economic Accounting*, edited by Robert Baldwin, Robert Lipsey, and J. David Richardson. Chicago: University of Chicago Press.

Dunne, T., and J. Schmitz. 1992. "Wages, Employer Size-Wage Premia and Employment Structure: Their Relationship to Advanced Technology Usage at U.S. Manufacturing Establishments," Center for Economic Studies Discussion Paper no. 92-15. Washington, D.C.: GPO.

Froot, Kenneth A., and Jeremy C. Stein. 1991. "Exchange Rates and Foreign Direct Investment: An Imperfect Capital Markets Approach," *The Quarterly Journal of Economics* 106(November):119-217.

Globerman, S., J. Ries, and I. Vertinsky. 1994. "The Economic Performance of Foreign Affiliates in Canada," *Canadian Journal of Economics* 27(1):143-156.

Graham, Edward M., and Paul R. Krugman. 1989. *Foreign Direct Investment in the United States*. Washington, D.C.: Institute for International Economics.

Howenstine, Ned G., and William J. Zeile. 1992. "Foreign Direct Investment in the United States: Establishment Data for 1987," *Survey of Current Business* 72(October):44-78.
———. 1994. "Characteristics of Foreign-Owned U.S. Manufacturing Establishments," *Survey of Current Business* 74(January):34-59.

McCulloch, Rachel. 1993. "New Perspectives on Foreign Direct Investment," in *Foreign Direct Investment*, edited by Kenneth A. Froot. Chicago: University of Chicago Press.

Troske, K. 1994. "Evidence on the Employer Size-Wage Premium for Worker-Establishment Matched Data," mimeo, Center for Economic Studies, Bureau of the Census, Washington, D.C.:GPO.

Vernon, Raymond. 1993. "Where Are the Multinationals Headed?" in *Foreign Direct Investment*, edited by Kenneth A. Froot. Chicago: University of Chicago Press, pp. 57-79.

APPENDIX: SUMMARY STATISTICS FOR REGRESSION ANALYSIS OF FOREIGN-OWNED PLANTS RELATIVE TO PLANTS OF U.S. MNCS WITH MORE THAN 500 EMPLOYEES AND FOREIGN ASSETS >10% OF TOTAL ASSETS BY TWO-DIGIT INDUSTRY (STANDARD ERRORS IN PARENTHESES)

2-Digit Industry	Log Prod. Work. Wages	Log Nonproduction Worker Wages		PW/TE		Log Capital/ Labor		Log Value Added/ Employee		Total Factor Productivity	
	(1)	(1)	(2)	(1)	(2)	(1)	(2)	(1)	(2)	R	FS
Ind. 20, Food	.031	.023	.000	-.026	.002	-.023	.029	.034	.087	-.015	.005
	(.018)	(.025)	(.024)	(.008)	(.009)	(.044)	(.044)	(.026)	(.026)	(.014)	(.018)
Ind. 21, Tobacco	D	D	D	D	D	D	D	D	D	D	D
Ind. 22, Textiles	-.034	-.019	-.090	-.040	.021	.118	.235	-.098	.018	-.003	-.058
	(.041)	(.057)	(.055)	(.019)	(.020)	(.103)	(.102)	(.060)	(.060)	(.033)	(.041)
Ind. 23, Apparel	-.056	.044	-.035	-.065	-.015	.321	.419	-.079	.018	-.027	.006
	(.061)	(.089)	(.087)	(.029)	(.029)	(.152)	(.152)	(.090)	(.089)	(.048)	(.060)
Ind. 24, Lumber	-.054	.242	.187	-.014	.036	-.172	-.073	-.088	.011	-.003	-.031
	(.040)	(.055)	(.054)	(.019)	(.019)	(.099)	(.099)	(.059)	(.058)	(.032)	(.039)
Ind. 25, Furniture/ Fixtures	-.048	-.066	-.083	-.010	.037	-.255	-.163	-.139	-.049	-.030	.043
	(.057)	(.078)	(.076)	(.027)	(.027)	(.142)	(.142)	(.084)	(.084)	(.045)	(.057)
Ind. 26, Paper Products	-.052	-.046	-.105	-.006	.043	-.213	-.124	-.229	-.139	-.079	-.062
	(.026)	(.036)	(.035)	(.012)	(.013)	(.065)	(.065)	(.038)	(.038)	(.021)	(.026)
Ind. 27, Printing/ Publishing	-.066	-.111	-.136	-.074	-.029	-.131	-.043	-.110	-.022	-.000	-.018
	(.022)	(.032)	(.031)	(.010)	(.011)	(.057)	(.056)	(.033)	(.033)	(.018)	(.022)
Ind. 28, Chemicals	.031	-.020	-.037	-.010	.001	.002	.010	.041	.048	-.007	.018
	(.015)	(.021)	(.021)	(.007)	(.007)	(.038)	(.038)	(.022)	(.022)	(.012)	(.015)
Ind. 29, Petroleum Products	.019	.094	.039	.035	.046	-.197	-.188	.073	.083	-.036	.013
	(.030)	(.047)	(.046)	(.014)	(.015)	(.075)	(.075)	(.044)	(.044)	(.024)	(.030)
Ind. 30, Rubber and Plastics	-.027	.007	-.043	-.023	.014	.064	.131	-.103	-.036	-.030	-.068
	(.022)	(.031)	(.030)	(.010)	(.011)	(.055)	(.055)	(.033)	(.033)	(.018)	(.022)
Ind. 31, Leather Goods	-.094	-.239	-.345	-.002	.048	-.177	-.078	-.324	-.225	-.096	-.128
	(.066)	(.092)	(.090)	(.031)	(.032)	(.166)	(.166)	(.098)	(.096)	(.053)	(.066)
Ind. 32, Stone, Clay, Glass	-.084	.037	.023	.014	.041	-.328	-.277	-.128	-.077	-.065	.004
	(.018)	(.026)	(.026)	(.008)	(.009)	(.045)	(.044)	(.026)	(.026)	(.014)	(.018)
Ind. 33, Primary Metals	-.030	-.033	-.080	-.025	.001	-.060	-.005	-.121	-.067	-.054	-.054
	(.028)	(.039)	(.038)	(.013)	(.014)	(.070)	(.070)	(.041)	(.041)	(.022)	(.028)
Ind. 34, Fabricated Metals	-.052	-.006	-.048	-.045	-.011	.019	.084	-.124	-.060	-.013	-.022
	(.023)	(.032)	(.031)	(.011)	(.011)	(.058)	(.057)	(.034)	(.034)	(.018)	(.023)
Ind. 35, Industrial Machinery	-.017	.008	-.043	-.060	-.022	-.041	.030	-.131	-.060	-.058	-.025
	(.020)	(.028)	(.027)	(.009)	(.010)	(.050)	(.050)	(.030)	(.030)	(.016)	(.020)
Ind. 36, Electrical Machinery	-.088	-.032	-.055	.004	.036	-.040	.026	-.201	-.136	-.067	-.070
	(.022)	(.031)	(.030)	(.010)	(.011)	(.055)	(.055)	(.032)	(.032)	(.017)	(.022)
Ind. 37, Transportation Equipment	-.070	.069	.003	-.027	.013	-.091	-.0167	-.190	-.115	-.074	-.059
	(.038)	(.053)	(.051)	(.018)	(.018)	(.095)	(.095)	(.056)	(.056)	(.030)	(.038)
Ind. 38, Scientific Instruments	-.055	-.020	-.059	-.035	.002	.121	.184	-.100	-.037	-.067	-.079
	(.029)	(.040)	(.039)	(.014)	(.014)	(.072)	(.072)	(.043)	(.043)	(.023)	(.029)
Ind. 39, Miscellaneous	-.117	-.041	-.060	-.050	-.011	.177	.252	-.095	-.018	-.003	-.094
	(.042)	(.058)	(.057)	(.020)	(.020)	(.106)	(.106)	(.062)	(.062)	(.034)	(.042)

4

Takeovers and Transplants: Reassessing FDIUS

Edward J. Ray

INTRODUCTION

The purpose of this chapter is to provide a comprehensive summary and analysis of foreign direct investment in the United States (FDIUS) between 1979 and 1990.[1] This period covers the historic surge in foreign ownership that sparked much of the debate during the late 1980s and early 1990s. The research extends beyond the earlier analyses of FDIUS and its economic characteristics (Graham and Krugman 1989; Glickman and Woodward 1990). This study includes evidence of the concentration of foreign direct investment (FDI) by industry and location for each source country. Industry, state, and macroeconomic factors are identified to explain takeovers as well as new capital investment by source countries. Principal findings not reflected in earlier studies include evidence that Japanese new plant investment in U.S. manufacturing (transplants) has been stimulated both by existing trade restrictions and the threat of new protectionist measures in the United States and by a desire to install new technology into U.S. manufacturing plants. Generally, acquisitions (takeovers) are associated with management-intensive industries in which rents associated with administrative know-how are likely to be greatest. Differences in workforce characteristics across states, but not tax and business incentive programs or the availability of labor, play a significant role in determining the location of new plant and expansion FDIUS.

The scope of this study is unique in several respects:

1. The sources of investment include all countries and, separately, the United Kingdom (U.K.), the European Community[2] (EC), Canada, Japan, and the rest of the world;
2. FDI is divided into acquisitions or equity investments (takeovers) and new plant expansions or investments (transplants);
3. FDI activity is sorted by four-digit Standard Industrial Classification (SIC) industry as well as by the state in which the investment is located; and
4. Regression analysis is used to assess the impact of industry structure, production characteristics, trade policies, macroeconomic variables (including real exchange rates and relative economic growth), technology, and state characteristics (including taxes, business

incentive programs, workforce characteristics, and unemployment) on FDI activities of each of the investing countries.[3]

The data used in the study include four-digit SIC data, for all industries as well as for manufacturing, and information concerning annual macroeconomic variables and state level measures. Samples range from 600 for the geographical analyses to over 3,000 for the industrial characteristics studies.

The second section of the chapter offers a brief summary of information regarding the year-to-year concentration of FDI in the United States for all industries, for manufacturing, and by geographic location. The section summarizes the relative importance of investment from the U.K., the EC, Canada, Japan, and the rest of the world in all industries and manufacturing for all types of FDI including, separately, new plant and expansion activity. The geographical location of all industry, manufacturing, and new plant and expansion FDI for each source country are summarized as well.

The third section of the chapter provides evidence from regression analyses regarding the industry, macroeconomic, and state-specific factors that explain equity as well as new plant and expansion FDI activity in manufacturing in the United States during the 1979-1990 period. Regression analyses are also applied to the relationship between the geographical distribution of foreign direct investment across states throughout the 1979-1990 period and state workforce, tax and incentive policies, and industry and national economic conditions. The last section provides concluding remarks.

SOURCES AND USES OF FDIUS

The purpose of this section is to provide a context for and complement to the regression analyses in the following section. Here, extensive information is provided regarding the time profile, industry concentration, and location of new plant and expansion FDI activity in the United States from each of the source countries identified earlier.

Tables B.1 and B.2 in appendix B provide annual figures for FDI activity in the United States for all industries and across manufacturing industries, respectively, between 1979 and 1990. In all, $447 billion in overall FDI activity in the United States during the period and $216 billion in manufacturing FDI are documented. These tables reflect that the pace of FDI investment doubled between the first and second halves of the 1980s. For the 1979-1990 period as a whole, a dozen of the nearly 1,000 four-digit SIC industries accounted for one-third of overall FDIUS, while ten among the 469 four-digit SIC manufacturing industries accounted for 37 percent of all FDI activity in manufacturing.

The overall FDI figures are dominated by investments in natural resource-based industries (such as Crude Petroleum and Natural Gas, Petroleum Refining, Bituminous Coal and Lignite, and Copper Ore) and by service industries (like Hotels and Motels, Motion Picture and Video Production, Department Stores, Depository Institutions, and Insurance Carriers). The leading sectors for manufacturing FDI activity comprise a diverse group ranging from Petroleum Refining, Plastics Materials and Resins, Motor Vehicles and Car Bodies, and Tires and Inner Tubes to Book

Publishing, Dry, Condensed and Evaporated Products, and Prepared Flour Mixes and Doughs.

Table B.3 provides a time profile of all industry and manufacturing sector FDI activity by state within which the investment occurred in the United States from 1979 to 1990. Ten states accounted for 69 percent of all industry FDI and 71 percent of manufacturing FDI. Nine of the ten leading states for each type of investment activity are the same: California, New York, Texas, Ohio, Pennsylvania, Illinois, Connecticut, New Jersey, and Massachusetts. Between 1979 and 1990, Florida is a top ten state in overall, but not manufacturing, FDI activity, while Minnesota is a top ten state for manufacturing, but not overall, FDI.

The table dramatizes the fact that the pace of FDI activity in the United States during the fast growth period of the 1980s quickened and was highly concentrated in terms of the industries and states within which investment occurred. One view to explain the rapid expansion of FDI activity in the United States that gained some currency during the last half of the 1980s was that the activity reflected an effort by foreigners to buy U.S. industry at bargain basement prices as a result of the depreciation of the U.S. dollar against major currencies.[4] The fact that both overall investment and manufacturing investment were highly concentrated in terms of both industry and location suggests that a more subtle process was at work.

Tables B.4 through B.6 provide information on the concentration of FDIUS for all industries, for manufacturing industries, and for new plant and expansion investment across manufacturing industries, with summaries for all industries according to the source country or region for the investment. Each table indicates the leading industries within which investment activity was located from all sources and, separately, the amount and rank of the investment in each of those industries for each of the source countries.

The twelve industries that accounted for one-third of all FDI activity in the United States during the period 1979-1990 were among the leading investment target areas for each of the countries considered separately. Japan invested heavily in Motion Picture and Video Production and Hotels and Motels. Canada invested heavily in Department Stores. The U.K. had substantial investments in Pharmaceutical Preparations and Petroleum Refining. The EC put a large share of its money in Crude Petroleum and Natural Gas. The rest of the world invested heavily in natural resource-based industries, including Bituminous Coal and Lignite, Crude Petroleum and Natural Gas, and Petroleum Refining. Together, the U.K., Japan, Canada, and the EC accounted for $372.8 billion (83.4 percent) of the total $447.1 billion in FDI in the United States during the 1979-1990 period. The U.K. was the leading source of FDI in the United States, with $114.5 billion in investments, followed by the EC, Japan, and Canada.

Each of the countries considered in this study served as a major source of investment funds in one or more of the manufacturing industries in which FDI was concentrated, as indicated in table B.5. Japan invested heavily in Motor Vehicles and Car Bodies, Tires and Inner Tubes, and Electronic Computing Equipment. Canada invested heavily in Plastics Materials and Resins and Book Publishing. The U.K. invested substantial sums in Pharmaceutical Preparations, Petroleum Refining, Prepared Flour Mixes and Doughs, and Book Publishing. At the same time, Toilet

Preparations, Plastics Materials and Resins, and Tires and Inner Tubes were targets for significant EC FDI activity in U.S. manufacturing. Together, Japan, Canada, the U.K., and the EC accounted for $182.3 billion (84.4 percent) of the total of $216.1 billion in FDI in U.S. manufacturing between 1979 and 1990. Again, the U.K. was the leading source of FDI activity in the manufacturing sector in the U.S. with $70 billion in investments, followed by the EC, Japan, and Canada.

Table B.6 provides information on the leading sectors within which FDI took the form of real capital formation through new plant construction and expansion in manufacturing industries, with summaries for all industries. There are several points worth noting. First, new plant and expansion investment accounted for only $36.3 billion (8.1 percent) of all industry FDI activity and $31.3 billion (14.5 percent) of manufacturing industry FDI activity. Second, Japan accounted for $17.9 billion (49.4 percent) of new plant and expansion FDIUS and $16.9 billion (53.9 percent) of new plant and expansion FDI activity in U.S. manufacturing. Those figures suggest that, if there were much content to the charge that FDIUS during the 1979-1990 period was motivated by desires to buy up the United States on the cheap, the label would appear to be less applicable to Japan than to our other major industrial trading partners. Moreover, these facts partially explain the results concerning operating characteristics for Japanese MNCs in 1987 presented by Doms and Jensen in the previous chapter. Much of Japanese investment was of recent vintage, new plant investment (transplants), not takeovers of existing plants. Takeovers of existing companies would not be as likely to involve startup costs that would explain lower productivity, as would be the case when new plants have just been constructed.

Third, the top ten share of all FDI activity is generally more concentrated for new plant and expansion FDI activity for all industries and manufacturing than for overall FDI activity with respect to all industries and manufacturing. Further, new plant and expansion FDI activity was more concentrated in terms of source countries than overall FDI activity. Japan, Canada, the U.K., and EC accounted for $32.9 billion (90.5 percent) of all industry new plant and expansion FDI and $29.0 billion (92.6 percent) of manufacturing new plant and expansion FDI.

Tables B.7 and B.8 in appendix B provide information on the top ten states within which FDI activity was located throughout the 1979-1990 period and the contribution of each of the source countries to that concentration of activity for each of our four investment aggregates (all industries, manufacturing, new plant and expansion in all industries, and new plant and expansion in manufacturing). California, Ohio, and Texas are among the top ten states for FDI activity for all four industry investment measures. New plant and expansion investment is more concentrated in Midwestern (Indiana, Ohio, Tennessee, Kentucky, Michigan) and southern (Alabama, Georgia, North Carolina) states than is overall FDI activity. The relative concentration of investment in the top ten states was more variable for manufacturing and for both measures of new plant and expansion FDI than for overall FDI from the source countries.

DETERMINANTS OF FDI ACTIVITY IN THE UNITED STATES

The purpose of this section is to explore alternative explanations for the extraordinary level of FDI activity in manufacturing in the United States during the 1979-1990 period and to examine the explanatory power of factors that have been proposed to explain the industry, geographical location, and source country or region concentration of overall investment and investment in new plant and expansions. This effort is uniquely comprehensive. It examines the explanatory power of industry, macroeconomic, and location factors for FDI activity in manufacturing as well as all industries; and provides an assessment of factors contributing to equity FDI in manufacturing and new plant and expansion investment in manufacturing over an extended period.

For the sake of brevity, the regression analyses focus on new plant and expansion FDI activity in the United States between 1979 and 1990.[5] Nevertheless, regression analyses of equity and new plant and expansion FDI activity are compared and contrasted to assess the likely impact of FDI activity on technology flows to and from the United States during the period with respect to the source countries included in this study.

In the regression analyses, a set of five variables capture the relevance of industry-specific characteristics and macroeconomic measures to decisions by companies in foreign source countries to undertake FDIUS during the 1979-1990 period.[6] Industry-specific measures include the rate of growth in the value of shipments in the United States during the 1980s within the industry in which the investment occurred; the size of the industry, as measured by the value of shipments within the industry in the United States that is targeted for the investment; and a measure of whether the industry within which the investment occurs is the same at the four-digit SIC level as the industry of the parent company in the source country or region.[7]

The two macroeconomic variables common to the regressions are U.S. GNP growth relative to growth in the home country or region of the investing parent company and the real exchange rate between the U.S. dollar and the currency of the country or region of the investing parent company country or region.[8] The exchange rate is expressed as the real dollar price of the foreign currency. A higher value of the real exchange rate corresponds to a depreciation of the U.S. dollar relative to the home country currency of the investing firm.

The strongest link between industry characteristics and both equity and new plant and expansion FDI activity is the positive and significant relationship between the investment activity and the size of the market in the United States. The relevance of market size is consistent with the presumption that FDI is most likely to be attractive to a potential investor if it provides access to large local markets for goods and services.

Almost as strong and certainly as consistent a finding with respect to the determinants of FDI in manufacturing is the positive and significant link between the value of investment and the indicator that the parent and subsidiary are in the same manufacturing industry, whether equity or new plant and expansion FDI (Caves 1971; Horstmann and Markusen 1987; Markusen 1995; Ray 1989; Ray 1995; Rugman 1980; Vernon 1966). The positive relationship, found in earlier studies, is related to the fact that foreign investors face disadvantages in terms of uncertainties regarding legal standing, supplier connections, customer needs, competitive challenges, and the like, in trying to compete through subsidiaries in distant markets. The presumption is that those disadvantages are likely to be minimized if the parent company invests in local manufacturing abroad in product lines that are well known to the investing firm and within which the parent has had marketing success in the home country or region.

The relative growth in shipments within a given industry in the United States was found to have a negative impact on or to be unrelated to FDI in U.S. manufacturing for both equity and new plant and expansion FDI. Simple intuition would lead one to expect investment of all kinds including FDI to be associated with rapid growth industries. One could construct somewhat tortured explanations for the negative relationship found in some cases.[9]

U.S. relative GNP growth compared to real aggregate economic growth in the source country or region of the parent investing company was found, generally, to be unrelated to FDI activity, although new plant and expansion by Japanese companies in the United States is consistently and positively related to relative GNP growth in the United States. That finding is worth noting since the overall explanatory power of all of the regression runs proved greatest for Japanese FDIUS. Japan accounted for the majority of new plant and expansion FDI activity in manufacturing in the United States during the period analyzed.

The real effective exchange rate proved positively related to equity and new plant and expansion FDIUS from Japan, for equity investment from the EC, and for new plant and expansion FDI from the U.K. Those positive linkages imply that FDIUS for those forms of investment and from those countries was stimulated by a depreciation of the U.S. dollar relative to the home country currency of the investing parent company. The explanation for such a relationship could be bargain shopping, in the case of equity investment, and timing of physical capital investment to keep costs down, in the case of new plant and expansion investments. Those findings are consistent with some earlier studies but are not consistent with the results of several recently published papers.[10]

Table 4.1 includes several variables intended to reflect the market characteristics of industries in which new plant and expansion FDI activity might be concentrated. If one were to use the early literature on U.S. FDI in Europe as a guide to predicting the industry targets for FDIUS, one would expect to find investment concentrated in industries producing consumer goods that are produced by a few oligopoly firms with a highly unionized workforce (Caves 1971; Gruber, Mehta, and Vernon 1967; Hymer 1960; Vernon 1966). The concentrated nature of production and unionization would presumably signal the existence of oligopoly industry quasi-rents to be captured by entering the market. The results in table 4.1 suggest that FDI in new plant and expansions in the United States were primarily associated with intermediate goods that were not particularly heavily unionized. There is evidence that FDI activity by Japan and from all sources is positively related to production concentration.

Table 4.2 provides information on the relationship between various measures of protection within manufacturing industries and new plant and expansion FDI from source countries. Specifically, the regressions include as separate measures tariffs,

Table 4.1
Market Structure and the Value of New Plant and Plant Expansion FDIUS:
1979-1990
(Tobit Regressions with Absolute t-Statistics in Parentheses)

Independent Variables	Dependent—New Plant & Plant Expansion FDIUS ($ million)				
	All Countries	U.K.	EC	Japan	Canada
Constant	-4.80	-5.19	-4.43	-5.15	-5.06
	(19.04)	(9.04)	(11.64)	(15.01)	(4.18)
Consumer Goods	-0.38	-0.56	-0.38	-0.21	-0.58
	(4.45)	(2.71)	(3.10)	(2.02)	(2.69)
Unionization	0.001	-0.004	-0.002	-0.0008	0.004
	(1.14)	(1.53)	(1.16)	(0.53)	(1.48)
Four-Firm Concentration Ratio	0.006	0.003	0.002	0.004	-0.002
	(4.48)	(1.13)	(1.21)	(2.14)	(0.74)
Within Parent Industry	0.001	0.02	0.009	0.008	0.07
	(5.20)	(5.60)	(5.97)	(10.55)	(3.59)
Log Value of Shipments	0.40	0.27	0.32	0.31	0.26
	(15.65)	(5.56)	(9.28)	(9.31)	(5.35)
U.S. Industry Growth	-0.002	-0.003	-0.003	-0.003	-0.0006
	(2.03)	(1.49)	(2.17)	(2.60)	(0.34)
U.S. Relative GNP Growth	0.01	0.04	-0.01	0.20	-0.16
	(0.89)	(0.77)	(2.07)	(2.54)	(0.57)
Effective Exchange Rate	0.41	0.006	0.006	1.70	0.01
	(1.98)	(2.99)	(1.31)	(6.49)	(0.85)
R-square	0.19	0.01	0.12	0.43	0.01
Number of observations	3048	3048	3048	3048	3048

a dummy variable for the presence of nontariff barriers to trade (NTBs), and a joint tariff-NTB measure. Earlier studies have documented that the most highly protected industries in the United States enjoy both tariff and NTB protection (Ray and Marvel 1984). Industries that are protected only with tariffs are industries that have experienced the greatest loss of protection through the postwar GATT rounds of trade liberalization. Industries protected only with NTBs are industries that have acquired protection during the postwar period, because innovations in nontariff protective measures have expanded the reach of protectionism to politically weaker industries. The evidence in table 4.2 suggests industries that have systematically experienced declining protection, those protected with tariffs only, and relatively newly protected industries have not been targets for new plant and expansion FDI from any of the source countries or regions. However, industries that maintained or even gained protection throughout the trade liberalization period after World War II were more likely to attract real capital investment from all sources, Japan, and Canada. These

Table 4.2
U.S. Protectionism and the Value of New Plant and Plant Expansion FDIUS:
1979-1990
(Tobit Regressions with Absolute t-Statistics in Parentheses)

Independent Variables	Dependent—New Plant & Plant Expansion FDIUS ($ million)				
	All Countries	U.K.	EC	Japan	Canada
Constant	-4.49	-5.62	-4.28	-5.07	-5.56
	(16.50)	(8.85)	(10.22)	(13.69)	(4.17)
Tariff Barriers	-0.03	0.02	0.0004	-0.03	-0.12
	(2.28)	(1.03)	(0.02)	(1.89)	(3.10)
Nontariff Trade Barriers	-0.38	-0.18	0.003	-0.58	-0.84
	(3.52)	(0.84)	(0.02)	(3.96)	(3.79)
Tariff and Nontariff Trade Barriers	0.05	-0.007	0.007	0.05	0.14
	(3.18)	(0.27)	(0.33)	(2.57)	(3.42)
Trade Balance	0.00009	0.00012	0.0004	-0.0003	-0.000001
	(3.43)	(0.86)	(2.03)	(2.27)	(0.16)
Within Parent Industry Investment	0.001	0.02	0.008	0.008	0.08
	(5.40)	(4.43)	(5.09)	(11.15)	(3.69)
Log Value of Shipments	0.41	0.28	0.30	0.33	0.31
	(14.78)	(5.26)	(8.01)	(9.11)	(5.84)
U.S. Industry Growth	-0.001	-0.002	-0.002	-0.003	-0.0008
	(1.40)	(1.02)	(1.40)	(2.12)	(0.40)
U.S. Relative GNP Growth	0.01	0.01	-0.01	0.22	-0.10
	(1.04)	(0.22)	(1.62)	(2.64)	(0.34)
Effective Exchange Rate	0.45	0.007	0.005	1.73	0.02
	(2.01)	(3.04)	(0.94)	(6.23)	(1.30)
R-square	0.18	0.007	0.13	0.44	0.01
Number of observations	2556	2532	2532	2544	2544

results contrast with earlier evidence implying there are no protection-jumping invest-ment incentives based on data for the 1979-1985 period (Ray 1989; Ray 1995).[11]

Furthermore, table 4.2 includes a measure of the difference between the industry-specific trade balance and the overall trade balance for the United States. That variable is intended to reflect which industries are relatively most vulnerable to imports and therefore most likely to be candidates for future protection. The trade balance effect is positive for all sources and negative for Japan. Given the majority role of Japan in new plant and expansion FDI activity in manufacturing in the United States, it is interesting to find that Japan did invest in real capital formation in subsidiaries in U.S. industries from which pressure for protectionist measures might be expected to increase over time. Clearly, this is an area of inquiry that bears revisiting as more data become available.

Table 4.3
Production Characteristics and the Value of Equity FDIUS: 1979-1990
(Tobit Regressions with Absolute t-Statistics in Parentheses)

Independent Variables	Dependent—Equity FDIUS ($ million)				
	All Coun- tries	U.K.	EC	Japan	Canada
Constant	-5.54	-5.79	-5.93	-5.92	-5.68
	(21.01)	(13.09)	(13.95)	(14.87)	(5.48)
Midpoint Plant Shipments	-0.0008	-0.002	-0.003	-0.0004	-0.001
	(1.69)	(2.86)	(3.67)	(0.65)	(1.69)
Management Intensity	3.25	3.78	3.45	2.17	2.04
	(8.38)	(7.07)	(6.45)	(3.86)	(2.99)
Origin R&D	-0.0004	-0.0003	0.001	-0.00002	-0.0008
	(1.37)	(0.65)	(2.25)	(0.04)	(1.13)
Within Parent Industry	0.002	0.02	0.01	0.003	0.08
	(8.80)	(6.52)	(6.76)	(3.15)	(4.82)
Log Value of Shipments	0.42	0.38	0.32	0.34	0.37
	(15.20)	(9.64)	(8.22)	(8.48)	(7.65)
U.S. Industry Growth	-0.002	0.0004	-0.001	-0.002	0.0001
	(1.86)	(0.39)	(0.87)	(1.46)	(0.10)
U.S. Relative GNP Growth	-0.01	0.07	-0.0003	-0.05	-0.04
	(0.92)	(1.97)	(0.05)	(0.60)	(0.16)
Effective Exchange Rate	1.49	0.003	0.02	2.26	0.005
	(7.44)	(1.78)	(5.19)	(8.07)	(0.50)
R-square	0.15	0.02	0.04	0.03	0.008
Number of observations	2700	2700	2700	2700	2700

Tables 4.3 and 4.4 contain the same set of explanatory variables. The dependent variable in table 4.3 is equity FDIUS (takeovers), and the dependent variable in table 4.4 is new plant and expansion FDIUS (transplants). FDI activity is generally presumed associated with the existence of quasi-rents that can be captured to offset the natural disadvantages of attempting to operate a business in a foreign country. Therefore, it is interesting to inquire if differences in the sources of quasi-rents could help to explain whether an investment would be in the form of an equity position or in the form of new physical capital investment.

To the extent that the source of quasi-rents from FDI is associated with administrative know-how, one might expect to find such investment concentrated in management-intensive industries in which scale economies are not significant and that it would take the form of equity investments, which are, again, primarily takeovers of existing companies. The evidence in table 4.3 suggests that equity FDI is associated with management-intensive industries with a bias toward small-scale plant operations.

Consequences for the Economy

Table 4.4
Production Characteristics and the Value of New Plant and Plant Expansion FDIUS: 1979-1990
(Tobit Regressions with Absolute t-Statistics in Parentheses)

Independent Variables	Dependent—New Plant & Plant Expansion FDIUS ($ million)				
	All Coun-tries	U.K.	EC	Japan	Canada
Constant	-3.66	-6.25	-4.43	-4.70	-5.54
	(13.50)	(8.94)	(10.51)	(12.53)	(4.32)
Midpoint Plant Shipments	0.001	-0.0006	-0.001	0.001	-0.0001
	(2.18)	(0.67)	(1.57)	(1.89)	(0.14)
Management Intensity	0.59	3.87	1.84	0.82	-0.71
	(1.41)	(4.92)	(3.28)	(1.49)	(0.81)
Origin R&D	0.002	-0.00007	0.001	0.001	-0.0003
	(6.64)	(0.10)	(2.67)	(2.89)	(0.44)
Within Parent Industry	0.0005	0.02	0.008	0.004	0.08
	(2.02)	(5.69)	(5.02)	(4.63)	(3.75)
Log Value of Shipments	0.26	0.26	0.29	0.22	0.29
	(9.21)	(4.30)	(7.09)	(5.75)	(5.26)
U.S. Industry Growth	-0.001	-0.001	-0.003	-0.001	-0.0006
	(1.20)	(0.63)	(2.28)	(1.12)	(0.32)
U.S. Relative GNP Growth	0.01	0.03	-0.01	0.20	-0.12
	(1.05)	(0.61)	(1.64)	(2.53)	(0.43)
Effective Exchange Rate	0.36	0.007	0.004	1.72	0.02
	(1.65)	(3.24)	(0.78)	(6.24)	(1.16)
R-square	0.30	0.02	0.13	0.44	0.004
Number of Observations	2700	2700	2700	2700	2700

If the source of quasi-rents is to be found embodied in new capital equipment, one would expect FDI to be concentrated in capital-intensive industries that are research and development (R&D) intensive, rather than management intensive, and to take the form of new plant and expansion FDI. Table 4.4 indicates that scale effects are insignificant, except in the "all sources" case, where it is positive. Management intensity, except for the U.K. and the EC, is not significant; and R&D intensity in production is positive for all sources, EC, and Japan with respect to new plant and expansion FDI. While far from conclusive, the results presented in tables 4.3 and 4.4 provide some support for the argument that equity FDI may reflect attempts to capitalize on managerial know-how and that physical, capital investments in subsidiaries through FDI activity, which Japan dominated, may reflect efforts to capture quasi-rents by introducing new technology into subsidiaries.[12] The latter results are broadly consistent with Doms and Jensen's findings presented in the previous chapter. Further analysis of technology effects can be found in subsequent chapters. The evidence here would suggest that Japanese FDI in new plant and expansions in the United States resulted in a transfer of technology *into* U.S. industry rather than a transfer of technology *out of* U.S. industry. If one wanted to acquire U.S. technology to ship it abroad, equity and not new plant and expansion investment would be the simplest way to accomplish that end.

Tables 4.5 and 4.6 provide regression analyses of the relationship between new plant and expansion FDIUS across states throughout the 1979-1990 period. Both tables include U.S. relative GNP growth and the real effective exchange rate as explanatory variables. The relative growth rate was not significantly related to the timing of investments across states, but the real exchange rate results indicate that Japan timed its real capital investments in U.S. subsidiaries in all industries and in manufacturing to take advantage of U.S. dollar depreciation. FDI in new plant and expansions in manufacturing from all sources was timed to take advantage of U.S. dollar depreciation, too.

Both tables indicate that FDI was not attracted to states based on the availability of labor (as measured by state unemployment rates), income per capita, or business incentive programs. That last result contrasts with earlier work and is important enough in its implications for state policy to warrant more systematic investigation.[13]

State unionization rates had a consistent, negative impact on FDI in new plant and expansions for all sources, the U.K., and the EC. State tax collections per capita had a positive impact on all source and U.K. new plant and expansion investment in all industries.

Based on the earlier discussion of the industries in which various countries invested in new plant and expansion FDIUS, it would not be surprising to find that Japanese new capital FDI was located in states with relatively greater numbers of auto workers, while the U.K. and the world in general invested in states with a relative abundance of petroleum workers. However, there may be a point to the relationship between workforce characteristics and the location of FDI within the United States that has not been appreciated. Foreign subsidiaries need local workers with the job-specific skills relevant to their line of business. FDI activity in auto states with ready supplies of petroleum and steel workers. In short, there may be a message here that the characteristics of the local workforce are more important to attracting FDI to a particular industry than such measures as state-based tax incentives or general labor availability, as measured by the state unemployment rate. Further analysis of the spatial distribution of FDIUS by source country is presented in Cletus Coughlin's contribution to this volume.

Table 4.5
FDI in New Plants and Plant Expansion in the United States 1979-1990: Across States, All Industries
(OLS Regressions with Absolute Value of t-Statistics in Parentheses)

Independent Variables	Dependent—New Plant & Plant Expansion FDIUS ($ million)				
	All Countries	U.K.	EC	Japan	Canada
Constant	-44.68	-34.69	4.60	-35.87	-44.73
	(0.66)	(1.28)	(0.21)	(0.78)	(1.33)
State Unemployment Rates	3.16	1.44	1.15	-0.72	1.51
	(1.05)	(1.38)	(1.28)	(0.35)	(2.06)
State Unionization Rates	-2.07	-0.71	-0.51	-0.62	-0.28
	(2.97)	(2.79)	(2.45)	(1.30)	(1.51)
State Steel Employment	1.99	0.49	0.43	0.22	0.93
	(1.87)	(1.26)	(1.36)	(0.30)	(3.24)
State Auto Employment	0.90	0.02	0.12	0.73	0.008
	(6.63)	(0.50)	(3.09)	(7.92)	(0.21)
State Petroleum Employment	1.44	0.59	0.36	-0.16	0.002
	(2.36)	(2.66)	(2.00)	(0.39)	(0.02)
State Income Per Capita	-3.07	-0.73	0.38	-2.27	0.75
	(0.72)	(0.48)	(0.30)	(0.78)	(0.67)
State Tax Collections Per Capita	0.05	0.04	0.0008	0.006	0.006
	(2.39)	(4.85)	(0.12)	(0.40)	(1.06)
State Business Incentives	0.03	-0.15	-0.18	0.22	0.17
	(0.07)	(0.81)	(1.20)	(0.63)	(1.23)
U.S. Relative GNP Growth	4.88	3.10	-0.32	10.63	-7.50
	(1.97)	(1.51)	(1.13)	(1.61)	(0.98)
Effective Exchange Rate	65.84	0.03	-0.02	118.20	0.35
	(1.46)	(0.35)	(0.11)	(3.81)	(1.06)
R-square	0.16	0.06	0.06	0.17	0.04
Number of Observations	600	600	600	600	600

Table 4.6
FDI in New Plants and Plant Expansion in the United States 1979-1990: Across States, Manufacturing Industries
(OLS Regressions with Absolute Value of t-Statistics in Parentheses)

Independent Variables	Dependent—New Plant & Plant Expansion FDIUS ($ million)				
	All Countries	U.K.	EC	Japan	Canada
Constant	-0.82	-0.10	0.75	-28.88	-18.14
	(0.02)	(0.008)	(0.04)	(0.64)	(0.59)
State Unemployment Rates	-0.08	-0.41	1.16	-0.66	1.01
	(0.03)	(0.85)	(1.43)	(0.33)	(1.50)
State Unionization Rates	-1.34	-0.29	-0.48	-0.47	-0.11
	(2.31)	(2.43)	(2.57)	(1.02)	(0.65)
State Steel Employment	1.80	0.20	0.46	0.31	0.99
	(2.04)	(1.12)	(1.62)	(0.43)	(3.75)
State Auto Employment	0.83	0.03	0.13	0.70	-0.033
	(7.43)	(1.31)	(3.51)	(7.75)	(1.00)
State Petroleum Employment	1.26	0.54	0.32	-0.28	-0.09
	(2.48)	(5.27)	(1.92)	(0.69)	(0.59)
State Income Per Capita	-2.80	0.13	-0.18	-2.79	0.60
	(0.79)	(0.18)	(0.16)	(0.98)	(0.57)
State Tax Collections Per Capita	0.01	0.003	0.004	0.005	0.0004
	(0.62)	(0.68)	(0.62)	(0.32)	(0.07)
State Business Incentives	0.11	-0.11	-0.15	0.29	0.17
	(0.27)	(1.32)	(1.07)	(0.83)	(1.35)
U.S. Relative GNP Growth	2.54	0.02	-0.33	11.62	-15.01
	(1.24)	(0.02)	(1.27)	(1.81)	(2.13)
Effective Exchange Rate	79.37	0.03	0.07	108.74	0.22
	(2.11)	(0.88)	(0.38)	(3.61)	(0.72)
R-square	0.19	0.08	0.07	0.17	0.04
Number of Observations	600	600	600	600	600

CONCLUSION

The results of this inquiry confirm a number of observations regarding the nature of FDIUS. Direct investment tends to be concentrated in a small number of relatively large states, in a relatively small number of industries, and sourced in major industrialized countries. However, several findings are not consistent with earlier studies and shed light on the relevance of popular perceptions concerning the motives behind FDIUS.

There is no evidence that state-based business incentive schemes have stimulated FDI in real capital formation within states. Further, real U.S. dollar depreciation did stimulate FDIUS; but the concentrated nature of that investment by industry and location tends to undermine the once popular perception that foreigners were simply trying to buy U.S. industry at bargain basement prices.

Perhaps the most interesting results and the ones that deserve the greatest scrutiny include the finding that takeovers, or equity investment, are consistent with attempts to capture quasi-rents associated with administrative know-how, while transplants, or real physical FDI investment, are consistent with capturing quasi-rents that are associated with embodied technological change.

Furthermore, there is evidence to suggest that Japanese new plant and expansion FDI transferred new technology into the United States. One of the major factors explaining the inflow of real foreign capital investments by states may be the skill mix in the workforce rather than the general availability of labor, as reflected by state unemployment rates. A more extensive analysis of FDIUS and its state and regional characteristics by source country follows in the next chapter.

NOTES

1. An investment is categorized as a foreign direct investment if it involves more than a 10 percent position in the firm in question. Most actual foreign direct investment (FDI) activity involves a majority interest and, often, wholly owned positions in the subsidiary firm.

2. Throughout the chapter, EC is defined as the European Community excluding the United Kingdom.

3. Definitions and sources for all of the variables used in the regression analyses are provided in appendix A of this chapter.

4. A major theme of the Dukakis campaign for the presidency in 1988 was that foreign interests and particularly the Japanese were buying up U.S. manufacturing firms at bargain-basement prices as a result of the depreciation of the U.S. dollar relative to major currencies beginning in the mid-1980s (Glickman and Woodward 1990).

5. Apart from a desire to keep the chapter manageable in size, the focus on new plant and expansion investment in U.S. manufacturing is coincident with most people's concept of real investment. For example, states bidding for foreign investment activity are looking for new physical capital formation and not simply the acquisition of U.S. companies by foreign multinationals.

6. The regressions were estimated using tobit to adjust for the estimation problems associated with the use of limited dependent variables.

7. The value of shipments data are for 1987. The industry growth measure is the percentage change in the value of shipments within the industry from 1982 to 1987. The within-parent measure consists of the percentage of investments in an industry representing a matched pair of parent and subsidiary in terms of their four-digit SIC classification for 1979-1985. After 1985, industry matching rates for the parent and subsidiary firms were assumed

to equal the average of the actual 1979-1985 average matches.

8. The exchange rate used for the EC regressions was the real effective exchange rate for the U.S. dollar and the DM (deutsche mark).

9. To the extent that most FDIUS took the form of equity investment, it is conceivable that foreigners saw an opportunity to turn around firms in slow-growth industries that could be acquired at relatively low prices because of the administrative know-how of the parent company management team.

10. A positive link between FDIUS and U.S. dollar depreciation was found in studies by Klein and Rosengren (1994), Mann (1989), and Ray (1989, 1995). Goldberg (1993) provided evidence that FDIUS was encouraged by U.S. dollar depreciation in the 1970s but not in the 1980s. Campa (1993) found that exchange rate variability, which is not considered here, discouraged FDIUS.

11. The positive link between protection and FDI, first documented by Horst (1972), is prominent in models of FDI including Bhagwati (1987), Brander and Spencer (1987), Helpman (1984), and Markusen (1995).

12. These results are consistent with those presented in Ray (1995) that were based on a shorter time span. Kogut (1991) found contradictory evidence that differences in R&D activity within an industry in the United States compared to Japan were not positively related to plant FDIUS by Japan.

13. These results are in contrast to Coughlin, Terza, and Arromde (1992), based on estimates of factors influencing the probability of FDI within states for the 1981-1983 period. They found FDI in manufacturing positively related to state income per capita, unemployment, government incentives, and unionization but negatively related to taxes.

REFERENCES

Bhagwati, Jagdish N. 1987. *The Theory of Political Economy, Economic Policy and Foreign Investment*. New York: Columbia University Discussion Paper Series 386, December.

Brander, James S., and Barbara J. Spencer. 1987. "Foreign Direct Investment with Unemployment and Endogenous Taxes and Tariffs," *Journal of International Economics* 22(May):257-279.

Bureau of the Census. 1972. "Industry Series," *Census of Manufactures*. Washington, D.C.: GPO.

———. 1982. "Industry Series," *Census of Manufactures*. Washington, D.C.: GPO.

———. 1984. *Statistical Abstract of the United States*. Washington, D.C.: GPO.

———. 1987a. "Concentration Ratios in Manufacturing," *Census of Manufactures*, Subject Series MC87-S-6. Washington, D.C.: GPO.

———. 1987b. "Industry Series," *Census of Manufactures*. Washington, D.C.: GPO.

———. 1987c. *Statistical Abstract of the United States*. Washington, D.C.: GPO.

———. 1988. *Current Population Survey*. Washington, D.C., GPO, March.

———. 1989. *Statistical Abstract of the United States*. Washington, D.C.: GPO.

———. 1991. *Statistical Abstract of the United States*. Washington, D.C.: GPO.

Campa, Jose M. 1993. "Entry by Foreign Firms in the United States under Exchange Rate Uncertainty," *Review of Economics and Statistics* 75(4):614-622.

Caves, Richard E. 1971. "International Corporations: The Industrial Economics of Foreign Investment," *Economica* 38(149):1-27.

Coughlin, Cletus C., Joseph V. Terza, and Vachira Arromde. 1992. "State Characteristics and the Location of Foreign Direct Investment within the United States," *Review of Economics and Statistics* 73(4):675-683, November.

Department of Commerce. 1985. *Foreign Direct Investment in the United States: Completed Transaction 1974-1983, Volume II: Industry Sector*, International Trade Administration. Washington, D.C.: GPO.

Department of Labor. 1990. "Geographic Profile of Employment and Unemployment," Bulletin 2381, Table 12, pp. 35-48.

Federal Trade Commission. 1974. *Line of Business Survey*. Washington, D.C.: Federal Trade Commission.

Freeman, Richard B., and James L. Medoff. 1979. "New Estimates of Private Sector Unionism in the United States," *Industrial and Labor Relations Review* 32(2):143-173, January.

Glickman, Norman J., and Douglas P. Woodward. 1990. *The New Competitors: How Foreign Investors Are Changing the U.S. Economy*. New York: Basic Books.

Goldberg, Linda S. 1993. "Exchange Rates and Investment in United States Industry," *Review of Economics and Statistics* 75(4):575-588, November.

Graham, Edward M., and Paul R. Krugman. 1989. *Foreign Direct Investment in the United States*. Washington, D.C.: Institute for International Economics.

Gruber, W., D. Mehta, and Raymond Vernon. 1967. "The R&D Factor in International Trade and the International Investment of United States Industries," *Journal of Political Economy* 75(1):20-37.

Helpman, Elhanan. 1984. "A Simple Theory of International Trade with Multinational Corporations," *Journal of Political Economy* 92(3):451-471.

Horst, Thomas. 1972. "Firm and Industry Determinants of the Decision to Invest Abroad: An Empirical Study," *Review of Economics and Statistics* 54(3):258-266.

Horstmann, Ignatius J., and James R. Markusen. 1987. "Licensing versus Direct Investment: A Model of Internationalization by the Multinational Enterprise," *Canadian Journal of Economics* 20(3):464-481.

Hufbauer, Gary C., Diane T. Berliner, and Kimberly A. Elliott. 1986. *Trade Protection in the U.S.: 31 Case Studies*. Washington, D.C.: Institute for International Economics.

Hymer, Stephen H. 1960. "The International Operations of National Firms: A Study of Direct Foreign Investment," doctoral dissertation, Massachusetts Institute of Technology (published by Cambridge, Mass.:M.I.T. Press, 1976).

Industrial Trade Commission. 1975. *Industrial Characteristics and Trade Performance Data Bank*. Washington, D.C.: GPO.

Klein, Michael W., and Eric Rosengren. 1994. "The Real Exchange Rate and Foreign Direct Investment in the United States," *Journal of International Economics* 36(3-4):373-389.

Kogut, Bruce, and Sea Jin Chang. 1991. "Technological Capabilities and Japanese Direct Investment in the United States," *The Review of Economics and Statistics* 73(3):401-413.

Mann, Catherine L. 1989. *Determinants of Japanese Direct Investment in U.S. Manufacturing Industries*, International Finance Discussion Paper 362. Washington, D.C.: Board of Governors of the Federal Reserve System, September.

Markusen, James R. 1995. "The Boundaries of Multinational Enterprises and the Theory of International Trade," *Journal of Economic Perspectives* 9(2):169-189.

Office of Economic Research. 1988. International Trade Commission data. Washington, D.C.

Office of the President. 1981. *Economic Report of the President*. Washington, D.C.: GPO.

———. 1987. *Economic Report of the President*. Washington, D.C.: GPO.

———. 1991. *Economic Report of the President*. Washington, D.C.: GPO.

Ray, Edward J. 1989. "The Determinants of Foreign Direct Investment in the United States: 1979-1985," in *Trade Policies for International Competitiveness*, edited by Robert Feenstra. Chicago, Ill.: University of Chicago Press, pp. 53-77.

———. 1995. "Old Myths and New Realities in Foreign Direct Investment in the United States," *International Trade Journal* 9(2):225-246.

Ray, Edward J., and Howard P. Marvel. 1984. "The Pattern of Protection in the Industrialized World," *Review of Economics and Statistics* 66(3):452-458.

Rugman, Alan M. 1980. *Multinationals in Canada: Theory, Performance, and Economic Impact.* Boston, Mass.: Martinus Nijhoff.

Scherer, Frederic M. 1984. "Using Linked Patent and R&D Data to Measure Interindustry Technology Flows," in *R&D, Patents and Productivity*, edited by Zvi Griliches. Chicago: University of Chicago Press.

Vernon, Raymond. 1966. "International Investment and International Trade in the Product Cycle," *Quarterly Journal of Economics* 80(2):190-207.

APPENDIX A: VARIABLES, DESCRIPTIONS, AND SOURCES

Variable (Variable Name)	Description and Source
Foreign Direct Investment (FDISICA, FDISICJ, etc.)	Foreign Direct Investment into the United States by industry in millions of U.S. dollars. Data have been aggregated by 4-digit SIC (unless elsewhere noted) or by state where appropriate. Data for 1984 and 1985 were extracted from tape data received from the International Trade Administration. Data were compiled from the series "Foreign Direct Investment in the United States." Source: Department of Commerce (1985).
Consumer Goods	Output attributed to personal consumption expenditures divided by total output. Source: Industrial Trade Commission (1975).
Unionization	Percentage of production workers covered by collective bargaining, by 3-digit 1967 SIC code attributed to component 4-digit industries. Computed from 1968-1972 surveys by Freeman and Medoff (1979).
Four-Firm Concentration Ratio	Percentage of value of shipments accounted for by the four largest companies. Source: Bureau of the Census (1987a).
Within Parent Industry	Within Parent Foreign Direct Investment is measured as the value of FDI received by an affiliate firm in the same 4-digit SIC industry as the parent source of the FDI. Two additional years were extracted from the ITA tape. After 1985, the value of within parent investment takes on the average value of within parent investment in industries with FDI for that year. Within parent investment was also computed for investments from specific countries, such as JWPINVST for Japan, CWPINVST for Canada, etc. Source: Department of Commerce (1985).
Log Value of Shipments	Source: Bureau of the Census (1987b).
U.S. Relative GNP Growth: All Country Regressions	Growth Rates in Real GNP, percentage change. Source: Table B-110 (Office of the President 1991, 411), Tables B5 and B106 (Office of the President 1987, 251), and Table B-107 (Office of the President 1981).
Individual Country Regressions	Ratio of Real U.S. GNP growth to Country growth rates. EC stands for EC-12. Source: Table B-110 (Office of the President 1991, 411), Tables B5 and B106 (Office of the President 1987, 251), and Table B-107 (Office of the President 1981).

U.S. Industry Growth	(LNVS87-LNVS82)/LNVS82. Growth in Value of Shipments between 1982 and 1987. Source: Bureau of the Census (1982; 1987).
Exchange Rates	Foreign Exchange Rates in cents/unit of foreign currency. EC Regressions use the exchange rate between the $ and the DM (ANEXUSGN). Source: Table B-109 (Office of the President 1991), Table B-105 (Office of the President 1987).
Tariff Barriers	Post Tokyo Round, 1986, Nominal U.S. Tariff Rates. Averaged for 4-digit SIC categories. Source: Office of Economic Research (1988).
Nontariff Barriers	A dummy variable that takes on a value of one if there exists a nontariff barrier for that industry for 1975 and zero otherwise. Updated to 1984 using Hufbauer, Berliner, and Elliott (1986).
Tariff and Nontariff Trade Barriers	An interactive term that takes on the value of the tariff if there exists a non-tariff barrier and zero otherwise.
Midpoint Plant Shipments	This variable is constructed from Bureau of the Census data (Bureau of the Census 1972).
Management Intensity	Percentage of workers in an industry who are reported as being in management or professional occupations (occupation codes 3-199). Compiled data had to be converted from census industry code to 2- or 3-digit SIC codes and then 3-digit data is applied to each 4-digit industry. Compiled from Bureau of the Census data (Bureau of the Census 1988).
Origin R&D	The dollar value of investment in R&D by industry of origin based on 1974 data from the Federal Trade Commission (Federal Trade Commission 1974; Scherer 1984).
State Unemployment Rates	Annual Unemployment Rates, Percentage, 1979-1990. Source: Bureau of the Census (1991, 405; 1989, 396; 1987c, 393; 1984, 224) and Department of Labor (1990).
State Unionization Rates	Union membership as percentage of employed in manufacturing 1988. Source: Bureau of the Census (1991, 424; 1989, 415).
State Steel Employment	Number of establishments with 20 or more employees in a state. Source: Bureau of the Census (1987, 33a-8, 33a-9).
State Petroleum Employment	Number of establishments with 20 or more employees in a state. Source: Bureau of the Census (1987, 9A-10).
State Auto Employment	Number of establishments with 20 or more employees in a state. Source: Bureau of the Census (1987, 37a-8, 37a-9).

State Income per Capita   Per Capita income 1987, $ Thousand. Source: Bureau of the
                               Census (1991, 461).

State Tax Collections   State Tax collections divided per capita by population, in dollars
                               per capita. Source: Bureau of the Census (1991, 292, 20-21).

State Business Incen-   1987 Ranking of the willingness of a state to offer incentives to
tives   attract and expand manufacturing businesses. Source: Grant
                               Thornton, *Manufacturing Climates Study,* July 1988.

Table B.1
Leading Sectors for FDIUS: 1979-1990 (All Industries, $US Millions)

Top 12 Industries	1979	1980	1981	1982	1983	1984	1985	1986	1987	1988	1989	1990	Total
Crude Petroleum & Natural Gas (1311)	118.4	454.3	1,165.3	2,134.4	2,956.1	8,479.7	2,524.4	708.4	628.4	2,028.5	745.9	39.8	21,983.6
Hotels & Motels (7011)	87.8	60.0	659.3	229.1	138.1	519.5	1,072.9	1,586.3	1,977.0	1,466.9	4,958.3	3,702.7	16,457.9
Petroleum Refining (2911)	34.0	10.6	295.4	6.6	564.9	1,106.6	800.0	540.0	8,183.9	3,378.5	378.0	711.5	16,010.0
Pharmaceutical Preps. (2834)*	121.3	19.0	138.0	31.7	98.5	101.8	44.3	1,191.4	34.6	687.8	9,648.8	3,810.0	15,927.2
Motion Picture & Video Prod. (7812)	0.0	0.0	0.0	0.0	0.0	0.0	0.0	0.0	2.4	70.0	5,494.4	9,120.0	14,686.8
Department Stores (5311)	68.1	0.0	37.2	365.3	0.0	135.0	0.0	4,310.6	1.0	8,800.0	453.0	0.0	14,170.2
Depository Institutions (6000)*	894.4	1,450.9	1,034.2	1,272.6	2,055.8	826.7	20.9	60.8	1,660.9	750.0	101.1	840.5	10,968.8
Insurance Carriers (6300)*	627.4	326.9	284.5	10.0	57.0	25.0	891.3	727.0	30.0	0.0	1,552.5	4,330.2	8,861.8
Bituminous Coal & Lignite (1211)	18.1	1609.0	1163.1	224.7	2,471.0	2,082.0	42.0	73.7	31.6	0.0	0.0	0.0	7,715.2
Plastics Materials & Resins (2821)*	471.0	267.0	2,580.0	126.4	0.0	25.6	5.4	74.0	1,498.2	69.8	411.0	1610.8	7,139.2
Copper Ores (1021)	2.2	233.5	3,973.3	87.5	87.5	67.8	55.0	295.0	1,551.2	0.0	175.4	0.0	6,528.4
Motor Vehicles & Car Bodies (3711)	258.0	445.5	1,155.7	65.0	258.4	971.0	628.5	850.8	435.5	419.5	690.1	131.1	6,309.1
Top 10 Share	15%	30%	39%	26%	45%	33%	29%	30%	28%	32%	33%	42%	33%
Total Value	17,972.5	16,103.3	31,879.5	17,723.3	19,388.3	43,013.5	21,062.1	35,505.9	58,069.0	54,503.8	74,715.4	57,213.2	447,149.8

*These industries had to be grouped at the 2-digit level to calculate the top 10 industry share of all industry FDI. Therefore, the top twelve industries are given.

Table B.2
Leading Sectors for FDIUS: 1979-1990 (Manufacturing Industries, $US Millions)

Top 10 Industries	1979	1980	1981	1982	1983	1984	1985	1986	1987	1988	1989	1990	Total
Petroleum Refining (2911)	34.0	10.6	295.4	6.6	564.9	1,106.6	800.0	540.0	8,183.9	3,378.5	378.0	711.5	16,010.0
Pharmaceutical Preparations (2834)	121.3	19.0	138.0	31.7	98.5	101.8	44.3	1,191.4	34.6	687.8	9,648.8	3,810.0	15,927.2
Plastics Materials & Resins (2821)	471.0	267.0	2,580.0	126.4	0.0	25.6	5.4	74.0	1,498.2	69.8	411.0	1,610.8	7,139.2
Motor Vehicles & Car Bodies (3711)	258.0	445.5	1,155.7	65.0	258.4	971.0	628.5	850.8	435.5	419.5	690.1	131.1	6,309.1
Tires & Inner Tubes (3011)	100.0	0.0	0.0	52.0	52.0	0.0	0.0	245.0	625.0	2,887.0	615.0	1,500.0	6,076.0
Book Publishing (2731)	5.2	60.0	61.0	0.0	0.0	15.0	90.0	760.2	22.8	3,401.9	1,479.3	121.0	6,016.4
Toilet Preparations (2844)	96.5	15.0	7.8	100.0	0.0	146.0	25.0	0.0	3,116.5	341.6	2,159.5	3.0	6,010.9
Dry, Condensed & Evaporated Products (2023)	0.0	0.0	0.0	0.0	0.0	3,000.0	3,000.0	0.0	0.0	0.0	0.0	0.0	6,000.0
Prepared Flour Mixes & Doughs (2045)	0.0	0.0	0.0	0.0	0.0	0.0	0.0	0.0	0.0	0.0	5,800.0	0.0	5,800.0
Electronic Computing Equipment (3573) *	210.4	17.9	244.2	239.7	22.0	445.2	223.0	248.3	994.8	1,345.2	745.7	869.7	5,606.1
Top 10 Share	18%	17%	49%	14%	23%	41%	40%	25%	38%	36%	47%	35%	37%
Total Value	6,405.7	5,549.8	9,260.2	4,449.7	4,285.9	14,103.1	11,782.2	15,676.1	38,088.5	35,157.7	46,191.4	25,111.1	216,061.4

*Data given are categorized by old SIC 3573, the corresponding new SICs are 3571, 3572, 3575, 3577.

Table B.3
Leading States Receiving FDIUS: 1979-1990

Top 10 States	1,979.0	1,980.0	1,981.0	1,982.0	1,983.0	1,984.0	1,985.0	1,986.0	1,987.0	1,988.0	1,989.0	1,990.0	Total
All Industries, $US Millions													
California	5,023.4	3,550.1	5,597.3	2,255.2	4,222.9	8,741.9	6,335.6	3,296.1	5,267.4	3,324.5	9,519.9	20,194.6	77,328.9
New York	1,742.0	1,371.4	3,189.4	2,739.2	1,753.0	1,741.7	995.0	11,714.9	13,973.4	9,578.8	13,889.1	5,106.7	67,794.6
Texas	1,661.2	1,237.7	3,723.0	2,860.6	720.9	8,160.5	2,974.7	3,447.5	1,006.4	3,599.9	4,427.6	3,460.0	37,280.0
Ohio	307.2	348.1	735.3	430.2	171.8	1,122.1	485.0	1,203.3	10,184.8	12,776.8	2,615.9	2,723.2	33,103.7
Pennsylvania	672.6	374.0	543.9	808.7	607.4	601.4	486.4	227.6	487.1	1,702.4	10,348.2	3,988.5	20,848.2
Illinois	595.2	178.3	477.6	729.5	662.1	3,207.8	1,896.6	1,936.1	1,630.0	5,500.1	3,113.5	837.7	20,764.5
Connecticut	389.2	62.8	3,470.7	229.5	157.9	511.6	774.7	1,199.0	4,507.3	1,544.4	2,452.9	388.3	15,688.3
New Jersey	378.5	462.9	311.7	309.6	602.0	378.8	1,309.2	882.8	1,054.5	2,484.1	2,974.6	2,516.3	13,665.0
Florida	1,120.8	1,107.6	1,487.3	344.4	1,400.8	760.1	235.0	409.2	1,157.8	2,451.7	2,312.9	479.4	13,267.0
Massachusetts	847.7	905.0	354.7	404.0	391.6	284.0	177.3	276.6	994.0	1,239.4	1,033.8	3,381.1	10,289.2
Top 10 Share	71%	60%	62%	63%	55%	59%	74%	69%	69%	81%	71%	75%	69%
Total Value	17972.5	16103.3	31879.5	17723.3	19388.3	43013.5	21062.1	35505.9	58069.0	54503.8	74715.4	57213.2	447149.8
Manufacturing Industries, $US Millions													
New York	532.3	673.0	768.9	602.5	356.6	697.0	674.9	3,429.1	8,751.8	8,578.4	5,174.6	2,563.1	32,802.2
California	466.5	257.6	423.1	83.1	1,018.9	5,877.1	3,873.0	1,020.0	1,551.1	535.9	5,453.3	3,846.0	24,405.6
Ohio	201.2	254.0	685.4	238.1	135.0	949.2	370.1	1,159.8	9,678.0	3,963.0	2,312.0	2,606.8	22,552.6
Pennsylvania	566.0	180.5	410.2	643.0	541.2	421.4	449.2	129.3	70.8	1,653.3	9,828.2	3,893.5	18,786.6
Illinois	284.7	171.4	86.2	88.0	105.5	1,042.7	1,235.2	1,670.8	1,486.6	4,474.5	1,961.5	121.7	12,728.8
Connecticut	367.4	62.8	32.5	29.5	30.4	503.3	742.7	1,095.5	4,449.0	1,423.6	2,452.9	335.3	11,524.9
Texas	847.6	501.8	392.4	299.0	339.0	658.3	205.2	970.7	310.9	2,385.0	887.5	1,108.8	8,906.2
Minnesota	9.1	33.0	46.0	21.4	0.0	28.8	5.3	184.7	796.3	35.7	6,362.1	110.0	7,632.4
New Jersey	353.8	453.5	102.0	63.0	51.6	119.5	1,194.1	150.6	215.0	2,238.2	1,029.6	1,465.3	7,436.2
Massachusetts	46.0	81.2	263.7	394.1	149.6	42.5	122.8	76.6	329.7	456.1	753.1	3,054.9	5,770.3
Top 10 Share	57%	48%	35%	55%	64%	73%	75%	63%	73%	73%	78%	76%	71%
Total Value	6405.7	5549.8	9260.2	4449.7	4285.9	14103.1	11782.2	15676.1	38088.5	35157.7	46191.4	25111.1	216061.4

Table B.4
Leading Sectors for FDIUS, by Country and Rank: 1979-1990 (All Industries, $US Millions)

Top 12 Industries (SIC in Parentheses)	All	Rank	Japan	Rank	Canada	Rank	U.K.	Rank	EC	Rank	Other	Rank
Crude Petroleum & Natural Gas (1311)	21,983.6	1	529.9	23	2,285.5	4	3,828.1	4	11,209.8	1	4,130.3	2
Hotels & Motels (7011)	16,457.9	2	8,262.0	2	427.8	18	3,424.4	7	1,718.1	13	2,625.6	5
Petroleum Refining(2911)	16,010.0	3	10.0	250	718.1	11	9,744.1	2	1,464.4	17	4,073.4	3
Pharmaceutical Preparations (2834)*	15,927.2	4	1,298.4	14	93.5	60	10,016.5	1	2,019.7	9	2,499.1	6
Motion Picture & Video Production (7812)	14,686.8	5	13,210.0	1	0.0	-	10.4	283	1,360.0	18	0.0	-
Department Stores (5311)	14,170.2	6	0.0	-	13,100.0	1	365.0	64	167.7	77	0.0	-
Depository Institutions (6000)*	10,968.8	7	1,922.5	12	557.7	14	3,722.5	5	1,614.1	15	3,152.0	4
Insurance Carriers (6300)*	8,861.8	8	97.5	90	247.4	31	1,852.3	11	4,838.6	3	1,826.0	8
Bituminous Coal & Lignite (1211)	7,715.2	9	1.0	349	38.7	84	1,037.2	23	1,716.3	14	4,922.0	1
Plastics Materials & Resins (2821)*	7,139.2	10	1,135.8	15	2,647.3	2	388.2	61	2779.5	6	188.4	21
Copper Ores (1021)	6,528.4	11	477.0	25	135.0	53	1,298.1	19	2,590.5	7	2,027.8	7
Motor Vehicles & Car Bodies (3711)	6,039.1	12	4,851.2	4	0.7	204	0.0	-	1,350.3	20	0.0	-
Top 12 Share	33%		33%		33%		31%		33%		34%	
Total Value	447,149.8		97,546.8		62,587.2		114,464.6		98,229.8		74,321.4	

*These industries are aggregated by 2-digit SIC to calculate the top ten industry share of all industry FDI. Therefore, the top twelve industries are given.

Table B.5

Leading Sectors for FDIUS, by Country and Rank: 1979-1990 (Manufacturing Industries, $US Millions)

Top 12 Industries (SIC in Parentheses)	All	Rank	Japan	Rank	Canada	Rank	U.K.	Rank	EC	Rank	Other	Rank
Petroleum Refining (2911)	16,010.0	1	10.0	166	718.1	7	9,744.1	2	1,464.4	10	4,073.4	1
Pharmaceutical Preparations (2834)	15,927.2	2	1,298.4	8	93.5	32	10,016.5	1	2,019.7	6	2,499.1	2
Plastics Materials & Resins (2821)	7,139.2	3	1,135.8	9	2,647.3	1	388.2	36	2,779.5	3	188.4	14
Motor Vehicles & Car Bodies (3711)	6,309.1	4	4,851.2	1	0.7	114	0.0	-	1,350.3	12	0.0	-
Tires & Inner Tubes (3011)	6,076.0	5	3,644.0	2	0.0	-	0.0	-	2,432.0	4	0.0	-
Book Publishing (2731)	6,016.4	6	0.0	-	1,198.0	4	3,504.4	4	1,064.4	16	0.0	-
Toilet Preparations (2844)	6,010.9	7	374.1	24	3.0	100	210.0	63	5,418.0	1	5.8	29
Dry Condensed & Evaporated Products (2023)	6,000.0	8	0.0	-	0.0	-	0.0	-	0.0	-	0.0	-
Prepared Flour Mixes & Doughs (2045)	5,800.0	9	0.0	-	0.0	-	5,800.0	3	0.0	-	0.0	-
Electronic Computing Equipment (3573)*	5,606.1	10	2,607.5	3	24.7	52	342.9	39	2,205.3	5	425.7	8
Top 10 Share	37%		33%		26%		43%		35%		21%	
Total Value	216061.4		41874.4		17801.9		69974.0		52640.1		33771.0	

*Data given are categorized by old SIC 3573; the corresponding new SICs are 3571, 3572, 3575, 3577.

Table B.6
Leading Sectors for New Plant and Plant Expansion FDIUS, by Country and Rank: 1979-1990 (Manufacturing Industries, $US Millions)

Top 10 Industries (SIC in Parentheses)	All	Rank	Japan	Rank	Canada	Rank	U.K.	Rank	EC	Rank	Other	Rank
Motor Vehicles & Car Bodies (3711)	4,789.7	1	4,192.3	1	0.7	50	0.0	-	564.8	2	0.0	-
Motor Vehicle Parts & Accessories (3714)	2,432.2	2	2,163.9	2	85.5	9	72.6	9	78.2	19	32.0	3
Semiconductors & Related Devices (3674)	1,711.5	3	1,381.3	3	3.0	37	0.0	-	261.2	5	0.0	-
Pulp Mills (2611)	1,337.8	4	500.0	8	562.8	2	0.0	-	0.0	-	0.0	-
Plastics Materials & Resins (2821)	1,119.6	5	161.1	21	2.2	42	388.2	1	379.7	3	188.4	2
Paper Mills (2621)	905.5	6	0.0	-	883.9	1	0.0	-	21.6	47	0.0	-
Petroleum Refining (2911)	808.3	7	0.0	-	0.9	48	116.6	6	640.8	1	0.0	-
Blast Furnaces & Steel Mills (3312)	732.6	8	185.4	19	250.0	5	22.0	24	44.1	31	231.1	1
Pharmaceutical Preparations (2834)	677.0	9	133.5	23	0.0	-	349.0	2	119.0	14	0.0	-
Electronic Computing Equipment (3573)*	573.4	10	531.0	5	0.0	-	4.9	42	37.5	34	0.0	-
Top 10 Share	48%		55%		50%		39%		36%		20%	
Total Value	31273.2		16868.1		3599.7		2473.8		6019.3		2312.3	
For All Industries												
Top 10 Share	48%		49%		46%		54%		38%		13%	
Total Value	36299.1		17918.5		4278.7		4038.0		6624.1		3349.8	

*Data given are categorized by old SIC 3573; the corresponding new SICs are 3571, 3572, 3575, 3577.

Table B.7
Leading States Receiving FDIUS, by Country and Rank: 1979-1990

Top 10 States	All	Rank	Japan	Rank	Canada	Rank	U.K.	Rank	EC	Rank	Other	Rank
All Industries, $US Millions												
California	77,328.9	1	26,732.1	1	8,864.6	2	10,188.2	4	13,025.8	3	18,518.2	1
New York	67,794.6	2	17,727.6	2	7,161.0	3	19,674.8	1	13,598.3	2	9,632.9	2
Texas	37,280.0	3	2,430.7	8	6,001.2	4	4,830.4	8	14,636.8	1	9,380.9	3
Ohio	33,103.7	4	6,345.7	3	9,823.5	1	11,102.1	3	3,633.0	7	2,199.4	7
Pennsylvania	20,848.2	5	1,741.9	12	1,304.0	9	11,270.7	2	5,732.2	5	799.4	19
Illinois	20,764.5	6	4,825.4	6	3,490.4	6	5,845.2	7	2,745.8	9	3,857.7	5
Connecticut	15,688.3	7	473.3	26	1,663.8	8	3,812.0	10	7,990.0	4	1,749.2	11
New Jersey	13,665.0	8	2,353.2	10	847.1	19	5,871.8	6	2,851.3	8	1,741.6	12
Florida	13,267.0	9	1,130.6	18	3,766.4	5	3,096.8	12	1,795.8	16	3,477.4	6
Massachusetts	10,289.2	10	845.6	22	970.9	18	4,014.0	9	3,965.1	6	493.6	22
Top 10 Share	69%		66%		70%		70%		71%		70%	
Total Value	447149.8		97546.8		62587.2		114464.6		98229.8		74321.4	
Manufacturing Industries, $US Millions												
California	24,405.6	2	5,848.3	3	1,391.7	4	3,429.4	6	2,639.6	6	11,096.6	1
Ohio	22,552.6	3	6,299.8	1	817.5	9	10,568.9	2	3,131.4	5	1,735.0	5
Pennsylvania	18,786.6	4	1,580.4	10	884.4	8	10,328.5	3	5,510.9	2	482.4	11
Illinois	12,728.8	5	3,485.5	4	175.7	19	5,045.1	5	1,326.3	11	2,696.2	3
Connecticut	11,524.9	6	468.3	18	1,414.5	3	2,622.1	8	5,387.5	3	1,632.5	6
Texas	8,906.2	7	1,017.5	12	447.7	15	1,729.3	9	1,548.5	10	4,163.2	2
Minnesota	7,632.4	8	114.0	27	455.7	13	6,076.2	4	959.1	15	27.4	28
New Jersey	7,436.2	9	478.6	17	64.1	23	3,382.6	7	2,372.3	7	1,138.6	9
Massachusetts	5,770.3	10	303.4	22	205.2	18	1,696.6	10	3,301.1	4	264.0	17
Top 10 Share	71%		61%		43%		82%		71%		74%	
Total Value	216061.4		41874.4		17801.9		69974.0		52640.1		33771.0	

Table B.8
Leading States Receiving New Plant and Plant Expansion FDIUS, by Country and Rank: 1979-1990

Top 10 States	All	Rank	Japan	Rank	Canada	Rank	U.K.	Rank	EC	Rank	Other	Rank
For All Industries, $US Millions												
California	3,624.8	1	2,129.5	2	364.5	6	169.5	5	642.9	1	318.4	4
Kentucky	2,934.4	2	1,547.0	4	33.5	19	33.9	21	288.0	11	1,032.00	1
Ohio	2,782.2	3	2,186.7	1	43.2	16	231.4	4	211.4	15	109.5	8
Texas	2,474.9	4	730.4	10	201.2	8	639.5	2	344.0	7	559.8	2
North Carolina	2,309.9	5	1,140.1	7	158.9	11	513.7	3	402.5	4	94.7	9
Tennessee	2,119.1	6	1,985.2	3	11.2	26	52.9	15	42.8	26	27.0	14
Michigan	1,817.8	7	1,409.2	5	3.8	30	10.0	27	389.8	5	5.0	19
Alaska	1,474.1	8	65.4	24	167.6	10	1,233.1	1	3.0	38	5.0	19
Georgia	1,375.7	9	706.1	11	422.1	4	45.0	16	157.3	18	45.2	10
Indiana	1,319.4	10	1,187.8	6	40.0	17	25.0	24	48.4	25	18.2	16
Top 10 Share	**61%**		**73%**		**34%**		**73%**		**38%**		**66%**	
Total Value	**36299.1**		**17918.5**		**4278.7**		**4038.0**		**6624.1**		**3349.8**	
For Manufacturing Industries, $US Millions												
California	3,060.8	1	1,892.1	3	63.5	10	156.2	5	630.6	1	318.4	2
Ohio	2,748.1	2	2,186.7	1	43.2	13	221.3	3	211.4	14	85.5	7
Texas	2,424.3	3	724.0	9	201.2	7	627.0	1	312.3	7	559.8	1
North Carolina	2,284.9	4	1,140.1	7	158.9	9	495.7	2	402.5	3	87.7	6
Tennessee	2,119.1	5	1,985.2	2	11.2	21	52.9	11	42.8	26	27.0	11
Kentucky	1,866.9	6	1,488.5	4	33.5	15	24.9	20	288.0	10	32.0	9
Michigan	1,778.4	7	1,387.1	5	0.0	-	10.0	23	379.8	4	0.0	-
Indiana	1,319.4	8	1,187.8	6	40.0	14	25.0	19	48.4	24	18.2	13
Georgia	1,318.2	9	704.1	10	422.1	4	45.0	12	130.3	17	16.7	14
Alabama	1,259.2	10	101.4	20	703.3	1	4.0	27	300.0	8	150.5	3
Top 10 Share	**65%**		**76%**		**47%**		**67%**		**46%**		**56%**	
Total Value	**31273.2**		**16868.1**		**3599.7**		**2473.8**		**6019.3**		**2312.3**	

5

Cross-Country Locational Differences of Foreign Manufacturers in the United States

Cletus C. Coughlin

INTRODUCTION

Potentially, nationality affects all aspects of the behavior of multinational corporations. A myriad of economic effects have been covered in previous chapters. The focus of the present chapter is one specific aspect of the behavior of foreign-owned firms in the United States: location decisions. The fundamental goal is to identify differences in the location of foreign-owned manufacturers from different countries.

The attempt to identify a role for nationality in the location of foreign-owned manufacturers across states proceeds directly from conventional theories of foreign direct investment (FDI). Multinational enterprises tend to develop in industries in which firms possess unique ownership advantages. The profit-maximizing exploitation of these advantages entails production of goods and services in various locations. The attractiveness of a particular location depends on the characteristics of that location relative to other locations. If multinational firms from different countries tend to generate different types of firm-specific advantages, it is reasonable to expect that the desired locations for their foreign production would differ because the firms would differ in their evaluations of the characteristics associated with potential locations.[1]

In the present research, differences in FDI in manufacturing throughout the United States among the four leading countries—Canada, Germany, Japan, and the United Kingdom—in terms of industrial composition and location are identified.[2] Using data compiled by Arpan and Ricks (1993) covering the mid-1970s to the early 1990s, the industrial composition at the two-digit Standard Industrial Classification (SIC) level and the location across states of the leading investors is compared using various measures to identify differences. Prior to the analysis, however, some of the key literature relevant to the issue of whether and how nationality affects the location of foreign manufacturers throughout the United States is reviewed.

THE DETERMINANTS OF THE LOCATION OF FOREIGN MANUFACTURERS ACROSS STATES

Literature directly related to the approach of this chapter is scarce. Most studies of FDI by individual countries in the United States (Rugman and McIlveen 1986; McClain 1986; Wheeler 1986) do not examine the location of this activity across the United States, but rather seek to identify reasons for investing in the United States.[3] These studies do, however, rely upon the idea that FDI activity requires firm-specific advantages and the United States must have some location-specific advantages. The studies do not extend this idea to identify how the location-specific advantages possessed by different regions in the United States affect the decision of where to locate within the United States. Furthermore, even though many studies have examined the dynamic pattern of FDI, direct comparisons of the determinants of FDI location across states based on the nationality of the investor are scarce. Oftentimes, studies have focused on a specific investor, especially the Japanese, but it is not easy to find comparisons across countries.

In a recent article, Coughlin (1995) reviewed the literature based primarily on conditional logit models to identify the determinants of the location of FDI in manufacturing across states. A number of statistically significant determinants of the spatial distribution of manufacturing FDI were identified. First, the size of a state's market and its position relative to other state markets is positively related to FDI in a state (Woodward 1992; Head, Ries, and Swenson 1994). Second, agglomeration economies are also positively associated with the location of foreign-owned plants (Head, Ries, and Swenson 1994; 1995). On the other hand, higher wage rates and taxes deter foreign direct investment. Finally, states with larger promotional efforts have attracted more foreign direct investment.[4]

Few of the studies surveyed in Coughlin (1995) provided findings about the differences across investor countries. Even when differences were found, the studies did not address whether the determinants or the parameter values associated with these determinants have changed over time. Thus, the focus of this chapter is restricted to the identification of statistically significant determinants.

Friedman, Gerlowski, and Silberman (1992) provide evidence on differences and similarities of Japanese and European investors. The major difference in determinants involves labor market conditions. For Japanese-owned manufacturing firms in the United States, the following variables (with their coefficient signs in parentheses) were statistically significant determinants of the location of these firms across states: manufacturing wage (-), unionization rate (+), and productivity (+). On the other hand, these variables were not statistically significant determinants of the location of European-owned manufacturing firms. Variables that were statistically significant for both Japanese and European investors are: demand (+), access to ports (+), state and local taxes (-), and promotional expenditures (+). The authors note that the magnitudes differ across investors. For example, European investors seem more responsive to port access and demand than Japanese investors. No evidence, however, is provided to conclude whether the differences are statistically significant.

In this volume, Ray (chapter 4) examines the spatial distribution of FDI in new plants and plant expansions. Restricting attention to manufacturing, Ray found that higher unionization rates deterred FDI from all sources collectively as well as from the United Kingdom (U.K.) and the European Community (EC) individually. Unionization rates were not related to FDI from Japan and from Canada. Obviously, these findings conflict with those of Friedman, Gerlowski, and Silberman (1992) just listed. Ray also found workforce characteristics to be statistically significant variables. For example, FDI was attracted to states with more automobile employment. This result held individually for investment from Japan as well as from the EC. Finally, neither per capita state tax collections nor state business incentives contributed to explaining the pattern of FDI.

Additional evidence on location decisions by investors from specific countries was generated by Ondrich and Wasylenko (1993), who used dummy variables to capture regional preferences among source regions. The authors found that European firms, relative to Canadian firms, prefer the Midwest to the Northeast, Mountain-Pacific, and California regions, but were indifferent between the Midwest and Southern regions. Comparing Canadian and Asian firms, Asian firms tended to prefer the Midwest and to avoid the Northeast and the South.[5]

The possibility of regional preferences varying across countries has also been explored by Ó hUallacháin and Reid (1992). They argue that regional preferences are related to the differential stocks of information that foreign investors have about states in the United States. First, all foreign investors are relatively more knowledgeable about investment opportunities and input sources in large states than in small states. Second, there are knowledge differences across foreign investors stemming from so-called "border effects." For various reasons, foreign investors are more likely to know more about the states to which they are geographically closer.

Ó hUallacháin and Reid (1992) generate evidence on this hypothesis in many ways, but the present discussion focuses on their results with respect to manufacturing employment in 1987 by Canadian, German, Japanese, and British firms. The authors found that the distribution of Canadian manufacturing employment in the United States mirrored the distribution of U.S. manufacturing jobs. The other three countries, especially Japan and Germany, showed a disproportionate concentration of manufacturing employment in the largest manufacturing states. Little support for border effects was found. Only Japanese manufacturing employment exhibited such an effect.

In a final noteworthy study, Hines (1993) found that state taxes in combination with the tax system of the source country affected the distribution of FDI in the United States (FDIUS). Specifically, investors from countries with foreign tax credit systems, such as Japan and the U.K., are less likely to be deterred from investing in high-tax states than investors from other countries with different tax systems. The reason is that they have less economic incentive to avoid the tax obligation in the United States because they would be liable for the taxes in their home countries.

THE LOCATIONAL PATTERNS OF FOREIGN MANUFACTURERS

Prior to examining the location of foreign manufacturers throughout the United States, the data used in the following analysis will be briefly discussed. Five editions of the *Directory of Foreign Manufacturers in the United States* by Arpan and Ricks

(1975; 1979; 1985; 1990; 1993) are used to generate summary information on the location of foreign manufacturers for all countries and for Canada, Germany, Japan, and the United Kingdom separately. This reference is far from ideal for present purposes, especially as it does not allow one to differentiate on the basis of mode of entry. Greenfield investments as opposed to acquisitions increase the location possibilities for foreign firms, and it is reasonable to think that the determinants and, consequently, the locational patterns vary across modes of entry.[6] Another limitation is that this reference is not strictly a plant location directory. On the other hand, it covers a reasonably long time period that allows for a rough assessment of changing locational patterns. For analyses focusing on recent years, data on the location of foreign-owned plants that are available through the Department of Commerce are likely to be more useful. However, the current analysis is for a longer time period.[7]

To determine how closely related were the measures based on Arpan and Ricks to those of the Department of Commerce, simple correlations were calculated between the number of manufacturing plants across states according to the Department of Commerce (1993) and the number of foreign-owned manufacturers according to Arpan and Ricks for a specific year, 1989. The use of 1989 assumes that the 1990 edition of the *Directory of Foreign Manufacturers in the United States* provides a snapshot of foreign-owned manufacturers for the preceding year. Statistically significant correlation coefficients at the 0.01 level are found for: *(i)* all foreign manufacturers ($r = 0.80$); *(ii)* Canadian manufacturers ($r = 0.60$); *(iii)* German manufacturers ($r = 0.86$); *(iv)* Japanese manufacturers ($r = 0.79$); and *(v)* U.K. manufacturers ($r = 0.78$). Thus, one may be reasonably confident that the locational patterns used in the present analysis are consistent with reality. Such confidence, however, must be tempered by an observation made by Glickman and Woodward (1988), who concluded that dynamic patterns of FDI are sensitive to the data and how the data are normalized as well as the time period examined.

Locational Patterns over Time for Individual Countries

To examine the effects of nationality, the analysis focuses on foreign manufacturers from Canada, Germany, Japan, and the U.K. The first exercise uses the rank of each state in terms of the number (count) of foreign manufacturers to calculate rank correlation coefficients over time and across countries. These results are listed in the appendix in table 1. Overall, none of the four countries exhibited much change in the locational pattern of its foreign manufacturers between 1978 and 1992. As shown in panel A of table 1, the rank correlation coefficient between these two years is 0.75 or higher, which is statistically significant at the 0.01 level, for each country.[8] The two countries exhibiting substantial change, Canada and Japan, do so between 1974 and 1978. Germany and the U.K. show little change over time, as their rank correlation coefficients between 1974 and 1992 were 0.84 and 0.79, respectively.

Relative to the (unadjusted) count data, the count data per dollar of manufacturing gross state product exhibit much more change over time for the four countries. Panel A of table 2 in the appendix reveals that generally the bulk of the changes occurred between 1974 and 1978; however, substantial changes continued to occur between 1978 and 1992. For example, no country had a rank correlation that exceeded 0.60 between 1978 and 1992. In fact, the rank correlation of 0.34 for Canada indicates that the hypothesis of no statistical association cannot be rejected at the 0.01 level. Between 1974 and 1992, the coefficient ranged from 0.48 for Germany to 0.07 for Canada. Thus, for both Canada and Japan the hypothesis of no statistical association between 1974 and 1992 could not be rejected.

Concentration Coefficients for Foreign Manufacturers

The focus now shifts to the degree of concentration of foreign-owned manufacturers. That is, what is the degree of concentration, and have the changes identified above tended to make the distribution of foreign manufacturers more or less concentrated? To examine the degree of concentration of foreign-owned manufacturers, concentration coefficients were calculated using the count data scaled by manufacturing gross state product.[9] Analogous to income inequality measured by Gini coefficients, states were ranked from lowest to highest based on the ratio of their percentage of the total number of foreign manufacturers divided by their percentage of total manufacturing gross state product. This order was used to construct Lorenz curves. The resulting concentration coefficients are presented in table 5.1 and selected Lorenz curves are plotted in figure 5.1.

Table 5.1
Concentration of Foreign Manufacturers
(Concentration Coefficients: Count Data per Dollar of Manufacturing GSP)

	All Countries	Canada	Germany	Japan	United Kingdom
1974	0.43	0.45	0.55	0.71	0.50
1978	0.31	0.44	0.32	0.48	0.39
1984	0.33	0.48	0.36	0.39	0.38
1989	0.28	0.45	0.35	0.36	0.36
1992	0.32	0.44	0.38	0.36	0.36

Looking at all foreign manufacturers, one sees a large decrease in inequality or concentration between 1974 and 1978, with little change thereafter. In 1974 the concentration coefficient was 0.43, and for all other years its value ranged from 0.28 to 0.33. Another view of concentration is provided by looking at the ten states with the highest ratios of their percentage of the total number of foreign manufacturers divided by their percentage of total manufacturing gross state product. For each year, the share of foreign-owned manufacturers located in the top ten states was more than double the share of manufacturing gross state product. The composition of the top ten states has varied over time. Only four of the top ten states in 1974 were also in the top ten in 1992.

Next consider individual countries. The concentration coefficients for Canada reveal virtually no change in the degree of inequality of the distribution of foreign-owned manufacturers between 1974 and 1992. For the top ten states in 1974 and in 1992, their shares of foreign manufacturers exceeded two and one-half times their shares of gross state product. Only four of the top ten states in 1974, however, were also in the top ten in 1992. New York appears both times. In 1992, New York's share of manufacturing gross state product was 6.4 percent, while 19.7 percent of foreign-owned manufacturers were located within its borders.

For Germany, the concentration coefficient declined from 0.55 in 1974 to 0.32 in 1978, with only small changes thereafter. For the top ten states, their share of foreign manufacturers exceeded two times their share of manufacturing gross state product in every year. Five of the top ten states in 1974 were also in the top ten in 1992. One of the leading states in both of these years was South Carolina. In 1992, South Carolina's share of manufacturing gross state product was 1.7 percent, while 4.9 percent of foreign manufacturers were located within its borders.

Figure 5.1
Concentration of Foreign Manufacturers: Lorenz Curve

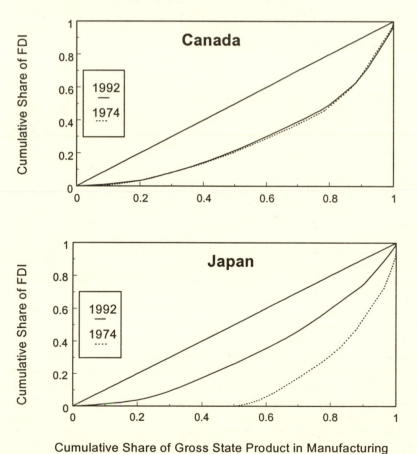

Cumulative Share of Gross State Product in Manufacturing

Figure 5.1 (continued)
Concentration of Foreign Manufacturers: Lorenz Curve

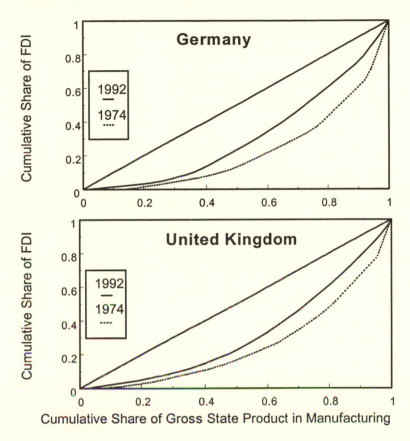

Cumulative Share of Gross State Product in Manufacturing

For Japan, the concentration coefficients reveal a relatively sharp decline in inequality between 1974 and 1978, a smaller decline between 1978 and 1984, and virtually no change thereafter. For the top ten states, their shares of foreign manufacturers always exceed two times their shares of manufacturing gross state product. Accompanying the change in concentration were substantial changes in the leading states. Only four of the top ten states in 1974 appeared in the top ten in 1992. California was notably absent from the top ten in 1992.

Similar to that of Germany, the distribution of British foreign manufacturers became less unequal between 1974 and 1978, with virtually no change thereafter. For the top ten states, their shares of foreign manufacturers was more than double their shares of manufacturing gross state product in all years. Five of the top ten states in 1974 were also in the top ten in 1992. All five of these states are located on the East Coast.

Concentration and Spatial Autocorrelation

In this section, the analysis considers whether states with proportionately larger shares of foreign-owned manufacturers tend to be clustered geographically. That is, do states with proportionately larger shares of foreign-owned manufacturers tend to be located near each other, and do states with proportionately smaller shares tend to be located near each other? The basic issue is whether foreign capital attracts additional foreign capital and whether this attraction has a nationality dimension. That is, does an investment by a German firm in one location spur investments in nearby locations by other German firms? If so, an increasing concentration of German FDI in a specific area could occur over time. Such a dynamic, which might operate at the industry level for a specific country, will be examined for the four individual countries as well as for all countries together.[10]

Evidence on this issue is generated by the use of Moran's I.[11] Values of Moran's I are provided in table 5.2. Combining all foreign manufacturers, Moran's I does not provide strong statistical evidence to indicate a clustering of foreign manufacturers in either 1974 or 1992.[12] In other words, as represented in figure 5.2, states with higher levels of foreign manufacturers relative to their respective manufacturing gross state products do *not* tend to be nearer each other rather than interspersed with states having lower levels of foreign manufacturers relative to gross state products in manufacturing.

Table 5.2
Spatial Autocorrelation of Foreign Manufacturers (Moran's I: Count Data per Dollar of Manufacturing GSP)

	All Countries	Canada	Germany	Japan	United Kingdom
1974	0.102	- 0.027	0.220*	0.022	0.240*
1992	0.167	0.087	0.194	0.028	0.338*

* Statistically significant at the 0.01 level.

Geographic clustering, however, does hold in selected cases at the level of individual countries. While Canadian manufacturers show some tendency to cluster, using the data for 1992, statistical tests do not permit rejection of the hypothesis of no clustering at the 0.01 level. An examination of figure 5.3 reveals the lack of a clear-cut pattern for Canadian manufacturers. A pattern of clustering is much more pronounced for German manufacturers (supported in table 5.2 and depicted in figure 5.3). For both years, higher values tend to be clustered in the eastern half of the United States. Despite major changes in the level of Japanese ownership of production facilities in the United States, in neither 1974 nor 1992 was statistically significant spatial autocorrelation detected.[13] Figure 5.4 reveals no clear-cut patterns for Japanese manufacturers. Finally, British manufacturers were concentrated geographically in both 1974 and 1992, according to table 5.2; however, the pattern

Figure 5.2
Location of Foreign Manufacturers

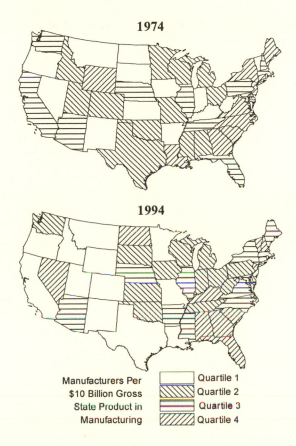

1974

1994

Manufacturers Per	Quartile 1
$10 Billion Gross	Quartile 2
State Product in	Quartile 3
Manufacturing	Quartile 4

did change over time. Generally speaking, the concentration of British manufacturers tended to move eastward (figure 5.4).

Locational Patterns across Countries

The next question is whether the changing patterns for individual countries had any systematic effect on the degree of similarity across countries. In other words, did the locational pattern of foreign direct investors become more or less alike over time? Using the (unadjusted) count data, the location of foreign direct investors tended to become more similar over time. In pairwise calculations of rank correlation coefficients, for *every* pair of countries, the coefficient increased between 1974 and 1992. As shown in panel B in table 1 of the appendix, the largest increase occurred between Germany and Japan, with the coefficient increasing from 0.45 in 1974 to 0.76 in 1992. Generally speaking, the bulk of the convergence occurred between 1974 and 1978; yet even between 1978 and 1992, convergence continued in five

Figure 5.3
Location of Canadian and German Manufacturers, 1974 and 1994

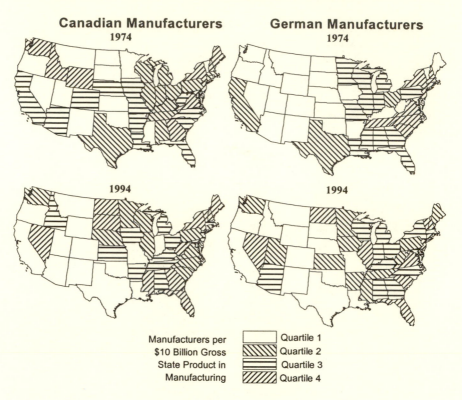

of the six cases. In addition, by 1992 the coefficient exceeded 0.70 in each case, ranging from 0.71 between Canada and Japan to 0.92 between Germany and the United Kingdom. Each of these coefficients is statistically significant at the 0.01 level.

Using the count data per dollar of manufacturing gross state product, the rank correlation coefficients in table 5.2 provide evidence that, generally speaking, the location pattern of foreign manufacturers (among source countries) tended to become more similar between 1974 and 1992. In three of the six cases, the coefficient increased by at least 0.18; and it declined slightly in two other cases. Only in the Japan–United Kingdom case did the rank correlation coefficient decline substantially. In 1992, the correlation coefficient ranged from a low of 0.23 between Canada and Japan to a high of 0.68 between Germany and the United Kingdom.

Industrial Locational Patterns across Countries

Another way to view the pattern of FDI is to examine the pattern using individual industries for the four leading investor countries. Using the number of foreign

Figure 5.4
Location of Japanese and United Kingdom Manufacturers, 1974 and 1994

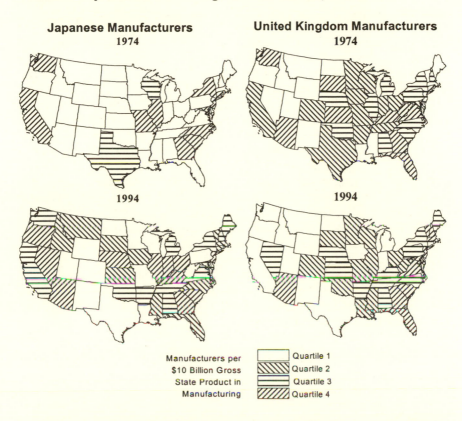

Japanese Manufacturers 1974

United Kingdom Manufacturers 1974

1994

1994

Manufacturers per
$10 Billion Gross
State Product in
Manufacturing

Quartile 1
Quartile 2
Quartile 3
Quartile 4

manufacturers at the two-digit SIC industry level, a rank correlation coefficient over time and across countries was calculated (see table 3 in the appendix). For individual countries, the pattern identified in 1974 remained relatively stable over time. The industrial composition of Japanese investment changed the most; however, the rank correlation coefficient between 1974 and 1992 was 0.57, which is statistically significant at the 0.01 level. The industrial composition of investment from other countries changed little, as the rank correlation coefficient between 1974 and 1992 was 0.81 for Canada, 0.85 for Germany, and 0.78 for the United Kingdom.

Even though the industrial composition changed little in terms of rank, the concentration of foreign manufacturers tended to decline, although not substantially, in each country. For example, in 1992 the five leading industries for Canada accounted for 53 percent of all the Canadian manufacturers in the United States, while in 1974 these same industries accounted for 57 percent of all Canadian manufacturers. Performing the same calculation for the other countries revealed the following: Germany was 69 percent in 1992 and 77 percent in 1974; Japan moved from 60 percent in 1992 to 64 percent in 1974; and the United Kingdom changed from 55 percent in 1992 to 61 percent in 1974.

Across countries, the pattern of industrial composition was roughly similar in 1974 and has become more similar over time. For 1992, the rank correlation coefficient ranges from 0.69 between Canada and the United Kingdom to 0.94 between Germany and Japan. In five of the six cases, the coefficient increased between 1974 and 1992. In these five cases, the smallest increase was 0.10 between Canada and Germany and the largest increase was 0.66 between Germany and Japan. In the exceptional case involving Canada and the United Kingdom, the rank correlation in 1974 of 0.70 was virtually identical to its 1992 value of 0.69.

Given the preceding results, it is natural to explore the pattern of location for a specific industry across the four leading countries. SIC 35, industrial and commercial machinery, was chosen because it is the leading industry for Germany, Japan, and the United Kingdom and the second leading industry for Canada. Table 4 in the appendix contains rank correlation coefficients that allow a comparison of the state location of foreign manufacturers in SIC 35 for 1992 across countries. The results indicate that in three of the six pairwise cases there is a statistically significant relationship. The patterns for Canada–Germany, Germany–Japan, and Germany–United Kingdom are similar in a statistically significant sense, while Canada–Japan, Canada–United Kingdom, and Japan–United Kingdom are weakly related, but not statistically significant.

Figure 5.5 shows the distributions of SIC 35 manufacturers for Canada, Germany, Japan, and the United Kingdom. The extent of clustering is not strong. Table 5.3 shows that spatial autocorrelation exists in a statistical sense at the 0.05 level only for German manufacturers.

Figure 5.5
Location of Manufacturers in SIC 35

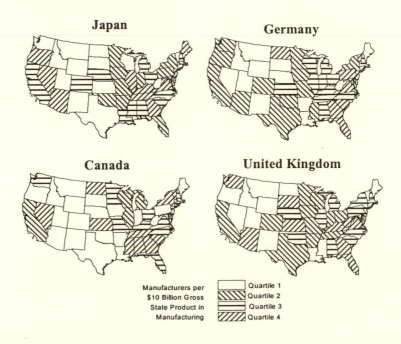

Japan

Germany

Canada

United Kingdom

Manufacturers per
$10 Billion Gross
State Product in
Manufacturing

Quartile 1
Quartile 2
Quartile 3
Quartile 4

Table 5.3
Spatial Autocorrelation of 1992 Foreign Manufacturers in SIC 35
(Moran's I Using Count Data per Dollar of Gross State Product)

Canada	Germany	Japan	United Kingdom
0.001	0.173*	0.045	- 0.005

* Statistically significant at the 0.05 level.

SUMMARY

The literature on the location of foreign operations in the United States reveals little about distinctions among different source countries. This analysis, which examined the distribution of foreign manufacturers throughout the United States between 1974 and 1992 using a variety of statistical measures, identified a number of observations about these patterns. The results are sensitive to whether the number of foreign manufacturers is adjusted for manufacturing activity. The time-series and cross-section analyses highlighted numerous similarities as well as differences across countries.

Using the count data, no country exhibits much change in locational patterns across states between 1978 and 1992. The changes that occurred, however, tended to increase the similarity of locational patterns across countries. Using count data per dollar of manufacturing gross state product, each country exhibits much more change, not only between 1974 and 1978, but also between 1978 and 1992. In fact, both Canadian and Japanese changes were so large that a hypothesis of no statistical association between the locational patterns in 1974 and 1992 could not be rejected. In contrast to the results using the unadjusted count data, these changes tended to increase the similarity of locational patterns across countries in some cases and to decrease the similarity in other cases.

The degree of concentration of foreign manufacturers in 1992 as measured by concentration coefficients was similar across countries. Excluding Canada, which exhibited virtually no change in concentration between 1974 and 1992, the other countries showed large declines in concentration between 1974 and 1978, with relatively small changes thereafter. The concentration, however, does not have a strong geographic dimension. Excluding the United Kingdom in 1992, the other countries did not exhibit a pattern of clustering such that states with proportionately larger shares of a country's foreign-owned manufacturers tended to be located near each other while states with proportionately smaller shares tended to be located near each other. In the British case, the clustering tended to occur in the eastern half of the United States.

Differential behavior across countries could be due to differences in the industrial composition of manufacturers from these countries. A number of findings were generated by disaggregating to the two-digit level. First, for individual countries there was little change in the industrial composition of investment, in terms of ranks, for Canada, Germany, and the United Kingdom between 1974 and 1992. This distribution for Japanese manufacturers changed relatively much more. The changes for each country, no matter how small, tended to lessen the degree of industrial concentration. These changes also tended to make the industrial composition across countries much more similar.

For a particular manufacturing industry, industrial and commercial machinery, the pattern of state location across countries is similar by varying degrees, with Japan relative to the United Kingdom having little similarity. In terms of spatial autocorrelation, statistically significant clustering occurred only for German manufacturers.

Future research possibilities abound. One possibility would be to use different measures of FDI to confirm the results identified above. The data from the FDIUS Data Link Project discussed in earlier chapters would, no doubt, be best suited for this purpose. A second research direction would be to estimate econometric models of the location of foreign manufacturers of the leading countries across states for key industries. Such cross-section, time-series models might provide insights about determinants that are statistically significant, the sizes of parameters, and the change over time in these determinants and parameters. This information would lead to more definitive statements about the role of nationality, especially with respect to generating explanations of the observed patterns.

NOTES

1. Cantwell and Hodson (1991), using patent statistics, conclude that firms from different countries possess different competitive advantages. For example, in the 1980s, Japanese firms tended to generate relatively more advances than firms from other countries in office machinery, photographic equipment, and robotics, while British firms were more productive in generating advances in pharmaceuticals.

2. See Dunning's chapter in this volume stressing the implications that stem from the proliferation of numerous forms of international business.

3. Occasionally, these studies make geographic observations. For example, Wheeler (1986) commented that Japanese FDI did not appear to have a Sunbelt bias, while Rugman and McIlveen (1986) suggested that Canadian proximity to the United States was a reason for Canadian multinational activity in the United States in resource-based industries.

4. The focus of both the Woodward (1992) and the Head, Ries, and Swenson (1994; 1995) studies is Japanese FDI in the United States (FDIUS).

5. Woodward (1992) found that region-specific control variables were statistically significant in his analysis of Japanese manufacturing start-ups in the United States.

6. Relatively speaking, Japanese investors engage in greenfield investments more than investors of other countries. Young and Hood (1980) argue that British firms, lacking monopolistic advantages in technology and marketing, seek acquisitions where their experience in the management of large enterprises may be utilized profitably.

7. See Ray in this conference volume for additional information on the geographic distribution of FDIUS between 1979 and 1990. Ray uses both a different data set and a different approach to describing and summarizing that make his chapter and the current chapter complementary.

8. The actual values of the rank correlation coefficients using 1978 and 1992 are Canada 0.75, Germany 0.89, Japan 0.79, and the U.K. 0.89.

9. See Ray in this conference volume for the FDI shares unadjusted for state size between 1979 and 1990.

10. See Klier (1995) for an industry-based argument for clustering stemming from "lean" manufacturing. Clustering occurs because efforts to reduce inventories and arrange for just-in-time deliveries work best when supplying and receiving plants are located near each other. Klier examines the clustering of supplier plants in the I-75/I-65 automobile corridor associated with recently opened automobile assembly plants.

11. Moran's I is calculated as follows: $I = (n/\Sigma\Sigma w_{ij})(\Sigma w_{ij}z_i z_j/\Sigma z_i^2)$, where the subscripts denote individual states; n = number of states; w is a weighting matrix equaling one if states are adjacent and zero otherwise; $z_i = x_i - \bar{x}$; and x = number of foreign manufacturers per gross state product. See Cliff and Ord (1973) for additional details on the moments of Moran's I and hypotheses testing.

12. This statement is based on a significance level of 0.01. Using a cutoff of 0.05, however, one could conclude that clustering does exist.

13. See Reid (1991) for an overview of Japanese FDI in manufacturing in the United States. The automobile sector has been an especially dynamic one for Japanese investors. See Florida and Kenney (1991) for a discussion of the developments involving Japanese FDI in automobile production and Smith and Florida (1994) for an econometric study of the Japanese-affiliated manufacturing establishments in automotive-related industries.

REFERENCES

Arpan, Jeffrey S., and David A. Ricks. 1975. *Directory of Foreign Manufacturers in the United States*. Atlanta: Georgia State University Business Press.

————. 1979. *Directory of Foreign Manufacturers in the United States*. Atlanta: Georgia State University Business Press.

————. 1985. *Directory of Foreign Manufacturers in the United States*. Atlanta: Georgia State University Business Press.

————. 1990. *Directory of Foreign Manufacturers in the United States*. Atlanta: Georgia State University Business Press.

————. 1993. *Directory of Foreign Manufacturers in the United States*. Atlanta: Georgia State University Business Press.

Cantwell, John A., and C. Hodson. 1991. "Global R&D and British Competitiveness," in *Global Research Strategy and International Competitiveness*, edited by Mark C. Casson. Oxford: B. Blackwell, pp. 133-182.

Cliff, Andrew D., and J. Keith Ord. 1973. *Spatial Autocorrelation*. London: Pion.

Coughlin, Cletus C. 1995. "The Spatial Distribution of Foreign-Owned Firms in the United States: The Current State of Knowledge," in *International Business in the Twenty-First Century, Volume II: International Finance*, International Trade and Finance Association proceedings, edited by Khosrow Fatemi and Susan Nichols. Laredo, Texas: Texas A&M International University, May, pp. 493-507.

Department of Commerce. 1993. *Foreign Direct Investment in the United States: Establishment Data for Manufacturing, 1989*, Bureau of Economic Analysis and Bureau of the Census, September. Washington, D.C.: GPO.

Florida , Richard L., and Martin Kenney. 1991. "Japanese Foreign Direct Investment in the United Sates: The Case of Automotive Transplants," in *Japan and the Global Economy: Issues and Trends in the 1990s*, edited by Jonathan Morris. London: Routledge, pp. 91-114.

Friedman, Joseph, Daniel A. Gerlowski, and Jonathan Silberman. 1992. "What Attracts Foreign Multinational Corporations? Evidence from Branch Plant Location in the United States," *Journal of Regional Science* 32(November):403-418.

Glickman, Norman J., and Douglas P. Woodward. 1988. "The Location of Foreign Direct Investment in the United States: Patterns and Determinants," *International Regional Science Review* 11(2):137-154.

Head, Keith, John Ries, and Deborah Swenson. 1994. "The Attraction of Foreign Manufacturing Investments: Investment Promotion and Agglomeration Economies," *NBER* Working Paper No. 4878 (October).

_____. 1995. "Agglomeration Benefits and Location Choice: Evidence from Japanese Manufacturing Investment in the United States," *Journal of International Economics* 38(May):223-247.

Hines, James R., Jr. 1993. "Altered States: Taxes and the Location of Foreign Direct Investment in America," *American Economic Review* 86(5):1076-1094.

Klier, Thomas H. 1995. "The Geography of Lean Manufacturing: Recent Evidence from the U.S. Auto Industry," Federal Reserve Bank of Chicago, *Economic Perspectives* 19(November/December):2-16.

McClain, David. 1986. "Direct Investment in the United States: The European Experience," in *Uncle Sam as Host*, edited by H. Peter Gray. Greenwich, Conn.: JAI Press, pp. 309-343.

Ó hUallacháin, Breandán, and Neil Reid. 1992. "Source Country Differences in the Spatial Distribution of Foreign Direct Investment in the United States," *Professional Geographer* 44(3):272-285.

Ondrich, Jan, and Michael Wasylenko. 1993. *Foreign Direct Investment in the United States: Issues, Magnitudes and Location Choice of New Manufacturing Plants.* Kalamazoo, Mich.: Upjohn Institute for Employment Research.

Reid, Neil. 1991. "Japanese Direct Investment in the United States Manufacturing Sector," in *Japan and the Global Economy: Issues and Trends in the 1990s*, edited by Jonathan Morris. London: Routledge, pp. 61-90.

Rugman, Alan M., and John McIlveen. 1986. "Canadian Foreign Direct Investment in the United States," in *Uncle Sam as Host*, edited by H. Peter Gray. Greenwich, Conn.: JAI Press, pp. 289-307.

Smith, Donald F., Jr., and Richard L. Florida. 1994. "Agglomeration and Industrial Location: An Econometric Analysis of Japanese-Affiliated Manufacturing Establishments in Automotive-Related Industries," *Journal of Urban Economics* 36(June):23-41.

Wheeler, J. W. 1986. "Japanese Foreign Direct Investment in the United States," in *Uncle Sam as Host*, edited by H. Peter Gray. Greenwich, Conn.: JAI Press, pp. 345-375.

Woodward, Douglas P. 1992. "Locational Determinants of Japanese Manufacturing Start-ups in the United States," *Southern Economic Journal* 58(January):690-708.

Young, Stephen, and Neil Hood. 1980. "Recent Patterns of Foreign Direct Investment Activity by British Multinational Enterprises in the United States," *National Westminster Bank Quarterly Review*, May, pp. 20-32.

APPENDIX: CORRELATION TABLES

Table 1
State Locational Patterns of Foreign Manufacturers, Unadjusted, Panel A (Rank Correlation Coefficients: Count Data)

	CAC74	CAC78	CAC84	CAC89	CAC92
CAC74	1.00	0.70	0.67	0.63	0.59
CAC78		1.00	0.93	0.85	0.75
CAC84			1.00	0.93	0.81
CAC89				1.00	0.85
CAC92					1.00

	GEC74	GEC78	GEC84	GEC89	GEC92
GEC74	1.00	0.86	0.83	0.89	0.84
GEC78		1.00	0.96	0.92	0.89
GEC84			1.00	0.94	0.92
GEC89				1.00	0.97
GEC92					1.00

	JAC74	JAC78	JAC84	JAC89	JAC92
JAC74	1.00	0.59	0.55	0.44	0.44
JAC78		1.00	0.92	0.78	0.79
JAC84			1.00	0.83	0.84
JAC89				1.00	0.92
JAC92					1.00

	UKC74	UKC78	UKC84	UKC89	UKC92
UKC74	1.00	0.85	0.81	0.81	0.79
UKC78		1.00	0.95	0.94	0.89
UKC84			1.00	0.95	0.93
UKC89				1.00	0.96
UKC92					1.00

NOTE: CA, GE, JA, and UK refer to Canada, Germany, Japan, and the United Kingdom, respectively. The "C" in each abbreviation identifies count data, while 74, 78, 84, 89, and 92 refer to the year the data cover. Correlation coefficients exceeding 0.35 indicate statistical significance at the 0.01 level.

Table 1 (continued)
State Locational Patterns of Foreign Manufacturers, Unadjusted, Panel B (Rank Correlation Coefficients: Count Data)

	CAC74	GEC74	JAC74	UKC74
CAC74	1.00	0.64	0.56	0.75
GEC74		1.00	0.45	0.75
JAC74			1.00	0.58
UKC74				1.00

	CAC78	GEC78	JAC78	UKC78
CAC78	1.00	0.78	0.74	0.73
GEC78		1.00	0.72	0.87
JAC78			1.00	0.76
UKC78				1.00

	CAC92	GEC92	JAC92	UKC92
CAC92	1.00	0.83	0.71	0.81
GEC92		1.00	0.76	0.92
JAC92			1.00	0.78
UKC92				1.00

NOTE: CA, GE, JA, and UK refer to Canada, Germany, Japan, and the United Kingdom, respectively. The "C" in each abbreviation identifies count data, while 74, 78, 84, 89, and 92 refer to the year the data cover. Correlation coefficients exceeding 0.35 indicate statistical significance at the 0.01 level.

Table 2
State Locational Patterns of Foreign Manufacturers, Adjusted, Panel A (Rank Correlation Coefficients: Count Data per Dollar of Manufacturing GSP)

	CAC$74	CAC$78	CAC$84	CAC$89	CAC$92
CAC$74	1.00	0.44	0.29	0.20	0.07
CAC$78		1.00	0.78	0.60	0.34
CAC$84			1.00	0.87	0.56
CAC$89				1.00	0.75
CAC$92					1.00

	GEC$74	GEC$78	GEC$84	GEC$89	GEC$92
GEC$74	1.00	0.50	0.32	0.57	0.48
GEC$78		1.00	0.69	0.52	0.51
GEC$84			1.00	0.70	0.71
GEC$89				1.00	0.93
GEC$92					1.00

	JAC$74	JAC$78	JAC$84	JAC$89	JAC$92
JAC$74	1.00	0.41	0.39	0.17	0.20
JAC$78		1.00	0.82	0.54	0.58
JAC$84			1.00	0.56	0.58
JAC$89				1.00	0.84
JAC$92					1.00

	UKC$74	UKC$78	UKC$84	UKC$89	UKC$92
UKC$74	1.00	0.53	0.49	0.41	0.37
UKC$78		1.00	0.89	0.75	0.60
UKC$84			1.00	0.78	0.65
UKC$89				1.00	0.85
UKC$92					1.00

NOTE: CA, GE, JA, and UK refer to Canada, Germany, Japan, and the United Kingdom, respectively. The "C$" in each abbreviation identifies count data per dollar of gross state product in manufacturing, while 74, 78, 84, 89, and 92 refer to the year the data cover. Correlation coefficients exceeding 0.35 indicate statistical significance at the 0.01 level.

Table 2 (continued)
State Locational Patterns of Foreign Manufacturers, Adjusted, Panel B (Rank Correlation Coefficients: Count Data per Dollar of Manufacturing GSP)

	CAC$74	GEC$74	JAC$74	UKC$74
CAC$74	1.00	0.26	0.27	0.26
GEC$74		1.00	0.30	0.44
JAC$74			1.00	0.51
UKC$74				1.00

	CAC$78	GEC$78	JAC$78	UKC$78
CAC$78	1.00	0.13	0.24	0.24
GEC$78		1.00	0.26	0.54
JAC$78			1.00	0.51
UKC$78				1.00

	CAC$92	GEC$92	JAC$92	UKC$92
CAC$92	1.00	0.44	0.23	0.45
GEC$92		1.00	0.26	0.68
JAC$92			1.00	0.36
UKC$92				1.00

NOTE: CA, GE, JA, and UK refer to Canada, Germany, Japan, and the United Kingdom, respectively. The "C$" in each abbreviation identifies count data per dollar of gross state product in manufacturing, while 74, 78, 84, 89, and 92 refer to the year the data cover. Correlation coefficients exceeding 0.35 indicate statistical significance at the 0.01 level.

Table 3
Industrial Composition of Foreign Manufacturers, Panel A (Rank Correlation Coefficients: Count Data)

	CAI74	CAI78	CAI84	CAI89	CAI92
CAI74	1.00	0.77	0.80	0.77	0.81
CAI78		1.00	0.97	0.96	0.93
CAI84			1.00	0.98	0.97
CAI89				1.00	0.98
CAI92					1.00

	GEI74	GEI78	GEI84	GEI89	GEI92
GEI74	1.00	0.78	0.84	0.89	0.85
GEI78		1.00	0.96	0.88	0.91
GEI84			1.00	0.95	0.95
GEI89				1.00	0.97
GEI92					1.00

	JAI74	JAI78	JAI84	JAI89	JAI92
JAI74	1.00	0.69	0.59	0.65	0.57
JAI78		1.00	0.96	0.83	0.83
JAI84			1.00	0.89	0.90
JAI89				1.00	0.96
JAI92					1.00

	UKI74	UKI78	UKI84	UKI89	UKI92
UKI74	1.00	0.86	0.88	0.80	0.78
UKI78		1.00	0.97	0.88	0.88
UKI84			1.00	0.94	0.94
UKI89				1.00	0.98
UKI92					1.00

NOTE: CA, GE, JA, and UK refer to Canada, Germany, Japan, and the United Kingdom, respectively. The "I" in each abbreviation identifies that the count data are by SIC code rather than by state, while 74, 78, 84, 89, and 92 refer to the year the data cover. Correlation coefficients exceeding 0.56 indicate statistical significance at the 0.01 level.

Table 3 (continued)
Industrial Composition of Foreign Manufacturers
Panel B (Rank Correlation Coefficients: Count Data)

	CAI74	GEI74	JAI74	UKI74
CAI74	1.00	0.61	0.49	0.70
GEI74		1.00	0.28	0.63
JAI74			1.00	0.51
UKI74				1.00

	CAI78	GEI78	JAI78	UKI78
CAI78	1.00	0.50	0.56	0.62
GEI78		1.00	0.84	0.78
JAI78			1.00	0.67
UKI78				1.00

	CAI92	GEI92	JAI92	UKI92
CAI92	1.00	0.71	0.72	0.69
GEI92		1.00	0.94	0.92
JAI92			1.00	0.86
UKI92				1.00

NOTE: CA, GE, JA, and UK refer to Canada, Germany, Japan, and the United Kingdom, respectively.
The "I" in each abbreviation identifies that the count data are by SIC code rather than by state,
while 74, 78, 84, 89, and 92 refer to the year the data covers. Correlation coefficients exceeding
0.56 indicate statistical significance at the 0.01 level.

Table 4
State Locational Patterns of Foreign Manufacturers in SIC 35 (Rank Correlation
Coefficients: Count Data per Dollar of SIC 35 GSP)

	CAC$92	GEC$92	JAC$92	UKC$92
CAC$92	1.00	0.43	0.22	0.27
GEC$92		1.00	0.49	0.43
JAC$92			1.00	0.08
UKC$92				1.00

Note: CA, GE, JA, and UK refer to Canada, Germany, Japan, and the United Kingdom, respectively.
The "C$" in each abbreviation identifies count data per dollar of gross state product, while 92
refers to the year that the data cover. Correlation coefficients exceeding 0.35 indicate statistical
significance at the 0.01 level.

6

Intrafirm Trade and FDIUS

Simon Reich

The trade surpluses create a huge imbalance in foreign-exchange markets that inevitably raises the yen's value and subverts the competitiveness of Japanese industry. . . . The message is that unless Japan acts *effectively* to reduce its trade surpluses, economic forces will ultimately act for it.
—Robert J. Samuelson, 1986

Japan's huge trade surpluses are unsustainable. If they aren't corrected, the cycle of stagnation may continue, and the Japanese will have only themselves to blame.
—Robert J. Samuelson, 1995

INTRODUCTION

This chapter tackles one of the most vexing issues in the debate over foreign direct investment in the United States (FDIUS): The Japanese trade imbalance and its relationship to the Japanese investment surge over the past twenty years. Earlier analyses of FDIUS (notably, Graham and Krugman 1989; Glickman and Woodward 1990) detected peculiarities in the pattern of Japanese trade and investment that do not appear with other countries. Yet, to date, no one has provided a full explanation for these peculiarities, and mainstream opinion has largely ignored the issues.

Robert J. Samuelson's quotes above expressed well the conventional wisdom about U.S. trade with Japan during the 1980s and 1990s. In 1986, the yen value then stood at approximately 170 to the dollar. The yen's exchange rate had risen from 238 to the dollar the prior year when Japan earned a $50 billion current account surplus, the overwhelming proportion in trade exports. That year, the bilateral trade deficit was $4.7 billion. The bilateral annual merchandise trade deficit for that year was $54.4 billion. The conventional prescription was for Japan to grow faster at home, to cut domestic interest rates, and to import more (Samuelson 1986).

Nearly a decade later, relatively soon after an announcement that Japan's January bilateral trade surplus with the United States had reached over $14.7 billion, the yen reached eighty to the dollar. By then Japan's monthly surplus with the United States had grown significantly. In 1993, the annual U.S. trade deficit with Japan had reached $60.5 billion. Between the mid-1980s and mid-1990s, the deficit grew despite the policies of successive Republican and Democratic administrations in raising and then lowering interest rates, strengthening the dollar's value and then letting it weaken, introducing and then discarding various forms of protectionist trade measures, and despite seemingly innumerable rounds of bilateral negotiations between successive United States governments and their Japanese counterparts.

Meanwhile many economists assured an impatient U.S. public that the balance of trade would soon take effect. Politicians promised that, if elected, they would get something done to alleviate the problem.[1] U.S. corporate executives complained about market access, while balking at investing in Japan.

Why was the trade deficit able to take on a life of its own that defied government policies within the world's largest economy? One explanation focused on U.S. consumers. U.S. consumers are known for their propensity to spend rather than save. This leads to a trade deficit because of the consistently higher quality of Japanese goods and the lack of substitutability for many consumer products.

Yet this kind of explanation confronted a major problem: The deficit continued to grow as U.S. firms became more competitive in sectors that offered rival products to those made by Japanese firms. These sectors largely accounted for the deficit itself. Two U.S. automotive companies (Chrysler and Ford), for example, offered competitive, quality products and revitalized the domestic industry in the early and mid-1990s. Even General Motors—the largest U.S. automotive firm—managed to introduce new models and increase its dividends for shareholders by 50 percent as the market share of Japanese firms in the United States suffered their first hiatus in almost three decades. This led some to suggest that Japanese firms could now be written off as competitors.[2] Nevertheless, the automotive sector still comprised three-quarters of the bilateral deficit between the United States and Japan. By the mid-1990s, negotiations between the two countries stalled. The promise of the agreement that President Bush had reached with Japanese government officials in the late 1980s inspired great hopes among U.S. officials at the start of the Clinton round of negotiations. By the beginning of Clinton's second term, these hopes had faded.

Perhaps what better explains the resilience of the deficit is the contrasting policies of multinational corporations (MNCs) based in the two countries. Traditional British and U.S. economics, which focuses on the substitutability of trade and investment, is largely based on empirical evidence drawn from studies of British and U.S. firms. Trade theory predicts a fall in the deficit in the context of a series of macroeconomic changes and, failing that, governmental interventions to engineer agreements that would rig the market outcome. What conventional approaches fail to recognize is the strategic relationship between trade and investment, which replaces the focus on substitutability with a focus on intrafirm trade (IFT).

A corporate strategy centered around IFT has distinct advantages. IFT can be seen as a way of overcoming trade barriers while potentially maintaining control over distribution. Furthermore, for the country, it is seen as a way of preserving high wage jobs at home, as well as the technologies that are increasingly important in driving the competitiveness of firms. The first company to create a new market and thus fill a niche in demand is critical. It remains a major source of a firm's competitive advantage in the new global economy, one in which the old manufacturing assumptions about mass production and economies of scale have receded. Despite the macroeconomic changes wrought by government policies on the behavior of firms, these factors often remain marginal. They may not affect the new thrust of firm behavior.

The most extensive and effective proponents of IFT strategies in the 1980s were the largest Japanese firms, where local market laws and a lack of informal political pressure allowed Japanese firms to cut costs at home in the face of successive *endakas* (yen currency appreciations) through faster research, development, and engineering cycles and through cost offsets onto third- and fourth-ranked suppliers by demanding cheaper products and enhanced productivity from them. Simultaneously, Japanese firms shifted increasing proportions of the manufacturing processes offshore in the 1980s (primarily to the United States and Southeast Asia), although taking care—whenever possible—to minimize technology transfer and export of the high-value end of manufacturing production. Wherever they invested, Japanese firms maintained the high-value production elements of their manufacturing processes, if possible, unlike British and U.S. firms had historically done. Thus, despite the much-publicized discussion about the "hollowing out" of the Japanese economy, technology development and the most fundamental, technologically sophisticated aspects of the production processes remained firmly rooted in Japan.[3]

Clearly, Japanese firms did transfer some technology abroad, predominantly in the form of process technology. The much-vaunted case of the introduction of "Toyota-ism" to the United States—"lean production" systems and just-in-time inventory systems—was consistently singled out by advocates of the benefits of Japanese investments as an example of how foreign multinationals enhanced U.S. competitiveness.[4] But while Japanese firms have clearly contributed to the vibrancy of the U.S. economy, the simple fact is that Japanese firms had to transfer such manufacturing processes to their foreign subsidiary plants if they wanted to replicate their economic success at home. Succinctly stated, Toyota could not build a foreign plant without its competitive advantages, without "Toyota-ism"—a form of process technology inseparable from assembling its cars. By the mid-1990s, the more meaningful question was whether the more valuable components of a Toyota product were manufactured in its new plant in Kentucky or its traditional ones in Nagoya. A second order question largely became whether these same companies chose to purchase components from domestic U.S. suppliers or from the transplanted subsidiaries of their traditional suppliers from Japan who had established themselves as a "second wave" in the United States. Much public debate and little empirical study were stimulated by these subjects.[5]

The key to the persistence of the bilateral deficit lies in the policies of Japanese corporations and their apparent refusal to conform to the laws of orthodox economic theory. But this chapter is not simply about that deficit, nor just about the United States and Japanese trade relations. The bilateral deficit simply represents the most acute and perhaps important example of the wider phenomenon of how little is collectively understood about diverse multinational corporate behavior; how, correspondingly, different firms (largely but not exclusively based on nationality) tend to behave; and the significance of these differences for foreign relations and the stability of the global economic system.

The focus of this chapter is therefore about how differences in multinational corporate behavior influence the contours of global trade and investment— and how little governments understand, or can control, that process. The failure to understand such distinctions or to ignore them has significant, broad, unsettling implications. At present, Japanese firms provide a stellar example of a contrasting approach to the relationship between trade and investment generally pursued by British and U.S. firms. Interviews conducted in gathering data, however, suggest that these firms are not alone in pursuing this course. Other non-Japanese firms have clearly suggested that they intend to follow suit in the future (Pauly and Reich 1997).

It is not that MNCs are impervious to macroeconomic forces or that governments can do nothing to influence the behavior of multinational firms. The capacity of both macroeconomic forces and governments to influence corporate behavior remains highly circumscribed. Failure to understand fully the limits of state policy, the behavior of firms, and, accordingly, the leverages of power in a new, globalizing economy will result in enhanced frustration.

This chapter therefore addresses the questions of if and how firms depart from the behavior predicted by traditional Anglo-American models of corporate behavior in the realms of trade and investment, whether any behavioral fissures are fading, and what the broader implications are for government policy. In doing so, the traditional product cycle model is outlined and an alternative pattern presented, before aggregate data are provided that examine the behavior of MNCs from across the advanced industrial countries, particularly Europe, Japan, and the United States. Finally, this chapter will examine how these firms behave in the context of the U.S. market.

In this chapter, a composite picture is built that profiles how firms behave collectively—within and between sectors, and across nations. The argument is based on a combination of aggregate data and individual firm cases. This comparative corporate strategy in the U.S. market is important because of what it reveals. Despite some counterclaims, the U.S. market remains, arguably, the most open, unregulated market for foreign direct investors among any major market in the Triad (the countries of Japan, North America, and Western Europe).[6] In the absence of political strictures (the Exon-Florio provision being the most significant exception), one should best be able to observe the "natural" behavior of foreign multinationals, that is, the strategies that they prefer to adopt without intervening factors. Their actions in the most open market therefore may come closest to identifying the core of corporate strategy.

Product Cycle as the Traditional Model of Trade and Investment

The function of foreign direct investment (FDI) really defines the MNC, distinguishing it from a national corporation, whether the investment is in the form of acquiring wholesale or manufacturing facilities. The first wave of multinationals (Dutch and British) were largely trading companies that invested in extractive plants for natural resources and in wholesale and service facilities. Theories, however, about multinational corporate behavior focused increasingly on the subsequent patterns of corporate investment in manufacturing facilities, with an emphasis on the transplant of manufacturing facilities abroad, to what was alternatively described as the Third World, the underdeveloped world, the lesser-developed countries, the periphery, or, in contemporary parlance, the emerging markets.

Early debates focused on the distributional consequences of such development: primarily, whether the investing First World country or the recipient Third World country benefited more, and secondarily, what the distributional consequences of investment were between classes within the First World (Hobson 1938; Lenin 1977; Kautsky 1915). The liberal response was encapsulated in the theory of the product cycle, which, in contrast to these earlier formulations that stressed the divisive and zero-sum effects of FDI, emphasized the mutually beneficial, cyclical, routinized pattern of foreign investment.

In theory, the product cycle is quite straightforward. When MNCs establish affiliates in a foreign country, these new firms tend to pursue a familiar, consistently replicated strategy. Initially firms tend to export finished products to foreign markets. These are produced in the First World and sold in (successively) other markets of the advanced industrialized world and then, as economies of scale bring the product price down, in limited Third World markets.

As competition develops from other firms in advanced industrial states, producers have to cut prices and thus seek to reduce costs by developing production facilities offshore. Initially, the aspects of the manufacturing process that are relocated to foreign plants are the most simple assembly jobs, with more sophisticated production processes that require intensive capitalization remaining within, broadly speaking, the advanced industrialized world. As a result, multinationals heavily import intermediate goods early in the FDI cycle, since they have more developed business relations, established standards and certification procedures, and secure supply sources in the home market.

Critically, however, foreign affiliates can be expected to increase local sourcing over time, as they become more deeply integrated into the local economy and consequently can realize the efficiencies of local sourcing. Eventually, product sales will service both local markets and export markets, the production plants of the affiliate serving as the primary manufacturing base of individual products as the home plants of the MNC move on to the production of new, more technologically sophisticated goods. The development of the consumer electronics industry provides an example of this pattern, as production shifted from within the Triad to facilities in Southeast Asia.

Anomalies for Theorists and Policy Makers

The product cycle was popularized in recent decades by the work of liberal political economists, who have continued to focus on patterns of investment between the Advanced Industrialized and Third World countries. Among the most vocal and eloquent proponents of this theory have been Raymond Vernon and, in continuing work built upon these basic assumptions to form more sophisticated formulations, John Dunning.[7]

In practice, however, there are a series of problems in observing or operationalizing the theory. First, there is no standard expectation regarding the amount of time that firms need to operate in local markets before high degrees of local content are expected. By this explanation, Japanese affiliates in the United States have different sourcing patterns from their European counterparts because Japanese investment in the United States is relatively new. Over time, the theory predicts, the volume of Japanese IFT will decrease and local content will increase as Japanese affiliates become more deeply embedded in the U.S. economy.

Second, data limitations make it difficult to measure local content, particularly in industries that produce goods with large numbers of complex manufactured parts and components. It can become further complicated when it is unwieldy to define local content in industries that include a large number of foreign affiliates that produce or assemble intermediate goods locally. So the arrival of a "second wave" of affiliates of the traditional suppliers to the parent of the multinational corporation in the country of origin presents problems for evaluating local production.

Last, the product cycle theory often assumes the investing firm is based in the advanced industrialized world and the recipient in the less-developed countries, with little consideration given to differing factors that may apply when investment remains within the Triad (or, more broadly, the Organisation for Economic Co-operation and Development). Europe generally accounted for about 37 percent of inward investment in the 1980s and early 1990s, however, and Japan for less than 1 percent, while the U.S. percentage grew from 16.4 percent to 22.0 percent (Organisation for Economic Co-operation and Development 1993, 54).

It is important to note that, even as the world's stock of FDI grew in the 1980s and early 1990s, the proportion of global FDI in the Triad countries also grew (International Trade Administration 1988; United Nations Conference on Trade and Development 1993).[8] Attention was often shifted away from intra-Triadic investment. But, given that the overwhelming percentage of inward investment came from other parts of the Triad and that this Triad investment accounted for an increasing majority of total FDI, the renewed attention to "emerging market" investment is seen in proper perspective. Discussion about investments in the Third World shifted focus away from considering whether any contrasting dynamic applied in the case of intra-Triadic investment.

Data limitations ensure local content estimates remain inherently problematic. Consequently, the product cycle theory is difficult to confirm by analyzing the sourcing behavior of foreign affiliates. Further, indicators that focus on the output of affiliates provide important, but often stubbornly inconclusive, evidence.

These problems will be assessed in greater detail in the later sections of this chapter. At this juncture, let us simply suggest that problems are evident. First, they exist in the formulation and operationalization of the product cycle theory; second, concerns remain about whether the same conditions apply in the case of intra-Triadic FDI as apply to outward investment to the rest of the world's economies; and, finally, a series of empirical anomalies (that are discussed at greater length in the ensuing analysis) collectively raise a series of theoretical and empirical challenges to the generalizability of product cycle theory. Yet, this theory continues to underlie the thinking of much conventional policy.

An Alternative Formulation of the Trade-Investment Relation

In the product cycle formulation, investment and trade are interchangeable, with investment substituting for trade over time. Substitutability between the two, however, need not be guaranteed. Nearly three decades ago, Japanese economists, notably Kojima, wrote about a different relationship between trade and investment (Gilpin 1989).

In a study of the investment behavior of Japanese MNCs abroad, Kojima concluded that at least two forms of relationship exist between trade and investment. The first specified relationship, implicit in traditional product cycle theory, suggested that investment was "trade-destroying." This means that, over time, investment abroad would result in a reduction in exported goods (first finished goods, then intermediate goods). The process would gradually extend from the firm to the macroeconomic level. Thus "when FDI in manufacturing replaces domestic production followed by export to a foreign market, FDI substitutes for trade and could be termed 'trade-destroying'" (Gilpin 1989).

In his study of the behavior of Japanese firms, however, Kojima suggested that a second pattern of FDI existed—one that was "trade-creating," rather than trade-destroying. In this context, MNCs used their FDI as a conduit for, if not the creation of more exports, then certainly the maintenance of those exports. In this formulation, therefore, investment was not a substitute for trade but a supplement to trade.

Kojima was initially ignored in Anglo-American circles. Some argued that "trade-creating" FDI was a vestige of a mercantilist approach that an evolving Japanese economy would have to discard. The product cycle theory, developed in the study of British and U.S. firms, suggested that every firm would come to behave the way British and U.S. firms did.

Western critics noted that Kojima's analysis was focused on the behavior of Japanese multinationals in the context of their accumulation of extractive resources in Southeast Asia. Accordingly, the critics dismissed the applicability of this alternative trade-creating model to the general behavior of Japanese (or any other) MNCs within the advanced industrialized world. In this chapter, Kojima's model is not considered to be a purely "Japanese model." Instead, the adaptation of this model for application in the context of the 1980s and 1990s is examined.

No doubt, Japanese firms have been the most common practitioners of trade-creating FDI. The key additional component to that model, which distinguishes it from product cycle theory, is the use of intrafirm trade, or IFT, as the mechanism for a trade-creating strategy. This may have been, in part, what Akio Morita, former president of the Sony Corporation, meant in observing that Japanese MNCs have institutional characteristics that encourage them to behave differently from their European and U.S.-based counterparts (Morita 1992).

As international trade and investment expanded throughout the 1970s and 1980s, IFT increased in tandem (albeit unevenly) across the Triad. Indeed, by the early 1990s, IFT within MNCs accounted for more trade within the Triad than interfirm trade. At its most extreme, this reached startling proportions. For example, U.S. IFT with Japan comprises a much larger proportion of all U.S.–Japanese merchandise trade than does interfirm trade. IFT constituted an average of 71 percent of all merchandise trade between 1983 and 1992 (Department of Commerce 1983-91a; 1983-91b; 1993a). Furthermore, over the same period, Japanese MNCs and their affiliates were responsible for an average of 92 percent of all U.S.–Japanese IFT. This asymmetry is even more pronounced than that associated with the bilateral United States–Japan imbalances in direct investment and merchandise trade. Taken together, the two statistics indicate that most U.S. trade with Japan takes place within and is dominated by affiliated networks of Japanese MNCs.

The ability to pursue strategies with high levels of IFT is, of course, contingent on the capacity to invest freely, as is the traditional form of FDI. Thus, both are circumscribed when direct investment is limited or heavily regulated. But, in practice, this "trade-creating" form of FDI may require a greater degree of freedom, notably from domestic content regulations. Thus, while firms advocating this strategy may seek to adopt this approach in differing markets, the firms are as limited by governmental regulation as by the peculiarities of sectoral requirements.

Yet the atmosphere of the 1980s and 1990s, with a focus on deregulation, liberalization, and globalization, has generated an environment in which such an approach has more latitude for application by MNCs. As will be demonstrated, some firms have used that opportunity to pursue such a strategy, and others have suggested that it is a model they intend to pursue. The consistent distinction among firms, in terms of which model they adopt, lies in their country of national origin.

NATIONAL VARIATIONS IN A GLOBALIZING ECONOMY

If the proponents of globalization are correct, then the world's major multinationals should be converging in their behavior—away from the trade-creating model and toward the trade-destroying variant outlined by product cycle theory. Yet there is little evidence of such convergence. Indeed, arguably, any movement in corporate behavior is away from the product cycle pattern and toward the trade-creating model, as countries seek to replicate the success of Japanese firms, given the palpable impact of such investment strategies on national trade balances.[9]

At this point, an empirical baseline or benchmark needs to be established that justifies the distinction between multinational firms that practice differing approaches. The attempt begins with the broadest of comparative data about firm behavior (that is, regional IFT flows within the Triad) and sequentially works through specific cross-national comparison, to an examination of the behavior of individual firms in the same market.

Regional Trade, Investment, and Intrafirm Trade Flows

This section compares levels of direct investment, the proportion of IFT, and bilateral trade during the 1980s and early 1990s, when trade and investment became intrinsically related (as the alternative model suggests). In the case of Europe and the United States, reciprocal investment is relatively balanced, as is trade. The two regions do not have a perfect balance of trade (with the U.S. running a deficit from the middle of the 1980s into the early 1990s) or of investment, but variations may be explained by cyclical factors (such as the effect of recessions in demand and changes in exchange rates) consistent with conventional economic models. Indeed, the characteristic feature of the economic figures on trade and FDI is how unexceptional they are, conforming to the conventional expectations of economists.

As figures 6.1 and 6.2 on FDI in both directions reveal, investment between the two regions is relatively balanced, following similar patterns of growth in the 1980s and 1990s. Furthermore, the largest proportion of both European investment in the United States and, conversely, U.S. FDI in Europe is in the manufacturing sector. Services and service-related goods such as insurance and banking comprise most of the remainder, with wholesaling a relatively small percentage of overall investment for both.

Figure 6.1
Europe's Direct Investment Position in the United States by Sector, 1984-1993 (Historical Cost)

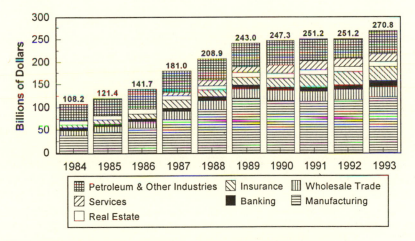

Note: Bureau of Economic Analysis statistics on services available only as of 1987.

Source: Office of Technology Assessment based on data from Bureau of Economic Analysis, *Survey of Current Business* 73(7):65-67, July 1993; 71(8):51-54, August 1991; 69(8):52-53, August 1989; 77(8):90, August 1987; Department of Commerce press release, June 28, 1994, table 3.

Figure 6.2
U.S. Direct Investment Position in Europe
by Sector, 1984-1993 (Historical Cost)

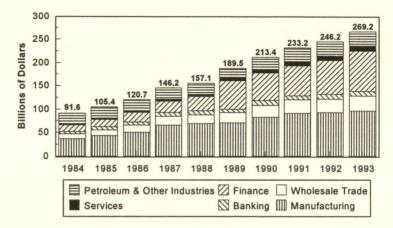

Note: Bureau of Economic Analysis statistics on services available only as of 1987.

Source: Office of Technology Assessment based on data from Bureau of Economic Analysis,
    Survey of Current Business 73(7):97-100, July 1993; 71(8):86-88, August 1991; 69(8):67-69,
    August 1989; 77(8):63-65, August 1987; Department of Commerce press release, June 28,
    1994, table 2.

The direct investment markets of the United States and Western Europe are often characterized as relatively mature. Analysts contend that these are long-standing reciprocal investments.[10] It is important to note, however, that (as indicated by the numbers on the left-hand scale in figures 6.1 and 6.2) the historical cost value of investments suggests that the majority of investment in both directions took place over the course of the last decade. Certainly, investment in both directions appears to conform to the pattern outlined by product cycle theory.

Likewise, intrafirm trade within MNCs across the Atlantic conforms with conventional expectations. Between 1983 and 1992, IFT accounted for an average of 43 percent of U.S.-Europe merchandise trade (Department of Commerce 1983-1991a; 1983-1991b; 1993a). Of that IFT, 43 percent was conducted by U.S.-based MNCs and 57 percent by European-based MNCs—certainly not equal but comparable. When one examines the direction of IFT, rather than the nationality of the parent firm responsible for the IFT, the figures for the United States and Europe maintain a proximate status quo over time, as reflected in figure 6.3.

Furthermore, the aggregate IFT figures remain reasonably balanced, U.S.-based MNCs having transferred roughly the same amount of merchandise to their European affiliates as European-based MNCs have transferred to their U.S. affiliates. This fact is reflected in figure 6.4 which illustrates the volume and direction of U.S.-European IFT for the same period.

Figure 6.3
U.S. Merchandise Trade Balance with Europe,
1983-1992 (Constant 1987 Dollars)

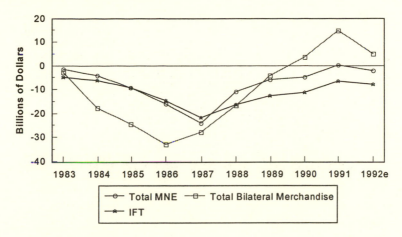

Note: 1992 data are preliminary.

Source: Office of Technology Assessment, based on data from Bureau of Economic Analysis,
   FDIUS, table G-4 (1983-1986) and table G-2 (1987-1992); *USDIA* revised 1983-1991 estimates
   and preliminary 1992 estimates, tables 50 (1983-1988) and III.H.1 (1989-1992) *Survey of Current
   Business* 72(6):88-90, table 2, June 1992; 73(3):90-91, table 2, March 1993; 74(3):68-69, table 2,
   March 1994.

As indicated, U.S.-European IFT has been relatively symmetrical over the past
decade, despite having grown as a percentage of all trade. Most trade has flowed
from the parent firm to its overseas affiliate—but again, in fairly comparable
proportions between U.S. parents and their affiliates in Europe and between European
parents and their affiliates in the United States.

Notably, trade, investment, and IFT rates for Europe and the United States,
collectively, are correlated and remain consistent with the expectations of the
conventional economic propositions integrated in product cycle theory. IFT rates
moderate at a stable level, divided (comparably, if not equally) between MNC parents
in the two continents; and the composition of investment is diffused, despite the fact
that manufacturing represents the largest proportion of FDI. The collective profile
of the effect of this combination of factors on the total merchandise trade balance
during the 1980s and early 1990s is reflected in figure 6.5.

As figure 6.5 indicates, the United States ran an IFT trade balance deficit with
Europe, but still had a total positive merchandise trade balance by the end of the
1980s because nearly 60 percent of trade is conducted between firms, not within
them. The profile of trade, like the composition of investment, is therefore widely
diffused. This fragmentation allows the U.S. economy to compensate for the fact
that European firms send more (in terms of the value of goods and services) to their
U.S. affiliates than U.S. parents send to their affiliates in Europe.

Figure 6.4
Volume and Direction of U.S.-European Intrafirm Trade,
1983-1992 (Constant 1987 Dollars)

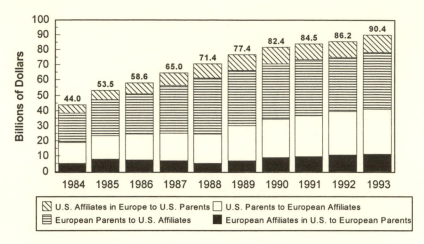

Note: 1992 data are preliminary.

Source: Office of Technology Assessment, based on data from Bureau of Economic Analysis,
     FDIUS, table G-4 (1983-1986) and table G-2 (1987-1992); *U.S. Direct Investment Abroad:*
     Operations of U.S. Parent Companies and their Foreign Affiliates revised 1983-1991 estimates
     (Washington, D.C.: GPO 1986-1994), tables 50 in 1983-1988 and III.H.1 in 1989-1991; *Survey of*
     Current Business 73(6):78, table 2, June 1993.

Stated more broadly, balanced investment between the United States and Europe
is widely diffused across a number of sectors of the recipient economy in both cases.
Coupled with a relatively low proportion of IFT as a percentage of all trade, this
leads to apparent cyclical changes in the total merchandise trade balance. Sometimes
the U.S. economy primarily benefits, sometimes the European economy does. A
liberal economist would argue that both do, at least, most of the time.

Furthermore, these figures support the proposition that, overall, trade patterns
respond to varied exogenous forces, including fluctuations in exchange rates and
changes in firm calculations about economies of scale as consumer demand for
products rise or decline. An interesting example of these forces coming into play
was the decision by Volkswagen to invest in manufacturing facilities in New Stanton,
Pennsylvania, and subsequently to withdraw from the United States within a decade.[11]
Similarly, corporate executives from other German manufacturing firms, in confidential interviews, suggested that their recent decisions to invest in U.S. plants was
heavily influenced by shifts in exchange rates which had raised the price of their
goods in the United States and reduced demand accordingly. In this case, the assumptions of the product cycle theory and, indeed, conventional investment theory seemed
justified.

Such a comment cannot be made in the case of comparable U.S. economic
relations with Japan. The composition of investment and pattern of flows, the huge

Figure 6.5
Total Merchandise and Intrafirm Exports and Imports: Europe and the United States, 1983-1992 (Constant 1987 Dollars)

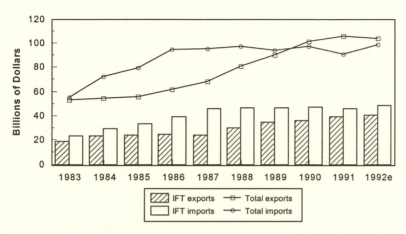

Note: 1992 data are preliminary.

Source: Office of Technology Assessment based on data from Bureau of Economic Analysis,
   FDIUS, table G-3 (1983-1986) and table G-1 (1987-1992); *USDIA,* table 50 (1983-1988) and
   table III.H.1 (1989-1992); *Survey of Current Business* 73(10):54, table 1, October 1993; 73(3):90-
   91, March 1993.

trade imbalances, and the degree of IFT between Japan and the United States starkly contrast with those outlined between the United States and Europe. With respect to the United States–Japan relationship, broad differences persist in the scale and composition of Japanese investment in the United States as compared to U.S. direct investment in Japan. Far from being relatively balanced, even after some positive moves toward greater equity in the early 1990s, Japanese investment in the United States still exceeds U.S. investment in Japan by a factor of 3 to 1, with only nominal signs of a movement toward balanced investment in the long term.

The slow-paced but eventual deregulation of foreign investment in Japan has only led to further frustration as it has revealed innumerable private sector barriers. Many analysts and managers of U.S.-based MNCs argue that official government restrictions have been supplanted by "private sector impediments" emanating from an "interior layer of business practices" (Johnson 1982).[12] Managers of U.S.-based MNCs suggest that U.S. government efforts to overcome these barriers, such as the Structural Impediments Initiative, have had only limited success in making the Japanese domestic market more receptive to foreign products. In a 1993 article, for example, Akio Morita, then chairman of the Sony Corporation, confirmed the continued discrimination. "It is clear," he wrote, "that many foreign products still have trouble with entry into and distribution in the Japanese market" (Morita 1993). Both U.S. and Japanese governmental officials and U.S. corporate officials contend that structural, cultural, and Japanese governmental limitations on investment practices by U.S. firms still exist.[13]

Despite the global explosion of FDI in the 1980s (especially elsewhere within the Triad), U.S. direct investment in Japan remained disproportionately small, relative to Japanese investment in the United States, to U.S. investment in Europe, and to European investment in the United States. In sum, as figure 6.6 indicates, the size and pattern of U.S. FDI in Japan is an anomaly among U.S. bilateral investments within the Triad.

Figure 6.6
Total Direct Investment Positions: U.S.-Europe and U.S.-Japan,
1984-1993 (Historical Cost)

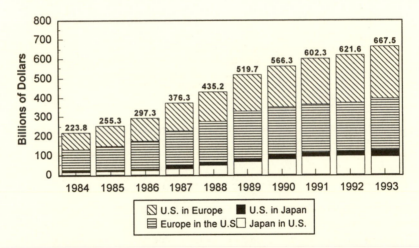

Source: Office of Technology Assessment, based on data in Bureau of Economic Analysis,
   Survey of Current Business 73(7):65-67, 97-100, July 1993; 71(8):51-54, 86-88, August 1991;
   69(8):52-53, 67-69, August 1989; and 77(8):63-65, 90, August 1987; and "U.S. Department of
   Commerce News," press release, June 28, 1994, tables 2 and 3.

Not only is Japanese-U.S. FDI heavily imbalanced in terms of size; it is also skewed in terms of composition, as reflected in comparing figures 6.7 and 6.8 on the relative distribution of bilateral investment in the United States and in Japan.

Unlike reciprocal U.S.-European investments and U.S. investment in Japan, in which (in all three cases) manufacturing investment is always the largest proportion and wholesale trade is relatively small, the largest component of Japanese investment in the United States is composed of wholesale trade. By way of comparison, Japanese investment in wholesale trade in the United States had grown to 49.8 percent by 1993, up from 40.6 percent in the mid-1980s. In the same period, the German proportion had fallen from 15.2 percent to 10.5 percent, and the British (the largest European investors) proportion from 13.9 percent to 9.9 percent.[14] The significance of these figures lies in the relationship between wholesale trade and imports. Wholesaling

Figure 6.7
U.S. Direct Investment Position in Japan by Sector,
1984-1993 (Historical Cost)

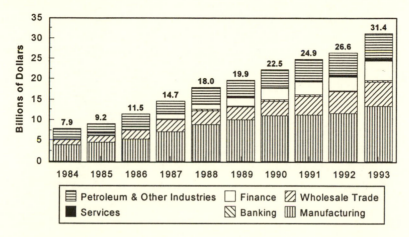

Note: Bureau of Economic Analysis statistics on FDI position include figures for services available
    only as of 1987.

Source: Office of Technology Assessment based on data from Bureau of Economic Analysis,
    Survey of Current Business 73(7):97-100, July 1993; 71(8):86-88, August 1991; 69(8):67-69,
    August 1989; and 77(8):63-65, August 1987; and "U.S. Department of Commerce News,"
    press release, June 28, 1994, table 2.

is the major conduit for organizing imports—either through affiliates or, often, related
(cross share-holding) firms.

Japanese investment in wholesale facilities is therefore potentially indicative
of a strategy that defies the process outlined in product cycle theory. Japanese
investment in U.S. wholesale facilities was the largest percentage of all their investment and grew throughout the 1980s and into the 1990s, when product cycle
theory would expect it to have declined (albeit slowly) as affiliate manufacturing
production replaced production at the parent's home plants with production overseas.

Economists, justifying this growth in Japanese wholesaling investment, have
argued that there are no indicators to signal when wholesale investment as a
percentage of all FDI or the percentage of intermediate goods as a proportion of all
imports should start to fall. Economists expect it to initially rise as manufacturers
export intermediate goods along with assembly and then capital machinery to affiliates. But, even if true, this highlights two problems—one theoretical and the other
empirical. The theoretical one is that a fair "test" of such a theory needs some form
of independent indicator. If wholesale exports to the country receiving investment
were expected to decline over time, then a means of assessing how long it should
take is required to return a fair test of the theory. Second, an empirical problem
appeals to our common sense: Japanese investment in the United States has now
been going on for three decades—a significant period of time. Furthermore, even

Figure 6.8
Japan's Direct Investment Position in the United States by Sector, 1984-1993
(Historical Cost)

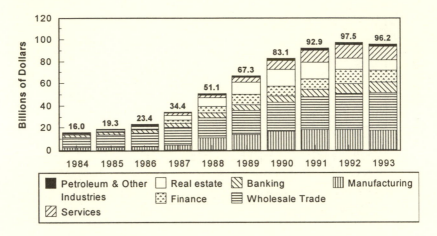

Note: Bureau of Economic Analysis statistics on FDI position include figures for services only
      as of 1987.

Source: Office of Technology Assessment based on data from Bureau of Economic Analysis
      Survey of Current Business 73(7):65-67, July 1993; 71(8):51-54, August 1991; 69(8):52-53,
      August 1989; and 77(8):90, August 1987; and "U.S. Department of Commerce News," press
      release, June 28, 1994, table 3.

if we accept the argument that the largest proportion of that investment has taken
place over the last fifteen years, the same is true of European investment. It is
therefore hard to accept the argument that time explains the different composition
of investment in the United States between, for example, Japan on the one hand and
Britain on the other.

The significance of this asymmetry in investment and, correspondingly, the
differing composition of FDI becomes more apparent in analyzing the contrasting
levels of IFT between MNCs located in the different regions of the Triad. Certainly,
compared with Europe, U.S. IFT with Japan displays anomalies. First, IFT comprises
a much larger part, 71 percent on average between 1983 and 1992, of all United
States–Japan merchandise trade (Department of Commerce 1983-91a; 1983-91b;
1993a). Second, over the same period, Japanese MNCs and their affiliates conducted
an average of 92 percent of all U.S.-Japan IFT. These figures are presented in
figure 6.9.

The data in figure 6.9 are important for several reasons. The relatively small
gap between the top of the bar chart and the point on the line above it illustrates the
overwhelming proportion of merchandise trade accounted for by non-intrafirm trade.
Furthermore, figure 6.9 demonstrates that the overwhelming percentage of all
merchandise trade was conducted within, and thus dominated by, Japanese firms,

Figure 6.9
Total Merchandise and Intrafirm Trade: Japan and the United States,
1983-1992 (Constant 1987 Dollars)

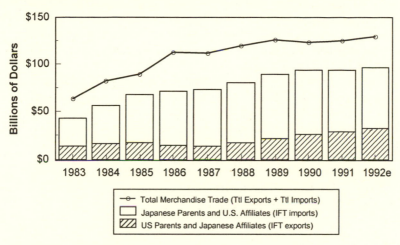

Note: 1992 data are preliminary.

Source: Office of Technology Assessment based on data from Bureau of Economic Analysis,
     FDIUS, table G-3 (1983-1986) and table G-1 (1987-1992); *USDIA*, table 50 (1983-1988)
     and table III.H.1 (1989-1992); *Survey of Current Business* 73(10):54, table 1, October 1993;
     73(3):90-91, table 2, March 1993.

regardless of the direction of the flow between the two countries. Notably, time-series data show that Japanese IFT as a proportion of all bilateral merchandise trade is growing when product cycle theory would expect it to decline. Furthermore, it is important to note that the flow within Japanese firms is not increasingly balanced over time in terms of direction. Japanese firms exported far more to the United States from Japan than they did from the United States to Japan. But, it is further worth noting (as a sign of just how little in IFT exports U.S. firms send to the affiliates in Japan) that Japanese affiliates still managed to export more to their parent firms in Japan than the U.S. parents did to their affiliates there.[15] Unfortunately, exports as a percentage of sales of Japanese affiliates in North America consistently fell in the decade of the 1980s, before recovering at the end of the decade (but still not reaching the peak of 1983 by the early 1990s)—a pattern at odds with the expectations of product cycle theory.[16] In sum, Japanese firms essentially controlled the bilateral flow of trade between the two countries. Moreover, their large investments in wholesale facilities in the United States, coupled with the private (and any nominal public) sector barriers to trade or investment in Japan, were the conduits for this phenomenon.

In tandem, the asymmetry in both investment and IFT has major consequences for the balance of trade between the two countries. As discussed earlier, product cycle theory assumes that investment supplants trade: A firm sells into a market, and when

the demand for a product generated in local markets combined with competition'
is sufficient to warrant FDI, firms will invest in manufacturing facilities. But the
failure (or inability) of U.S. firms to invest in Japan (regardless whether they are
correct in claiming that they only bear the most limited responsibility for that development), the composition of Japanese direct investment in the United States, the
overwhelming degree to which Japanese firms control trade in both directions, and,
finally, the unusually high degree of Japanese IFT all combine to exert enormous
influence on bilateral trade flows.

As figure 6.10 indicates, whereas there are significant differences in the levels
of IFT balances, of total affiliated trade balances, and of total merchandise trade
balances between the United States and Europe, these follow a remarkably close
correlation in the case of United States–Japan trade—to the detriment of the United
States.

Figure 6.10
U.S. Merchandise Trade Balance with Japan,
1983-1992 (Constant 1987 Dollars)

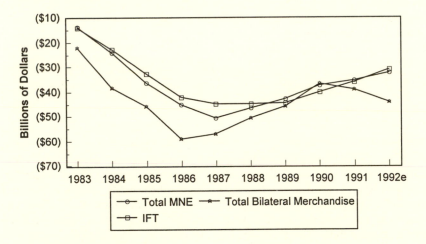

Note: 1992 data are preliminary.

Source: Office of Technology Assessment based on data from Bureau of Economic Analysis,
FDIUS, table G-4 (1983-1986) and table G-2 (1987-1992); *USDIA*, table 50 (1983-1988) and
table III.H.1 (1989-1992); *Survey of Current Business* 72(6):88-90, table 2, June 1992;
73(3):90-91, table 2, March 1993; 74(3):68-69, table 2, March 1994.

This relationship and its consequences for the United States are discussed at
greater length subsequently. Suffice it to note at this stage that U.S. trade, IFT, and
investment patterns with Europe look different from counterpart statistics with Japan.
In part, the large-scale U.S. trade deficit with Japan in the 1980s can be explained
by the high dollar-yen exchange rate, a decline in the growth rate of U.S. productivity, and higher Japanese rates of savings and investment. But its persistence into the

1990s, especially in light of the Plaza Accord and the prominent role of United States–Japan IFT, suggests that the relatively low level of direct investment in Japan is important. In the absence of massive investment by U.S.-based firms in Japan, the U.S. merchandise trade deficit with Japan will not likely be substantially reduced.

Although a complete picture of bilateral flows would include the third leg of the Triad, Japan and Europe, comparable data do not exist. The previous two sets of bilateral relationships suggest, in support of an initial and plausible statement, that all MNCs do not behave in the same way. Most firms are investing in manufacturing facilities; some are concentrating on wholesale facilities. Given the fact that most of this investment took place in the last decade-and-a-half, the age of investment cannot explain the enormous discrepancy in these aggregated patterns of behavior.

NATIONAL PATTERNS: HOST-ECONOMY REGULATION, SECTORAL VARIATIONS, AND TIMING OF INVESTMENT

The aggregate data on regional trade flows across the Triad suggest that firms, according to their country of origin, behave in differing ways. In particular, the data suggest that Japanese firms behave differently in the case of their trade and investment in the United States. But the discussion reveals nothing about unique elements of the U.S. market that could account for such behavior or about sectoral variations, and nothing definitive about the difference that the timing of investment may make (although it suggests that time was not a critical variable here).

This section begins by considering the question of whether there are general patterns of trade and outward investment behavior that can be consigned to the MNCs of individual countries, regardless of context, or whether MNC behavior is more heavily influenced by the policies of recipient countries, the sectoral characteristics of investment, or the age of investment.

The prior section clearly suggests that Japanese firms might be an exception to the general pattern of behavior ascribed to European and U.S. firms by product cycle theory and supported by empirical data. This begs the question of identifying broader evidence to support the general propositions outlined. Certainly, the commentary on the behavior of Japanese MNCs as potential outliers encourages further scrutiny in different contexts to see how their behavior varies across differing regulatory environments.

Next consider the findings of a broad study by Japan's Ministry of International Trade and Industry (MITI): Japanese firms do have an exceptionally high level of IFT as a percentage of exports (refer to table 6.1). These figures are revealing on several points. First, there is significant variation across sectors. Across countries, IFT is most common in both science-based industries and scale-intensive industries with highly differentiated products.

Science-based industries, such as pharmaceuticals, computers, and semiconductors, are characterized by high research and development (R&D) costs, low transport costs, and relatively high profit margins. Consequently, foreign affiliates have a strong incentive to import intermediate goods from their parent firm. Scale-intensive industries with highly differentiated products, such as motor vehicles and consumer

Table 6.1
Value of Exports and Share of Infrafirm Trade of Japanese MNE Parent
Companies by Sector, 1988 and 1991

	1988		1991	
Industry	Exports (billions of nominal yen)	IFT as Percentage of Exports	Exports (billions of nominal yen)	IFT as Percentage of Exports
All industries	46,694.2	35.5	52.586.3	27.5
All manufacturing	28,907.8	42.0	32,782.6	40.2
Chemicals	1,454.6	27.7	1,512.2	18.7
Nonferrous metals	328.1	23.0	259.2	21.0
Machinery	2,307.5	31.5	1,528.5	34.7
Electric machinery	9,550.9	46.0	10,706.7	45.5
Transport equipment	9,565.2	48.4	13,078.9	41.3
Commerce	17,099.5	25.6	18,772.5	6.4

Note: Commerce includes wholesale and retail trade to distributors and dealers.

Source: Ministry of International Trade and Industry, Industrial Policy Bureau, International Business
Affairs Division, *Kaigai Toshi Tokei Soran: Dai 3-kai Kaigai Jigyo Katsudo Kihon Chosa*
(Tokyo: MITI, 1989), tables 1-19, 20, 23, and 24; and *Kaigai Toshi Tokei Soran: Dai 4-kai
Kaigai Jigyo Katsudo Kihon Chosa* (Tokyo, MITI, 1991), tables 1-22, 23, 25, 26, and 27.

electronics, typically produce complex consumer goods that use large quantities of
manufactured parts, components, and subassemblies. In these industries, firms
frequently source components from within their MNC networks. By contrast, IFT
is usually quite low in resource and labor-intensive industries, such as nonferrous
metals, steel, and textiles. These sectors are characterized by high transportation costs
and lower levels of manufactured, intermediate goods (Organisation for Economic
Co-operation and Development 1993, 7, 28). In essence, the more technologically
sophisticated the sector and the individual product (and the higher the value added),
the more likely intermediate goods will be produced in the MNC's home country
and then shipped to foreign affiliates for final assembly.

Some of these tendencies explain variation in the data on Japanese IFT percentages in table 6.1. Chemicals, for example, is a sector with high transportation costs,
where the movement of intermediate goods often carries environmental risks and
where the high value elements of production must, by necessity, often be conducted
toward the end of the process. Chemicals has a relatively low and precipitously declining level of IFT. A second, contrasting point that is consistent with the author's
expectations, however, is the magnitude and relative stability of Japanese IFT exports
in some scale-intensive industries where highly valued components can be manufactured and shipped overseas for final assembly—most notably electric machinery,
which analysts regularly (and, according to these numbers incorrectly) claim is an
area of the economy that has been subject to a process of "hollowing out" by virtue
of overseas investment.[17] These figures would suggest, in contrast, that a large percen-

tage of the manufacturing process in this important area of the Japanese economy remains firmly embedded in Japan. Indeed, although it covers a relatively short period, a third point emerging from this data is that the percentage of IFT exports in the machinery sector has grown—any tendency toward off-shore production by Japanese MNCs being reversed here.

Overall, these figures seem to defy the expectations of the product cycle. Their virtue lies in the breadth of the figures, providing a profile of the major export sectors of the Japanese economy. The figures generate the interesting empirical conclusion that, in the early 1990s, IFT still accounted for over 40 percent of all exports by Japanese MNCs. The failure of these figures, clearly, is their lack of sufficient time dimension. As a snapshot, however, they still indicate that IFT remains a surprisingly high percentage of the global exports of Japanese MNCs in the context of the huge foreign investments of Japanese firms dating from the late 1970s.

But do variable factors in the investment climate of the recipient country affect IFT levels? If so, which factors? In addressing these questions, one must consider how global Japanese figures look when compared to Japanese investment in Europe at about the same time. In comparing the global pattern of IFT to the European one, the answer, found in table 6.2, is that some interesting variations are present. First, Japanese IFT exports are markedly lower in sectors where regional regulation or agreements between European governments and the government of Japan has forced Japanese MNCs to expand local production. Transportation equipment, which accounts for the majority of the U.S. bilateral trade deficit with Japan and averages over 40 percent in IFT as a proportion of all Japanese sectoral exports, had only a 23.2 percent IFT level to Europe by the end of the 1980s— bringing down the all-manufacturing level to 43.1 percent, comparable to the global average for manufacturing.

The same, however, was not true of major sectors of the Japanese economy. Notably different are sectors in which Japanese investors have not been subject to pressure by European governments. In electric machinery, for example, IFT to Europe by Japanese MNCs still accounted for nearly 60 percent of the value of all exports by that sector. The chemical and general machinery figures were also notably higher, the latter approaching 50 percent.

Comparing Japanese IFT figures for Europe and global figures to those for Japanese IFT figures for North America (the third region of the Triad) adds further complexity. The most startling departure from the average of the figures outlined for all Japanese IFT in table 6.1 are the IFT figures for Japanese parents to their affiliates in North America for the same years as those for Europe. While the figures for Europe vary on both sides of the "global norm," the IFT statistics for North America are consistently higher than the norm, as reflected in table 6.3.

Here, the growth of investment between the mid-1980s and late-1980s was accompanied by an enormous growth in IFT. The causes and consequences of this disparity will be revisited in the following section. Suffice it to say that the absence of any regulation or any serious informal political pressure on this issue did not "encourage" Japanese firms to reduce levels of IFT as they may have done in Europe. Certainly, the disparity in Japanese IFT patterns between Europe and the United States cannot be explained by the age of investment. While oft-voiced Japanese

Table 6.2
Value of Exports and Share of Intrafirm Trade of Japanese MNE Parent
Companies to Europe by Sector, 1986 and 1989

	1986		1989	
Industry	Exports (billions of nominal yen)	IFT as Percentage of Exports	Exports (billions of nominal yen)	IFT as Percentage of Exports
All industries	9.712.6	36.0	12,080.2	30.5
All manufacturing	5,618.2	43.4	5,403.0	43.1
Chemicals	128.0	14.0	227.9	27.1
Nonferrous metals	48.7	12.4	37.4	20.1
Machinery	409.7	44.3	357.3	47.8
Electric machinery	1,885.2	50.6	2,118.8	59.8
Transport equipment	1,609.9	33.7	1,691.6	23.2
Commerce	3,748.2	24.4	7,005.6	20.2

Note: The source's definition for commerce includes wholesale and retail trade to distributors and dealers.

Source: Ministry of International Trade and Industry, Industrial Policy Bureau, International Business Affairs Division, *Kaigai Toshi Tokei Soran: Dai 3-kai Kaigai Jigyo Katsudo Kihon Chosa* (Tokyo: MITI, 1989), tables 1-19, 20, 23, and 24; and *Kaigai Toshi Tokei Soran: Dai 4-kai Kaigai Jigyo Katsudo Kihon Chosa* (Tokyo, MITI, 1991), tables 1-22, 23, 25, 26, and 27.

claims in the 1980s that U.S. auto component suppliers were inferior (and thus Japanese firms were forced to buy from home or from the affiliates of traditional suppliers) seem plausible, it is far-fetched to argue that Japanese firms were better able to locate competent suppliers and employ better workers in every major manufacturing industry covered in MITI's study. Here, the lack of local laws or political pressures on Japanese investors apparently proved decisive.

Unfortunately, IFT figures for exports by European or U.S. parent MNCs to other parts of the Triad are neither readily available nor comparably calculated. The relevant data for U.S. IFT levels are not sector specific and do not replicate the method used by MITI. But, recalling that IFT accounted for 43 percent of all U.S.-European merchandise trade, with the U.S. MNCs comprising 43 percent of that amount, creates the impression (at least) that Japanese practices vary from those of their U.S. counterparts (Department of Commerce 1983-91a; 1983-91b; 1993a). OECD data directly comparing investment practices also indicate that U.S.-based affiliates of Japanese MNCs use their investment in the United States as a conduit for trade to a greater degree than do U.S. firms in foreign markets. The IFT average for U.S. firms was stable at about a third between 1977 and 1989 (Organisation for Economic Co-operation and Development 1993, 16).

Certainly, anecdotal data on individual corporate histories are consistent with these assessments about the proclivities of U.S. firms to have lower IFT levels. U.S.

Table 6.3
Value of Exports and Share of Infrafirm Trade of Japanese MNE Parent
Companies to North America by Sector, 1986 and 1989

Industry	1986		1989	
	Exports (billions of nominal yen)	IFT as Percentage of Exports	Exports (billions of nominal yen)	IFT as Percentage of Exports
All industries	17,626.6	21.2	17,026.4	52.2
All manufacturing	10,374.0	25.6	9,190.0	63.4
Chemicals	83.3	3.8	223.9	48.8
Nonferrous metals	41.9	2.0	90.7	29.2
Machinery	452.4	18.6	443.2	67.2
Electric machinery	2,811.7	25.7	3,126.9	65.5
Transport equipment	5,971.6	32.7	4,020.9	64.6
Commerce	7,396.6	16.2	7,509.3	34.6

Note: Commerce includes wholesale and retail trade to distributors and dealers.

Source: Ministry of International Trade and Industry, Industrial Policy Bureau, International Business
Affairs Division, *Kaigai Toshi Tokei Soran: Dai 3-kai Kaigai Jigyo Katsudo Kihon Chosa*
(Tokyo: MITI, 1989), tables 1-19, 20, 23, and 24; and *Kaigai Toshi Tokei Soran: Dai 4-kai
Kaigai Jigyo Katsudo Kihon Chosa* (Tokyo, MITI, 1991), tables 1-22, 23, 25, 26, and 27.

automobile firms, for example, historically have had low levels of exports, dating
from their initial European investments in the early twentieth century.[18]

While not definitive, the data concerning the sectoral behavior of Japanese firms
on a global basis, compared to their IFT patterns in Europe and in North America,
generate some interesting observations. First, there is notable sectoral variation.
Nevertheless, Japanese firms demonstrate a general proclivity toward high levels
of IFT, regardless of the location of investment. Certainly, IFT is much more
significant as a percentage in U.S.-Japanese merchandise trade than in U.S.-European
merchandise trade. Moreover, the absolute volume of IFT between the United States
and Japan is greater than that between the United States and all of Europe. In 1992,
United States–Japan IFT totaled $97.0 billion, compared to $90.4 billion for United
States–Europe IFT. In terms of volume in 1992, Japan-based MNCs accounted for
$88.5 billion of a total $97.0 billion in IFT with the United States, while Europe-
based MNCs accounted for $49.3 billion of a total $90.4 billion in IFT with the
United States.

Furthermore, this emphasis on IFT by Japanese firms is most relevant in sectors
that have formed the backbone of the Japanese economy's success during the last
three decades such as autos, consumer electronics, and electrical machinery. Indeed,
Japanese IFT levels look relatively high even in sectors where they have traditionally
been low among foreign investors, such as the chemical industry.

Second, there is enormous variation in behavior by Japanese MNCs across
regulatory environments—reflected in universally gross disparities in IFT levels

across sectors. It is difficult to reconcile the disparity of these IFT figures by sector in Europe with those in the United States. This variation seems better explained by differences in formal laws or informal agreements—the contrasting degrees of political pressure in Europe and the United States. Confidential interviews with French and German corporate officials confirmed the oft-repeated claim that it has been made clear to Japanese investors that there are acceptable limits to both their production figures and import practices in the European Union (EU). Simply stated, Japanese investors in Europe respond to a series of limitations by increasing their level of domestic content and, correspondingly, reducing their IFT levels. Although part of the variation could be explained, as Japanese investors have claimed, by the superior quality of European suppliers in some industries (notably, Japanese corporate officials make that claim about European automobile suppliers), it is difficult to believe that U.S. industry could not provide suppliers in any industrial sector of the economy qualified comparably to their European counterparts.

The final observation is that the variable of time does not seem to play the role predicted by product cycle theory. Japanese investment dating from similar time periods shows marked diversity in IFT levels across the two regions. Sometimes IFT levels rise when they might reasonably be expected to decline; and, albeit rarely, sometimes they decline dramatically.

While no single factor explains all this variance, one persuasive factor seems to be the importance of the regulatory and political climate of the recipient region. When interviewed, European bureaucrats consistently stressed the liberalizing investment climate in Europe. Yet, neither interviews with European corporate executives nor the findings of a 1990 study of investment barriers in the countries of the EU by Coopers and Lybrand confirmed that view (Commission of the European Communities 1993, 51).

In these interviews, U.S. and European investors repeatedly stressed, for example, that joint ventures were preferred because takeovers may be precluded through national laws and practices. Among European countries, investors associated this problem most closely with Germany, a country where the dominant form of corporate governance differs from the United States and the United Kingdom. As the Coopers and Lybrand study further notes:

> Many contested takeovers do not take place for the simple reason that nobody really believes that they can happen. For example, the unsuccessful hostile bid by Italy's Pirelli for Germany's Continental Tyre Company in 1991 may confirm the view that German companies are impregnable as long as they have the support of big German banks. (Commission of the European Communities 1993, 51)

A 1990 report identifies two types of barriers to takeovers of public companies in the EU. The first is "structural," such as impediments that arise from the ownership structure and the cultural characteristics of individual markets. For example:

> In Italy . . . only eight out of over 200 listed companies have issued more than 50 percent of their shares to the public. That means that they remain tightly controlled by small cabals of like-minded industrialists and financiers who are not minded to give up control.[19] (Commission of the European Communities 1993, 51)

Among the major European economies, the study found the strongest structural barriers in France, Germany, Italy, and Switzerland.

The second impediment to acquisitions identified by the report was a series of technical barriers that inhibit or prevent the transfer of control by contested takeover. For example, in Germany, Switzerland, and the Netherlands, companies often restrict the voting rights of ordinary shareholders and concentrate voting power in the hands of shareholder groups that are friendly to management. Among EU members, the United Kingdom has relatively weak structural and technical barriers. As a result, management in the United Kingdom is much more likely to be responsive to shareholders' short-term interests. In addition, the value and number of cross border acquisitions in the United Kingdom often exceed those found in the rest of the EU (Commission of the European Communities 1993, 51-52).

Although these are only examples of impediments to acquisitions by foreign investors in Europe, they provide insight about the general investment environment. How does the European context compare to the situation for foreign investors in the United States? Thomsen (1994) suggests, in relation to foreign direct investment regulations, that:

> non-EC firms face national restrictions within the Community even though the EC has no community-wide restrictions on the establishment of foreign companies through greenfield investment or acquisition. To suggest that the absence of restrictive Community policies makes the EC more open than the U.S.A. is clearly far-fetched. Each and every member state in the Community has potentially more restrictive policies toward investors than does the U.S.A. under the Exon-Florio amendment. (Thomsen 1994)

In this climate, it is therefore plausible to contend that the variance in Japanese IFT patterns between Europe and the United States can be better explained by these regulatory and political influences than by the age of an investment or sectoral factors.[20] If that is the case, then the true "test" of whether there are divergent patterns of trade and investment behavior among MNCs should be a study of what MNCs do in the context of the United States. If the United States is the least regulated of the three Triad regions, then companies there have the greatest latitude in strategy. The following section is an examination of the comparative trade and investment behavior of foreign affiliates.

U.S. Government Principles, Policies, and Practice

While hardly the perfect test, the consensus that the U.S. market is the least regulated of the major Triadic markets, coupled with the fact that it remains the largest single location for investment in the world, seems to qualify the United States as the basis for a comparative analysis of the behavior of foreign MNCs. Indeed, to put the growth and contemporary importance of the U.S. market as a location for FDI in some perspective, the United States was the largest recipient of FDI during the 1980s, accounting for more than 40 percent of global FDI, with Britain in second position at 15 percent.[21] The United States thus became the world's largest importer of capital in the 1980s. The gross total of FDIUS grew from $83 billion to $185 billion between 1981 and 1985, increasing at an annual rate of 17 percent. The rate of FDIUS growth accelerated between 1985 and 1989, averaging 21 percent.[22]

How did the U.S. government respond to the influx of FDI that dated from the 1970s? The answer is "favorably," with only nominal institutional constraints on investment flows. At the federal level, the institution directly responsible for addressing issues relating to FDIUS is the Committee on Foreign Investment in the United States (CFIUS). Created by President Gerald Ford as an oversight body in 1975, CFIUS monitors and regulates FDIUS from the standpoint of protecting national security. It is an interagency body composed of officials from the Departments of State, Commerce, Defense, and Justice, the Office of the United States Trade Representative, the Office of Management and Budget, and the Council of Economic Advisers; it is usually chaired by a Treasury official.

Most CFIUS authority comes from the Exon-Florio provision in the *Omnibus Trade and Competitiveness Act of 1988*, which empowers the president to veto any takeover of a U.S. firm on national security grounds. Agency officials see the mandate of CFIUS as being consistent with a broader U.S. policy "to welcome direct investment and to support free and open FDI among all nations" (Canner 1992). They have stated that the Exon-Florio provision is a statute that protects national security without compromising an open investment policy (Wethington 1992).

The Treasury officials who have headed the agency have adopted a narrow definition of threats to national security.[23] Laura Tyson, formerly president of the Council of Economic Advisors and head of the National Economic Council, a prominent critic of existing CFIUS practices, noted that U.S. FDI policy does not distinguish between purchases made by foreign investors from the private sector and those made by foreign governments, whose motives might not be "market-driven." Tyson then offered three policy prescriptions: advocate that the U.S. government routinely examine all prospective purchases involving foreign governments; suggest that the definition of national security be clarified to include a list of critical military technologies that would not be available for foreign purchase; and argue that the definition of national security be expanded to include elements of economic security (Tyson 1992).

However, with few notable exceptions, CFIUS has adopted a passive role in policy formulation and implementation. Agency officials have "received over 700 notices since the inception of Exon-Florio in August 1988. Of that total, 13 transactions have been subject to a 45-day extended review. Nine of those reached the President's desk for decision. In eight of those nine transactions, he decided to take no action" (Canner 1992). The only recorded case of a sale blocked by a president after CFIUS review was the purchase of Mamco Manufacturing of Seattle by the China National Aero-Technology Import and Export Corporation. According to a former director of CFIUS (and a contributor to this book), the agency "is achieving its goal of protecting the national security without discouraging foreign direct investment" (Canner 1992).[24] The limited use to date of the legislative provisions under which CFIUS operates therefore does not appear to represent as significant a barrier to foreign direct investors in the mid-1990s as it had appeared to some in 1990.

This begs the question of how foreign investors have responded in the context of this still largely unfettered regulatory structure. Certainly, their collective response has been impressive in terms of the sheer volume of investment, as previously discussed. The importance of these foreign investors in the U.S. economy is perhaps better illustrated by considering the impact of the combined volume of trade and investment.

When foreign investment is coupled with trade through finished imports (or "effective penetration"), foreign investors exert a significant influence on the domestic market. For example, in the automotive industry, foreign producers control about 31 percent of the U.S. market (measured as transplanted production plus imports). In the merchant semiconductor market, the figure was about 30 percent in 1991 (Semiconductor Industry Association 1991); and, in the chemical industry, the foreign share was about 26 percent (Department of Commerce 1992a; *U.S. Industrial Outlook* 1992; 1993). Furthermore, by the end of the 1980s, foreign firms accounted for an estimated 72,200 automotive-industry jobs in the United States (Economic Strategy Institute 1992), 280,800 jobs in the chemical industry (Office of the Chief Economist 1991), and 51,500 jobs in the steel industry (Office of the Chief Economist 1991).

In this context, the largest growth was in Canadian, Japanese, and European investment. But, both the absolute amount and percentage of Japanese growth were most notable. Overall, Japan's FDIUS rose from $4.7 billion in 1980 to $69.7 billion in 1989, increasing an annual average of 32.5 percent between 1980 and 1985, and accelerating to 37.8 percent between 1985 and 1989. Putting these figures in comparative perspective, the EU countries' expansion of FDIUS, although notable, was much slower than Japan's.[25]

By the early 1990s, Japan therefore vied for the title of largest investor in the United States. How did this growth influence the composition of investment by Japanese firms? In other words, which model of investment did Japan investors subscribe to—"trade-creating" or "trade-destroying"—and, crucially, how did their behavior compare to that of investors from other countries?

To answer these questions, we compare the behavior of the largest foreign investors according to four major indicators: employment patterns, strategic manufacturing linkages, the ratio of imports to sales, and IFT levels as measured by intermediate goods purchases. Collectively, the evidence generated by these statistics give a profile of the pattern of investment, providing insight into the question of which kind of strategy firms pursue—"trade-creating" or "trade-destroying."

Employment data show that, although British investors employ nearly a quarter-million more people, they employ over 90,000 fewer in wholesaling than Japanese investors (Department of Commerce 1992b, table F.3). Given that wholesale trade is directly related to the import of goods, rather than their domestic manufacture, this statistic suggests that, for Japanese investors, a large percentage of their affiliates' workers are primarily devoted to the import of products. These figures therefore suggest that Japanese investment has a greater degree of vertical integration than that of other major investors, as it links the import of intermediate products to assembly, distribution, and sales processes.

The second consideration is the question of strategic horizontal manufacturing linkages, that is, the distribution of investment across sectors and whether these sectors seem to be strategically integrated. Here, Japanese manufacturing investment in the United States also differs from traditional patterns of investment by other foreign affiliates because of its horizontal linkages. This is reflected in the profile of the investment figures for the manufacturing affiliates of Japanese MNCs in the 1990s. During the 1980s, for example, Japanese firms invested heavily in steel, rubber, and automobiles as one complex, or "triangle," of investment (consumer electronics, semiconductors, and computers being another). This manufacturing integration appears to be more coherent, comprehensive, and strategic than European patterns of FDIUS, such as heavy British investments in the disparate sectors of chemicals, medical instruments, and publishing. Indeed, Japanese investment also appears to demonstrate a greater degree of horizontal integration than that of other major investors (Department of Commerce 1992b, table B-5).

Third, consider the issue of the import, export, and sales patterns of U.S. affiliates of the four major foreign direct investors (which is one measure of IFT), as reflected in table 6.4.

Table 6.4
Selected Financial Data for U.S. Affiliates of Foreign Companies, 1990

	Japan	United Kingdom	Nether- lands	Ger- many
Number of affiliates	2,142	1,161	346	1,144
Total assets ($ billion)	370	262	91	101
Sales ($ million)	313,138	188,852	72,819	107,521
Net income ($ million)	(2,191)	2,406	32	219
Number of employees (thousands)	616.7	1,039.2	290.2	513.3
Average compensation ($/per employee)	37,203	32,036	34,290	34,307
Exports by affiliates ($ million)	39,155	7,926	2,829	7,041
Imports to affiliates ($ million)	87,712	13,225	6,588	17,858
Ratio of imports to sales	0.28	0.07	0.09	0.17
Ratio of exports to imports	0.45	0.60	0.43	0.39

Source: Department of Commerce, *Foreign Direct Investment in the United States: Operations of U.S. Affiliates of Foreign Companies, Preliminary 1990 Estimates*, August 1992, table A-2; *Foreign Direct Investment in the United States: An Update*, June 1993.

Consistent with the earlier analysis of IFT, these data seem to support the proposition that Japanese investment is more "trade-creating" than "trade-destroying," with a ratio of imports to sales (0.28) more than three times that of Dutch investment and four times that of British investment. This table therefore supports the view that Japanese-based MNCs tend to use their U.S. affiliates as a conduit for the sale of products made in Japan, rather than as facilities to replace Japanese-made goods with U.S.-made goods. A higher proportion of goods sold by Japanese firms seem to be assembled in the United States either from components built in Japan or in third countries by other Japanese affiliates, relative to U.S. affiliates of other foreign firms.

Finally, consider the issue of IFT levels from a comparable but more specific angle: Examine the intermediate goods purchases of foreign affiliates. Recalling the data presented in table 6.3 on Japanese investment in the United States, the percentages of IFT exceeded the Japanese global norm and far exceeded the relevant IFT percentages for Europe. However, no meaningful comparison with MNCs based in other countries was made because a suitable methodology upon which to base such a comparison is not available. Examining data on intermediate goods imports into the United States by country, however, does provide a valid means of comparison because it focuses specifically on purchases of the type of goods most crucial to a "trade-creating strategy." The findings are depicted in table 6.5.

Table 6.5
Foreign Content of Intermediate Goods Purchased by Foreign Affiliates in the United States by Sector and Country, 1990 and 1991

Industry	All Countries		France		Germany		Japan		United Kingdom	
	90	91	90	91	90	91	90	91	90	91
All industries	19.4	19.6	12.1	10.7	21.6	19.9	30.2	31.7	9.6	9.2
All manufacturing	16.7	17.3	17.3	16.2	21.4	20.9	28.4	28.0	9.4	10.0
Chemicals & Allied Products	12.1	13.2	9.6	9.5	18.4	18.5	5.1	7.2	11.6	13.2
Primary and Fabricated Metals	14.0	14.1	7.3	6.9	20.0	21.4	6.6	5.9	7.2	7.3
Non-electrical Machinery	31.0	30.4	NA	20.3	25.9	25.5	48.5	45.3	12.9	9.5
Electric & Electronic Equipment	30.7	28.6	NA	37.5	43.7	39.2	41.4	38.1	11.3	14.3
Motor Vehicles & Equipment	40.4	45.1	NA	NA	NA	NA	49.3	52.8	NA	NA
Wholesale Trade	32.3	33.9	11.6	12.1	39.9	39.6	34.6	38.3	15.3	12.2

Source: Adapted from Department of Commerce, *Survey of Current Business* 73(10):64, table 10, October 1993.

As shown, the foreign content of all intermediate goods purchased by manufacturing foreign affiliates in the United States averaged 17.3 percent in 1991. In 1991, the foreign content among manufacturing affiliates varied significantly by sector, ranging from 13.2 percent in chemicals to 45.1 percent in autos.[26] However, table 6.5 also shows considerable variation by country. Among all foreign manufacturing affiliates in the United States, Japanese affiliates have the highest foreign content at 28.0 percent in 1991; German affiliates have the second highest foreign content at 20.9 percent, while French and British affiliates have considerably lower foreign shares at 16.2 percent and 10.0 percent, respectively.

Across sectors, Japanese affiliates have the highest foreign content in the non-electrical machinery and motor vehicles and equipment sectors, while German affiliates have the highest foreign shares in chemicals, electric and electronic equipment, and primary and fabricated metals. This confirms anecdotal data gathered in interviews with German executives,[27] in which they suggested that they did and would maintain high levels of IFT to their U.S. affiliates to sustain high value-added employment and a trade surplus at home—and thus, according to them, domestic political tranquillity. In their comments, these executives clearly recognized the pattern of Japanese investment in the United States and the utility of a trade-creating strategy for them for both economic and political reasons.

The substantial variations in foreign content across sectors indicate that Japanese affiliates in the United States rely more on foreign suppliers than do European affiliates. French and British affiliates import a relatively low percentage of intermediate goods, while German affiliates import substantial percentages of intermediate goods across several manufacturing sectors.

The higher reliance of Japanese manufacturing affiliates in the United States on imported intermediate goods helps to explain their high ratio of imports to exports. In 1991, the average ratio for all foreign manufacturing affiliates was 1.22:1, while the ratio for Japanese manufacturing affiliates was 2.29:1, indicating that the Japanese manufacturing affiliates imported more than twice as much as they exported.[28] By comparison, German manufacturing affiliates imported only slightly more than they exported, while French and British manufacturing affiliates actually ran trade surpluses (Department of Commerce 1993b, 58, table 4).

While not definitive, the data obtained by considering these four indicators suggest a clearly divergent approach to FDI by the parents and affiliates of foreign MNCs operating in the United States. The affiliates of British firms pursue a strategy consistent with the "trade-destroying" approach encapsulated in product cycle theory. They invest in a variety of manufacturing industries in which they substitute U.S. production for British production. Meanwhile their nonmanufacturing investment is designed to make these firms more competitive in service industries, rather than support affiliate imports through wholesaling. The ratio of imports to sales, percentage of intermediate good purchases, and proportion of investments allotted to wholesaling remain relatively small.

Many senior executives of leading British companies suggested in interviews that they only maintain their head offices in Britain for public relations reasons. They confided that the British and European markets were too small to support their growth and that they felt their future sales expansion involved focusing on the United States. The volume of their stocks transacted on Wall Street often exceeded those in Britain, and many had relocated research and development facilities to the United States.

The behavior of Japanese firms represents the opposite end of this spectrum. The more specific findings of these four indicators are consistent with the raw IFT data on a global and regional basis presented earlier in this chapter. This wealth of data confirms the view that Japanese firms, as studied both in aggregate and by sector, have chosen to pursue a "trade-creating" strategy that uses their U.S. investment as a conduit for sales rather than a "trade-destroying" one that substitutes goods produced offshore for exported products.

German, French, and Dutch firms represent interesting "mixed" cases according to these data. The proportion that German firms allocate to manufacturing as a percentage of all investment distinguished them from Japanese firms. Like their major European counterparts, German firms invest heavily in manufacturing and a small percentage in wholesaling. Yet, in the context of manufacturing investment, the IFT levels of German firms approach the high IFT levels of Japanese firms. Similarly, the German firms share with Japanese firms a high propensity toward high levels of intrafirm exports as a percentage of all exports, and a comparably high level of foreign content purchases of intermediate goods.

In other words, the profile of the behavior of German firms is clearly distinct from Japanese firms and comparable to other major European investors in terms of the percentage of their direct investment devoted to non-manufacturing activities. But German firms do reflect comparable strategies and practices of Japanese firms, if not always to the same degree, when it comes to the manufacturing investment. Illustrating this point is the fact that German affiliates were exceptional among European firms in their high IFT propensity, heavily skewed toward the automobile industry (Department of Commerce 1994a, 58).[29]

Finally, French and Dutch firms offer a similarly "mixed" picture. But both, overall, approach the British pattern in terms of their large investments in the United States with significant manufacturing positions. It is worth noting that Dutch firms have both significantly reduced their manufacturing and increased their wholesaling position in the course of the last decade. This has, at least, the appearance of approximating the behavior of German affiliates in the United States (Department of Commerce 1994a, table 3; 1987, 90, table 10).

Foreign Affiliates and Intrafirm Trade: How It Works in Practice

Most of the discussion to this point has focused on firm behavior in an aggregate sense. Yet it seems inappropriate not to take the analysis one stage further by briefly analyzing the ways and means by which the increasingly complex relationship between trade and investment unfolds in the United States. In doing so, the focus is on the behavior of Japanese automobile firms in the United States. The reason for their selection is as powerful as it is simple: Automobile trade is responsible for the majority of the bilateral trade deficit. It is therefore as important as it is likely that evidence for the trade-creating pattern of investment in this instance will be found. In sum, autos are both a most-likely case study and a crucial one—a rare confluence.

By the end of the 1980s, foreign firms accounted for an estimated 72,200 automotive-industry jobs in the United States (Economic Strategy Institute 1992). The Japanese percentage of that figure had grown considerably, as first traditional Japanese producers set up affiliates and manufacturing plants in the United States and then traditional suppliers followed suit.[30]

Initial investments by Japanese auto transplants had high levels of IFT and, correspondingly, low levels of domestic content. Proponents of such investment, however, pointed to the product cycle effects, arguing that, over time, the volume of Japanese IFT would diminish, reflecting an increase in the local sourcing of

Japanese affiliates. The data on this point, a decade-and-a-half after this process began, are mixed. For example, Japanese auto transplants—that produce cars in the United States—report their percentage of locally sourced parts has increased significantly in recent years.

This evidence seems to support the proponents of product cycle theory. But the debate does not end at this point; there are at least two major problems. The first is the reliability of this kind of data. For example, the Honda Corporation made similar claims about domestic content before a U.S. Customs Service audit of the U.S. affiliate in 1990 concluded that the legitimate domestic content was considerably less than the company reported. Indeed, the audit suggested that the appropriate figure was less than 20 percent.[31]

But even if the reliability of such data is not questioned as it was in the Honda case, its interpretation and utility remain issues, prompted by contrasting interpretations of what constitutes "domestic content" and "local production." New affiliates certainly face major problems in establishing local sourcing for parts and components. Switching from traditional to new suppliers can be costly and time-consuming. It requires new standards and certification procedures, creates uncertainties regarding the reliability and quality of supplies, often introduces new price differentials, and may damage existing relations with traditional suppliers.

Certainly, as these affiliates have increased U.S. production capacity, they have correspondingly increased the volume of purchases from domestic parts suppliers. Toyota, for example, will have increased its local purchases from $800 million in 1988 to a projected $3.8 billion in 1994, as its U.S. production will have grown from 164,500 to 600,000 vehicles—impressively rapid growth in domestic sourcing by any measure. According to Toyota, the local content rate for its U.S. production currently ranges from a high of 75 percent for the Camry to a low of 60 percent for the Hilux truck, based on EPA CAFE measurement standards (Toyota Motor Corporation 1994).

In the face of all the data, however, a series of issues remain unresolved. Specifically, how much of this constitutes increased domestic manufacturing? Local content does not necessarily mean local manufacturing, and estimates of the latter vary greatly, due to difficulties in determining the national origin of complex components, many of which contain imported parts. While Toyota and Honda, for example, claim domestic content levels of 75 percent and 70 percent, respectively, the Bureau of Economic Analysis (BEA) estimates that Japanese affiliates in the automotive sector purchase, on average, approximately 50 percent of their inputs from domestic suppliers (Office of Technology Assessment 1994, 141, table 6.1), revealing an apparent discrepancy.[32]

These issues have primarily emerged because what has been termed a "second wave" of component suppliers arrived in the United States from Japan, either accompanying or in the aftermath of the establishment of new production facilities by the major Japanese producers, heavily concentrated in the 1980s.[33] As a result of this second wave, 43 percent of all U.S. suppliers to the three major Japanese automobile transplant assemblers—Toyota, Honda, and Nissan—are themselves affiliates of Japanese-based MNCs. Moreover, 53 percent of those suppliers have an equity link with one or more of the three Japanese transplant assemblers in the

United States.[34] Some analysts have responded to these data by noting that transplants purchase a large percentage of their local parts and components from affiliates of Japanese supplier firms, often ones within the same *keiretsu* (or network of firms) (Howes 1993).

This raises the broader and related issue of the replication of *keiretsu* relations in the United States and its solidification of a linkage between trade and investment. *Keiretsu* relations are widely regarded as restrictive in Japan and the prospect of their being transferred to the United States or Europe raises concern that they might convey unfair competitive advantages to Japanese automotive assemblers and suppliers, whether transplanted or not. Even normally reticent Japanese government officials have conceded that such behavior constitutes an impediment to competition within Japan and to market access for foreigners.[35] Further, there is evidence to suggest that *keiretsu* relations are being replicated beyond both the United States and the automotive industry. Although sourcing relationships are difficult to trace, for example, one study indicates that *keiretsu* linkages are common among Japanese affiliates in the European automotive and semiconductor sectors (Mason and Encarnation 1994).

In the context of these interfirm linkages, domestic content becomes increasingly difficult to measure and interpret. While there is therefore arguably greater benefit to foreign investment than an alternative of the import of finished products, the replication of such kinds of *keiretsu* linkages among the affiliates of Japanese firms does not augur well in attempting to maximize the benefit of FDI for the U.S. economy.

The Consequences: Linking Trade, Investment, and Deficits

At the outset of this chapter, a relationship was specified between how firms linked trade and investment strategies and the likely effect of asymmetrical patterns on national trade balances. Then followed a discussion of this pattern's effect on broad trade flows among three regions of the Triad, contrasting the U.S. experience with that of Japan and of Europe.

Certainly, it would be remiss to overlook completely the issue of the effects of this pattern on the U.S. economy. And while there are undoubted benefits to some forms of foreign investment in the United States, and many foreign investors do generate jobs and transfer technology to the U.S. economy, the data suggest that this pattern of unremitting benefits is not universal. Specifically, foreign investors who do adopt trade-creating strategies materially and adversely influence the present U.S. merchandise trade deficit.

As may be expected, foreign affiliates have consistently imported into the United States far more than they have exported. In 1991, the ratio of imports to exports was 1.83:1, after having peaked at 2.98:1 in 1987 (Department of Commerce 1993b, 54, table 1). Characteristically, from the middle of the 1970s until the most recently available figures, the trade deficit of foreign affiliates has amounted to more than 50 percent of the entire U.S. merchandise trade deficit, and their proportion of this deficit has steadily risen since the *endaka* of the mid-1980s.[36] In 1987, the trade deficit of all foreign affiliates in the United States was equivalent to 53 percent of the total trade deficit; that level rose steadily to peak at 120 percent in 1991. In 1992, foreign affiliates ran a trade deficit of $70.7 billion in real terms, compared to a deficit of $6.1 billion run by U.S. firms.[37]

Much of the trade deficit can be accounted for by IFT. Not surprisingly, variations in the proportion of IFT to total trade were found that may indicate that Japanese affiliates in the United States have a stronger propensity to trade through IFT channels than their European counterparts (with the exception of German firms). German and Japanese affiliates have a powerful tendency to import from their parent groups, their respective IFT imports averaging 82.6 percent and 80.5 percent of total imports from 1981 to 1991. French and U.K. affiliates import noticeably less from their parent groups, averaging 67.1 percent and 43.2 percent, respectively, over the same time period (Department of Commerce 1993b, 57, table 3).

The flow of this trade, furthermore, was heavily skewed toward imports into the United States through IFT. From 1981 to 1991, the average IFT export propensity for all foreign affiliates in the United States was 42 percent, compared to 71 percent for imports through IFT. Consistent with my general proposition, national variations are evident in the percentage of exports accounted for by IFT. As with import propensity, France and the United Kingdom have the lowest IFT export propensity. German firms import a great deal through IFT; however, their exports lacked the same characteristic during the same time period. Japan's exports reflected the same elements as their imports, being largely through IFT at an average of 61 percent (Department of Commerce 1993b, 57, table 3).

These statistics substantiate the claim that Japanese affiliates consistently have demonstrated a strong tendency to trade within MNC networks.[38] German affiliates have had a higher propensity to import than to export within MNC networks, while French and British affiliates consistently have had a lower than average propensity to do either. Overall, the tendency is toward increased IFT imports, from 63.5 percent in 1981 to 74.1 percent in 1991. By contrast, IFT exports have fluctuated slightly but increased little over the decade, from 42.0 percent of all trade in 1981 to 42.3 percent in 1991.

While it is difficult to explain this large imbalance in the growth in IFT imports as opposed to exports, some analysts suggest that the gradual rise in IFT imports is mostly due to the increased wholesale trading activity of Japanese and Korean affiliates in the United States, primarily in the automotive sector (Organisation for Economic Co-operation and Development 1993, 16). The pattern of Japanese investment in the automotive sector outlined in the previous section adds credence to their claim.

There appears to be a link between the composition and pattern of FDI and the bilateral trade balances between the United States and its major trading partners. The findings presented in this chapter indicate that the trading behavior of foreign-owned affiliates varies by national origin. Japanese affiliates in the United States consistently have run the largest trade deficit, often with an extraordinary differentiation between the figures for Japanese firms and those from the rest of the world. For example, the affiliate deficit in 1992 was $37.4 billion, which was equivalent to 49 percent of the total merchandise trade deficit that year (Department of Commerce 1993b, 57, table 3; 1991-1992, table G-2).

German and U.K. affiliates also have run deficits, although considerably smaller at $9.6 billion and $4.1 billion, respectively, in 1992. French affiliates tend to run small trade surpluses, amounting to $3.1 billion in 1992 (Department of Commerce 1993b, 57, table 3; 1991-1992, table G-2). The suggestion that Japanese firms are simply "better" or more competitive than their European rivals seems indefensible. Germany, it should be noted, has twice been the largest exporter in the world in the last half-dozen years. Yet the merchandise trade deficit for its affiliates with U.S. affiliates in Germany, as these figures indicate, is only approximately 25 percent of that for Japanese firms. The dramatic difference in the trade balances of foreign affiliates by country of origin is reflected in figure 6.11.

Figure 6.11
Trade Balances of Foreign Subsidiaries in the United States by Nationality of Ownership, 1982-1992 (Constant 1987 Dollars)

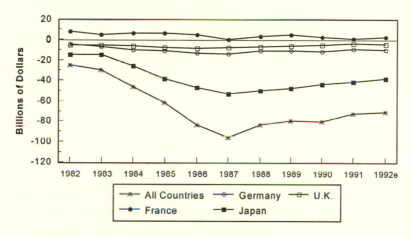

Note: 1992 data are preliminary.

Source: Bureau of Economic Analysis, *Survey of Current Business* 73(10):57, table 3, October 1993; *FDIUS*, table G-2, 1992-1992.

Key in explaining this variation is the composition of investment, especially the Japanese focus on wholesaling discussed earlier. The concentration of Japanese FDIUS on wholesale trade shows up clearly in the aggregate trade data of Japanese affiliates in the United States. Since the mid-1980s, Japanese affiliates consistently have accounted for 40 percent of the exports and 50 percent of the imports of all foreign affiliates in the United States. All but a small share of their trade has been by wholesale trade affiliates (Department of Commerce 1993b, 53).

This form of affiliates has particularly strong tendencies toward IFT, reflecting their role as distributors for their parent's products. Although at lower levels than in wholesale trade, affiliates in manufacturing industries also have high import tendencies, largely due to IFT imports of parts, components, and subassemblies.

In sum, the bilateral distribution of FDI clearly affects the relative symmetry of bilateral trade flows. This is most evident in the United States–Japan economic relationship, where significant asymmetries in investment have contributed to an imbalanced trading relationship marked by consistent Japanese trade surpluses, most of which can be associated with flows of merchandise from Japanese MNC parents to their affiliates in the United States.

Certainly, the trade deficit is affected by a broad range of factors, including exchange rates, variations in national growth and productivity rates, and different rates of domestic savings and investment. It cannot reasonably be claimed that foreign affiliates in the United States are wholly responsible for the trade deficit. Furthermore, these factors may reduce the deficit in some cases by partially producing goods in the United States that might otherwise have been produced entirely abroad and imported as finished products.

The fact remains, however, that the majority of the merchandise trade deficit is accounted for by IFT, that Japan has the highest levels of IFT imports in absolute and relative terms, that the largest component of the overall trade deficit is accounted for by Japan, and that Japanese firms have the heaviest reliance on a wholesale investment strategy. The argument for a causal relationship looks persuasive, the linkages between the composition of trade and investment and the trade deficit appear compelling, and the consequences for the developing patterns of the U.S. economy significant.

CONCLUSION

This chapter began with a discussion of the components of product cycle theory. It was noted that much of its preeminence could be explained by historical factors: the fact that the world's largest and most dominant MNCs from the late eighteenth century onward were, with few exceptions, first British and then American. Furthermore, this historical dominance was coupled with the growing acceptance of an Anglo-American version of economics in the Western social sciences.[39] As Anglo-American firms dominated the globe economically, Western economists dominated Western thought intellectually. The latter therefore studied the former, and one of the first "products" was product cycle theory.

An alternative formulation was then offered—one that was more mercantilistic in both tone and substance and emphasized a different kind of relationship between trade and investment. Instead of characterizing direct investment as a substitute for trade, it emphasized a complementary relationship between the two. Investment in this formulation focused on wholesaling rather than manufacturing and on assembly plants instead of production facilities within manufacturing. This approach could be made to increase domestic exports while taking advantage of the cost reductions and skirting many protectionist barriers.

Of course, such differentiation, if empirically verified, worked in contrast to the assumption of convergence. This alternative formulation led to the suggestion that, far from a replication of the pattern of investment depicted by product cycle theory, MNCs from a variety of countries might sustain their different patterns or, at least conceivably, might be moving further apart.

Is this "trade-creating" theory of investment empirically justifiable? Do some MNCs pursue strategies that are consistent with this approach, and, if so, what types of firms do so? Answers to these questions have been offered in this chapter.

The author's research indicates that the formulation of an alternative theory of trade-promoting investment is indeed an accurate description of the behavior of *some* MNCs, even if the theory is not as coherent or comprehensive as product cycle theory. Three observations are derived.

First, there are distinct, identifiable patterns of behavior in the realm of trade and investment among the world's MNCs that approximate the expectations generated by either the trade-promoting or product cycle formulations. These differences are most clearly reflected in IFT levels and are consistent, whether examined on an (aggregate) interregional level, a bilateral cross-national level, or at the individual firm level.

Second, while there are differences, these are based on the nationality of the firms. Thus, although IFT levels may vary across sectors, the nationality of the firm appears most determinative as an indicator of behavior. Some industries have lower levels of IFT as a result of their peculiarities. But there is a consistent trend in which Japanese firms generally maintain the highest IFT levels within sectors, especially those sectors in which Japanese firms are most competitive such as automobiles and consumer electronics.

Third, little evidence suggests that Japanese MNCs are converging toward a pattern of behavior that conforms with product cycle theory. It remains to be seen whether this pattern will change over time. As noted at the outset, however, while product cycle theory assumes change over time, it is vague about indicators for timing. Japanese affiliates may also begin to export a larger percentage of their sales as they become more embedded in foreign markets and become more fully integrated and establish independent production facilities. To date, however, there is no evidence that Japanese affiliates are exporting more and contradictory data about the extent of their efforts to become more deeply rooted in the U.S. economy and to exhibit production and trade tendencies similar to most European affiliates.[40]

Indeed, the patterns of global and Triadic investment of Japanese affiliates confirm the view that they continue to pursue trade-creating strategies, conditioned by the exigencies of host government regulations and sectoral prerequisites. The evidence in support of this contention is provided by limited comparative data across countries, coupled with detailed data about the behavior of foreign affiliates in the United States and a case study of the behavior of affiliates of Japanese automobile firms in the United States.

The final observation is that Japanese firms are not alone in pursuing such strategies, although they may be the most comprehensive and effective exponents of a trade promoting strategy that uses investment as a conduit for trade on a global basis. German firms, for example, provide some evidence of pursuing comparable strategies in the United States—a view given credence by their comments in interviews. Furthermore, although not the primary focus of attention in this analysis, new investors, such as Korean firms, show preliminary signs of following the Japanese pattern of investment in the United States (Organisation for Economic Co-operation and Development 1993, 16). Indeed, even Dutch firms, that traditionally have been associated most closely with Anglo-American patterns of behavior among Continental European countries, show signs of shifting their pattern of U.S. investment away from a traditional product cycle strategy toward a trade-promoting strategy.[41]

In contrast, little evidence suggests that Anglo-American multinationals are abandoning their traditional form of behavior. The composition of their investment remains diffuse, with little evidence of strategic elements of horizontal or vertical integration, and relatively low levels of IFT. And this is not an exclusive universe of British and U.S. firms. Data on other European producers suggest that some, such as French firms, appear to follow variants of the same pattern, one consistent with product cycle theory.

Such evidence therefore supports the inference not only that differences in strategic approaches are being maintained but also that the behavior of MNCs may be diverging. Japan is not alone in pursuing this strategy. Some Western countries and emerging, new multinational firms from outside the Triad appear to find the alternative of the "trade-creating" model more appealing.

Of course, there must be a further set of limits to this pattern of behavior, those imposed by macroeconomic factors. The appreciation of the yen, discussed at the outset of this chapter, would inevitably constrain the behavior of Japanese MNCs, forcing them to invest an increasing portion of the production process abroad, and thus forcing them to shift from assembly to high value-added manufacturing components production.

However, Japanese MNCs have not discovered those limits yet, despite two *endakas*. Indeed, Japanese firms often defy the boundaries specified by macroeconomic theory.

NOTES

This chapter was originally presented at a conference held at Georgetown University in September 1995 entitled "Between Us and Them: Foreign Ownership and U.S. Competitiveness in the 1990s." The author is indebted to Douglas Nigh, Douglas P. Woodward, Davis B. Bobrow, William Keller, Louis Pauly, and Paul Doremus for their comments. All responsibility for the final product rests with the author.

1. This kind of argument has been used about Japan in a variety of recent contexts. Edward Graham and Naoki Anzai (1994), for example, suggest the yen's overvaluation will reduce manufacturing in Japan and make Japanese firms "less competitive, and a little more like everyone else."

2. For a recent journalistic discussion of this tendency, complete with a survey of opinions among executives in high technology manufacturing industries, see *San Jose Mercury News*, April 30. 1995; and for a more detailed assessment, see Eamonn Fingleton, *Blindside: Why Japan Is Still on Track to Overtake the U.S. by the Year 2000* (Boston: Houghton Mifflin Co., 1995).

3. For an extensive critical assessment of the rectitude of the claim of the "hollowing out" of the Japanese economy, see Mark Tilton, *Restrained Trade: Cartels in Japan's Basic Materials Industries* (Ithaca, New York: Cornell University Press, 1995). On page 12, for example, Tilton suggests that "Although the Japanese talked about hollowing out as domestic production was replaced by imports, that event only happened in aluminum smelting, apparel, and to a very limited degree, lumber and furniture."

4. See, for example, Martin Kenney and Richard Florida, "How Japanese Industry Is Rebuilding the Rust Belt," *Technology Review*, 1991: 25-33. On this general issue of the contribution of Japanese investment to the welfare of the U.S. economy, see also Robert R. Rehder, "What American and Japanese Managers Are Learning from Each Other," *Business Horizons* 24 (March/April) 1981, pp. 63-70, and Kazuhiko Nagato, "The Japan-United States Savings Rate Gap," in *Inside the Japanese System*, edited by Daniel Okimoto and Thomas Rohlen (Stanford, Calif.: Stanford University Press, 1988), pp. 64-70.

5. As an exception to this comment see, for example, Richard G. Newman, "The Second Wave Arrives: Japanese Strategy in the Auto Parts Market," *Business Horizons* 23, 4 (July/August) 1990, pp. 24-30.

6. For an example of such a dissident voice (albeit one born of political reasons), see a European assessment of the constraints on foreign direct investment in the United States (FDIUS), in Services of the Commission of the European Communities, *Report on United States Trade and Investment Barriers: Problems of Doing Business with the U.S.* (Brussels, Belgium: Commission Services, April 1993), pp. 82-90.

7. One of the early, most comprehensive formulations of the FDI life cycle theory by an economist was offered by John Dunning as the "eclectic theory" of FDI (Dunning 1977). See also, in more recent work, J. H. Dunning, *Japanese Participation in British Industry* (London: Croom Helm, 1986) and J. H. Dunning, *Multinational Enterprises and the Global Economy* (Wokingham, United Kingdom: Addison-Wesley, 1993). Raymond Vernon's major contributions include *Sovereignty at Bay* (New York: Basic Books, 1971) and *The Storm over the Multinationals: The Real Issues* (Cambridge, Mass.: Harvard, 1977). But Vernon's most succinct and perhaps widest-read analysis of this issue is in an article entitled "International Investment and International Trade in the Product Cycle" (*Quarterly Journal of Economics* 80(2):190-207, 1966). Other notable contributions on this issue are J. Hennert, *A Theory of Multinational Enterprise* (Ann Arbor, Mich.: University of Michigan Press, 1985); and Richard J. Barnet and Ronald E. Müller, *Global Reach: The Power of the Multinational Corporations* (New York: Simon and Schuster, 1974).

8. Inward investment refers to the flows of foreign direct investment into a given country. Outward investment refers to the flows of direct investment abroad from a given country. In principle, world inflows and outflows should balance. In practice, however, they often do not (as is the case with other balance-of-payments items). Reasons for the discrepancy between total inflows and outflows of investment include cross-national differences in accounting for unremitted branch profits, capital gains and losses, reinvested earnings, real estate and construction investment, and the transactions of offshore enterprises.

9. For an interesting analysis, questioning the whole concept of convergence in national models, see Suzanne Berger, "Introduction" in *National Diversity and Global Capitalism*, edited by Suzanne Berger and Ronald Dore (Ithaca, New York: Cornell University Press, 1996, pp. 1-25).

10. For an example of studies that omit this aspect, see Charles Lipson, *Standing Guard: Protecting Foreign Capital in the Nineteenth and Twentieth Centuries* (Berkeley: University of California Press, 1985).

11. For details concerning the initial decision to invest in U.S. plants, see Wolfgang Streeck, *Industrial Relations in West Germany: A Case Study of the Car Industry* (New York: St. Martin's Press, 1984).

12. For evidence in support of this view, see the American Chamber of Commerce in Japan, *The United States–Japan White Paper 1993* (Tokyo: American Chamber of Commerce in Japan, 1993).

13. Analysis in support of this view comes from a number of sources. See Office of the United States Trade Representative, *1993 National Trade Estimate Report on Foreign Trade Barriers* (Washington, D.C.: GPO, 1993), pp. 79-94, 143-170; for a Japanese

perspective in support of this finding, see the Report of the Ad-Hoc Committee on Foreign Direct Investment in Japan, Keidanren Committee on International Industrial Cooperation, Committee on Foreign Affiliated Corporations, *Improvement of the Investment Climate and Promotion of Foreign Direct Investment into Japan*; see also House Wednesday Group, *Beyond Revisionism: Toward a New U.S.–Japan Policy for the Post–Cold War Era* (Congress of the United States, March 1993).

14. Figures based on data in Department of Commerce, *Foreign Direct Investment in the United States: Preliminary 1992 Estimates* (Washington, D.C.: GPO, 1994), table 3: and Department of Commerce, *Survey of Current Business*, August 1987, table 10, p. 90.

15. See Office of Technology Assessment Report, *Multinationals and the U.S. Technology Base*, OTA-ITE-612 (Washington, D.C.: GPO, September 1994), figure 6-9, p.137. Data from Department of Commerce, *Foreign Direct Investment in the United States: An Update* (Washington, D.C.: GPO, June 1993), table G-4 (1983-1986) and table G-2 (1987-1992); Department of Commerce , *U.S. Direct Investment Abroad* (Washington D.C.: GPO, various years), table 50 (1983-1988) and table III.H.1 (1989-1992); Department of Commerce, *Survey of Current Business* 73(6); 78, table 2, June 1993.

16. In the case of Japanese manufacturing affiliates in North America, exports have increased as a percentage of all sales since the late 1980s, yet they were the highest in 1983 at 12.8 percent and actually decreased from then until 1988, when they hit a low of 6.2 percent. For further details, see Office of Technology Assessment, *Multinationals and the U.S. Technology Base*, OTA-ITE-612 (Washington, D.C.: GPO, September 1994), figure 6-16, p.149.

17. For a critical assessment of this claim, see Mark Tilton, *Restrained Trade: Cartels in Japan's Basic Materials Industries* (Ithaca, New York: Cornell University Press, 1995).

18. For a historical analysis of U.S. investment in Europe, see Simon Reich, *The Fruits of Fascism: Postwar Prosperity in Historical Perspective* (Ithaca, New York: Cornell University Press, 1990), and Mira Wilkins and Frank E. Hill, *American Business Abroad: Ford on Six Continents* (Detroit, Mich.: Wayne State University Press, 1964).

19. This image of Italy is consistent with broader data on inward FDI flows, which remain small and relatively volatile. While the stock of investment grew in the late 1980s and early 1990s, the flow was uneven, peaking in 1988 and 1990, and dropping substantially in subsequent years. For further discussion and data on FDI flows in and out of Italy, see Commission of the European Communities 1993 (p. 61, table 14).

20. For a discussion of the issue of the contrasting regulations and their effect on foreign investment, see Robin Gaster, "Protectionism with Purpose: Guiding Foreign Investment," *Foreign Policy*, no. 80 (Fall 1992), pp. 96-100, and "The Enemy Within," *The Economist*, June 12, 1993, pp. 67-68.

21. In contrast, the Federal Republic of Germany attracted investments totaling $19 billion in the same period ("Study: U.S. Leads, Germany Trails, in Attractiveness to Direct Investors" 1992).

22. For these and other relevant figures, see Office of the Chief Economist, *Foreign Direct Investment in the United States: Review and Analysis of Current Developments* (Washington, D.C.: GPO, August 1991).

23. For example, see Statement of Peter Mills, Former Chief Administrative Officer of Sematech, at Hearing before the Subcommittee on International Finance and Monetary Policy on June 4, *Foreign Acquisition of U.S. Owned Companies* (Washington, D.C.: GPO, 1992), pp. 15-18. Some analysts argue that, without change, the Exon-Florio legislation would support much more restrictive policies toward FDIUS (Graham and Ebert 1991).

24. For details of the review process undertaken by CFIUS, see statement of Frederick Volcansek, Acting Assistant Secretary for Trade Development, U.S. Department of Commerce, in Hearing before the Subcommittee on International Finance and Monetary Policy on June

4, *Foreign Acquisition of U.S. Companies* (Washington, D.C.: GPO, 1992), pp. 10-11.

25. European FDIUS rose from $47.3 billion in 1980 to $234.8 billion in 1989, an annual increase of 17.8 percent between 1980 and 1985, and 21.6 percent between 1985 and 1989. For figures, see Department of Commerce, *Foreign Direct Investment in the United States: Review and Current Developments*, August 1991, table 2-4; Department of Commerce, *Foreign Direct Investment in the United States: An Update* (Washington, D.C.: GPO, June 1993); and Department of Commerce, "U.S. Net Investment Position, 1992," press release, June 30, 1993, p. 8 and table 3. For a more recent discussion of preliminary figures, see "Japan Keeps Cash at Home," *Financial Times*, June 15, 1993, p. 4.

26. Table 6.5 shows only selected manufacturing industries.

27. In general, foreign content is highest in industries that purchase a lot of manufactured intermediate goods, such as the machinery and transportation equipment industries. Foreign content is generally the lowest in industries that use raw materials subject to high transportation costs, such as beverages, primary ferrous metals, and stone, clay, and glass products (Department of Commerce 1993b, 64-65).

28. This imbalance between imports and exports for Japanese MNCs is reflected in their ratio of exports as a percentage of all sales over time. Product cycle theory predicts that foreign affiliates will shift over time from purely domestic to more internationally diversified sales. In the case of Japanese manufacturing affiliates in North America, exports have increased as a percentage of all sales since the late 1980s, yet they were the highest in 1983 at 12.8 percent and actually decreased from then until 1988, when they hit a low of 6.2 percent at the end of the 1980s (Office of Technology Assessment 1994, 149, figure 6-16).

29. There is one other exception to the generally moderate proportion of wholesale trade to total trade among European affiliates: Fifty percent of the exports by French affiliates were shipped by wholesale trade affiliates in 1991; most were in farm-product raw materials (Office of Technology Assessment 1994, 140, footnote 13).

30. See, for example, Richard G. Newman, "The Second Wave Arrives: Japanese Strategy in the Auto Parts Market," *Business Horizons* 23(4):24-30, July/August 1990.

31. For a discussion of the different estimates of Honda's local content, see Office of Technology Assessment, *Multinationals and the National Interest: Playing by Different Rules*, OTA-ITE-569 (Washington, D.C.: GPO, September 1993), pp. 96-97. The enterprise-level data needed to completely assess the local content rates of individual firms are not publicly available due to disclosure restrictions.

32. In 1990, the local content for all Japanese automotive affiliates was 50.7 percent; in 1991, it was 47.2 percent (Office of Technology Assessment 1994, 146, footnote 25).

33. Note that Honda began production in Ohio in 1982; Nissan began truck production in 1983 and automobile production in 1985 in Tennessee; and Toyota began automobile production in 1988 in Kentucky (after having established the NUMMI joint venture with GM).

34. These figures are based on data calculated from ELM International, Inc., *The ELM Guide to U.S. Automotive Sourcing* (East Lansing, Mich.: ELM International, Inc., 1992), and ELM International, Inc., *The ELM Guide to Japanese Affiliated Suppliers in North America*, Fourth Ed. (East Lansing, Mich.: ELM International, Inc., 1993).

35. According to Jotaro Yabe of Japan's Fair Trade Commission, "It makes economic sense for auto-makers to organize their distributors into keiretsu. For example, it contributes to maintaining after-sales service and to raising sales efficiency. On the other hand, it prevents the entry of foreign cars into the market, and is thus seen as a problem. . . . Business practices, however, restrict the freedom of dealers to handle other manufacturers' cars, including foreign cars" (Yabe 1993).

36. The two exceptions were 1984 and 1985, two years that coincided with Japanese MNCs adjustment to monumental changes in the value of the yen.

37. Data compiled from Department of Commerce, *Survey of Current Business* (Washington, D.C.: GPO 1993), table 1, p. 54.; 73(3): 90-91, table 2, March 1993; and 74(3): 68-69, table 2, March 1994; Department of Commerce, *Foreign Direct Investment in the United States and U.S. Direct Investment Abroad: Operations of U.S. Affiliates of Foreign Companies*, revised 1983-1991 estimates and preliminary 1992 estimates (Washington, D.C.: GPO, 1986-1994), table G-3 (1982-1986) and table G-1 (1987-1992).

38. OECD data also indicate that U.S.-based affiliates of Japanese MNEs use FDIUS as a conduit for trade to a greater degree than do U.S. firms in all foreign markets (Organisation for Economic Cooperation and Development 1993, 16).

39. This point is discussed extensively in James Fallows, *Looking at the Sun: The Rise of the New East Asian Economic and Political System* (New York: Pantheon Books, 1994).

40. This process may be taking place within individual Japanese firms that have been in the U.S. economy for some time. For instance, Honda, which began U.S. production in 1983, recently announced plans to expand its North American car and engine manufacturing facilities, use the increased capacity to boost regional exports from 43,000 to 150,000 units by the end of the decade, and generally accord the region greater independence within Honda's global business (Griffiths 1994).

41. Between 1985 and 1993, the shift by Dutch firms in industrial investment as a percentage of all investment fell from 20.1 percent to 14.7 percent. In that same period, their percentage invested specifically in manufacturing fell from 22.4 percent to 13.7 percent. Finally, their proportion of wholesale trade as a percentage of all investment rose from 7.4 to 11.1 percent (Department of Commerce 1994, table 3; 1987, 90, table 10). These represent significant shifts in a large investment position over an eight year period.

REFERENCES

Canner, Stephen J. 1992. Report of the Treasury Official Director for International Investment before the Defense Policy Panel and Investigations Subcommittee of the Armed Services Committee, U.S. House of Representatives, May 14.

Commission of the European Communities. 1993. *Panorama of EC Industry 1993*. Brussels, Luxembourg: Office for Official Publications of the European Communities.

Department of Commerce. 1983-91a. *Foreign Direct Investment in the United States*, Bureau of Economic Analysis, Washington, D.C.: GPO.

———. 1983-91b. *U.S. Direct Investment Abroad*, Bureau of Economic Analysis. Washington, D.C.: GPO.

———. 1987. *Survey of Current Business*, Bureau of Economic Analysis, August. Washington, D.C.: GPO.

———. 1991-1992. *Foreign Direct Investment in the United States and U.S. Direct Investment*, Bureau of Economic Analysis. Washington, D.C.: GPO.

———. 1992a. *Survey of Current Business*, Bureau of Economic Analysis. Washington, D.C.: GPO.

———. 1992b. *Foreign Direct Investment in the United States: Operations of U.S. Affiliates of Foreign Companies, Preliminary 1990 Estimates*, August. Washington, D.C.: GPO.

———. 1993a. *Survey of Current Business*, Bureau of Economic Analysis, June. Washington, D.C., table 2, p. 78.

———. 1993b. *Survey of Current Business*, Bureau of Economic Analysis, October. Washington, D.C.: GPO.

———. 1994. *Foreign Direct Investment in the United States: Establishment Data for Manufacturing 1991*, Bureau of Economic Analysis, April. Washington, D.C.: GPO.

Dunning, John H. 1977. "Trade, Location of Economic Activity and MNE: A Search for an Eclectic Approach," in *The International Allocation of Economic Activity: Proceedings of a Nobel Symposium Held at Stockholm* edited by B. Ohlin, P.-O. Hesselborn, and P.M. Wijkman. London: Macmillan, pp. 395-418

Economic Strategy Institute. 1992. "The Case for Saving the Big Three," interim report. Washington, D.C., monograph, p. 56.

Gilpin, Robert. 1989. "Where Does Japan Fit In?" *Millennium: Journal of International Studies* 18(3):337.

Glickman, Norman J., and Douglas P. Woodward. 1990. *The New Competitors: How Foreign Investors Are Changing the U.S. Economy.* New York: Basic Books.

Graham, Edward M., and Paul R. Krugman. 1989. *Foreign Direct Investment in the United States.* Washington, D.C.: Institute for International Economics.

Graham, Edward M., and Michael E. Ebert. 1991. "Foreign Direct Investment and U.S. National Security," *World Economy* 14(3):245-268.

Graham, Edward M., and Naoko T. Anzai. 1994. "The Myth of a de Facto Asian Economic Bloc: Japan's Foreign Direct Investment in East Asia," *Columbia Journal of World Business,* Fall, pp. 6-20.

Griffiths, J. 1994. "Honda to Spend $310m on Bolstering US Plants," *Financial Times,* July 20, p. 1.

Hobson, John A. 1938. *Imperialism: A Study.* London: George Allen and Unwin.

Howes, C. 1993. *Transplants and the U.S. Automobile Industry.* Washington, D.C.: Economic Policy Institute.

International Trade Administration. 1988. *International Direct Investment: Global Trends and the U.S. Role.* Washington, D.C.: GPO, table 2, p.90.

Johnson, Chalmers. 1982. *MITI and the Japanese Miracle: The Growth of Industrial Policy, 1925-1975.* Stanford, Calif.: Stanford University Press, p. 200.

Kautsky, Karl. 1915. *Nationalstaat, Imperialistischer Staat und Staatenbund.* Nuremberg, Germany: Fränkische Verlagsanstalt.

Lenin, Vladimir I. 1977. *Imperialism, the Highest Stage of Capitalism: A Popular Outline.* New York: International Publishers.

Mason, Mark, and Dennis J. Encarnation, eds. 1994. *Does Ownership Matter? Japanese Multinationals in Europe.* Oxford: Clarendon Press, pp. 147, 156, 314.

Morita, Akio. 1992. "Nihon-gata Keiei ga abunai," *Bungei Shinju,* pp. 94-103, February.

———. 1993. "Toward a New World Economic Order," *Atlantic Monthly,* June, pp. 90 and 96.

Office of the Chief Economist. 1991. *Foreign Direct Investment in the United States: Review and Analysis of Current Developments,* August. Washington, D.C.: GPO, p. 68.

Office of the President. 1991. *Economic Report of the President,* transmitted to Congress, February, together with the *Annual Report of the Council of Economic Advisors,* Washington, D.C.: GPO, p. 262.

Office of Technology Assessment (OTA). 1994. *Multinationals and the U.S. Technology Base,* OTA-ITE-612, September. Washington, D.C.: GPO.

Organisation for Economic Co-operation and Development (OECD). 1993. *Globalization of Industrial Activities: Background Synthesis Report,* Directorate for Science, Technology, and Industry. Paris: OECD.

Pauly, Louis W., and Simon Reich. 1997. "National Structures and Multinational Corporate Behavior: Enduring Differences in the Age of Globalization," *International Organization* 51(1):1-30.

Samuelson, Robert J. 1986. "The Japanese Blindness," *Newsweek,* May 5, p. 59.

———. 1995. "The Japanese Miracle Is a Myth," *Los Angeles Times,* March 29.

Semiconductor Industry Association. 1991. *Annual Data Book,* p. 12.

"Study: U.S. Leads, Germany Trails, in Attractiveness to Direct Investors." 1992. *This Week in Germany,* October 23, p. 5.

Thomsen, S. 1994. "Comment," in *Does Ownership Matter? Japanese Multinationals in Europe*, edited by Mark Mason and Dennis Encarnation. Oxford: Clarendon Press, p. 203.

Toyota Motor Corporation. 1994. Press release, June 14, p.13.

Tyson, Laura D'Andrea. 1992. Statement at Hearing before the Subcommittee on International Finance and Monetary Policy on June 4, *Foreign Acquisition of U.S. Owned Companies*. Washington, D.C.: GPO, pp. 18-19.

United Nations Conference on Trade and Development (UNCTAD). 1993. *World Investment Report 1993: Transnational Corporations and Integrated International Production*, Division on Transnational Corporations and Investment. New York: United Nations. table I.1, p.14.

U.S. Industrial Outlook. 1992. January. Washington, D.C.: GPO.

————. 1993. Washington, D.C.: GPO, January.

Wethington, Olin. 1992. Statement of Assistant Secretary for International Affairs, U.S. Department of the Treasury, at Hearing before the Subcommittee on International Finance and Monetary Policy on June 4, *Foreign Acquisition of U.S. Owned Companies*. Washington, D.C.: GPO, pp. 5-6.

Yabe, J. 1993. "Freedom of Distributors Restricted: Problems Including Rebates for Reaching Goals," *Nihon Keizai Shimbun*, October 11, p.14.

Part III

R&D and High-Technology Effects

7

Foreign R&D Facilities in the United States

Donald H. Dalton and Manuel G. Serapio, Jr.

INTRODUCTION

Every serious analysis of foreign direct investment's effects on a host country must consider research and development (R&D). Previous chapters on economics have already alluded to R&D effects. This chapter provides a much more detailed examination of the topic, using the best available data for the United States. The data underlying the chapter's analysis combine official government sources on R&D and the authors' own compilation of information on foreign R&D facilities in the United States. Some interesting comparisons of R&D by source country emerge in the chapter.

In recent years, R&D expenditures by foreign-owned businesses in the United States[1] have increased at a much faster pace than total R&D expenditures within the United States by U.S. firms. This chapter documents that R&D spending in the United States by foreign-owned companies is now large enough to have an influence on the overall growth rate of total private R&D in the United States. In the high-technology sector, R&D expenditures by foreign companies account for one of every five dollars spent on corporate R&D in the United States. The growth in R&D spending by foreign companies in the United States can be attributed largely to the expansion of R&D expenditures by the U.S. affiliates of multinational companies from six countries: Switzerland, Japan, United Kingdom, Germany, France, and Canada.

TRENDS IN U.S. R&D EXPENDITURES BY FOREIGN-OWNED COMPANIES

Data on R&D spending by U.S.- and foreign-owned companies are collected through surveys of companies by the Bureau of Economic Analysis (BEA) (Department of Commerce annual-a) and the National Science Foundation (NSF) (National Science Foundation annual). BEA data are based on annual surveys of the R&D

expenditures of U.S. affiliates of foreign companies in the United States. The NSF publishes two series of industry R&D statistics: *(i)* Total funds (company, federal, and other) and *(ii)* Company and other (except federal) funds. The term "company-funded" R&D refers to the NSF industry R&D series excluding federal funds and covers R&D performed within the United States by both U.S.-owned and foreign companies.

Both the BEA and NSF surveys use similar Standard Industrial Classification (SIC) industry groups (3-digit) for their enterprise-based surveys, although some companies perform R&D in various industries. Because the BEA and NSF surveys limit their definition of R&D expenditures by foreign-owned companies to funds spent at company-operated R&D facilities, the data from both surveys are conservative estimates of R&D expenditures. Both surveys exclude other types of foreign sponsored R&D, such as foreign company–sponsored research at U.S. universities. However, the NSF conducts (at two year intervals) a separate survey of contract research in the United States. Based on the BEA and NSF data, several important trends are brought to light in the next part of this chapter.

Rising Share of Foreign Funding of U.S. R&D

According to BEA estimates, R&D spending by U.S. affiliates of foreign companies more than doubled from $6.5 billion in 1987 to $15.6 billion in 1994. R&D expenditures by U.S. affiliates of foreign companies have increased at a rate of 15 percent or more per year since 1987, with the exception of the years 1991 and 1993. The significant expansion of foreign R&D expenditures in the United States could be attributed partially to several major acquisitions of U.S. firms by foreign multinationals. Although there was a widespread surge in the late 1980s in acquisitions in all industries, such as computers, semiconductors, steel, and tires, the largest impact on R&D funding was in the acquisition by foreign multinational companies of U.S. pharmaceutical and biotechnology firms with large R&D budgets. Ciba Geigy's purchase of a 49.9 percent stake in Chiron and Hoffman LaRoche's investment in Genentech are examples of these acquisitions.

As previously mentioned, R&D expenditures by foreign companies in the United States have grown much faster than total R&D expenditures by U.S.-owned firms within the United States. Total R&D spending within the United States by U.S. firms rose about 59 percent from $61 billion in 1987 to $97 billion in 1994. In comparison, R&D expenditures by U.S. affiliates of foreign companies increased by 240 percent during the same period. As shown in figure 7.1, the foreign share of total company spending in R&D reached a plateau of about 9 percent from 1981 to 1985, but then quickly increased in the second half of the 1980s.

In 1991, a slowdown in foreign R&D spending due to the decline in new foreign investment in the United States and the upward revision in the NSF survey data of U.S. R&D led to the first decline in the foreign R&D share since 1980. The substantial increase in the level of U.S. R&D could be attributed largely to a sharp jump in reporting of nonmanufacturing R&D. Although the *revised level* of R&D spending in the NSF survey is larger since 1990, the growth rate has been sluggish, and the foreign share has increased at a much slower pace, reaching 16.1 percent in 1994.

Figure 7.1
Foreign Affiliated Companies' Share of U.S. R&D
(Company-Funded R&D)

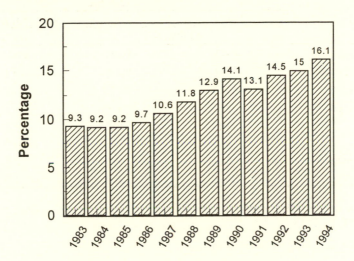

Source: Bureau of Economic Analysis (foreign) and National
Science Foundation (total).

Country Shares

R&D spending within the United States by foreign-owned businesses increased $9.1 billion between 1987 and 1994. Most of the growth in R&D expenditures by foreign companies in the United States has come from an increase in R&D spending by U.S. affiliates of multinational companies from four countries: Japan, United Kingdom, Switzerland, and Germany (table 7.1). Japanese-funded R&D in the United States, which increased from $307 million in 1987 to $2 billion in 1994, experienced the most rapid rate of growth among the large countries.

Japan ranked fifth in total U.S. R&D spending by affiliates in 1994, behind the United Kingdom, Germany, Switzerland, and Canada. Japan's share of the U.S. total R&D expenditures by foreign-owned companies in the United States (12.9 percent) trailed the shares of the United Kingdom (15.9 percent) and Germany (15.7 percent), but was significantly larger than the shares of France (8.9 percent) and the Netherlands (4.6 percent). Other countries ranked in the top ten were Sweden, Italy, and Korea. U.S. R&D expenditures by Korean companies soared to $167 million in 1994 from $55 million in 1993.

Industry Distribution

Foreign-affiliated companies are concentrating their U.S. research activities in a few U.S. industry sectors, reflecting to a large degree the industry concentration of their direct investments in the United States. In 1994, U.S. R&D spending by

Table 7.1
R&D Expenditures and Employment by Affiliates of Foreign Companies, 1994

Country	Expenditures		R&D Employees
	1987	1994	
	$ millions		(000's)
All Countries	6,521	15,602	108.0
United Kingdom	833	2,479	19.1
Germany	1,139	2,450	20.8
Switzerland	765	2,409	14.4
Japan	307	2.013	12.5
France	366	1,385	10.0
Netherlands	542	723	6.3
Canada*	1,666	2,363	11.1

*Canadian affiliates include a major U.S. chemical company with a minority Canadian investment.

Source: Department of Commerce (annual-a).

foreign-owned companies was concentrated in three industries: drugs, electronics, and industrial chemicals. These accounted for more than 60 percent of R&D expenditures by foreign-owned companies in the United States. These companies spent far less of their U.S. R&D funds on machinery, excluding computers, and transportation equipment (aerospace and motor vehicles) than did U.S. companies. About 14 percent of R&D funds by affiliates of foreign companies were allocated to nonmanufacturing—services and wholesale trade. Foreign-owned companies spent nearly $1 billion on R&D service industries, primarily computer and data processing services and accounting, research, and management services.

Another measure of the concentration of the R&D expenditures of U.S. affiliates of foreign companies in high-technology industries is the amount of spending relative to the NSF survey data for R&D by all companies (table 7.2). U.S. affiliates accounted for 45 percent of total private R&D funding in industrial chemicals and plastics and synthetics, and 38 percent of all funding in drugs and medicines (including biotechnology), and 33 percent of communications equipment, audio and video.

High concentrations of foreign-funding in R&D in these industries generally reflect the concentration of foreign ownership of businesses in these industries, as measured by sales or employment. Establishment data on foreign-owned shares of U.S. industries, from a joint survey program by BEA and the Bureau of the Census for 1991, show that foreign-owned establishments accounted for nearly 30 percent of shipments for industrial inorganic chemicals, 40.5 percent of plastic materials, 37.4 percent of drugs, 11.7 percent of computer equipment, 25.3 percent of communications equipment, 71.5 percent of household audio and video, 13 percent of electronic components, and 12.8 percent of instrumentation.

Table 7.2
Ratio of R&D Expenditures of U.S. Affiliates to R&D of All Companies for
Selected High-Technology Industries, 1994

Industry	U.S. Affiliates ($ millions)	All Companies ($ millions)	Percentage of Total R&D
Industrial chemicals	1,993	4,780	41.7
Drugs and medicines	4,526	9,625	47.0
Computers and office equipment	628	4,078	15.3
Communications equipment, television	1,356	5,003	27.1
Electronic components	294	5,870	5.0
Scientific and professional instruments	635	8,058	7.9

Source: Department of Commerce (annual) for U.S. affiliates. National Science Foundation (annual)
for all companies, company-funded R&D.

FOREIGN R&D FACILITIES IN THE UNITED STATES

This section is based on the detailed information compiled by the authors on 641 foreign-owned research and development (R&D) facilities in the United States. The Office of Business and Industrial Analysis of the Economics and Statistics Administration, Department of Commerce, compiled the listing from several sources. Most of the information on foreign R&D facilities in this listing was provided by companies through directory surveys and public announcements, although the authors did not attempt to verify the accuracy of every listing and generally relied on company classification and definition of an R&D facility. The full list of foreign-owned R&D facilities in the United States is in an earlier publication (Dalton and Serapio 1995).

Definition of a Foreign R&D Facility in the United States

For purposes of this report, we define a foreign R&D facility in the United States (also referred to as an R&D center, R&D company, R&D laboratory) as a free-standing R&D company (in other words, a company engaged mainly in R&D) of which 50 percent or more is owned by a foreign parent company. The R&D facility typically operates under its own budget, is overseen by its own group of officers, and is located in a free-standing facility outside and separate from the other U.S. facilities (such as sales and manufacturing facilities) of the parent company.

This definition of an R&D facility excludes R&D departments or sections within the U.S. affiliates (such as marketing offices and manufacturing plants) of foreign-owned companies.[2] For example, Toyota Motor Corporation conducts R&D at Toyota Technical Center in Torrance, California. Toyota's manufacturing affiliate, New

United Motor Manufacturing, Inc. (NUMMI). NUMMI also conducts R&D on a limited basis in its plant in Fremont, California. The former (Toyota Technical Center in Torrance) is defined as a foreign R&D facility and the latter (NUMMI) as a U.S. affiliate of a foreign company.

This definition of an R&D facility also excludes R&D performed by third-party organizations, such as R&D conducted by U.S. research universities or third-party contractors that are financed by a foreign company. In addition, this definition only includes those foreign R&D facilities in the United States of which 50 percent or more are owned by the foreign parent company. Because we rely on company classifications of R&D facilities, the range of activities may vary across industries and nationalities and includes activities that are not strictly R&D, such as product customization, design centers, and technology scanning.

R&D Facilities by Country and by Industry

The classification of R&D facilities by country of ownership is shown in table 7.3, based on wholly or partially owned facilities of 308 foreign companies. The 224 Japanese R&D facilities in the United States far outnumber the U.S. R&D facilities of other countries, accounting for nearly 35 percent of the 641 total foreign-owned facilities. The United Kingdom was second with 109 facilities, followed by Germany (95), France (52), and Switzerland (45). South Korea has a rapidly growing R&D presence in the United States with 27 R&D facilities. The large number of U.S. R&D laboratories of Japanese companies is partly due to the relatively large number of Japanese parent companies with R&D facilities in the United States—107 companies in 1994, compared with 61 British parent companies, 32 German parent companies, and 22 French parent companies.

In terms of industry distribution, the industries with the largest number of foreign-owned R&D centers in the United States are drugs and biotechnology (113 facilities), chemicals and rubber (109 facilities), automotive (53 facilities), computer software (44 facilities), and computers (39 facilities). Japanese companies account for most of the R&D centers in the electronics and automotive industries, while European companies have far more drugs and chemicals R&D laboratories (table 7.3).

Size of R&D Facilities

Table 7.4 lists the thirty-five largest foreign research centers in the United States in terms of staff size. The largest foreign laboratories are concentrated in pharmaceuticals, automotive, and electronics. Of the thirty-five foreign R&D facilities listed in table 7.4, twenty-four are owned by European companies. The majority of these European R&D facilities are in pharmaceuticals and biotechnology. Japanese companies account for about 20 percent of the companies listed in table 7.4, mostly in the automotive industry.

Although staff size is not available for all of the 641 R&D facilities, the available data indicate that the pharmaceutical, biotechnology, and automotive R&D laboratories are much larger than the electronics R&D facilities. In the electronics industry,

Table 7.3
U.S. R&D Facilities of Foreign Companies, 1994

Industry	Japan	Ger-many	Korea	Nether-lands	U.K.	Switzer-land	Sweden	France	Others
Computers	2	2	4	7	3				3
Computer Software	28	4	1	1	6			3	1
Semiconductors	19	3	10	3					
Telecommunications	14	4	1		2	1	2	2	3
Optoelectronics	11	3			2		1		
HDTV, other electronics	33	9	4	4	10	5		4	
Drugs, biotechnology	24	18	1	5	23	17	5	11	9
Chemicals, rubber, mat'ls	23	28		4	19	10		17	8
Metals	5	1			3	1	1	4	
Automotive	34	11	3		1		2	2	
Machinery	7	2			4		6	3	
Instrumentation, controls	1	3		3	23	4	1	5	
Foods, consumer goods, misc.	7	6		5	19	6	1	2	7
Total Companies	107	32	10	10	61	16	15	22	35
Total Facilities	224	95	27	26	109	45	22	52	42

Source: Dalton and Serapio (1995).

the available data also indicate that Japanese R&D centers in the United States are much smaller than their European counterparts. This finding could be explained by the fact that several of the Japanese laboratories are much newer and have not yet reached full staffing. In addition, the disparity in staff size between the European and Japanese companies could be attributed to a difference in research focus. Japanese electronics companies tend to focus their R&D on a single technology at each site in the United States,[3] while European firms tend to establish large central laboratories covering many technologies. However, it is important to note that some Japanese companies (such as Sony) are consolidating their electronics R&D operations in fewer locations in California.

Location

Foreign R&D facilities in the United States are highly concentrated in some areas of the country. California ranks first with 158 R&D facilities, followed by New Jersey with 63 labs, and Michigan with 41 facilities (table 7.5).

Table 7.4
Largest Foreign Research Centers in the United States

Company	Location	Professional Staff
1. Pharmacia (SWE)	Upjohn Laboratories, Kalamazoo MI	1,318
2. Northern Telecom (CAN)	Research Triangle Park NC	1,260
3. SmithKline Beecham (UK)	King of Prussia PA	1,198
4. Philips (NE)	Magnavox, Fort Wayne IN	1,100
5. Siemens (GER)	Iselin NJ	1,100
6. Glaxo (UK)	Research Triangle Park NC	1,000
7. Burroughs Wellcome (UK)	Research Triangle Park NC	891
8. Honda (JA)	Marysville OH (2); Torrance CA; Denver CO	800
9. Hoechst (GER)	Somerville NJ	716
10. Hoffman-LaRoche (Swiss)	Genentech, San Francisco CA	672
11. Sony (JA)	San Jose CA	600
12. Toyota (JA)	Ann Arbor MI; Calif. (4)	513
13. Nissan (JA)	Mich. (2), Calif. (2), Ariz., Mass.	509
14. Bayer (GER)	Milies, West Haven CT	500
15. Glaxo (UK)	Sterling Drug, Rensselaer NY	450
16. Hoechst (GER)	Marion Merrell Dow, Kansas City MO	411
17. Nestle (Swiss)	Westreco, New Milford CT	410
18. Nestle (Swiss)	Alcon Labs, Fort Worth TX	404
19. Rhone-Poulenc (FR)	Fort Washington PA	400
20. Bayer (GER)	Miles, Pittsburgh PA	389
21. Hoffman-LaRoche (Swiss)	Nutley NJ	350
22. Rhone-Poulenc (FR)	Research Triangle Park NC	350
23. Unilever (NE/UK)	Edgewater NJ	329
24. Northern Telecom (CAN)	San Ramon CA	319
25. Northern Telecom (CAN)	Rochester NY	280
26. PA Consulting (UK)	Hightstown NJ	250
27. Zeneca (UK)	Wilmington DE	245
28. Moore (CAN)	Grand Island NY	235
29. Thomson (FR)	Indianapolis IN	230
30. Mazda (JA)	Flat Rock, Ann Arbor MI; Irvine CA	213
31. Racal (UK)	Sunrise FL	209
32. Goldstar (KO)	United Micro Tech, NJ	200
33. Siemens (GER)	Gammasonics, Hoffman Estates IL	200
34. Siemens (GER)	Rolm, Boca Raton FL	200
35. OSRAM (GER)	Sylvania, Danver MA	200

Source: Compiled by the authors from *Directory of American Research and Technology* 1994, R.R. Bowker, Inc.

Table 7.5
States with the Most Foreign R&D Facilities

State	Number of Facilities
California	158
New Jersey	63
Michigan	41
Ohio	38
Massachusetts	36
North Carolina	36
Pennsylvania	29
Illinois	27

Source: Compiled from R&D facilities lists in Dalton and Serapio 1995.

Japanese companies initially established R&D laboratories in California and more recently are moving east, while European companies began on the East Coast and are moving west. The largest concentration of R&D facilities is in California's Silicon Valley, which attracted large numbers of laboratories in computers, semiconductors, computer software, and biotechnology. The Los Angeles metropolitan area has a smaller number of R&D facilities, with a more diverse group of companies, including auto design and styling centers.

Another major cluster of R&D centers is in New Jersey, especially around Princeton University. Many of the major European drug and chemical companies have located near U.S. drug company research centers in New Jersey and, to a lesser degree, in Pennsylvania, North Carolina, and Connecticut. New Jersey also attracted a large number of electronics R&D facilities from European and Japanese companies. The Research Triangle Park in North Carolina is a center for biotechnology and telecommunications research for both U.S. and foreign companies. The Boston area ranks high, especially for its proximity to computer companies and access to Massachusetts Institute of Technology (MIT) faculty.

Some areas are highly specialized in certain industries, such as Detroit for automotive laboratories and Richardson, Texas, for telecommunications research facilities. Specialized expertise in certain university departments has attracted biotechnology laboratories to the Seattle (University of Washington) area and Silicon Valley (Stanford and Berkeley), while the Boulder-Denver-Longmont (University of Colorado) area has attracted computer disk drive labs.

Nature and Scope of Operations

Automotive Industry. Of the fifty-three automotive R&D facilities listed in the appendix, thirty-four are Japanese companies, sixteen are European companies, and three are South Korean companies. The U.S. R&D facilities of automotive companies—Japanese automotive companies in particular—conducted little R&D when they first started operations in the United States. Instead, their main activities were testing emissions for certification requirements and scanning the regulatory environment. They also evaluated the performance of their own and competitors' vehicles and monitored U.S. automotive design and styling trends.

Since the late 1980s, the foreign automotive companies, especially Toyota, Nissan, Mazda, and Honda, have expanded the scope of their R&D activities in the United States. Several facilities have undertaken projects in advanced concept design (in other words, the design of future vehicles), joint research, and vehicle prototype production. Also, these facilities have become more involved in parts and materials design and evaluation from local suppliers. An example of such higher-valued-added activities is the lead involvement by Toyota's Research Design Center (California) in the exterior design of the Lexus/Soarer Coupe. Mazda's design center in California also assisted in developing the Miata sports car, and Honda's U.S. research facilities in Ohio played a major role in developing a new Accord model for the U.S. market.

Drugs and Biotechnology. The pharmaceutical and biotechnology industries account for the largest number of foreign R&D facilities in the United States, with 113 facilities in 1994. These industries also have the largest (in terms of staff size) foreign-owned R&D facilities in the United States and the primary area for basic research by foreign companies. Most of the facilities are owned by European companies, with high concentrations of German, Swiss, and British drug companies. In addition, many of the European drug companies have large operations in the chemicals markets, such as BASF and Hoechst.

Foreign investment in U.S. R&D in drugs and biotechnology has been characterized by acquisitions of U.S. firms. A new wave of mergers is occurring in the industry. In 1995, several major mergers and acquisitions were announced: Hoechst's decision to acquire Marion Merrell Dow, the merger of two large British companies, Glaxo and Burroughs Welcome, and the merger of Upjohn with a Swedish company, Pharmacia. In 1994, Ciba Geigy, a Swiss company, increased its stake in Chiron, a U.S. biotech company, to 49.9 percent, and Roche Holding, another Swiss company, acquired Syntex. Major acquisitions of U.S. companies in earlier years include Roche's purchase of a majority stake in Genentech and the acquisition of Rorer by Rhone-Poulenc, a French company. In 1987, the British firm Beecham acquired SmithKline Beckman.

In the biotechnology industry, foreign R&D facilities fall into two basic groups: laboratories that conduct research in recombinant DNA and monoclonal antibody technologies, and R&D centers involved in pharmaceuticals, chemicals, and agribusiness. The former are small laboratories with capitalization of $50 million or less; the former are among the largest foreign R&D facilities in the United States.[4]

Electronics. Foreign-owned facilities in the electronics area reflect a diversity of corporate interests and strategies across many industries, from the giant European telecommunications equipment and electronics company facilities to many small single technology labs operated by Japanese companies. Japanese R&D facilities far outnumber the R&D facilities of other countries in computers, semiconductors, and computer software. Most of the foreign-owned R&D facilities in electronics conduct applied research with some activities in developing new applications of existing technologies or products or tailoring products to customer needs. A small group of facilities conduct basic research. These facilities include the NEC Research

Institute (Princeton, New Jersey), Philips, Siemens, Canon, and Panasonic Technologies (Matsushita).

Investment Motives

Foreign companies have invested in R&D facilities in the United States for different reasons. Table 7.6 lists ten reasons cited by senior R&D/technical executives of foreign R&D facilities in the automotive, biotechnology, and electronics industries. Of these, two reasons were cited as important by most R&D facilities, namely, to acquire technology and to keep abreast of technological developments in the United States. As could be expected, firms that deal with technologies where U.S. firms conduct leading research (such as biotechnology, software design, certain new materials) cite these two reasons as important. Companies that deal with technologies where foreign companies lead or are equal to U.S. firms (such as consumer electronics) cite the reasons mentioned above as unimportant.

The growth of foreign R&D investments in the U.S. automotive industry is directly linked to the expansion of Japanese and European automotive manufacturing facilities in the United States. Two reasons cited as important by automotive firms were *(i)* assisting the parent company in meeting U.S. environmental regulation and *(ii)* assisting the parent company in meeting U.S. customer needs. Other important reasons for investing in U.S. R&D facilities were "assisting the parent company's U.S. manufacturing plants in local procurement" and "keeping abreast of technological developments in the United States."

In the biotechnology industry, "taking advantage of a more favorable environment for research," "cooperating with other U.S. R&D laboratories," and "engaging in basic research" were cited as important factors influencing the decision of foreign firms to invest in U.S. R&D facilities. Other studies have also noted that "access to U.S. research universities," "availability of scientists for employment by foreign-owned employers," and "spillovers from U.S. private research" are prime inducements for the growth in foreign-owned R&D centers in biotechnology and drugs. In particular, Japanese drug companies appear motivated in their U.S. R&D investments mostly in gaining access to U.S. biotechnology discoveries, partly because of relative weakness in their domestic biotechnology research capabilities. Japanese drug companies have established a U.S. presence for other reasons, including conducting their own clinical testing for new drugs for the U.S. market and to acquire U.S. technology to bolster competitiveness in the Japanese market (Roehl 1994).

The most important aspect of the favorable research environment in the United States is a U.S. policy encouraging research in biotechnology and related fields. Robert Fujimura of the U.S. Food and Drug Administration, a leading expert in biotechnology, attributes the excellent environment for research in his field to leading-edge research in life sciences now being conducted in the United States. He believes that this has been due in part to the substantial and sustained support of the U.S. government and the participation of top scientists and researchers from all over the world. In contrast, European firms, and German companies in particular, have maintained that the biotechnology research environment has been largely unfavorable in Europe.

Table 7.6

Reasons for Foreign R&D Investments in the United States Given by Senior R&D and Technical Executives
(1 = extremely important, 2 = important, 3 = neutral, 4 = unimportant)

	Electronics	Autos	Biotechnology
Acquire technology	1	2	1
Keep abreast of technological developments	2	2	1
Assist parent company in meeting U.S. customer needs	1	1	3
Employ U.S. scientists & engineers	2	3	2
Follow competition	3	3	4
Take advantage of favorable research environment	4	4	1
Cooperate with other U.S. R&D labs	2	3	2
Assist parent company in meeting U.S. environmental regulations	4	1	4
Assist parent company's U.S. manufacturing plants in procurement	4	2	4
Engage in basic research	3	4	2

Source: Interview survey of Japanese companies by author, Manuel G. Serapio, Jr., published in the present authors' article, "Foreign R&D Facilities in the United States," *Research Technology Management*, November-December 1993.

In the electronics industry, "assisting the parent company in meeting U.S. customer needs" was cited as an important motive for investing in R&D facilities in the United States. These firms have relied upon their U.S. R&D facilities in monitoring technological developments in the United States, customizing products to the specifications of U.S. customers, and facilitating concurrent design and development. Another important factor influencing the decision by foreign electronics companies to establish R&D facilities in the United States is the growing complexity and speed of innovation in new technologies. A senior executive of a Japanese company told the authors, "Acquiring technology has become a more complex task. Without an actual presence in the United States, it is difficult for us to judge what technology is worth buying from U.S. companies. We built our R&D centers in the United States to establish a base that will help us make these decisions." Another executive from a software company expressed a similar opinion. The rapidity of technological change in the computer software industry dictated the company's presence in the United States which enables them to "keep up with day to day developments" in the U.S. software industry.

U.S. R&D FACILITIES ABROAD: A COMPARISON

Are European, Japanese, and other foreign companies the only organizations expanding their overseas R&D operations? As shown by figure 7.2, U.S. companies are also increasing their R&D activities abroad. According to the National Science Foundation, R&D expenditures by U.S. multinational companies have more than doubled in less than a decade, increasing from $3.6 billion in 1985 to $9.4 billion in 1994. R&D expenditures by U.S. companies abroad accounted for an additional 9.8 percent of all company-financed U.S. expenditures on R&D in 1994, up from 6.4 percent in 1985 and 9 percent in 1989.[5]

Figure 7.2
U.S. R&D Abroad

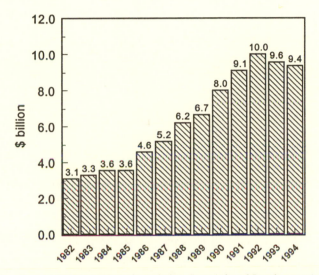

Source: National Science Foundation, *Research and Development in Industry*, 1994.

In 1994, most of the expenditures on U.S. R&D abroad were concentrated in drugs, industrial chemicals, automotive, and services, according to NSF survey data. The largest R&D expenditures by U.S. multinationals in 1993, the latest available data from BEA, were in Germany ($2.6 billion), United Kingdom ($1.6 billion), Canada ($1.0 billion), and France and Japan with $0.9 billion each. U.S. R&D investments in newly industrializing countries have increased significantly, with Singapore ranked tenth in U.S. R&D expenditures abroad, followed by Brazil, ranked twelfth.

Direct investments by U.S. multinational companies are nothing new. U.S. multinational firms such as IBM, Caterpillar, and Union Carbide have operated R&D facilities abroad for many years. In a pioneering study of R&D abroad by U.S. multinational companies, Ronstadt (1977) noted that IBM spent about $200 million (roughly 30 percent of its budget) in 1974 in overseas R&D. Other companies, such as Otis Elevator, CPC International, and Exxon, spent 50 percent, 38 percent, and 25 percent of their R&D budgets, respectively, in overseas R&D during the same period (Ronstadt 1977).

An NSF study identified seventy U.S. R&D facilities in Japan, including joint ventures, which employed over 5,000 people (National Science Foundation 1991). Of these facilities, more than half had been established or acquired during the previous seven years. Some of the newly established U.S. R&D facilities in Japan include R&D centers of U.S. companies such as Apple Computers and Texas Instruments. General Motors recently expanded its technical center, GM Asian Technical Center, in Japan. Likewise, Ford Motor Company has announced plans to expand its R&D presence in Japan. Other companies with a longstanding presence in Japan include IBM, DEC, and Caterpillar.

The authors have compiled a new database on U.S. R&D facilities abroad (Dalton and Serapio 1995). Of the over 108 U.S. R&D facilities on our list, sixty-two are located in Europe, twenty-nine in Japan, fourteen in Canada, two in Brazil, and one in Singapore. These R&D facilities cover a wide range of industries including computer hardware, software, consumer electronics, automotive, pharmaceuticals, consumer products, and chemicals.

Comparison of Investment Motivations

A recent study published by the Japan Technology Program of the U.S. Department of Commerce compared the motivations and activities of U.S. electronics R&D facilities in Japan and Japanese R&D facilities in the United States. The most important investment motives cited in the interview study of both U.S. R&D in Japan and Japanese R&D in the United States were *(i)* to assist the parent company in meeting the host country company needs, *(ii)* to monitor technological developments, and *(iii)* to acquire or generate new technology. The most important location decision for U.S. R&D in Japan and Japanese R&D in the United States was "availability of scientists and engineers," and the majority of facilities focused primarily on applied research and development (Serapio 1994).

R&D GLOBALIZATION ISSUES

Rapid growth of foreign R&D in the United States has led to concerns about an erosion of U.S. science and technology leadership, industrial competitiveness, and the clustering of foreign R&D centers around major U.S. research universities that receive large shares of their funding from federal grants and other support from taxpayers. Some observers have questioned the quality of the research effort by foreign companies, and some studies have raised doubts about the importance of the globalization of R&D.

One area of consensus concerns the short term benefits. Direct benefits include funding for R&D within the United States and employment opportunities for U.S. scientists and engineers. In 1994 foreign companies spent $15.6 billion in the United States on R&D and employed 108,000 R&D workers. Without the foreign spending in recent years, U.S. company-funded R&D performed in the United States might have declined. Foreign funding of academic research and equipment purchases has been welcomed by university researchers in a period of declining federal funding. The know-how and expertise developed by U.S. scientists, engineers, technicians, and auxiliary workers employed by foreign R&D companies will remain in the United States to be utilized by other employers.

In addition, foreign-funded R&D has similar local spillovers and indirect benefits compared with U.S. R&D.[6] Local communities benefit from the presence of highly paid scientists and engineers and spinoffs of research into new companies. Other U.S. companies in the same industry may benefit from U.S.-based research by foreign companies from the new products and processes developed from basic research, such as biotechnology. Coe and Helpman (1993) suggest that international R&D may lead to an increase in economic growth. The National Research Council study on foreign R&D also emphasizes the role of local benefits of R&D, regardless of nationality: "If a large share of the returns to R&D investments is captured by those proximate to the R&D activity, and these returns are beneficial, clearly it is better to have R&D performed within one's borders than beyond them."

However, some observers have argued that the U.S. research centers of foreign companies are merely "listening posts" that focus on technology scanning with only a small research effort. Although this description may have applied to the early stages of U.S. research by affiliates, foreign firms have committed substantial resources, $15.6 billion in 1994, at their U.S. research facilities. The ratio of manufacturing R&D to sales of U.S. affiliates of foreign companies was 3.0 percent in 1994, compared with 2.9 percent for all U.S. company-funded R&D in manufacturing. However, ratio of the R&D to sales varies across industries and was much larger in the computer industry, 7.9 percent for U.S. companies in 1994, compared with 6.2 percent for affiliates. The ratios were nearly equal in the drug industry. In our study, we found that Japan's automotive R&D has moved from an early stage of design work and emissions testing to more value-added research in developing new vehicles for the U.S. market. A major effort in basic research is conducted by affiliates in the chemicals, drugs, and biotechnology industries.

Another issue in the debate about the quality of U.S. R&D by foreign companies is based on studies that question whether globalization of R&D is an important source of generating new technology. A recent report by the Office of Technology Assessment (1994) concluded from an interview study of U.S. R&D managers that leading-edge R&D or a company's "core" technology is performed only at a company's central labs in the home country.[7] Some empirical research by Patel and Pavitt (1991) on the location of patents by large multinational companies shows that most of their patents are filed in the home country. The results from patent data are supported by the expenditure data on U.S. firms R&D abroad, which shows that about 90 percent of R&D expenditures by U.S. companies are spent at their facilities in the United States.

New research has begun to look at some indirect benefits that may accrue from the cross-fertilization between foreign-owned R&D facilities and the U.S. research community. More than two-thirds of the foreign-affiliated R&D labs are engaged in cooperative research with U.S. universities, according to a survey by Florida (1996). Other results from the survey indicate that about 10 percent of the staff at the U.S. R&D centers of foreign companies were transferred from the parent lab. Florida's survey also found that the foreign-owned R&D facilities published over 1,800 research papers, and many were joint papers with U.S. researchers. The interaction between the R&D of the parent and its U.S. affiliate may have long-term benefits for the U.S. R&D community because 90 to 95 percent of the affiliates' R&D employees are U.S. scientists and engineers who can transfer this experience to other U.S. R&D companies.

SUMMARY

In summary, foreign R&D in the United States has clear benefits by taking up the slack from the cutbacks of large U.S. R&D firms and federal funding. The foreign share of U.S. company–funded R&D has grown with the foreign ownership share in the U.S. economy. Foreign-owned companies account for about 15 percent of U.S. manufacturing output (Department of Commerce 1994), and their share of U.S. company–funded R&D is in the same range. The real issues underlying the debate about the globalization of R&D are perhaps more about foreign ownership of intellectual assets and about the realization that foreign companies have a much more optimistic view of the potential rewards to the firm from R&D performed in the United States than do U.S.-owned companies. A microeconomic look at R&D strategies by foreign firms in the United States is provided by Lois Peters in chapter 9.

NOTES

1. Foreign-owned businesses are defined here, as elsewhere in this book, as U.S. affiliates of foreign firms in which a foreign parent company owns at least 10 percent of the affiliate's equity.

2. R&D expenditures performed by U.S. affiliates of foreign-owned businesses are discussed in the first part of this chapter.

3. For a discussion of single-technology facilities by Japanese companies see Eleanor Westney, "Cross-Pacific Internationalization of R&D by U.S. and Japanese Firms," *R&D Management* 23(2), 1993.

4. For more details, see the authors' article, "Foreign R&D in the United States," *IEEE Spectrum*, November 1994.

5. Both the NSF and the BEA publish annual data on U.S. R&D abroad based on company surveys. The NSF data series provides data only for industry classifications, while the BEA series publishes separate data for industries and countries. U.S. R&D abroad is not included in the NSF series on company-funded R&D because it is not performed within the United States.

6. For a detailed analysis of local R&D spillovers, see Jaffe, Trajtenberg, and Henderson (1993).

7. For a discussion of a survey of U.S. firms about their "core" technology, see Office of Technology Assessment (1994).

REFERENCES

Bowker, R.R., Inc. 1994. *Directory of American Research and Technology*. Twenty-eighth edition, New Providence, NJ.

Cheng, Joseph, and Douglas S. Bolon. 1993, "The Management of Multinational R&D: A Neglected Topic in International Business Research," *Journal of International Business Studies*, first quarter, p. 1-18.

Coe, David T., and Elhanan Helpman. 1993. *International R&D Spillovers*. National Bureau of Economic Research, Working Paper No. 4444, August.

Dalton, Donald H., and Manuel G. Serapio, Jr. 1995. *Globalizing Industrial Research and Development*, Department of Commerce, Technology Administration, Office of Technology Policy, NTIS PB96-119201. Washington, D.C.: GPO, October.

Department of Commerce. annual-a. *Foreign Direct Investment in the United States*. Bureau of Economic Analysis, Washington, D.C.: GPO.

——. annual-b. *U.S. Direct Investment Abroad*. Bureau of Economic Analysis, Washington, D.C.: GPO.

——. 1994. *Foreign Direct Investment in the United States: Establishment Data for Manufacturing 1991*, Bureau of Economic Analysis. Washington, D.C.: GPO, April.

Fahim-Nader, Mahnaz, and William J. Zeile. 1996. "Foreign Direct Investment in the United States," *Survey of Current Business*, Department of Commerce, Bureau of Economic Analysis. Washington, D.C.:GPO, 76(July).

Florida, Richard L. 1996. "Foreign Direct Investment in Research and Development: Scope, Performance, and Activities of Foreign-Affiliated R&D Laboratories in the United States," Center for Science and International Affairs, John F. Kennedy School of Government, Harvard University, draft, January.

Jaffe, Adam B., Manuel Trajtenberg, and Rebecca Henderson. 1993. "Geographic Localization of Knowledge Spillovers as Evidenced by Patent Citations," *Quarterly Journal of Economics*, August.

Japan Economic Institute. monthly. *Japan–U.S. Business Report*, Washington, D.C.

Miller, R. 1993. "Global R&D Networks and Large-Scale Innovations: The Case of the Automobile Industry," *Research Policy*, May.

National Science Foundation. annual. *Research and Development in Industry*, Division of Science Resource Studies. Arlington, Va.: National Science Foundation.

——. 1991. *Survey of Direct U.S. Private Capital Investment in Research and Development Facilities in Japan*, NSF 91-312. Arlington, Va.: National Science Foundation, January.

Office of Technology Assessment (OTA). 1994. *Multinationals and the U.S. Technology Base*, OTA-ITE-612. Washington, D.C.: GPO, September.

Patel, Pari, and Keith L. R. Pavitt. 1991. "Large Firms in the Production of the World's Technology: An Important Case of 'Non-Globalization'," *Journal of International Business Studies* 22(1):1-21.

Pearce, Robert D. 1989. *The Internationalization of Research and Development by Multinational Enterprises*. New York: St. Martin's Press.

Reid, Proctor P., and Alan Schriesheim, eds. 1996. *Foreign Participation in U.S. Research and Development—Asset or Liability?* Washington, D.C.: National Academy Press.

Roehl, Tom. 1994. *The Role of International R&D in the Competence-Building Strategies of Japanese Pharmaceutical Firms*, College of Commerce and Business Administration, University of Illinois at Urbana-Champaign, CIBER Working Paper No. 94-008.

Ronstadt, Robert C. 1977. *Research and Development Abroad by U.S. Multinationals*. New York: Praeger.

Serapio, Manuel G., Jr. 1993. "Macro-Micro Analysis of Japanese Direct R&D Investments in the U.S. Automotive and Electronics Industries," *Management International Review* 33(3).

——. 1994. *Japan-U.S. Direct R&D Investments in the Electronics Industries*. NTIS PB94-127974, June. Springfield, Va.: National Technical Information Service.

Serapio, Manuel G., Jr., and Donald H. Dalton. 1993. "Foreign R&D Facilities in the United States," *Research Technology Management*, Industrial Research Institute, November-December.

——. 1994. "Foreign R&D in the United States," *IEEE Spectrum*, November 1994.

Weiss, Juri. 1994. "Firms Active in R&D at U.S. Universities," *Nikkei Weekly*, July 18.
Westney, Eleanor. 1993. "Cross-Pacific Internationalization of R&D by U.S. and Japanese Firms," *R&D Management* 23(2).

8

Foreign Direct Investment in the United States and U.S. Technology Development

Sumiye Okubo

INTRODUCTION

The rapid growth of foreign direct investment in the United States (FDIUS) has raised concerns about the impact on technology development. In the 1980s' wave of FDIUS, some authors emphasized negative effects on U.S. productive capacity, technological capability, and threats to our national security (Tolchin and Tolchin 1988; Choate 1990). Others concluded that FDIUS promotes U.S. competitiveness and technological progress (Graham and Krugman 1991; Becker 1989; Glickman and Woodward 1990).

Recent studies, like Doms and Jensen's chapter in this book, using establishment (plant) level data, support the conclusion that FDIUS has had a net positive impact on the U.S. economy. Compared to U.S.-owned firms, U.S. affiliates of foreign firms (hereafter referred to as "U.S. affiliates") in manufacturing industries are more capital intensive, pay higher wages, employ higher-skilled workers, and have higher productivity (see also Howenstine and Zeile 1993; 1994). Even after differences in size, age, industry, and location are considered, foreign-owned plants are found to pay higher wages, to be more capital intensive, and to be more productive than the average U.S.-owned plant. However, as Doms and Jensen document in chapter 2, when only plants of multinational corporations (MNCs)—U.S.- and foreign-owned—are considered, foreign-owned plants in the United States lag slightly behind those of U.S. multinationals. Moreover, an analysis of the use of advanced technologies in U.S. manufacturing establishments indicates that foreign-owned plants, although they are similar to plants of U.S. MNCs, adopt more advanced technologies than the average U.S.-owned plant (Doms and Jensen 1995).

These studies, however, do not directly address the effect of these investments on U.S. science and technology development. Do foreign-owned firms contribute to U.S. technological capability? Even if they do, are their parent firms acquiring or establishing U.S. firms to acquire U.S. high technologies? Are the research and development (R&D) facilities established in the United States intended to boost sales in the United States—as facilities for tailoring products and services to the U.S. market and laboratories for developing new products and processes? Are they also listening posts for gaining access to U.S. scientific and technological developments to aid the parent firms? Are they a source of technology that "spills over" to aid the development and use of technology by U.S.-owned firms?

Relying on several technology indicators, this chapter addresses these questions. Using the concentration of investment and market shares of foreign affiliates in U.S. high-technology industries, the chapter begins by looking for evidence that foreign firms may have pursued strategies to acquire U.S. technologies. Then attention is focused on their R&D spending and other R&D activities in the United States to assess the possible impact on U.S. technology development. The chapter also examines data on royalties and license fees to determine the extent to which U.S. affiliates of foreign firms are sending technology to their foreign parents or are receiving technology from them. Finally, future research directions are discussed.

The sources of data are the Bureau of Economic Analysis (BEA), foreign direct investment (FDI) surveys, and establishment level data from the BEA–Census Data Link Project for 1987 and 1992, and the BEA–Bureau of Labor Statistics (BLS) Data Link Project for 1989. Data on R&D spending and technology transfer are aggregated by industry, rather than by product. Much of the increase in R&D spending by affiliates reflects additions to the data set of existing U.S. firms acquired by foreign owners and increased spending of existing foreign-owned firms. Comparisons of activities by U.S.- and foreign-owned firms over time are difficult because R&D expenditures of newly acquired, foreign-owned firms cannot be separated easily from that of existing foreign-owned firms.

Despite data limitations of analyzing FDIUS and U.S. technology developments, especially those affecting detailed industry and product data, this chapter provides several key conclusions:

- Foreign-owned firms have concentrated their investments in manufacturing, primarily non-high-technology industries. Nonetheless, their share of total U.S. investment in U.S. non-high-technology and high-technology industries is rising.
- The concentration of U.S. affiliates' sales in high-technology and non-high-technology manufacturing industries changed little between 1987 and 1994. U.S. affiliates' sales are slightly more concentrated in high-technology industries than are U.S.-owned firms. Moreover, their share of *total* U.S. high-technology manufacturing sales has risen rapidly over the past seven years, while the corresponding share held by U.S.-owned firms has shrunk.
- Foreign firms appear to have invested in high-technology industries, not so much to acquire U.S. technology as to exploit a competitive advantage of the parent firms' technology. Foreign parent firms have tended to concentrate investments in the same industries as the strong export industries of their home countries, both high-technology and non-high-technology. One example is the U.S. audio and video equipment industry, in which U.S. affiliates of internationally-competitive Japanese firms have a dominant share of FDI in the United States.
- U.S. affiliates have contributed to overall U.S. technological development, doubling their R&D spending over the past five years. In U.S. manufacturing in 1994, U.S. affiliates' R&D intensity almost equaled that of U.S.-owned firms. Among the high-technology industries, U.S. affiliates' R&D intensity was greater in drugs and audio,

video, and communications equipment and lower in the others than that of U.S.-owned firms.
- Affiliates in high-technology manufacturing industries account for the bulk of R&D expenditures (over three-quarters) by *all* foreign-owned affiliates and, thus, probably have the greatest impact on U.S. technological capability in those industries.
- U.S. affiliates appear to import substantial technology from their foreign parents, as their payments of royalties and licensing fees overwhelmingly exceed their receipts.

DEFINITION OF HIGH-TECHNOLOGY INDUSTRIES

One approach to examining the relationship between FDIUS and U.S. technology development is comparing the performance of foreign-owned and U.S.-owned firms in high-technology goods and services industries. High-technology industries are those that use new, advanced, or leading-edge technologies. Industries are frequently classified as high-technology using the scheme developed by the Department of Commerce for studying U.S. high-technology, goods-producing industries (DOC-3) (Davis 1982).[1] To reflect the growing importance of technology embodied in the U.S. services sector and among foreign-owned U.S. firms, three high-technology service industries are also included with the DOC-3 industries: Computer and Data Processing Services (SIC 737); Engineering, Architectural, and Surveying Services (SIC 871); and Research and Testing Services (SIC 873) (table 8.1).

Table 8.1
High-Technology Industries

Sector	SIC Class
Industrial chemicals and synthetics	281, 282, 286
Drugs and medicines	283
Computers and office machines	357
Video, audio, and communications equipment	365, 366
Electronic components	367
Instruments and related products	38
Other transportation equipment	372-376, 379
Computer and data processing services	737
Engineering, architectural, surveying services	871
Research and testing services	873

Detailed establishment-level data, classified by industry, are used when available, such as data from the 1987 BEA-Census Data Link Project. But, time series data on FDIUS published by the BEA are not separately available for each of the original DOC-3 detailed industry groups. Therefore, several industries have been aggregated, and several DOC-3 industry groups have been excluded.[2]

EXTENT OF FOREIGN DIRECT INVESTMENT IN HIGH-TECHNOLOGY INDUSTRIES

The FDIUS position rose rapidly in the 1980s, especially in the second half of the decade, and tripled between 1985 and 1995 (figure 8.1). During this period, foreign-owned firms have invested most heavily in the U.S. manufacturing sector, increasing their share of total FDIUS position in this sector, as well as the finance and insurance sectors, and have reduced their shares in the petroleum and real estate sectors. Foreign-owned forms comprise a small, but rising, share of the U.S. manufacturing sector—their shares of assets and of value added growing from 8.3 percent and 7.9 percent, respectively, in 1980 to 18.0 percent and 13.2 percent, respectively, by 1995 (table 8.2). As a group, these foreign-owned firms do not appear to be more significantly concentrated in U.S. high-technology industries than in other industries.

Figure 8.1
FDIUS Position by Industry of Affiliate, 1985 and 1995

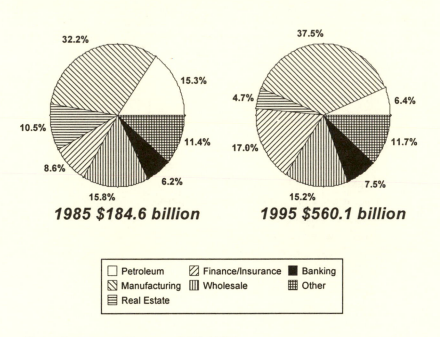

Source: Department of Commerce (1988, 1997c).

Table 8.2
Estimated Shares of Assets and Gross Product of Nonbank Affiliates of Foreign Companies in U.S. Manufacturing
(Percentage)

	1980	1987	1990	1992	1993	1994
Assets	8.3	13.2	18.6	16.9	17.6	17.7
Gross Product (value added)	7.9	10.5	13.8	13.9	12.8	13.2

Source: Department of Commerce (1993b; 1996), Bureau of Census, *Quarterly Financial Report for Manufacturing, Mining and Trade Corporations*.

Concentration of Foreign-Owned Firms in U.S. High-Technology Industries

High-technology industries comprise a small share of all U.S. manufacturing, and U.S. affiliates of foreign firms account for a relatively small share of all U.S. manufacturing and of U.S. high-technology manufacturing industries (figure 8.2). These U.S. affiliates are more concentrated in high-technology industries than are U.S.-owned firms (figure 8.3). U.S. affiliates have significantly increased their share of all U.S. manufacturing sales (figure 8.4). Their share of high-technology sales doubled between 1987 and 1994, rising from 12 percent to 22 percent. Similarly, their share of all U.S. manufacturing sales grew from 2.2 percent in 1987 to 3.9 percent in 1994.[3]

Figure 8.2
Manufacturing Sales of U.S. Affiliates and U.S.-Owned Firms, 1992

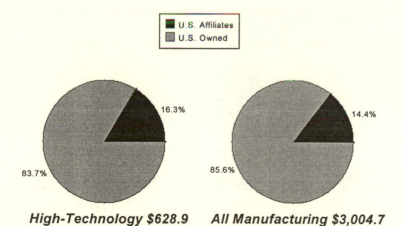

■ U.S. Affiliates
▨ U.S. Owned

16.3%

83.7%

14.4%

85.6%

High-Technology $628.9   *All Manufacturing $3,004.7*

Source: Department of Commerce (1997a).

Figure 8.3
High-Technology Manufacturing Sales as Share of Total
Manufacturing Sales: U.S. Affiliates and U.S.-Owned Firms,
1992

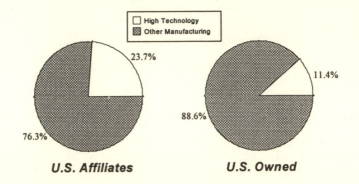

U.S. Affiliates   **U.S. Owned**

Source: Department of Commerce (1997a).

Figure 8.4
U.S. Affiliates' Share of High-Technology Manufacturing and Total U.S.
Manufacturing Sales: 1987, 1992, and 1994

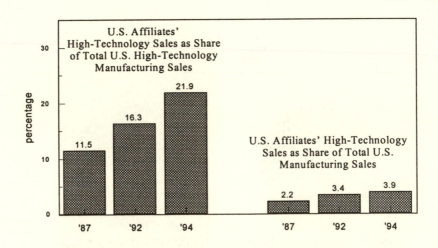

Source: Department of Commerce (1990; 1995a).

Although sales data indicate a growing importance of U.S. affiliates in high-technology industries, other data suggest that foreign firms have not given significantly greater priority to direct investment in U.S. high-technology industries over U.S. non-high-technology industries. Even during the latter half of the 1980s, when total FDIUS surged, the share of foreign investment and their operations in U.S. high-technology industries changed relatively little compared to that of other industries, in terms of FDI position, asset values, and property, plant, and equipment for U.S. affiliates. The share of high-technology industries rose slowly in terms of FDI position and was relatively stable in terms of assets and property, plant, and equipment (table 8.3).

Table 8.3
High-Technology Affiliates' Share of FDIUS Position, All U.S. Affiliates' Assets and Property, Plant, and Equipment
Accumulated Value of FDIUS (Percentage)

Type of Investment	1987	1990	1992	1993	1994
All Industries:					
FDI Position	14.2	14.6	14.9	14.9	15.4
Assets	10.3	11.2	6.8	10.3	10.3
Property, plant, and equipment	18.5	17.3	18.1	18.2	17.9
Manufacturing Industries:					
FDI Position	35.8	36.2	37.8	39.5	40.1
Assets	40.4	38.3	39.9	38.9	39.4
Property, plant, and equipment	48.0	43.0	43.5	43.2	42.9

Source: Department of Commerce (1990; 1993b; 1995a; 1996; 1997b).

The BEA–Census Data Link Project provides a detailed picture of the extent to which U.S. affiliates account for the operations of all U.S. high-technology industries. Foreign-owned U.S. firms represent a small, rising share of operations of all U.S. firms in high-technology manufacturing industries. In 1992,[4] their share reached 13.5 percent of total U.S. high-technology industries' employment, 13.2 percent of payroll, and 16.6 percent of sales. U.S.-owned firms dominate the sales of all U.S. high-technology industries, except for the *audio and video equipment* industry (table 8.4). Foreign-owned U.S. firms have long dominated U.S. sales in this industry, with their share of total U.S. industry sales rising from 53 percent in 1987 to more than 60 percent in 1992. Foreign-owned U.S. firms also have increased their market shares of total U.S. industry sales in three other U.S. high-technology industries between 1987 and 1992:

- In *plastics and synthetics*, the share rose from 34 percent to 40 percent.
- In *industrial inorganic chemicals*, the share grew from 25 percent to 30 percent.
- In *drugs and medicines*, the share increased from 24 percent to 33 percent.

In 1992, the smallest participation was in *aircraft and parts*,[5] with less than 3 percent of total industry sales, and in *high-technology services* industries, with about

Table 8.4
High-Technology Establishment of Foreign-Owned Affiliates as a Share of All U.S.
Business in 1987 and 1992
(Percentage)

Industry	1987				1992		
	No. of establish-ments	Employ-ment	Payroll	Sales	Employ-ment	Payroll	Sales
All U.S. Businesses	1.1	3.7	4.7	N/A	6.6	8.3	11.6
All High-Technology Industries (manufacturing & services)	1.8	7.1	8.5	9.9	10.4	10.6	13.9
High-Technology Manufactur-ing	4.9	9.0	11.4	11.5	13.5	13.2	16.6
Inorganic chemicals	23.8	19.3	18.9	25.2	21.8	21.0	29.6
Plastic materials & synthetics	18.4	38.2	37.9	34.2	41.2	41.5	39.9
Drugs	8.0	19.4	21.6	23.6	33.4	36.1	32.9
Ordnance & accessories	3.2	7.6	7.2	9.2	11.8	10.3	12.9
Engines & turbines	4.5	6.0	5.7	3.7	5.7	6.0	4.2
Computer & office equipment	2.7	7.0	6.4	5.7	12.7	13.2	11.7
Household audio & video equipment	2.8	33.8	35.1	52.8	39.7	41.8	64.0
Communications equipment	5.9	13.9	12.3	14.7	16.3	17.1	18.9
Electronic components & access.	3.1	9.2	9.1	9.2	12.6	12.8	13.0
Aircraft & parts	2.5	1.9	1.6	1.7	4.1	3.5	2.6
Guided missiles, spacecraft	2.8	(D)	(D)	(D)	0.7	0.6	(D)
Instruments & related parts	3.1	7.4	6.9	7.2	11.7	11.3	11.8
High-Technology Services:					5.3	6.3	6.4
Computer & data processing	1.1	3.5	4.4	3.9	4.9	5.9	5.6
Engineering & architectural	0.6	2.1	2.7	3.6	5.4	6.4	7.2
Research & testing	2.5	4.0	4.8	4.0	6.6	7.6	7.3

Note: (D)—Suppressed so that confidential information on individual companies would not be divulged.

Source: Department of Commerce (1992; 1997a).

6 percent of total sales. This low participation pattern is also reflected in the correspondingly low shares of total employment in these two industries.

U.S. affiliates accounted for a rising share of the employment in all U.S. high-technology industries, growing from 7.0 percent in 1987 to 10.4 percent in 1992. Employment by high-technology affiliates grew by 13 percent between 1987 and 1992, from 489,100 to 554,542 workers, compared to the 6 percent growth in all U.S. high-technology firms, from 4.9 million to 5.2 million workers. Much of this increase in employment share might be attributed to the large number of foreign acquisitions of U.S. high-technology firms, and not necessarily to growth of employment in existing U.S. affiliates. According to unpublished BEA data, foreign acquisitions accounted for one-fourth to three-fourths of the total annual increases in employment in high-technology industries in each of the years 1987 to 1990.

Among the high-technology industries, the U.S. affiliates' shares of total employment and growth of the total number of workers varies widely. The largest shares are in *inorganic chemicals*, *plastics and synthetics*, *drugs*, and *audio, video, and communications equipment* industries; and the fastest growing shares are in the *aircraft and parts*, *drugs*, *instruments*, and *electronic components* industries. Although growing rapidly, the share for *aircraft and parts* remains small. The share for high-technology services industries remains less than 10 percent, but employment in these industries is also rising relatively quickly (figure 8.5).

The employment of workers in high-skilled categories by U.S. affiliates and U.S.-owned firms is the only available basis for estimating the corresponding differences in the relative importance of research activities in these firms. This basis has been adopted by other researchers on this issue. U.S. affiliates employ a higher proportion of high-skilled workers[6] than U.S.-owned firms, on average, across *all* manufacturing, but a lower proportion across all high-technology manufacturing industries, according to the data link between BEA and the Bureau of Labor Statistics (BLS) data. There are significant differences in these proportions among individual high-technology industries. U.S. affiliates employ a higher proportion of high-skilled workers than U.S.-owned firms in *plastics and synthetics*, *audio and video equipment*, *communications equipment*, and *instruments*, and a lower proportion in other manufacturing industries.

Differences in Concentration among Affiliates by Country of Parent

Data on FDIUS by country of ownership suggest that foreign parent firms have tended to concentrate their FDI in the same high-technology and non-high-technology industries in which these parent firms' exports are concentrated.[7] This conclusion is supported by data on U.S. affiliates owned by parents in the United Kingdom, Japan, and Germany, three of the five largest investing countries (in terms of FDIUS). Although the Netherlands and Canada also rank among the top investors, publicly available data on their direct investments in U.S. high-technology industries have been suppressed.[8]

U.S. affiliates of Japanese, U.K., and German parent firms account for a large share of all U.S. high-technology affiliates' sales. Broad industry (but not establishment) level data for 1994 show that U.S. affiliates of these three countries accounted

Figure 8.5
U.S. Affiliates' Share of High-Technology Manufacturing Employment, 1987 and 1992

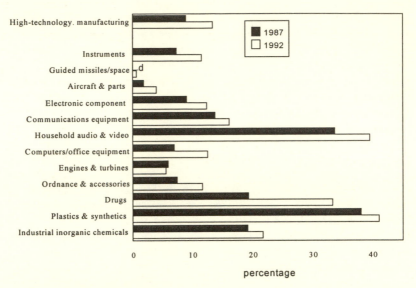

Note: "d" denotes supressed data.

Source: Department of Commerce (1992; 1997a).

for more than 50 percent of all high-technology affiliates' sales (table 8.5). Even though these three countries' affiliates, as a group, represent a high share of all U.S. affiliates' high-technology sales, the share of any one country is small. Japan has the lowest share at 8 percent, followed by the United Kingdom at 14 percent, and Germany at 17 percent.

The BEA–Census Data Link provide additional detailed information about the extent of concentration of U.S. affiliates of foreign firms in each industry (U.S. affiliates' share of total industry sales). The data link shows that in 1991, affiliates of Japanese, German, and British parents had 5 percent or less of *total* U.S. sales in each of five high-technology industries, with seven exceptions:

- Japanese-owned affiliates had 11.1 percent of total industry sales in *electronic components* and 8.2 percent of sales in *computers*. They also had 50 percent of total industry sales in the *audio and video equipment* industry and 11.1 percent of total industry sales when sales in the *audio and video equipment* industry are combined with sales in *communications equipment*.
- German-owned affiliates had 7.5 percent of total industry sales in *computers* and 11.8 percent of *industrial chemicals* (inorganic chemicals and plastics and synthetics) and, within the latter, 10.8 percent of total industry sales in *plastics and synthetics* industry.
- British-owned affiliates had 12.3 percent of total industry sales in *drugs*,[9] and a 9.1 percent share of total industry sales in the *industrial inorganic chemical* industry.

Table 8.5
Sales of Affiliates in High-Technology Industries: Selected Countries, Industry Sales, 1994
(billions of dollars)

Industry	All Countries	Japan	Ger-many	United Kingdom
High-Tech Manufacturing:				
Industrial chemicals & synthetics	50.5	3.7	11.9	7.2
Drugs	30.4	1.2	4.7	10.6
Computers	10.6	5.2	0.4	0.2
Audio, video, & communications equipment	24.0	7.6	1.8	0.7
Electronic components	13.4	6.5	1.0	1.9
Instruments	19.5	2.3	4.0	5.8
Other transportation equipment	5.6	0.2	0.5	2.0
High-Tech Services:				
Computer & data processing services	9.0	1.0	0.3	1.7
Engineering & architectural services	7.3	0.7	1.6	1.1
Research & testing services	6.8	1.2	0.3	2.9
All High-Tech Goods & Services	177.2	29.6	26.4	34.0
All manufacturing	505.1	114.3	62.6	82.1
All industry	1447.6	388.7	152.6	243.7
High-technology manufacturing as percentage of all manufacturing	30.5%	23.3%	38.7%	34.4%
High-technology manufacturing & services as percentage of all	12.2%	7.6%	17.3%	13.9%

Source: Department of Commerce, 1997b.

In all high-technology industries, the most dramatic increase in share of total industry sales was in the Japanese-owned affiliates' share of all U.S. industry sales in the *video and audio equipment* industry, rising from 32.2 percent in 1987 to 50 percent in 1991. The Data Link, however, cannot provide information about foreign parents' strategies, that is, whether they sought to gain major market shares in any single high-technology industry or to exploit a competitive advantage in that sector.

R&D ACTIVITIES OF FOREIGN-OWNED FIRMS

One way of gauging the strategies of foreign-owned firms and their contribution to U.S. science and technology development is to examine the extent of their R&D efforts in the United States and their international technology transfer activities. Available data on R&D expenditures by foreign-owned firms in the United States suggest they make a net contribution to the aggregate U.S. technological capability.

Undoubtedly, many of the foreign parents of these affiliates are also benefitting from the technological achievements of these affiliates.

The data on royalties and license fees show that U.S. affiliates have established a number of in-house R&D facilities in the United States and pay for research done by other U.S. firms. The data also indicate that there is a large net outflow of technology payments by affiliates to their foreign parents, suggesting that there is a corresponding net inflow of the underlying technology.

Foreign-owned U.S. firms have increased their R&D spending at a faster rate than U.S.-owned firms, especially in high-technology industries. Their ratios of R&D spending to sales have almost equaled the average of U.S.-owned firms in manufacturing industries, and particularly those in high-technology manufacturing industries. The affiliates' ratios of R&D spending to sales are higher than the average for U.S.-owned firms in *drugs* and *industrial chemicals* and are approaching those in *computers* and *audio and video equipment* and *communications equipment*.

R&D Spending in High-Technology Industries

R&D spending by U.S. affiliates of foreign firms has comprised a small, but rapidly rising share of total spending by all companies. Data from the National Science Foundation (NSF) show an average annual increase in R&D spending by *all U.S. firms* of 6.8 percent between 1987 and 1994, from an aggregate of $61.4 billion in 1987 to $97.4 billion in 1994 (National Science Foundation 1994).[10] In contrast, R&D spending by *U.S. affiliates* rose at twice the average rate for all U.S. firms, more than doubling from $6.5 billion in 1987 to $15.6 billion in 1994. Their spending rose at an average annual rate of 13 percent. This substantial rise in affiliates' R&D spending reflects in part large numbers of acquisitions of existing U.S. firms, along with increases in R&D by existing U.S. affiliates.[11] The difference in the extent of the two separate sources cannot be determined from available data.

The more rapid increase in R&D spending by U.S. affiliates, relative to all U.S. firms, is reflected in the affiliates' share of total U.S. company-funded R&D expenditures (figure 8.6). Affiliates of two countries, Japan and Switzerland, accounted for most of the growth during this period, followed by U.K.-owned, German-owned, and French-owned affiliates.

The U.S. affiliates' share of R&D spending in all high-technology, manufacturing industries increased from 13 percent in 1987 to 24 percent in 1994. In some high-technology industries, affiliates' R&D spending represents a relatively high share of total U.S. company-funded R&D spending, but shares vary widely (figure 8.7).

- Affiliates accounted for a large, but declining, share of total R&D expenditures in the *industrial chemicals and synthetic materials* industry: 54 percent in 1987 and 42 percent in 1994.
- In the *drugs* industry, affiliates' share of total R&D spending grew from 27 percent in 1987 to 47 percent in 1994.
- The share of R&D spending in the *audio, video, and communications equipment* industry almost tripled between 1987 and 1992, from 10.7 percent to 27 percent.

Figure 8.6
U.S. Affiliates' Share of All Company R&D Performed in the United States

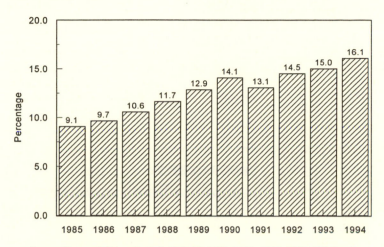

Source: Bureau of Economic Analysis (1988, 1990, 1993b, 1995a, 1996, 1997b) and National Science Foundation (1996).

- Affiliates in the *computer and office equipment* industry tripled their share of R&D spending from 4.5 percent in 1987 to 15 percent in 1994.
- In the *electronic components* industry, affiliates' share remained relatively stable from 1987 to 1994, at 10.6 percent and 11 percent, respectively.
- In each of the other high-technology industries, U.S. affiliates' share of R&D spending in 1992 was relatively small (less than 10 percent).

These differences are reflected in the distribution of R&D spending across industries by U.S. manufacturing affiliates and all U.S. manufacturing firms (figure 8.8). Of total affiliates' R&D spending in manufacturing in 1994, U.S. affiliates devoted much more to chemicals—21 percent in *industrial chemicals* and 47 percent in *drugs*—than all U.S. manufacturing companies, which devoted a total of 33 percent to these two industries. U.S.-owned firms spend considerably more than foreign-owned firms in *electronic components, other transport, instruments*, and *computers and office equipment*.

Comparison of R&D Intensities of Foreign-Owned and U.S.-Owned Firms

U.S.-owned and foreign-owned firms also differ in the proportion of resources devoted to R&D, typically compared in terms of the ratio of R&D to sales, or the R&D intensity ratio.[12] Compared to U.S.-owned manufacturing firms,[13] which had a 2.9 percent R&D intensity ratio in 1994, U.S. manufacturing affiliates, with a

Figure 8.7
Affiliates' Share of R&D in U.S. High-Technology Industries, 1987 and 1994

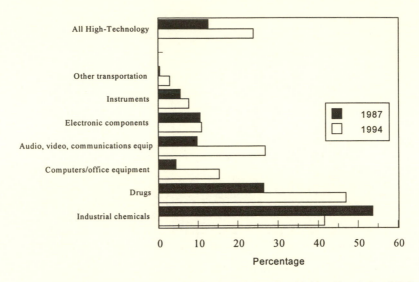

Source: Department of Commerce (1990; 1997b) and National Science Foundation (1996).

2.4 percent R&D intensity ratio, were not far behind. The difference in the ratios for firms in high-technology manufacturing industries was negligible in 1994: 6.4 percent for U.S.-owned firms compared to 6.2 percent for U.S. affiliates, closing the 2.0 percentage point difference that existed in 1992.

Significant differences in intensity ratios exist among the high-technology industries (figure 8.9). U.S. affiliates devote relatively more resources to R&D than do U.S.-owned firms in *drugs* (U.S. affiliates' ratio of R&D to sales was almost 50 percent higher than that of U.S.-owned firms) and in *industrial chemicals*. For the remaining five high-technology industries, U.S.-owned firms have higher R&D intensities, with ratios of R&D to sales double those of U.S. affiliates in *electronic components* and *instruments*. Among the high-technology industries, the ranking of R&D intensities for U.S. affiliates is similar to that for U.S.-owned firms. In 1994, the R&D intensity of U.S. affiliates is highest in the *drugs* industry, followed by those in *computers, audio, video, and communications equipment, industrial chemicals and synthetics*, and *instruments*. The R&D intensity of U.S.-owned firms is highest for *drugs, computers and office equipment*, and *audio, video, and communications equipment*, followed by *electronic components*.

Between 1987 and 1994, the R&D intensities of U.S. affiliates, as a whole, changed little. The ratio of R&D to sales for U.S. affiliates in *all* industries remained unchanged at 1.0 percent. For high-technology industries as a whole, the ratio rose slightly from 5.2 to 6.2 percent (figure 8.10). Among the industries, the ratio changed dramatically between the two years. The R&D ratios increased significantly in *drugs*

Figure 8.8
Distribution of High-Technology R&D Spending by All U.S. Firms and U.S. Affiliates, 1994

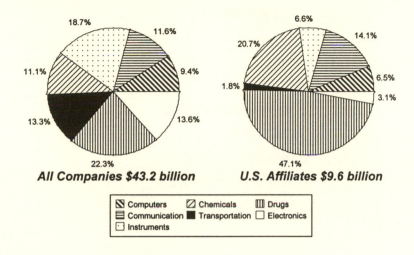

All Companies $43.2 billion   **U.S. Affiliates $9.6 billion**

⧅ Computers	▨ Chemicals	▥ Drugs
⊟ Communication	■ Transportation	☐ Electronics
⊡ Instruments		

Source: Department of Commerce (1997b) and National Science Foundation (1996).

Figure 8.9
U.S.-Owned Firms' and U.S. Affiliates' Ratios of R&D to Sales, 1994

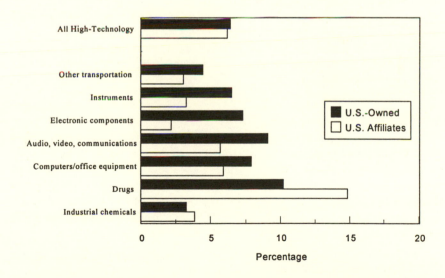

Source: Department of Commerce (1997b) and National Science Foundation (1996).

Figure 8.10
U.S. High-Technology Affiliates' Ratio of R&D to Sales, 1987 and 1994

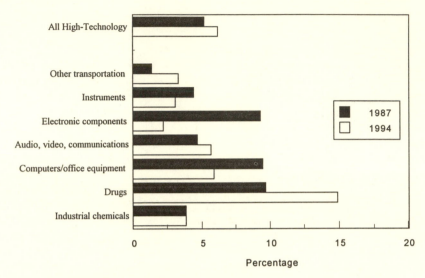

Source: Department of Commerce (1990; 1997b).

and *other transport* and modestly in *audio, video, and communications equipment.* The ratios in other high-technology industries decreased, except in *industrial chemicals,* which remained unchanged, over this period. However, the extent to which these changes are due to changes in the activities of existing U.S. affiliates versus changes in ownership (in other words, from domestic to foreign and vice versa) cannot be readily determined.

R&D Facilities

Another way that U.S. affiliates contribute to U.S. technological capability is through their establishment or acquisition of R&D facilities in the United States. In the same way that output of U.S. affiliates are a part of total U.S. output, their R&D performed in the United States is a part of U.S. technology capability. The impact of their contribution on overall U.S. technology capability, however, depends on a number of key factors, including the purpose of the facilities. Their R&D activities may be grouped into four types (Dunning 1994):

• A firm may adapt, improve, and test products or processes needed to meet local market conditions and standards, that is., to tailor the products for local market needs.
• A firm may establish research facilities because some inputs are produced overseas, for example, as in the case of mining (materials research) or because close contact with the customer is required.

- A firm may rationalize research activities, domestically and internationally, to take advantage of economies of scale and scope. In addition, more U.S. and foreign firms are setting up cross-border alliances to lower competitive pressures and R&D costs.
- A firm may need to maintain an R&D presence near major U.S. innovating centers, that is, the foreign parent wants to have access to results from nearby U.S. research centers of universities, corporate laboratories, or other research institutions.

A recent study of foreign-owned R&D laboratories in the United States found that investments in these facilities were technology and marketing driven (Florida 1996). Among the most important activities of the laboratories, survey respondents listed developing new product ideas; obtaining information on developments in U.S. science and technology; gaining access to high-quality scientists, engineers, and designers; and, though not as important, customizing products for the U.S. market. Moreover, sources of innovation for foreign-owned laboratories are, in order of importance, in-house research staff, customers, sister R&D facilities, competitors, and joint venture partners.

Reasons for setting up R&D facilities frequently differ by industry of U.S. affiliates. Technology-driven activities are important to high-technology industries, such as biotechnology and computer software, while market-driven activities are important to industries with high levels of investment in manufacturing and consumer products (Florida 1996). For example, universities are more important to the biotechnology industry, while manufacturing plants and suppliers are more important to the auto industry (Florida 1996). Moreover, the purpose for having U.S. affiliates with R&D facilities in the United States appears to have changed over time. For example, R&D activities of Japanese-owned auto firms have shifted from mainly meeting environmental regulations and gaining U.S. auto design capability to other purposes that include research in new materials and electric vehicles. Electronics companies have been locating their R&D laboratories near customers, close to U.S. research universities and in areas with large numbers of scientists and engineers, such as in Silicon Valley or the Research Triangle in North Carolina (Dalton and Serapio 1995). European firms (particularly German firms) are moving biotechnology research to the United States because of an unfavorable regulatory environment for biotechnology research and manufacturing in Europe (Arakaki 1991).

The number and size of R&D facilities of U.S. affiliates differ significantly by country of foreign parent (table 8.6). Japanese-owned companies have the most R&D facilities, in total and in most industries.

- In 1994, 107 Japanese parent firms had R&D facilities in the United States, compared to 61 U.K. firms, 32 German firms, and 22 French companies.
- Correspondingly, Japanese parents had more U.S. R&D facilities (224) than did other countries. In the aggregate, European companies have 348 R&D facilities in the United States, Korean companies 27, and Canadian companies 8 (Dalton and Serapio 1996).[14]
- There are more R&D centers in each industry owned by Japanese firms than owned by firms from other countries, except in the biotechnology industry, which is dominated by European companies. Several Japanese electronic firms have more R&D facilities than other foreign companies.

Technology Transfer between U.S. Affiliates and Their Foreign Parents

Proxy variables, such as royalties and license fees,[15] are often used to estimate transfers of technology between companies. Royalties and license fees are annual payments for the sale and use of intangible property rights, such as patents, industrial processes, trademarks, copyrights, franchises, know-how, and other *intellectual property* rights. Some observers, however, believe U.S. and foreign MNCs also use these fees to minimize tax obligations by shifting costs from affiliates in a low-tax country to those in a high-tax country. To the extent that these fees reflect such transfer pricing, this measure of technology transfer (payments and receipts) between foreign parents and their U.S. affiliates is misstated.

The data on royalty and license fees suggest there has been an overwhelmingly large *net* inflow of technology to U.S. affiliates from their foreign parents. Net payments by U.S. affiliates to their foreign parents have increased from $426 million in 1980 to $4,718 million in 1995 (table 8.7).

Payments by U.S. high-technology affiliates represent more than half of the total payments to foreign parents by all U.S. affiliates in the manufacturing and services sectors. In contrast, receipts of high-technology affiliates from their foreign parents are about one-fourth of the total receipts by all U.S. affiliates (table 8.8). British, German, and Japanese multinationals account for almost 60 percent of total royalties and license fee payments by U.S. affiliates in high-technology industries. In 1994, the United Kingdom received the largest payments of royalties and license fees, followed closely by Japan, Switzerland, and Germany.

Much of the attention given the issue of technology transfer has focused on Japanese firms because of Japan's history of ready adoption of and dependence on foreign technology and because of the high profile given by the media to the rapid growth in Japanese acquisition of U.S. firms in the last half of the 1980s.

Royalties and license fees data indicate wide differences in high-technology industries by country of parent:

- Net payments (payments minus receipts) in *all* industries in 1995, by Japanese-owned affiliates ($784 million) are almost double those by German affiliates ($389 million) or Swiss affiliates ($349 million) but are two-thirds that of British affiliates ($1,170 million).
- For high-technology manufacturing affiliates, net payments varied widely. In 1995, for Japanese affiliates were $36; for German affiliates, $99 million; and for Swiss affiliates, $164 million. In 1994, net payments were for Japanese affiliates, they were $78 million; for British affiliates, $6 million; for German affiliates, $192 million; and for Swiss affiliates, $136 million.

A recent survey of all Japanese manufacturing companies by Japan's Science and Technology Agency (*Survey Report on Research Activities in Private Enterprises* 1992) indicates that attitudes about technology transfer from the United States are changing: 36 percent of the firms surveyed indicate no technology transfer would occur if they did not own U.S. firms; 36 percent expect technology to be both exported and imported; and the balance of the Japanese firms are almost equally divided between solely importing and solely exporting technology.

Table 8.6
U.S. R&D Facilities of Foreign Companies: Selected Industries and Companies, 1992

Industry	Japan	Germany	Korea	Nether- lands	United Kingdom	Swiss	Sweden	France	Others
Computers	22	4	7	3					3
Software	28	4	1	1	6			3	1
Semiconductors	19	3	10	3					
Telecommunications	14	4	1		2	1	2	2	3
Optoelectronics	11	3			2		1		3
HDTV, electronics	33	9	4	4	10	5		4	3
Drugs, biotechnology	24	18	1	5	23	17	5	11	9
Chemicals, rubber, materials	23	28		4	19	10		17	8
Metals	5	1			3	1	1	4	
Automotive	34	11	3		1		2	2	
Machinery	7	2			4		6	3	
Instrumentation	1	3	3	3	23	4	1	5	
Foods, consumer goods	7	6	5	5	19	6	1	2	7

Source: Donald H. Dalton and Manuel G. Serapio, Jr., "Foreign Research Centers in the U.S. and U.S. R&D Abroad," U.S. Department of Commerce, Technology Administration, Japan Technology Program, draft, November 1996.

Table 8.7
Payments and Receipts of Royalties and License Fees between
U.S. Affiliates and Foreign Parents (millions of dollars)

Year	Payments	Receipts	Net Payments
1980	426	48	378
1981	487	74	413
1982	394	69	325
1983	465	60	405
1984	665	68	597
1985	568	102	466
1986	799	180	619
1987	1,083	150	933
1988	1,244	122	1,122
1989	1,632	349	1,283
1990	1,967	383	1,584
1991	2,830	576	2,254
1992	3,191	793	2,398
1993	3,130	771	2,359
1994	3,562	998	2,564
1995	4,718	1,439	3,279

Note: Receipts and Payments are before deduction of withholding tax.

Source: Department of Commerce, *Survey of Current Business*, various issues.

Table 8.8
Royalties and License Fees: Payments to and Receipts from Foreign Parents by
U.S. Affiliates in All Industries and in High-Technology Industries,
1983-1994 (millions of dollars)

	1983		1987	
	Payments	Receipts	Payments	Receipts
Manufacturing	234	33	755	94
Of which high-technology is	98	4*	371	11*
Services	14	2	41	3*
Of which high-technology is	0	0	3*	8*
	1991		1995	
	Payments	Receipts	Payments	Receipts
Manufacturing	1,771	200	2,921	550
Of which high-technology is	921	101	1,696	157
Services	104	102	250	177
Of which high-technology is	10*	6*	75	37

*Number understated because industry data have been suppressed to maintain confidentiality
of company information.

Source: Bureau of Economic Analysis, unpublished data.

There is little evidence that foreign acquisitions of small, high-technology U.S. firms have resulted in large scale technology transfer abroad. The data on royalties and license fees provide no information on the importance of the particular technologies transferred, such as whether the technology is "key" or "critical." Views about technology transfer vary among U.S. industries. There is a consensus that affiliates of Japanese firms are bringing advanced process technology into the United States in the steel and auto industries (Florida and Kenney 1992). In contrast, with respect to technologies in which Japan lags, such as in computer software and biotechnology, some studies suggest significant technology may have been transferred from the United States to Japan through affiliates as well as by other types of strategic alliances (National Research Council 1992). One study of Japanese investments into the United States shows Japanese firms tend to establish more new plants in R&D-intensive industries than in other industries, but joint ventures are preferred if U.S. technology is sought (Kogut and Chang 1991).

Technology Spillover Effects

Technological innovations and knowledge generated by one firm's research often flow to other firms within and outside its industry. There is anecdotal evidence that U.S. affiliates of foreign firms provide benefits to other U.S. firms and the U.S. economy in general, in the form of technology spillovers from the foreign-owned U.S. affiliates R&D facilities to U.S.-owned facilities, and that these spillovers are sizeable. Clearly, the magnitude of license fees indicates these spillovers are large. The magnitudes and the channels of transmission of these spillover effects, however, are not clear.

There is a large body of literature on the techniques of estimating technology spillovers. Economic researchers have employed various models and techniques in their studies. For example, a Cobb-Douglas type of production function is often the starting point for the estimation of intra- and interindustry effects of technology growth on total factor productivity growth (Terleckyj 1984; Griliches 1979; Griliches and Lichtenberg 1984). In their simplest form, these models explicitly incorporate the total level of technology capital (knowledge) in the industry as one of the factors of production. Another estimate of the spillover effect is a cost function estimation (Bernstein and Nadiri 1989; Mohnen and Lepine 1988), which has the advantage of estimating the separate impacts of both total costs and the demand of labor and other inputs such as R&D. Yet another method is the use of patents granted in other industries as an explanation of R&D productivity growth in a particular industry (Schankerman 1979). So far, no single approach has established superiority over the others.

A number of studies have attempted to gauge the extent and magnitude of technology spillovers for all U.S. firms, and the approaches used could also be applied to foreign-owned firms. So far, no efforts have been made to distinguish spillovers from U.S.-owned and foreign-owned firms. As foreign direct investment in the U.S. increases, the impact of foreign firms on the U.S. economy will also rise. Thus, the need for better understanding technology spillovers is increasingly important. A contribution can be made by refining and extending these models and techniques for estimating the technology spillover effects of foreign-owned companies.

FUTURE RESEARCH

Better quality data made available in the mid-1990s enable us to investigate technology development and FDIUS with far greater depth and accuracy. Yet, a number of key issues on the relation between FDI and technology development remain to be addressed. Research on these issues has still been hampered in part by data limitations.

• Separate data on output, employment, R&D spending, and other performance measures for acquisitions of existing high-technology affiliates versus newly created establishments are lacking.
• The role of U.S. affiliates in high-technology niche markets (in other words, 4-digit SIC versus 3-digit SIC categories) is lacking.
• Existing data cannot be used to identify corporate linkages, and thus the extent to which differences in performance are fostered by corporate linkages (such as *keiretsu* relationships) among foreign firms and the affiliates cannot be determined.
• The size of acquired firms cannot always be readily determined and therefore cannot be used as an indicator of motive for accessing U.S. technology. Some observers have concluded that the size of the affiliate, at least in the electronics industry, indicates why the foreign firm is motivated to acquire the U.S. firm and its technology.[16]

In addition, questions about differences in Japanese company strategies versus European or Canadian firms' strategies to access U.S. technology similarly remain unaddressed. Finally, additional research is needed to estimate the impact of FDIUS on U.S. technological capability in terms of the technology spillover effects between foreign-owned and U.S.-owned firms.

NOTES

This chapter builds on the analysis and updates data presented in "Influence of Foreign Direct Investment on the Development and Transfer of U.S. Technology," published in *Foreign Direct Investment in the United States: An Update* (Washington, D.C.: U.S. Department of Commerce, June 1993), pp. 52-76. The author wishes to thank Lewis Alexander, Lester Davis, and William Brown for helpful comments and suggestions. The views expressed are those of the author and should not be interpreted as the official views of the U.S. government or the U.S. Department of Commerce.

1. This classification scheme is often referred to as the "DOC-3" definition.

2. The FDI in high-technology industries is understated by *excluding* the "ordnance" industry, "engines, turbines, and parts" industry, and "research and testing services" and is overstated by *including* some low-technology industries, such as "industrial organic chemicals" under industrial chemicals and "ship and boat building, railroad equipment, and miscellaneous transport equipment" under the broad "other transportation equipment" category. Although classified as high-technology under DOC-3, the "engines, turbines, and parts" (SIC 351) industry and the "ordnance and accessories" (SIC 348) industry are excluded because FDI data for these industries are not collected separately but are combined with data for two other three-digit industries within the metal products group (SIC 34). The engines, turbines, and parts industry is excluded because the FDI data for this industry are suppressed in some years

to avoid disclosure problems. On the other hand, "other transportation equipment" has been included in its entirety because over 70 percent of this group is accounted for by "aircraft and parts" (SIC 372) and "guided missiles and spacecraft" (SIC 376). Similarly, "industrial organic chemicals" represents 40 percent of industrial chemicals and synthetics. These percentages are based on sales data reported by the Department of Commerce (1992). In addition, for FDI analysis, the DOC-3 sector, SIC 365-367 has been disaggregated to show FDI performance separately for electronic components (SIC 367). Moreover, data on the high-technology *services* industries are available only after 1983, and "research and testing services" are not reported separately over time. The latter is included in the analysis when data are available.

The BEA-Census Data Link Project helps resolve these aggregation problems by providing data on the number, sales, payroll, and employment of establishments (plants) of U.S. affiliates of foreign firms at detailed four-digit SIC categories in 1987 and 1992.

3. The shares for 1994 are based on classification of U.S. affiliates by industry of sales, which approximate data by establishment from the BEA-Census Data Link Project, but are not exactly equivalent. BEA data on employment and sales are collected on both industry of affiliate and an industry of sales bases. The latest year for which data from the Data Link Project are available is 1992. Industry classifications for data published under the Data Link Project are more detailed than the annual FDIUS data. The shares for 1994 are estimated, using industry of sales data and detailed information from the Data Link, 1987 and 1992. See William J. Zeile, "Foreign Direct Investment in the United States: 1992 Benchmark Survey Results," *Survey of Current Business* (vol. 74, July 1994) for definitions. U.S.-owned sales are derived by subtracting U.S. affiliates' sales from all U.S. sales.

4. The latest data available from the BEA-Census Data Link Project are for 1992.

5. U.S. firms in *aircraft and parts* and *guided missiles and spacecraft* are shielded from foreign acquisition by, among other factors, the Exon-Florio amendment to the Defense Production Act. Moreover, data on *guided missiles and spacecraft* have been suppressed to avoid disclosure.

6. High-skilled workers are defined in this chapter to include managerial and administrative workers plus professional, paraprofessional, and technical workers. BLS provides data for three-digit manufacturing industries by major occupational group: managerial and administrative workers; professional, paraprofessional, and technical workers; sales and related workers; clerical and administrative support workers; service workers; production and related workers; agricultural, forestry, fishing, and related workers. The only year for which these data are available is 1989. Most studies only divide workers into production and nonproduction workers as proxies for high and low skills.

7. See Dorothy B. Christelow, "U.S.-Japan Joint Ventures: Who Gains," *Challenge* (November-December, 1989), pp. 29-38, for estimates of changes in comparative advantage and patterns of industry specialization for the United States and Japan between 1974 and 1989 and for an analysis of joint venture decisions by Japanese firms in sectors in which they have a comparative advantage. See also John H. Dunning, "Multinational Enterprises and the Globalization of Innovator Capacity," *Research Policy* (vol. 23, 1994), pp. 67-88.

8. Sales of high-technology affiliates of Canadian and Dutch parents in a number of these industries are suppressed to avoid divulging confidential information on individual companies. The five countries, Japan, the United Kingdom, the Netherlands, Canada, and Germany, represented over 70 percent of total FDIUS in 1994.

9. Although data for Swiss firms are not available separately, it is likely that those firms also account for a large share of total industry sales in drugs.

10. Both BEA and NSF survey data used here are collected at the enterprise level and exclude contract research by companies at universities and private laboratories. NSF, but not BEA, also collects and reports data that include contract research.

11. The R&D spending by manufacturing affiliates may be understated, because of industry classification problems. BEA's R&D expenditures are classified by primary industry of sales. Thus, R&D spending by some industries may be grouped in wholesale trade even though a relatively large (though less than the largest) proportion of an affiliate's business may be in manufacturing. To account for this possibility, in this chapter, R&D spending of the wholesale trade of motor vehicles and equipment has been included with manufacturing of motor vehicles and equipment, especially since the reported value of their R&D spending is far greater in wholesaling than in manufacturing. However, including R&D spending by motor vehicle wholesalers could overstate U.S. affiliates' spending relative to that of all U.S. companies. Available data cannot be used to determine the extent of this problem.

12. For some purposes, a better indicator of resources devoted to R&D efforts is the ratio of R&D to value added, but value added data are not available on a comparable basis for U.S. affiliates and U.S. companies.

13. U.S.-owned R&D spending and sales have been derived by deducting U.S. affiliates' R&D spending and sales from total U.S. R&D spending and sales, respectively.

14. These data include design studios, which are not considered research facilities by the NSF and thus may represent a significant overstatement of actual research facilities located in the United States—as much as 80 percent above actual R&D facilities, according to one NSF analyst.

15. Ideally, royalties, which include payments for copyrights to books, musical recordings, trademarks, and franchises, but not necessarily technical know-how of industrial processes, should be deducted from the sum of royalty and licensing fees. However, the data are not available separately for *affiliated* parties. Patent licensing fees represent about 70 percent of total royalties and license fees paid between *unaffiliated* parties, and thus the values discussed in this section are overstated to the extent that they include royalty payments not related to technology transactions. Moreover, how well patents measure outputs of technology and how well licenses measure payments for this know-how are problematic. These issues are extensively discussed in the literature on the economics of R&D and technical change. For a discussion on the limitations of these data, see Mary Ellen Mogee, "Toward International Licensing by U.S.-based Firms: Trends and Implications," *Technology Transfer*, Spring 1991, pp. 14-19.

16. For one point of view, see Phyllis A. Genther and Donald H. Dalton, *Japanese-Affiliated Electronics Companies: Implications for U.S. Technology Development* (Economics and Statistics Administration and Technology Administration, Department of Commerce, NITS, March 1991).

REFERENCES

Arakaki, Emily. 1991. "Trends in Foreign Direct Investment in U.S. Biotechnology," in
    Foreign Direct Investment in the United States, Department of Commerce, Economics
    and Statistics Administration, August.
Becker, Michael. 1989. *Myths about Foreign Investment*. Washington, D.C.: Citizens for a
    Sound Economy Foundation.
Bernstein, J. I., and M. I. Nadiri. 1989. "Research and Development and Intra-industry
    Spillovers: An Empirical Application of Dynamic Duality," *Review of Economic Studies*
    56:249-269.
Choate, Pat. 1990. *Agents of Influence: How Japan's Lobbyists in the United States Mani-
    pulate America's Political and Economic System*. New York: A.A. Knopf.
Dalton, Donald H., and Manuel G. Serapio, Jr. 1995. "Foreign Research Centers in the U.S.
    and U.S. R&D Abroad," Department of Commerce, Technology Administration, Japan
    Technology Program, Washington, D.C., draft, June.

Davis, Lester A. 1982. *Technology Intensity of U.S. Output and Trade,* Office of Trade and Investment Analysis, Department of Commerce, International Trade Administration, July.

Department of Commerce. 1988. *Foreign Direct Investment in the United States: Operations of U.S. Affiliates of Foreign Companies, Revised 1985 Estimates*, Economics and Statistics Administration, Bureau of Economic Analysis, June. Washington, D.C.: GPO.

———. 1990. *Foreign Direct Investment in the United States: 1987 Benchmark Survey, Final Results*, Economics and Statistics Administration, Bureau of Economic Analysis, August. Washington, D.C.: GPO.

———. 1991. *Foreign Direct Investment in the United States: Review and Analysis of Current Developments*, Economics and Statistics Administration, September. Washington, D.C.: GPO.

———. 1992. *Foreign Direct Investment in the United States: Establishment Data for 1987*, Bureau of Economic Analysis and Bureau of the Census, June. Washington, D.C.: GPO.

———. 1993a. *Foreign Direct Investment in the United States: An Update*. Economics and Statistics Administration, June. Washington, D.C.: GPO.

———. 1993b. *Foreign Direct Investment in the United States: Operations of U.S. Affiliates of Foreign Companies, Revised 1990 Estimates*, Economics and Statistics Administration, Bureau of Economic Analysis, June. Washington, D.C.: GPO.

———. 1995a. *Foreign Direct Investment in the United States: 1992 Benchmark Survey, Final Results*, Economics and Statistics Administration, Bureau of Economic Analysis, August. Washington, D.C.: GPO.

———. 1995b. *Foreign Direct Investment in the United States: An Update*, Economics and Statistics Administration, January. Washington, D.C.: GPO.

———. 1996. *Foreign Direct Investment in the United States: Operations of U.S. Affiliates of Foreign Companies, Revised 1993 Estimates*, Economics and Statistics Administration, Bureau of Economic Analysis, July. Washington, D.C.: GPO.

———. 1997a. *Foreign Direct Investment in the United States: Establishment Data for 1992*, Economics and Statistics Administration, Bureau of Economic Analysis, May. Washington, D.C.: GPO.

———. 1997b. *Foreign Direct Investment in the United States: Operations of U.S. Affiliates of Foreign Companies, Revised 1994 Estimates*, Economics and Statistics Administration, Bureau of Economic Analysis, September. Washington, D.C.: GPO.

———. 1997c. *Foreign Direct Investment in the United States: Preliminary 1995 Estimates*, Economics and Statistics Administration, Bureau of Economic Analysis, June. Washington, D.C.: GPO.

Doms, Mark E., and J. Bradford Jensen. 1995. "A Comparison between Operating Characteristics of Domestic and Foreign Owned Manufacturing Establishments in the U.S.," paper prepared for the Conference on Research in Income and Wealth, Geography and Ownership as Bases for Economic Accounting, May.

Dunning, John H. 1994. "Multinational Enterprises and the Globalization of Innovatory Capacity," *Research Policy* 23:67-88.

Florida, Richard L. 1996. "Foreign Direct Investment in Research and Development: Scope, Performance, and Activities of Foreign-Affiliated R&D Laboratories in the United States," Center for Science and International Affairs, John F. Kennedy School of Government, Harvard University, draft, January.

Florida, Richard L., and Martin Kenney. 1992. "Restructuring in Place: Japanese Investment, Production, Organization, and the Geography of Steel," *Economic Geography* 68(2):146-173.

———. 1992."The Japanese Transplants: Production, Organization, and Regional Development," *Journal of the American Planning Association* 58(1):21-38.

Glickman, Norman J., and Douglas P. Woodward. 1990. *The New Competitors: How Foreign Investors Are Changing the U.S. Economy*. New York: Basic Books.

Graham, Edward M., and Paul R. Krugman. 1991. *Foreign Direct Investment in the United States*. Second edition. Washington, D.C.: Institute for International Economics.

Griliches, Zvi. 1979. "Issues in Assessing the Contribution of Research and Development to Productivity Growth," *Bell Journal of Economics* 10(1):92-116.

Griliches, Zvi, and F. Lichtenberg. 1984. "Interindustry Technology Flows and Productivity Growth: A Reexamination," *Review of Economics and Statistics* 66:324-329.

Howenstine, Ned G., and William J. Zeile. 1993. "Foreign Direct Investment in the United States: The Data Link Project and Establishment Data for 1987," in *Foreign Direct Investment in the United States: An Update*, Department of Commerce, Economics and Statistics Administration, June. Washington, D.C.: GPO.

————.1994. "Characteristics of Foreign-Owned U.S. Manufacturing Establishments," *Survey of Current Business* 74(January):34-59.

Kogut, Bruce, and Sea Jin Chang. 1991. "Technological Capabilities and Japanese Direct Investment in the United States," *Review of Economics and Statistics* 73(3):401-413.

Mohnen, P., and N. Lepine. 1988. "Payments for Technology as a Factor of Production," Paper No. 8818, Department of Economics, University of Montreal.

National Research Council. 1992. Office of Japan Affairs, *U.S.-Japan Technology Linkages in Biotechnology; U.S.-Japan Strategic Alliances in the Semiconductor Industry*. Washington, D.C.: National Academy Press.

National Science Board. 1996. *Science and Engineering Indicators, 1996*, NSB 96-21. Washington, D.C.: GPO.

National Science Foundation. 1994. *Research and Development in Industry*, Division of Science Resources Studies.

Schankerman, M. 1979. "Essays on the Economics of Technical Change: The Determinants, Rate of Return and Productivity Impact of Research and Development," doctoral dissertation, Harvard University.

Survey Report on Research Activities in Private Enterprises. 1992. Science and Technology Agency, Tokyo, February, translated in *Science and Technology, Japan*, JPRS-JST-92-021, August 12.

Terleckyj, N. 1980. "Direct and Indirect Effects of Industrial Research and Development on the Productivity Growth of Industries," in *New Development In Productivity Measurement and Analysis*, edited by J. Kendrick and B. Vaccara. Chicago: University of Chicago Press, pp. 359-377.

Tolchin, Martin, and Susan Tolchin. 1988. *Buying into America: How Foreign Money Is Changing the Face of Our Nation*. New York: Times Books.

9

Strategies of Foreign Corporate R&D Investment and Sourcing in the United States

Lois S. Peters

INTRODUCTION

The globalization of markets has drawn much attention over the last decade (Peters and Rufer 1995; Bartlett and Ghoshall 1989; Erickson 1991). Empirical observations of firm actions suggest that competitive success in global markets requires direct investment.

Accompanying this market globalization is the internationalization of technology (Perrino and Tipping 1989), but the capability for generation of this technology is not the same everywhere. Associated with the growth in the importance of having access to sources of technology has been the growth of private sector technical alliances and expansion of the foreign research and development (R&D) sites of multinational corporations (MNCs). The growth of such activities has been docu-mented in many different technology-based industries over the last decade (Hagedoorn and Schakenraad 1990; Peters 1987; 1988; 1990; 1991a; 1991b; 1992a; 1992b; 1993a). The previous two chapters of this volume provide a broad empirical overview of the phenomenon. It is abundantly clear that research and development is a prominent extension of growing multinational networks. This chapter takes a microeconomic view of globalization in technology and R&D, examining cases of R&D strategies, including technical alliances and university linkages, that are often ignored.

Investment and sourcing of technology have been discussed extensively in the literature, and ample theoretical frameworks have been advanced to guide decision making (Dunning 1988; 1992; Porter 1990; Dosi et al. 1988; Granstrand, Håkanson, and Sjölander 1993; Mutinelli and Piscitello 1995). A less-developed literature is that regarding the generation of technology, or R&D sourcing and investment (Cheng and Bolon 1993). Much work has focused on U.S. overseas investment (Mansfield, Teece, and Romeo 1979; Pearce 1988). While overseas R&D investment has occurred since the early part of the twentieth century when internal R&D laboratories of firms were first established, only recently has there been significant increase of such activity (Peters 1991b; 1992a).

A perplexing issue is that, as the technology generation gap appears to have been reduced at least among the industrialized nations, there is increased global siting of such activity, as made clear in the previous chapter. If there is equal technology (know-how) generation capacity, why not trade know-how capability that is developed in the home base? Furthermore, if technology generation is the seed of future growth, are not firms putting themselves at risk by locating such activity in situations over which they may have less control?

Researchers focusing on the process of internationalization at the firm level (de Meyer and Mizushima 1989; Howells 1990; Wortmann 1990; Juul and Walters 1987; Håkanson 1981; Behrman and Fischer 1980; Ronstadt 1977; Cordell 1971) have primarily focused on a small group of multinationals from one region (de Meyer interviewed European multinationals) or country, such as Sweden (Håkanson 1981), Norway (Juul and Walters 1987), the United States (Rondstadt 1977; Creamer 1976), Canada (Cordell 1971), and Germany (Wortmann 1990). The last comprehensive review covering overseas laboratories of U.S. MNCs was for the period 1966-1975 (Creamer 1976). The focus in all these studies primarily has been from the perspective of headquarters as opposed to that of the R&D subsidiary. The recent expansion of Japanese multinationals and the extensive worldwide merger and acquisition activity experienced in the 1980s, especially in the United States, has raised interest in the increase in ownership of U.S. laboratories by non-U.S.-based multinationals. Recent studies have explored this phenomenon from the perspective of general processes of internationalization and its impact on the national interests of the United States (Dalton and Serapio 1993; Kenney and Florida 1993). As effective technology management becomes increasingly critical to a firm's international competitiveness, a focus on the decision-making processes about foreign R&D and its value to the firm would be beneficial.

The basic question of many researchers interested in the internationalization of R&D has been why firms internationalize. What are the determinants of internationalization of R&D, and what are the modes of entry? Much of the research has been based on aggregate data and focused on economic variables such as the scale of R&D required for global competition, appropriatability of internal R&D investments, and economic efficiency. Process models of internationalization of R&D focusing on behavioral variables exist but are less well developed than recent economically oriented models such as Dunning's eclectic theory of internationalization or models based on transaction cost theory. Few have questioned how firms internationalize beyond whether it was by acquisition, strategic alliances, or greenfield investment. What types of choices do experienced multinational firms with long histories of investment in R&D face? An also less emphasized question is what types of technology generation organization and technology are integral to achieving successful competition in current global markets? Research aimed at mapping out what is going on by country and industry, with an eye toward contextual situations, effects and policy implications suggest that this may be an important question (Peters 1992a; Dalton and Serapio 1993; Kenney and Florida 1993; Granstrand, Håkanson, and Sjölander 1993) . In particular, much interest has been raised about the reversal from outward investment in technology and R&D by U.S. multinational firms to inward U.S. FDI in technology and R&D by non-U.S. firms (Peters 1993a).

Therefore, the objective of this chapter is to improve our understanding of the decision making and management of the initiation, strategy, procedures, and effectiveness of foreign R&D activity in the United States. Compared with the previous chapters, this chapter takes a managerial perspective. A description of different modes of entry to the U.S. R&D system is discussed first. Then the strategies and management issues of five non-U.S. multinational corporations with considerable histories of R&D activity are explored. The chapter ends with comments about policy and managerial efficiency. Throughout, special care is taken to make comparisons between the Japanese and European experience, different types of industries and technology climates, and parent versus subsidiary perspectives.

The chapter draws on material gathered in a continuing program to examine the nature, procedures, and impact of R&D activities conducted by MNCs in countries other than the home country of the corporate management. Structured interviews with ample time for open-ended discussion were conducted during 1994 at a U.S. laboratory site of ABB, Philips, Matsushita, Thomson, and Bayer.

FOREIGN MODES OF PARTICIPATION IN THE U.S. R&D SYSTEM

The large U.S. markets, the dynamic advance of high-tech industries in biotechnology and electronics, and the unique strength of the U.S. research universities are powerful attractions for European and Japanese corporations to establish laboratories in the United States. In recent years, European and U.S. corporations have added laboratories in Japan for similar reasons.

The United States, as a host country for foreign laboratories, is of particular interest because of the sophistication and size of its markets and technical base, its leadership in many areas of high technology, and the unique strengths of its research universities. Market opportunities alone were sufficient reasons for foreign corporations to initiate U.S. laboratories after World War II. In more recent years access to technical advances seems an increasingly important factor in that decision. However, it is unlikely that proximity to technical resources alone is sufficient reason for a foreign corporation to establish a laboratory in the United States. There are less expensive ways to keep informed about and make contacts with those advances.

The relative importance of multiple objectives of foreign corporations concerning their U.S. laboratories cannot be discerned from the statistics about these laboratories, such as those offered by Dalton and Serapio in this book. Nor do the numbers provide insight on the effectiveness of these laboratories in achieving corporate objectives. Those insights can only come from examining individual corporate experiences.

Establishments of R&D Laboratories

The United States has a long history of serving as host to laboratories of European multinationals. In 1913, Unilever conducted research in a laboratory in Cambridge, Massachusetts. The Philips laboratory in Briarcliff, New York, was initiated 40 years ago; Hoffman-LaRoche began research activity in New Jersey in

1921 with the Roche Institute for Molecular Biology. Tables 9.1 and 9.2 present some characteristics of recent foreign-owned laboratories in the United States. These tables contain details on facilities from the author's database. Wholly-owned foreign R&D facilities, however, are only part of overall foreign R&D activity, as the next section reveals.

Table 9.1
Summary R&D Statistics for Selected MNCs with R&D Investment in the United States

	Sales (Million)	R&D (Million)	R&D/ Sales (%)	Employ-ees World-wide	Re-search-ers World-wide	Re-search-ers in United States	Total Re-search-ers/ To-tal Em-ployees (%)
British Telecom.	22,516	394	1.75	210,500 (192)	4,000		
ELF Acquitaine	38,989	874	2.24	94,000	5,480	590	5.83
ENICHEM	10,873	331	3.04	52,656	300	35	0.57
Hitachi	60,515	4,025	6.65	330,637	12,500	25	3.78
Hoffman LaRoche	8,020	1,210	15.09	55,134	4,000	1,017	7.85
Honda	33,183	1,600	4.82	91,300	7,500	290	8.21
L.M. Ericsson	7,657	1,170	15.28	69,597			
NEC	28,225	2,208	7.82	147,910	15,000	36	10.14
Northern Telecom.	8,376	949	11.33	60,293	5,100	599	11.82
Royal Dutch/Shell Oil	97,174	881	0.91	117,000		2,000	
Elf Sanofi	4,060	393	9.68	38,500		235	
SmithKline Beecham	9,261	864	9.33	51,900		2,083	
Toshiba	37,159	2,503	6.74	175,000			

Source: Business Week, June 27, 1994; "Fortune's Global 500," Fortune, 1994; Directory of Corporate Affiliations, 1993; IEEE Spectrum 27(10), October 1990; Wall Street Journal, May 24, 1993; Standard & Poor's Register: Corporations, 1994; America's Leading Public and Private Companies, 1994.

Other lists of R&D facilities, like those found in the chapter by Dalton and Serapio, may miss some significant activity of European-based firms. For example, the U.S. R&D activity of Shell, a British and Dutch company, is sometimes not listed for either country (Dalton and Serapio 1993), nor are the U.S. R&D activities of ABB. Dalton and Serapio's (1993) statement that the 155 Japanese facilities in the United States outnumber the U.S. R&D facilities of other countries combined was misleading. The European R&D facilities in the United States are generally much larger than those of the Japanese. Many of the Japanese facilities are focused on technical services and design. Differences in estimates of the total number of laboratories under foreign ownership can be explained by differing definitions of

Table 9.2
Case Study Company Summary Statistics 1993

	Sales (Million)	R&D (Million)	R&D/Sales (%)	Employees World-wide	Researchers World-wide	Researchers in United States	Total Researchers/Total Employees (%)	Percent Researchers, U.S.-to-Worldwide
Asea Brown Boveri	28,300	2,300	7.93	206,490	11,000	1,588	5.33	14.4
Bayer	27,334	1,958	7.27	151,900	13,500	2,575	8.89	19.1
Matsushita	56.659	3,227	5.70	254,059	14,200	200	5.59	1.4
Philips	33,571	2,087	6.22*	238,500	13,000 ††	1,700	5.45	13.1
Thomson	11,917	1,700	14.3**	99,900	12,000	430	12.1	3.58
Thomson-CSF	6,476	527	8.14 †					

*Annual report estimates this to be 5.8%.
**Other estimates suggest this is closer to 10%.
†Other estimates suggest this was as high as 18.4% in 1988.
††Annual reports stated there was an average of 25,651 employees in research and production in 1993.

Source: Interviews; Annual reports; *Business Week,* June 27, 1994; *Global Company Handbook,* 1992; "Fortune's Global 500," *Fortune,* 1994;
    Directory of Corporate Affiliations, 1993.

ownership. Nevertheless, the general thrust of the investigation highlighting the recent increase of Japanese foreign R&D laboratory investment in the United States and the importance of investment in U.S. biotechnology R&D for foreign companies is correct.

Technical Alliances

In chapter 1, Dunning emphasized that alliances are key features of globalization. The alliances that take place through R&D include technical alliances, university ties, and participation in U.S. government programs. First, consider technical alliances. The expansion of technical alliance activity within a company is frequently as vigorous as its internal R&D expansion. For example, in recent years, Siemens established a corporate R&D laboratory in the United States, to bring its total number of laboratories to thirty-five. During the same period, Siemens has set up significant R&D joint ventures with Philips and IBM. Worldwide, Siemens has an estimated 300 technical links with other firms (Hagedoorn and Schakenraad 1990).

NEC has expanded R&D laboratory activities in the United States by establishing a basic research laboratory in Princeton, New Jersey, and has, at the same time, negotiated extensive strategic alliances with both European and U.S. firms. For example, NEC signed a contract with AT&T for a comprehensive package in semiconductor development for the next five years. NEC also entered joint development agreements with Hewlett Packard to develop tools for microprocessors and microcomputers. Other companies having joint technology agreements with NEC include Grumman (supercomputer), American Microsystems (microprocessors), 3M (optical memory system), Summit Micro Circuit (a venture company to develop high-speed SRAMS), Huges (weather satellite), Adobe Systems (desktop publishing software), General Electric (international PC network), and Tektronix (gate array design software). What is noteworthy about these alliances is the array of companies and technologies covered. Corporations therefore seek to improve their competitive advantage through expanding their foreign R&D sites and establishing a variety of linkages to external technical resources. Other examples include the relationship between Siemens (Germany), Toshiba (Japan), and IBM (U.S.) in electronics and joint ventures like those between Astra (Sweden) and Merck (U.S.), Sumitomo Electric Industries partnering with AT&T (Litespec, Inc.), Alcan (Alcan-Sumitomo Electric, Inc.), Lucas Industries (Lucas Sumitomo Brakes, Inc.) and Eaton (Engineered-Sintered Components, Inc.), and Sanofi (France) and Sterling, a subsidiary of Kodak (U.S.). The latter two companies formed a global strategic alliance aimed at establishing joint ventures for the development and marketing of pharmaceutical consumer health products. This alliance was seen by both as providing a critical mass on R&D. The picture was complicated in 1995 when Bayer bought part of Sterling's assets from Smith-Kline-Beecham, now an English company that bought Sterling from Kodak.

Success stories of joint ventures are atypical; the failure rate in joint venturing is high. GE's experience is typical. In the case of both the CAT scanner and Magnetic Resonance Imaging, GE developed the technology and licensed it to the joint venture. The Japanese partner (Yokogawa) refined the design and developed a lower cost product. The GE joint venture with Fanuc in machine tool controls is an excellent organization, and both have shared in the outcomes. Sumitomo's experience is that the international joint venture with U.S. firms is a powerful means, combining technical skills of parties where both parties learn.

One company in one field can have a spectrum of alliances. Figure 9.1 illustrates the array of alliances in biotechnology and the mean for one company. Alliances within one company can cover a broad array of fields. During the period 1982-1989, Du Pont technical alliances fell into seven broad categories (figure 9.2). Figure 9.1 also emphasizes that the form of linkages is varied even in one company within one field. Some of the relationships provide for close interaction; in others, the organization for technology flow is much looser. For example, Mazda and Ford have had interactions over two decades, while the relationship between Ford and Nissan is less than five years old. In characterizing the relationship with Mazda, the CEO of Ford said, "It is one of the family, the others are just friends."

Figure 9.1
Array of Alliances in Biotechnology

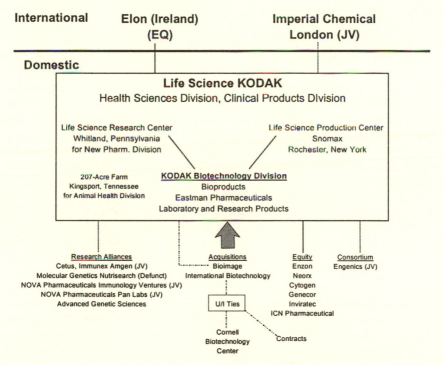

Source: L.S. Peters, unpublished database on technical alliance, Center for Science and Technology Policy, School of Management, Rensselaer Polytechnic Institute.

Figure 9.2
Du Pont Technical Alliances by Industrial Group

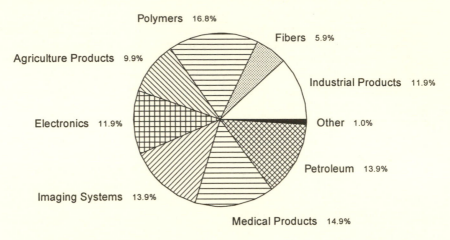

Source: Derived from data in Du Pont annual reports.

There is a long history of technical alliances between the United States and Japanese-based firms (Peters 1987). Originally much of the technical know-how transfer flowed from the United States to Japan. The nylon industry in Japan was built upon technology imported from the United States. The microelectronics industry in Japan as well as in the United States arose from technology licensing activities of U.S. firms, such as Bell Laboratories and RCA. In about 1973, Japan started selling technology.

Data based on statistics collected by the Japanese government illustrate the growth of technical alliances in various industrial sectors since 1950. These are cases of technology importation, but a closer review indicates that many involve technical exchange. Technology importation in the high-tech sectors indicates the increasing prevalence of ties even in these extremely competitive fields (Peters 1987).

United States–Japan technical alliances represent a significant portion of technical alliances in many industries: semiconductors, machine tools, communication equipment, computer-related technology, agrichemicals, and pharmaceuticals. But, as table 9.3 emphasizes, if all European-based firms are considered, the European-U.S. technical connection is still the most significant.

Previous studies show that we are approaching a technical parity between the two countries, the United States and Japan (Peters 1987). Of consequence is that the number of U.S.-Japanese technology agreements continues to rise, despite the fact that the technology gap continues to narrow. During the 1980s, Japanese companies were increasingly interested in investing in young R&D biotechnology ventures. A substantial acquisition was Chugai Pharmaceutical Company's $100 million purchase of Gen-Probe, Inc. Sumitomo Chemical invested $10 million in Regeneron Pharmaceuticals, a company that is studying ways to treat neurological

Table 9.3
Percentage of Total International Technical Alliances Recorded in the Dialog
Database for Japan, the United States, and Europe for Two Time Periods

Region	January 1979-1983	January 1984-1988
U.S.-Japan	24%	28%
U.S.-Europe	65%	61%
Europe-Japan	11%	11%

Source: L.S. Peters, unpublished database on technical alliance, Center for Science and Technology
   Policy, School of Management, Rensselaer Polytechnic Institute.

problems. Mygogen, a company developing biopesticides, has joint ventures with Japan Tobacco and Kubota.

The prevalence of types of technical alliances can be associated with industry sector. In pharmaceuticals, licensing is the predominant form of technical alliance. In the chemical industry, major technical alliance activities are licensing and joint ventures. In telecommunications, joint ventures are far more important than licensing arrangements (Peters 1987; Peters 1997).

University-Industry Research Ties

Another source of R&D not often considered in analyses of foreign firms is university-industry research. U.S. universities have attracted significant non-U.S. corporate support. Shiseido of Japan, for example, in 1989, contracted to provide $85 million over a period of ten years to Harvard's Massachusetts General Hospital, and Hoechst of Germany made a similar contract with Mass General in the early 1980s. In 1990, Ciba-Geigy of Switzerland agreed to fund University of California-San Diego $20 million during six years for research on arthritis. More recently in 1992, Sandoz of Switzerland made a ten year arrangement with Scripps Research Institute promising $300 million over a period of ten years to conduct research in immunology, nervous system, and cardiovascular disease and for exclusive rights to research outcomes. Supported by Hoffman-La Roche, researchers at the University of Texas' Anderson Cancer Center are collaborating with Mexican researchers on a new cancer therapy. BASF has established a biotechnology unit in a Biotechnology Park associated with universities in Worcester, Massachusetts.

A survey of 110 Japanese subsidiaries operating in the United States revealed that about 40 percent of the participants had collaborative activities with U.S. universities. This survey also found that Japanese corporations intend to increase their ties with foreign academic institutions (Peters 1991b). The Center for Public Integrity reported that, during the period 1986-1991, nearly 100 U.S. academic institutions received money from Japanese services. Harvard University received the most, over $93 million.

European companies, especially German companies, look toward U.S. research universities because, according to European company representatives, professors in the United States are used to designing research projects with a goal and benchmark toward reaching that goal. The excellence of continental research is recognized, but the structure and priorities are not deemed to be as conducive to research cooperation as is the U.S. system.

There is a continuing ambiguity regarding the nature of the university as a resource for industrial innovation. Governments support university research on the premise that universities will be the basis for industries of the future. Academic researchers frequently see their connections to companies as a way for companies to access new products or processes. Companies see their connections with university research as a vehicle for pointing them in the right direction or steering them away from venues that may not be fruitful to pursue, at least in terms of return on investment. Firms view university-industry connections as a help in the progress of innovation, but not as a driver.

Turning to issues of an international scope, we must reconcile the essentially domestic character of universities with the current influx of international activity. Many research universities believe they should not accept funding from foreign sources, either from foreign governments or companies, because it may result in conflicts over intellectual property. Universities would be selling themselves to the highest bidder. People fear that their nation could lose control of its most valuable resource—its research universities. But now, as research funding becomes more difficult to obtain, universities may be cutting off a major financial source, which could threaten their capacity to remain in the forefront of science and technology scholarship. Furthermore, strong international university-industry relations contribute to the general reservoir of technology and science and engineering knowledge. These industry-university relationships also provide students with a greater understanding of the changing character of the international workplace.

Public opinion and government policies are ambivalent about interactions of foreign companies with U.S. universities, and statements by officials and the media are inconsistent. Are foreign laboratories in the United States getting cheap access to scientific advances funded by U.S. taxpayers, or are U.S. universities strengthened by the added financial support and exposure to international technical developments provided by foreign laboratories? The subject should be considered in more detail than is possible here (Peters 1993b; Fusfeld 1994, 201-206; Peters 1995b).

In practice, U.S. universities are generally receptive to cooperative working relationships with foreign laboratories, recognizing the professional value of the interaction as well as the access to added funds. The foreign laboratory does obtain some leverage from the broad range of activity at the university supported by other funding sources, as is equally true for universities of its home country, and therefore has an obligation to conduct its interaction as a two-way street with reasonable limitations on exchanging proprietary information.

University cooperation can be influenced by government agencies that fund nationally about 85 percent of all university R&D. The federal government, providing

55 percent to 60 percent, has concerns for national security that have in the past raised questions about foreign participation in areas of supercomputing and advanced materials. The states, however, which account for 25 percent to 30 percent of university R&D support, emphasize their interest in regional economic development, an objective to which foreign laboratories can contribute.

Participation in National Programs

Next consider foreign participation in federal R&D programs. Here foreign firm alliances in the United States have been minimal. Indeed, federal programs for support of industrial R&D activity can be ambiguous with regard to participation by foreign laboratories. An initiative in the early 1990s by the Defense Advanced Research Projects Agency (recently reconverted from DARPA to ARPA) to provide technical advances that might stimulate a U.S. HDTV industry was not receptive to proposals from U.S.-based foreign-owned technical groups. However, the Advanced Technology Program (ATP) of the Department of Commerce, a major effort to encourage new and exploratory concepts for commercial application, does permit support for U.S.-based industrial R&D that can lead to U.S. manufacture if successful. Units of foreign companies can be funded in this program. The funding, which reached about $850 million in the mid-1990s, was often attacked as "corporate welfare" and threatened by Congress.

Government encouragement for cooperative R&D by industry has been demonstrated for specific industries by the use of major government funding to match equal funds from a consortium of companies. The best known of these is Sematech to advance semiconductor manufacturing processes. Initially funded at $200 million annually, half from industry and half from ARPA, this program was not open to foreign companies. Its objectives were to improve the competitiveness of the U.S. semiconductor industry and to insure a U.S.-based capability for the manufacture of fabrication equipment. This mixture of economic and defense objectives was not a receptive base for foreign participation.

Somewhat different motivations have stimulated government matching funds for consortia in the auto industry, including the U.S. Advanced Battery Consortium to stimulate development of electric vehicles and the initiative to develop a "car of the future" that will vastly increase the miles per gallon performance. The principal force behind these activities is environmental and energy conservation. It is not clear that the aim is to benefit U.S.-owned companies, since there is now widespread recognition and acceptance of the substantial manufacturing facilities within the United States of Japanese and German auto companies. There would appear to be no critical objections to participation by these companies in the government-supported R&D consortia.

There is great pressure to use the advanced facilities and technical personnel of the national laboratories on behalf of industry. The missions of these laboratories in defense and energy require less effort today than during the Cold War period. Nevertheless, those missions are still important, and there is strong political opposition to major reduction or elimination of such large facilities as Oak Ridge, Argonne, Livermore, or Sandia.

Cooperative R&D programs with industry are therefore encouraged and pursued vigorously, notably by Argonne. Since economic growth is the key objective, there is no technical objection to participation in such programs by foreign laboratories. There is, however, great sensitivity to the enormous public investment in the facilities and staff at these laboratories and to the fact that much scientific knowledge and technical know-how were developed within highly classified programs. This sensitivity may continue to limit great activity or very large programs with foreign companies.

STRATEGIES OF FOREIGN SUBSIDIARIES

The previous section discussed aspects of foreign R&D not typically found in other analyses. This section continues to narrow the focus to specific R&D strategies of MNCs operating in the United States. The MNCs studied were ABB, Bayer, Matsushita, Philips, and Thomson. All have distinct technology management and reporting relationships. All companies have long histories and, except for ABB and Matsushita, were founded in the last half of the nineteenth century. ABB was created in 1987 through a merger of Asea (Sweden) and Brown Boveri (Switzerland). Each of the two merged companies was also founded in the last quarter of the twentieth century. Thomson was originally a U.S. company. Thomson-House and Edison merged to form GE in 1892. During the depression of 1893, the international divisions were sold off, and the French arm became Thomson. Other divisions were sold to Britain and Brazil. Thomson grew in France in parallel to GE's growth in the United States.

All companies studied have extensive and long-term commitments to R&D. They are all in multiple businesses that require excellence in several technologies. Corporate research facilities in the firm's national home base were an important feature of each of the companies studied, but each of the firms studied had multiple foreign R&D sites. All companies except Matsushita secured at least part of their global technical facilities through acquisition. Table 9.2 above gives summary statistics such as sales, R&D intensity, and number of research personnel for each company studied.

U.S. laboratories of the corporations studied covered a broad spectrum of U.S. experience and capability. All companies except Matsushita had corporate-like R&D activities in the United States. Only Philips and Bayer said they were explicitly interested in new product development as well as supporting existing businesses. The R&D efforts of the other three companies were primarily directed at supporting existing businesses in their home base as well as the United States.

For all the companies studied, only one (Philips) conducted significant R&D activity in the United States before 1980. Three initially established their U.S. R&D activity through acquisition of U.S. companies, and two initially entered through greenfield investment in R&D. The three companies that initially came to the United States because of U.S. R&D strengths already had significant presence in the United States when they established their R&D activity, except perhaps for Philips. Philips concurrently established R&D in the United States and an operating presence through acquisition. Bayer originally was most focused on market access when it acquired a U.S. technology company and only later focused on building up a U.S. R&D capability as they recognized the strength of U.S. R&D capabilities in particular areas. ABB was focused on its own globalization as it acquired U.S. companies with R&D capabilities. It does not plan to invest in new U. S. R&D sites but is using some of the R&D sites as an extension of corporate R&D, which is primarily conducted in Switzerland and Germany. Only one company (Philips) had a dedicated corporate R&D laboratory in the United States.

The size of U.S. laboratories varied from 15 to 330. Bayer had the largest research laboratory (330), similar in size to the Philips laboratory (300), and also had the largest number of scientists in the United States: 2,575. While each Matsushita laboratory was small, in total they had over 200 researchers in the United States.

Steering committees composed of researchers and business representatives were all part of the project selection procedures of case-study firms. In all companies, there has been recent effort to set up special projects, seminars, and meetings to facilitate developing synergies among the diverse technologies and global assets supported by each corporation. An additional objective of these efforts was to assist in company coordination of R&D. Each company has found such coordination to be difficult.

ANALYSIS OF CASES

The one finding that can be used to describe the R&D operations in the United States for the five MNCs examined in detail is that each is unique. The organizational structure and the functions conducted by the U.S. technical organizations are determined by *(i)* the origin of each unit, *(ii)* the structure of the parent corporation, and *(iii)* the strategic growth plans of the parent company, particularly with regard to the United States. No two of the companies studied are alike in these three conditions. There are indications in several cases of the role of the chief technical officer, which is unique in each case. Nevertheless, a number of observations that bear on managerial choices and therefore on managerial efficiency are useful.

Origin: Acquisition or Expansion

Decision making regarding the establishment of each laboratory was complex. The extent of relevant technology activity, the existence of manufacturing capabilities, the availability of high quality technical professionals and the open U.S. culture, as well as the universality of English, were all aspects of the desirability of establishing a U.S. laboratory.

Nevertheless, special circumstances in each case propelled the companies studied to set up U.S. foreign R&D. Whether the U.S. technical activities are principally due to being part of an acquisition or to a planned expansion as part of the parent corporation's strategy is a matter of degree. ABB established itself in the United States by acquisition, particularly of Combustion Engineering, but then initiated a laboratory in the Research Triangle. Bayer also moved into U.S. markets by acquisition but then proceeded to expand R&D within those acquisitions. None of the companies studied had initiated a laboratory outside of an operating unit except for the long-term contractual arrangement of Thomson with the David Sarnoff Laboratory, which Thomson inherited as part of the acquisition of the consumer electronics business of GE. While that relationship appears to be serving an important function for Thomson, it is not likely that it would have been initiated except for the acquisition.

Control: Central Research or Business Group

Only Philips has a major U.S. research laboratory reporting to the corporate chief technical officer of the parent company. This is a recent organizational change, as the Briarcliff laboratory grew within North American Philips (NAP), and its mission was primarily to support the product lines of NAP. Bayer has all U.S. research activities within operating divisions; but the growth of a research center near Yale University and the major commitment in biotechnology, while part of the Pharmaceuticals Division of Miles, were both pursued in close cooperation with the corporate central research group in Germany. The U.S. technical groups of ABB, Matsushita, and Thomson, including the programs at the David Sarnoff Laboratory, report to business groups.

R&D Directors: United States or Home Country

Bayer is the only one of the five cases that had transferred a research executive from the parent company to head a U.S. research center, and that was the one most closely related to corporate central research. Most technical groups of Bayer in the United States and all R&D activities in the United States of the other companies are headed by U.S. citizens. That statement does not necessarily hold for the top business executives of U.S. operations, but it is generally true in that area as well. For years, NAP always had a chief executive from the Netherlands, but that changed several years ago when Stephen Tumminello, a twenty-five-year executive at NAP, was named chief executive officer. The prevalence of U.S. research directors is consistent with the fact that the research groups fall within business units that were acquired.

Interactions with U.S. Universities

All companies viewed interactions with U.S. universities as desirable. Bayer has substantial interactions in biotechnology, partly due to history, partly to the nature of the field. The fact that George Scangos came to Bayer from a professorship at Johns Hopkins is another factor. On the other hand, Matsushita and Thomson have minimal interactions with U.S. universities. Philips maintains reasonable contact with universities, as expected in a rapidly advancing technical area. The U.S. group at Briarcliff has a particular responsibility to maintain awareness of U.S. technical and policy developments as a function of the corporate central research staff. ABB has established an R&D group in the Research Triangle, which may encourage interactions with the three universities there, but there are not extensive university relations generally on the part of ABB, Matsushita, and Thomson. Since Matsushita has much of its technical activity headquartered at Panasonic near Princeton, it may be assumed that members of the technical staff maintain some interactions with both Princeton and Rutgers.

Technical Alliances

Philips and many other similar multinationals like to consider their technology base as proprietary. Therefore, they consider technological cooperation with suspicion. Despite these doubts, Philips is engaged in a substantial number of alliances for direct business reasons as well as to obtain indirect benefits. The advantages and disadvantages of participation in any one agreement shift over time, in part because of dynamic technological environments. Of nine joint ventures referred to in a 1987 speech by the then Philips research director P. Kramer, none have survived, although a few new joint ventures have been established.

Two categories of technological cooperation were distinguished. The first category is cooperation involving mutual goals, most often between enterprises. Also in this category is cooperation with universities and scientific institutes. The second category is cooperation involving government control and funding. Included in these programs are the U.S. Advanced Technology Program (ATP) program, Eureka, and the European Union programs. Philips' experiences suggest that, while government subsidies are important catalysts for cooperation, business aspects come first when deciding on participation. This can be complicated by various kinds of political constraints. Such constraints can affect openness in choice of partner and content or methodology.

Mobility of Technical Personnel

All the companies studied encourage extensive communication between U.S. technical groups and their counterparts in the parent company. Personal travel is also encouraged, though limited by the greater expense. Perhaps surprisingly, there are no substantial exchanges of technical personnel wherein a number of researchers on one side of the Atlantic or Pacific are stationed for a year or more on the other side. Where some individuals have had such assignments, it has usually been from the parent corporation to the U.S. technical group. The assignment of George Scangos to Bayer in Germany is a notable exception. There are several such instances in companies not among the five cases studied, as for example at Hoechst. One U.S. citizen from Hoechst Celanese headed a major division of the central research laboratory in Germany, while another headed a Hoechst laboratory in Japan. However, these are exceptions, and there have not been any significant exchanges of research personnel to or from the U.S. laboratories.

Corporate Strategies and Management

The interrelationship between the management structure of U.S. technical activities and corporate strategy is complex and changing. In terms of subsidiary strategy to ensure longevity, the initial objective tends to be directed toward developing a distinctive competence that is recognized globally. For example, early on, Philips developed a more efficient ballast for its lighting business, and Matsushita developed expertise in digital time based correction. Then Matsushita leveraged that knowledge to become the company champions for digital based picture tube development. ABB's combustion engineering and Thomson's picture tube laboratory in liaison with the David Sarnoff Research Center already had a technological competence that the rest of the company did not have.

The challenge remains to maintain that competence. Bayer's West Haven and California laboratories became the world technological centers for Bayer's biotechnology efforts. Gaining distinctive competence is usually followed by an effort to gain legitimacy for that competence. Lobbying about these capabilities over and above mere communication with the business groups and the corporate center back home has proven to be essential. With the exception of Thomson, R&D groups in the United States are mainly intended to strengthen global corporate business operations. This is frequently accomplished by first supporting requirements for operating in the United States.

All the companies attempt to decentralize their business operations, which in turn exercises control over their own technical groups required for their current business and future growth. The direct relation between each U.S. technical group and an existing business activity is most clear-cut in the case of Matsushita, reasonably so for Thomson, but somewhat more complex for Philips, ABB, and Bayer. Both ABB and Bayer work at obtaining benefits for worldwide corporate interests from the technical developments conducted by U.S. groups. Even though those groups are responsible to U.S. business executives, their technical expertise is counted on for corporate-wide contributions when this is relevant. ABB uses a detailed network of Technology Program Areas to involve necessary skills throughout the company, and Bayer has broad corporate business groups that encompass U.S. activities. The present chief executive officer of Bayer's Pharmaceutical Division once headed the research center in West Haven. The programs headed by George Scangos in biotechnology, while administratively within Miles, Inc., are intended to support broader corporate interests in Bayer. Recent restructuring at Philips integrated the U.S. Briarcliff laboratory with the corporate research activity in Eindhoven, but the U.S. group still feels responsible for supporting U.S. operating groups.

The management principle of decentralization of business units, implying a degree of self-sufficiency of resources to pursue the business of each unit, is compromised to a degree by another management principle. This principle is the increasingly critical determination to obtain the most effective use of all technical resources within the corporation for the benefit of the entire corporation. The U.S. technical groups examined in this study are directly concerned with the U.S. business objectives, except for Philips, but are expected to contribute to corporate-wide business groups (such as Thomson Consumer Electronics in France or Bayer Pharmaceutical Division in Germany) or to programs of corporate central research (such as projects in an ABB Technology Program Area). There is potential conflict in this attempt to superimpose corporate R&D requirements on divisional responsibilities, but the cost of technical advances and the complex demands of global marketing require flexibility in the management and coordination of foreign laboratories. The success of the overall system depends strongly on the personality and leadership of the chief technical officer, clear directives from the corporate chief executive officer, and good working relationships among the group executives of the corporation. While a weakness in any of these criteria can do damage even to a purely domestic corporation, it can do irreparable harm to an MNC seeking market share in foreign markets that require strengths in rapidly changing technologies.

Each of the companies studied has established a system that fits its corporate strategy, structure, and technical base. One element common to all cases is the sense of continuing adaptation to changing conditions. Restructuring R&D to address global change is a continuing activity at ABB, Philips, Matsushita, Thomson, and Bayer. They are all concerned with making more effective use of global technical resources. International strategic alliances with U.S. companies as well as universities were frequently a part of this thrust. Matsushita, Thomson, ABB, Philips, and Bayer focused on global markets as part of their R&D strategies, and all except perhaps Thomson and Matsushita were explicitly internationalizing their R&D activities. Each company studied, except Bayer, had recently undergone restructuring in its corporate R&D department as a response to changing technological environments. In each case, the restructuring seemed to result in establishing closer ties of the U.S. laboratory to home base corporate research activities and in maintenance or growth of the U.S. R&D capability. In the case of Philips, there have been major corporate changes in the past few years, resulting in a U.S. citizen coming to Eindhoven as chief technical officer, followed by a shift in having the Philips Laboratories report to the CTO directly. ABB also brought a U.S. citizen to Zurich as CTO, and his focus has been on effective coordination of all technical resources.

Thomson and Matsushita, together with Philips, are running hard to keep up with the demands and opportunities of the fast-moving electronics fields. Bayer's moves reflect comparable changes in biotechnology. One interesting note, possibly related to the need to sense changing conditions and adapt, is that there is no intention to reduce significantly R&D activity in the U.S. for the companies studied, despite pressures in the home country on costs and profits. Indeed, there seems to be a predisposition to refrain, if possible, from cutting U.S. R&D operations. The stability and even growth of the U.S.-based R&D can be based on the size of the U.S. market and the new health of the U.S. economy, the continuing leadership of U.S. science and technology in many fields, and possibly a concern with public relations and the potential impact of U.S. policies on foreign laboratories. This subject will be discussed separately in the next section.

Technology

Another general observation is that the history and the technology cores of the multinational constrain as well as provide opportunities for the subsidiary R&D. In choosing a technological competence for the foreign laboratory, one has to balance the needs of the local laboratories with the technical capabilities of the home laboratory. There are constraints on the scope of technological possibilities for the foreign laboratory. The power balance of the importance of the home laboratory usually must be maintained. In addition the administrative heritage of the home company needs to be communicated to facilitate technology transfer and harmonization of strategies. Travel budgets must be adequate, and exchanges must be frequent to accomplish this. One manager spent two years in the company's home country base to be able to lead the U.S. laboratory and felt that more time would have to be spent there if his responsibilities were to be increased.

The companies studied covered a broad range of technologies from chemicals to electronics to power generation. The organization of R&D was always in some manner related to the type of technology and the stage of its development as well as the political and social characteristics of its use. When companies such as Bayer successfully cover a diverse technology base, there is similar diversity in R&D structure and management. In Bayer, the organization of biotechnology research was entrepreneurial. In agricultural pesticide research, it was more traditional and focused on testing. Different kinds of infrastructure were needed for each. The influence of social and political factors is demonstrated by the activities and organization of the three laboratories we studied involved in HDTV research. The U.S. FCC nonacceptance of either a Philips-based or a Japanese-based standard and new research discoveries by AT&T refocused R&D efforts in this area on the U.S. market and encouraged foreign company laboratories to tie their research efforts to the U.S. technical institutional base.

Cultural Considerations

Managers must take into account cultural differences in innovation behavior in the host country and home country. Discussion with the laboratory directors highlighted some of these differences. For example, the Japanese initial response to a problem is to find specific solutions, whereas U.S. citizens are more apt to solve the general problem and later address the specifics. Staffing must therefore be considered within the context of the characteristics of the innovation style of the host nation as well as in terms of laboratory and company objectives. The individualistic style and the value placed on autonomy in the U.S. culture is embodied in a greater predisposition to flexible management procedures such as allowing funding off budget, loose monitoring, and the acceptance of bootstrap operations. Such approaches are extremely valuable for the beginning stages of innovation. Where the desire for radical innovation is part of the corporate strategy, then U.S. cultural control of the laboratory can be important. Bayer's interest in new biotechnology products and appointment of a U.S. citizen to run its U.S. biotechnology operations is an example. Where the objective is technology transfer from the home company, tight control from the home operation is important. Matsushita management style is an example.

An advantage of the United States is that its history of providing a home to many cultures provides a diversity of culturally related behaviors. Differences in innovation behavior can be a barrier to efficient technology transfer and communication of objectives between the home laboratories and the U.S.-based laboratories. The Japanese apparent need for a consensus building approach to development sometimes leads to a failure either to accept or to reject a project. The predisposition of U.S. citizens to expect immediate response creates frustration. Without an immediate "go ahead," U.S. citizens begin to devise alternative solutions or devise new objectives only to be surprised when the home country managers come back in full support of the initial approach.

Managers have to devise programs to take advantage of the innovation styles and institutional technological base of the host country. With regard to the companies studied, tying into the institutional base of the United States was somewhat problematic. Some of the laboratories studied were not tied into the U.S. university system to the extent desired. In most cases, this was related to time constraints and a lack of explicit company policy regarding technological networking, but not always. A Philips objective is to increase ties with U.S. government laboratories and universities. Yet they were not allowed to participate in some instances, because of export control regulations and issues related to "national treatment" and maintaining the competitiveness of U.S. firms.

Measuring the Value of Foreign-Owned U.S. R&D Laboratories

The success of the U.S. laboratory in part depends on management's effective use of U.S. attributes but also depends upon the laboratory continually positioning itself to be responsive to U.S. resources and policy change. Evaluating the success of each of these laboratories studied seems related in part to communication concerning their distinctive competencies. Each of the laboratories is probably too new to determine its overall value to the survival of the corporation, except perhaps for the Philips laboratory, which continues to be invaluable to Philips by maintaining a balance among supplying support to local operations, being a resource for new corporate initiatives, and rescuing the corporation from a Eurocentric technological view. It appears that foreign laboratories, even more than the home-based corporate laboratories, must on the whole be more opportunistic and adept at information brokering than the corporate laboratories at home, to be truly and continually an asset for the corporation.

CONCLUDING COMMENTS ON MANAGERIAL EFFICIENCY AND POLICY

Gray (1995) has suggested the importance of considering managerial efficiency in the next generation of articulating Dunning's (1988) eclectic theory of multinational firms. This chapter has thus gone inside the black box to consider what some elements of managerial efficiency might entail regarding the internationalization of R&D.

Consideration of the evidence presented suggests that behavioral models developed to explain the internationalization of R&D must consider an association between information cost reduction and technology generation capabilities. This generation capacity apparently is increasingly required in some industries in order to obtain information about markets and government policy (such as standard setting and regulation) as well as about technology per se. There is a political economic ring to all this. One has to have new information to get more new information. It is not a matter merely of trading, but of being at a level that helps the organization seek out and understand what is important. The type of technology and character of technology–market development affects the processes of R&D internationalization.

Firm technology and administrative legacies limit management choices about international R&D structure. Accumulation of technical know-how is important (Peters, 1992a), and we expect this is increasingly true in sophisticated technical markets.

But information cost reduction is not sufficient. Activities aimed at efficient use of information are required. For an R&D subsidiary, this is often manifested in gaining distinctive competence apart from the home R&D organization. Information gathering alone is not enough to maintain internationalization. Packaging the information is part of the job. We expect that the balancing requirements for information cost reduction, use, and packaging with technology generation is different for determining managerial efficiency at home and abroad. Thus, managerial efficiency for R&D internationalization is tied to location and markets. There is an international science and technology tax that is reduced by investment in R&D and is affected by national innovation systems.

Multiple modes of activity at least by experienced firms suggest that the level of R&D investment is not the only story. A projection can be made that R&D activity portfolios can be as important as magnitude of R&D investment. Managing these activities to efficiently source and use information must be a managerial objective. The next step thus requires exploration of how the number of R&D projects and character of the R&D portfolio impact managerial efficiency and are associated with information sourcing, use, and packaging.

The policy implications of these observations are complex. The results of the author's study point to an existing complex network of technology generation capability within the United States that foreign firms are free to access and source information. But these firms also contribute to the network. Japanese firms may be more likely to emphasize information sourcing than information investment, but they also appear to be entering the U.S. innovation system through new investment as opposed to acquisition, which is the main route for European-based internationalization of R&D. The global economy can lead to a situation in which a U.S. company can benefit from a foreign technical advance or that technical alliances and global networks can add to the technical base of the United States. Yet, the perception of the United States that often permits its own technical strengths, assisted by public funds, to benefit foreign companies to the detriment of U.S. industry must be considered by policy makers. Related policy issues are considered in depth in the final part of this book.

NOTE

Data on the international R&D activity of multinational firms primarily rely on the author's data on more than 5,000 technical alliances, on materials assembled about the characteristics of R&D activities of 400 leading MNC R&D spenders, and on research begun in 1979 when site visits were conducted at more than 100 universities and companies to explore their motivations for participating in university-industry research relationships (Peters and Fusfeld 1982). The database was assembled using ABI Inform, Dialog Predicast Prompt information sources, The Funk and Scott Index of Corporate Change, and information from industrial R&D associations and corporate directories. This material was supplemented with information from company annual reports and structured interviews with top level technical executives representing more than 100 companies having a home base in either the Pacific Rim, the United States, or Europe. Multiple interviews were conducted at more than twenty sites over a period of ten years. Interviews with company representatives focused on the characteristics of the R&D conducted at different sites, the functions of different types of laboratories, reporting procedures, management coordination techniques, external sourcing of technology and research, mechanisms used for transferring and commercializing laboratory results, and outcomes and changes in these factors over time. Among the topics discussed was the value of academic institutions as an external source of technology and the intensity of the firms' connections with universities.

REFERENCES

Bartlett, Christopher A., and Sumantra Ghoshal. 1989. *Managing Across Borders: The Transnational Solution*. Boston, Mass.: Harvard Business School Press.

Behrman, Jack N., and William A. Fischer. 1980. "Transnational Corporations: Market Orientations and R&D Abroad," *Columbia Journal of World Business*, Fall, pp. 55-60.

Cheng, Joseph L. C., and Douglas S. Bolon. 1993. "The Management of Multinational R&D: A Neglected Topic in International Business Research," *Journal of International Business Studies*, 24(1):1-18.

Cordell, A. J. 1971. *The Multinational Firm, Foreign Direct Investment and Canadian Science Policy*, Special Study. Ottawa: Science Council of Canada.

Creamer, Daniel B. 1976. *Overseas Research and Development by United States Multinationals 1966-1975: Estimates of Expenditures and a Statistical Profile*. New York: The Conference Board.

Dalton, Donald H., and Manuel G. Serapio, Jr. 1993. *U.S. Research Facilities of Foreign Companies*, Department of Commerce, Technology Administration, Japan Technology Program. Washington, D.C.: GPO.

de Meyer, Arnoud, and Atsuo Mizushima. 1989. "Global R&D Management," *R&D Management* 19(2):135-146.

Dosi, Giovanni, C. Freeman, R. Nelson, G. Silverberg, and Luc Soete, eds. 1988. *Technical Change and Economic Theory*. London: Pinter Publishers, Ltd.

Dunning, John H. 1988. *Multinationals, Technology and Competitiveness*. London: Unwin Hyman, p. 280.

———. 1993. *Multinational Enterprises and the Global Economy*. Wokingham: Eddison-Wesley.

Erickson, Tamara J. 1991. "Competing with Technology in the World Arena," *Journal of Business Strategy* 12(March/April):11-16.

Fusfeld, Herbert I. 1994. *Industry's Future: Changing Patterns of Industrial Research*. Washington, D.C.: American Chemical Society (Books).

Granstrand, O., Lars Håkanson, and S. Sjölander. 1993. "Internationalization of R&D—A Survey of Some Recent Research," *Research Policy* 22:413-430.

Gray, H. Peter. 1995. "The Eclectic Paradigm: The Next Generation," to be presented at the Meetings of the European International Business Association, Urbino, December.

Hagedoorn, John, and Jos Schakenraad. 1990. "Technology Cooperation, Strategic Alliances and Their Motives: Brother, Can You Spare A Dime, Or Do You Have a Light?" Paper presented at Strategic Management Society Conference, Stockholm, September 24-17.

Håkanson, Lars. 1981. "Organization and Evolution of Foreign R&D in Swedish Multinationals," *Geografiska Annaler* 63B:47-56.

Hirschey, R. C., and Richard E. Caves. 1981. "Research and Transfer of Technology by Multinational Enterprises," *Oxford Bulletin of Economics and Statistics* 43:115-130.

Howells, Jeremy. 1990. *The Location and Organization of Research and Development: New Horizons*. New York: Elsevier Science Publisher B.V., pp. 133-146.

Juul, M., and Peter G.P. Walters. 1987. "The Internationalization of Norwegian Firms—A Study of the U.K. Experience," *Management International Review* 27:58-66.

Kenney, Martin, and Richard L. Florida. 1993. "The Organization and Geography of Japanese R&D: Results from a Survey of Japanese Electronics and Biotechnology Firms," *Research Policy* 23:305-323.

Mansfield, Edwin, David J. Teece, and Anthony Romeo. 1979. "Overseas Research and Development by U.S. Based Firms," *Economica* 46(May):187-196.

Mutinelli, M., and Piscitello, P. 1995. "Foreign Direct Investment and Entry Mode Choice: The Influence of Factors Related to Information Costs," in *International Business in the Twenty-First Century, Volume II, International Finance*, edited by Khosrow Fatemi and S. Nichols. Laredo: Texas A&M International University, pp. 405-418.

Office of Technology Assessment (OTA). 1993. *Multinationals and the National Interest: Playing by Different Rules*, OTA-ITE-569. Washington, D.C.: GPO.

Pearce, Robert D. 1988. *The Determinants of Overseas R&D by U.S. MNCs: An Analysis of Industry Level Data*, Department of Economics, June. University of Readings, England.

Perrino, Albert C., and James W. Tipping. 1989. "Global Management of Technology," *Research Technology Management* 32(May/June):12-19.

Peters, Lois S. 1987. "Technical Network between U.S. and Japanese Industry," Center for Science and Technology Policy, Rensselaer Polytechnic Institute, p. 242.

———. 1988. "Export Controls and the International Technical System: The U.S. Agrichemical Industry," Center for Science and Technology Policy, School of Management, Rensselaer Polytechnic Institute, p. 300.

———. 1990. "Export Controls and the International Technical System: The U.S. Pharmaceutical Industry," Center for Science and Technology Policy, School of Management, Rensselaer Polytechnic Institute, p. 300.

———. 1991a. "Internationalization Corporate Telecommunication Alliances: Expanding Our Views of Technology, Organization and National Technical Capability," in *Proceedings of the Congress of Political Economists Convention*, January 9-12, 1991. Boston: Congress of Political Economists.

———. 1991b. "Management of Technology and MNC Globalization," in *Proceedings of the International Trade and Finance Association Conference*, May 31-June 2, 1991. Marseille, France.

———. 1992a. "Technology Management and the Research and Development Activities of Multinational Enterprises," in the *Academy of International Business Northeast U.S.A. Region Best Paper Proceedings*, June 1-2.

———. 1992b. "Technology Strategies of Japanese Subsidiaries and Joint Ventures in the United States," in *Proceedings of the International Trade and Finance Association*, May 31-June 2, 1991. Marseille, France.

———. 1993a. "Technology Strategies of Japanese Subsidiaries and Joint Ventures in the United States," in *International Commercial Policy*, edited by Mordechai E. Kreinin. Bristol, Pa.: Taylor and Francis, p. 221-231.

———. 1993b. "The Multinational and Its Foreign University Connections," in *Proceedings of the Purchase Conference on Academic Industry Relationships*, May. Purchase, New York: Purchase University.

———. 1995a. "Dimensions of Strategic Leadership in Hybrid and Network Organizations," in *Strategic Alliances in High Technology*, vol. 5, edited by Gomez-Mejia and Lawless. Greenwich, Conn.: JAI Press, pp. 172-200.

———. 1995b. "MNC University Collaboration," in *Issues in Commercial Policy*, edited by Mordechai Kreinin. New York: Oxford University Press, pp. 203-210.

————. 1997. "International Technology Cooperation: Generation and Policy," in *International Trade in the 21st Century*, edited by Khosrow Fatemi. Tarrytown, New York: Pergamon, pp. 285-302.

Peters, Lois S., and Herbert I. Fusfeld. 1982. "Current U.S. University-Industry Research Connections," in *University Industry Relationships*. Washington, D.C.: National Science Board, pp. 1-161.

Peters, Lois S., and R. Rufer. 1996. "Competitive World Marketing Strategies: An Evaluation of Strategic Paradigms," in *Proceedings of the International Academy of Business Disciplines*, April 10-14.

Porter, Michael E. 1990. *The Competitive Advantage of Nations*. New York: Free Press, p. 855.

Ronstadt, Robert C. 1977. "International R&D: The Establishment and Evolution of Research and Development Abroad by Seven U.S. Multinationals," *Journal of International Business Studies* 9:7-24.

Wortmann, Michael. 1990. *Multinationals and the Internationalization of R&D: New Developments in German Companies*. New York: Elsevier Science Publishers B.V., pp. 175-183.

Part IV

Corporate Behavior: Political, Social, and Managerial

10

Politically Active Foreign-Owned Firms in the United States: Elephants or Chickens?

Kathleen A. Getz

INTRODUCTION

Scholarly considerations of government relations in international business typically focus on political risk and the need for firms to analyze and guard against it. Recently, however, a number of scholars have broken away from this way of thinking. They suggest that government and its actions are malleable, at least to some extent. Firms can and should try to influence government policies that have potential effects on their operations and profits. To the extent that scholars have attempted to describe and prescribe multinational corporation's political behavior with respect to foreign governments, they have focused primarily on U.S.-based firms operating abroad.

This chapter addresses the question: In what ways is political activity different for foreign multinational corporations (MNCs) operating in the United States? The answer to this question is developed theoretically. Using Dunning's eclectic theory as a guiding framework, the relationships and explanations inherent in five broad social science theories (resource dependency, collective action, transaction cost, agency, and institutions) that have been applied to corporate political strategy are integrated. The analysis yields a general model of corporate political action within which we can begin to understand differences in political action related to the nationality of an MNC's owners.

INTERNATIONAL BUSINESS-GOVERNMENT RELATIONS

Most international business-government relations (IBGR) research assumes that government actors and policies are exogenous to the firm and, therefore, beyond its control. The literature thus stresses identifying governmental constraints, potential areas of conflict, and appropriate business responses (de la Torre 1981; Gladwin and Walter 1980). Much of the research in the area addresses political risk (Behrman 1986; Kobrin 1979, 1982; Kobrin et al. 1980; Raddock 1986; Root 1968), while some empirical work specifically links governmental policies with firms' investment decisions (Contractor 1990; Nigh 1985; Fatehi-Sedeh and Safizadeh 1988; Scholl-hammer and Nigh 1984). In addition, conceptual and empirical works describe the business-government relationship and business structures intended to improve firms' reactions and responses to governmental actions (Baker, Ryans and Howard 1988; Behrman and Grosse 1990; Mahini and Wells 1986; Schollhammer 1975).

Recently some scholars have suggested that business can control or influence government actions, to create economic opportunities or reduce political risk. Conceptual, empirical, and normative works highlight such opportunities and exhort business to include the political environment in their strategic planning (Boddewyn 1975, 1991; Boddewyn and Brewer 1994; Brewer 1992a, 1992b; Toyne 1989). The relationship between the political environment and managerial practices, the interactions between firms and host country governments, and the bargaining power of foreign companies are also topics that have been researched (Fagre and Wells 1982; Jain and Nigh 1989; Kobrin 1987; Poynter 1982, 1986).

In both bodies of work, there has been a tendency for scholars to focus on U.S. companies operating outside the United States. Also, none of the work has acknowledged that business involvement might entail participation in the public policy process. Rather, the general approach has been that policies are immutable. To the extent that business can influence government, the domain of influence is limited to a bilateral relationship (a firm and the government). Thus IBGR research generally focuses on issues such as government requests for increases in local value added, demands for local ownership, and so forth. The specific topic of corporate political action is not addressed.

At least one international business scholar has tried to integrate the political environment into scholarly understanding of the multinational firm (Boddewyn 1988). "Explicit integration of political elements into MNE theory may provide a better understanding of why particular MNEs have succeeded where a purely economic analysis may fail to account for their success" (Boddewyn 1988, 342). While Boddewyn's analysis borrows from several literatures (international economics, political economy, political science, sociology, anthropology, and organization theory), the focus is on eclectic theory (Dunning 1980, 1981, 1988).

This is perhaps the most promising piece in the IBGR literature to serve as a basis for an exploration of the relationship between firm ownership and political action. Though Boddewyn does not focus directly on corporate political action, his effort to relate political involvement to broader theories of international business is interesting. Dunning's (1980, 1981, 1988) eclectic paradigm is now the dominant view of the multinational enterprise, though others have offered alternative or complementary analyses (Knickerbocker 1973; Rugman 1979; Vernon 1974). Thus, we can consider aspects of the eclectic theory, together with literature on corporate political action, to develop an understanding of the political activity of foreign-owned multinational enterprises (MNEs) in the United States. According to Dunning (1988, 5), it is "the juxtaposition of the ownership-specific advantages of firms contemplating foreign production, or an increase in foreign production, the propensity to internalize the cross-border markets for these, and the attractions of a foreign location for production which is the gist of the eclectic paradigm of international production." In the situation under consideration here, location advantages are not of interest, since all firms being considered operate in the United States (that is, there is no variability in location). We thus begin with ownership and internalization advantages, particularly in light of extant theories of U.S. corporate political action.[1]

OWNERSHIP

In the eclectic paradigm, ownership advantages are those characteristics of the firm that are "specific to the nature or nationality of their ownership" (Dunning 1988, 2) and typically include technology and management skills. As Boddewyn (1988) makes clear, ownership advantages may also include political knowledge or expertise. Boddewyn specifies three types of advantage: *(i)* intelligence about political situations, *(ii)* access to political decision makers, and *(iii)* influence skills. For the present purposes, ownership advantages can be broadly defined to include any firm-specific characteristics that may facilitate corporate political activity (CPA), since such attributes may enhance a firm's influence skills. These typically do not derive from nationality of ownership, though there may be some correlation between ownership and the possession of some of the advantages.

Firm Characteristics

The literature of CPA identifies many firm-specific variables that affect a firm's political involvement (both strategic choices and successes). Rehbein and Schuler (1995) suggest that the firm should be viewed as a filter. That is, certain characteristics of the firm influence its interpretation of external variables, thereby altering its choice of political strategy. Although Rehbein and Schuler identify just five such variables, the potential list is quite long: corporate strategy (Buchholz 1990; Gale and Buchholz 1987; Mahini and Wells 1986; Mahon and Waddock 1991; Marcus, Kaufman, and Beam 1987; Shipper and Jennings 1984; Yoffie 1987); firm size (Andres 1985; Baysinger, Keim, and Zeithaml 1987; Boddewyn 1975; Brenner 1980; Epstein 1969; Hillman 1995b; Keim, Zeithaml, and Baysinger 1984; Masters and Baysinger 1985; Masters and Keim 1986; Salamon and Siegfried 1977); firm age, experience, or traditions (Boddewyn 1975; Hillman 1995b; Rehbein and Schuler 1995); profitability (Boddewyn 1975; Salamon and Siegfried 1977); structure, such as existence of government-relations office or locus of control for business government decisions (Brenner 1980; Mahini and Wells 1986; Rehbein and Schuler 1995); resources (Hillman 1995b; Rehbein and Schuler 1995; Yoffie 1987); issue salience (Rehbein and Schuler 1995); diversification (Rehbein and Schuler 1995); and stakeholder dependence (Rehbein and Schuler 1995). The rationale for consideration of these variables typically derives from resource dependency theory, though many scholars have not so specified.[2] One characteristic not included in the list is ownership. Ownership can be characterized in several ways: corporation, partnership, or proprietorship; closely-held or openly-traded; public- or private-sector; and so forth. For this paper, the dichotomy of interest is U.S.-owned versus foreign-owned.

Industry Characteristics

In addition to firm-specific characteristics, there are some industry-level characteristics that affect firms' political behavior. These include concentration (Andres 1985; Masters and Keim 1986; Munger and Rehbein 1988; Pittman 1977; Olson 1965; Salamon and Siegfried 1977; Yoffie 1987) and extent of regulation (Andres 1985; Masters and Baysinger 1985; Masters and Keim 1986; Sabato 1985). The rationale for consideration of these variables typically derives from collective action theory or resource dependency theory. Rehbein and Schuler (1995) show that firm and industry characteristics affect either a firm's willingness or its capability to be politically active (shown in table 10.1).

Table 10.1
Effects of Firm and Industry Characteristics on Willingness and Ability to Engage in Political Activity

Characteristic	Willingness	Ability
Size	+	+
Profitability		+
Resources	X	+
Competitive strategy	X	
Diversification	X	+
Structures	X	X
Experience/traditions	X	X
Issue salience		+
Stakeholder dependence	+	
Industry concentration	+	
Industry regulation	+	

Note: + indicates positive relationship; X indicates nonlinear relationship.

There are many interactions among the firm- and industry-level variables listed herein. Of particular interest in this chapter are the relationships between ownership and each of the other variables. There are some expected differences that may affect political action. For example, U.S.-owned firms are likely to have better developed structures for government relations than those of foreign-owned firms (Mahini and Wells 1986; Schollhammer 1975).

INTERNALIZATION

In the eclectic paradigm, "It must be in the best interests of enterprises that possess ownership-specific advantages to transfer them across national boundaries within their own organizations rather than sell them, or their right of use, to foreign based enterprises" (Dunning 1988, 3). Thus, internalization entails a firm using whatever advantages it has itself, rather than attempting to benefit from those advantages by selling them. Eclectic theory thus is related to traditional transaction cost economics (Williamson 1985), but turns the "make or buy" decision into a "make or sell" decision. In applying eclectic theory to international business-government relations, Boddewyn (1988, 349) reverts to the "make or buy" question by considering whether a firm should perform government relations itself or contract with another actor to do it.

Transaction Cost Theory

This is precisely the question addressed by Kaufman, Englander, and Marcus (1987), as they explicitly apply the logic of transaction cost theory to political action. Transaction cost economics is concerned with identifying the organizational arrangement that most efficiently economizes on transaction costs (Williamson 1985). Using two variables pertinent to the theory (specificity and frequency), Kaufman, Englander, and Marcus (1993) suggest there are four governance structures for political action (see table 10.2). For specific issues (that is, firm and industry interests diverge) that recur with some frequency, a firm should create or enhance its internal issues management/government relations staff. For specific issues that occur only occasionally, a firm should contract out for the services of specialized intermediaries, such as public relations firms or lobbyists. For issues that are non-specific (that is, firm and industry interests converge), a firm should rely on its trade association to manage political action. The trade association can either engage in political action itself (for recurrent issues) or contract out to intermediaries (for occasional issues).

Table 10.2
Issue Characteristics and Structural Choices

	Issue Specificity	
	Nonspecific (Firm and Industry Interests Converge)	Specific (Firm and Industry Interests Diverge)
Issue Frequency		
Recurrent	Firm relies on trade association	Firm relies on internal staff
Occasional	Trade association contracts with specialized intermediaries	Firm contracts with specialized intermediaries

Source: Kaufman, Englander, and Marcus (1987, 158).

The Kaufman, Englander, and Marcus (1987) analysis of political action from the perspective of transaction cost economics is a good start, but the four approaches defined are not exhaustive of all options available to a firm. An important form of collective action, the temporary coalition, is left out. Littlejohn (1986) has noted a trend toward greater use of cooperative activities as firms have begun to define their objectives more precisely. Firms feel free to form coalitions with other actors around specific issues. Coalitions differ from trade association activities in that coalition partners may be drawn from among all groups interested in the issue: there need be no direct linkage with industry members. Therefore, the interests of coalition members are likely to be heterogeneous, with overlap on just a single issue (Wexler 1982). Also, the existence of a coalition can be fleeting. With the resolution of the specific issue, the coalition is likely to dissolve (Oberman 1993).

A second problem with using transaction cost theory to analyze and describe political action is noted: "The power of transaction cost economics derives from its simplifying assumptions and narrow economizing focus, and because of this it ignores important political factors" (Kaufman, Englander, and Marcus 1987, 159). In addition, other noneconomic factors, especially societal factors, are ignored by the transaction cost approach. Kaufman, Englander, and Marcus suggest using agency theory to consider political factors. Institutions theory may also be also to address noneconomic factors, especially with regard to foreign firms engaging in political action in the United States. First, agency theory perspectives on political action are considered, followed by institutions theory perspectives.

Agency Theory

Agency theory deals with relations in which one party acts for another and examines the problems inherent in principal-agent relationships (Mitnick 1984). It has been applied to a wide variety of organizational and interorganizational behaviors. A relation need not be formalized for it to be considered an agency relationship, characterized by agency problems and principal efforts to mitigate those problems (Getz 1993b; Jensen and Meckling 1976). In suggesting that agency theory be used to complement transaction cost theory, Kaufman, Englander, and Marcus (1987) are concerned primarily with the relationship in which the firm is principal and a collective (such as trade association) is agent. This agency relationship has been addressed in the literature on political action (Wahn 1992). Another agency relation in political action that has been considered is that in which the firm is principal and the government official is agent (Getz 1991, 1993a, 1993b; Keim and Baysinger 1988; Weingast 1980). This relationship is the current focus.

There are likely to be problems in an agency relationship (Eisenhardt 1989; Mitnick 1984; Getz 1991, 1993b). The basic problem is failure of perfect agency to occur (Mitnick 1984). Building on the work of Mitnick, Getz (1991; 1993b) focuses on the agency relationship between a firm and government decision makers (whom she terms targets of corporate political action) and highlights problems that can occur as the relationship is created and maintained.

Four agency problems are knowledge (target does not know or understand the position of the firm), skill (target does not understand the issue itself), disposition (target disagrees with the position of the firm), and effort (target does not place high priority on the issue). Getz (1991) explains the conditions under which these problems would occur. Briefly, knowledge problems are likely when a firm has difficulty articulating its position on an issue, when its position is narrow rather than broad in focus, and when information about the issue is complicated. Skill problems are likely when the issue is complex. Disposition problems are likely when there are multiple principals for a target whose interests diverge and when the issue or policy is viewed as having an inherent moral or value component. Disposition problems may be mitigated by a consistency between a firm's interests and the larger public interest and by dependence by the target on the firm for information regarding the issue. Effort problems are likely when a target faces multiple policy problems, as well as when there are multiple principals whose interests diverge. Getz (1991; 1993b) asserts that the occurrence of different agency problems leads to the selection of particular political tactics, since different tactics are useful in resolving particular problems. She lists seven tactics in different combinations for the various problems. Getz's list of tactics, though derived from a review of the literature, is unsystematic. Here we substitute the tactics typology systematically developed by Oberman (1993), linking the tactics to problems (as shown in table 10.3).

Table 10.3
Agency Problems and Political Tactics

Problem Type	Tactics
Knowledge	Lobbying
	Testimony
	Collegial persuasion
Skill	Policy analysis
Disposition	Constituency influence
	Collective organizing
	Advocacy advertising
	Litigation
	PAC contributions
Effort	Constituency influence
	Collective organizing
	PAC contributions
	Litigation
	Advocacy advertising

Source: Getz (1993b) and Oberman (1993).

Institutions Theory

Hillman (1995b) asserts that Getz assumes too much rationality on the part of firms making decisions about political involvement and, most notably, ignores institutional variables that might affect a firm's political behavior. Indeed, institutions theory provides an important complement to both transaction cost and agency theories in understanding fully a firm's choices in the political arena. While transaction cost theory highlights economic considerations and agency stresses political concerns, institutions theory underscores societal factors.

There is no clear and concise definition of the term *institution*.[3] However, the functions of institutions seems to be well-comprehended: institutions "define conditions and set limits for maintaining a stable system; they regulate social relations to maintain conformity with existing value patterns and consistency among these patterns themselves" (Oberman 1993, 215). Examples of institutions are government, education systems, and churches and religions. Hillman (1995b) and Oberman (1993) consider the effects of institutions on corporate political action.

Hillman (1995a) categorizes political behaviors in two ways: strategies and approaches. Following Berry (1977), she divides specific political activities into four strategies or tactics groups: information, direct pressure/access, constituency building, and cooperative (see table 10.4). She also provides the unique insight that a firm's general approach to affecting public policy has a time horizon. With long-term, or relational, approaches, firms are concerned with government relations across issues and across time. With short-term, or transactional, approaches, firms focus on a single issue and single policy. Firms that take this approach may be expected to enter and exit the political arena, rather than sustain a political presence. Hillman notes that this distinction is especially critical to understanding political behavior in cross-national comparisons, given different political institutions and cultures. Hillman (1995a) develops hypotheses regarding three institutional features of countries: corporatism versus pluralism, strong versus weak party control, and tenure of public officials. Expected relationships are shown in table 10.5.

In a more systematic analysis, Oberman (1993) presumes that firms compete within an institutional framework and the framework itself can be appropriated by a firm as a competitive resource. Table 10.6 presents Oberman's typology of resources. He classifies political resources along three dimensions: actor-controlled/institutional, formal/informal, and structure/content. Then he describes political activity as "the attempted transformation of political resources, the ultimate aim of which being an increase (or a prevention of a decrease) in the actor's stock of formal institutional resources (in other words, advantageous government structure or policy)" (Oberman 1993, 216). He then defines political strategy as "the course . . . by which this attempted transformation proceeds" (Oberman 1993, 218). In other words, political activity is the use (or acquisition and use) of political resources to establish desirable political institutions (that is, formal and informal rules, procedures, and norms).

Oberman (1993) goes on to describe political action as communications phenomena aimed at obtaining favorable decisions from policy makers. He identifies eight types of tactics based on three key dimensions: avenue of approach to decision maker (direct or indirect), breadth of transmission (public or private), and content

Table 10.4
Hillman's Political Strategies and Tactics

Strategy	Tactics
Information	Lobbying
	Reporting research and survey results
	Testimony
	Supplying position papers and technical reports
Direct Pressure /Access	Providing financial support through PACs or other means
	Personal service
	Hiring personnel with direct political experience
Constituency Building	Grassroots mobilization of individuals linked to the firm
	Advocacy advertising
	Public image advertising
	Economic or political education
Cooperative	Forming coalitions with other interest groups
	Joining trade associations

Source: Hillman (1995a).

Table 10.5
Institutional Variables and Political Tactics

Variable	Tactics
Corporatist government	Relational approach
	Constituency building
	Cooperative
Pluralist government	Transactional approach
	Information
	Direct pressure/access
Strong party	Cooperative
Weak party	Direct pressure/access
	Constituency building
Tenure of public officials	Relational approach

Source: Hillman (1995a).

Table 10.6
Typology of Political Resources

		Actor Controlled	Institutional
Formal			
		examples	examples
Objective	Structure	formal organization	courts, agencies, legislatures
	Content	material resources	policies, laws, constitutions
Mixed	Structure	informal organization	iron triangles, policy networks
	Content	ideology, group values	political culture, societal values
Subjective	Structure	patterns of group behavior	communication networks
	Content	group perceptions	public opinion
Informal			

Source: Oberman (1993, 217).

of communication (information or pressure). This typology is shown in table 10.7. Institutional rules and norms and possession of institutional resources affect which political tactics a firm can and may employ. For example, effective direct communication requires access that is based on the possession of considerable institutional resources; actors that do not have such resources may be forced to use indirect communication. Furthermore, the particular tactic or combination of tactics used by a firm is also dependent on its policy preference and on the relative strength and resources of the opposition. When the firm is in a position of strength, direct and/or private tactics are expected. In defensive situations in which the challenger has strength, the firm will probably use indirect and public activities, especially if stakes are high.

APPLYING THEORIES TO PROBLEMS

The three theoretical approaches described here have been developed primarily in the context of the political action of U.S. companies and U.S. government (although Hillman does specifically consider governmental institutions outside the United States). In the analysis that follows, these approaches are applied to the question of the political action of foreign MNEs operating in the United States.

The transaction cost approach (Kaufman, Englander, and Marcus 1987) focuses on issue specificity and frequency. U.S.-owned and foreign-owned firms might be expected to face equivalent (though not identical) arrays of recurrent and occasional issues. Regarding issue specificity, there may be some differences based on ownership. In particular, foreign firms may have the same general perspective on issues as the industry as a whole, but there may be certain aspects of the foreign

Table 10.7
Typology of Tactics

Avenue of Approach to Decision Maker	Breadth of Transmission	Content of Communication	Typical Influence Activity
Direct	Public	Information	Official testimony
			Policy analysis
		Pressure	Civil disobedience
	Private	Information	Lobbying
		Pressure	PAC contributions
			Bribery
Indirect	Public	Information	Advocacy advertising
		Pressure	Public exposure
			Constituency influence
	Private	Information	Collegial persuasion
		Pressure	Litigation
			Collective organizing

Source: Oberman, 1993, p. 235.

firms' views that are different. If those aspects are perceived as critical, the firm may feel compelled to break away from the trade association in political action on the issue. Thus, more occasions in which foreign firms experience economic pressure to act alone in the political arena are likely. Of course, the possibility for coalitional collective action exists, provided coalition partners are available.

A key element of agency theory has to do with agency problems. The occurrence of agency problems is likely to vary based on ownership. Knowledge problems are likely when a firm has difficulty articulating its position on an issue or when its position is not broadly shared by other interest groups. Foreign-owned firms may have more difficulty articulating their position to targets because of poor access. Getz (1991) describes access to targets as internal or external. Internal access occurs when the firm is part of a target's "natural" constituency—that is, when the target believes, for whatever reason, that it ought to represent the firm. With internal access, the target may make an effort to learn about the firm's interest in issues or simply may have a better understanding based on knowledge of and experience with the firm in other situations. For foreign-owned firms, access is less likely to be internal than for U.S.-owned firms, though the problem may mitigate over time.

There ought to be few systematic differences based on ownership for the occurrence of skill problems. Skill problems occur most often with complex issues, because targets fail to understand the issue itself. There is no a priori reason to expect that complex issues are more likely to be of interest to either U.S.-owned or foreign-owned firms.

Differences based on ownership are likely to be pronounced for disposition problems, if we assume that government officials act in the public interest. Recall that disposition problems are likely both when there are multiple principals and when the issue is seen as having an inherent value component. Given a public perception that government officials ought to act in the interest of U. S. citizens and a pronounced concern that foreign-owned firms' interests are not consistent with the U.S. public interest (Choate 1990; Olen 1990), there may well be a tendency for targets to prefer courses of action different from those preferred by foreign-owned firms. A key issue here is perceived legitimacy (which, of course, relates to institutions, discussed below). The lower the legitimacy of a firm, the more likely there will be disposition problems in its relation with government officials. The legitimacy of foreign-owned firms operating in a host country varies according to the impetus for foreign production (Behrman and Grosse 1990). Legitimacy is most likely to be questioned for natural resource-seeking firms (such as logging concerns), since they exploit the U.S. natural heritage. For efficiency-seeking firms, legitimacy will be questioned to the extent the firm's policies appear to be determined by the foreign parent. Whatever the reason for foreign investment, the actions of foreign-owned firms are likely to be viewed more skeptically than for U.S.-owned firms.

Effort problems occur when targets fail to consider the interests of the firm important enough to work on, which might occur when there are multiple principals. Though Mitnick (1984) suggests that effort problems occur due to agent laziness, it is possible, at least in the political arena, that opportunism contributes to effort problems. If targets are exclusively or primarily self-interested, as public choice theory suggests (see Buchanan 1984), they may choose to pursue policy only for principals (firms or other interest groups) that can provide some sort of reward. To the extent that foreign firms are perceived as unable to deliver desired rewards, effort problems are more likely for foreign than for U.S. firms.

Two aspects of institutions theory are important. First, do institutional expectations vary depending on ownership? And second, is the ability to obtain and use institutional resources (Oberman 1993) different based on ownership? Although institutions theory has been widely discussed, there is no schedule of acceptable and unacceptable behavior. Behavioral expectations, though stable, are somewhat fluid. Expectations regarding compliance with formal rules (such as laws and regulations) should be the same for both U.S. and foreign firms, with the exception of extra-territorial application of U.S. laws, which, outside the United States, apply only to U.S.-based firms (such as the U.S. Foreign Corrupt Practices Act or various U.S. antitrust laws). Hillman (1995a) implies that at least some informal institutional expectations may be universally applied, though in a different context than is considered here. Other norms and expectations may vary based on ownership, perhaps because of prejudices held by either the public or government decision makers.

A second element of institutions theory is the ability to obtain and use institutional resources (Oberman 1993). As shown in table 10.6, there are numerous institutional resources in the environment, ranging from formal (such as courts, laws) to informal (such as communications networks, public opinion). Oberman suggests that acquisition of informal resources is an instrumental step toward the surer protections of formal institutional resources. Given the legitimacy concerns, described above, foreign MNCs may have more difficulty in obtaining informal institutional resources, such as favorable public opinion. Again, as mentioned above, legitimacy problems need not be everlasting. Over time, with political and social experience, foreign firms may well become accepted by the general public. But so long as they are viewed as foreign, full legitimacy will be difficult to obtain.

CONCEPTUAL MODEL

The analysis thus far can be depicted graphically as shown in figure 10.1, which presents a conceptual model of corporate political action based on the five theoretical perspectives of transaction cost, agency, institutions, resource dependency, and collective action. The effects of collective action and resource dependency are shown to moderate the effects of transaction costs, agency, and institutions. The conceptual model presents a broad theory of political action applicable to all firms and perhaps applicable in all democratic countries. It does not specifically highlight differences in expected corporate political action between U.S.-owned and foreign-owned firms. However, those differences can be discerned by looking beneath the surface simplicity of this model.

Given the analysis, what sort of political behavior might we expect by foreign-owned MNEs operating in the United States? Transaction cost theory, as expounded

Figure 10.1
Conceptual Model of Corporate Political Activity Derived from Five Theoretical Perspectives

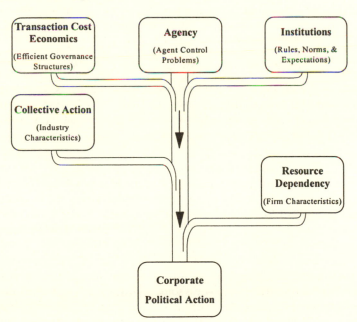

by Kaufman, Englander, and Marcus (1987), suggests there might be a slight tendency for a foreign firm to engage in independent political action, due to the probability that within a given issue the foreign firm's interest will diverge somewhat from that of other industry members. Whether this action is carried out internally or through intermediaries depends on whether the issue is recurrent or occasional.

Proposition 1:   Foreign-owned firms are more likely to use independent political action than are U.S.-owned firms.

Using agency theory, we see that there is a slight tendency for knowledge problems to occur more frequently for foreign-owned firms and a marked tendency for disposition and effort problems to occur. The tactics to be used to mitigate these agency problems are lobbying, testimony, collegial persuasion, constituency influence, collective organizing, advocacy advertising, litigation, and PAC contributions (Getz 1993b; Oberman 1993).

Proposition 2a: Foreign-owned firms are more likely to experience knowledge problems in their relationships with targets in government than are U.S.-owned firms.

Proposition 2b: Foreign-owned firms are likely to use information tactics (lobbying, testimony, and collegial persuasion) to mitigate knowledge problems.

Proposition 3a: Foreign-owned firms are more likely to experience disposition problems in their relationships with targets in government than are U.S.-owned firms.

Proposition 3b: Foreign-owned firms are likely to use pressure tactics (constituency influence, collective organizing, advocacy advertising, litigation, and PAC contributions) to mitigate disposition problems.

Proposition 4a: Foreign-owned firms are more likely to experience effort problems in their relationships with targets in government than are U.S.-owned firms.

Proposition 4b: Foreign-owned firms are likely to use pressure tactics (constituency influence, collective organizing, PAC contributions, litigation, and advocacy advertising) to mitigate effort problems.

Hillman's (1995b) interpretation based in institutions theory dictates that a politically active firm in the United States (regardless of ownership) would tend toward transactional relationships with targets, using information, pressure, or constituency-building tactics.

Proposition 5:   Foreign firms operating in the United States are likely to use transactional approaches in political action.

Proposition 6:   Foreign firms operating in the United States are likely to use information tactics (lobbying, reporting research and survey results, testimony, supplying position papers), pressure/access tactics (PAC contributions, personal service, hiring politically experienced personnel), and constituency building tactics (grassroots mobilization, advocacy advertising, public image advertising, economic/political education).

Finally, Oberman (1993) suggests that firms attempt to obtain formal institutional resources. Firms that do not already possess some such resources (formal or informal) must expend material resources to get desired institutional resources. Thus tactics such as PAC contributions, advocacy advertising, and constituency influence would be appropriate for foreign-owned firms operating in the United States.

Proposition 7:   Foreign-owned firms are more likely to use tactics that are dependent on economic resources (PAC contributions and advocacy advertising) than are U.S.-owned firms.

Proposition 8:   Foreign-owned firms are more likely to use tactics that are dependent on informal institutional resources (constituency building) than are U.S.-owned firms.

On the whole, then, we see that there are reasons related to transaction cost economics, agency theory, and the particular nature of U.S. political institutions that would seem to dictate that foreign-owned firms act independently in the political arena and use political tactics such as PACs (to pressure or gain access to government officials) or lobbying (to provide information to public officials). As can be seen from table 10.8 the range of appropriate tactics for foreign firms does not appear to be extremely limited. That is, to address issues of concern (reduce transaction costs, mitigate agency problems, match tactics with institutional constraints, and obtain institutional resources) the foreign-owned firm would ideally avail itself of practically the full range of political tactics. To some extent firms' ability to implement these tactics is affected by the firm-specific characteristics mentioned previously (see table 10.9). However, these effects are not directly related to ownership.

The Caveat: Legitimacy

Formal constraints on political action for foreign-owned firms are virtually the same as they are for U.S.-owned firms (lobbyists must be registered, PAC contributions are limited, and so on). Informal constraints, however, may be somewhat more restrictive. In particular, the legitimacy of foreign-owned firms is more likely to be questioned. The greater the firm's use of pressure tactics, the greater the risk to legitimacy. Thus, until a given foreign-owned firm earns legitimacy in the U.S. economic, political, and social environment, the wiser course of action may well be to participate in collective political action.[4]

Proposition 9:   Foreign-owned firms are more likely to use collective tactics than are U.S.-owned firms.

While participating in collective efforts, the foreign-owned firm ought also to continue trying to obtain informal institutional resources, such as favorable public opinion and strong relationships with government officials (by, for example, providing employment and paying taxes or by engaging in social outreach activities, such as philanthropy or community service). Even though Hillman (1995b) suggests that in the United States, transactional approaches to political action are more appropriate than relational approaches (as compared to processes in other countries), broader institutions theory emphasizes the importance of relationship- and network-building (Dahl 1956; Knoke 1990; Oberman 1993). Indeed, building good relationships with elected and appointed policymakers is a critical part of political activity (Bagby, Wartick, and Stevens 1987).

Given the suggestion that foreign-owned firms may be more likely to engage in collective than independent political action, two issues remain. What sort of

Table 10.8
Appropriate Tactics for Foreign-Owned Firms

Tactics	Transaction Cost Theory	Agency Theory	Institutions Theory (Hillman)	Institutions Theory (Oberman)
Independent	X			
Lobbying		X	X	
Testimony		X	X	
Reporting research results			X	
Policy analysis/technical reports		X		
Collegial persuasion		X	X	
Hiring former government employees				
PAC contributions		X	X	X
Bribery				
Public exposure				
Civil disobedience				
Advocacy advertising		X	X	X
Public image advertising				
Economic/political education			X	
Litigation				
Collective				
Constituency building/grassroots		X	X	X
Collective organizing		X		

collective is appropriate, and what should be the firm's level of participation? Again, Oberman (1993) provides answers. In another systematically developed typology, he classifies collective action along two dimensions: extent of issue overlap and level of participation (see table 10.10). Issue overlap is the extent to which members of the collective share interests on multiple issues (similar to the transaction cost distinction between convergence and divergence of interests). For high overlap, it is probable that the members of the collective are obvious, such as the firm's own constituency or an existing trade association. For low overlap, partners in the collective action may be less obvious, such as firms in other industries or nonbusiness interest groups.[5] Level of participation can range from initiating through free-riding (Yoffie 1987). The higher a firm's stakes in an issue and the greater the expected benefit of political action, the greater the expected level of participation (see also Olson 1965).

Determining the appropriate collective participation for foreign-owned firms from among these choices highlights again the issues of convergence of interests and exposure to accusations of illegitimate efforts to influence public policy. Foreign-owned firms' interests are expected to diverge from broader industry interests somewhat more frequently than would be the case for U.S.-owned firms, thereby reducing the probability that participation in trade association activity would be a viable option. Foreign-owned firms are expected to prefer participating rather than

Table 10.9
Relationship between Firm Characteristics and Tactics

Tactics	Size	Profit-ability	Resources	Diversi-fication	Stru-ctures	Expe-rience
Lobbying		+	+		+	+
Testimony		+	+		+	+
Reporting research results		+	+			+
Policy analysis		+	+		+	+
Collegial persuasion		+	+			+
PAC contributions		+	+		+	+
Advocacy advertising		+	+			+
Economic/political education		+	+		+	+
Grassroots	+			+		
Collectives		-	-		-	-

Note: + indicates positive relationship; - indicates inverse relationship.

Table 10.10
Typology of Collective Tactics

Corporate Role		Multi-Issue Interest Overlap	
		Low	High
Active	Initiating	Coalition Building	Constituency Building
	Participating		
	Existing collectivity	Encompassing business organization	Trade association
	Emergent collectivity	Coalition membership	Constituency membership
Nonactive		Free rider	

Source: Oberman (1993, 237).

initiating activities, because of their desire to minimize visibility in activities that may be viewed with skepticism by the general public (as much political action is). This, then, would push the firm toward coalition membership rather than coalition-building.

Proposition 10: Foreign-owned firms are more likely to be part of single-issue than multiple-issue collectives.

Proposition 11: Foreign-owned firms are more likely to participate in coalitions than to initiate coalitions.

Conclusion and Implications

The analysis began with a review of the literature on international business-government relations, which barely speaks to the issue of participation in the public policy process (corporate political action) in host countries. The analysis developed using the framework of the eclectic theory of international business (Dunning 1980; 1981; 1988), with a discussion of possible firm-level advantages and efforts to internalize. This led through three different theoretical approaches to political involvement: transaction cost theory, agency theory, and institutions theory.

While each of these theories helps to understand differences in the political action of U.S.-owned and foreign-owned firms, the key difference in the U.S. political arena is the greater risk for foreign-owned firms due to lack of legitimacy. Note, of course, that the legitimacy of business political action is questioned in any case (Parenti 1988; Rauch 1994; Schlozman and Tierney 1986). For this reason, foreign firms are expected to approach political action cautiously, to take "back-seat" roles, to be joiners and followers. Legitimacy problems may well abate with time, as the "liability of newness" is overcome (Baum 1994). With time and experience, foreign firms can earn legitimacy and thus will be less reluctant to avail themselves of the full range of political tactics. Once legitimacy is fairly well established (on a more-or-less equal footing with U.S.-owned firms), there should be no significant ownership-based differences between the political behavior of foreign firms and that of U.S.-owned firms.

The conceptual model presented herein can and should be further developed through empirical testing. Such testing should begin with a broad-based, cross-sectional survey of the political activities of foreign-owned firms. In addition, longitudinal research (or more likely case studies that take into account past activities) ought to be done to assess changes over time in the political behavior of foreign-owned firms.

The immediate policy implications of this analysis are not overwhelming. With regard to political behavior, foreign-owned firms behave as much as possible like U.S.-owned firms and thus should be accorded national treatment. Given the open, pluralist political system of the United States, no actor affected by public policy ought to be systematically handicapped in its efforts to influence policy.[6]

This, of course, leaves the larger question of the legitimacy of corporate political action in general, a question that, at its most basic, addresses the fear that business organizations with control over massive economic resources may be able to convert those resources to political ends so as to obtain unfair advantages over nonbusiness interests. This question has been addressed by Epstein (1969) and Salamon and Siegfried (1977), among others. In reviewing the concept of pluralism in Epstein's work, Barry M. Mitnick wrote,

> We acknowledge that the playing field is tilted. We see elephants among the chickens. But instead of throwing up our theoretical hands, we simply elect to call for better rules of the game for our playing field, but just the minimal rules necessary to make it level and give the chickens (and any would-be barnyard participants) an even chance. (Mitnick 1993, 61)

There is no reason for us to expect that foreign-owned firms are more likely to be elephants than other firms. Thus we do not need additional rules to control their political action.

NOTES

1. Dunning's eclectic paradigm is used only as a general framework to help categorize variables. Claiming that the approach in this chapter blends into or extends eclectic theory would be a gross distortion.

2. On resource dependency, see Pfeffer and Salancik (1978).

3. Parsons and Smelser (1956, 102) define institutions as the "ways in which the value patterns of the common culture of a social system are integrated through the concrete action of its units in their interaction with each other through the definition of role expectations and the organization of motivation."

4. Proposition 9 is exactly opposite of Proposition 1. Proposition 1 is offered assuming other things are equal. Proposition 9 is offered upon consideration that legitimacy is not likely to be equal early in the tenure of foreign-owned firms in the United States.

5. For an intriguing interpretation regarding "manufacturing" agents in nonbusiness interest groups, see Mahon (1993).

6. Periodically, it is proposed that restrictions be placed on the political action of foreign firms. For example, in 1990, the Senate approved a measure sponsored by then-Senator Lloyd Bentsen that would have banned political action committees operated by companies that are more than 50 percent foreign-owned. The measure died with campaign-reform legislation (Olen 1990). To date, no restrictive law has been implemented.

REFERENCES

Andres, Gary J. 1985. "Business Involvement in Campaign Finance: Factors Influencing the Decision to Form a Corporate PAC," *PS* 18:213-220, Spring.

Bagby, J. W., S. L. Wartick , and J. M. Stevens. 1987. "Cooperative Approaches to Business-Government Relations," in *Business Strategy and Public Policy: Perspectives From Industry and Academia*, edited by Alfred A. Marcus, Allen M. Kaufman, and David R. Beam. New York: Quorum Books, pp. 283-291.

Baker, James C., John K. Ryans, Jr., and Donald G. Howard, eds. 1988. *International Business Classics*. Lexington, Mass.: Lexington Books.

Baum, J. 1994. "Organizational Niches and the Dynamics of Organizational Mortality," *American Journal of Sociology* 100:346-380.

Baysinger, Barry D., Gerald D. Keim, and Carl P. Zeithaml. 1987. "Constituency Building as a Political Strategy in the Petroleum Industry," in *Business Strategy and Public Policy: Perspectives From Industry and Academia*, edited by Alfred A. Marcus, Allen M. Kaufman, and David R. Beam, New York: Quorum Books, pp. 223-238.

Behrman, Jack N. 1986. "The Future of International Business and the Distribution of Benefits," *Columbia Journal of World Business* 24 (4):15-22.

Behrman, Jack N., and Robert E. Grosse. 1990. *International Business and Governments: Issues and Institutions*. Columbia, S.C.: University of South Carolina Press.

Berry, Jeffrey M. 1977. *Lobbying for the People: The Political Behavior of Public Interest Groups*. Princeton, N.J.: Princeton University Press.

Boddewyn, Jean J. 1975. "Multinational Business-Government Relations: Six Principles for Effectiveness," in *Multinational Corporations and Governments: Business-Government*

Relations in an International Context, edited by Patrick M. Boarman and Hans Scholl-hammer. New York: Praeger, pp. 193-202.

———. 1988. "Political Aspects of MNE Theory," *Journal of International Business Studies* 19(3):341-363.

———. 1991. "International-Business Political-Behavior Research: Patterns and Directions," paper presented at the Academy of Management Annual Meeting, Miami.

Boddewyn, Jean J., and Thomas L. Brewer. 1994. "International-Business Political Behavior: New Theoretical Directions," *Academy of Management Review* 19(January):119-143.

Brenner, Steven N. 1980. "Corporate Political Activity: An Exploratory Study in a Developing Industry," in *Research in Corporate Social Performance and Policy*, edited by Lee E. Preston. Greenwich, Conn.: JAI Press, pp. 197-236.

Brewer, Thomas L. 1992a. "An Issue-Area Approach to the Analysis of MNE-Government Relations," *Journal of International Business Studies* 23(2):295-309.

———. 1992b. "MNE-Government Relations: Strategic Networks and Foreign Direct Investment in the United States in the Automotive Industry," *International Executive* 34(2):113-129.

Buchanan, James M. 1984. "Politics without Romance," in *The Theory of Public Choice—II*, edited by James M. Buchanan and Robert D. Tollison. Ann Arbor: University of Michigan Press, pp. 11-22.

Buchholz, Rogene A. 1990. *Essentials of Public Policy for Management*. Englewood Cliffs, N.J.: Prentice-Hall.

Choate, Pat. 1990. *Agents of Influence: How Japan's Lobbyists in the United States Manipulate America's Political and Economic System*. New York: A. A. Knopf.

Contractor, Farok J. 1990. "Ownership Patterns of U.S. Joint Ventures Abroad and the Liberalization of Foreign Government Regulations in the 1980s: Evidence from the Benchmark Surveys," *Journal of International Business Studies* 21(1):55-73.

Dahl, Robert A. 1956. *A Preface to Democratic Theory*. Chicago: University of Chicago Press.

De la Torre, J., Jr. 1981. "Foreign Investment Conflict, Regulations and Negotiation," *Journal of International Business Studies* 12(2):9-32.

Dunning, John H. 1980. "Toward an Eclectic Theory of International Production: Some Empirical Tests," *Journal of International Business Studies* 11(1):9-31.

———. 1981. *International Production and the Multinational Enterprise*. London: George Allen and Unwin.

———. 1988. "The Eclectic Paradigm of International Production: A Restatement and Some Possible Extensions," *Journal of International Business Studies* 19(1):1-31.

Eisenhardt, Kathleen M. 1989. "Agency Theory: An Assessment and Review," *Academy of Management Review* 14(January):57-74.

Epstein, Edwin M. 1969. *The Corporation in American Politics*. Englewood Cliffs, N.J.: Prentice-Hall.

Fagre, N., and Louis T. Wells, Jr. 1982. "Bargaining Power of Multinationals and Host Governments," *Journal of International Business Studies* 13(2):9-23.

Fatehi-Sedeh, K., and M. Hossein Safizadeh. 1988. "Sociopolitical Events and Foreign Direct Investment: American Investments in South and Central American Countries," *Journal of Management* 14(1):93-107.

Gale, Jeffrrey, and Rogene A. Buchholz. 1987. "The Political Pursuit of Competitive Advantage: What Business Can Gain from Government," in *Business Strategy and Public Policy: Perspectives From Industry and Academia*, edited by Alfred A. Marcus, Allen M. Kaufman, and David R. Beam. New York: Quorum Books, pp. 31-41.

Getz, Kathleen A. 1991. "Selecting Corporate Political Tactics: The Montreal Protocol on Substances That Deplete the Ozone Layer," doctoral dissertation, University of Pittsburgh.

————. 1993a. "Corporate Political Tactics in a Principal-Agent Context: An Investigation in Ozone Protection Policy," in *Research in Corporate Social Performance and Policy*, vol. 14, edited by James E. Post. Greenwich, Conn.: JAI Press, pp. 19-55.

————. 1993b. "Selecting Corporate Political Tactics," 242-273 in *Corporate Political Agency: The Construction of Competition in Public Affairs*, edited by Barry M. Mitnick. Newbury Park, Calif.: Sage, pp. 242-273.

Gladwin, Thomas N., and Ingo Walter. 1980. *Multinationals under Fire: Lessons in the Management of Conflict*. New York: Wiley.

Hillman, Amy. 1995a. "The Choice of Corporate Political Tactics: The Role of Institutional Variables," paper presented at the Sixth Annual Meeting of the International Association for Business and Society, Vienna, Austria.

————. 1995b. "Political Strategy Formulation for International Firms: The Role of Firm, Industry, and Institutional Variables," unpublished dissertation proposal, Texas A and M University.

Jain, Arvind K., and Douglas Nigh. 1989. "Politics and the International Lending Decisions of Banks," *Journal of International Business Studies* 20(2):349-359.

Jensen, M. C., and W. H. Meckling. 1976. "Theory of the Firm: Managerial Behavior, Agency Costs, and Ownership Structure," *Journal of Financial Economics* 3(4):305-360.

Kaufman, Allen M., Ernie J. Englander, and Alfred A. Marcus. 1987. "Selecting an Organizational Structure for Implementing Issues Management: A Transaction Costs and Agency Theory Perspective," in *Corporate Political Agency: The Construction of Competition in Public Affairs*, edited by Barry M. Mitnick. Newbury Park, Calif.: Sage, pp. 148-168.

Keim, Gerald D., and Barry D. Baysinger. 1988. "The Efficacy of Business Political Activity: Competitive Considerations in a Principal-Agent Context," *Journal of Management* 14(2):163-180.

Keim, Gerald D., Carl P. Zeithaml, and Barry D. Baysinger. 1984. "New Directions for Corporate Political Strategy," *Sloan Management Review* 25(3):53-62.

Knickerbocker, Frederick T. 1973. *Oligopolistic Reaction and Multinational Enterprise*. Boston: Harvard University.

Knoke, David. 1990. *Political Networks: The Structural Perspective*. Cambridge: Cambridge University Press.

Kobrin, Stephen J. 1979. "Political Risk: A Review and Reconsideration," *Journal of International Business Studies* 10(1):67-80.

————. 1982. *Managing Political Risk Assessment: Strategic Response to Environmental Change*. Berkeley: University of California Press.

————. 1987. "Testing the Bargaining Hypothesis in the Manufacturing Sector in Developing Countries," *International Organization* 41(Autumn):609-638.

Kobrin, Stephen J., J. Basek, S. Blank, and J. LaPalombara. 1980. "The Assessment and Evaluation of Noneconomic Environments by American Firms: A Preliminary Report," *Journal of International Business Studies* 11(1):32-47.

Littlejohn, Stephen E. 1986. "Competition and Cooperation: New Trends in Corporate Public Issue Identification and Resolution," *California Management Review* 29(1):109-123.

Mahini, Amir, and Louis T. Wells, Jr. 1986. "Government Relations in the Global Firm," in *Competition in Global Industries*, edited by Michael E. Porter. Boston: Harvard Business School Press, pp. 291-312.

Mahon, John F. 1993. "Shaping Issues/Manufacturing Agents: Corporate Political Sculpting," in *Corporate Political Agency: The Construction of Competition in Public Affairs*, edited by Barry M. Mitnick. Newbury Park, Calif.: Sage, pp. 187-212.

Mahon, John F., and Sandra A. Waddock. 1991. "Strategic Issues Management: An Integration of Issue Life Cycle Perspectives," paper presented at the Academy of Management Annual Meeting, Miami.

Marcus, Alfred A., Allen M. Kaufman, and David R. Beam, eds. 1987. *Business Strategy and Public Policy: Perspectives From Industry and Academia*. New York: Quorum Books.

Masters, Marick F., and Barry D. Baysinger. 1985. "The Determinants of Funds Raised by Corporate Political Action Committees: an Empirical Examination," *Academy of Management Journal* 28(Sep):654-664.

Masters, Marick F., and Gerald D. Keim. 1986. "Variation in Corporate PAC and Lobbying Activity: An Organizational and Environmental Analysis," in *Research in Corporate Social Performance and Policy*, vol. 8, edited by Lee E. Preston. Greenwich, Conn.: JAI Press, pp. 249-271.

Mitnick, Barry M. 1984. "Agency Problems and Political Institutions," paper presented at the Annual Research Conference of the Association for Public Policy Analysis and Management, New Orleans.

————. 1993. "Political Contestability," in *Corporate Political Agency: The Construction of Competition in Public Affairs*, edited by Barry M. Mitnick. Newbury Park, Calif.: Sage, pp. 11-66.

Munger, M. C., and Kathleen A. Rehbein. 1988. "On the Political Participation of Manufacturing Industries in the Electoral Process," paper presented at the Academy of Management Annual Meeting, Anaheim, Calif.

Nigh, Douglas. 1985. "The Effect of Political Events on United States Direct Foreign Investment; A Pooled Time-Series Cross-Sectional Analysis," *Journal of International Business Studies* 16(1):1-17.

Oberman, William D. 1993. "Strategy and Tactic Choice in an Institutional Resource Context," in *Corporate Political Agency: The Construction of Competition in Public Affairs*, edited by Barry M. Mitnick. Newbury Park, Calif: Sage, pp. 213-241.

Olen, H. 1990. "Fed Weighs Outlawing PACs Operated by Concerns over 50% Foreign-Owned," *Wall Street Journal*, November 7, p. A18.

Olson, Mancur, Jr. 1965. *The Logic of Collective Action*. Cambridge: Harvard University Press.

Parenti, Michael. 1988. *Democracy for the Few*. Fifth edition. New York: St. Martin's Press.

Parsons, Talcott, and Neil J. Smelser. 1956. *Economy and Society: A Study in the Integration of Economic and Social Theory*. Glencoe, Ill.: Free Press.

Pfeffer, Jeffrey, and Gerald R. Salancik. 1978. *The External Control of Organizations*. New York: Harper and Row.

Pittman, R. 1977. "Market Structure and Campaign Contributions," *Public Choice* 31:37-52.

Poynter, Thomas A. 1982. "Government Intervention in Less Developed Countries: The Experience of Multinational Companies," *Journal of International Business Studies* 13(1):9-25.

————. 1986. "Managing Government Intervention: A Strategy for Defending the Subsidiary," *Columbia Journal of World Business* 21(4):55-65.

Raddock, David M., ed. 1986. *Assessing Corporate Political Risk*. Totowa, N.J.: Rowman and Littlefield.

Rauch, Jonathan. 1994. "Suckers!" *Reason*, May, pp. 20-24.

Rehbein, Kathleen A., and Douglas A. Schuler. 1995. "The Firm as a Filter: A Conceptual Framework for Corporate Political Strategies," in *Academy of Management Proceedings*, edited by Dorothy P. Moore. The Citadel, pp. 406-410.

Root, Franklin R. 1968. "U.S. Business Abroad and Political Risks," *MSU Business Topics*, Winter, pp. 73-80.

Rugman, Alan M. 1979. *International Diversification and the Multinational Enterprise*. Lexington, Mass.: Lexington Books.

Sabato, Larry J. 1985. *PAC Power*. New York: W.W. Norton.

Salamon, Lester M., and John J. Siegfried. 1977. "Economic Power and Political Influence: The Impact of Industry Structure on Public Policy," *American Political Science Review* 71:1026-1043.

Schlozman, Kay L., and John T. Tierney. 1986. *Organized Interests and American Democracy.* New York: Harper and Row.

Schollhammer, Hans. 1975. "Business-Government Relations in an International Context: An Assessment," in *Multinational Corporations and Governments: Business-Government Relations in an International Context,* edited by Patrick M. Boarman and Hans Scholl-hammer. New York: Praeger, pp. 217-222.

Schollhammer, Hans, and Douglas Nigh. 1984. "The Effects of Political Events on Foreign Direct Investments by German Multinational Corporations," *Management International Review* 28(1):18-40.

Shipper, Frank, and Marianne M. Jennings. 1984. *Business Strategy for the Political Arena.* Westport, Conn.: Quorum Books.

Toyne, Brian. 1989. "International Exchange: A Foundation for Theory Building in International Business," *Journal of International Business Studies* 20(1):1-17.

Vernon, Raymond. 1974. "The Location of Industry," in *Economic Analysis and the Multinational Enterprise,* edited by John H. Dunning. London: Allen and Unwin, pp. 89-114.

Wahn, Judith. 1992. "Trade Association Participation in Government Policy Formation," paper presented at the Academy of Management Annual Meeting, Las Vegas.

Weingast, Barry R. 1980. "Regulation, Reregulation, and Deregulation: The Political Foundations of Agency-Clientele Relationships," working paper #62. St. Louis: Center for the Study of American Business of Washington University.

Wexler, Ann. 1982. "Coalition Building: How to Make It Work for You Now and in the Future," *Public Affairs Review* 3(1):56-76.

Williamson, Oliver E. 1985. *The Economic Institutions of Capitalism.* New York: Free Press.

Yoffie, David B. 1987. "Corporate Strategies for Political Action: A Rational Model," in *Business Strategy and Public Policy: Perspectives From Industry and Academia,* edited by Alfred A. Marcus, Allen M. Kaufman, and David R. Beam. New York: Quorum Books, pp. 43-60.

11

Corporate Citizenship: Comparing Foreign Affiliates and Domestic Subsidiaries

Tammie S. Pinkston

INTRODUCTION

The collective wisdom among most international business scholars is that, overall, foreign direct investment in the United States (FDIUS) has a positive net impact on the host country. A study by McKinsey's Global Institute (Thompson and Rehder 1995) has said that Japanese investments in particular have played an instrumental role in increasing the productivity and competitiveness of its domestic industry counterparts. Yet, polls continually show that some source countries, notably Japan, raise concerns by citizens who feel threats to national sovereignty and autonomy.

Still, many U.S. citizens remain skeptical of the foreign presence. In the early 1990s, their concern primarily revolved around the high visibility of foreign direct investment. Such visibility could not have come at a worse time. As the United States found itself in a deep recession, the U.S. public was concerned about the increasing dependence on imports and the future economic prosperity of individual U.S. citizens. The United States appeared to be investing less in foreign markets as the dollar weakened. The imbalance of trade, particularly with Japan, continued to grow. Most important, even U.S. corporations were faltering in the area of corporate citizenship, with downsizing, permanent displacement of workers, extensive retraining, intensifying job entry requirements, plant closings, and the collapse of several savings-and-loan institutions. Many people attributed the domestic difficulties to the increasing foreign presence. "Buy American" quickly became a significant grassroots campaign. Perceptions were promoted that foreign firms and domestic firms were significantly different in terms of operating philosophy. Inferences were made that foreign firms were not "good citizens," produced offshore, evaded taxes, discriminated, and utilized "hollow-factories."

The current study attempts to determine if allegations like these are warranted by comparing the corporate citizenship of foreign affiliates with that of domestic subsidiaries. Executives located in the U.S. subsidiaries of chemical firms headquartered in England, France, Germany, Japan, Sweden, and Switzerland, along with a sample of domestic subsidiaries, were asked to respond to a mail survey designed to elicit responses concerning four areas of corporate citizenship: *(i)* the orientations of top management toward corporate citizenship; *(ii)* an assessment of the organizational stakeholders considered to be of critical importance to the continuing operations of the firm; *(iii)* an identification of the corporate citizenship issues brought to bear on the firm by these stakeholders; and *(iv)* the determination of the degree of corporate citizenship decision-making autonomy delegated to the subsidiaries located in the United States by their foreign parents. The data collected from the executives of the foreign-based facilities were compared to the results obtained from the mail survey administered to a sample of U.S. chemical subsidiaries to determine if differences in corporate citizenship do exist between the foreign affiliates and their U.S. counterparts.

CORPORATE CITIZENSHIP

There appears to be no major distinction between the concepts of corporate citizenship and corporate social responsibility. *The Corporate 500: The Directory of Corporate Philanthropy* (1985, xiii) defines corporate citizenship as being "the notion that a company, like an individual, has duties to society." It goes on to say that corporate citizenship is also called corporate social responsibility. For the purpose of this research, corporate citizenship was equated with corporate social responsibility. Research in the area of corporate social performance (Carroll 1979; Sethi 1975; Wartick and Cochran 1985; Wood 1990) provided a framework by which to examine corporate citizenship.

Corporate Citizenship Orientations

In academic literature, corporate social responsibility (CSR) has been identified as a critical dimension of the broader concept of corporate social performance (CSP). Carroll (1979) provided a conceptual model of corporate social performance. The three primary dimensions of his model were *(i)* social responsibility categories, *(ii)* philosophies of social responsiveness, and *(iii)* social issues involved. The category of social responsibility included economic, legal, ethical, and discretionary or philanthropic aspects.

Aupperle (1982) surveyed 818 firms to determine how CSR was interpreted by various U.S. corporations. Aupperle's research was grounded on the four-part definition of the CSR construct developed by Carroll (1979) and supported the existence of the four components of CSR—economic, legal, ethical, and discretionary—in order of importance. Although Aupperle (1982) investigated only domestic firms, it is asserted here that the construct could be applicable to a sample including both domestic and foreign firms. It was assumed that the four responsibility categories proposed by Carroll would also exist and be representative of an organization's definition of corporate citizenship, regardless of country of origin.

Several authors have examined CSR or CSP within a number of specific countries (Clarkson 1988; Cowton 1987; Dierkes 1980; MacMillan 1980; Mafune 1988; Moore and Richardson 1988; Rey 1980; Wokutch 1990). Their general findings indicate that economic considerations were of primary importance. However, the studies also indicated that corporate concern for employees and the environment were of growing importance. Some researchers have addressed CSR/CSP across more than one country, providing some cross-cultural comparisons (Hargreaves and Dauman 1975; Preston, Rey, and Dierkes 1978; Sethi 1978). Hofstede (1980), for instance, recognized that nationality had the potential to influence people's thinking. These studies have collectively demonstrated the existence of notably different attitudes or practices with respect to corporate citizenship across countries.

Although much of this research recognizes the importance of economic responsibilities, there are differences that imply that an organization's orientation toward corporate citizenship will be derived from its home country business environment. Within the context of the current study, it is anticipated that the priorities of corporate citizenship orientations will be different for domestic subsidiaries compared to foreign affiliates.

Organizational Stakeholders and Corporate Citizenship Issues

Within the context of multinational corporation (MNC) citizenship, little research has directly addressed the issue of stakeholder management. More often, research has focused on the issues of concern to the stakeholder groups. By grouping similar issues together, one can infer which stakeholders have the highest impact on the organization's operations. Accordingly, the priority of the corporate citizenship issues would be difficult to divorce from the priority of the organizations' stakeholder groups.

Organizational Stakeholders. The stakeholder groups most consistently cited throughout the literature includes owners, consumers, employees, communities, and government (Freeman 1984; Tuleja 1985). The priority of these stakeholders may not be consistent for long periods of time, but some stability in the pattern was apparent by specific industry. Researchers cited within the body of literature on CSR across nationalities have found employees to be of primary importance with the environment increasingly important. Other stakeholder groups did not appear to be ranked with as much consistency across countries.

The scant literature on the relationship between business and society in different cultures indicates that businesses operating in different countries experience different expectations and degrees of involvement from stakeholder groups. Since these relationships can vary by country, the stakeholder priorities were expected to vary for the sample organizations.

Corporate Citizenship Issues. Several attempts have been made to catalog the corporate citizenship issues that MNCs must address. A 1990 conference sponsored by Vesper International brought academicians and practitioners together to draft guidelines for the socially responsible operations of international corporations. Nearly half of the issues of concern centered around employees—employee safety, employee rights, employee welfare in the form of job security, nondiscriminatory practices, layoffs, or plant closings. Other issues included cooperation with host governments, disclosure of information, environmental protection, product safety, profitability, fair pricing, community interest, and legal and ethical behavior.

Bob (1990) and Gladwin and Walter (1979) analyzed MNC operations in the United States from the perspective of social responsibility. Both studies found environmental protection and labor relations as the two critical concerns. Other studies (Gelsanliter 1990; Rehder 1990) have focused on the lobbying practices of the foreign affiliates. As a result of their lobbying efforts, significant incentives have been offered to the foreign companies; and some believe that these incentives are given to foreign firms at the expense of the competitiveness of the domestic industry participants. Averyt (1990) and Choate (1990) have investigated an increasingly important extension of lobbying efforts in Washington—"grassroots lobbying"—concluding that the Japanese effort at this activity is far more extensive than that of other countries represented in the United States.

Langlois and Schlegelmilch (1990) compared corporate codes of ethics of U.S. and European firms and identified topics that were common to both continents' business organizations. Typical concerns common to both European and U.S. firms were the protection and safety of the environment, donation to charities, dialogue with special interest groups, cultural activities, and pledges recognizing and accepting social responsibility.

While their specific research is too recent to have been substantially corroborated, it has supported the notion that the perceived importance of corporate citizenship issues may be contingent on the organization's country of origin. In addition, the corporate citizenship issues of primary interest may vary as organizations invest in new countries. The issues associated with the new host markets may be different from the issues with which any particular organization is familiar within its home country, such as German issues in Germany versus issues in the United States faced by German foreign affiliates. Although this research does not specifically address this topic, it is pertinent to the current study in the determination of whether an organization has the ability to adapt its orientation or mode of behavior or simply attempts to transfer corporate citizenship from its home country to the host country.

At a minimum, if the priority of the stakeholder groups was assumed to differ across country of origin, the issues that these groups brought to bear on the organization should also differ.

MNC Headquarters and Subsidiary Relations

In prior research, Blake (1981) confirmed the difficulty in determining the role of headquarters and the role of the individual subsidiaries in the management of international public affairs. The primary results, from the headquarters managers' perspectives, indicated that neither headquarters nor subsidiary managers were specifically involved in the management—formulation, implementation, and evaluation—of international public affairs. In addition, Behrman (1988) suggested that headquarters would take the leading responsibility only if the policies developed at headquarters would in no way interfere with the competitiveness of the subsidiary.

One of the interesting findings from the research of Bob (1990) is that there was little support or autonomy given to the Japanese affiliates by their headquarters in Japan. Over 50 percent of the firms engaged in corporate citizenship activity indicated that the primary decision-making responsibility resided at corporate headquarters in Japan. Only a minority of the largest, most powerful Japanese subsidiaries have any significant level of autonomy with respect to corporate citizenship.

Although the research findings remain mixed in the area of decision-making autonomy, the subsidiary's degree of autonomy may vary. Country of origin is believed to be one of the mediating factors in the degree of autonomy that a subsidiary can anticipate having with respect to corporate citizenship decision making.

RESEARCH METHODS AND FINDINGS

Sample Description and Research Methods

Several industries were considered as potential samples for the study. The first criterion was that a significant level of FDI existed in the industry. Three industries have consistently received the most significant levels of FDIUS over the last twenty years: industrial machinery and equipment, chemicals and allied products, and electrical equipment and electronic components. Only the chemicals and allied products industry received significant investment from multiple countries of origin. By focusing on one industry, industry effects could be minimized. Potential country effects were controlled by focusing on a single host country. Given the availability of data and existence of FDI, the United States was considered an appropriate host country. In addition, a considerable amount of the previous research on international business has taken the perspective of U.S.-based MNCs investing into other countries. Relatively few prior studies have focused on FDI coming into the United States.

Using the *International Directory of Corporate Affiliations* (1990/1991), six countries were identified as the principal foreign direct investors in the U.S. chemical industry: England, France, Germany, Japan, Sweden, and Switzerland. The *International Directory of Corporate Affiliations* (1990/1991) was then used to construct a list of 591 subsidiaries of chemical firms originating from these six countries or constituting a subset of U.S.-based chemical facilities. These chemical firms received a mail survey supplemented with one follow-up mailing. The surveys were sent to the chief executive officers (CEOs) or presidents of the sample firms' headquarters in the United States or to general managers or plant managers at various plant locations. The coding of the surveys provided reasonably effective check for converging or differing responses for various levels within one organization. The number of useable responses was 131, yielding a response rate of 22 percent. Respondents included 56 CEO or presidents, 47 general or plant managers, 5 public affairs officers, 7 administrative assistants to the CEO, and 16 other management positions.

While the response rate was modest, the responding sample was distributed across these demographic characteristics in a manner that resembled the population of firms surveyed. Based on secondary country of origin, annual sales, and age data collected from the *International Directory of Corporate Affiliation* (1990/1991) and *The Merger Yearbook* (annual), no discernible pattern of nonresponse was evident.

Variable Measurement and Data Analysis

Four areas of interest served as the primary foci of this research study in the attempt to assess or ascertain the "corporate citizenship" of both the foreign affiliates located in the United States and their domestic counterparts. These were: *(i)* corporate citizenship orientations, *(ii)* organizational stakeholders, *(iii)* corporate citizenship issues, and *(iv)* corporate citizenship decision-making autonomy.

Corporate Citizenship Orientation. The orientations toward "corporate citizenship" of the top management in the foreign affiliates and their domestic counterparts were measured utilizing a fifteen-item forced-choice questionnaire designed by Aupperle (1982) and also employed by Aupperle, Carroll, and Hatfield (1985). The four-part definition of CSR put forth by Carroll (1979) served as the basis of the questionnaire. The four parts that Carroll argued constituted CSR were economic, legal, ethical, and discretionary (philanthropic). The orientations were evaluated based on the Aupperle instrument originally designed to measure each of the four components of corporate social responsibility (Carroll 1979; Smith and Blackburn 1988).

The respondents were asked to allocate points representing the priority of those four components in given situations. The questionnaire was designed for the respondents' allocation of no more than ten points to each forced-choice set. The point allocation forced respondents to indicate the relative importance of the items provided, within each question set, relating to the four CSR components.

Table 11.1 presents the mean scores by country of origin. There appear to be no significant differences in the corporate citizenship orientations between foreign affiliates and their domestic counterparts.

Table 11.1
Corporate Citizenship Orientations by Country of Origin

Country of Origin	Economic Orientations	Legal Orientations	Ethical Orientations	Philanthropic Orientations
England	3.49	3.15	2.29	.98
France	3.60	3.04	2.35	.98
Germany	2.86	3.21	2.46	1.42
Japan	3.34	2.76	2.42	1.41
Sweden	3.27	3.30	2.43	1.00
Switzerland	3.11	3.04	2.70	1.10
U.S.	3.31	2.96	2.48	1.19
All Non-U.S.	3.28	3.10	2.40	1.19

Key: 1 = greatest degree of importance
      5 = least degree of importance

Note: Scores are calculated means of relative importance.

Organizational Stakeholders. Freeman (1984) and Tuleja (1985) both provided interpretations about most universal and most common stakeholder groups. Freeman

(1984) cited twelve stakeholder groups: owners, financial community, activist groups, customers, customer advocate groups, unions, employees, trade associations, competitors, suppliers, government, and political groups. Tuleja (1985) identified five primary stakeholder groups: owners, employees, consumers, community, and society. To reduce the complexity and increase the manageability of the number of groups, the latter five stakeholder groups were identified in the questionnaire.

To determine the priorities of the various stakeholders and the social issues that they may bring to impact the corporate citizenship decisions of the organizations, the questionnaire recipients were asked to prioritize the five stakeholder groups (employees, communities, government, consumers, and owners) using a ranking procedure.

With respect to organizational stakeholders, no significant differences between the foreign affiliates and their domestic counterparts were found. By looking at the mean scores for each organizational stakeholder presented in table 11.2, two levels emerged. Consistently, the stakeholder groups of employees, owners, and consumers were perceived as being of more importance than the stakeholder groups of communities and government.

Table 11.2
Organizational Stakeholders by Country of Origin

Country of Origin	Employees	Community	Government	Consumers	Owners
England	2.13	4.13	4.00	2.13	2.61
France	2.09	4.27	4.09	2.45	2.09
Germany	2.43	3.61	4.26	2.35	2.35
Japan	1.56	4.11	4.44	2.56	2.33
Sweden	1.71	4.43	4.00	2.43	2.43
Switzerland	1.89	4.00	4.11	2.22	2.78
U.S.	2.29	4.12	4.16	2.31	2.12
All Non-U.S.	2.09	4.01	4.12	2.31	2.46

Note: Scores are calculated mean rankings.

Corporate Citizenship Issues Assessment. As a result of the previous definition of corporate citizenship, it was argued that the primary stakeholders, with the most direct ties to the organization, were the community and employees. With corporate citizenship defined broadly as a sense of concern and responsibility to one's community, the greatest contribution of the business to the overall society affected primarily the immediate, surrounding community area. Employees of the organization would most often be members of that same surrounding community. Neither owners nor consumers had as much likelihood of being found in this immediate local area.

In light of the great proportion of the social issues associated with the legal environment of the MNC, the third stakeholder of primary importance to the study of citizenship was the government. If the assumption could be made that government represented the citizenry, then the government became a stakeholder in the operations of the MNC with more immediate impact on its operations than society in general. In addition, societal concerns are often channelled through governmental legislation. Therefore, from Tuleja's framework, owners, consumers, and society as stakeholders were eliminated from the central focus of this study of corporate citizenship issues. More detailed attention of corporate citizenship issues was given to the three primary and immediate benefactors of an organization's corporate citizenship. Accordingly, the primary stakeholders with respect to "corporate citizenship" issues for this research became employees, communities, and governments.

Just as these key stakeholder groups were derived from the literature, the social issues most often associated with each group were also drawn from a thorough review of the literature. Once the primary issues had been identified, a group of chemical industry experts were asked to confirm the issues as being of critical importance. These experts were also asked to provide any additional issues that should be further explored. This was accomplished through a pilot study in which a sample of organizations and industry experts were sent the preliminary questionnaires and asked for comments and opinions. This test group was asked to validate the questionnaire and make changes that they considered appropriate, particularly with respect to the corporate citizenship issues.

Following the pilot study with industry experts, in which some issues included on the original survey were deleted while others were reworded, the final set of issues was categorized for each of the three key stakeholder groups (employees, communities, and government) and incorporated into the mail survey instrument. The respondents were asked to indicate the degree of importance (using a 4-point Likert scale) that their subsidiary placed on the various corporate citizenship issues. The degrees of importance ranged from unimportant (1) to critically important (4). Table 11.3 presents the sixteen corporate citizenship issues categorized by organizational stakeholder.

Table 11.3
Corporate Citizenship Issues by Organizational Stakeholders

Employees	Community	Government
• Employee health & safety in the workplace	• Environmental protection	• Regulatory compliance
• Representation and participation of minorities	• Contribution to philanthropy	• Political action contributions
• Job security	• Community outreach programming	• Adaptation to local business practices
• Payment of a fair living wage	• Employee volunteerism	• Local government incentives
• Protection of personal privacy	• Minority development	• Representation in Washington, D.C.
		• Grass-roots lobbying

The primary purpose of the research was to determine whether the priorities of the corporate citizenship issues would be different between foreign affiliates and their domestic counterparts. Individual responses were combined for each country of origin. The mean scores appear to vary somewhat by country; however, it is not possible to determine if there are significant differences between foreign affiliates and their domestic counterparts with respect to the corporate citizenship issues because of the lack of statistical power to test for differences across the sample. Table 11.4 presents the mean scores by country of origin.

Table 11.4
Corporate Citizenship Issues by Country of Origin

	Eng-land	France	Ger-many	Japan	Swe-den	Switz-erland	U.S.	All Non-U.S.
1. employee health and safety in the workplace	3.87	3.82	3.91	3.67	3.71	3.78	3.88	3.79
2. representation and participation of minorities	2.57	2.82	3.00	2.67	2.14	2.78	2.90	2.68
3. job security	2.79	2.73	2.83	3.33	3.14	3.00	3.10	2.88
4. payment of a fair living wage		3.28	3.17	3.22	3.14	3.00	3.20	3.11
5. protection of personal privacy	2.83	3.00	3.22	2.89	2.86	2.67	2.92	2.90
6. environmental protection	3.61	3.64	3.74	3.44	3.57	3.67	3.73	3.61
7. contribution to philanthropy	1.70	1.73	2.04	2.11	1.71	2.11	2.02	1.90
8. community outreach programming	1.74	1.64	2.35	2.33	2.00	2.33	2.02	2.04
9. employee volunteerism	1.87	2.00	2.43	2.22	1.86	2.22	2.12	2.11
10. minority development	2.09	2.55	2.65	2.44	1.71	2.67	2.59	2.35
11. regulatory compliance	3.83	3.91	3.74	3.56	3.57	3.78	3.78	3.70
12. political action contributions	1.39	1.73	1.57	1.44	1.14	1.67	1.82	1.51
13. adaptation to local business practices	2.39	2.55	2.43	2.78	2.14	2.44	2.35	2.45
14. local government incentives	1.74	2.00	1.78	2.72	2.00	1.67	1.82	1.85
15. representation in Washington, D.C.	1.70	2.28	2.26	1.78	1.57	2.33	2.22	1.99
16. grassroots lobbying	1.70	2.09	2.09	1.67	1.43	2.33	1.94	1.89

Note: Scores are calculated means of relative importance.

Within the sixteen corporate citizenship issues, differences appeared to exist. Three specific issues—employee health and safety in the workplace, environmental protection, and regulatory compliance—were cited as the three most important issues consistently across the sample, although their actual ranking was somewhat different across individual countries of origin. The priorities of the remaining issues appeared to be less consistent across respondents. The patterns for the issues appear to be relatively stable from country to country. Although the mean scores for the individual issues are different, these differences do not appear to result from any organization's "foreignness."

Corporate Citizenship Decision-Making Autonomy. To assess the degree of autonomy of the subsidiaries with respect to the development of corporate citizenship policies, the respondents in the sample organizations were asked to indicate the perceived responsibility of both their subsidiary and headquarters in the corporate citizenship decision-making process. Respondents were asked to indicate the degree of headquarters and subsidiaries involvement in formulating and implementing corporate citizenship decisions, using a 5-point Likert scale where 1 indicated sole responsibility of the subsidiary, 3 indicated that the responsibility was shared by the subsidiary and headquarters, and 5 indicated sole responsibility of headquarters. Activities involved in both areas are presented in table 11.5. These particular activities were similar to those used by Blake (1981) when he developed a survey to measure the degree to which headquarters or subsidiary managers were involved in the various aspects of public affairs management. This set of questions was believed to determine implicitly whether the decision-making responsibility with respect to corporate citizenship had been delegated to the subsidiaries or whether the responsibility remained at headquarters.

Table 11.5
Corporate Citizenship Decision-Making Activities

Formulation Activities	Implementation Activities
1. the identification of corporate citizenship issues	6. developing tactics for dealing with specific corporate citizenship issues
2. gathering information about corporate citizenship issues	7. executing corporate citizenship policies and tactics
	8. determining budgets for subsidiary corporate citizenship efforts
3. setting objectives for corporate citizenship activities	9. integrating corporate citizenship concerns and efforts with the planning process
4. devising strategies for managing corporate citizenship issues	10. organizing and coordinating corporate citizenship efforts and concerns with operating functions
	11. participating in the selection of personnel (staff or line) with corporate citizenship responsibilities
5. establishing general policies for dealing with corporate citizenship issues	12. training personnel to be more effective with corporate citizenship issues

The ANOVA, testing whether differences in corporate citizenship decision-making autonomy existed across countries of origin, revealed significant differences ($p < .0004$). Since there was an overall significant main effect for country of origin, it was helpful to identify where specific differences existed (table 11.6).

Multiple Comparison Procedure. Duncan's New Multiple Range Test was performed to reveal whether significant differences could be found. According to the results presented in table 11.7, the United States was significantly more centralized, and Sweden was significantly more decentralized. With the exception of the United States and Sweden, the other sample countries were relatively similar in corporate citizenship decision-making autonomy given to their subsidiaries.

Table 11.6
Corporate Citizenship Decision-Making Autonomy

Country of origin	Mean Score*
England	3.11
France	3.13
Germany	2.22
Japan	2.77
Sweden	1.92
Switzerland	2.71
USA	3.40
All Non-US	2.60

KEY: 1 = Subsidiary is solely responsible
2 = Subsidiary is primarily responsible; headquarters contributes
3 = Subsidiary and headquarters are equally responsible
4 = Headquarters is primarily responsible; subsidiary contributes
5 = Headquarters is solely responsible

* Mean score calculated from survey responses.

Table 11.7
Duncan's New Multiple Range Test

	Alpha= .05 df= 124 MSE= 1.545223				
	Means with the same letter are not significantly different.				
Duncan grouping			Mean	N	Country
	A		3.403	588	United States
B	A		3.129	132	France
B	A		3.109	276	England
B	A	C	2.769	108	Japan
B	A	C	2.713	108	Switzerland
B		C	2.221	276	Germany
		C	1.917	84	Sweden

CONCLUSION

For foreign affiliates to successfully adapt to local U.S. conditions may be a larger task than had first been thought. A recent study by Calori and Dufour (1995) postulates that there is a "European" management philosophy. Through extensive interviews with 52 European executives, the authors found four commonalities among the European business executive: a greater orientation toward people; a higher level of internal negotiation; greater skill at managing diversity; and managers capable of managing between extremes. The combination of these practices may result in different approaches to doing business; in other words, differences in corporate citizenship. For instance, the CEO of Solvay was quoted as saying, "The British, like the Americans, are more oriented toward short-term and quick financial profits than the Germans, or even other nationalities on the continent" (Calori and Dufour 1995, 61). Another executive, who even referenced the church, discussed the process of closing a plant in Italy, France, Spain, or Germany and the multitude of stakeholders which intervene in the process.

The European firms tend to practice dialogue and negotiation between management and workers. France experiences more confrontation, while Germany focuses on building consensus, and Sweden mirrors the societal view of egalitarianism. A former executive at Volvo acknowledged inviting employees to sit on the board, prior to being legally required to do so.

Such differences in home country environments might be expected to result in different orientations or differences in the priorities of stakeholders at a minimum. But, the Europeans in particular apparently recognize that they must overcome such differences when they operate outside the European Community. The Europeans see themselves as being less "imperialistic than the Americans and the Japanese who may still have a tendency to export their [management] models" (Calori and Dufour 1995, 61).

> We have been very careful that the board's structure reflects both the legal requirements, the culture of the countries in which they operate and what we consider to be good business practice there. We have been very keen to see that the top management of the company reflects the nationality of the country in which they operate. (Calori and Dufour 1995, 65)

It is believed that the willingness of Europeans to adjust to local management practices ultimately decentralizes its foreign operations. Given the results of the current study, the Japanese appear to be practicing some of the same principles.

> The great strength of foreign-owned companies in the United States is that they make a determined effort to "fit in," adopt established values, and develop programs that address community needs....Foreign-owned companies that operate in the United States live within its laws and cultural norms and it is this physical presence in U.S. society that gives rise to the need for companies to consider their role as corporate citizens, not just "portfolio" investors. (Logan 1994, 8-9)

While one must recognize the limitations of the current study—small sample size, self-reported data, single industry focus, lack of rigorous statistical analysis—the conclusion was that foreign affiliates are similar to domestic entities in this sample. There appeared to be no cause for concern over the increasing foreign investment as foreign affiliates and domestic subsidiaries in the U.S. chemical industry were similar on two of the four dimensions; namely, corporate citizenship orientations and organizational stakeholders. Economic responsibilities were found to be the most important followed by legal, ethical, and philanthropic respectively. The exceptions were Germany and Sweden where legal responsibilities were the highest priority followed by economic, ethical, and philanthropic responsibilities. Still, there were no significant differences.

The sample did not appear to have significant differences in the priority of organizational stakeholders. Consistently, employees, consumers, and owners were cited as more important than community or government. There also appeared to be little cause for concern over the fourth dimension, corporate citizenship decision-making autonomy. In general, foreign affiliates in the sample appeared to be more decentralized than their domestic counterparts. This can be interpreted in three ways. First, the sample was drawn in the United States, and, as a result, the physical proximity of subsidiary to headquarters for the domestic firms may encourage more centralized decision-making. Second and more directly tied to the implication of this study, the foreign affiliates appear to be more decentralized allowing their subsidiaries to respond to local conditions in their host countries. Logan (1994, 7) also found "no evidence that overseas corporate headquarters seek to control everyday community involvement activities." In fact, much of the community involvement begins as employee initiatives, not as philanthropic, strategic decisions. This would seem to contradict the general concern of increasing foreign investment in "small-town" U.S.A. Third, the chemical industry is a global industry. As a result, subsidiaries have been given tremendous authority to "think globally and act locally."

One of the explanations for the overall lack of differences may be found in the nationality of the affiliates' top executives. Although in many cases it has proven difficult to effectively integrate local managers into foreign affiliates, Rhone-Poulenc and Asea Brown Boveri are two foreign firms which emphasize the importance of doing just that (Rosensweig 1994). By placing local managers into high level decision-making positions, foreign affiliates are able to act locally and blend into host communities. In many cases, this spills over into the corporate citizenship issues which the subsidiary addresses.

It is this third dimension of corporate citizenship, corporate citizenship issues, which appeared to be the only area where concern may be justified. However, this concern was not necessarily tied to a foreign affiliate's country of origin. Logan (1994) found that, in the area of community involvement, foreign firms contributed at an average level in contrast to other companies their size. In addition, Logan asserts that, in many cases, these foreign firms seem to be doing more in the United States than they do in their home countries. However, Logan's study also revealed that there may be differences in the focus of discretionary giving based on the home country environment. For instance, attention to the physical environment in the United States may be a result of the public support for environmental protection in the crowded Japanese and European home markets. In addition, while European and Japanese firms also favor education, domestic firms tend to focus more on health and human services. Overall, while the focus of philanthropic responsibilities may differ, the relative giving does not seem to vary due to a firm's "foreignness."

While findings such as Logan (1994) would imply differences among foreign and domestic firms, the current study found similar attention given to the three issues consistently cited as critical issues—employee health and safety in the workplace, environmental protection, and regulatory compliance. As these three primary issues are all protected under U.S. law, it can be assumed that all corporations operating within U.S. boundaries must address these issues. The concern, then, must focus on what has been done in those areas not yet governed by legislation. These areas would be at the heart of "corporate citizenship" as organizations respond without legal mandates. In general, society demands that corporations meet economic and legal responsibilities. Society also has significant expectations with respect to ethical behavior of corporations. Corporations exercise discretion in philanthropy, among other responsibilities.

While positive economic conditions do not guarantee good corporate citizenship, they certainly enable it. Executive after executive acknowledged that "You need money to obey the law and you have to follow the law to make money. Anything left over can go toward promoting good corporate citizenship" (Pinkston and Carroll 1995) . While this response is not enlightened to the point that it recognizes good corporate citizenship as providing economic returns and potentially avoiding legal difficulties, it presents an interesting position, especially in light of the citations which indicate a downturn in the economic performance of foreign affiliates in the United States.

> After increasing significantly through the 1980s, the growth of foreign direct investment in the United States peaked in 1989, then fell sharply in 1990 and again in 1991. This drop in the rate of investment reflected recession and a slow recovery, continued low earnings of many foreign-owned U.S. affiliates, and a reduced need and ability of foreign investors, especially British and Japanese, to expand their U.S. operations. (Arpan and Ricks 1986, vii)

From 1983 to 1991, FDIUS has experienced an average rate of return of approximately 2.6 percent. During the same period, the average rate of return for all-U.S. businesses was 8.4 percent while U.S. business investing abroad earned 8.7 percent (Landefeld, Lawson, and Weinberg 1992). There are many explanations for this difficulty experienced by the foreign affiliates—recency of investments, acquisitions of distressed firms, scale effects, and competitive responses (Rosenswieg 1994). The impact of economic difficulties, particularly on the area of philanthropic responsibilities, can not be dismissed. The question is whether the foreign affiliates, given their unique situation in the U.S. market, are hit harder by U.S. economic and global downturns, and if this will, in turn, result in differences between the foreign affiliates and their domestic counterparts' corporate citizenship. It is a question which merits further investigation.

REFERENCES

Arpan, Jeffrey S., and David A. Ricks. 1986. "Foreign Direct Investment in the U.S.: 1974-1984," *Journal of International Business Studies* 17(Fall):149-153.

Aupperle, Kenneth E. 1982. "An Empirical Inquiry into the Social Responsibilities as Defined by Corporations: an Examination of Various Models and Relationships," Doctoral dissertation, University of Georgia, 239 pages.

Aupperle, Kenneth E., Archie B. Carroll, and John D. Hatfield. 1985. "An Empirical Examination of the Relationship Between Corporate Social Responsibility and Profitability," *Academy of Management Journal* 28(June):446-463.

Averyt, William F. 1990. "Managing Public Policy Abroad: Foreign Corporate Representation in Washington," *The Columbia Journal of World Business* 25(Fall):32-41.

Behrman, Jack N. 1988. *Essays on Ethics in Business and the Professions*. Englewood Cliffs, New Jersey: Prentice-Hall.

Blake, D.H. 1981. "Headquarters and Subsidiary Roles in Managing International Public Affairs—a Preliminary Investigation," in *The Management of Headquarters-Subsidiary Relationships in Multinational Corporations*, edited by L. Otterbeck. New York: St. Martin's Press.

Bob, Daniel E. 1991. *Japanese Companies in American Communities: Cooperation, Conflict and the Role of Corporate Citizenship*. New York: Japan Society.

Calori, Richard, and Bruno Dufour. 1995. "Management European Style," *Academy of Management Executive* 9(August):61-73.

Carroll, Archie B. 1979. "A Three-Dimensional Model of Corporate Performance," *Academy of Management Review* 4:497-505.

Choate, Pat. 1990. "Political Advantage: Japan's Campaign for America," *Harvard Business Review* 68(Sept.-Oct.):87-103.

Clarkson, M. 1988. "Corporate Social Performance in Canada, 1976-1986," in *Research in Corporate Social Performance and Policy, Vol. 10*, edited by Lee E. Preston. Greenwich, Conn.: JAI.

Corporate 500: The Directory of Corporate Philanthropy, The. 1985. Detroit: Gale Research.

Cowton, Christopher. 1987. "Corporate Philanthropy in the United Kingdom," *Journal of Business Ethics* 6(7):553-558.

Dierkes, M. 1980. "Corporate Social Reporting and Performance in Germany," in *Research in Corporate Social Performance and Policy, Vol. 2*, edited by Lee E. Preston. Greenwich, Conn.: JAI.

Freeman, R. Edward. 1984. *Strategic Management—A Stakeholder Approach*. Boston: Pitman.

Gelsanliter, David. 1990. *Jumpstart: Japan Comes to the Heartland*. New York: Farrar, Straus, Giroux.

Gladwin, Thomas N., and Ingo Walter. 1980. *Multinationals under Fire: Lessons in the Management of Conflict*. New York: Wiley.

Hargreaves, Basil J. A., and Jan Dauman. 1975. *Business Survival and Social Change: A Practical Guide to Responsibility and Partnership*. New York: John Wiley and Sons.

Hofstede, Geert H. 1980. *Culture's Consequences: International Differences in Work-Related Values*. Beverly Hills, Calif.: Sage Publications.

International Directory of Corporate Affiliations, Vol. 1-2. 1990/91. Wilmette, Ill.: National Register Publishing Co.

Landefeld, J. Steven, Ann M. Lawson, and Douglas B. Weinberg. 1992. "Rates of Return on Direct Investment," *Survey of Current Business* 72(August):79-86.

Langlois, Catherine C., and Bodo B. Schlegelmilch. 1990. "Do Corporate Codes of Ethics Reflect National Character? Evidence from Europe and the United States," *Journal of International Business Strategy* 4:519-539.

Logan, David. 1994. *Community Involvement of Foreign-Owned Companies*. New York: The Conference Board, Report Number 1089-94-RR.

MacMillan, I. 1980. "Corporate Social Responsiveness to the Unemployment Issue: a British Perspective," in *Research in Corporate Social Performance and Policy, Vol. 2*, edited by Lee E. Preston. Greenwich, Conn.: JAI.

Mafune, Y. 1988. "Corporate Social Performance and Policy in Japan," in *Research in Corporate Social Performance and Policy, Vol. 10*, edited by Lee E. Preston. Greenwich, Conn.: JAI.

Merger Yearbook, The (vol. 1-7). annual. Ipswich, Mass.: Cambridge.

Moore, C., and J. Richardson. 1988. "The Politics and Practice of Corporate Responsibility in Great Britain," in *Research in Corporate Social Performance and Policy, Vol.10*, edited by Lee E. Preston. Greenwich, Conn.: JAI.

Pinkston, Tammie S., and Archie B. Carroll. 1995. "A Retrospective Examination of CSR Orientations: Have They Changed?" *Journal of Business Ethics* 15:199-206.

Preston, L. E., F. Rey, and M. Dierkes. 1978. "Comparing Corporate Social Performance: Germany, France, Canada, and the U.S." *California Management Review* Summer, pp. 40-49.

Rehder, Robert R. 1990. "Japanese Transplants: After the Honeymoon," *Business Horizons*, 33(January/February):87-98.

Rey, F. 1980. "Corporate Social Performance and Reporting in France," in *Research in Corporate Social Performance and Policy, Vol. 2*, edited by Lee E. Preston. Greenwich, Conn.: JAI.

Rosenszeig, Philip M., 1994. "The New 'American Challenge': Foreign Multinationals in the United States," *California Management Review* 36(Spring):107-123.

Sethi, S. P. 1975. "Dimensions of Corporate Social Performance: an Analytical Framework," *California Management Review* 17:58-64.

———. 1978. "An Analytical Framework for Making Cross-cultural Comparisons of Business Responses to Social Pressures: the Case of the United States and Japan," in *Research in Corporate Social Performance and Policy, Vol.2*, edited by Lee E. Preston. Greenwich, Conn.: JAI.

Shear, J. 1990. "Foreign Investment Is Making Borderless Corporate World," *Insight* pp. 40-42, July 2.

Smith, W.J., and R.S. Blackburn. 1988. "CSR: a Psychometric Examination of a Measurement Instrument," *Proceedings of the Southern Management Association*, November, pp. 293-295.

Thompson, Judith K., and Robert R. Rehder. 1995. "Nissan U.K.: A Worker's Paradox?" *Business Horizons* 38(January-February):48-58.

Tuleja, Tad. 1985. *Beyond the Bottom Line: How Business Leaders are Turning Principles into Profits*. New York: Facts on File.

Vesper International. 1990. *Just Profits: Wending Our Way Through the Moral Maze*, Working draft from the Annual Conference in San Francisco, August 7-9.

Wartick Steven L., and Philip S. Cochran. 1985. "The Evolution of the Corporate Social Performance Model," *The Academy of Management Review* 10:758-769.

Wokutch, Richard E. 1990. "Corporate Social Responsibility Japanese Style," *Academy of Management Executive* 4(May):56-74.

Wood, Donna J. 1990. *Business and Society*. Glenview, Ill.: Scott, Foresman.

12

Top Management Turnover: Comparing Foreign and Domestic Acquisitions of U.S. Firms

Jeffrey A. Krug and Douglas Nigh

INTRODUCTION

In this chapter, we examine the turnover of top executives of U.S. companies that have been acquired by other firms. Of particular interest is the extent to which the nationality of the acquiring company has an effect on top management turnover. What is the nature of the differences, if any, in top management turnover for acquisitions by companies who call the United States home versus those whose domicile is a foreign country? In what ways, if any, do the national cultural values of the United States and the home country of the acquiring firm affect top management turnover following acquisition?

A growing body of literature in strategic management has documented higher than "normal" turnover rates among top managers in U.S. firms acquired by other U.S. firms (Cannella and Hambrick 1993; Furtado and Karan 1990; Hayes 1979; Hayes and Hoag 1974; Martin and McConnell 1991; Walsh 1988). Turnover rates are highest in the first year following the acquisition, and the full effect of the acquisition is generally captured within four years. Subsequent studies in the domestic literature have led to speculation regarding the origins of this higher-than-normal turnover, including characteristics of the merger and acquisition (M&A) process (Walsh 1989), communications between management teams during the post-acquisition integration process (Schweiger and DeNisi 1991), agency theory and the market for corporate control (Walsh and Ellwood 1991; Walsh and Kosnik 1993), and the "relative standing" of target company managers following the acquisition (Hambrick and Cannella 1993). However, the extant literature in this area remains speculative, and the origins of this high postacquisition turnover are still not fully understood.

Analysis of foreign acquisitions and their effects on acquired U.S. top management teams has, to date, been limited. The evidence, based on five years of post-acquisiton data, indicates that both foreign and domestic acquisitions of U.S. firms lead to higher-than-normal turnover. Further, foreign acquisitions exhibit a higher rate of turnover than domestic acquisitions, but not until the fifth year after the acquisition (Krug and Hegarty 1997). These results raise the question of differences in executive turnover beyond the fifth year.

The importance of examining the role of foreign companies in the U.S. economy is underscored by the increased importance of foreign firms in U.S. merger and acquisition activity, as well as in U.S. industrial production. In 1983, foreign firms accounted for approximately 4 percent of the total value of all mergers and acquisitions in the United States. By 1990, this value had increased to 27 percent (*Mergers and Acquisitions* 1990). This is consistent with the pattern of manufacturing output in the United States during the last fifteen years. Between 1977 and 1993, U.S. manufacturing output by foreign-based multinational corporations (MNCs) increased from 4 percent to approximately 20 percent. Foreign MNCs employed 2.2 million U.S. workers in 1991, or 12 percent of the U.S. industrial workforce, about four times the 1977 level. During the same period, industrial jobs offered by U.S.-based manufacturing firms fell by nearly 3.9 million employees, a 16 percent drop in employment (Chetwynd 1994).

Further, the focus on top management teams of business organizations in this international context is important because top management teams hold the key to many strategic decisions that influence the competitiveness of both companies and countries. Top management teams decide whether to expand production facilities, for one example, and whether to invest in new technologies or training programs, for another example. Most pointedly, top management teams decide the country location of investments in physical and human resources and provide crucial leadership in implementing such key decisions.

Below, theoretical arguments are offered about why turnover of acquired executives will be higher when the U.S. firm is acquired by a foreign-owned (as opposed to domestic) company. Both the magnitude and timing of these differences are addressed. There follows consideration of foreign country cultural values and their influence on top management turnover in U.S. companies acquired by foreign companies. Hypotheses are tested using eight years of data on turnover after acquisition, rather than the five years reported in previous studies. Acquisitions by companies from specific countries and certain regions of the world are explored and compared to the acquisitions by U.S. companies.

PREVIOUS RESEARCH AND THEORETICAL DEVELOPMENT

The existing literature on top management turnover following mergers and acquisitions has focused almost exclusively on U.S. acquisitions of other U.S. firms. Hayes and Hoag (1974) and Hayes (1979) surveyed fifty managers who had been involved in acquisitions by sixteen acquiring firms from the Fortune 500 between 1967 and 1971. They found that 58 percent of the managers had left the acquired firm within five years of the acquisition. In two subsequent empirical studies, Walsh (1988; 1989) examined turnover among acquired executives in manufacturing and mining companies during the 1975-1979 time frame. Walsh found that about 60 percent of the acquired managers had departed within five years of the acquisition. The turnover rate in a control group of nonacquired U.S. firms was 33 percent.

Similar results were found in subsequent studies (Cannella and Hambrick 1993; Furtado and Karan 1990; Martin and McConnell 1991; Walsh and Ellwood 1991).

To examine the effects of "foreignness," Krug and Hegarty (1997), examining turnover among U.S. top management teams in 270 cross-border and purely domestic acquisitions and 120 nonacquired U.S. firms, found that turnover was significantly higher in firms acquired by both foreign and domestic acquirers. By the fifth year following the acquisition, turnover of acquired U.S. executives reached 69 percent in the purely domestic acquisitions, 75 percent in the foreign acquisitions, and 37 percent in the 120 nonacquired firms. Turnover rates in both foreign and domestic acquisitions rose at about the same rate through the third year. Beyond the third year, turnover rates in the purely domestic acquisitions rose at about the same rate as turnover in the nonacquired firms. This is consistent with existing studies of purely domestic acquisitions. However, turnover in the foreign acquisitions continued to rise and became significantly higher than turnover in the purely domestic acquisitions in the fifth year following the acquisition.

A variety of theories have been put forward to explain a company's motivation for investing abroad. Early theories emphasized the manager's perception of international business as risky. International business resulted from an unsolicited order from abroad (Aharoni 1966); was undertaken incrementally, with the firm increasing its involvement in international business as its experience grew (Johanson and Vahlne 1977); or was driven by a desire to take advantage of disequilibria in financial markets (Johnson 1970; Ragazzi 1973). More recently, foreign direct investment (FDI) has been viewed as a means by which firms exploit monopolistic advantages such as technology or marketing know-how (Caves 1971; 1974; Graham 1974; Hymer 1960; Kindleberger 1969; Knickerbocker 1974). Finally, internalization theory (Buckley and Casson 1976; McManus 1972; Rugman 1986) and transaction cost theory (Coase 1937; Williamson 1975) have suggested that firms engage in FDI because it is a more cost-effective means of exploiting a comparative advantage than other means, such as trade, licensing, or joint ventures. Dunning (1973; 1980) expanded these views by arguing that three criteria were necessary for FDI to take place: *(i)* a firm-specific advantage enables the firm to compete with local firms; *(ii)* internalization is the most cost-effective means of conducting business abroad; and *(iii)* there is a location-specific advantage associated with the proposed FDI site.

Surveys of foreign firms indicate that a major motivation of many foreign firms investing in the United States during the 1970s and 1980s was to break into the U.S. market for the first time, to take advantage of the large U.S. market, or to acquire U.S. technological, managerial, or marketing know-how (Ajami and Ricks 1981; Daniels 1971; Kim and Lyn 1987; Sametz and Backman 1974; Sokoya and Tillery 1992). In many cases, the objective of foreign firms is to learn the acquired technology or know-how and repatriate it back to the home country (Franko 1976). Kim and Lyn (1987) found that foreign firms are most attracted to industries that enable them to gain access to U.S. technology and innovation. In addition, foreign investments tend to be concentrated in a small number of industries, suggesting that the high political stability of the U.S. market, the highly developed U.S. capital market, and other environmental factors are not major motivations for foreign firms. A later study by Sokoya and Tillery (1992) suggested that the large size of the U.S. market and U.S. technology continue to be important motives for investment, though U.S. technology is a less important motivator for firms from countries with a history of technological innovation, such as Germany and Japan.

In cases where a foreign acquirer makes an acquisition to break into the U.S. market for the first time, the foreign acquirer may be inclined to operate the acquired U.S. business largely as an autonomous subsidiary until the acquirer becomes more comfortable operating in the U.S. environment. Additionally, a foreign acquirer investing to acquire U.S. technological, managerial, or marketing know-how may be inclined to run the U.S. business largely as an independent unit until the acquirer has sufficiently learned the acquired technology or know-how. Thus, foreign acquirers may be less inclined to integrate or make changes in the U.S. business during the early years following the acquisition. In fact, retention of U.S. managers may be an important element in the foreign firm's strategy of learning the market and acquired technology or know-how.

However, while the acquired unit may be run somewhat autonomously from a strategic point of view, the parent may nevertheless institute certain controls (such as accounting, financial, or MIS) to improve communications and the flow of resources between the two merging units. Even in the absence of such controls, the acquiring company is likely to send personnel to the acquired subsidiary to learn the U.S. mode of operations. Therefore, certain "linkages" will likely be developed, even though the U.S. subsidiary may retain a certain degree of strategic or operational autonomy.

In the case of foreign companies investing to acquire technology or know-how, particularly when the foreign company is a first-time investor in the United States, the process of building linkages may be particularly acute, and policies may be slower to change when compared to purely domestic acquisitions. Retention of top managers with strong ties to stakeholder groups may be critical to acquisition success in the early stages of the postacquisition period. However, once the foreign acquirer's knowledge of the U.S. operation reaches a higher level, retention of U.S. managers may become less critical for success. As time passes, the success of the acquired company may be less dependent on the tacit knowledge embedded in the acquired executives. Then, strategic and operational changes become more likely.

Arguably, foreign firms will be inclined to integrate the acquired U.S. business at a slower rate when compared to U.S. firms acquiring other U.S. businesses. Therefore, the full turnover effects of purely domestic acquisitions should occur at an earlier stage following the acquisition (that is, within four years of the acquisition, which is consistent with existing studies on domestic acquisitions) and much later in the case of foreign acquisitions (that is, beyond four years).

The process of merging two companies has been shown to be a great source of stress and uncertainty for employees in the acquired firm (Buono and Bowditch 1989; Marks and Mirvis 1985; Schweiger and Walsh 1990). The primary source of stress during the postacquisition process appears to be the many organizational changes that alter people's work and personal situations (Levinson 1970; Marks 1982; Schweiger, Ivancevich, and Power 1987). In the absence of communication mechanisms designed to reduce uncertainties among target company personnel during the merger process, target company employees often experience increased levels of stress, lower job commitment, lower job satisfaction, and higher intent to turnover (Schweiger and DeNisi 1991). Hambrick and Cannella (1993) hypothesized that the tendency of acquired executives to quit the new organization is a function of the executive's "relative standing" in the new organization. As a manager's job status and decision-making authority within the organization decline (whether real or perceived), the manager's inclination to leave the organization increases.

The success of an acquisition is often a function of the successful integration of the target and acquiring firms. Pablo (1994, 806) defined integration as the "degree of postacquisition change in an organization's technical, administrative, and [corporate] cultural configuration." Successful integration may be especially difficult in the face of organization fit problems (Jemison and Sitkin 1986) and differences in strategies, structures, and corporate cultures between the merging firms (Mirvis 1985). Differences in corporate culture are particularly problematic as they may lead to polarization, anxiety, and ethnocentrism within the acquired management team (Sales and Mirvis 1984) and to power struggles between the target and acquiring management teams (Mirvis 1985). Weber and Schweiger (1989) determined that positive attitudes of acquired executives decline with increasing perceptions of cultural differences between the merging top management teams. Negative attitudes within the acquired top management team often lead to lower commitment to the new organization and less cooperation with the acquiring company.

The importance of the successful management of differences in corporate cultures between the merging firms during the integration process is underscored by evidence that acquiring firm performance following an acquisition varies significantly as a function of cultural fit. Chatterjee et al. (1992) demonstrated that stock market gains of acquiring firms are positively and significantly correlated with investors' perceptions of cultural similarities between the two merging top management teams. While corporate cultural differences may hinder the successful integration of two firms regardless of their nationality, the integration of two firms of different nationalities may be exacerbated by cross-national cultural differences. Organizational fit and communication problems may be created by different organizational and administrative practices and employee expectations that result from differences in national cultures (Kogut and Singh 1988). National culture significantly affects managers' responses in certain situations, though it appears to affect managers differently depending on the national origin of the manager (Kelley, Whatley, and Worthley 1987). Moreover, relationships among managers tend to deteriorate when interpersonal differences become apparent. Li and Guisinger (1991) found that a sample of subsidiaries of foreign firms in the United States failed at a greater rate as a function of the cultural distance between the home country and the United States. Therefore, postacquisition turnover rate among acquired executives may be a function of the cultural distance between the acquiring and U.S. target firms.

The review of previous studies and the authors' theoretical development in this area are summarized by the following three propositions that are empirically examined in this chapter.

Proposition 1:   Postacquisition turnover rates in U.S. companies acquired by foreign firms are higher than postacquisition turnover rates in purely domestic acquisitions.

Proposition 2:   The full turnover effects of foreign acquisitions occur later than those of purely domestic acquisitions.

Proposition 3:   Postacquisition turnover rates of U.S. acquired firms are positively related to the cultural distance between the United States and the home country of the acquiring firm.

RESEARCH APPROACH

Sample and Procedure

Mergers and Acquisitions publishes quarterly data on all mergers, acquisitions, and divestitures involving U.S. firms with a transaction value of $1 million or more. There are few other restrictions for inclusion in the database. For example, acquisitions of service as well as manufacturing and mining firms are included, as are publicly traded, private, and subsidiary targets. Acquisitions are categorized by *(i)* U.S. acquisitions of U.S. targets, *(ii)* foreign acquisitions of U.S. targets, and *(iii)* U.S. acquisitions of foreign targets. A pooled sample was drawn from *Mergers and Acquisitions* for the period 1986-1988.

Krug and Hegarty (1997) sampled 648 acquisitions of U.S. firms during the 1986-1988 time frame. These data were also used in this research. However, Krug and Hegarty (1997) analyzed turnover among acquired executives for five years following the acquisition. Their data were augmented to analyze turnover for an eight-year period following the acquisition. Before the sample was drawn, the population of foreign acquisitions of U.S. firms was segmented into culturally similar regions based on the typology developed by Ronen and Shenkar (1985). A random sample, drawn from each of these segments, permitted a statistical analysis of cultural differences between the United States and numerous countries in which the foreign acquirers were based. The sample included 340 purely domestic acquisitions and 308 foreign acquisitions by firms headquartered in sixteen regions including Europe, Canada, Australia, Japan, and Hong Kong. Acquisitions from Arabic countries, Africa, Latin America, and Southeast Asia were numerically small or non-existent during this period.

Standard and Poor's Register of Executives, Directors, and Corporations (*Register*), Dun and Bradstreet's *Million Dollar Directory*, and the *Polk Financial Institutions Directory* were used to identify U.S. top management teams in place prior to the acquisition in each of the 648 acquired U.S. entities. Annual reports, 10-K reports, *Directory of Corporate Affiliations*, *International Directory of Corporate Affiliations*, *Ward's Business Directory*, and *Corporate Technology Directory* were used to check the accuracy of the data in the primary reference sources. Of the 648 acquisitions, complete data were found for 363 target companies.

Each target company was tracked in the reference source for eight years following the acquisition. The reference source stopped reporting data on 130 of the target companies during this eight-year postacquisition period. Each of these 130 target companies was then followed in the NEXIS/LEXIS database to determine its status. Telephone calls were also made to fifty target companies to solicit information on the employment status of the top managers still working with the company at the time of the last published record in the reference source. In 51 cases, complete data were obtained through either the NEXIS/LEXIS search or phone conversations with target company personnel. In the other 79 cases, the firm had declared bankruptcy during the period, the firm's phone had been disconnected, or the firm refused to answer questions pertaining to the study. Therefore, complete data for 284 or 78.2 percent of the 363 identifiable target companies were available for up to eight years following the acquisition.

Each of the 284 firms was tracked in the annual *Merger and Acquisition* almanacs to identify other acquisitions of the firms during a four-year period surrounding the acquisition identified in the sample. Twenty target firms were eliminated from the sample because they had been acquired by more than one company headquartered in different countries during the period. Additionally, each target firm was identified in the *Directory of Corporate Affiliations* or *International Directory of Corporate Affiliations* just prior to the acquisition to verify the headquarters location of the acquiring firm listed in *Mergers and Acquisitions*. One reclassification was made. The final sample included 264 acquired U.S. targets: 101 U.S. acquisitions (38.3 percent of the total) and 163 foreign acquisitions (61.7 percent of the total).

A control group of 600 nonacquired U.S. companies was randomly sampled from the *Register* during the 1986-1988 time frame. At some point during the eight-year period following the firm's initial observation, 484 or 80.7 percent of the firms were dropped from the reference source as a result of bankruptcy, acquisition, or other reasons. This left 116 control firms in the sample. Analysis of the annual *Merger and Acquisitions* almanacs revealed that three additional control firms were involved in an acquisition during the study period. These, too, were excluded from the control group, leaving 113 firms that were operational and not involved in an acquisition during the eight-year research period. Table 12.1 summarizes the merger and acquisition and the control group samples.

Measures

Top Management Turnover. Annual and cumulative top management turnover rates for each acquired firm were calculated in each of the eight years following the acquisition. Annual rates were calculated by dividing the number of managers constituting the U.S. target company top management team just prior to the acquisition (base top management team) into the number of managers from the base top management team who left during the year. Cumulative turnover rates were calculated by dividing the base top management team into the total number of managers from the base top management team who had left the firm since the acquisition. These calculations are consistent with previous work on domestic acquisitions and top management turnover. Managers who joined the firm during the postacquisition period and subsequently left were not measured in the turnover calculation.

Cultural Distance. Kogut and Singh (1988) examined the relationship between a foreign firm's entry mode (in other words, acquisition, greenfield, or joint venture) and *(i)* the cultural distance between the country of the investing company and the United States and *(ii)* the uncertainty avoidance characterizing the investing firm relative to the United States. Both cultural measures were based on Hofstede's

Table 12.1
Sample and Control Group

	U.S. M&As	Foreign M&As	Total M&As	Control Group	Total Sample
Initial Sample	340	308	648	600	1248
Identifiable Management Teams	153	210	363	600	963
% Sample	45.0%	68.2%	56.1%	100.0%	77.2%
Complete 8-Year Data	109	175	284	116	400
% Identifiable Management Teams	71.2%	83.3%	78.2%	19.3%	42.9%
Exclusions (1)	-7	-13	-20	-3	-23
Reclassifications (2)	-1	1	0	0	0
Final Sample	101	163	264	113	377
% Total M&As	38.3%	61.7%	100.0%		

(1) Exclusions: Target companies acquired by two or more acquirers from different countries within a four-year period surrounding the sampled acquisition.

(2) Reclassifications: Analysis of the headquarters location of the ultimate owner of each acquiring firm revealed that one U.S. acquiring company listed in *Mergers & Acquisitions* was owned by a company headquartered outside the United States. The acquisition was reclassified as a foreign acquisition.

(1980a; 1980b) four cultural dimensions (power distance, masculinity-femininity, individualism-collectivism, and uncertainty avoidance). A composite index measuring "cultural distance" was constructed based on the deviation of each country's index from the U.S. index along each of Hofstede's four cultural dimensions. Kogut and Singh's methodology has subsequently been used in a variety of empirical studies analyzing the effects of cultural distance on various dependent variables (for example, Benito and Gripsrud 1992; Li and Guisinger 1991; 1992). This research utilizes Kogut and Singh's measure of cultural distance between the United States and a foreign country.

Methods of Analysis

To test for differences in magnitude and timing of turnover in domestic versus foreign acquisitions, cumulative turnover rates for each of the eight years following acquisition were used, and t-tests were calculated for each of the eight years to examine mean cumulative turnover differences between the two groups. The turnover rates of the control group were compared to the turnover rates of nonacquired U.S. companies.

To test the relationship between turnover in the acquired U.S. firms and national cultural differences between the United States and country of origin of the acquiring firm, cumulative turnover rates for each of the eight years were correlated with a composite index of cultural distance based on Kogut and Singh's (1988) analysis. As a follow-up test, one-way analyses of variance were conducted for each of the eight years following the acquisition to test for mean cumulative turnover differences across different acquiring groups based on the methodology of Ronen and Shenkar (1985).

RESULTS

The results of the cumulative turnover calculations for eight years after the acquisition are shown in table 12.2. Table 12.2 provides data segmented by the culturally similar regions developed by Ronen and Shenkar (1985) and breaks data down to the country level. This table provides the mean cumulative target company top management turnover rates for each year through the eighth year following the acquisition. It also provides summary cumulative rates for domestic and foreign acquisitions and for the control group of U.S. companies that were not acquired.

Cumulative turnover rates for the nonacquired U.S. firms, as seen at the bottom of table 12.2, are much lower than the rates for either foreign or domestic acquisition rates in each of the eight years. The rates of this control group start out lower and remain so. These nonacquired firms provide some measure of the "normal" rates for executive turnover in U.S. companies. The differences between nonacquired and foreign acquired turnover rates and between nonacquired and domestic acquired rates are statistically significant. These results are quite consistent with previous comparisons of turnover rates in acquired and nonacquired companies.

A different pattern of results across the eight years is evident in cumulative turnover rates in foreign versus domestic acquisitions. The results of the t-tests of mean cumulative turnover differences between the foreign and domestic acquisitions show that cumulative turnover in both instances is not significantly different for years 1, 2, 3, or 4 (table 12.3). However, cumulative rates for foreign acquisitions are significantly higher than for domestic acquisitions in years 5 and 6 following the acquisition. For years 7 and 8, there are no significant turnover differences.

This pattern of results over time can be seen clearly in figure 12.1, which shows turnover rates among executives in U.S. firms acquired by foreign and domestic acquirers, as well as "normal" turnover rates in nonacquired U.S. firms. For years 1 through 3, the rates for foreign and domestic acquisitions are quite close. After year 3, they diverge. Turnover rates in the domestic acquisitions rise at a lower rate that parallels the rate of the nonacquired firms. However, turnover in the foreign acquisitions continues to rise at a higher rate after year 3 through year 6 following the acquisition.

The evidence of table 12.3 and figure 12.1 supports propositions 1 and 2. First, foreign acquisitions have a higher cumulative turnover rate than domestic acquisitions, a difference that becomes significant for years 5 and 6. While the turnover rate for domestic acquisitions levels off in year 4 and equals that of the nonacquisitions, the turnover rate for foreign acquisitions continues to outpace that of domestic acquisitions through year 6, before tapering off and resembling that of the nonacquisitions. The foreign acquisitions take longer to exhibit the full effect of the acquisition than do domestic acquisitions.

Table 12.4 shows the correlations between cumulative turnover in the acquired firms in each of the eight years following acquisition and the measure of national culture distance between the United States and the country of origin of the acquiring

Table 12.2
Cumulative Postacquisition Top Management Turnover Rates

Acquiring Country	# Firms	Year Following the Acquisition							
		1	2	3	4	5	6	7	8
Denmark	1	0.0	0.0	58.3	58.3	91.6	91.6	91.6	91.6
Finland	4	6.3	27.7	58.9	86.0	86.0	89.6	95.8	95.8
Sweden	7	28.9	58.2	66.1	70.4	73.3	78.5	88.1	89.2
Nordic Region	12	19.0	43.2	63.1	74.6	79.1	83.3	90.9	91.6
Germany	14	18.3	40.3	61.1	67.6	84.4	86.2	90.3	90.7
Switzerland	5	9.5	57.5	63.5	77.8	77.8	77.8	83.8	83.8
Germanic Region	19	16.0	44.8	61.7	70.3	82.6	84.0	88.6	88.9
Belgium	2	22.2	27.8	56.3	56.3	88.9	88.9	88.9	94.4
France	11	36.2	42.6	65.1	69.4	70.0	76.2	76.2	76.2
Italy	3	26.0	26.0	54.9	57.4	60.0	87.2	94.9	94.9
Monaco	1	0.0	0.0	100.0	100.0	100.0	100.0	100.0	100.0
Latin Europe	17	30.6	35.4	64.3	67.6	72.2	81.0	82.4	83.0
Netherlands	7	25.9	51.8	61.6	74.7	81.4	88.0	88.0	89.5
United Kingdom	45	16.3	32.4	50.1	62.1	70.8	77.8	79.6	81.9
Europe	100	19.7	37.9	57.1	67.0	75.0	80.9	83.7	85.1
Europe excluding U.K.	55	22.4	42.4	62.8	70.9	78.5	83.4	87.1	87.7
Canada	23	23.1	53.6	65.7	77.9	80.9	85.0	89.1	90.1
Australia	10	26.6	44.1	79.5	80.0	92.9	92.9	92.9	92.9
Venezuela	1	0.0	16.7	33.3	33.3	33.3	50.0	50.0	100.0
Hong Kong	4	24.6	48.8	71.9	73.7	78.6	78.6	78.6	81.7
Japan	25	27.4	44.0	61.1	64.1	66.8	77.0	78.3	81.2
Anglo Region	179	20.6	40.2	57.6	66.2	71.7	77.2	80.4	83.2
Non-Anglo Region	85	22.7	41.0	59.6	65.5	71.2	77.3	79.9	81.8
Total Foreign Acquisitions	163	21.8	41.6	60.5	68.8	75.5	81.4	83.9	85.7
Total U.S. Acquisitions	101	21.7	41.0	58.0	65.2	69.3	75.2	79.2	82.9
Total Acquisitions	264	21.7	41.4	59.5	67.5	73.1	79.0	82.1	84.6
Nonacquired U.S. Firms (Control Group)	113	8.0	16.1	23.8	31.8	37.2	42.0	47.8	50.6
Total Firms	377								

Table 12.3
T-Tests: Top Management Turnover in Foreign versus Domestic Acquisitions

	Number of cases	Mean turnover	Standard deviation	t-value	One-Tail Probability
Year 1 following acquisition					
Foreign acquired firms	163	21.8	30.34	0.01	0.497
U.S. acquired firms	101	21.7	28.67		
Year 2 following acquisition					
Foreign acquired firms	163	41.6	33.67	0.14	0.445
U.S. acquired firms	101	41.0	33.96		
Year 3 following acquisition					
Foreign acquired firms	163	60.5	30.40	0.64	0.262
U.S. acquired firms	101	58.0	33.06		
Year 4 following acquisition					
Foreign acquired firms	163	68.8	27.71	0.99	0.161
U.S. acquired firms	101	65.2	30.25		
Year 5 following acquisition					
Foreign acquired firms	163	75.5	25.54	1.73	0.043
U.S. acquired firms	101	69.3	29.94		
Year 6 following acquisition					
Foreign acquired firms	163	81.4	22.25	1.88	0.031
U.S. acquired firms	101	75.2	27.89		
Year 7 following acquisition					
Foreign acquired firms	163	83.9	21.25	1.54	0.063
U.S. acquired firms	101	79.2	25.75		
Year 8 following acquisition					
Foreign acquired firms	163	85.7	19.82	1.05	0.147
U.S. acquired firms	101	82.9	23.12		

Figure 12.1
Postacquisition Target Company Turnover Rates

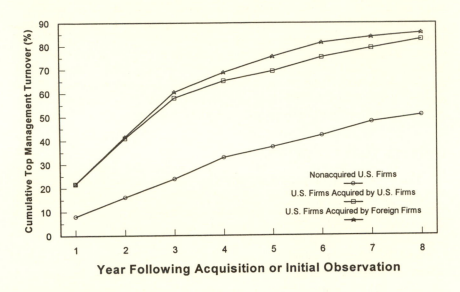

Table 12.4
Correlations among the Variables

Cumula-tive Turnover		C1	C2	C3	C4	C5	C6	C7	C8
Year 1	C1	--							
Year 2	C2	0.57 **	--						
Year 3	C3	0.32 **	0.55 **	--					
Year 4	C4	0.31 **	0.49 **	0.86 **	--				
Year 5	C5	0.23 **	0.45 **	0.76 **	0.86 **	--			
Year 6	C6	0.20 *	0.37 **	0.68 **	0.75 **	0.85 **	--		
Year 7	C7	0.18 *	0.33 **	0.61 **	0.71 **	0.80 **	0.92 **	--	
Year 8	C8	0.17 *	0.31 **	0.57 **	0.66 **	0.76 **	0.86 **	0.93 **	--
Cultural Distance	CD	0.07	0.02	0.05	-0.01	-0.04	-0.01	-0.04	-0.02

$*p < 0.01$; $**p < 0.001$

firm. No relationship between turnover and cultural distance was found. One-way analyses of the variance were conducted for each of the eight years following the acquisition to test for cumulative mean turnover differences across culturally similar acquiring groups. The 264 acquisitions were segmented into six groups: *(i)* Nordic, *(ii)* Germanic, *(iii)* Latin European, *(iv)* Anglo, *(v)* the United States, and *(vi)* others (Ronen and Shenkar 1985). Although the United States is categorized as an "Anglo" country in Ronen and Shenkar's analysis, it was separated from other Anglo acquirers to retain the distinction between foreign and domestic acquisitions. Nevertheless, no differences were found across these categories. Therefore, proposition 3 was rejected. The evidence of this study provides no support for a positive effect of cultural distance on the acquired firm's executive turnover.

DISCUSSION AND CONCLUSION

This research provides the first analysis of the long-term comparative effects of foreign versus domestic acquisitions on U.S. target company top management turnover. Turnover was analyzed for eight years following the acquisition. Previous work in this area has been limited to analyses of one to five years following the acquisition.

Results indicated that, consistent with previous research, the greatest turnover effects occur within three years of the acquisition, regardless of the nationality of the acquiring firm. Turnover in the foreign and purely domestic acquisitions rose at about the same rate through the third year following the acquisition. Beyond the third year, turnover in the domestic acquisitions rose at about the same rate as turnover in the control group of nonacquired U.S. firms. However, cumulative turnover in the foreign acquisitions continued to rise at a higher rate beyond the third year and became significantly higher compared to turnover in the purely domestic acquisitions in the fifth and sixth years following the acquisition. No differences were found beyond the sixth year.

An intriguing finding of this study was that turnover rose at about the same rate in both foreign and domestic acquisitions during the first three years after the acquisition. This is contrary to the literature, which suggests that foreign firms are often motivated to invest in the United States to break into the U.S. market for the first time or to acquire U.S. technology and know-how. This would suggest that retention of U.S. managers during the first few years following the acquisition would be an essential element in the foreign firm's ability to learn the U.S. market and acquired technology and know-how. Possibly, acquisitions by foreign firms are transacted through U.S. affiliates of the foreign firm, which are manned by U.S. personnel. Also possibly, foreign acquirers with experience in the U.S. acquisition market already feel comfortable making changes in the acquired U.S. entity immediately following the acquisition. In these cases, foreign acquisitions may share many of the characteristics of purely domestic acquisitions. However, such a scenario still does not explain the fact that turnover in foreign firms persists through the sixth year after the acquisition, while turnover returns to a relatively "normal" rate in the purely domestic acquisitions. Additional research examining acquisition motivations and acquirer experience in the U.S. market may shed light on this issue.

There was no support for proposition 3, that turnover in acquired U.S. firms would vary as a function of the cultural distance between the U.S. and the country of origin of the acquiring firm. Moreover, when the acquisition sample was segmented by groups of countries based on cultural similarity, no differences in turnover were found. This result is particularly intriguing given evidence that differences in national culture have been associated with a foreign firm's choice of entry mode in the United States (Kogut and Singh 1988) and higher failure rates of U.S. affiliates (Li and Guisinger 1991). A partial explanation may be found in the level of internationalization of the acquiring firm. Li and Guisinger (1992) found that cultural distance between the home and host countries inversely affects FDI of service MNEs in the early stage of internationalization. However, once a firm has reached a higher level of internationalization, the effect of cultural distance is no longer evident. Cho and Padmanabhan (1996) argue that decision-specific experience (such as acquisition experience) has a greater influence than either general international or country-specific experience. Both acquisition experience and general international experience may enable acquiring firms to overcome the cultural barriers faced by first-time U.S. investors. These experienced firms have learned how to retain executives in foreign acquisitions, even without U.S. (country-specific) experience.

A second possible explanation may be found in differences between intracultural and cross-cultural behavior among executives conducting business abroad. Adler and Graham (1989) found that businesspeople tend to adapt their behaviors to the culture of the people with whom they are dealing. Possibly, foreign businesspeople operating in the United States have developed a high level of knowledge of the U.S. culture and can make sufficient adaptations to U.S. business practices. In such cases, cultural differences may no longer be a major cause of turnover among acquired executives. The increased level of internationalization among firms in the industrialized countries during the last ten years suggests that research on the motivations of foreign firms investing in the U.S. market may have become outdated. The country-specific experience level may be generally high among foreign acquiring firms. More timely research on this issue may be warranted.

The objective of this research was to examine the long-term comparative effects of foreign versus domestic acquisitions on U.S. target company top management turnover and to explore the cross-national cultural determinants of this turnover. The evidence indicates that foreign and domestic acquisitions both lead to widespread turnover in acquired U.S. entities. The pattern of turnover is somewhat different for acquisitions by foreign-owned firms compared to domestic firms. Turnover in foreign acquisitions rises at about the same rate as domestic acquisitions through the third year, rises at a higher rate from the fourth through the sixth years, then tapers off during the seventh and eighth years following the acquisition. Therefore, foreign ownership does matter when it comes to turnover rates of executives of acquired firms, but it matters only in the later years, particularly years 4, 5, and 6 after the acquisition. For the first three years, foreign and domestic acquisitions are quite similar in the turnover of top executives. The most significant finding is that they both differ from turnover in nonacquired U.S. firms.

The results offered no evidence to suggest that cross-national culture differences between the United States and the foreign acquirer's home country are associated with postacquisition top management turnover. When confronted with differences in nationality, national cultural differences easily serve as explanatory factors. Yet companies differ in many ways other than the national cultural values of their home country. Other factors may be more relevant and shed more light on the differences in top management turnover rates. Attention should be given to such factors as the acquiring firm's acquisition experience, international business experience, country-specific (U.S.) experience, acquisition motives, and industry globalization. Future research is needed to examine the role of such factors in acquisitions by foreign firms and the consequent turnover of the acquired firm's top managers.

NOTE

A detailed discussion of the sample development is provided by Krug and Hegarty (1997).

REFERENCES

Adler, Nancy J., and John L. Graham. 1989. "Cross-Cultural Interaction: The International Comparison Fallacy?" *Journal of International Business Studies* 20(3):515-537.

Aharoni, Yair. 1966. *The Foreign Investment Decision Process*. Boston, Mass.: Harvard University.

Ajami, Riad A., and David A. Ricks. 1981. "Motives of Non-American Firms Investing in the United States," *Journal of International Business Studies* 12(3):25-34.

Benito, Gabriel R. G., and Geir Gripsrud. 1992. "The Expansion of Foreign Direct Investments: Discrete Rational Location Choices or a Cultural Learning Process?" *Journal of International Business Studies* 23(3):461-476.

Buckley, Peter J., and Mark C. Casson. 1976. *The Future of the Multinational Enterprise*. London: Macmillan Press.

Buono, Anthony F., and James L. Bowditch. 1989. *The Human Side of Mergers and Acquisitions*. San Francisco, Calif.: Jossey-Bass Publishers.

Cannella, Albert A., Jr., and Donald C. Hambrick. 1993. "Effects of Executive Departures on the Performance of Acquired Firms," *Strategic Management Journal* 14(special issue):137-152.

Caves, Richard E. 1971. "International Corporations: The Industrial Economics of Foreign Investment," *Economica* 38(149):1-27, February.

———. 1974. "Causes of Direct Investment: Foreign Firms' Shares in Canadian and United Kingdom Manufacturing Industries," *Review of Economics and Statistics* 56(August):272-293.

Chatterjee, Sayan, Michael H. Lubatkin, David M. Schweiger, and Yaakov Weber. 1992. "Cultural Differences and Shareholder Value in Related Mergers: Linking Equity and Human Capital," *Strategic Management Review* 13(5):319-334.

Chetwynd, J. 1994. "Foreign Firms Produced 20% of '93 U.S. Output," *Wall Street Journal*, December 1, p. A4.

Cho, Kang Rae, and P. Padmanabhan. 1996. "The Role of Decision-Specific Experience in Foreign Establishment Mode Choice of Multinational Corporations," UCD-CBA Working Paper 1996-01, University of Colorado, Denver.

Coase, Ronald H. 1937. "The Nature of the Firm," *Economica* 4(November):386-405.

Daniels, John D. 1971. *Recent Foreign Direct Manufacturing Investment in the United States: An Interview Study of the Decision Process*. New York: Praeger.

Dunning, John H. 1973. "The Determinants of International Production," *Oxford Economic Papers*, pp. 289-336.

———. 1980. "Toward an Eclectic Theory of International Production: Some Empirical Tests," *Journal of International Business Studies* 11(1):9-31.

Franko, Lawrence G. 1976. *The European Multinationals: A Renewed Challenge for American and British Big Business*. Stamford, Conn.: Greylock Publishers.

Furtado, Eugene P. H., and Vijay Karan. 1990. "Causes, Consequences, and Shareholder Wealth Effects of Management Turnover: A Review of the Empirical Evidence," *Financial Management* 19(2):60-75.

Graham, Edward M. 1974. "Oligopolistic Imitation and European Direct Investment in the United States," doctoral dissertation, Harvard Business School.

Hambrick, Donald C., and Albert A. Cannella, Jr. 1993. "Relative Standing: A Framework for Understanding Departures of Acquired Executives," *Academy of Management Journal* 36(4):733-762.

Hayes, Robert H. 1979. "The Human Side of Acquisitions," *Management Review* 68:41-46.

Hayes, Robert H., and Gerald H. Hoag. 1974. "Post Acquisition Retention of Top Management: A Research Study," *Mergers and Acquisitions* 9(2):8-18.

Hofstede, Geert H. 1980a. *Culture's Consequences: International Differences in Work-Related Values*. Beverly Hills, Calif.: Sage.

———. 1980b. "Motivation, Leadership, and Organization: Do American Theories Apply Abroad?" *Organizational Dynamics* 9:42-63.

Hymer, Stephen H. 1960. "The International Operations of National Firms: A Study of Direct Foreign Investment," doctoral dissertation, Massachusetts Institute of Technology (published by Cambridge, Mass.:M.I.T. Press, 1976).

Jemison, David B., and Sim B. Sitkin. 1986. "Corporate Acquisitions: A Process Perspective," *Academy of Management Review* 11(1):145-163.

Johanson, Jan, and Jan-Erik Vahlne. 1977. "The Internationalization Process of the Firm: A Model of Knowledge Development and Increasing Foreign Market Commitments," *Journal of International Business Studies* 8(1):23-32.

Johnson, Harry G. 1970. "The Efficiency and Welfare Implications of the International Corporation," in *The International Corporation*, edited by Charles P. Kindleberger. Cambridge, Mass.: MIT Press.

Kelley, Lane, Arthur Whatley, and Reginald Worthley. 1987. "Assessing the Effects of Culture on Managerial Attitudes: A Three-Culture Test," *Journal of International Business Studies* 19(2):17-32.

Kim, Wi Saeng, and Esmeralda O. Lyn. 1987. "Foreign Direct Investment Theories, Entry Barriers, and Reverse Investment in U.S. Manufacturing Industries," *Journal of International Business Studies* 19(2):53-66.

Kindleberger, Charles P. 1969. *American Business Abroad: Six Lectures on Direct Investment*. New Haven, Conn.: Yale University Press.

Knickerbocker, Frederick T. 1973. *Oligopolistic Reaction and Multinational Enterprise*. Boston, Mass.: Harvard University.

Kogut, Bruce, and Habir Singh. 1988. "The Effect of National Culture on the Choice of Entry Mode," *Journal of International Business Studies* 19(3):411-432, Fall.

Krug, Jeffrey A., and W. Harvey Hegarty. 1997. "Postacquisition Turnover among U.S. Top Management Teams: Analysis of the Effects of Foreign versus Domestic Acquisitions of U.S. Targets," *Strategic Management Journal* 18(8):667-675.

Levinson, H. 1970. "A Psychologist Diagnoses Merger Failures," *Harvard Business Review* 48:138-147.

Li, Jiatao, and Stephen Guisinger. 1991. "Comparative Business Failures of Foreign-controlled Firms in the United States," *Journal of International Business Studies* 22(2):209-224.

———. 1992. "The Globalization of Service Multinationals in the 'Triad' Regions: Japan, Western Europe and North America," *Journal of International Business Studies* 23(4):675-696.

Marks, Mitchell L. 1982. "Merging Human Resources: A Review of Current Research," *Mergers and Acquisitions* 17(2):38-44.

Marks, Mitchell L., and Philip Mirvis. 1985. "Merger Syndrome: Stress and Uncertainty," *Mergers and Acquisitions* 20(2):50-55.

Martin, Kenneth J., and John J. McConnell. 1991. "Corporate Performance, Corporate Take-overs, and Management Turnover," *Journal of Finance* 46:671-688.

McManus, J. C. 1972. "The Theory of the International Firm," in *The Multinational Firm and the Nation State*, edited by C. Paquet. Toronto: Collier-Macmillan, pp.66-93.

Mergers and Acquisitions. 1979-1995. New York: MLR Publishing Company.

Mirvis, Philip H. 1985. "Negotiations after the Sale: The Roots and Ramifications of Conflict in an Acquisition," *Journal of Occupational Behavior* 6:65-84.

Pablo, Amy L. 1994. "Determinants of Acquisition Integration Level: A Decision-Making Perspective," *Academy of Management Journal* 37(4):803-836.

Ragazzi, G. 1973. "Theories of the Determinants of Direct Foreign Investment," *IMF Staff Papers.* Washington, D.C.: International Monetary Fund, pp. 471-498.

Ronen, Simcha, and Oded Shenkar. 1985. "Clustering Countries on Attitudinal Dimensions: A Review and Synthesis," *Academy of Management Review* 10(3):435-454.

Rugman, Alan M. 1986. "New Theories of the Multinational Enterprise: An Assessment of Internationalization Theory," *Bulletin of Economic Research* 38(2):101-118.

Sales, Amy L., and Philip H. Mirvis. 1984. "When Cultures Collide: Issues in Acquisition," in *New Futures: The Challenge of Managing Corporate Transitions*, edited by John R. Kimberly and Robert E. Quinn. Homewood, Ill.: Dow Jones-Irwin, Inc., pp. 107-133.

Sametz, Arnold, and Jules Backman. 1974. "Why Foreign Multinationals Invest in the United States," *Challenge* 17(1):43-47.

Schweiger, David M., and Angelo S. DeNisi. 1991. "Communication with Employees Following a Merger: A Longitudinal Field Experiment," *Academy of Management Journal* 34:110-135.

Schweiger, David M., and James P. Walsh. 1990. "Mergers and Acquisitions: An Interdisciplinary View," in *Research in Personnel and Human Resource Management*, edited by Kendrith M. Rowland and Gerald R. Ferris. Greenwich, Conn.: JAI Press, pp. 41-107.

Schweiger, David M., John M. Ivancevich, and Frank R. Power. 1987. "Executive Actions for Managing Human Resources Before and After Acquisition," *Academy of Management Executive* 1(2):127-138.

Sokoya, Sesan K., and Kenneth R. Tillery. 1992. "Motives of Foreign MNCs Investing in the United States and the Effect of Company Characteristics," *The International Executive* 34(1):65-80.

Walsh, James P. 1988. "Top Management Turnover following Mergers and Acquisitions," *Strategic Management Journal* 9(2):173-183.

———. 1989. "Doing a Deal: Merger and Acquisition Negotiations and Their Impact upon Target Company Top Management Turnover," *Strategic Management Journal* 10(4):307-322.

Walsh, James P., and John W. Ellwood. 1991. "Mergers, Acquisitions, and the Pruning of Managerial Deadwood," *Strategic Management Journal* 12(3):201-217.

Walsh, James P., and Rita D. Kosnik. 1993. "Corporate Raiders and Their Disciplinary Role in the Market for Corporate Control," *Strategic Management Review* 36(August):671-700.

Weber, Yaakov, and David M. Schweiger. 1989. "Implementing Mergers and Acquisitions: The Role of Cultural Differences and Level of Integration," unpublished paper, The Darla Moore School of Business, University of South Carolina.

Williamson, Oliver E. 1975. *Markets and Hierarchies: Analysis and Antitrust Implications.* New York: Free Press.

Part V

Policy Implications

13

Nations, Nationality, and Transnational Enterprises: Policy Choices for Defining Corporate Nationality

John M. Kline

INTRODUCTION

With this chapter, the focus of the book's concern over national ownership and its consequences shifts to policy. The growing dichotomy between territorially based nation-states and globally integrated transnational enterprises (TNEs) poses difficult issues regarding whether, how, and when to apply concepts of corporate nationality to public policies and programs. Driven by the seemingly compelling imperative to boost national economic competitiveness, some governments seek to develop business promotion initiatives that aid national companies while denying benefits to foreign firms. These distinctions between "us" and "them" (Reich 1990; 1991; Tyson 1991) appear necessary due to the increased local presence of foreign enterprises following recent surges in foreign direct investment (FDI), including the spread of low or nonequity ventures as well as international strategic alliances (ISAs) (Office of Technology Assessment [OTA] 1993; 1994). Most threatened by concern over issues of corporate nationality is the fundamental principle of national treatment for foreign investment—an important cornerstone of an open world economic system (Organisation for Economic Co-operation and Development [OECD] 1993).

Nearly a quarter century has passed since Vernon's (1971) path-breaking book described the spread of U.S. multinational corporations (MNCs), raising initial questions about the link between those firms and national political authorities. His portrayal of a radical new form of MNC now appears surprisingly simple, in hindsight, when viewed against the current complexity of global business networks. Contemporary enterprises have evolved intricate forms of internal coordination and external cooperation that respond to continually changing international market conditions, in contrast to the relatively fixed circumstances of national political identity (United Nations 1993; Dunning 1993; Boyd 1995). Resurgent and newly developing economies have also expanded the number of nations spawning TNEs to contest the initial dominance of U.S. corporations. The result yields a diverse array of contemporary TNEs with multiple and mixed nationality characteristics that call into question easy assumptions about their responsiveness to national political direction as well as the basic compatibility between TNE goals and those of individual nation-states.

Issues of corporate nationality take on practical meaning primarily in relation to national government efforts to distinguish between foreign and domestic enterprises with the intention to discriminate against "them" in favor of "us." If foreign business elements are insignificant within a country or if there is no intent to favor national over nonnational firms, there is no reason to draw nationality distinctions. Thus, growth in government interventions to promote national economic competitiveness combined with increased FDI and the evolution of complex TNE networks raise public policy issues of corporate nationality. When such programs discriminate against foreign investors, the national treatment standard is violated.

This chapter attempts to clarify corporate nationality issues and options by *(i)* identifying major policy and program areas where nations employ corporate nationality distinctions, examining both motivations and implementation methods; *(ii)* analyzing how corporate nationality definitions function in governmental programs that seek competitive national advantage; *(iii)* exploring the role of corporate nationality in reciprocal investment policies; and *(iv)* clarifying important policy choices and possible trade-offs, especially where the unilateral pursuit of national advantage may adversely affect fundamental international economic principles and multilateral cooperation.

THE RISE OF CORPORATE NATIONALITY ISSUES

In the 1980s issues of corporate nationality gained prominence from the convergence of several FDI trends. An accelerated liberalization of foreign investment regulations expanded cross-investment, particularly among the industrialized countries where restrictive foreign exchange and capital controls were virtually eliminated (United Nations 1995). Globally, nations engaged in a growing competition for investment funds with even previously hostile developing countries and formerly communist nations adopting liberal regulatory regimes to attract foreign investors (United Nations 1994). This increasingly "open door" attitude began to shift the need for negotiating more liberal entry conditions for FDI to a follow-on objective of ensuring nondiscriminatory national treatment for foreign investors once established.

The unprecedented growth of FDI in the United States during the 1980s carried special significance for the evolution of policy debates over corporate nationality issues. With FDI inflows exceeding outflows throughout the decade, the nation's stock of inward and outward FDI were brought into rough balance. Traditionally focused on issues of concern to investors abroad, U.S. government officials now faced a growing domestic debate over the impact of FDI in the United States (Tolchin and Tolchin 1988; Graham and Krugman 1989). This development undoubtedly drew additional attention because many major new investments during this period came from Japan, which was both a nontraditional, non-Western investor in the U.S. economy and the United States' greatest economic rival, perceived by the U.S. public to rival the former Soviet Union in terms of the threat posed to the country (*Americans Talk Security* 1988).

The U.S. Congress responded to this unfamiliar challenge by championing initiatives to boost U.S. competitiveness while, in seemingly logical fashion, often denying programmatic advantages to foreign investor firms from competitor trading nations. These moves shifted U.S. attitudes from a decidedly unidimensional focus on promoting the interests of outward investors to an approach with a more notably restrictionist tinge. This process thrust the United States into the atypical role of posing active threats to the national treatment standard by considering new policies and programs that would overtly deviate from the principle (Kline and Wallace 1992).

Corporate nationality issues appear more starkly in U.S. policy debates than elsewhere because inward FDI increased so quickly and dramatically over the past decade and because the U.S. policy-making system is so publicly open in its deliberative processes. Other nations deal with similar issues, and some have been doing so for many years. However, even experienced host nations confront a set of altered circumstances where old answers and approaches may no longer suffice. Spreading global economic interdependence and the deeper integration of foreign investors into domestic economies make traditional attempts to distinguish corporate nationalities difficult and often counterproductive to achieving specific goals (United Nations 1993).

The dilemma for national governments, particularly in the advanced industrialized countries, is clear. They face an increasingly competitive economic environment that pushes them to intervene to advance national goals, especially in critical high technology areas. At the same time, key private sector TNEs are spreading their assets globally, adopting more complex organizational arrangements, and diversifying or decentralizing coordination and control functions in ways that often ignore their assumed national identities, with resulting indeterminate impacts on political jurisdictions.

The inescapable conclusion is that expanded FDI and strategic alliance networks present a range of new challenges to defining corporate nationality when government policies or programs seek to favor companies that promote national competitiveness goals. Resulting discrimination against firms defined as noneligible "foreign" corporations can pose a potentially serious threat to the national treatment principle as a guarantor of an open and equitable international investment system.

NATIONAL TREATMENT AND RECOGNIZED EXCEPTIONS

Virtually all nations confront corporate nationality issues when they choose to depart from the national treatment standard in dealing with foreign investors. Although somewhat different problems arise depending on particular national situations and characteristics, the national treatment standard offers a common principle whose adherence and exceptions to it form a central part of the debate over international FDI policy. The Organisation for Economic Co-operation and Development (OECD) provides the best instrument for evaluating the importance of the national treatment principle and actual practice of adherence (or nonadherence) to it, based on the Decision on National Treatment, adopted as part of the 1976 Declaration on International Investment and Multinational Enterprises (OECD 1993).

The National Treatment decision reaffirmed OECD member nations' support for the national treatment principle and established a commitment to report exceptions to the standard, providing a means to examine these measures while encouraging their removal. This agreement covers the major home and host countries to the vast majority of the world's FDI; it also creates an officially recognized set of policies and identifies national programs that depart from the national treatment standard (and therefore must employ some corporate nationality definition to distinguish between national and foreign firms).

The corporate nationality concept bears an instrumental relationship to national treatment exceptions. Where the standard is upheld, there is no need for corporate nationality distinctions. However, wherever policies or programs depart from national treatment, corporate nationality distinctions provide a necessary implementation device to distinguish (and discriminate) between favored national and disfavored nonnational firms. In practice, some distinctions may be based more on the defined nationality of a TNE's product rather than the enterprise itself. For example, government procurement and trade financing determinations are often deal-specific, relying on domestic content valuations of the products involved in a particular transaction. On the other hand, if such actions treat foreign investors less favorably than domestic enterprises in similar situations, the practice constitutes a departure from the national treatment standard.

In order to understand and evaluate current multilateral adherence to national treatment, it is necessary to recognize that motivation matters. In general, nations deviate from national treatment and thereby discriminate against foreign investors for three broad reasons: *(i)* to preserve fundamental public order and national security interests, *(ii)* to gain or reserve special benefits or advantages over other nations, and *(iii)* to respond to perceived unfair treatment by other countries.

The OECD divides reported departures from the national treatment principle into only two distinct categories by combining measures inspired by motivations number two and three. Actions based on public order or essential security interests are regarded as inherent limitations on applying the national treatment principle and therefore are not considered exceptions to the standard, even if they openly discriminate against foreign investors. It is important however, that policies and programs motivated by such interests are still reported for transparency purposes. The results help identify national differences, showing how the same sector or activity may be unrestricted in some countries, while in others the government departs from national treatment, sometimes based on security interests and sometimes in pursuit of other objectives. Also reported for the sake of transparency are so-called "corporate organization" measures, where governments restrict the nationality of management or director positions without directly affecting an enterprise's ownership or operation (OECD 1993).

In clarifying public order and essential security interests, the OECD imposes several important limitations. First, discriminatory actions taken in pursuit of national cultural interests are not included in this category; instead they are considered clear departures from national treatment and must be reported and dealt with as exceptions.

Similarly, the pursuit of national geopolitical or economic interests also falls outside public order and essential security justifications.

Political debates over departures from the national treatment standard often describe proposals in terms similar to national security motivations, citing the importance of significant foreign political goals, the maintenance of a country's "economic security," or the preservation of cultural values that shape national identity. Nonetheless, these arguments are not recognized by the OECD as legitimate limitations on the national treatment principle, and related discriminatory policies are deemed departures from the accepted standard. Although nations can still attempt to present such policies under the national security umbrella, transparency reporting requirements subject these measures to the scrutiny of other OECD members who will seek to restrict overly broad applications of this classification.

The OECD's decision to define the national treatment principle separate from actions motivated by national security and public order recognizes the practical limits of international agreement under prevailing political conditions. These motivations will claim special deference as long as contemporary nation-state security concerns prevail, which appears likely into the indefinite future. Therefore, rather than debating the justification for discriminatory actions motivated by security concerns, the more productive alternative is to investigate, define, and seek to reduce non-security-based motivations. This approach provides a comparative standard against which claimed security justifications can be evaluated while also clarifying and challenging nonsecurity rationales for discrimination against foreign investors.

All governmental measures that discriminate against foreign investors and are not justified by essential national security or public order motivations are classified by the OECD as exceptions to the national treatment standard. Five topical subgroups are used to organize these measures: *(i)* investment by established foreign-controlled enterprises, *(ii)* official aids and subsidies, *(iii)* tax obligations, *(iv)* government purchasing, and *(v)* access to local finance. A separate category is provided for reported exceptions by territorial subdivisions because OECD members have undertaken "to endeavor to ensure" that their subdivisions also apply the national treatment standard (OECD 1993).

Although the OECD does not formally differentiate among nonsecurity motivations for discriminatory treatment of foreign investors, both programmatic experience and the tenor of recent national policy debates suggest it is important to recognize two major distinctions. Most policies and programs reported as exceptions to national treatment derive from a desire to gain or retain exclusive national benefits or values by granting advantages to local firms while denying them to foreign investors. By contrast, reciprocity-based motivations seek to remove or offset advantages granted firms based in other nations by discriminatory foreign government policies. The former seems proactive and aggressive, while the latter appears reactive and defensive. Although this characterization is far too simplistic, examining this motivational distinction helps clarify the origins of certain policies; it can also help evaluate the policies' impact and how they might be approached in international negotiations.

NATIONAL ADVANTAGE AND CORPORATE NATIONALITY

Many departures from the national treatment standard stem from a desire to promote a nation's competitive advantage by gaining or reserving important resources and assets for use by national enterprises. The operative assumption underlying this approach is that the nation-state will accrue special benefits resulting from its corporations' exclusive or preferential use of these assets. Corporate nationality definitions can function as the instrumental link between intention and result. Determining which enterprises are treated as favored national firms in governmental policies and programs can shape business dealings and affect the geographical distribution of resultant benefits among territorially based political jurisdictions.

In a simpler past, a corporation's national identity might be treated as "self-evident." When definitions were needed, ownership often served as a logical and convenient proxy for citizenship. Gradated ownership levels could be used for joint venture operations, providing adjustable cutoff points below which an enterprise would be judged "foreign." One potential weakness of this approach emerges as ownership becomes increasingly dispersed through global stock exchanges. Another serious problem results from the growth of strategic alliances, wherein the role and influence of multiple partners on business decision-making may not be reflected clearly in their overt equity positions.

With more complex international business networks, the critical element for determining how corporate operations will affect national advantage is an understanding of the basis for corporate decision-making relative to the specific benefit being sought. Generalized notions of citizenship, or even defined levels of ownership, are increasingly dubious guarantors of specified national outcomes.

An assessment conducted in the Council of Economic Advisers (CEA) of foreign participation in U.S. government research and development (R&D) projects recognized that "ownership serves as a rough proxy" for where the most and highest-value-added jobs will likely be located. However, it also noted, the proxy's value varies by industry and is weakening as TNEs diversify their employment base. "As this trend continues, it will become necessary for policymakers to examine directly the number and quality of jobs generated by specific producers, rather than rely on a proxy measure such as nationality of ownership" (Stowsky 1994).

Greater specificity is also required when selecting the desired benefits expected from policies and programs that seek national advantage by discriminating against foreign investors. The problem with selecting clear program objectives stems from the multiplicity of benefits sought by different societal groups and the difficulty a democratic political process often has in choosing among potentially competing or conflicting goals. A generalized objective such as "enhancing national competitiveness" may garner widespread support precisely because it is indistinct and can therefore mean all things to all people. Naturally, realistic projections of the program's eventual results will be indeterminate without more specific guidelines or measurements to shape the outcome.

A seemingly more measurable yet still generalized goal would be improving the total effect on U.S. national income over the long run. This concept provides a composite measure of benefit to workers, producers, and consumers. Near-term priorities might favor actions that increase local value-added and linkages through purchased intermediate inputs (Stowsky 1994). Nevertheless, the complexities of national income accounting would likely prove daunting in applying this measure to practical government programs.

Other, more discrete goals could be chosen from among the many potential benefits commonly discussed in relation to national advantage policies. The list includes items such as increased employment, exports, market share, corporate or shareholder income, tax revenue, production output, local sourcing, technological advances, and balance of payments gains. Unfortunately, actions promoting one goal may have counterproductive effects on other objectives. For example, in deciding where to manufacture a new product derived from technological advances, cost factors in a competitive global economy may dictate a trade-off between employing high-wage domestic workers and utilizing local procurement versus expanding a TNE's global market share and increasing shareholder income.

At times, government programs do indicate priority goals. The U.S. Department of Energy provided one such guideline in a restatement of technology transfer policy on U.S. competitiveness regarding the negotiation of Cooperative Research and Development Agreements (CRADAs). Because the technology being transferred resulted from research funded by U.S. taxpayers, the department sought to ensure a return for the taxpayer on this investment. The principal message was clear: "We have identified perhaps the most desirable return or dividend as increased jobs" (Lewis 1993). Nevertheless, recognizing that proposed projects might not always be able to identify job gains, the department provided a "U.S. Competitiveness Work Sheet" with the following guidelines:

> The preferred benefit to the U.S. economy is the creation and maintenance of manufacturing capabilities and jobs within the U.S. . . . . Appropriate recognition of U.S. taxpayer support for the technology, e.g., a quid-pro-quo commensurate with the economic benefit that would be domestically derived by the U.S. taxpayer from U.S.-based manufacture must be demonstrated. Such benefits may include one or more of the following:
> - Direct or indirect investment in U.S.-based plant and equipment.
> - Creation of new and/or higher quality U.S.-based jobs.
> - Enhancement of the domestic skills base.
> - Further domestic development of the technology.
> - Positive impact on the U.S. balance of payments in terms of product and service exports as well as foreign licensing royalties and receipts.
> - Cross-licensing, sublicensing, and reassignment provisions in licenses which seek to maximize the benefits to the U.S. taxpayer.
> - Leveraging government resources in furtherance of DOE program goals.
>
> (Lewis 1993)

These criteria, of course, do not presume a necessary distinction or resulting discrimination between local and foreign investors; they rely instead on performance characteristics designed to address identified priority goals related to program objectives.

When policies and programs that seek national competitive advantage specify the types of benefits to be gained, implementing definitions can be formulated that address and promote those particular results. Policies can pursue national advantage without violating the national treatment principle. If discrimination against foreign investors takes place, the definition of corporate nationality employed should at least bear a direct relationship to the benefits desired, or else the discrimination is both arbitrary and indeterminate regarding its programmatic results. Where corporate nationality definitions are employed in addition to performance-based criteria, the restriction again would appear arbitrary as well as potentially counterproductive by excluding otherwise qualified firms from participation.

An examination of national treatment exceptions reported to the OECD reveals that most corporate nationality definitions, when specified, are stated in terms of ownership, control, and citizenship (OECD 1993). This traditional approach assumes national benefit will result from the exclusion or discriminatory treatment of "foreign" enterprises as defined by generalized proxy characteristics. Interestingly, in the relatively new realm of technology-promotion programs, most countries appear to rely primarily on national economic benefit standards that are applied equally to domestic and foreign firms.[1] Where stated eligibility criteria are not based on the actual demonstration of how a firm's participation or proposed projects would meet national benefit goals, the most commonly used corporate nationality characteristic is defined as the presence of research facilities or capabilities in the host country—an attribute logically and substantively related to a results-oriented goal of achieving technological advances (Tarullo 1994).

The central issue regarding corporate nationality as applied to governmental policies and programs that seek national competitive advantage is therefore the degree to which the concept and its definition can serve effectively as a direct link between specified national benefits and the achievement of those goals. Citizenship, ownership, or control criteria presume that domestic firms will act in the national interest. But, as various commentators have observed, the actual behavior of TNEs shows that they are often guided by motivations other than national loyalty (Reich 1990; Belous and McClenahan 1991; Kobrin 1995). The most surprising aspect of this observation may be that so many people and governments, nevertheless, still act as though *they* assume TNEs are motivated by national rather than corporate interests.

The more ambiguous a national advantage program's goal, the less easily the program's success can be guided and assured. When program objectives are specified, performance criteria and corporate characteristics clearly related to the achievement of those goals offer the most reasonable approach. Lacking clear evidence that general corporate nationality distinctions serve as a good proxy for goal-oriented results, there is little rationale for relying on corporate nationality definitions such as citizenship, ownership, and control. The OECD nations have already endorsed the gradual removal or narrowing of existing national treatment exceptions. Certainly the primary targets for this exercise should be those measures that rely on generalized proxies such as ownership for their definition of corporate nationality.

RECIPROCITY AND CORPORATE NATIONALITY

The primary justification for reciprocity-based exceptions to national treatment is the argument that such measures aim at liberalizing FDI restrictions by forcing open otherwise closed foreign markets. Perceptions that your own firms face unfair or at least unequal treatment in other nations can lead to the imposition of reciprocity requirements that use local foreign investors as proxies for their home-based national governments. These measures would deny national treatment only to foreign investors whose defined home countries engage in similar discrimination (or sometimes where equivalent treatment is simply deemed to be precluded, regardless of direct foreign government action).

Air travel, banking, and other financial services traditionally have been the areas most subject to reciprocity provisions, especially where institutional financial structures vary widely among different nations. This problem was partly addressed in 1991 by an OECD agreement that recognized that particular national situations could justify different treatment so long as foreign investors received "equivalent" treatment that did not unfavorably affect the equality of competitive market opportunities (OECD 1993). More recently, governmental support programs for advanced technology sectors have become high-profile targets of reciprocal access provisions.

Tyson (1991) acknowledged the dangers of pursuing a selective reciprocity principle and urged its use "sparingly and only under exceptional circumstances." However, she endorsed U.S. reciprocity policies in important industrial sectors to counteract disadvantages faced by U.S. producers from long-term foreign government actions that benefit local producers through targeted industrial promotion while restricting U.S. sales and investment. Specifically, she discussed using reciprocity in relation to intellectual property standards, merger and acquisition policy, and public support for R&D (Tyson 1991).

Already beguiled by the appeal of reciprocity concepts in trade policy, the U.S. government (especially Congress) seems prone to incorporate investment-related reciprocity requirements in new or reformulated programs to promote U.S. technological competitiveness. During 1991-1993, at least a half dozen new laws contained reciprocity restrictions making the participation of non-U.S. firms contingent on whether U.S. enterprises had access to comparable opportunities in the parent firm's home country (Stowsky 1994). In most cases, the reciprocity provisions were added on top of other participation criteria, ranging from a general determination of U.S. economic interest to more specific requirements such as having significant research and production facilities in the United States. Several laws also incorporate intellectual property rights (IPR) standards as an additional participation criteria.

For example, the Advanced Technology Program (ATP) was established by the Omnibus Trade and Competitiveness Act of 1988 to provide financial assistance to U.S. businesses to foster the development of high-risk, enabling technologies. All applicants must show how their proposal would be in the U.S. economic interest. However, Congress mandated an additional eligibility provision to govern participation by non-U.S.-owned enterprises, specifying that a foreign firm's self-identified country of origin must offer comparable opportunities to U.S. companies to invest locally and to participate in similar technology joint ventures as well as providing adequate and effective IPR protection. This additional eligibility criteria caused the United States to take a reservation for the Program in the OECD's National Treatment instrument.[2]

The 1991 "National Critical Technologies Act" and "Advanced Manufacturing Technology Act," as well as the 1993 "National Defense Authorization Act," also incorporate reciprocity restrictions. Under these programs, all participating companies must conduct significant R&D and manufacturing in the United States. In addition, foreign firms must be incorporated in nations that encourage U.S. companies to participate in R&D consortia receiving government funding as well as providing adequate and effective IPR protection for U.S. enterprises.

Incorporating reciprocity criteria into these laws can be a misleadingly simple act. Implementing such provisions can require evaluating comparable treatment or opportunities under complex criteria and administrative processes. For instance, would reciprocal access to R&D support programs require an exact matching of the required national benefit criteria as well as defined corporate nationality characteristics for participating enterprises? Where two national programs similarly require participating firms to have "significant" local research and manufacturing capabilities, are the criteria understood and applied using comparable measurements? Even the relatively simple ATP reciprocity criteria require obtaining a variety of published documents and expert opinion and gathering information and advice from several U.S. government agencies, overseas commercial and science offices and embassies, foreign embassies in the United States, and foreign managers of counterpart programs.

In debating whether or when to adopt reciprocity restrictions, the United States should first consider the extent to which its firms are being denied comparable opportunities abroad. Some analyses suggest that meaningful discrimination against U.S. TNEs appears minimal in the technology promotion programs that are the most common current target for U.S. reciprocity restrictions. One assessment, based on reports from U.S. embassies, concluded that "The overall picture suggests that U.S. firms generally do not face serious problems of discrimination or restricted access to foreign governments' technology/R&D programs" (Tarullo 1994). Japan was the major exception (although foreign firms' access there has improved in recent years), while Taiwan presented some lesser obstacles.

Minor discrimination occurs in some countries, but most nations that sponsor significant R&D and technology programs permit or even encourage U.S. TNE participation, especially in basic research projects. All firms must generally demonstrate at least local research capability, and projects must meet some form of national benefit criteria. National firms may enjoy an easier initial presumption that participation will result in beneficial national impacts, but foreign firms do not appear seriously disadvantaged. Occasionally U.S. companies receive better than national treatment, such as when French subnational governments provide special incentives to attract U.S. technology-oriented investments (Tarullo 1994).

Sometimes U.S. TNE disinterest or reluctance to participate, rather than foreign discriminatory restrictions, accounts for the absence of U.S. firms in foreign government programs. Foreign financial support is lower, with the total expenditures of all other governments together only about equal to U.S. government spending on R&D and technology programs (with the bulk of foreign funds concentrated in Europe and Japan). A desire to benefit from sophisticated technological input from foreign partners also limits the number of programs that would attract U.S. corporate participation. Other reasons include a desire to guard strategic business plans, inconsistency between corporate and government program goals, and the inadequacy of IPR protection for technological inputs and results (Department of State 1994).

The international reality, therefore, may not match the rhetorical image created by policy debates that demand reciprocity conditions for U.S. programs to ensure comparable treatment abroad. A State Department analysis concluded that "Outside Japan, there are insufficient 'market-opening' justifications for including reciprocity provisions in U.S. technology programs" (Tarullo 1994). Certainly if market-opening objectives are limited to one or even a few countries, the problems could be addressed bilaterally rather than writing an across-the-board reciprocity requirement into U.S. law.

U.S. tactics could actually prove counterproductive. No other major country currently applies a reciprocity test to foreign corporate participation in R&D and technology programs. As U.S. programs become increasingly restrictive, with reciprocity conditions generally added to other types of requirements, other major nations might adopt their own reciprocity conditions, constricting the range of current participation by U.S. firms. Business representatives have expressed concern that the European Union or individual nations could adopt retaliatory reciprocity provisions that would restrict U.S. corporate access and significantly harm their business interests (Tarullo 1994).

The OECD treats reciprocity-motivated policies in the same way as other exceptions to the national treatment standard and encourages their removal. The organization's analysis concludes that, in the short term, such policies lead the host country to forgo the benefits of additional competition; "in the long run, reciprocity measures are incompatible with a multilateral approach to liberalization" (OECD 1993).

CONCLUSION

Motivation matters—in understanding the origin of policy discrimination against foreign investors; in evaluating the results and impact of those policies; and in choosing approaches to address them nationally and internationally. Setting aside the area of special actions taken to protect public order and national security interests, governmental policies and programs departing from the national treatment standard stem largely from the pursuit of national competitive advantage or the use of reciprocity instruments to remove or offset the effects of discriminatory foreign policies. The analysis above suggests that neither motive provides a convincing, internally consistent case for discriminating against foreign investors, particularly not when "us" versus "them" distinctions are made using corporate nationality definitions based on generalized concepts such as citizenship, ownership, or control.

This conclusion leads to the reaffirmation of policy positions taken in the OECD National Treatment Decision and point toward the importance of expanding and strengthening this effort in negotiations on the Multilateral Agreement on Investment (MAI) (see chapter 16). Primary objectives should be to achieve a true "standstill" commitment from OECD member nations to refrain from adopting any new departures from national treatment as well as a renewed, more vigorous effort to "roll back" existing exceptions by reducing or removing discriminatory policies and programs.

Greater detail should also be sought on reported exceptions, including particularly the specification of corporate nationality definitions and other implementation criteria used to administer the reported exceptions. This additional information would increase transparency regarding why the exception exists and how it functions. Aggrieved foreign enterprises and governments could be expected to increase pressures for the exception's modification or removal. A related benefit might arise if this new requirement also brought greater clarity and the opportunity for critical evaluation of the policy within the adopting nation itself. At least for programs that seek national competitive advantage, further debate on how well chosen corporate nationality definitions link purported goals with their likely attainment could increase internal pressures to adopt more coherent and efficient implementation mechanisms.

The challenge of pursuing this approach should not be underestimated despite the fact that a good foundation already exists in terms of an agreed basic principle and a multilateral negotiating mechanism to expand and apply it. The tenor of national political debates over international competitive imperatives weighs against forswearing the option to blame and penalize "foreign" corporations while assisting domestic enterprises. However, forces driving the internationalization of business are clearly making it more difficult to actually carry out discrimination against "foreign" enterprises by increasing the difficulty of distinguishing between "them" and "us." As the CEA assessment of R&D support policy concluded, "The debate over whether foreign firms can or should participate in U.S. government-sponsored technology programs may be superseded eventually by the conclusion that it is impossible with certainty to determine the nationality of a company" (Stowsky 1994). The interim question therefore may be whether governments have the wisdom and the will to abandon ill-conceived discriminatory policies and programs before they collapse under the weight of their own inoperability.

NOTES

1. The U.S. government is somewhat an exception, as described in the next section of this chapter.

2. No foreign firm has been denied participation in the ATP because of these restrictions, and a British and a Dutch firm received approval in 1993. It is less clear whether some firms did not apply because of the criteria or whether other firms whose proposals failed the technical performance review might have been denied at the later eligibility review.

REFERENCES

Americans Talk Security. 1988. Boston: Martilla & Kiley, Inc.

Belous, Richard S., and Kelly L. McClenahan, eds. 1991. *Global Corporations and Nation-States: Do Companies or Countries Compete?* Washington, D.C.: National Planning Association.

Boyd, Gavin, ed. 1995. *Competitive and Cooperative Macromanagement: The Challenges of Structural Interdependence.* Cornwall, United Kingdom: Edward Elgar Publishing.

Department of State. 1994. "U.S. Access to Foreign Industrial Technology Initiatives." Economic Bureau. Washington, D.C.: GPO.

Dunning, John H. 1993. *The Globalization of Business: The Challenge of the 1990s*. London: Routledge.

Graham, Edward M., and Paul R. Krugman. 1989. *Foreign Direct Investment in the United States*. Washington, D.C.: Institute for International Economics.

Kline, John M., and Cynthia D. Wallace. 1992. *EC 92 and Changing Global Investment Patterns: Implications for the U.S.-EC Relationship*. Washington, D.C.: Center for Strategic and International Studies.

Kobrin, Stephen J. 1995. "Global Firms Are Here Again," in *Multinational Enterprises and the Global Economy*, edited by Lee E. Preston. College Park, Md.: CIBER Maryland. pp. 3-14.

Lewis, Roger A. 1993. "Restatement of Department Technology Transfer Policy on U.S. Competitiveness." Memorandum. U.S. Department of Energy, February 10.

Office of Technology Assessment (OTA). 1993. *Multinationals and the National Interest: Playing by Different Rules*. OTA-ITE-569, Washington, D.C.: GPO.

————. 1994. *Multinationals and the U.S. Technology Base: Final Report of the Multinationals Project*. Washington, D.C.: GPO.

Organisation for Economic Co-operation and Development (OECD). 1993. *National Treatment for Foreign-Controlled Enterprises*. Paris: OECD.

Reich, Robert B. 1990. "Who Is Us?" *Harvard Business Review* 68(January-February):53-64.

————. 1991. "Who Do We Think They Are?" *The American Prospect*, Winter, p. 49-53.

Stowsky, Jay. 1994. "Assessing the Benefits of Foreign Participation in U.S. Government-Funded R&D Projects." Memorandum. U.S. Council of Economic Advisers, March 25.

Tarullo, Daniel K. 1994. "Preliminary Findings on U.S. Firms' Access to Foreign Governments' Technology/R&D Programs." Memorandum. U.S. Department of State, Assistant Secretary for State for Economic and Business Affairs, November 17.

Tolchin, Martin, and Susan Tolchin. 1988. *Buying into America: How Foreign Money Is Changing the Face of Our Nation*. New York: Times Books.

Tyson, Laura D'Andrea. 1991. "They Are Not Us: Why American Ownership Still Matters," *The American Prospect*, pp. 37-49, Winter.

United Nations Conference on Trade and Development (UNCTAD). 1993. *World Investment Report 1993: Transnational Corporations and Integrated International Production*, Division on Transnational Corporations and Investment, New York: United Nations.

————. 1994. *World Investment Report 1994: Transnational Corporations, Employment and the Workplace*, Division on Transnational Corporations and Investment. New York: United Nations.

United Nations (UNTCMD). 1995. *World Investment Report 1995: Transnational Corporations and Competitiveness*, Department for Economic and Social Development, Transnational Corporations and Management Division. New York: United Nations.

Vernon, Raymond. 1971. *Sovereignty at Bay: The Multinational Spread of U.S. Enterprises*. New York: Basic Books.

14

Foreign Acquisition of Defense-Related U.S. Firms: Concentration, Competition, and Reality

Robert T. Kudrle and Davis B. Bobrow

INTRODUCTION

The national security debate over the impact of foreign direct investment in the United States (FDIUS), begun in earnest with the investment surge of the 1980s, has continued through the 1990s. This chapter considers one persistent part of that debate: the national security implications of foreign acquisition of firms conducting defense-relevant production or research and development (R&D) in the United States. Research on R&D and high-technology presented in Part III of this book suggests that the potential for FDIUS to involve important U.S. defense-related activities is growing. In this chapter, particular attention is given to the usefulness of national security approaches based on competition policy, in general, and market concentration, in particular, for arriving at those implications and formulating a desirable policy for dealing with them.

Much of the following discussion will critically examine some major policy analyses of FDIUS and national security inspired by competition policy thinking (Moran 1990, 1993a; Graham and Krugman 1995;[1] Graham and Ebert 1992). Yet the fundamental starting point is the same as that of those authors—autarkic impulses more than naive internationalism pose a serious challenge to the treatment of FDIUS to serve the U.S. defense industrial and technology base. Exclusionary nationalism cannot maximize that base and may damage it.

The generally accepted objective is to have the highest quality, appropriate defense at the most reasonable cost while avoiding any grave risks from foreign dependency. This complex objective requires that the United States take advantage of foreign-produced goods and services, allowing foreign resources to flow into the domestically sited defense industrial and technology base through foreign-owned or controlled subsidiaries. Pure autarky in defense would be unsustainably costly and inferior in result (Moran 1990; Adelman and Augustine 1990). Policy analysis must balance those risks on one side of the ledger against those from excessive, avoidable foreign dependency on the other.

Before turning the focus to the application of competition policy approaches, it is important to clarify the meaning of the defense industrial and technology base. Indistinct bounds for that base lead to much broader domains of comprehensive industrial and science and technology policy. The feasibility and desirability of particular policies toward FDIUS then would be no longer specific to national security with an emphasis on defense. With respect to the bounded base, those issues that are particularly sensitive to FDIUS are distinct from those that have other drivers and call for attention whatever happens to FDIUS.

The next section of this chapter addresses those matters. Subsequent sections address five central questions in that context. The questions are: What is industrial concentration, how can it be measured, and how important is it as a guide to monopoly power? How does the analysis change when the character of purchasing by the government is considered? How does the special character of defense products condition an evaluation of industrial performance? How does foreign ownership and control affect the analysis? How should U.S. policy toward FDIUS in defense industries be designed?

SETTING THE STAGE

The arguments for and against a fully national defense industrial and technology base are well established in ceteris paribus terms. Those in favor emphasize reliability of supply to the nation that both owns and hosts and thus is relatively invulnerable to supply obstacles. Often discussed obstacles include blockage in transit, denial on policy grounds, exposure to leveraged bargaining by a foreign-owned or located source, or simple neglect of relevant production and technology development for commercial reasons by foreign-owned firms. Proponents of defense techno-industrial nationalism also commend the possibilities it presents to control the supply available to others, at least compared with a situation of foreign-located and foreign-owned defense industry and technology.

Those against autarky and in favor of internationalization of supply emphasize improved access to technology, cost containment through competition, bonding among alliance partners—and suggest that acceptance of FDIUS can provide, through indigenous siting, those benefits to a substantial degree while limiting possible threats to reliability of supply and unwanted diffusion to foreigners.

As a practical matter, the U.S. defense industrial and technology base can be spread across the four categories shown in figure 14.1. These are United States (U.S. owned and located); United States overseas (U.S. owned and foreign located); foreign owned (foreign owned and U.S. located); and foreign overseas (foreign owned and located).

The policy issue for the United States thus involves, for particular pieces of the defense industrial and technology base, answering questions about the benefits and costs of location in one or another cell in figure 14.1. That is, the real world choices are not necessarily between foreign owned and U.S. owned—and the real world choices are not blanket, comprehensive ones but rather of specific industrial and technological endeavors.

Figure 14.1
Categories of Defense Industrial and Technology Base

Location	Ownership	
	U.S.	Foreign
U.S.	United States	Foreign-Owned
Foreign	U.S. Overseas	Foreign Overseas

A complete map would plot the universe of what is and will be sought and invested in for defense purposes by U.S. government departments and agencies, especially the Defense and Energy Departments and the Central Intelligence Agency (CIA). Relevant purchases or investment may be made by those agencies or by intermediaries, one or more levels removed, to generate goods and services used by direct suppliers in the course of meeting military demand. The industrial base then is not limited to prime contractors, but includes subcontractors and their vendors. Firms are or will be in the base as they provide systems, subsystems, components, elements, material, or even raw material (as clarified in table 14.1). The current or prospective base may vary in strength with respect to goods and services in each of these categories. The technology base consists of technology currently used and prospectively relevant to the provision of goods and services in any of those categories.

To make matters more complicated, but realistically so in security terms, the contents of the defense industrial and technology base are appropriately thought of in three temporal slices: current, surge, and emergent. In principle, the current defense industrial and technology base is equivalent to the list of all items and suppliers of items in all categories that are part of military or military intelligence government purchases and the technologies now used to produce them. Items in that list could be assigned to sublists for each cell in figure 14.1. In practice, such a comprehensive list is not available to develop and execute policy, in spite of several decades of recommendations to compile it (General Accounting Office 1994). As a corollary, the comprehensive sublists also do not exist for the status quo.

The difficulties of bounding the present defense industrial and technology base stem from the possibility of alternative definitions as well as from a dearth of information. Moreover, whatever definition is employed, uncertainty increases as these boundaries are forecast and the time horizon considered extended.

The surge industrial and technology base can be thought of as identical to that of the present in the content of goods and services, but different in the quantity needed and the time urgency of receiving that quantity. This is the nest of industrial mobilization and conversion-to-defense production problems. The United States might need just what it already has and is getting, but much more of it in a short period of time—or it might not. The defense industrial and technology base then expands to include suppliers that may be diverted to military purposes. Uncertainty surrounds occurrences of war, military consumption rates, warning lead-times, and

Table 14.1
Tiers of the Defense Industrial Base

Tier	Name of product	Product definition	Product examples	Key activity at each level
I	System	The end product	Ship, aircraft, tank, missile	Assembling system
II	Subsystem	A subassembly of the end product; a major subdivision of the end product	Engine, bilge, air-conditioning unit, gun, avionics	Assembling subsystem
III	Component	A fundamental constituent of a system or an end product; a number of elements joined together to perform a specific function and capable of disassembly	Carburetor, pump, heat exchanger, audio-frequency amplifier	Assembling component
IV	Element	A fundamental constituent of a component or a subsystem; one piece or a number of pieces joined together that are not normally subject to disassembly without destruction	Screw, gear, rotor, front wheel bearing frame	Making element
V	Material	The basic ingredient (material) from which an element is produced	Fuel, oil, wire, casting	Refining and/or forming material
VI	Raw material	The mined (or untransformed) material	Ore mineral, crude oil	Extracting raw material

Source: General Accounting Office 1994.

acceptability of substitute products. These are not simple matters or ones of expert consensus. FDIUS has relevance because it bears on the availability of reallocatable U.S.- or foreign-owned capacity as part of the responsiveness of firms to sharp increases in U.S. military needs.

Uncertainties become more profound when they involve changes in the nature of relevant goods and services following from innovation in technology, and the future is especially opaque with respect to the consequences of emerging generic areas of technology. Here, one considers demand for hitherto nonexistent goods and services that are to be provided by technological capacities whose existence, as a practical manufacturing or operational application, ranges from "gleam in the eye" to embryonic.

Attempts to bound militarily relevant generic technologies are then highly speculative and subject to special pleading—pleading in which a number of government bureaus, firms, laboratories, and think tanks stand to benefit from being within the "critical technology" tent. It is hardly surprising that there are numerous, nonidentical critical generic technology lists in circulation and that most have their critics with respect to coverage and degree of (un!) specificity. Relevant FDIUS policies must be developed then on the basis of highly conjectural scenarios or general articles of faith about risk avoidance priorities.

Whatever one decides to include in the current, surge, or emergent defense base will be affected by some general developments. Firms and governments have no choice but to navigate the waves generated by those developments. For the purposes of this chapter, some of these factors and how they relate to FDIUS concerns are briefly noted.

First, defense industries in the advanced industrialized countries are concentrating substantially at the system level and in parts of lower levels as well. This concentration responds to reductions in current and expected military demand and the upward pressures of costs driven by technological change and specialized military-only requirements. Accordingly, leaving FDIUS aside, there may be fewer and fewer U.S. suppliers. An acquisition (or merger) via FDIUS could mean sole sourcing from a foreign-owned firm (albeit sited in the United States). Preventing the acquisition of a troubled U.S. firm through FDIUS could mean that there would be only a U.S. overseas or a foreign supplier—or perhaps none at all.

Second, remaining U.S. firms are increasingly driven to a variety of survival strategies that work to diminish the restraints on supply to others ostensibly associated with autarky. The survival strategies include strategic alliances and teaming with foreign firms, off-shore sourcing, and technology transfers to facilitate badly needed foreign sales (direct and indirect offsets integral to purchase, sourcing, coproduction, and codevelopment agreements). Such survival strategies can raise, in principle, many of the same concerns as FDIUS. They may carry increased dependency on external sources of supply, whether U.S. overseas or foreign overseas. They may involve at least some strengthening of the defense industrial and technology base of the participating foreign firm and country, thus facilitating future commercial competition or even military threat. The survival strategies may involve reduced U.S. government control over the transfer of critical products, technologies, and know-how to third parties. Yet, barriers to the activities that may carry these risks can themselves weaken the U.S. defense industrial and technology base. Clearly, even the most restrictive U.S. posture on FDIUS does not eliminate these effects from the international activities of U.S. firms.

Third, firms increasingly find the military market less attractive and less important than civil markets (Adelman and Augustine 1990). This is partly the result of forecasts for flat or reduced military spending with the attendant incentives to switch to commercial activities. It is also driven by the increased attractiveness to defense customers of materials, elements, and components developed and produced for civil markets, whose size dwarfs military markets. The appeals (in cost and technical capacity terms) of supplies and suppliers with deep commercial roots have been recognized by U.S. Department of Defense officials (such as the Perry-Deutch-Kaminski initiatives for procurement and R&D). This amounts to the pursuit of "spin-on" from commercially oriented technical and product innovations to military applications (Bryant 1996). In effect, the military "piggybacks" on commercially motivated activities, as in electric and hybrid-electric vehicle development.[2]

Many G-7 firms hitherto focused on defense now seek to diversify away from it *at the same time* that firms not focused on defense are sought as suppliers of attractive dual-use technologies and products. These developments mean that defense-relevant FDIUS will be increasingly indistinct from commercial FDIUS. Maintaining a defense industrial and technology base may increasingly involve efforts to induce firms to retain militarily relevant interests, product lines, and production capacities. Increasingly, real choices may lie not between U.S. versus foreign-owned suppliers, but among foreign-owned, U.S. overseas, and foreign overseas suppliers.

Fourth, nations other than long-established allies are pressing ahead with the development of a modern defense industrial and technology base (such as China) and providing formidable competition in non-U.S. markets for relatively inexpensive, penultimate generation military products. The erstwhile Warsaw Pact defense sectors continue to have the most urgent motivations for success in foreign markets, low price thresholds to attain profits, and even current generation military products and technologies. The United States and its closest allies may have a "club interest" in a pooled, more integrated defense industrial and technology base as a way to maintain military advantage at a sustainable cost—and as an alternative to off-shore procurement from and dependency on nonclub members. FDIUS is a possible instrument for pooling and integration.

These realities argue that the content of the defense industrial and technology base is elusive and amoeba-like. That fuzziness does not obscure serious threats to its vigor. Yet, many of the hazards are neither uniquely associated with FDIUS practices nor predominantly affected by them.

An important defense concern with FDIUS (aside from political posturing) arises if the firm in question makes something of serious military value that is hard to get elsewhere. Military undergarments may be vulnerable, but not to foreign dependency, given the enormous number of firms and locations of manufacture. A collusive cut-off is hard to imagine and, even if tried, would hardly affect the "balance of forces"; dependency on other than "U.S.-owned" and "U.S. made" seems innocuous. Production of advanced weapons and intelligence systems and of process equipment to manufacture key elements, components, and subassemblies may present a sharply different picture.

The defense relevance of foreign dependency, through FDIUS or other economic arrangements, can only be established by first employing some sort of screening methodology to determine defense relevance.[3] Applications of competition policy thinking have a special defense rationale only for goods and services that are found, one way or another, to be critical for present or future military or military intelligence capability.

For those goods or services that pass these tests, competition policy approaches have been suggested as a way to balance the risks and benefits of FDIUS. The risks include lessened competition with its costs and possible quality implications; information and technology transfer less controllable by the U.S. government; and the danger of competing sovereignties. Possible benefits from FDIUS include increased competition with lower costs and possibly higher quality implications and a larger U.S.-sited industrial and technology base.

Several authors have attempted to analyze the costs and benefits of foreign sourcing and foreign-owned production in the United States by relying on ideas clearly drawn from competition theory in microeconomics. The purpose of this chapter is to examine critically those attempts and to suggest what the appropriate contribution of such thinking is to an overall evaluation of foreign acquisition of U.S. defense-related industries.

CONCENTRATION AND COMPETITION

For decades, economists have recognized that, when a small number of sellers dominate a market, they may behave in a "monopoloid" fashion. Chamberlin (1929) explicitly demonstrated the recognized futility of price-cutting below the monopoly level set in a market for a standardized good, where one firm's price cut would affect another's sales so much that a responsive cut is inevitable. In such a situation, one can expect nominal competitors to refrain from competing on price. In sharp contrast, as the number of sellers increases and any one firm's price cut will imperceptibly affect any other's sales, each may be expected to try to expand its market share through such cuts. As each seller cuts price, however, the price moves toward the competitive level. If sellers are few, mutual forbearance will suffice to hold prices up; if they are many, self-interest suggests price-shading, regardless of formal agreement, absent an effective enforcement mechanism.[4]

Focusing on Foreign Concentration

What level of "concentration" (in other words, share of the market by the largest firms) suggests a danger from "monopoloid" behavior? In an influential 1990 article, Moran suggests a "4/50" rule of thumb: "No four countries or four companies supply more than fifty percent of the arm's length world market." Foreign takeovers would be allowed if the market did not fall under the constraint of the rule; otherwise they should be blocked by the Committee on Foreign Investment in the United States (CFIUS).[5]

In our view, Moran's argument (1990; 1993a) provides a simple, devastating, and wholly positive approach to dealing with protectionist supplications from U.S. industries with low concentration nationally and worldwide. Such industries are nearly always highly competitive by any standard, and their dispersion argues against supply manipulation for either economic or political purposes. Nevertheless, the rule is seriously incomplete as a general guide to policy.

First, the context (and Moran's subsequent use of the term "external concentration") implies that, while the market is global, the only agents under consideration for concentration attention are foreign.[6] However, focusing on only the share of the largest foreign firms leads to odd results. Consider three situations, in each of which the four-firm "external" concentration ratio for some good is 51 percent, all sales are "arm's length," and there is approximate equality in market size between the United States and the rest of the world. In the first case, suppose a domestic firm that completely monopolizes the U.S.-market accounts for 49 percent of the world market. The danger of allowing the acquisition of the U.S. firms seems obvious. In a second case, however, imagine that the U.S. market consists wholly of domestic firms, none of which has more than a small percentage of the market and again the external concentration ratio is 51 percent. Even the smallest foreign firm in the external group (or, depending on one's interpretation of Moran's intent, any foreign firm) would be unable to acquire any U.S. firm—even if such an acquisition were the most efficient means of entry and increased competition. In a third case, assume a U.S. firm with a 44 percent world market share, two other U.S. firms with a 2.5 percent market share each, all three of which sell only in the United States. Four foreign firms that sell a negligible amount in the United States have again a combined world share of 51 percent. This could well be a case in which direct investment is essential for serving a market satisfactorily. Assuming again that the U.S. market is only slightly less than the rest of the world market, the larger U.S. firm would hold more than 88 percent of the domestic market while the other two firms would command only a bit more than 5 percent each. The Moran rule suggests that, no matter how poorly the large firm or the two smaller ones are performing, neither of the small firms could be acquired by any of the four foreign-owned firms, no matter how small one of the latter may be.[7]

In a fourth possible case, if all world production takes place in the United States, then, by definition, there cannot be any foreign threat, no matter what the level of domestic concentration. But if Moran is concerned with corporate collusion unconnected with foreign military advantage, as some of his discussion implies (Moran 1990, 83), the absence of any discussion of domestic competition policy or the threat of domestic monopoly is not satisfactory. Much of what the Pentagon buys is purchased from domestic suppliers in industries where four firms hold much more than 50 percent of the United States or world market.[8] An explicit consideration of domestic concentration would have complicated Moran's argument because he would have been obliged either to propose remedies for domestic or world dominance by U.S. firms or to defend the innocuousness of some very high concentration levels.

One way or another Moran's rule seems incomplete even as a guide to firm concentration: The configuration of domestic production seems to provide neither assurance nor threat. Neither position is plausible. Another index that treats foreign and domestic concentration separately and then combines them in some way could be developed. That could be an improvement, but only if the relative weighting were persuasive and, more important, if the singular importance Moran attaches to concentration were accepted.

Using the same concentration screen for countries as for firms also needs defense. However approximate the "4/50" rule might be for private firms, they are out to make money. All U.S. rules of thumb about the dangers of concentration are based both on that assumption and on the absence of disciplined coordination among market participants (because such devices are illegal). Even though the example is unlikely, one can imagine eleven equal-sized firms in eleven different countries exhausting all world production of a product (perhaps made from a certain grade of a natural resource), effectively coordinated in their behavior by an overriding common goal of their parent governments that could dominate immediate financial profit. Indeed, this kind of eventuality appears to be precisely what Moran most fears, and thresholds drawn from other contexts do not persuade.[9]

Devising a concentration rule presumes a defined market to be measured. To determine BIC's marketshare, should its sales be denominated by cheap ballpoint pens, all ballpoints, all pens, or all writing instruments? And whatever the answer to that question, what geographic or jurisdictional boundaries are relevant? Such questions have vexed economists for decades, and conceptual innovations have recently modified government policy. Both the Federal Trade Commission (FTC) and the Antitrust Division of the Justice Department employ *Merger Guidelines* (Department of Justice 1982; 1984; 1992) for the enforcement of the antitrust laws that now define markets in a way that frequently corresponds poorly with any published data or other easily collected information.

The *Guidelines* attempt to determine the smallest number of firms and the smallest geographic area in which all sellers acting as one (including the firms considering merger) could raise prices by a certain amount (typically 5 percent) without losing sales for a period of one year. Concentration is then measured against this base, which allows for buyers to shift among products and for other suppliers to divert capacity quickly to take advantage of new profit opportunities. National boundaries do not constrain the analysis unless changes in trade barriers are anticipated (Abbott 1985). But this is not to say that national boundaries cannot impede smooth entry even where formal trade barriers are absent. This is an empirical issue that must be explored for each industry. Restriction on foreign acquisitions could obviously impede competition because such acquisitions might be the most effective means of entry. Presumably, if incumbents know that entry through acquisition by some or all of the best-placed entrants cannot take place, their behavior will be less restrained.

The *Guidelines* approach is predicated on the assumption that only analysis and not mere observation allows one to identify potential substitute products or potential new suppliers and hence to define the market in the first place.[10] If the 4/50 rule could be justified on other grounds, this problem adds considerable complexity to Moran's suggestion that all suppliers of defense-related goods be subject to a "monitoring exercise focusing on the 4/50 rule." While some notion of concentration among defense suppliers is essential for an understanding of the competitiveness of supply, anything close to accurate share estimates for many products would remain a tall order.[11]

In his original exposition, Moran notes that the 4/50 rule may well need refinement (Moran 1990, 82), but the problems go beyond the difficulties of market definition and the measurement of firm shares. The title of an industrial organization text that Moran cites as justification for concern about concentration, *Barriers to New Competition* (Bain 1956), suggests the inadequacy of using concentration alone for an evaluation of the competitiveness of industrial markets. If nothing prevents new sellers from swiftly entering a market, an extant monopolist dare not charge a monopoly price, or the market will be lost. Therefore, barriers to entry (and exit) rank with concentration as indices of competitive danger, and their role is enshrined in the *Merger Guidelines*. For example, under the 1984 guidelines, if excessive profits can be eroded by new entrants in less than two years, then, regardless of concentration, entry is "easy," and the antitrust enforcers will typically not challenge a merger regardless of concentration (Salop 1987, 7). One might argue that only immediate availability is germane for defense industries, but this makes little sense given the inventories and stockpiles that necessarily characterize much of defense procurement in an age of "come as you are" conflicts. Whether a different speed of entry standard is applied for a defense industry should therefore turn entirely on the use of the product and the scenario envisioned.

Many considerations in addition to concentration and barriers to entry are considered in evaluating government policy toward mergers (White 1987, 17). Consequently, unlike Moran's rule, the *Merger Guidelines* link government concern to various *ranges* of concentration, conditioned by entry and other factors.

Focusing on Domestic Concentration

In contrast to Moran's approach, some other treatments of the appropriateness of acquisitions from abroad appear to *begin* with *domestic* concentration and are less than clear about how far abroad their market analysis extends. Graham and Krugman (1995) argue that some emendation of the Sherman Act's stricture against monopolization might be appropriate for defense-related activities with more stringent but explicit standards applied.[12] The threshold level for single seller control would "surely be less than 100 percent but probably more than 25 percent" (Graham and Krugman 1995, 164). No discussion of concentration beyond this single-firm (or formally affiliated group) threshold is presented, but the new restriction is explicitly intended to apply to both foreign and domestic firms.[13] Graham and Krugman do not discuss the geographic or jurisdictional scope of the relevant market, but they express concern that product markets in antitrust cases are sometimes determined more broadly than is appropriate for "militarily critical goods" (Graham and Krugman 1995, 164).

In light of the considerable buying power exercised by the government and other defense purchasers, to be discussed below, the argument for a *more* stringent concentration standard needs explanation. This is an important issue because many defense markets, including distinct categories of military aircraft, have levels of domestic concentration in the range that Graham and Krugman (1995) find problematic, and experts have expressed doubts that the market can sustain as many firms as it now does (Kovacic and Smallwood 1994).

Graham and Krugman (1995) and Graham and Ebert (1991) see great merit in the policy approach of the British Monopolies and Mergers Commission in dealing with defense-critical industries. In sharp contrast to Moran, the British approach treats monopoly power in defense-related industries as seriously when it is posed by domestic as by foreign firms. Certain aspects of the British system and parts of the revision of FDIUS screening based on it that have been proposed by Graham and Ebert (1991, 264-266) appeared attractive. In particular, the treatment of national security issues as an integral part of the consideration of mergers and acquisitions has great merit. The commission's work clearly demonstrates the feasibility of using a different set of considerations to evaluate a merger's impact on defense-related products. The actual analysis displayed in the pair of cases that Graham and Ebert suggest as exemplary, those dealing with the unsuccessful hostile takeover attempt of the British electronics firm Plessey by GEC and the subsequently successful takeover by GEC and Siemens together, are less impressive (Monopolies and Mergers Commission 1986; 1989). The commission gives little attention to market definition in terms of product, geography, or jurisdiction. Further, the intermittent consideration of foreign competition is confusing. Without adequate explanation, the commission's discussion sometimes considered *domestic* concentration to be an overwhelmingly important consideration, while domestic monopoly for some products was accepted because of the scope for international discipline. Moreover, a deciding factor for or against the merger's acceptability for many products appears to have been the probable preservation of domestic technological capability, although the discussion often failed to make clear whether this goal was really necessary for defense purposes or was being pursued as part of broader industrial policy.[14]

MONOPSONY POWER IN DEFENSE PROCUREMENT

An appropriate consideration of market power cannot dwell on seller concentration to the exclusion of considerations on the buying side of the market. One of the explicit considerations of the *Merger Guidelines* is buyer concentration. In extreme cases of monopsony (single buyer), prices can be driven so low that supplying firms can be put out of business (Blair and Harrison 1993). Short of that unlikely possibility, the relative bargaining power of buyers and sellers is determined partly by relative concentration (Salop 1987, 11).

In considering defense purchases, U.S. government policy can benefit from at least two kinds of "countervailing power" (Galbraith 1952) that may be exercised against any market power by sellers. In many instances, government contractors are huge firms that successfully bargain for favorable prices with supplier industries that may be characterized by concentration and other features conducive to exploiting less powerful buyers. In other cases, the U.S. government deals directly with major firms, frequently as the only buyer of a product that the government has itself specified. Even if only a few firms are qualified to produce the product (or take charge of its production), the government bidding process may well result in a deal so "good" that the fortunes of the successful bidder are subsequently placed in jeopardy.[15]

Firms and the character of their products vary enormously among the defense industries. One typology (Adelman and Augustine 1990, 157-162) sees four main types of suppliers: *(i)* firms that sell largely "off the rack" products to the Defense Department or its suppliers and for which defense sales are typically a small part of total business; *(ii)* large firms with separate divisions or segments for defense production to government specification; *(iii)* highly specialized major firms—as in *(ii)* often "system-integrators"—that combine in-house expertise with the complex job of contracting with other, typically smaller firms, to produce finished products for defense purposes; and *(iv)* smaller manufacturers who supply components to *(ii)* and *(iii)*.

Some observers have suggested that the Pentagon's prime contractors were developed as private entities principally to avoid a layer of bureaucracy and its associated inefficiencies (Sacks 1994, 1022), and reduced defense demand can deliver a mortal blow to these repositories of rare human capital. The same is true of countless smaller specialized firms that serve the primes.

An additional dimension of variation relates to government restrictions on process and product. If we confine our attention only to "high-technology" sectors, restriction ranges from a level of security classification in which the existence of an activity is not acknowledged (let alone the precise nature of the product and the way it is made) through various levels of classification to "dual use" technologies in which a final product can be easily obtained and perhaps duplicated through "reverse engineering." The situation is further complicated by export restrictions on many technologies and products that are themselves not classified.

Most firms produce many products—sometimes in the thousands—and this can greatly complicate the application of policies necessarily focused on firms. Neither Moran nor Graham and his associates give definitive guidance about what products would be covered by their special competition concerns. Moran uses phrases such as "crucial to national security" (1990, 84) and "of direct importance to U.S. defense industries" (1990, 96), but perhaps the fairest reading of his intention is that the 4/50 rule be applied to anything purchased directly or indirectly for use by the defense establishment. Moran avoids discussing the kind of bounding discussed earlier, presumably because his approach is most powerful in rejecting special policy alternatives for many categories of purchase, such as military uniforms, that would also never make the explicit threat "cut" of the screening approaches anyway. But Moran fails to recognize that an investigation, perhaps frequently as elaborate and difficult as that proposed by some other analysts for criticality bounding, would be necessary to establish an appropriate market definition before a meaningful measurement of concentration could even take place. For example, Moran criticizes trade policy toward the machine tool industry for failing to focus "tariff relief on those subsectors where tight concentration ratios might show a genuine national security threat" (Moran 1990, 88). Apparently, his only criterion of "genuineness" is simply direct or indirect sales to the defense establishment, because otherwise he is involved in unacknowledged screening on other criteria. More importantly, he does not acknowledge that merely looking at the sales concentration figures would not make a case for monopoly power in the subsector. Only a knowledge of the speed and extent of sources of new supply in response to price hikes (or shortages) would give the concentration data meaning (Moran 1990, 87-88).[16]

Graham and Krugman (1995, 164) suggest that their special concentration concerns might apply to a "relatively short" list drawn up on the basis of "military importance" and "number and diversity of potential suppliers," although they confess, "We do not consider ourselves qualified to set precise criteria" (Graham and Krugman 1995, 163). Therefore, Graham and Krugman explicitly acknowledge the kind of bounding exercise discussed earlier, while a defensible application of Moran's approach would require detailed information about substitution in production and use for a huge range of goods and services. In fact, the range is so vast that bounding would be necessary to devote sufficient attention to the most critical defense purchases.[17]

In a world of increasing dual-use technologies and products, dividing noncritical sheep from critical goats within a particular firm would be enormously difficult and may become more so in the future as the Pentagon increases its "off the rack" purchases to save costs. Moreover, it is not at all clear that either a looser or a more stringent general *concentration* standard is appropriate for defense industries because it captures such a limited part of the picture. Only a detailed look at the specific conditions of the markets involved—one that would go well beyond a consideration of concentration in sales—could yield a defensible answer.

Concentration is particularly awkward to apply in contracting situations (McMillan 1984). *Ex ante*, the market defined in the *Merger Guidelines* sense may be highly concentrated. Once the contract is let, nominal concentration becomes 100 percent. But the buyer may still have the upper hand, depending on how the contract is written. Moreover, most such government contracting situations, particularly in the defense area, may be viewed as repeated play games, in which short-term opportunism by the seller, even if legal, would jeopardize the supplying firm's long term fortunes (Kovacic 1991, 583).

When these considerations are combined with the extraordinary level of continuous cost and price monitoring that characterize a typical defense supply contract, the role of a market's structural features, such as concentration and barriers to entry, lose much of its usual significance and thus greatly reduce the usefulness of standard competition analysis.[18]

Finally, something must be said about the "economies defense" in antitrust, which, even absent monopsony power, may be used to give the benefit of the doubt to levels of concentration that might be difficult to justify otherwise. The *Merger Guidelines* specifically recognize scale economies, which are important in much defense production, as are economies of cumulative output. Both tend to vitiate attempts to make procurement more competitive by assigning production to more than one firm (Burnett and Scherer 1989).

One of the greatest challenges facing defense procurement today is not suppliers' excess profits at taxpayers expense, but the extraordinary "deadweight losses" resulting from the monitoring aimed at avoiding such profits.[19] Because of the elaborate measures that the federal government exercises against excess profits for most goods and services supplied directly, the chief danger from monopoly may arise when these measures are exercised against firms who purchase for resale to the government. But competition in such markets appears adequately handled by antitrust policy.

Overall, the extreme variation among defense markets in such dimensions as relative seller-buyer concentration, barriers to entry, the use of contracting versus open market purchases, the role of inventories, and the pace of technical change makes us skeptical that anything would be gained by *generally* changing concentration standards for mergers in defense-related industries—or by making industries already concentrated above a certain level candidates for divestiture or dismemberment.

RELATIVE QUALITY

Thus far, the argument has questioned "concentration on concentration" as a dominant focus for determining the danger to national welfare. Not only are other considerations involved on the selling side, but the market power of the buyer must be considered as well. Arguably, the leverage of the major contractor or the government may often squeeze profits of sellers whose level of market concentration might otherwise permit excess earnings. But, there is a further critical consideration that distinguishes defense acquisitions from those made by governments for purely domestic purposes.

Rational government agents working on behalf of their principals (the voters' representatives) seek the most favorable combination of cost and quality from a menu of available options. In some cases, the best combination might be found from a foreign seller, but missing that option would not likely be a devastating mistake. In defense matters, it could be. By its nature, national security partakes of a zero-sum world, alien to the general prosperity goal of much other government activity. The availability of the latest technology in a certain defense area may be worth a great deal, even though the quality advantage is marginal (Adelman and Augustine 1990, 142). This critical difference from other markets has generated suggestions for a view of competition policy quite different from that which informs most of U.S. antitrust.

Shrinking defense budgets both at home and abroad give great urgency to the issue of admissible industrial combinations among defense firms, quite apart from the issue of foreign investment. In several persuasive articles, Kovacic (1990; 1991; Burnett and Kovacic 1989; Kovacic and Smallwood 1994) argues that mergers and acquisitions among major defense contractors should be viewed differently from those among other firms. Kovacic contends that the special competencies of firms within the same broad provision area (say, fighter aircraft) dictate careful attention to the impact of market withdrawals or mergers on the Defense Department's various "mission needs."

Kovacic joins several other analysts who conclude that the most critical resource in these considerations is the human capital developed over the years by the various contractors. Complete analysis of the probable results of mergers is greatly complicated by the current practice of "teaming;" in other words, joint ventures in which blame or credit is hard to assign; great uncertainties in the acquisition environment; and the unusual nature of regulation in Pentagon purchasing that drains much of the meaning from the usual preoccupation of merger analysis: market power (Kovacic and Smallwood 1994, 100-101).[20] One conclusion stands above all others from a mission-driven analysis: Two or even three potential contractors should be preserved not principally because of cost or price effects but to assure maximum ingenuity in the fulfillment of mission requirements (Kovacic and Smallwood 1994, 102), the qualitative edge in defense performance. This prime objective requires quite a different emphasis than is typical in the analysis of competition and may sometimes lead to the conclusion that, instead of being resisted or merely tolerated, concentration should be fostered by the government to generate and preserve expertise (Kovacic and Smallwood 1994, 94).

RELATIVE QUALITY AND FDIUS

Previous attempts to devise competition-based FDIUS policies have recognized the critical issue of relative quality in considering defense acquisitions. Both Moran and Graham-Krugman are anxious to encourage FDIUS in areas where foreigners might otherwise exploit defense-relevant monopoly advantages from an entirely foreign base. Unlike the case of a trading relationship, if there were a conflict of policies between the United States and a foreign subsidiary on U.S. soil, the issue would become an extraterritorial dispute rather than merely a cessation of supply.[21] Moreover, a complete pullout from U.S. operations for any reason—including a state of hostility between the United States and the home government—would leave the United States with some residual capacity.

And what happens to the concentration concerns in such cases? For Moran, a U.S. location appears to erase the danger, but Graham and Krugman express ambivalence. One policy option for the avoidance of a foreign-based monopoly might require the foreign holders of a key product or process to license U.S. producers. Although Graham and Krugman refer only to "a domestic producer" (1995, 164), perhaps enough licensees would be mandated to push concentration below some (unspecified) threshold. But Graham and Krugman realize that the compulsory patent licensing for government purposes (apparently legal under the Paris Convention) does not include any provisions for forcing disclosure of the knowledge necessary to make effective use. Hence, in many circumstances, Graham and Krugman believe that mandating the U.S. location of production and perhaps other activities such as R&D might be the best possible solution. This would be a condition for sales to the U.S. market. Graham and Krugman seem to regard such compulsory FDIUS by a monopoly a necessary exception to their preference for an acceptable concentration level. They are right. The only alternatives would be either a heavily subsidized and otherwise protected duplicative domestic effort or an attempt to dismember the monopolist's activities within U.S. jurisdiction—while threatening denial of access to the U.S. market as a penalty for not operating within that jurisdiction!

The authors agree with both Moran and Graham and Krugman that, if either Japan or Europe is developing a major technology with important defense implications, the United State must be developing it, too. This not only is prudent, but greatly increases U.S. bargaining power with foreign firms about mandated FDIUS and other performance requirements.

Graham and Krugman suggest that FDIUS performance requirements for foreign suppliers of defense relevant material should be incorporated into international agreements because states will generally want local competence in critical technologies (Graham and Krugman 1995, 164-165). The suggestion is worth exploring, but many difficulties are apparent. Most critical defense technologies have nonmilitary uses that typically swamp the military applications in magnitude. A policy nominally aimed as military assurance could effectively become a policy geared to commercial advantage. The United States could be the chief beneficiary of ambiguity because of superior bargaining power. U.S. threats to sponsor duplication of a technology would be more credible because of comprehensive know-how and the importance of military superiority. Moreover, access to the U.S. market would be hard to walk away from. Thus, the United States may expect others to insist that any mutually agreed upon performance requirements be narrowly drawn.[22]

THE DANGERS OF FOREIGN OWNERSHIP

In addition to the prime importance of relative quality, the very nature of defense activity suggests a concern with secrecy and conflicting sovereignty. Prior to 1984, firms owned[23] by foreigners and working on classified defense contracts were obliged to turn over control to U.S. trustees under either a proxy or voting trust agreement. To increase the meaningful participation of foreigners, a device known as a Special Security Arrangement (SSA) was introduced that allowed the foreign parent to retain what amounts to a minority position on the U.S. affiliate's board of directors. A review by the General Accounting Office (GAO) several years later found that objections to the new arrangements included concerns that SSAs were being granted more readily than intended by the rules and that some technical violations had occurred. Nonetheless, no evidence was found of significant breaches of security (General Accounting Office 1990). More generally, a literature search revealed no substantial security problems because of leakage of classified information to unauthorized personnel within foreign-owned firms. Given the need to find officers and other U.S. personnel who can obtain the necessary security clearances, one wonders how seriously disadvantaged some foreign firms continue to be.

Opponents of greater penetration of the U.S. defense-industrial base by foreign investors have not typically focused their concern on security issues. Instead, they have expressed alarm about the possible conflict of sovereignties posed by allowing a foreign firm to own a U.S. defense supplier. This concern, coupled with congressional doubts about the depth of foreign government pockets, led to a change in the Exon-Florio legislation that mandates monitoring FDIUS for threats to "national security"; since 1993, foreign-government-owned firms have been essentially blocked from participating in the defense-industrial base (Sacks 1994, 1055).

U.S. law controls the export of both products and technology, and a plausible "nightmare" scenario involves a conflict in foreign policy between the United States and the home country government about transfers to a third country. Moran described this problem in 1992 congressional testimony opposing the sale of LTV's missile and aircraft divisions to the French government-owned firm, Thomson (Moran 1992; 1993b).

In agreement with Moran, the sale to Thomson would have been unwise, given the available alternative buyer, a combination of Loral, Carlyle, and Northrup. In addition, the case illustrates a number of factors that cast doubt on the adequacy of any simple rule about foreign acquisitions.

First, Moran points out that several of the existing products of LTV would, if transferred abroad, create an external monopoly. But given the U.S. concern about military superiority, this must typically be the case for the transfer of property rights to foreigners of highly sophisticated weapons, which are typically *designed* to be in a class by themselves. The purpose of rules such as the *Merger Guidelines* "five percent test" for market definition rests on the difficulty of comparison of differentiated products (in other words, products that are either different or are perceived to be different). Yet, the application of such a test for leading edge weapons is extraordinarily difficult because directly competing products are seldom sold in competition with each other in relatively open markets. Thus, most modern weapon systems "monopolize" their own markets, if those markets are demarcated according to procedures resembling the *Merger Guidelines*.

The LTV case also obliges us to consider the ambiguity of treatment of permissible monopoly. While Moran may not be concerned with market definition and concentration for LTV's products when the firm is U.S.-owned, the Graham-Krugman approach raises the likelihood that some of LTV's products dominated their "markets" excessively even before the issues of foreign acquisition arose. Graham and Krugman might well respond that the lack of short-run substitutes for products made for government use at the government's request simply indicates a limitation of the use of concentration measures and not intolerable monopoly power. This is precisely the point.

Second, the acquiring firm was French. Moran reviews the long history of French subjection to U.S. extraterritorial interference that has resulted from the frequently diverging foreign policies of the two countries. One wonders if Moran would have had an objection to the sale to a French firm if the external concentration level had been below his threshold. Similar problems of conflicting sovereignty may still arise. Third, there was doubt about how much technology and other know-how Thomson was bringing to the deal. Finally, a more suitable U.S. buyer was available.

Arguably, if the situation had been different on all counts *except* nominal monopoly, the decision should have been decided the other way. Assume that some other unique set of defense products were produced by a U.S. firm that was not prospering, and the most technology-rich suitor (by a considerable margin) were a privately held British company. No serious risk of any kind is evident from the sale.

British and Canadian cooperation with the United States on defense production is long-standing and provides a high degree of assurance. Differential confidence is reflected in data. Of the 327 classified foreign defense contracts in force in 1989, 194 were held by British firms, and 108 involved Canadians. The French held one (General Accounting Office 1990, 8). The differences in defense production and R&D interdependence and, more generally, foreign policy consonance between the United States and particular foreign countries obviously cast doubt on the national security and political feasibility of a "four country" rule that ignores such considerations.[24]

Some object that high technology firms, particularly in the defense area, benefit from public expenditures on R&D, and this subsidy should preclude foreign acquisition. Two considerations cast doubt on this objection. First, profitability on defense sales is frequently highly regulated. Second, the anticipated profit streams from *previous* publicly financed efforts should not constitute a powerful objection to the sales of such firms to foreigners because those profits should be capitalized in the sales price of the firm.[25]

Some home countries may be unacceptable even if market power does not enter the analysis. Graham and Ebert counsel special attention to acquisitions from potential adversaries or from a "country of concern" under the Export Administration Act (Graham and Ebert 1991, 264).[26] This illustrates the basic point: High concentration is neither a necessary nor a sufficient condition for blocking a foreign acquisition.

CHANGING CURRENT POLICY

The brief recommendations for changes in current U.S. policy toward FDIUS in defense-related industries follow from the arguments and evidence just developed.

First, changes in Exon-Florio made in 1993 move CFIUS review in the direction of general technology protection and away from the restricted definition of national security protection that the authors would prefer. Suggestions that CFIUS consider "U.S. technological leadership in areas affecting national security" could be construed to prevent acquisitions in many areas because so many technologies have some utility for the military. Reciprocity in direct investment in high tech—especially programs that are publicly funded—presents public policy challenges, but the issues should not be grouped under a battle flag.[27]

Second, because the human capital embodied in teams of employees is regarded as the most important resource held by the targets of takeover, the government is justified in actively seeking appropriate means of preserving and building this capacity. In many cases, the search will be entirely national; in other cases, however, it is fully appropriate for foreign firms to play the invigoration role. Although specifying eligible home countries would be invidious, they would certainly include the United Kingdom and Canada. Apparent partiality to certain nationalities might spur bilateral agreements with other countries on extraterritorial issues.

Finally, the CFIUS review process needs further improvement in the meshing of expertise on competition policy with detailed knowledge of defense issues. Graham and Ebert (1991) make a powerful case for a more systematic role for competition experts in the administration of Exon-Florio. Some of their advice has been incorporated into proposed legislation (Graham and Krugman 1995, 167). If such observers as Kovacic and Smallwood are right, however—and the authors think they are—configuring defense suppliers for the future involves economic (and other) reasoning that moves beyond conventional competition analysis. The Pentagon thus faces a challenge to develop a powerful in-house capacity to present well-reasoned positions that may appear quite unusual to competition enforcers at Justice and the FTC (Kovacic and Smallwood 1994, 106-109).

CONCLUSION

Returning to the question with which this discussion began, careful analysis of defense acquisitions by foreigners must certainly include the best theory and empirical evidence from the industrial organization branch of microeconomic theory. In this thinking, market concentration plays an important role that has been operationalized by the U.S. government's *Merger Guidelines*[28] in a way that makes it far more defensible theoretically, but also much more difficult and subjective to estimate than when calculated from production and trade data, as in earlier years. Even as a guide to competition in ordinary industrial markets, however, concentration shares importance with barriers to entry and exit and several other characteristics, including concentration on the buying side.

When motivations related to national security are involved in either the selling or the buying side of a market, concentration may retain some heuristic merit. But an even greater range of additional considerations may dominate outcomes than those of commercial sphere. Internationally, access and denial issues may be instantly understood when concentration is low, but not dependably otherwise. Within the domestic economy, virtually any level of concentration in provision—and arguably foreign ownership as well—may serve the national interest.

Concentration is not an analytic silver bullet for the examination of national security concerns in FDIUS or in trade; it is better regarded as a hoe for the extirpation of nonsense. An approximate understanding of concentration may help focus serious attention on cases in need of further examination. But while low concentration may suffice to assure competitive supply, the upper limit for acceptable concentration in various situations of foreign ownership cannot be determined without detailed knowledge of other circumstances. Instead of devoting excessive attention to concentration, policy should be crafted toward foreign acquisitions of U.S. defense firms by drawing on comprehensive learning from industrial economics, an understanding of the special characteristics of various defense markets, and a consideration of the record of the acquiring firm and the host country. This view approximates current practice, and, while the procedures could be improved, CFIUS has yet to make any important mistakes.

NOTES

Some arguments and evidence in this chapter are anticipated in Bobrow and Kudrle (1994). Kudrle's research was sponsored by the Air Force Office of Scientific Research, Air Force Material Command, USAF, under grant number F49620-94-1-0461. The views expressed herein are those of the chapter authors and not necessarily of the Air Force Office of Scientific Research, the U.S. government, or the book editors.

1. The arguments were developed in the first edition of their book, which appeared in 1989.

2. For an example of the heavily, commercially-weighted consortia that may result, see "The Latest Innovations Developed by America's Leading Advanced Transportation Consortia" (1996).

3. For possible methodologies, see Institute for Defense Analysis (1990), The Analytic Sciences Corporation (1990), Libicki, Nunn, and Taylor (1987), and the summary of these studies in General Accounting Office (1994).

4. Under some circumstances, such "tacit collusion" can affect product development and promotional activity as well.

5. For an extensive discussion of the background enforcement of CFIUS and its role enforcing the Exon-Florio amendment to protect "national security," see Graham and Krugman (1995, 126-132).

6. The first section of Moran (1990) seems attentive to domestic concentration. His figure 1 clearly implies that "insecurity" attaches to high concentration of domestic ownership as well as foreign ownership, although the diagram also implies that the threat is lower when the concentration is in the control of domestic firms. The text of the article fails to discuss either the dangers of concentration in domestic hands or how it can be traded off against foreign concentration for a given level of security. The text expresses concern about "oligopoly-pricing and other (sic) predatory practices that discriminate among buyers (e.g., delayed delivery of new products . . .)" (Moran 1990, 83), but this apparently refers only to foreign firms.

7. Moran seems to offer an "out" when he writes: "A merger or acquisition among smaller firms in a concentrated industry might be permissible if it had the result of diluting the power of the four leaders" (Moran 1990, 97). But Moran does not otherwise consider domestic firms, so the "four leaders" must apparently be those with the 51 percent market share, whatever

the market power of larger domestic firms.

8. Moran cites figures of four-firm total sales concentration by defense suppliers as 54 percent in 1982, up from 33 percent in 1955 (1990, 90). These figures do not inform the present discussion, however, because market power turns on concentration at the individual product level (properly defined). In fact, under most circumstances, even the Department of Justice would find concentration meeting Moran's suggested standard too low to warrant investigation. The Department of Justice employs the Herfindahl-Hirschman (H-H) index of concentration rather than a four-firm concentration ratio, but four-firm ratios of 50 typically correspond to H-H values of 800 to 1000; official attention usually begins above that level (Scherer and Ross 1990, 195). For a discussion of present concentration levels, see Kovacic (1991, 575).

9. Although we will not pursue Moran's concentration rule with respect to countries, certain ambiguities are apparent. Are the "4" countries regarded as countries of location (as Moran suggests) or ownership (which would be the key to coordination)? And what is the significance of "country" in this context for the members of the European Union?

10. This casts doubt on Moran's claim that the concentration test is "objective" (1992, 313).

11. Among other problems, there are no published sources for the "arm's-length trans-actions" that Moran wants to measure, even on a national basis.

12. The *Merger Guidelines* were developed to enforce the Sherman and Clayton Acts but are not part of the law.

13. The *Guidelines* express special concern for mergers between firms with a combined market share of 35 percent or more.

14. Another troubling element of the activity of the Monopolies and Mergers Commis-sion is the extent to which a range of economic considerations beyond competition or national security appear to inform policy. The commission is directed to consider such issues as general industry employment and export earnings that move beyond either concern into the boundless expanse of "economic development." Graham and Ebert (1991) do not propose such an evaluative agenda for U.S. mergers.

15. Adelman and Augustine (1990) argue that monopsony in defense procurement gives the government a special responsibility. "To take advantage could indeed generate short-term benefits for the government and the taxpayer but in the long term could . . . (drive) would-be suppliers from the supplier base until a strong competitive situation no longer existed" (Adelman and Augustine 1990, 128). Fixed price contracts are held to be particularly dangerous (Adelman and Augustine 1990, 193).

16. Some readers may think we are making too much of defining the market correctly. Imagine there are only two cheap ballpoint pen firms (one of which makes pens with green barrels, the other with red barrels), and it takes a year for a new firm to get into the pen business. Suppose further that it takes each firm about one day to change barrel colors, if it chooses to. The *Merger Guidelines* suggest that it makes no sense to define the green barrel firm out of the relevant market in the first place by characterizing the other firm as a "monopolist" of red barrel pens. One learns nothing of policy importance from observing that red barrel pens are sold by only one firm.

17. This claim is made despite the fact that Moran does not explicitly acknowledge that his approach must rest on some screening system (General Accounting Office 1994, 43).

18. Kovacic (1991, 564, 586) also argues that collusion is unlikely because of the complexities of the products in question.

19. An additional challenge is letting supply contracts to a range of contending suppliers, even if a simpler approach would serve the ultimate buyer (in other words, the taxpayer) far more efficiently (Towell 1994).

20. Market power analysis is complicated not only by the monitoring of provider behavior but also by divisions within the Pentagon that may weaken the exercise of monopsony buying (Kovacic and Smallwood 1994, 101-102).

21. Supply delays and cutoffs from foreign sites as a *military* threat are also exaggerated and not necessarily well gauged by concentration. Much has been made of difficulties experienced by some private firms and government labs in obtaining semiconductor material and equipment and computer components from Japanese suppliers. The delays appear to have been entirely for reasons of commercial competition and involved no breach of contract (General Accounting Office 1991). The General Accounting Office has suggested that some attention to such behavior may have to be considered by CFIUS in assessing a firm's fitness to acquire under the Exon-Florio procedures (Mendelowitz 1992, 3). Nonetheless, if the delays had direct military significance, apparently the United States could have protested to the Japanese government under provisions of their 1983 security agreement.

22. There is considerable dispute about the extent to which various current and proposed discriminatory measures related to foreign direct investment are legal under current U.S. international obligations (Warner and Rugman 1994).

23. The requirements applied not just to ownership but also to "control" or "influence." For a discussion of these terms, see Rishe (1991), which also captures the complexity of security clearances for facilities and individuals.

24. This means that, even if we accepted Moran's "country concentration" test, we would not weight all countries equally.

25. Moreover, much ongoing excess profits from public funding should be recaptured by the Treasury in tax payments on income resulting from U.S. production *if* the international transfer price system within the firm is basically accurate. Unfortunately, this is an assumption about which there is currently great doubt (see, for example, Hufbauer 1992, chapter 6).

26. So far, the only case actually blocked under the Exon-Florio procedures was the acquisition of an aircraft parts firm by a Chinese-owned enterprise. The security stakes were apparently trivial, but the case gave the United States an opportunity to react sharply toward China in the aftermath of Tiananmen Square.

27. Not surprisingly, foreign observers view an expansive interpretation of "national security" with alarm, and various kinds of protectionism based on that pretext could be in violation of U.S. international obligations. For one interpretation, see Warner and Rugman (1994).

28. The term "government" is used because the FTC has joined the Justice Department in fully embracing the 1992 *Guidelines* in its enforcement activity (Arquit 1992).

REFERENCES

Abbott, Alden F. 1985. "Foreign Competition and Relevant Market Definition under the Department of Justice Merger Guidelines," *Antitrust Bulletin*, Summer, pp. 299-336.

Adelman, Kenneth L., and Norman R. Augustine. 1990. *The Defense Revolution: Strategy for the Brave New World*, Institute for Contemporary Studies. San Francisco: ICS Press.

Analytic Sciences Corporation, The. 1990. *Foreign Vulnerability of Critical Industries*. Arlington, Va.: The Analytic Sciences Corporation, March.

Arquit, Kevin J. 1992. "Perspectives on the 1992 U.S. Government Horizontal Merger Guidelines," *Antitrust Journal* 61:121-138.

Bain, Joe S. 1956. *Barriers to New Competition*. Cambridge: Harvard University Press.

Bergsten, C. Fred. 1992. "Statement" presented to Hearings before the Committee on Commerce Science and Transportation, United States Senate, One Hundred Second Congress, First Session, November 19, 1991. Washington, D.C.: GPO.

Blair, Roger D., and Jeffrey L. Harrison. 1993. *Monopsony: Antitrust Law and Economics*. Princeton, N.J.: Princeton University Press.

Bobrow, Davis B., and Robert T. Kudrle. 1994. "Economic Interdependence and Security: U.S. Trade and Investment Policy for a New Era," *Minnesota Journal of Global Trade* 3(1):61-96.

Bryant, Adam. 1996. "For Military-Industrial Complex, a New Reality," *New York Times*, November 18, p. C2.

Burnett, William B., and William E. Kovacic. 1989. "Reform of United States Weapons Acquisitions Policy: Competition, Teaming Agreements, and Dual Sourcing," *Yale Journal of Regulation* 6:249-317.

Burnett, William B., and Frederic M. Scherer. 1989. "The Weapons Industry," in *The Structure of American Industries*, Eighth ed., edited by Walter Adams. New York: Macmillan.

Chamberlin, Edward H. 1929. "Duopoly: Value where Sellers Are Few," *Quarterly Journal of Economics* 43(November):63-100.

Department of Justice. 1982. *U.S. Department of Justice Merger Guidelines* 47 Fed. Reg. 28,493.

―――. 1984. *U.S. Department of Justice Merger Guidelines* 49 Fed. Reg. 26,823.

―――. 1992. *U.S. Department of Justice Merger Guidelines* 57 Fed. Reg. 41,552.

Galbraith, John Kenneth. 1956. *American Capitalism; The Concept of Countervailing Power*. Boston, Mass.: Houghton Mifflin.

General Accounting Office. 1994. *Industrial Base: Assessing the Risk of DOD's Foreign Dependence*. Washington, D.C.: GAO, April.

―――. 1990. *Testimony on Defense Industrial Security: Special Security Agreements Permit Foreign Owned U.S. Firms to Perform Classified Defense Contracts (GAO/T-NSIAD-90-17)*. Washington, D.C.: GPO.

Graham, Edward M., and Michael E. Ebert. 1991. "Foreign Direct Investment and National Security: Fixing the Exon-Florio Process," *The World Economy* 14(3), September.

Graham, Edward M., and Paul R. Krugman. 1995. *Foreign Direct Investment in the United States*. Third edition. Washington, D.C.: Institute for International Economics.

Hufbauer, Gary Clyde. 1992. *U.S. Taxation of International Income: Blueprint for Reform*. Washington, D.C.: Institute for International Economics.

Institute for Defense Analysis. 1990. *Dependence of the U.S. Defense Systems on Foreign Technologies*, December.

Kovacic, William E. 1990. "Antitrust Analysis of Joint Ventures in Teaming Arrangements Involving Government Contractors," *Antitrust Law Journal* 58:1059-1115.

―――. 1991. "Merger Policy in a Declining Defense Industry," *Antitrust Bulletin*, Fall, pp. 543-592.

Kovacic, William E., and Dennis E. Smallwood. 1994. "Competition Policy, Rivalries, and Defense Industry Consolidation," *Journal of Economic Perspectives* 8(4):99-110.

"The Latest Innovations Developed by America's Leading Advanced Transportation Consortia." 1996. *DARPA Progress Report* 3(1), Spring.

Libicki, Martin, Jack H. Nunn, and Bill Taylor. 1987. *U.S. Industrial Base Dependence/Vulnerability: Phase II—Analysis*. Washington, D.C., November.

McMillan, Richard, Jr.. 1984. "Special Problems in Section Two Sherman Act Cases Involving Government Procurement: Market Definition, Measuring Market Power, and the Government as Monopsonist," *Public Contract Law Journal* 14(2):262-275.

Mendelowitz, Allen I. 1992. *Foreign Investment: Analyzing National Security-Related Investments under the Exon-Florio Provision, Testimony before the Subcommittee on International Finance and Monetary Policy, Committee on Banking, Housing and Urban Affairs, U.S. Senate*. Prepared by the General Accounting Office. Washington, D.C.: GAO.

Monopolies and Mergers Commission. 1986. *The General Electric Company PLC and The Plessey Company PLC: A Report on the Proposed Merger*. London: Her Majesty's Stationery Office.

———. 1989. *The General Electric Company PLC, Siemens AG and the Plessey Company PLC: A Report on the Proposed Merger*. London: HMSO.

Moran, Theodore H. 1990. "The Globalization of America's Defense Industries: Managing the Threat of Foreign Dependence," *International Security* 15(Summer):57-99.

———. 1992. Statement presented at Hearings before the Committee on Armed Services, United States Senate, One Hundred Second Congress, Second Session, April 30, 1992. Washington, D.C.: GPO.

———. 1993a. *American Economic Policy and National Security*. New York: Council on Foreign Relations Press.

———. 1993b. Statement presented at Hearings before the Investigations Subcommittee and the Defense Policy Panel of the Committee on Armed Services, United States House of Representatives, One Hundred and Second Congress, Second Session, June 25, 1992. Washington, D.C.: GPO.

National Defense University. 1987. *U. S. Industrial Base Dependence/Vulnerability*, November.

Rishe, Melvin C. 1991. "Foreign Ownership, Control, or Influence: The Implications for United States Companies Performing Defense Contracts," *Public Contract Law Journal* 20(2):143-187.

Sacks, Jeremy D. 1994. "Monopsony and the Archers: Rethinking Foreign Acquisitions after Thompson-LTV," *Law and Policy in International Business* 25:1019-1057.

Salop, Steven C. 1987. "Symposium on Mergers and Antitrust," *Economic Perspectives* 1(2):3-12.

Scherer, Frederic M., and David R. Ross. 1990. *Industrial Market Structure and Economic Performance*. Boston: Houghton Mifflin Company.

Towell, Pat. 1994. "Pentagon Banking on Plans to Reinvent Procurement," *Congressional Quarterly Weekly Report* 52(16):899-904.

U.S. House of Representatives. 1992. *Sale of LTV Missile and Aircraft Divisions: Hearings Before the Investigations Subcommittee and the Defense Policy Panel of the Committee on Armed Services*. Washington D.C.: GPO.

Warner, Mark A. A., and Alan M. Rugman. 1994. "Competitiveness: An Emerging Strategy of Discrimination in U.S. Antitrust and R.P.D. Policy?" *Law and Policy in International Business* 25:945-982.

White, Lawrence J. 1987. "Antitrust and Merger Policy: A Review and Critique," *Economic Perspectives* 1(2):13-22.

15

Foreign Investment Restrictions, National Treatment, and Telecommunications

Cynthia A. Beltz

INTRODUCTION

Since the late eighteenth century, the U.S. government has largely maintained that unfettered capital flows are in the national interest. Yet, is an open-door investment policy still rational for the United States at the end of the twentieth century? Or, does the United States need to institute a two-tier investment policy that holds foreign investors accountable for the regulatory and trade practices of the home government, as proposed by the proponents of managed trade and investment, reciprocal market access tests, and conditional national treatment? The answer argued here is that openness makes even more sense today than in years past.

Managed-investment proponents argue that the time has passed for an open-door policy. We are told that such an arrangement is no longer in the best interest of the United States because unilateral liberalization sacrifices the bargaining chips needed to force foreign governments to open their markets to the investments of U.S.-owned multinationals.

Such arguments are politically appealing because they play on one's sense of fairness. But, once the "us versus them" rhetoric is stripped away and the practical problems of implementation are examined, the managed-investment proposition loses much of its appeal. Technology, market, and policy trends also suggest that the debate is not about whether liberalization will occur but rather about the pace of reform. Advances in technology, consumer demands, the breakdown of monopolies in other markets, and institutional changes put intense pressure on national regulators to reform outdated systems and open economies to foreign investors.

Therefore, the essential question is, Can the United States speed the liberalization process in a cost-effective manner by using foreign investors as a crowbar? To answer, one also must ask what is likely to promote U.S. economic welfare in practice, not only what is possible in theory. It is a question of probabilities. That is, what is the probability a conditional national treatment rule will generate results superior to those that have been experienced under national treatment?

This chapter argues that the conditional national treatment (CNT) proposition in the area of investment is unlikely to generate superior results for U.S. economic welfare. In theory, a gain may be had from the closure of the U.S. market that is used as a means of opening a market that would otherwise have remained closed. Except for this assertion, however, there is little evidence to support an economic argument for foreign investment restrictions and CNT. Given current technology, market, and policy trends, the problems of accurately predicting foreign government behavior, and the problems of regulatory capture, this chapter concludes that an open door, based on the national treatment principle, remains the rational rule for practice.

To make the arguments more concrete, this chapter examines the case for foreign ownership restrictions in the telecommunication industry, with particular focus on three assumptions: *(i)* restrictions on foreign investment in the United States are needed to open foreign markets to competition, *(ii)* foreign governments will respond to U.S. regulatory pressure by opening their markets, and *(iii)* the Federal Communications Commission (FCC) and its foreign investment review process will promote the public interest and consumer economic welfare in pro-competitive policies.

The chapter concludes that, contrary to the assumptions that drive the conditional national treatment proposition, markets worldwide are already on a course toward increased competition, regardless of U.S. restrictions on foreign investment or U.S. reciprocity tactics. The U.S. experience demonstrates the benefits of unilateral liberalization as well as the multiplier role of that liberalization for other markets. Given the technology and market forces unleashed by deregulation in the United States and the fundamental, often unilateral, changes now taking place in the regulatory regimes of our major trading partners, the CNT proposition makes increasingly less sense.

A POSITIVE SUM GAME

Before turning to consider telecommunications, first consider the long-standing U.S. nondiscrimination policy. The United States has maintained an open door to foreign investors based on the hypothesis that an open door promotes domestic economic growth. In the late eighteenth century, America's first treasury secretary Alexander Hamilton argued that foreign investment "ought to be considered . . . precious because it permits an increased amount of productive labor and useful enterprise to be set to work" (Crowe 1978). Nearly two hundred years later, the Reagan administration set forth U.S. policy as one that "provides foreign investors fair, equitable, and nondiscriminatory treatment under our laws and regulations" (U.S. Trade Representative 1983, 174); or, as President Bush put it: foreign investment "is a positive sum game" (Office of the President 1991, 262).

The policy of nondiscrimination embraces two principles: the treatment of foreign investors that is no less favorable than *(i)* that accorded domestic investors (national treatment) and *(ii)* that accorded other investors (most favored nation [MFN]).[1] The MFN principle has often been described as the engine of multilateralism because it promotes liberalization and discourages discriminatory bilateral deal-making. Under the GATT, any trade concession accorded to one nation must be unconditionally extended to all other signatory countries. Although not bound by multilateral obligations, U.S. treatment of foreign investors has been so largely based on national treatment and the MFN principle that the United States has not discriminated among foreign investors, for the most part, except for reasons of national security.

Internationally, the United States has advanced these principles through friendship, commerce, and navigation treaties (FCNs) and bilateral investment treaties (BITs). The purpose is not only to protect the right of U.S. investors to be treated fairly around the world but also to build a body of practice in support of predictable and nondiscriminatory rules that protect the rights of investors from all countries.

The strategy has paid off. On the domestic side, the best companies in the world have been drawn to the United States, boosting productivity and economic welfare. In the case of the consumer electronics industry, foreign-owned firms purchased U.S. firms in the late 1970s. Since then, foreign-owned firms have played a vital role in the development of both cutting-edge technologies and new products such as digital television (Beltz 1992; Beltz 1994). Precisely when inward direct investment is "a threat to domestic competitors, it is most likely to be a source of future strength for the economy as a whole" (McCulloch 1993).

Foreign direct investment (FDI) has also generated positive externalities in the form of technological spillovers and increased competition that has put pressure on domestic firms to produce better products at lower costs. The economic growth literature has highlighted, in particular, the role of FDI in refreshing the domestic technology base, improving the efficiency of the innovation process, and boosting potential domestic growth rates (Grossman and Helpman 1991). Putting foreign- and U.S.-owned firms into more direct competition forces a continual upgrading to match best global practice, which has tended to boost productivity and U.S. economic welfare in the process. Far from the "sucker's payoff" claimed by open door critics, the U.S. open door on investment has generated a productivity payoff. A 1993 McKinsey Global Institute study found that FDI in the United States has played a powerful role in raising domestic productivity by increasing head-to-head competition with the best firms in the world. In contrast, those industries with less exposure to FDI and trade tended to be productivity followers rather than leaders (McKinsey Global Institute 1993, 4-5 and Exhibit 3-10). A 1993 report from the Department of Commerce found that foreign firms invested $14.3 billion in R&D, which is more than 15 percent of total company-funded R&D and accounted for 20 percent of private R&D spending in the high-tech sector (U.S. Department of Commerce 1993). Instead of getting stuck with a lopsided bargain or naively hosting the free ride of foreign firms, the study found that the United States has gained from "a very large *net* inflow of technology from foreign parent to their U.S. affiliates" (U.S. Department of Commerce 1993).

In the process, foreign investors have helped to transform the nation's rust belt into an export belt. Research on the Great Lakes region demonstrates that far from hollowing out the industrial base, FDI has helped to turn the region into a world leader in the export of high value-added manufacturing goods, has boosted exports to twice the national average, and thereby has helped make the United States once again the largest exporter in the world (Kenney and Florida 1991). Equally misguided is the assumption that foreign-owned firms import only low-paying jobs while keeping the high-skill, high-wage jobs at home. A 1992 report of the Federal Reserve Bank of St. Louis concluded there was no evidence to support this "screwdriver assembly" hypothesis (Coughlin 1992).

Taken together, the data suggest that foreign investors play a key role in updating and diversifying the technology base of the United States. Governments that discourage inward FDI under the guise of opening markets abroad or promoting growth at home, therefore, do so at their own expense (Worth 1994). Proposals to use investors in the United States as a trade tool or crowbar thus seem more likely to detract from than add to U.S. economic welfare. A key difference between import duties and investment restrictions is that the latter directly impacts American workers, suppliers, communities, and prospective corporate partners of foreign investors in the United States. Meanwhile, any negative impact only trickles back indirectly to the government or firm. This is not exactly a cost-effective technique for garnering leverage at the negotiating table or promoting economic growth at home.

There is also little evidence that unilateral liberalization has hurt the United States. In telecommunications, for example, most indicators (such as network development, the pricing of services, and investment efficiency) suggest that competitive market entries have benefited those countries where it is permitted. The cost of telecommunication services, such as high-speed leased lines, is five times as high in Germany as in the United States and twice as high as in Britain. For large commercial users, these prices can raise costs to 30 percent of turnover—double the proportion in the United States (see figure 15.1) ("The Last One to Draw" 1994; Crane 1995a). That difference is making and breaking the competitive edge of firms active in international markets.

The demonstrated benefits of competition in the United States have attracted the attention of developing countries, who are now moving at a record pace to open their doors and reduce foreign investment restrictions. In 1992 alone, more than forty nations moved in this direction, reflecting a fundamental shift away from a deep-seated suspicion of transnational investors to active solicitation of them. Demands for modern infrastructure and advanced communication systems also are driving liberalization plans to include areas, such as telecommunications, that are still restricted in many industrialized countries. Much more needs to be done to broaden, deepen, and secure these moves toward open investment regimes.

Ironically, just as other countries are moving to liberalize their FDI regimes, the United States is moving more toward nationality-based investment barriers. In the 1990s, restricting foreign investment for purposes other than national security has surged as frustrations over market access have increased. President Clinton stated in 1993 that the United States "will welcome foreign investment . . . But . . . we insist that our investors should be equally welcome in other countries."[2] Notions of bilateral reciprocity have become particularly popular in the contentious trade sectors of telecommunications and financial services, where existing and would-be foreign investors, as well as their U.S. partners in these sectors, have become high-profile bargaining chips.

The policy builds on the laws already in place that set the rules for access to federally funded technology programs such as the Advanced Technology Program,

Figure 15.1
Competition Pays

Telecommunications Costs as Percentage of Business Turnover*

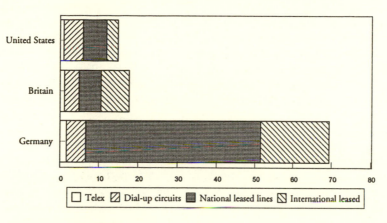

*Sample financial services company.

Source: PA Consulting.

the cornerstone of the Clinton technology plan. The policy shift further draws on the trade frustrations reflected in legislative proposals to link the treatment of foreign investors to the behavior of the home country government (conditional national treatment).

THE CONDITIONAL NATIONAL TREATMENT PROPOSITION

Those with an interest in promoting investment restrictions as a trade tool have claimed that, when other countries are closed or only partially opened to U.S. investors, an open door damages the U.S. economy. Proponents charge that the rest of the world is free-riding at our expense, leaving the United States with a "sucker's payoff" (Krasner 1986), and that the open-door, or national treatment, policy rule is based on outdated "ideological beliefs, not rational considerations" (Spencer 1991). Further, unhindered access of foreign investors is a luxury the United States can no longer afford when other nations do not play by our rules or when their economies are organized differently. Hence, a more discriminating or two-tier investment policy is recommended; one that opens the door wide to some investors and conditions the access of others from countries with offensive investment or trade barriers.[3]

"Conditional national treatment" (CNT), the general term used to describe this two-tier investment policy, indicates the treatment of foreign-owned firms that is less favorable than the treatment of domestic firms (Schwartz and Caplan 1994).

The term is useful because it recognizes that conditioning the treatment of foreign firms does not ensure reciprocity in any objective sense of the term. Conditioning takes the form of both general rules that the home country government needs to satisfy, such as an "adequate and effective" intellectual property standard, and specific reciprocity requirements.

Specific reciprocity is a key dimension of CNT proposals, especially in telecommunications, airline service, and access to international research and development (R&D) programs. The specific reciprocity principle is, If the home country government does not afford a U.S.-owned company "comparable" or "equivalent" opportunities to participate in public R&D programs, then firms from that country will be denied access to U.S. R&D programs (U.S. Office of Technology Assessment 1994, 28).

In the process, CNT substitutes a policy of discrimination and a managed gateway for an open-door policy. CNT rejects not only national treatment but also the unconditional MFN principle. Instead of according the same treatment to similarly situated investors regardless of nationality, the regime promotes discrimination both against foreign-owned firms operating in the United States and among them (conditional MFN). Gaster and Prestowitz (1994) argue that such discrimination is a practical alternative to an open door. What is needed, the argument continues, is a policy that promotes inward flows of "good" investment.

But how should "good" be defined? The standard offered by CNT and specific reciprocity is somewhat peculiar. Take, for example, access to U.S. R&D programs: Even if a foreign-owned multinational makes significant contributions to the U.S. economy and otherwise qualifies for participation, CNT advocates argue that the United States should consider excluding or placing more onerous requirements on the firm *if* the home country government "does not reciprocate in providing U.S.-based multinational enterprises (MNEs) with similar opportunities to invest overseas and derive benefits from those investments" (U.S. Office of Technology Assessment 1993a, 43). The "good" investment standard under such a regime is defined not by any reference to consumer welfare or the value of the firm's contributions to the U.S. economy, but by a political decision about whether the practices of the home government are objectionable.

Because of their political appeal, managed-investment ideas demand attention, even if they are devoid of economic merit. These ideas express, in part, the general ambivalence that exists toward any multinationals and the residual distrust of foreign-owned corporations, in particular. The general distrust is reflected in the rising interest in a national economic benefits test for firms (domestic and foreign-owned) who wish to participate in federal technology programs. The CNT movement also reflects the desire to impose a performance test on foreign governments in the form of a second eligibility test that firms from that country must pass.

As with managed-trade demands, managed-investment proponents are focused on results ("effective national treatment") over rules (legal obligations).[4] As two legal experts put it, "Conditional national treatment substitutes specific results, demanded by Congress, for treaty norms. Thus it devalues treaties, including those beneficial to U.S.-owned businesses" (Schwartz and Caplan 1994). Further, instead of the "you help me, and I'll help you" form of reciprocity associated with the GATT, the CNT approach is closer to the "unless you help me, I'll hurt you" form of reciprocity associated with Super 301.

CNT provisions also create new players in the trade arena. In a 1994 report, the Office of Technology Assessment (OTA) concluded that "in finding some countries eligible to participate in the ATP [Advanced Technology Program] and others ineligible, the Department of Commerce has taken an independent role in setting foreign economic policy" (Office of Technology Assessment 1994). In telecommunications, the FCC has been playing a similar role.

What divides the two sides of the debate over foreign investment restrictions is the faith of CNT proponents in the ability of the government to capture even greater gains for the United States by strategically managing the inward flow of foreign investment. Although plausible in theory, the marginal gains from such policies in practice seem more likely to be outweighed by the administrative burdens and abuses of the regulatory process.

Administrative Nightmares. The implementation of a policy based on CNT is fraught with political and practical problems. Objective definitions of "fair" and "reciprocal" treatment do not exist. Reciprocity, as a result, is easy to state as a proposition, but difficult, if not impossible, to implement (Noam 1995). The procedural problems are enormous. Implementation of the CNT tests in the technology programs has proven to be an administrative nightmare. Those charged with the task of reviewing the practices of foreign governments and the subsequent program eligibility of foreign-owned firms have faced a baffling array of international alliances as well as a series of "comparable" treatment definitions that vary by country and industry. Under the technology programs, federal agencies and courts have been free to apply inconsistent interpretations of congressional mandates or to reach inconsistent results. Program administrators would rather not deal with such restrictions because of the difficulty of defining a U.S. firm and the procedural problems that impede their R&D missions (Dover 1995).

In a recent review of the "comparable treatment" tests in U.S. R&D programs, the Office of Technology Assessment concluded that the tests had "extended the process of program implementation in both the Commerce and Energy Departments." The tests have "resulted in a large measure of bureaucratic interaction and a labored exchange of views in which little has been accomplished" (Office of Technology Assessment 1994). The report found that the administrators of the technology programs have insufficient expertise to assess the policies and practices Congress has mandated they review. As a result, decisions on foreign eligibility lack a uniform process of application and are often based on the "judgment calls" of administrators (Office of Technology Assessment 1994). Inconsistencies have also characterized the FCC's foreign investment review process and its interpretation of Section 310(b) of the Communications Act. The principles used by the FCC to determine whether this section should be waived for a foreign-owned carrier have been "utterly amorphous and thus amendable to any result that the FCC desires in a given case" (Sidak 1996).

Abuse of the Regulatory Process. In theory, CNT and specific reciprocity proposals could be used "prudently and conservatively" (Office of Technology Assessment 1993a, 19). Yet, implementation does not take place in a political vacuum. More often, outcomes reflect the relative power of the institutions, personalities, and firms involved rather than the original intent of the legislation or regulation.[5]

In practice, a foreign investment review process or reciprocity test can, as a result, be easily abused as a weapon to serve parochial interests rather than the "public interest." Even without blatant restrictions, an otherwise beneficial contribution to the domestic economy may be discouraged. The case of the CNT provisions in the ATP program in the Department of Commerce makes the point. Even if a foreign-owned firm passes the national benefits test required of all firms applying for an ATP grant, the firm still has to pass a CNT review that includes a specific reciprocity test (on the home country's local investment opportunities) and a fair treatment test (intellectual property). This two-step review process leaves the firm vulnerable to harassment by a domestic rival.

The potential for abuse in these circumstances has already been demonstrated, first by the Fujitsu case and more recently by the Exon-Florio national security review process, known as the "Pentagon Ploy." A domestic firm can invoke Exon-Florio and delay a hostile takeover for up to three months and potentially longer by refusing to provide the Committee on Foreign Investment in the United States (CFIUS) or the foreign firm with the required information. This process is now listed in securities law textbooks as a valid defense or delaying tactic against corporate takeovers. From 1975 to 1988, only thirty cases were reviewed for national security reasons under CFIUS. By contrast, in the five years after the enactment of Exon-Florio, more than seven hundred new cases were reviewed (Liebeler and Lash 1993; Alvarez 1989). Exon-Florio has also resulted in the imposition of de facto performance requirements as foreign firms have made local production concessions to win approval of the investment.

Missing the Target. The CNT approach is further prone to failure as a negotiating tactic because of the nature of many of the FDI barriers involved. Few developing countries have transnational firms operating in the United States. This leaves the U.S. government with few hostages to use as bargaining chips. In the case of industrialized countries, many of the investment barriers facing U.S. firms are structural in nature, difficult to change, and not under direct control of the national government. In Japan, for example, there is widespread agreement that many of the major barriers to FDI are private and structural in nature and therefore, by definition, difficult for the Japanese government to eliminate.[6]

THE CASE OF TELECOMMUNICATIONS

The telecommunications industry provides an instructive and timely case study of the conditional national treatment debate. A form of regulatory creep has hit the industry. In the past, national security was used to justify foreign ownership restrictions in telecommunications under Section 310(b) of the Communications Act. But, national security is no longer a credible justification for the Section 310(b) foreign investment restrictions.[7] Rather than eliminate the restrictions, trade objectives and foreign market access tests have been added to give the 310(b) statute new life. A couple of basic points on the structure of the industry and the evolution of competitive markets are necessary to put the debate over this development into perspective.

Market and Policy Trends

For over a century, the telecommunications industry has been controlled by monopolies at the national and international levels. The 1984 divestiture of AT&T touched off a revolution in innovative activity and competition, and this world started to crumble. Telecommunications is now part of the world's fastest growing industry—inforcommunications (telecommunications, computing, and audiovisual). In 1994, the information and communication industry grew at twice the pace of the overall world economy, which itself was on an upswing. Worldwide revenue in this industry rose to $1.4 trillion, which is 6 percent of world GDP. International telephone traffic in particular has grown at a record pace (17 percent annual rate) for the past decade (International Telecommunications Union 1995).

The growth is driven in part by the dramatic increase in world investment flows over the past decade and the demands of multinational corporations for reliable, seamless international networks. A second key factor in the growth is the liberalization tide sweeping the industry.

Market-Driven Liberalization. In developing countries, infrastructure demands and capital needs are driving an unprecedented shift toward market-opening strategies. The demand for telecommunication services is surging in response to strong economic expansion, population growth, and urbanization. To keep pace, the Asian Development Bank estimates that the Asian region alone will need to spend more than $1 trillion by the next decade to bolster infrastructure, with one-fifth of that expected to flow into telecommunications. Domestic capital pools and international institutions are incapable of meeting these demands, creating new opportunities for foreign investors. Left with few alternatives, national governments are breaking down formal barriers to trade and investment at an unprecedented rate. In addition, more than fifty telephone companies are scheduled to be privatized by the end of the decade (Arnst, et al. 1995).

Monopoly Breakdown. The privatization push reflects the growing recognition that the enormous inefficiencies associated with the century-old monopolistic structure of telecommunications are no longer affordable for either developing or industrialized economies. The large dividends from technological innovation, the pressures of competition, and the growth of alternative networks have worked together to undercut the financial and regulatory structure upon which that system was based.

The cracks in the monopoly structure first appeared in the 1950s with the development of microwave communications. This opened the door to the possibility of competition in long-distance service and substantially weakened the case for protecting the dominant national firm as a natural monopoly. Then, in the 1970s, advances in digital and fiber-optic technologies led to the emergence of high-capacity transmission systems, which in turn significantly reduced the marginal cost of transmission and led to convergence in switching and information-processing technology (Majone 1991; Cowhey 1990). Digital technology blurred the line between communications and data processing, making it possible for large commercial users, new electronic companies, and would-be providers of enhanced services to challenge national regulatory systems.

The experience with deregulation in the United States demonstrates the domino style of a monopoly breakdown once a breach in the wall occurs, as in this case with the breakup of AT&T in 1984.[8] Each subsequent decision to allow increased competition in a segment of the U.S. telecommunications market created additional business opportunities and new strains on the traditional regulatory system. Competition was transmitted, for example, to intermediate products and services as downstream firms worked to find new ways to improve products, cut costs, and gain competitive advantage. As a result, through consumer and market forces, competition in one segment worked to erode limitations on competition in adjacent market segments. For example, MCI used its initial private line services as a wedge to enter the U.S. domestic and international switched services market.

The breakup of AT&T worked to transfer pressure for liberalization not only to other parts of the domestic market, but to other national markets as well. Competition in United States brought lower prices and improvements in the quality and diversity of service offerings for telecommunications users. These benefits, in turn, gave commercial customers a significant competitive advantage in international markets. As users in the United States were enjoying innovative data services and a 50 percent reduction in the price of long-distance services, their rivals in Europe, where telecommunications monopolies still apply, were forced to pay telecommunications costs often ten times higher (Crane 1995a).

To keep pace with their U.S. rivals, European telecommunications users have started demanding lower prices as well as the advantages of intelligent networks such as audioconferencing on demand, calling cards, common cards, and short-code dialing. The globalization of major user markets such as financial services further intensified demands for more cost-effective communication systems and increased internal pressure for reform. As a result, the European Commission has targeted national monopolies for elimination. The commission is now pushing both privatization and foreign competition in an effort to upgrade Europe's second-rate telecommunications infrastructure and boost economic growth.

Moves to *open* markets in the United States have, therefore, helped open foreign markets as well. The interdependence stems not from heavy-handed reciprocity demands but from market forces and global competition. Indeed, U.S. reciprocity demand and foreign ownership restrictions could actually retard liberalization if other countries deter market-opening moves to gain bargaining power in future negotiations with the United States.

European Integration and Telecommunications Liberalization. Fortunately, fundamental political and institutional changes taking place in Europe add force to the market push for liberalization. Over the past decade, the European Union has taken an increasingly aggressive role in the telecommunications service sector as part of its broader push for the completion of the single market and the integration of economic activity (Sun and Pelkmans 1995). The first step involved extending the Single Market agenda to include telecommunications regulation and liberalization. By 1992, most services had been liberalized, but the largest segment of voice telephony remained a monopoly. The European Commission (EC) concluded that this monopoly and the supporting regulatory structure were responsible for the bottlenecks (lack of advanced services, scarce capacity of high-capacity leased lines, and high cross-border costs) that have blocked the development of the sector. The commission further argued that the bottlenecks had become "a virtual barrier to the future development of the Community" (European Commission 1992). The EC then issued an Open Network Provision Directive that requires member states to make leased lines available to customers. This move opened the door to the development of private networks to deliver voice and data services. Next, the EC adopted two major resolutions specifying that the members fully liberalize both telecommunications infrastructure and voice telephony by 1998.

The User Push and the Alliance Rush. The institutional changes in Europe reflect a fundamental shift in power from monopoly providers to users. Customers and corporate telecommunications managers in particular are quickly becoming the primary factors reshaping the industry worldwide. Thanks to the interplay of market, technology, and institutional forces, the options available to users are on the rise (Beltz 1996). If corporate customers' demands are not met by national telecommunications operators, they are starting to go elsewhere. In Europe, for example, the customers that account for the bulk of the telecommunications operator's profits are not waiting on their national operators. Exasperated by high costs and inadequate service, over fifty of the largest multinationals operating in Europe have joined forces to put pressure on, and bypass if necessary, the national operators. They have formed the European Virtual Private Network Users Association (EVUA), which has awarded contracts to Unisource/AT&T and British Telecommunications (BT) to construct two new virtual private networks (VPNs). These VPNs provide services over public networks that in the past were available only through private networks.

Users are on the move outside of Europe as well. Banacci, Mexico's biggest banking and stockbrokerage concern, is planning a long-distance phone business with MCI to reduce its reliance on Telefonos de Mexico (Telemex). Starting January 1, 1997, Banacci and MCI's Avantel SA venture will take on Telemex, connecting thirty-five cities through a fiber-optic network. Innovative services made possible by technological advances in the computer field are further cutting into monopoly profits. The growth of callback services, for example, is cutting into monopoly profits, particularly those in developing countries. These services let customers circumvent the higher rates of calling to the United States, which in many countries can cost more than making two international calls from the United States. In 1995, the volume of callback services grew by 63 percent. Governments in Argentina, China, South Korea, and Malaysia have tried to stop the service but, technically and logistically, the callback operators in the United States are beyond their grasp ("Don't Call Us" 1996). Technically, it is difficult to identify callback traffic as distinct from regular voice traffic. As a result, short of disconnecting a user's phone service, it is difficult for a government to block callback services.

In response to user demands, telecommunications operators are racing to form international alliances. For example, in developing countries, local operators are seeking international partners who can provide the pulling power to raise capital and boost competitive assets. On the other side of the equation, foreign firms are taking a minority stake in domestic operators or forming joint ventures to gain a strategic foothold in the markets that are starting to open. Italy's state-owned telecommunications monopoly, Societa Finanziaria Telefonica per Azioni, is seeking to buy into Bolivia's telephone monopoly, Cuba's phone system, and Chile's leading long-distance company Entel SA (*Wall Street Journal* 1995). And, Telefonica of Spain is becoming the biggest international player in Latin America ("*Financial Times* Survey" 1995). A growing number of second-tier operators have also hooked up with strategic partners. U.S. West took a 20 percent share in Malaysia's second network operator Binariang. Satelindo, Indonesia's second international operators and cellular service provider, has partnered with DeTeMobil, Deutsche Telekom's cellular subsidiary; and the Philippine cellular franchise has linked with Singapore Telecommunications.

Also driven by user demands and surging market for one-stop services for multinational companies, telecommunications operators in the OECD economies are rushing to gather partners and develop global network services (see appendix for detail). This super-carrier race has been marked by the competition between U.S. long-distance providers and their pursuit of European and Asian partners. MCI sold a $4.3 billion stake to British Telecom, Sprint sold a 20 percent stake to France Telecom and Deutsche Telekom (valued at $4.2 billion), and AT&T has a range of allies under its World Partners program. Some of the smaller European phone companies are also angling to join the race by seeking out international partners (figures 15.2a, 15.2b, 15.2c).

The globalization of the industry is also reflected in the changing orientation of domestic firms. Take U.S. West as one example. In the past ten years, U.S. West has gone from providing local telephone service in fourteen states to providing cellular telephone service, cable television, international call switching, standard telephone service, and advanced wireless communications in Hungary, Malaysia, the Czech Republic, Britain, Lithuania, France, Norway, Russia, Sweden, Slovakia, Poland, Japan, Brazil, Spain, the Netherlands, and India (Myerson 1995).

Most industry observers believe international alliances, although not free from risk, will become essential to winning the business of corporate customers in the future (Pope 1995). Eight more major international players based in the United States may, as a result, soon be joining the race. Regional players are expected to team with foreign partners after the Bell companies are released from the interexchange restrictions of the Modified Final Judgment and when GTE is released from its consent decree ("Global Ventures with Bells Seen Impaired by FCC, Senate Bill" 1995).

U.S. Regulatory Reform: Missing the Boat

National regulators worldwide are struggling to catch up with these economic and technological changes sweeping the industry. For its part, Congress passed a sweeping reform package that rewrote six decades of communications laws and creates a new regulatory landscape. The FCC for its part is experimenting with auctions and new administrative guidelines. Meanwhile, companies in the telephone,

Figure 15.2a
The Supercarrier Race: Sprint

Global One*

Global Partnership Board
Spring-Deutsche Telecom-France
Telecom
(equal votes)

Operational Units

Rest of World   Rest of Europe
50% Sprint   **33.3% Sprint**
50% DT & FT   **66.6% DT & FT**

Products in home markets to be offered by respective parent company.
Deutsche Telekom and France Telecom each to take 10% stakes in Sprint.
*Previously known under the working title Phoenix.

Source: International telecommunications map produced
by the *Financial Times* in association with Salomon
Brothers, October 3, 1995.

Figure 15.2b
The Supercarrier Race: MCI

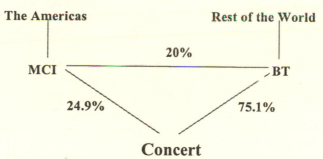

The Americas   **Rest of the World**

20%

MCI   BT

24.9%   75.1%

Concert

BT completed its 20% investment in the enlarged share capital of
MCI on September 30, 1994. BT has already established alliances
with operators in Denmark, Norway, Finland, Japan, and India. It has
also established joint ventures in Spain, Italy, Germany, Sweden,
India, and Japan.

Source: International telecommunications map produced
by the *Financial Times* in association with Salomon
Brothers, October 3, 1995.

Figure 15.2c
The Supercarrier Race: AT&T

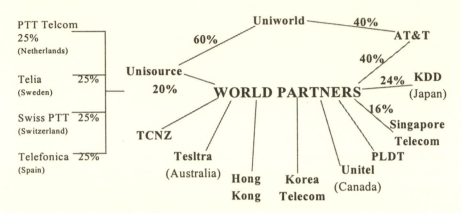

Source: International telecommunications map produced by the *Financial Times* in association with Salomon Brothers, October 3, 1995.

cable, entertainment, and computer businesses are furiously jockeying for position as they prepare for an intensive new race for customers and profit.

Yet for all this activity, a key element is noticeably absent. Despite the increased importance of foreign investment in the global strategies of U.S. telecommunications firms, a serious proposal to eliminate the restrictions that limit such opportunities under Section 310(b) is missing.[9] Its absence can be traced to the growing frustrations of U.S. trade negotiators and the need of the FCC to carve out a new purpose for itself and its regulations in the emerging global telecommunications arena. The impulse to regulate dies hard.

The broad powers of the FCC to limit the entry and expansion plans of a foreign carrier in the United States are well demonstrated by Section 310(b) (see appendix). Section 310(b) was originally intended to prevent foreign powers from gaining control of U.S. broadcasting during a war by providing a trigger for a national security review of the potentially harmful effects once foreign ownership reached 25 percent. The intent was for these investments to be approved under the waiver authority given to the FCC *unless* the public interest would be served by a refusal of the investment. But, instead of a trigger for a review, the FCC has interpreted the 25 percent baseline as a ceiling, with the burden of proof pushed onto the foreign firm to demonstrate that the waiver would be, rather than presumed to be, in the public interest (Sidak 1994).[10]

The shift has been permitted and perhaps encouraged by the broad level of discretion Congress tolerates at the FCC. The FCC asserts, for example, "the right to include any appropriate public interest factor" in its waiver decisions (FCC 1995d, at 39, para 93). As a result, the 310(b) waiver process is widely viewed as amorphous and amendable to any result the FCC desires in a given case. The waiver process has further been described as an "escape clause for any desired outcome."[11] Blessed with a reputation for ad hoc interpretation and the discretion to always add new factors to its analysis, the FCC has been relieved of the need to focus its "public interest" analysis under Section 310(b) on the consuming public's economic interests in lower prices and improved quality of service in the United States as the result of the foreign investment.[12]

With little accountability and vague guidelines, it no great surprise that the FCC review and licensing process— similar to the national security review process under Exon-Florio—has invited abuse as an anticompetitive device or harassment tactic.[13] Foreign firms also have not been the only ones harassed. Section 310(b) invites abuse as an anticompetitive device in the race among U.S. telecommunication carriers to serve the needs of transnational firms (see Sprint case below). Despite these problems, Section 310(b) has been added to the list of U.S. trade tools. FCC Chairman Hundt argues that linking "effective access to overseas markets to access to our own markets" not only is applicable but will more effectively serve the public interest (FCC 1995d, 1995f).[14] The FCC public interest review under 310(b) has accordingly included a wide range of judgments on the openness of the foreign carrier's home market to U.S. investors, on whether discrimination existed against U.S. carriers in that market, and on the nature of the regulatory regime of the home country government (FCC 1994).

AT&T has been the primary proponent in the business sector for adding a reciprocity rule to the public interest review under Section 310(b). In 1993, AT&T proposed a mirror image reciprocity rule whereby entry and expansion of foreign interest would be conditioned on comparable market access for U.S. carriers in the home market. Both MCI and Sprint were caught in the crossfire that followed during the FCC review of AT&T's petition over the 1993-1995 period.

Sprint, in particular, captured the media's eye in 1995 as it waited for the FCC to judge the merit of the proposed $4.2 million investment by France Telecom and Deutsche Telekom (Phoenix, later changed to Global One). In December 1995, the FCC gave its approval for the Global One venture based on the condition that the French and German governments open their telecommunications markets to U.S. companies. Until this happens, growth in trans-Atlantic phone service (the number of phone lines Global One can provide to Germany and France) will be frozen. Also, if France and Germany fail to keep their commitments to liberalize their telecommunications markets, the FCC can revoke its approval of the Global One deal. Other than a passing reference, national security was not even mentioned in the decision.

The FCC's current zeal for trade matters contrasts with its past reluctance to use its regulatory authority as a trade tool. In 1980, for example, the FCC rejected foreign ownership restrictions on cable operators as a means of leveraging open foreign markets to U.S. investment, concluding that it lacked the "responsibility for investment policy with respect to communications in foreign countries." The FCC continued, "We do not believe a desire for reciprocity in international investment policies by itself provides an adequate basis for action on our part. Nor are we, in any case, in a position to know if such a policy on our part would have the result intended or if, to the contrary, it would lead to increasing trade barriers in other areas."[15] Trade matters by the mid-1990s, however, had become an irresistible temptation.

The FCC Foreign Market Access Test. In December 1995, two weeks before the Sprint decision, the FCC announced its plans to interpret Section 310(b) as a trade statue "to encourage foreign governments to open their telecommunication markets to U.S. participation and investment." The rule adds an explicit market access test to the FCC's public interest review of foreign investments that exceed 25 percent in a U.S. wireless license (FCC 1995d, at 78-82). Under the new guidelines, absent other public interest factors, foreign investors will be permitted to increase their ownership stake above the 25 percent threshold in a common carrier wireless license if the home market (principle place of business) is judged to offer effective competitive opportunities (ECO) to U.S. telecommunications firms. Specific reciprocity is the guiding principle for the test, which will be applied on a service-by-service basis. The FCC will apply the ECO analysis, for example, "by comparing restrictions on U.S. participation in the home market for the particular wireless service in which a foreign investor seeks to participate in the U.S. market" (FCC 1995d, at 81, para 212).

A finding of "effective competitive opportunities," however, is neither necessary nor sufficient for the FCC to determine that the foreign investment is in the public interest. Market access is only one of several factors to be consulted in the evaluation process. "Other public interest factors" will come into play.[16] The new guidelines simply place trade objectives at the top of the laundry list of possible factors.

Precedent Setting Mistakes. The FCC's new market access test is based on the CNT reciprocity principle that foreign ownership interests in a U.S. market should be limited to the extent to which U.S. firms can take an equity stake in the same market segment in the home country of the parent firm. If the foreign government permits 30 percent ownership, absent other public interest factors, then the United States will permit 30 percent in that market. The FCC's goal is "to ensure that U.S. investors have similar opportunities to compete in foreign markets" (FCC 1995d, at 72, para 186; 81-82, para 213-214).

The prevailing assumption is that restrictions on foreign investment in the United States will produce a favorable economic outcome for the United States. This assumption in turn rests on three supporting propositions: (1) foreign investment in the United States by a monopoly will harm U.S. consumers; (2) restrictions on foreign investment in the United States are needed to open the foreign market to competition; and (3) the FCC is capable of discerning and promoting the public interest in international telecommunications markets. Another key assumption, which will come back to haunt U.S. negotiators in future negotiations, is the FCC's finding that it is appropriate to "hold foreign carriers accountable for the policies of their home governments" (FCC, 1995d, at 73, para 187). But, is this a practice the United States wants to encourage others to adopt? Can the United States afford to promote a practice that encourages others to hold U.S. carriers accountable for U.S. policies they consider to be unfair?

By claiming the right to make decisions unilaterally, the United States concedes the same right to others to decide what is fair and reciprocal treatment of transnational firms. The danger is that they may imitate us, as in the case of antidumping laws. Antidumping laws, which were initially promoted in the United States as a necessary "trade remedy," have spread around the world to the detriment of U.S.-owned multi-nationals. More than 40 nations—half of them developing countries—have adopted antidumping laws. There has also been a sharp increase in cases since 1990, with U.S. exporters the target more often than any other country. Discriminatory invest-ment measures could likewise become popular and lead to "a legislative crossfire inconsistent with today's global economy," curtailing rather than enhancing the access of U.S.-based transnationals to the resources and opportunities offered by foreign markets. Other examples include the introduction of quantitative restrictions (textiles, 1970s; cars, 1980s) and Europe's New Commercial Instrument, which is modeled on U.S. Section 301 of the trade laws.

Given the demonstrated boomerang effect of our trade policies, it is necessary to think beyond the specifics of an individual case or the importance of an individual firm to evaluate the longer-term implications. For example, do the specifics of the current telecommunications case warrant the institutional recasting of the FCC as some form of global trade cop in the area of investment policy? And, is it in the long-term interest of the United States to promote the linking of regulatory decisions to the current priorities and frustrations of our trade negotiators? "No" is the answer to both questions.

DOES CONDITIONING AN OPEN DOOR MAKE ECONOMIC SENSE?

Is Section 310(b) Really Needed to Protect U.S. Consumers?

In theory, it is possible a foreign monopoly operating in a protected home market could use this market power to disadvantage or displace more efficient firms operating in the U.S. market (sanctuary market thesis). But, even when this occurs the impact on telecommunications users and national welfare is ambiguous. What are consumers being protected from? Cross-subsidies could benefit U.S. consumers, and the competition between foreign and U.S. firms could help reduce any rents that may have existed previously in that U.S. market segment. Also, why would a foreign firm want to cross-subsidize when they have no hope of establishing a monopoly in the highly competitive U.S. market?

A policy rule that purports to promote public welfare must determine whether differences in access conditions injure domestic economic welfare. A claim of unfair trade (let alone the possibility) is not an economic case for restriction of trade or investment, a point even recognized by U.S. "unfair" trade laws. Return to the antidumping laws example. Antidumping laws require some demonstration both that "dumping" has taken place and that the domestic industry has been injured before any duties on imports can be imposed. At a minimum, a similar standard needs to be required on the investment side, in terms of injury not only to the domestic industry but to consumers as well.

Reciprocity demands for "equivalent competitive opportunities" cloud this debate by implying that those who do not open their markets gain at the expense of those who do. This is clearly not true from the perspective of telecommunications users, which include businesses whose ability to compete is impaired by poor service and artificially high costs. In addition, unilateral liberalization has benefited U.S. telecommunications providers, who are among the most competitive in the world and the most sought-after alliance partners because of their experience in competitive markets. U.S. firms are also the largest exporters of capital to the global telecommunications sector. They have capitalized on the global liberalization trend, entering and investing in foreign markets more extensively than foreign carriers have entered into the United States. There is also no indication that the large U.S. carriers that dominate the U.S. market are likely to be displaced by foreign entrants. There is also little evidence foreign entry or acquisitions have led to anticompetitive practices and significant injury.

Advances in technology, the development of alternative networks, and the globalization of the industry also cut into the revenue base of foreign monopolies, eroding any previously existing "sanctuary." Any forward-looking policy rule that presumes to look past the immediate circumstances of an individual case would, therefore, need also to address the sustainability of whatever cross-subsidies currently exist and the potential for future injury as well.

To the extent there is a problem with anticompetitive behavior that negatively impacts U.S. consumers, it is difficult to understand why more elaborate FCC regulations are the answer to this problem. The FCC is not exactly known as a bastion for pro-consumer competitive policies in the United States (Hazlett 1995; Waverman 1995). Further, regarding international markets, the FCC has argued in past decisions that neither foreign investment restrictions nor reciprocity rules were needed to address concerns about anticompetitive behavior.[17]

Section 310(b) is also not the only defense. The European Commission (Directorate General IV) uses its rules on competition under the Treaty of Rome to block deals or prospective alliances that threaten competition, such as the proposed pay TV joint venture that involved Bertlesmann and Deutsche Telekom. Multilateral rules are also being shaped that would establish ground rules for both nondiscriminatory access under the World Trade Organization and a process of dispute settlement. If the political will does not exist to eliminate Section 310(b) and if guarding against anticompetitive behavior is the intent, then the FCC review should at least be kept as simple as possible, limiting FCC decisions to the impact of the proposed investment on U.S. consumers irrespective of reciprocity or foreign market access concerns.

Will the Market Access Test Promote Competition?

Although the stated intent of Section 310(b) is to promote competition in telecommunications, the FCC's interpretation undercuts this objective. Most U.S. carriers, apart from AT&T, require financing outside traditional financial markets to expand their networks and position themselves in the international marketplace. Foreign telecommunications firms are important sources of such capital. Smaller firms are particularly dependent on equity relationships as they tend to lack the clout or leverage of an AT&T, which has been able to secure the necessary partnership with more arm's-distance, alliance relationships. By artificially limiting the opportunities for international partnerships and prolonging the monopoly life of some carriers, Section 310(b) tends to retard rather than to promote competition. The review process delays access to foreign capital of would-be international competitors and raises transaction costs.

It may also be argued that the 310(b) market test benefits AT&T more than any other carrier. The potential for anticompetitive behavior due to the monopoly power of a foreign firm is not limited to equity relationships. Other forms of strategic alliances and joint ventures also can give rise to anticompetitive behavior and discrimination against an unaffiliated U.S. carrier.[18] But, since the FCC rule applies only to equity arrangements, the AT&T World Partners alliance is excluded, and potential foreign partners are given an added incentive to partner with AT&T over U.S. rivals. Section 310(b) thus makes the point that the "us versus them" analysis typical of CNT propositions is hopelessly out of date. The race for international partners and the competition between global agendas are shrinking the common ground between U.S. firms while expanding it internationally.

Without Investment Restrictions, Will Foreign Markets Stay Closed?

The argument is often made that without a reciprocal market access test, or if Section 310(b) is eliminated, foreign governments will have no incentive to open their markets. But such logic, particularly in telecommunications, underestimates the power of the technology, market, and institutional forces at work and over-estimates the leverage of the United States. Foreign-market-opening decisions have tended to rely more on local political-economic concerns than on U.S. regulatory pressure. The countries that have significantly liberalized their markets (Canada, United Kingdom, New Zealand, Australia, Sweden, and Chile) have done so unilaterally. Canada, for example, opened most market segments to competition, in some cases doing so in advance of the United States. Few, if any, countries have increased the openness of their markets in response to regulatory pressures exerted by another country.

Instead, the combination of technology, consumer demand, and institutional changes has put intense pressure on national regulators to reform outdated systems and open sectors to competition. A report from the Office of Technology Assessment concluded, for example, that U.S. trade policy is not likely to be as effective as pressure from users and actions of the European Commission in terms of market opening because the decision to liberalize is often determined by these other economic and political factors (U.S. Office of Technology Assessment 1993b).

Even the advocates of aggressive reciprocity rules have been forced to concede the power of market forces, acknowledging that "the sole impetus for telecommunications liberalization in most countries originates from foreign businesses fearing their firms will be less competitive relative to U.S. firms as a result of a less liberalized domestic telecommunications market" (Olbeter and Chimerine 1995). More than any 310(b) restriction, reciprocity rule, or "encouragement" provided by U.S. regulation of foreign investment, the practical power of competitive markets in countries like the United States are having the biggest impact. The proliferation of innovative bypasses around the overpriced networks of monopoly operators testify to the market-creating power of new technologies when combined with insistent consumers and creative entrepreneurs.

Yet it is this pivotal role of competition and frustrated consumers that is too often discounted by 310(b) and reciprocity enthusiasts, who have been preoccupied with the political mobilization of foreign providers. Worldwide liberalization of telecommunications has occurred first in those countries where the political mobilization of commercial users was the greatest: the United States, the United Kingdom, and Japan (U.S. Office of Technology Assessment 1993b, 135-137). By stirring up the competitive fears of foreign corporate consumers, the *elimination* of the remaining foreign investment barriers in U.S. telecommunications may do far more than any reciprocity test for advancing the cause of market opening.

The interplay of technology, market, and institutional forces also works to raise the price of procrastination. Insulated from competition, monopolies have failed to develop the flexibility and cost discipline necessary to respond to user demands for customized telecommunications solutions, mobility, and new services. Deutsche Telekom, for example, lagged behind its competitors in the United States and Japan by up to eight years, while the German telecommunications market was seriously underdeveloped. Past resistance to reform, rising market pressure, and recent institutional changes in Europe have come together to put those who resist competition in the unenviable position of having to rapidly make profound changes. Governments are trying to sell off pieces of their telecommunications monopolies in saturated equity markets, while corporate staffs are struggling to learn the mechanics of working in a competitive environment.

In Europe, the European Commission has added stress by cranking up the pace of reform. In 1995 and 1996, in response to business demands and corporate complaints, the European Commission accelerated the introduction of competition by opening the supply of alternative infrastructure (that is, networks other than a public-switched network) ahead of the January 1, 1998, deadline.

Deutsche Telekom has four competitors that are already investing heavily in the construction of fiber-optic and microwave networks. The engineering group Mannesmann has a prosperous mobile phone network with 1.3 million clients. The three other operators—RWE, Veba, and Viag—are cash-rich utilities. Thysesen, the German steel and engineering conglomerate, is working with domestic and foreign financial institutions to mount yet another attack (Lindemann 1995b). The opening of the German market is also generating new opportunities for foreign firms, with German firms busily forging alliances in particular with those who have valued experience in deregulated markets. Veba has a strategic alliance with Britain's Cable and Wireless, Viag with British Telecom, and Mannesmann with AT&T (Barnard 1996).

A glut of telecommunications issues further complicates the privatization process. In 1995, privatization hit a record high, with telecommunications one of the most active sectors. In addition, over fifty countries have announced plans to privatize their national firms over the next few years (table 15.1). With supply outstripping demand for the foreseeable future, investors are being selective. The reception for telecommunications offerings in Spain, Indonesia, and the Netherlands has been particularly poor. Indonesia was forced to significantly scale back its offering to $1.6 billion because of insufficient demand (Lindemann 1995a; Sharpe 1996).

How Will Foreign Governments Respond?

Given the widely acknowledged benefits of foreign investment, foreign investment restrictions in telecommunications are viewed in most cases as self-inflicted wounds (Globerman 1995; Waverman 1995; Cass and Haring 1996). Except for the assertion that a gain can be had from the closure of our market as a means of opening a market that would otherwise have remained closed, there is little evidence to support an economic argument for foreign investment restrictions in telecommunications.

The behavior of a foreign government *in response* to U.S. regulatory pressure is, therefore, the key factor in the welfare analysis of foreign investment restrictions and CNT propositions. Consider, for example, the payoff structure. Unless the foreign market is opened *as a result* of the U.S. restriction, an open-market policy is usually the best policy rule for U.S. economic welfare. An open market offers a payoff preferable to a war of investment restrictions, the closing of both markets, or the closing of the U.S. market while the foreign market is opened as a result of forces other than U.S. regulatory pressure.

If a reciprocity rule such as Section 310(b) is to have any hope of promoting economic welfare, it must, therefore, be based on a careful design and accurate predictions of foreign behavior. That behavior, however, is contingent on a wide variety of political and economic constraints that make it notoriously difficult to predict. The foreign government may refuse to "be encouraged" to open its market and may drag its feet instead. Or worse, it may emulate the United States and "hold foreign carriers accountable for the policies of their home governments" it considers to be unfair (FCC, 1995d, at 73, para 187).

The strategic closure argument for Section 310(b) assumes that foreign governments will respond to U.S. pressure by opening their markets. But this assumption underestimates the complexity of the political-economic environment in which foreign governments operate. Both theory and practice inform us that the strategic response of other governments will depend on, among other issues, domestic political pressures, relative bargaining strength, and the credibility of U.S. threats.

Even if a foreign supplier were willing to face greater competition in the home market in exchange for greater access to the U.S. market, its employees and labor union(s) may not favor such a deal (Bensen and Gale 1995). Eliminating Section 310(b) would deny foreign governments the political cover that has been used to placate unions and justify barriers to U.S. direct investment. AirTouch, one of the largest cellular telephony service providers in the United States, has argued that the 310(b) restriction of 25 percent has handed foreign governments an excuse for capping their ownership of foreign companies at 25 percent. The FCC concedes that foreign governments have taken Section 310(b) as a convenient "metaphor for a closed U.S. market" (FCC 1995b).

The point is that foreign governments and interests hostile to reform will protect their interests by using whatever tools are given them. Section 310(b) encourages

Table 15.1
Forthcoming Worldwide Telecom Privatizations

Country	Company	Country	Company
Western Europe		**Middle East/Africa (cont.)**	
Belgium	Belgacom	South Africa	Telkom SA
Germany	Deutsche Telekom	Turkey	Turk Telekom
France	France Telecom	Uganda	UPTC
Netherlands	KPN	Zambia	ZANTEL
Greece	OTE	**Latin America**	
Portugal	Portugal Telcom	Venezuela	CANTV
Italy	STET	Ecuador	EMETEL
Switzerland	Swiss PTT	Bolivia	ENTEL
Ireland	Telecom Eireann	Honduras	Hondutel
Spain	Telefonica de Espana	El Salvador	INTEL
Sweden	Telia	Panama	INTEL
Eastern Europe/Former CIS		Nicaragua	TELCOR
Albania	Albanian Telecom	Brazil	Telebras
Lithuania	Lithuania Telecom	Haiti	TELECO
Hungary	Matav	**Asia Pacific**	
Slovenia PTT	Slovenije	Fiji	FTPL
Romania	Romania Telecom	Japan	KDD
Russia	Rostelecom	Korea	Korea Telecom
Russia	Sviazinvest	India	MTNL
Poland	TPSA	Japan	NTT
Middle East/Africa		Indonesia	PT Telkom
Egypt	ARENTO	Pakistan	PTC
Israel	Bezeq	Sri Lanka	PTO
Ivory Coast	CITEL-COM	Singapore	Singapore Telecom
Ghana	Ghana-Telecom	Australia	Telstra
Cameroon	INTELCAM	Thailand	TOT/CAT
Kenya	Kenya PTT	India	VSNL
Morocco	ONPT		

Source: International telecommunications map produced by the *Financial Times* in
association with Salomon Brothers, October 3, 1995.

other nations to enact similar measures that might not be drafted to be administered
as judiciously. Other nations may, for example, use a broad definition of national
security to unfairly restrict access by U.S. firms to their telecommunications markets.
Similarly, even if the FCC is careful in weighing the range of factors before deciding
on a 310(b) waiver, those resisting reform in other countries may not be deterred
from making the argument, "They restrict; so should we." In particular, France will
try to keep foreign firms at a distance as France moves to privatize significant
segments of its state-owned economy. Plans for partial privatization (49 percent)
of France Telecom have been sharply criticized by trade unions that warn of job cuts
and a loss of public sector status for workers (Ridding 1995). Facing these protests

and more strikes, the French government will no doubt continue looking for ways to justify delays in the privatization and opening of the market to foreign investors. Section 310(b) provides them such an excuse.

Retaliation through Emulation

"Holding foreign investors accountable for the commercial policies of their home governments" in this context sets a particularly troubling precedent. What will happen if foreign governments retaliate by emulating the United States? There is far more U.S. investment in telecommunications overseas than there is foreign investment in U.S. carriers. This asymmetry in investment exposure makes the United States vulnerable. As a result, the United States may not gain leverage at the negotiating table, particularly if the field of play is expanded to include more than telecommunications. To the extent others can harass U.S. transnational corporations, the relative bargaining power of the United States will be reduced. With over 40 percent of the world's multinational corporations (roughly 3,000) headquartered in the United States, which is the leading supplier of foreign direct investment, there may be ample opportunity for such maneuvers on the part of foreign governments (United Nations 1994, 4, 17). Any regulatory crossfire of discriminatory investment measures would tend to cut against the interests of multinational firms in reducing, rather than increasing, the fragmentation of the global information infrastructure.

Is 310(b) a Credible Trade Tool?

A study commissioned by AT&T argues that "without a credible threat, the United States would have no bargaining leverage" (Strategic Policy Research 1993). But for the threat to be credible, the foreign government must believe the United States has both the will and the capability to carry it out. Foreign governments must expect that their firms will be denied entry to or restricted from expanding their U.S. telecommunications operations unless they fulfill the market-opening conditions demanded by the United States. To the extent these conditions are negotiable, the threat is less credible.

In this context, Section 310(b) suffers from a major credibility problem. The FCC is quite clear that the guidelines will be applied on a case-by-case basis with no general commitment to the market access test as the determining factor in the analysis. Instead, the market test on effective competitive opportunities (ECO) is only one of many factors that will be considered in the FCC's public interest review. Even if the ECO test has been satisfied, a foreign investment may still be denied. Or, on the flip side, even if the ECO conditions are not met, an investment may still be permitted (as in the case of Deutsche Telekom's and France Telecom's investment in Sprint).

As long as the FCC has the latitude to accept or reject a petition for a 310(b) waiver irrespective of the ECO test, it hardly seems rational to expect a major change in government policy merely to permit a minority investment in a U.S. carrier. A flexible rule or multifactor test allows the FCC the discretion to take into account other economic or national security concerns, but it also undercuts the strategic market-opening objective on which Section 310(b) is now justified.

How Strong Is 310(b) as a Bargaining Chip?

In addition to the credibility problem, Section 310(b) may not be a strong bargaining chip even when it is used. On the one hand, some telecommunications experts have argued that foreign governments have exaggerated the importance of section 301(b) as an investment barrier, labeling it instead "a mole hill" that can easily be circumvented (Noam 1995; Olbeter 1994-1995). On the other hand, some of the same experts also have argued that the 310(b) restriction is needed to give the United States significant new leverage at the bargaining table. But if the restriction is not significantly impairing the access of foreign telecommunications firms to the United States, how can it also be a significant bargaining chip?

The focus of 310(b) cases on investments that do not involve a controlling interest in a firm detracts from its strength as a bargaining chip. The smaller the level of investment, the smaller the payoff to the foreign firm and the less leverage the United States will have to influence the opening of the foreign market (Bensen and Gale 1995, 7). It seems a bit optimistic to conclude that a rule that allows carriers to make a small investment in the United States will be successful in getting a foreign government to open up a market faster than the pace determined by local political-economic forces.

With major new telecommunications markets opening up outside the United States (China, Central Asia, the Pacific, and Latin America) and the proliferation of international alliances, foreign carriers may not need to take a significant equity stake in a U.S. carrier to play an active role in the global telecommunications market. Of the monopoly or dominant foreign carriers that have joined AT&T World Partners and Unisource alliances, only Telefonica has found it necessary to invest directly in a U.S. carrier (FCC 1995c; 1995g, 18-19).

Who Is Us?

Proponents of market access tests and Section 310(b) also argue that it will "ensure fair competition in the United States" and the international telecommunications market (Olbeter 1994-1995, 63). But, fair for whom? The "us versus them" rhetoric assumes incorrectly that there are an "us" and a "them" defined by national boundaries. The global agendas and strategies of the major telecommunications firms, however, defy such simple classifications.[19] Section 310(b) ironically makes the point by providing a convenient tool U.S. firms have used to harass each other as well as foreign firms.

The 1994-1996 Sprint case provides a good example. The German and French governments may have been the stated targets, but Sprint was the one taken hostage by the FCC review process. In 1994, Sprint had over $4.5 billion in debt, with its expected cash flow depressed in part by the advertising war in long-distance services (Keller 1994, A4). The Deutsche Telekom and France Telecommunications investment offered Sprint a key opportunity to boost its competitive fortunes and gain a position in the super-carrier race with AT&T and MCI.[20] Sprint first, however, had to get over the 310(b) stumbling block, which represented a strategic opportunity for AT&T and MCI to delay the introduction of greater competition in the international market.

"The game," as the Chairman of BT put it, "is how you develop your pieces around the world. For once the squares are taken by rivals, your options are constrained" (FCC 1995g, iii). The best defense in this case is a good offense that curtails the options of your opponent (actual and potential) before they can limit yours. AT&T tried to secure an alliance with Deutsche Telekom and France Telecom as it was searching for European partners. But its efforts failed, in part because few expected the union of the largest telecommunications operators would be tolerated by regulatory authorities on either side of the Atlantic (Adonis 1994). Section 310(b), however, gave AT&T another defensive tool. By preventing or delaying the formation of international alliances such as Global One, Section 310(b) invites its use as an anticompetitive tactic to delay the creation of more potent rivals. By opposing Global One, for example, AT&T managed to delay entry of Sprint into the supercarrier race and thereby the creation of a more potent rival.

If, as seems likely, Section 310(b) is going to be with us for a while, let us at least dispense with the presumption of "us versus them" and get to a more interesting set of questions. For example, from whose perspective is the field allegedly being leveled? Or, who are the specific winners and losers if the investment is delayed or conditioned by market-opening moves in the foreign market?

Institutions Matter

The Worst-Possible Direction for the FCC. Any policy idea is bound to be modified by the specific political and institutional context in which it is carried out. Too often, however, the role institutions play in shaping the practical impact of a regulation is ignored or discounted by CNT advocates. Section 310(b) embodies the assumption that the public interest decisions of the FCC will be objective and informed by economic reasoning. But the nature of the FCC and the history of the public interest standard give little cause for such optimism.[21]

The political nature of the FCC compromises the quality of the appointments charged with implementing the rules. Henry Geller, former general counsel at FCC, noted that "FCC appointments are usually regarded as political plums. Looking over the history of appointments, I can only conclude that with enough political pull, anyone can be appointed to the FCC" (Geller 1995). The result is a growing gap between the competency of FCC appointments and the complexity of the rapidly changing and expanding field of telecommunications. Unlike the case of appointments to other agencies, the president is not under pressure to appoint those best qualified to the FCC because the president is not held accountable for the performance of independent agencies. But, industry is not indifferent about appointments. The result is that FCC members tend to be "over identified" with the regulated industries. Once the practice of members moving to work for industry after leaving the FCC is taken into account, the notion of independent or objective economic analysis becomes an even more improbable assumption (Geller 1995).

Also, after decades of regulation, licensing, adjudication, and rule making, the FCC has no idea what the public interest standard means. Even strong advocates of the public interest standard have concluded the FCC has done little to ensure public service. Some conclude"the public interest" has come to mean as little as any phrase

Congress could use and still comply with its constitutional authority to provide administrative guidance to the FCC.[22]

With an elastic standard that justifies just about any action the FCC collectively decides to take, the FCC has tended toward protection of incumbent interests over the rights of others to compete. Most FCC information is obtained from those who have the most to lose from competition. As a result, the public interest review tends to be driven not by any real effort to advance consumer welfare, but rather by the competitive interests of the incumbent firm.[23]

Adding a market access test to Section 310(b), therefore, moves the FCC and the United States in the worst possible direction by adding yet another objective (other than consumer welfare) and a global dimension to the public interest review process. The trade rhetoric on issues of "fairness" and "leveling the playing field" confuse an already Byzantine review process. A shift in focus further away from consumer welfare aggravates the FCC's regulatory capture problem, that is, strategic use of the public interest rhetoric and review process by an established or incumbent firm.

Politics and the Public Interest. The guidelines issued by the FCC on its market access test and Section 310(b) provide a timely illustration of the political nature of the review process. The process started in 1986, when an FCC notice announced an inquiry "to determine whether the public interest requires that telecommunications policies of foreign governments be considered in the formation of U.S. regulatory policies" (FCC 1986, 1). At the time, AT&T argued against the change, noting that "government-to-government discussions would risk changing the fundamental nature of international services from one of cooperation and collaboration to one of delay and confrontation" (FCC 1986, 11).

Since then, AT&T has become a primary proponent of these "discussions" and rules that minimize competitive pressure.[24] In particular, in 1993, AT&T proposed that the FCC include a mirror-image reciprocity test as part of its public interest review. Under this proposal, foreign governments would have been forced to demonstrate that comparable market opportunities exist for U.S. carriers in their markets before carriers from that country would be permitted to invest in U.S. telecommunications firms.

In 1993, while seeking to join forces with British Telecommunications to compete with AT&T, MCI opposed AT&T and the use of 310(b) as a trade statute. MCI argued that

> it is not necessary to bar foreign carriers from participating in U.S. international service markets . . . it would be wholly counterproductive for the Commission [FCC] to deny U.S. customers the immeasurable benefits that flow from alliances between U.S. and foreign carriers . . . U.S. carriers necessarily must enter into various relationships in order to compete with AT&T. The Commission should not deprive U.S. carriers of the flexibility to pursue a suitable relationship whose beneficiary would be the public. (FCC 1993a, 3-4, 24)

But after its deal with BT had been approved by the FCC, MCI switched sides. By 1995, MCI was arguing in favor of a market access test and the use of Section 310(b) "as leverage to encourage foreign administrators to open their markets to competition by U.S. carriers" (FCC 1995e, iii). MCI opposed the FCC's approval of the French and German investment in Sprint (Global One). For its part, on the proposed market access test, British Telecommunications argued it would be "wasteful" to apply the test retroactively to its recently approved investment in MCI. But, not surprisingly, BT further argued that the test should not be limited to equity alliances, but should be expanded instead to include co-marketing arrangements and nonequity alliances such as those of AT&T (FCC 1995a, 6, 18).

For its part, Sprint sided with AT&T in 1993 and favored a reciprocal market access test. In its comments to the FCC, Sprint opposed the then-proposed $4 billion BT investment in MCI, arguing that "*only* equivalent opportunity in overseas markets can provide any assurance that U.S. carriers will not be disadvantaged." Sprint argued in particular that comparable market access should have been required before the FCC granted a 310(b) waiver for BT's investment in MCI (FCC 1993b). But, like MCI, Sprint also reversed positions once it had a partnership pending with Deutsche Telekom and France Telecom. By May of 1995, Sprint was arguing there was good reason to question whether a market access test would have any beneficial effect on U.S. consumers and the broad U.S. public interest. Instead, Sprint concluded, it seemed more likely the U.S. market reciprocity test "would be ineffective in achieving the underlying policy objectives" because the pace of whatever liberalization occurs "will be governed by internal economic, political, and legal considerations" (FCC 1995g).

These comments demonstrate that simplistic notions of "us and them" no longer fit the political-economic realities of the telecommunications market. They further illustrate how bilateral deals and international alliances are changing the dynamics of the reform process. As more firms become incumbents and stakeholders in the global web of bilateral deals, the opportunities and momentum for removing foreign investment restrictions are reduced. The bilateral deal making that takes place under provisions like Section 310(b) may work to undermine the progress being made toward a multilateral agreement. The deals may fix enough of the specific problems that individual firms become less willing to make the necessary sacrifices to get a broader deal at the multilateral level (Cowhey, 1995, 197).

Therefore, given the political nature of the FCC, its vulnerability to regulatory capture, and the history of its public interest standard, the FCC is a strange choice for promoting consumer welfare and competition in the international marketplace and for speeding up the liberalization process. Even the healthiest of agencies would be hard pressed to do the political-economic calculus necessary to attain this objective.

Worst-Possible Timing. U.S. fascination with reciprocal market access tests could not come at a more inopportune time. Just as foreign governments are being forced by technology and economic pressures at home to open their markets more to competition and just as the interest in multilateral investment rules is starting to take off, the United States begins experimenting with nationality-based restrictions.

How can this be rational? U.S. carriers, often the dominant partners in global alliances, have been the principle beneficiaries of the global liberalization trend. They are entering and investing in foreign markets far more than foreign carriers have entered or invested in the U.S. market. Between 1990 and 1993, AT&T teamed with the governments of Spain, China, Taiwan, Chile, Poland, the Czech Republic,

Kazakhstan, Ukraine, Armenia, and Russia to modernize their telecommunications infrastructures.

LOOKING AHEAD

Barriers to transnational investment exist. But a U.S. retreat from an open-door policy to reciprocity mandates and conditional national treatment (CNT) experiments contribute to the problem, not to a solution. Reciprocity mandates and CNT experiments confuse and retard competition. They also conflict with long-term U.S. objectives to promote technological developments, domestic economic growth, and a stable system of nondiscriminatory investment rules that protect the rights of investors from all countries.

To compete effectively in the future, even more so than in the past, the United States will need a consistent policy framework that promotes both inward and outward investment flows. Nationality- or ownership-based definitions of U.S. interests (in public R&D programs or the shaping of an investment liberalization strategy) are simply too narrow to handle the world of complex interdependence that is growing up around transnational corporations. As one business executive commented, "Policy must be reshaped to fit the world as it is becoming, not as it was" (Worth 1994, 4). Clearly, much work remains to be done.

The telecommunications case demonstrates that the country with the environment most conducive to telecommunications for business sets the standard for others (Aronson and Cowhey 1988). Large users in Europe saw that to be competitive with U.S. firms, they needed to reduce costs, increase scale, and improve their ability to deliver flexible and timely services. Relative to the mobilization of these users, tools like Section 310(b) and foreign market access tests are likely to play at best a marginal role in speeding up the liberalization process and the development of competitive markets. Taking into account the practical problems of implementation, institutions, and politics further defeats the case for specific reciprocity rules and a managed investment policy.

An open-door policy based on unconditional national treatment is not a perfect policy rule or even the best one in theory. But it is the one most likely to promote U.S. economic welfare in practice. The institution of alternative rules invites regulatory capture and abuse. To expect otherwise is naive, particularly in the highly politicized matters of telecommunications and trade policy. Setting up a process that conditions foreign investment on the policies of foreign governments makes "the folly of others the limit of our wisdom."[25] This is hardly a rational response for a nation that wants to build a bridge into the twenty-first century.

NOTES

This chapter, which draws on *The Foreign Investment Debate*, edited by Cynthia Beltz (Washington, D.C.: AEI Press, 1995), was prepared in 1995 prior to the 1997 conclusion of the World Trade Organization (WTO) negotiations on basic telecommunication services. At the time it was written, Section 310(b), a national security provision of the 1934 Communications Act, was widely promoted as a trade tool that was needed to give the United States significant leverage at the WTO negotiating table. This strategy, however, failed, for reasons discussed in the chapter. By 1997 and the final stages of the WTO negotiations, Section 310(b) had been replaced in its trade policy role by a U.S. proposal to reform its international settlement policy. The use of Section 310(b) over the 1994-1996 period, as a result, did little to advance U.S. negotiating objectives. Instead, through the use of a national security provision (Section 310(b)) as a trade tool, the United States has endorsed a practice that will be sure to come back and haunt U.S. trade officials in future negotiations, particularly with developing countries.

1. U.S. investment obligations are also contained in the OECD Code of Liberalization and Capital Movements, the Uruguay Round Agreement on Trade Related Investment Measures, and the General Agreement on Trade in Services. See Kenneth J. Vandevelde, "The Bilateral Investment Treaty Program of the United States," *Cornell International Law Journal* 21 (1988):202-276; Jose Alvarez, *Virginia Journal of International Law* 30 (1989); Harvey E. Bale, "The U.S. Policy toward Inward Foreign Direct Investment," *Vanderbilt Journal of Transnational Law* 18 (Spring 1985):199-222.

2. Remarks by President Clinton at American University, February 26, 1993.

3. See Office of Technology Assessment, *Multinationals and the National Interest: Playing by Different Rules* (Washington, D.C.: Government Printing Office, September 1993), as well as *Multinationals and the U.S. Technology Base* (Washington, D.C.: Government Printing Office, October 1994), especially pp. 4, 25-27, 33.

4. For a discussion of the managed trade roots of the reciprocity push in national treatment see Cynthia Beltz, "Investors Make Lousy Crowbars," in *The Foreign Investment Debate*, edited by Cynthia Beltz (Washington, D.C.: AEI Press, 1995).

5. The U.S.–Japan Framework talks provide a useful illustration. In the planning stage on the U.S. side, a great deal of analytical work and review went into the drafting of a list of strategic sectors on the basis of economic criteria. But as other U.S. agencies got involved and attached their agenda, the list was twisted and extended. Autos, an industry not on the economists' lists, ended up winning the priority role in the now infamous trip of President Bush to Japan.

6. For example, much of Japanese R&D is not funded through the government. On the other problems associated with quick government fixes to increase FDI (business structures, factor costs, cultural differences), see papers sponsored by the U.S.–Japan Management Studies Center for the conference, "Foreign Direct Investment into Japan: Why So Small and How to Encourage?" October 7, 1994, The Wharton School of the University of Pennsylvania.

7. For discussion of Section 310(b) as an ineffectual instrument of national security, see Sidak (1996), chapters 2, 3.

8. On the transmission of competition from services to equipment and the process of regulatory breakdown, see Ronald Cass and John Haring, *International Trade in Telecommunications: Monopoly, Competition, and Trade Strategy* (MIT Press and AEI Press, 1996), pp. 154, 162. On the relationships between deregulation of U.S. telecommunication services, the equipment sector, and other national markets, see Leonard Waverman (1995). See also Aronson and Cowhey (1988) and Majone (1991) for the impact of U.S. regulatory reform on European telecommunication policies.

9. An amendment proposed by Congressman Oxley that would have eliminated Section 310(b) was rejected early in the legislative process. For history and discussion of treatment of 310(b) by the telecommunication bills in the 104th Congress, see Gregory Sidak (1996).

10. Even under newly issued Section 310(b) guidelines, the FCC puts burden on foreign firms to prove that investment would be in the public interest (FCC 1995d, 62 (para 179), 71 (para 183)).

11. Director-General Krenzler, cited by Greg Sidak (1996), 725.

12. In 1986, for example, the FCC denied license renewal to thirteen television stations partially owned by Mexican media firms. A review of those decisions found that there was no discussion or substantive explanation offered on how the investments hurt U.S. interests

or consumer welfare (Sidak 1996).

13. One-third of the cases notified to CFIUS between October 1988 and May 1994 did not raise national security concerns. They involved instead transactions in industries such as consumer products, entertainment, and real estate. See, the General Accounting Office (1995).

14. See also FCC (1994). In July 1993, the U.S. Trade Representative Micky Kantor also tied the FCC's approval of British Telecommunications 214 application to the concessions the United Stated was seeking from the EC in the Uruguay Round.

15. Second Cable Order, 77 FCC 2d at 79.

16. These include the general significance of the investment to the promotion of competition in the U.S. telecommunications market, any national security, law enforcement, foreign policy, and trade concerns raised by the Executive Branch, and the extent of alien participation in the applicant's parent corporation.

17. In TLD case and 1994 AmericaTel case, FCC declined a petition to impose a reciprocal market access test on Spain or Chile, reasoning that there were sufficient safeguards to protect U.S. firms from potential abuse of Telefonica's market power (AmericaTel 1992, 9 FCC Rcd 3993, 3994 (par 7) and 3995-96 (para 13-15) See also, BT/MCI case (9 FCC Rcd at 3965 (para 26) and 3964 (n. 45)).

18. See Fred Bergsten letter attachment to AT&T comments, p. 2.

19. Concerns that an affiliated U.S. firm may be favored over its unaffiliated U.S. rivals have, for example, become a key feature of FCC decisions in cases dealing with foreign investment restrictions and foreign monopolies. See case of British Telecom and MCI (FCC 1994).

20. The joint venture's products range from voice, data, and video services designed specifically for business customers and multinationals to worldwide telephone card services. It will also provide carrier services to telecommunication companies.

21. For a history of the public interest standard and its failures in broadcasting, see Hazlett (1995).

22. First General Counsel of the Federal Radio Commission, Louis G. Caldwell (Hazlett 1995, 14, 13-20).

23. In the international arena, FCC actions, decisions, and rules have further been targeted as the major reason that competition did not evolve (Waverman 1995).

24. AT&T has opposed 90 percent of the applications for international simple resale (Waverman 1995, 10).

25. Sir James Graham, British statesman, in 1849 as cited by Robert Keohane, "Reciprocity in International Relations," *International Organization* 40(1):15, Winter 1996.

REFERENCES

Adonis, Andrew. 1994. "AT&T's Hidden Global Agenda," *Financial Times*, June 24.

Alvarez, Jose. 1989. "Political Protectionism and U.S. Investment Obligations in Conflict: The Hazards of Exon-Florio," *Virginia Journal of International Law* 30(1):89, Fall.

Arnst, Catherine, Susan Jackson and Michael Shari. 1995. "The Last Frontier," *Business Week*, September 18, pp. 98-102.

Aronson, Jonathan D., and Peter F. Cowhey. 1988. *When Countries Talk: International Trade in Telecommunication Services*, Cambridge, Mass.: Ballinger Publishing Company.

Barber, Lionel. 1995. "Second-Rate EU Utilities Will Harm Economy," *Financial Times*, December 13.

Barnard, Bruce. 1996. "EU Braces for Telecom Invasion," *Journal of Commerce* 1407(28647):1A, January 25.

Beltz, Cynthia. 1992. 1991. *High Tech Maneuvers: Industrial Policy Lessons of HDTV.* Washington, D.C.: AEI Press.

————. 1994. "Lessons from the Cutting Edge and HDTV," *Regulation*, February.

————. 1996. "Talk Is Cheap," *Reason*, August.

Bensen, Stanley M., and John M. Gale. 1995. "A Game-Theoretic Analysis of the FCC's Proposed Reciprocity Rule," Charles River Incorporated, April 10, p. 9.

Cass, Ronald, and John Haring. 1996. *International Trade in Telecommunications: Monopoly, Competition, and Trade Strategy.* MIT Press and AEI Press, pp. 154, 162.

Coughlin, Cletus C. 1992. "Foreign-Owned Companies in the United States: Malign or Benign?" *Federal Reserve Bank of St. Louis Review* 74(May/June):17-31.

Cowhey, Peter F. 1990. "The International Telecommunications Regime: The Political Roots of Regimes for High Technology," *International Organization* 44 (Spring):169-199.

————. 1995. "Building the Global Information Highway: Toll Booths, Construction, Contracts, and Rules of the Road," in *The New Information Infrastructure: Strategies for U.S. Policy*, edited by William J. Drake. New York: Twentieth Century Fund Press, p. 197.

Crane, Alan. 1995a. "Competition Down the Line," *Financial Times*, January 19; *Wall Street Journal*, September 27.

————. 1995b. "Era of Intelligent Networks," *Financial Times*, March 1.

————. 1996. "Telecoms Competition Heats Up," *Financial Times*, January 21.

Crowe, Kenneth C. 1978. *America for Sale*, Garden City, N.Y.: Doubleday, p. 249.

"Don't Call US." 1996. *The Economist*, 338:55, January 6.

Dover, Agnes P. 1995. Deputy General Counsel, at U.S. Department of Energy at the National Research Council, "International Access to National Technology Promotion Programs," January 19.

European Commission. 1992. "Review of the Situation in the Telecommunications Services Sector." Communication by the Commission, SEC(92) 1048 (October 21):17-18.

"FCC Approves French, German Stake in Sprint." 1995. *Journal of Commerce*, December 18.

Federal Communications Commission (FCC). 1986. "Order on Reconsideration," adopted December 12, p. 1.

————. 1993a. "MCI Comments to FCC," RM-8355, November 10, pp. 3-4, 24.

————. 1993b. "Sprint Comments," RM-8355, November 1.

————. 1994. "Case of British Telecom and MCI," 9.

————. 1995a. "Comments of British Telecommunications of North America," RM-8355, May 12.

————. 1995b. "Comments of Deutsche Telekom," April 11, p. 33.

————. 1995c. "Comments of LDDS Communications, Inc.," IB Docket No. 95-22, RM-8355, April 11.

————. 1995d. "Market Entry and Regulation of Foreign-affiliated Entities," Notice of Proposed Rulemaking 10 (22). R. at 5263, note 16.

————. 1995e. "MCI Comments," RM-8355, May 12, p. iii.

————. 1995f. Reed Hundt, Chairman, in *Hearings on Section 310 of the Communications Act of 1934 before the Subcommittee. on Commerce, Trade, and Hazardous Materials of the House Committee on Commerce*, R at 1423, March 3.

————. 1995g. "Sprint Comments," RM-8355, April 11.

Financial Times. 1994. May 13.

————. 1995b. October 3.

"*Financial Times* Survey." 1995. International Telecommunications, *Financial Times*, October 3.

Gaster, Robin, and Clyde Prestowitz. 1994. *Shrinking the Atlantic: Europe and the American Economy*, Washington, D.C.: Economic Strategy Institute, June.

Geller, Henry. 1995. "Reforming the U.S. Telecommunications Policymaking Process," in *The New Information Infrastructure: Strategies for U.S. Policy*, edited by William J. Drake. New York: Twentieth Century Fund Press, pp. 115-136.

General Accounting Office. 1995. *Foreign Investment: Implementation of Exon-Florio and Related Amendments*. Washington, D.C.Government Printing Office, December.

"Global Ventures with Bells Seen Impaired by FCC, Senate Bill." 1995. *Washington Telecom Week*, November 24.

Globerman, Steven. 1995. "Foreign Ownership in Telecommunications: A Policy Perspective," *Telecommunications Policy* 19(1):21-28.

Grossman, Gene M., and Elhanan Helpman. 1991. *Innovation and Growth in the Global Economy*. Cambridge: MIT Press, chapter 7.

Hazlett, Thomas. 1995. "Is the Public Interest in the Public Interest: An Essay on the Broadcast License Bargain of 1927," working paper delivered at Western Michigan University, November 8.

International Telecommunications Union. 1995. *The World Development Report*. Geneva: ITV.

Keller, John J. 1994. "Sprint's 4th-Quarter Earnings Expected to Fall as Much as 10% below Estimates," *Wall Street Journal*. Eastern Edition, December 15, p. A4.

Kenney, Martin, and Richard L. Florida. 1991. "How Japanese Industry Is Rebuilding the Rust Belt," *Technology Review* 94(Feb-Mar):24-33.

Krasner, Stephen D. 1986. "Trade Conflicts and the Common Defense: The United States and Japan," *Political Science Quarterly* 101(5):787-806.

"The Last One to Draw." 1994. *The Economist*, August 13.

Lewis, James L. 1995. *PRNewswire*, December 15.

Liebeler, Susan W., and William H. Lash, III. 1993. "Exon-Florio: Harbinger of Economic Nationalism?" *Regulation* (Winter):44-51.

Lindemann, Michael. 1995a. "Sales Shortfall May Hit Deutsche Telekom Sell-off," *Financial Times*, December 1.

————. 1995b. "Thyssen seeks telecoms partner," *Financial Times*, December 7.

Majone, Giandomenico. 1991. "Cross-National Sources of Regulatory Policymaking in Europe and the United States," *Journal of Public Policy* 11 (1):92-93.

McCulloch, Rachel. 1993. "Foreign Investment in the United States: Source of Strength or Sign of Weakness," *Economic Directives* 3 (June):6.

McKinsey Global Institute. 1993. *Manufacturing Productivity*, Washington, D.C., October, pp. 4-5 and Exhibit 3-10.

Myerson, Allen R. 1995. "Investments Abroad Reach Record Pace," *New York Times*. Late New York Edition, November 24, p. D9+.

Noam, Eli. 1995. Testimony on foreign ownership reform before the U.S. Senate Committee on Commerce, Science, and Transportation on SR-253, March 21.

Office of the President. 1991. *Economic Report of the President*, Washington, D.C.: Government Printing Office, February, p. 262.

Office of Technology Assessment (OTA). 1993a. *Multinationals and the National Interest: Playing by Different Rules*. Washington, D.C.: GPO, September.

Olbeter, Erik. 1994-1995. "Opening the Global Market for Telecommunications," *Issues in Science and Technology*, pp. 63-64.

Olbeter, Erik, and Lawrence Chimerine. 1995. *Crossed Wires*, Washington, D.C.: Economic Strategy Institute, p. ix.

Pope, Kyle. 1995. "Cable and Wireless, Hurt by Tougher Rivals, is Losing Phone Wars," *Wall Street Journal*. Eastern Edition, September 27, p. A1+.

Reuter's News Service. 1996. January 31.

Ridding, John. 1995. "France Telecom May Face a Partial Sell-Off Next Year," *Financial Times*, December 4.

Schwartz, Robert, and Bennett Caplan. 1994. "Conditioning the Unconditional," *New York Law Journal*, August 19.

Sharpe, Antonia Sharpe. 1996. "Telecom Issues Pall," *Financial Times*, January 16.

Sidak, Gregory J. 1994. "Don't Stifle Global Merger Mania," *Wall Street Journal*, July 6.

———. 1996. *Foreign Investment in American Telecommunications*, Chicago: University of Chicago Press.

Spencer, Linda. 1991. *Foreign Investment in the United States: Unencumbered Access*. Economic Strategy Institute, May.

Strategic Policy Research. 1993. "The U.S. Stake in Competitive Global Telecommunication Services: The Economic Case for Tough Bargaining," p. 32.

Sun, Jeanne-Mey, and Jacques Pelkmans. 1995. "Why Liberalisation Needs Centralisation: Subsidiarity and EU Telecoms," *World Economy*, September 18, pp. 635-664.

United Nations Conference on Trade and Development (UNCTAD). 1994. *World Investment Report 1994: Transnational Corporations, Employment and the Workplace*. Division on Transnational Corporations and Investment, New York: United Nations, pp. 4, 17.

U.S. Department of Commerce. 1993. *Foreign Direct Investment in the United States: An Update*. Economics and Statistics Administration, Washington, D.C.: GPO, June, pp. 62, 70.

———. 1993b. *U.S. Telecommunication Services in European Markets*, OTA-TCT-548. Washington, D.C.: Government Printing Office, August, pp. 2-6.

———. 1994. *Multinationals and the U.S. Technology Base*. Washington, D.C.: GPO, October.

U.S. Trade Representative. 1983. *Annual Report of the President of the United States on the Trade Agreements Program: 1983*. Washington, D.C.: GPO, p. 174.

Washington Telecommunications Week. 1995. December 8, p.11.

Waverman, Leonard. 1995. "It Takes Two to Tango: Why Bilateral Relationships Dominate the International Telecommunications Market and What to Do about It," working paper for the American Enterprise Institute, June.

Williamson, John. 1995. "Virtual Private Networks: Big Benefits for Big Business," *Financial Times*, October 3.

Worth, Douglas C. 1994. Remarks of the Chairman of the Trade Committee Business and Industry Advisory Committee to the OECD Roundtable on the New Dimensions of Market Access in a Globalized World Economy, June 30-July 1.

APPENDIX
Conditional National Treatment Legislation

Law	*Eligibility Restrictions for Program Participants*
Stevenson-Wydler Technology Innovation Act of 1980 (As amended by Technology Transfer Act, ATP Act)	Home government of foreign parties must permit U.S. persons to enter into CRADAs and licensing agreements.
American Technology Preeminence Act, including the Technology Administration Authorization Act of 1991 (P.L. 102-45)	Home country of foreign-owned firm must afford U.S.-owned companies *(i)* opportunities comparable to those afforded to any other company to participate in joint ventures similar to those authorized under ATP; *(ii)* local investment opportunities; and *(iii)* "adequate and effective" protection for intellectual property rights of U.S.-owned companies.
Advanced Technology Program (ATP)	
Energy Policy act of 1992	ATP Conditions*
Defense Authorization Legislation of 1992	ATP Conditions*
National Cooperative Production Amendments of 1993	Foreign-owned company's parent country must grant "national treatment" to U.S. companies in its national competition law covering joint ventures.**

*Proposal****
Defense Appropriations of 1993	ATP Conditions*
Amendments to the Trade Act of 1974 (HR. 249). Introduced January 5, 1993	Actions by a foreign country denying national treatment in investment may be actionable under Section 301.
National Competitiveness Act of 1993 (HR 820). Introduced February 1993	Home government of the foreign-owned firm must *(i)* provide U.S. companies "comparable" opportunities and offer them "access to resources and information equivalent to opportunities" authorized under this legislation; and *(ii)* have "open and transparent standards-setting process that results in standards that are fair and reasonable."
Department of Commerce and National Science Foundation programs	

Manton Amendment	Plus the second and third ATP conditions. Note: Senate companion (S.4) does not contain this Manton amendment.
Aeronautical Technology Consortium Act of 1993 (S 419 /HR 1675). Introduced February 24, 1993, and April 2, 1993	Home country of foreign-owned firm must *(i)* afford U.S.-owned companies opportunities comparable to those afforded any other company in R&D consortia to which government of that country provides funding directly or indirectly through international organizations or agreements; and *(ii)* afford "adequate and effective" protection for intellectual property rights of U.S.-owned companies.
Hydrogen Future Act of 1993 (HR 1479). Introduced March 25, 1993	Restricted to U.S.-owned firms.
National Environmental Technology Act of 1993 (S 978). Introduced May 18, 1993	ATP Conditions*
National Aeronautics and Space Administration Authorization Act (HR 2200). Introduced May 20, 1993	See Aeronautical Technology Consortium Act Conditions.
Omnibus Space Commercialization Act of 1993 (HR 2731). Introduced July 23, 1993	ATP Conditions*
Fair Trade in Financial Services Act of 1993 (S.1527). Introduced October 7, 1993	Authorizes sanctions against firms from countries which deny national treatment to U.S. financial services firms.
Fair Trade in Services Act of 1993 (HR 3565). Introduced November 19, 1993	Authorizes sanctions against foreign governments restricting U.S. firms in telecommunications and financial services.
Authorizations for the Earthquake Hazards Reduction Act of 1977 (HR 3485). Introduced November 10, 1993	No contract/subcontract can be made with a company organized under laws of a foreign country unless that country affords comparable opportunities to U.S. companies.**

Hazardous Materials Transpor-   Waives mandatory filing requirement for person
tation Act Amendments of 1993   not domiciled in U.S. if the country where
(HR 2178). Passed by House   person is domiciled does not require a U.S.
November 21, 1993   domiciliary to file registration statements for
                                   same purpose. Also contains ATP Conditions.

*Contains reciprocity conditions and language identical or similar to that for the Advanced Technology
Program.
**Rule may be waived if it violates GATT or any international agreement.
***Unless noted otherwise, language is as originally introduced. CNT bills proposed as of June, 1994.

Source: Based on survey done by Caplan and O'Keefe of McDermott, Will & Emery. Chart created
by Cynthia Beltz.

Major Telecommunications Alliances (as of 11/1/95)*

AT&T • **Uniworld**: Joint venture of Unisource (Dutch, Swiss, and   12/19/94
          Swedish, Spanish phone companies) and AT&T to combine
          European data and business voice services.

      • **Unisource Group, KDD, Singapore Telecom**: Service   6/27/94
          agreement AT&T (50%), KDD (30%), Singapore Telecom
          (20%).

      • **Alfa** [Mexican steel, petrochemical, textile, and food con-   11/14/94
          sortium]: announced $1 billion joint venture to pursue na-
          tional and international services. AT&T (49%) and Alfa
          (51%).

      • **CNI**: Communications Network International (Deutsche   9/4/95
          Bank, Mannesman) signed letter of intent with AT&T and
          Unisource.

      • **Unitel** (Canada): AT&T w/ 3 Canadian banks to purchase   9/26/95
          $195 million equity stake.

      • **World Partners:** AT&T, PTT Telecom (Netherlands),
          Telia (Sweden), Swiss PTT (Switzerland), Telefonica
          (Spain), KDD (Japan), Singapore Telecom, TCNZ, Telstra
          (Australia), Hong Kong Telecom, Korea Telecom, Unitel
          (Canada), PLDT.

MCI   • **British Telecom**: 20% equity stake ($4.3 billion) in MCI

      • **Concert**: British Telecom (75.1%) MCI (24.9%).   7/18/94

      • **Belzie Telcomm**: MCI acquired 23.5% interest.   2/20/95

- **News Corp**: Entertainment and publishing company. MCI 5/15/95 to take a $2 billion equity.

- **SHL**: Canada's SHL Systemhouse Inc. acquired for $1 9/20/95 billion.

- **Mexican Financial Group Banacci**: MCI will invest $450 1/31/95 million and take 45% share, Banacci will invest $550 million and own a 55% share

Sprint • **Global One**: Joint venture with Deutsch -Telekom and 1/30/96 France Telecom (previously known as Phoenix) to provide global voice, data, and video services to businesses.

- **Grupo Iusacell**: have agreed to form venture to seek com- 8/1/94 petitive long distance license in Mexico. Iusacell will own at least 51%, and Sprint will own at least 33%.

- **Telefonos de Mexico**: have agreed to a strategic alliance 12/19/94 to provide cross-border service to Mexico and United States.

- **Call Net Telecommunications Ltd**: Canada's largest alternative producer of long distance services in which Sprint has a 25% equity stake.

* Sprint Global One alliance as of 1/30/96.

Source: *Washington Telecom Week*, November 24, 1995

U.S. Foreign Investment Restrictions in Telecommunications

The Communications Act of 1934—Foreign firms prohibited from holding a common carrier radio license, owning more than 20 percent of U.S. firms holding a radio license, or having representation on the board of a U.S. radio license holder. The subsidiary of a foreign firm can hold a common carrier radio license, but the parent firm is limited to 25 percent foreign stock ownership, foreign directors, and foreign officers (see also Section 310(b)).

Section 308(c) of the Communications Act of 1934—Permits FCC to impose a reciprocity condition when issuing radio license for an international route, can "impose any terms, conditions, or restrictions on the granting of a radio station license for commercial communications between the U.S. and a foreign country."

*Section 310(b) of the Communications Act***—Limits foreign ownership of broadcasters and common carriers using radio licenses to 25 percent of corporate stock unless the FCC finds that it would be in the public interest to waive the restriction. In the public interest review for common carrier licenses (not for broadcast or aeronautical licenses), the FCC will examine whether the home market (principle place of business) offers "effective competitive opportunities" to US firms in the particular service in which the foreign applicant seeks to participate in the US market.

Section 214 of the Communications Act**—Requires carriers to apply to FCC for license to provide services, based on whether the operation is necessary and convenient for the public. For foreign-owned firms, FCC will examine whether "effective competitive opportunities" exist for U.S. carriers in the destination markets of those carriers with market power seeking to enter the U.S. international service market either directly or through an affiliation with either a U.S. facilities-based or resale carrier.

1992 Regulation of International Common Carrier Services (FCC 92-463)—FCC decision requires foreign owned be considered a dominant carrier, which face stricter regulations than other carriers such as filing pricing plans and schedules with the FCC. "Foreign owned" is defined as any US carrier that is over 15% directly or indirectly owned by a foreign telecommunications entity or on whose board of directors a member of a foreign telecommunications firm sits.

The Communications Satellite Act of 1962—Created the private satellite corporation COMSAT and gave it exclusive rights to INTELSAT (provides global satellite connections for range of wireless services) and INMARSAT (provides global maritime satellite communication services), thereby limiting the access of foreign carriers to provide these services to the American market.

The Submarine Cable Landing Act of 1921 (made part of the Communications Act of 1934, 47 U.S.C. Section 34)—Requires that any foreign firm which wants to land submarine cables on US shores to first seek approval from the FCC. The FCC may withhold or revoke licenses if such action will assist in securing cable landing rights for US citizens in foreign countries.

The Telegraph Act of 1900—Prohibits foreign carrier from landing telegraph lines or cables in Alaska.

* As interpreted by the FCC.   **As of December 1995.

16

The Multilateral Agreement on Investment: The Next Challenge for Global Interdependence

Stephen J. Canner

INTRODUCTION

Foreign direct investment (FDI) has emerged as one of the most important issues in the post-Uruguay Round era of multilateral negotiations. Despite its importance, the international economic agenda for most of this postwar era has been limited to negotiation of rules to facilitate international trade, notably the General Agreement on Tariffs and Trade (GATT), now succeeded by the World Trade Organization (WTO). Yet, the growth of direct investment continues to outpace trade.

The critical role of direct investment in the modern economy is evident throughout this book. To remain competitive, business must function in a global marketplace in the design, development, production, and sale of goods and services. Succeeding in a global marketplace requires a company to establish a physical presence in overseas markets, hire local employees, participate in local research and development (R&D) consortia, access skills and technology not available in the home market, grow close to customers, and fully understand the needs of the local market. This can be achieved only through direct investment.

The ever-increasing role of technology in the global marketplace puts an even higher premium on the ability of firms to invest across borders. The pace and high cost of technology development compel companies to turn to business partners from other countries to develop new technologies. Direct investment provides the flexibility for U.S. firms to access critical technologies and to remain competitive. For example, building the Global Information Infrastructure (GII), which will provide for the borderless flow of information and data, will require an unparalleled level of international investment.

Direct investment is also critical to the globalization of services. Most service providers must establish a physical presence to gain market access. Although FDI is conventionally thought to be concentrated in manufacturing and extractive industries, services have come to account for a larger share of both trade and investment flows, comprising nearly 50 percent of total inward direct investment stocks in developed countries. As the liberalization of financial services, telecommunications, and transport progresses, services will account for an even greater percentage of FDI flows.

In May 1995, the governments representing the developed countries of the Organisation for Economic Co-operation and Development (OECD) took an important step in providing investors with a framework of disciplines for international investment by launching the negotiation of the Multilateral Agreement on Investment (MAI). Designed to reduce restrictions on international investment and provide investors with assurance about the treatment of their investment, the MAI was conceived to benefit firms competing in the global economy and to convey economic benefits to home and host countries. Critics of globlazation mobilized to defeat the MAI along battle lines similar to those during the debates over the Uruguay Round of GATT and the World Trade Organization. They argued that the treaty would subordinate the ability of national governments to set national economic policy. In particular, they objected to sections in the draft document that called for national treatment, disallowing governments the ability to discriminate between foreign investors based on their country of origin. As a result, an historic agreement among developed countries, not to mention developing countries, that would significantly liberalize investment flows remains far from assured as of this writing. Confusion about the specifics of the MAI spread as the rancorous debate unfolded in the late 1990s.

Whether or not the MAI negotiations are successful, direct investment liberalization will remain at the top of the agenda as economies continues to globalize. The purpose of this chapter is to review what a multilateral agreement would entail and why it remains the essential next step toward true global interdependence. This chapter takes a comprehensive look at the MAI, beginning with its historic roots. It then examines the potential obstacles and ultimate benefits of an agreement.

EARLY EFFORTS TO ESTABLISH RULES FOR DIRECT INVESTMENT

Investment in the Uruguay Round

In the Uruguay Round, the United States, Europe, and Japan were the principal proponents of incorporating new rules for investment in the GATT context. India and Brazil led a group of developing countries that strongly opposed the discussion of investment. These countries argue that international investment rules cut too deeply into their national sovereignty and lead to neocolonialism by multinational enterprises. As a result of this divide, GATT contracting parties could agree only to the discussion of investment as it relates to trade—trade-related investment measures (TRIMs). Accordingly, what had been seen as an opportunity for the creation of a multilateral agreement for the protection of investors quickly became a discussion only of trade-related investment measures.

In general, TRIMs are a subset of the performance requirements proscribed under many bilateral investment agreements. Performance requirements include stipulations that investors purchase from domestic sources, manufacture locally, or export at specified levels; restrictions on access to foreign exchange; requirements to transfer or license technologies to local entities; remittance restrictions; and requirements that local investors hold a minimum share of equity.

The TRIMs add no additional substantive rules to the GATT/WTO with respect to investment. Instead, the agreement clarifies the parties' existing GATT obligations by adding an illustrative list of measures that violate GATT articles. In general, the following are listed as prohibited TRIMs:

1. requirements to purchase from domestic sources;
2. limitations on the purchase or use of imported products tied to the volume or value of local products exported;
3. restrictions on importation, regardless of tie to the volume or value of local production exported;
4. restrictions on importation affected by restriction access to foreign exchange to an amount related to foreign exchange earnings; and
5. restrictions on exportation or sale for export.

This list represents a relatively narrow set of the issues identified as of concern to investors. WTO members are required to eliminate all TRIMs notified within two years for developed countries, five years for developing countries, or seven years for least-developed countries. WTO dispute settlement rules will apply for the resolution of disputes under the agreement.

The General Agreement on Trade in Services

A substantial number of services may be effectively delivered only through a local presence. To include locally provided services supplied by foreign-owned companies, the General Agreement on Trade in Services (GATS) defines "trade in services" to include supply of services through commercial presence (in other words, investment) in the territory of another member. In principle, the agreement also contains many obligations of importance to investors, including most-favored-nation (MFN) and national treatment, restrictions on quantitative limitations, prohibition of certain restrictions on transfers and payments, and requirements to publish government rules relating to trade in services. Thus, in many respects, the GATS is the WTO's real investment agreement. However, the structure of the GATS and the nature of many of these obligations are such that many investor concerns are not fully addressed and important service sectors are not covered. For example, the MFN treatment obligation, which applies to the establishment and operation of investment in all service sectors, does not currently apply to such important sectors as financial services and basic telecommunications.

Additionally, the structure of the GATS and the exemptions taken by individual members make it impossible to generalize about the level of protection investors may actually expect in any particular country. Some rules, such as MFN, apply to most services. Other rules, such as those providing for national treatment, limitations on quantitative restrictions, or the prohibition of restrictions on payments and transfers, apply only for sectors specifically listed by a member as part of its commitments. Even then, the country may have defined the sector or the application of the obligations in a way that limits its scope.

The GATS also lacks many important protections found in bilateral investment agreements. For example, the GATS does not contain an absolute ban on performance requirements. No provision is made to ensure that investments and investors are provided fair and equitable treatment under international law. No rules on expropriation are elaborated, and there is no provision for investor compensation. In contrast to the North American Free Trade Agreement (NAFTA) and bilateral investment agreements, investors do not have rights to initiate dispute settlements but instead must rely on their home governments to protect them in the case of disputes.

BUILDING A MULTILATERAL AGREEMENT ON INVESTMENT

Despite efforts to promote the liberalization of direct investment, restrictions abound. Companies seeking to establish and maintain access to a market through international investment may confront several barriers, including:

- outright prohibition on foreign investor participation in certain sectors of the economy such as telecommunications;
- licensing or economic screening of investment to limit access to certain sectors;[1]
- conditions on investment imposed by the host government such as a minimum investment level, employment requirements, transference of specific technology, and mandatory partnering;
- the lack of full commitment by the host government to treat foreign investors in the same manner as domestic investors[2]; and
- the absence of a dispute settlement mechanism that allows an investor to initiate a claim against a host government and to seek monetary damages if a host government violates commitments made in investment treaties.

These barriers posed a challenge to further liberalization. In turn, they also prompted the MAI initiative by the OECD. In 1994, the OECD with the cooperation of the business community began preparatory work on the multilateral agreement on investment. On May 24, 1995, the trade ministers of the OECD countries launched the MAI negotiations stating the agreement should:

> provide a broad multilateral framework for international investment with the liberalization of investment regimes and investment protection and with effective dispute settlement procedures; be a free standing international treaty open to all OECD members and the European Communities, and to accession by non-OECD Member countries, which will be consulted as the negotiations progress.
> (OECD Council of Ministers Communiqué, May 1995)

What are the key elements of a successful MAI? The following section, derived from the *Statement on the Multilateral Agreement on Investment* (U.S. Council for International Business 1995), provides a synopsis.

Broad Definition of Investment. The MAI must insure that "investment" is broadly defined to cover the multitude of ways in which investors access overseas markets and the types of assets that are considered to be an investment—physical structures, intellectual property, trademarks, and service and turnkey construction contracts.

The Right of Establishment. Under the MAI, firms must be free to "establish" a physical presence in foreign markets without being unduly burdened or restricted by bureaucratic regulations and restrictions. Moreover, investors must be free from the screening of their investment (except for national security reasons) and "performance requirements" that mandate a certain performance or outcome on the part of the investor.

National Treatment and Most Favored Nation Treatment. At the heart of the MAI must be a guarantee that foreign investors, either U.S. firms investing overseas or foreign-owned investors in the United States, are not discriminated against because of their nationality. As discussed in previous chapters, this is known as *national treatment.* The principle of national treatment provides that U.S. firms, both in seeking to establish an enterprise overseas and in operating the enterprise overseas, should receive treatment no less favorable than domestic enterprises in the countries in which the U.S. firms are investing. Any exceptions to this principle must be narrowly drawn. Furthermore, the MAI should provide for nondiscrimination among foreign investors by the host country. Each foreign investor is to be treated as favorably as every other foreign investor. This is known as the *most favored nation* (MFN) principle. In every respect, investors should receive the better of national treatment or MFN.

Transfer of Funds. Investors must be able to make an investment and any investment-related transfer of funds including profits, capital, royalties, and fees without being subject to government restriction or conditions. This provision covers investing capital in an overseas market as well as transferring funds out of that market.

Protection from Expropriation. Investors must be protected from the arbitrary seizure of their assets whether directly, through nationalization, or indirectly through costly discriminatory taxes or other measures. Any expropriation must provide for prompt, adequate, and effective compensation.

Dispute Settlement. All of these provisions will amount to little unless the investor is provided with a means to rectify violations of the agreement by a host government. If an investor is treated unfairly or discriminated against, the MAI will provide recourse to international binding arbitration in a number of possible forums, between the investor and the host government.

THE DIFFICULT ISSUES

Clearly, an MAI with these elements would greatly facilitate investment flows. Yet multilateral negotiations are never easy. As Beltz' chapter emphasized, although barriers to investment in developed countries have been reduced significantly in recent years, many remain. In some countries, entire sectors of the economy are off limits to foreign investors, or their equity participation is sharply constrained. Privatization of state-owned assets often restricts foreign participation. Some countries still screen takeovers of domestic firms for reasons of national security or national economic interest, and some countries still impose performance requirements as a condition of entry.

Liberalization of Barriers to Investment

A major issue that negotiators often confront is whether existing barriers will be liberalized "up front" as a condition of the agreement coming into force or subject to a standstill with some vague intention of liberalization to be implemented at a later date. The better argument is for liberalization up front. While it may be easier to conclude an agreement that simply calls for a freeze and standstill, approval for an agreement with "up front" liberalization will better serve business to enhance access to markets in the global economy.

Exceptions for National Security: Exon-Florio

National security exceptions are among the more common derogations to national treatment for foreign investors. For the United States, the national security exception is manifested primarily in the 1988 Exon-Florio provision of the Defense Production Act. This provision grants the president the authority to prohibit or suspend a merger, acquisition, or takeover that threatens the national security.

The Committee on Foreign Investment in the United States (CFIUS), an interagency committee chaired by the Treasury Department, administers the Exon-Florio provision. CFIUS utilizes a voluntary notification system with a thirty-day review procedure to identify national security concerns. If necessary, the review procedure may be extended to a formal forty-five-day investigation; in which case, the president must decide whether the transaction poses a national security threat and what action, if any, to take.

The president has used this authority sparingly and in a manner consistent with an open investment policy. Of the 978 notices filed with CFIUS, all but fifteen were found to be no threat to national security within the initial thirty-day review. Of the fifteen that were subject to the forty-five-day investigation, five were withdrawn by the parties to the transaction, nine were cleared by the president, and one was judged a threat to the national security.

Notwithstanding these results, the Europeans, Japanese, and Canadians may be expected to argue that Exon-Florio opens the door to protectionism in international investment. This concern is buttressed by the fact that national security is not defined in the statute or regulations. Absent a definition of national security, it is argued, Exon-Florio could be a Trojan horse for industrial policy, a tactic that has been resisted thus far, but that some in Congress may wish to foster.

Thus, Exon-Florio may take a turn for protectionism and be used as an element of industrial policy. But Exon-Florio has been relatively dormant in recent years, and, given the overall record of CFIUS not to use national security to embrace industrial policy, these concerns should not be taken too seriously. One must not lose sight of the fact that Europeans, Canadians, and Australians have formal or informal mechanisms for screening foreign investment that are more restrictive than Exon-Florio and that the standards for blocking (national interest, public interest) in these countries is much lower and less well-defined than the national security standard of Exon-Florio.

Conditional National Treatment

National treatment and MFN treatment are the core of any investment agreement. National treatment, discussed in detail in the last chapter, is the principle that governments must give foreign-owned or -controlled firms the same rights as national firms. Practically applied, host nations are obliged to treat foreign-owned businesses operating in their country no less favorably than comparable locally owned businesses. The obligation also goes to the investor seeking to establish a presence in a country. For establishment, the national treatment obligation also requires that, under law and policy, a foreign investor be treated no less favorably than a domestic investor.

Beltz's chapter provided an exhaustive review of departures from national treatment, or conditional national treatment, in setting telecommunications policy. In general, sectors of the government and business community in the United States have been concerned about the international competitiveness of U.S. high technology firms. The particular concern has been that the United States needs to work in partnership with its industries and universities to accelerate technology development, but foreign participation should be limited since the goal is to enhance international competitiveness. One result of this debate has been a departure in the long standing U.S. policy of national treatment.

Eligibility criteria for participation in several government R&D programs, such as the Advanced Technology Program (ATP) in the National Institute of Standards and Technology (NIST), and the programs in the Department of Energy (DOE) under section 2306 of the Energy Policy Act of 1992 were drafted to contain restrictive and discriminatory conditions. The American Technology Pre-eminence Act of 1991 established the ATP to fund business-related R&D in high-risk, high-potential commercial products. The ATP provides funding for up to five years on a cost-sharing basis to companies, universities, and federal laboratories to develop enabling technologies with widespread benefits for the U.S. economy and U.S. industry. ATP does not fund product development, but rather supports pre-product technologies that could underlie new products.

The ATP eligibility requirements consist of two stages. The first stage governs all potential applicants to the program and mandates that participation in the venture provide benefits to the U.S. economy. The second stage, however, applies only to U.S. affiliates of foreign enterprises and requires the firm to demonstrate that the home county of the foreign parent offers:

1. comparable opportunities for U.S. companies in similar joint ventures,
2. comparable investment opportunities for U.S. firms, and
3. effective intellectual property protection for U.S. companies.

Since the inception of the ATP, fifteen grants have been awarded to European-owned companies in the United States. The largest ATP award to date was given to Affymetrix, Inc., the U.S. subsidiary of the Dutch firm Affymax. NIST has asserted that no European-owned company has ever been blocked from ATP participation because of foreign ownership. In the two cases in which foreign ownership was a consideration, both firms were Japanese.

Continued funding for the ATP program has been challenged in Congress, and the program will likely be phased out. At most, funding may be provided for ongoing contracts, with no new awards being allowed. This funding posture is due not to national treatment concerns, but to a general reduction in U.S. R&D funding.

Additionally, section 2306 of the Energy Policy Act established eligibility criteria identical to those of the ATP. The DOE has not restricted any foreign firms from participating to date, although there was significant controversy over the DOE's decision to allow a Swiss firm (ABB) to compete in and win a competition with GE.

Containing and rolling back the "comparable opportunities" test for participation of foreign-owned companies in ATP programs (and, for that matter, similar restrictive provisions in counterpart programs in Europe, Canada, and Japan) may be viewed as one measure of conditional national treatment that could be viewed as a measure of success of the MAI.

Regional Economic Integration Organizations

The European Union (EU) Commission staff assert that the MAI must have a broad, generic economic integration clause that will allow members of an economic integration agreement, such as the EU, to apply to each other future (unspecified) liberalization measures without extending them to other parties to the MAI or violating the national treatment and MFN obligations of MAI. Stated another way, unless the EU obtains an exception for Regional Economic Integration Organizations (REIO), REIO measures would be in violation of the national treatment and MFN provisions generally contained in investment agreements. The U.S. government rejected a REIO clause in the Energy Charter negotiations (which the United States did not sign) and has told the EU that the United States will not accept a generic "carve out" or exception for REIO.

The EU Hydrocarbons Directive and the proposed Satellite Network Directive are oft-cited examples of EU actions that violate national treatment. In hydrocarbons, if the EU Commission finds that a third country does not accord comparable treatment to community firms in this sector, the commission may propose retaliatory measures, including precluding the third country from engaging in the hydrocarbons sector in the EU. The proposed Satellite Network Directive would go one step further to establish across-the-board limitations on foreign ownership.

The REIO issue involves a number of technical issues about EU competency on investment issues. Does the EU have the legal authority to establish community law and policy *in investment*? If it does, then the EU can speak for member states in seeking an exception for REIO. If EU does not have competency or shares competency with member states, the situation is more complicated. In shared competency, would the REIO be held responsible for adhering to the terms and conditions of MAI, or would the member states be responsible? Further, if a REIO violates MAI, how would the investor-to-state and state-to-state dispute settlement mechanisms be handled? How would they be enforced?

This will be one of the most difficult issues to resolve in the negotiation. It is unrealistic to expect one party to provide a blank check "carve out" to another party.

Exceptions that are narrowly drawn, transparent, and not prone to proliferation may be acceptable.

Forum for Investment Negotiations

Although negotiations among the developed countries are underway in the OECD, some observers argue that, insofar as the majority of investment barriers are in the LDCs, the LDCs should be at the negotiating table, and the correct forum is the WTO. A large part of this argument is based on "turf." In the OECD, member states speak for themselves rather than through the commission, although the commission maintains observer status. If investment negotiations were held in the WTO, the commission would have a larger role than the member states, even though the commission does not enjoy full authority over the issue.

Negotiating in the OECD makes sense for several reasons. First, it is critical that the MAI articulate the needs of *providers of capital*, not the minimum acceptable to the largest number of recipients. This can be achieved best in the OECD. Unlike trade negotiations (where all parties make trade concessions), an investment agreement should be a clear statement of the conditions needed to attract capital. Since the flow is from capital providers to capital recipients, only an agreement that reflects the needs of the providers would produce the flow needed by the recipients. An agreement that is less than that needed to produce the flow would interest neither party. Moreover, any attempts to hasten the negotiations, with a view toward bringing the negotiations prematurely to the WTO, would only encourage negotiators to hold back on their offers. In this scenario, a shift of venue to the WTO would enable the LDC governments to water down their obligations.

There are other reasons to support negotiations in the OECD. The OECD Secretariat has much experience in investment issues (whereas the WTO Secretariat has little or no experience in investment issues). OECD member countries have spent several years in preliminary work to lay the groundwork for the MAI (but the WTO has undertaken no preliminary work for an international investment agreement).

Many LDCs will wish to accede to the MAI because it will serve as a "seal of approval" to signal developed countries that, in their search for capital to finance their growing needs for investment, LDC signatories to the agreement are committed to providing world class standards to protect investors. This should not come as a surprise. Many LDCs have bilateral agreements with the United States and other OECD countries, such as Chile, Argentina, Ecuador, Jamaica, Turkey, Costa Rica, Poland, the Czech Republic, Hungary, and others. In fact, there are about 600 bilateral treaties in place among developed and developing countries, albeit with somewhat different standards. The MAI offers the opportunity for these countries to consolidate and reaffirm their commitment to *common* high standards for international investors and their investments.

BENEFITS FROM THE MAI

A successful MAI will enable U.S. firms to compete more effectively in the global marketplace by reducing and eliminating barriers to investment and by facilitating the entry and operation of U.S. firms in overseas markets that historically have been closed or restricted. By establishing investor protection against discriminatory and other government actions, MAI will reduce the cost of investing and operating in overseas markets. A transparent agreement will also reduce investor uncertainty because it will establish the rules of the game and how they may be enforced. Provisions for an effective investor-to-state dispute settlement mechanism will lower the risk associated with overseas investments. In general, it will work to promote high-productivity, high-wage operations of U.S. MNCs and affiliates of foreign companies in the United States, as documented in the chapter by Doms and Jensen.

Not only large MNCs stand to gain from the creation of multilateral rules on investment. The MAI will reduce risk and add a significant degree of predictability to entering new markets, thereby making it easier for small- and medium-sized enterprises (SMEs) to become more integrated in the global economy. Once overseas, SMEs thrive. A study by McKinsey and Company (1987) found that SMEs compete successfully in foreign markets; and that their performance, in terms of sales and operating income from foreign markets, most often was greater than their performance in their home market.

Significant returns, the direct monetary gains from investment overseas, are another tangible benefit to the home economy. In today's global economy, a U.S. company may have from 50 percent to 60 percent or more of its annual revenue produced by sales, profits, royalties, and returns on overseas investment. Nearly 80 percent of international payments for royalties and fees take place on an intrafirm basis. In 1994, royalties, fees, and profits from overseas affiliates yielded $90 billion (Department of Commerce 1995). Of this total, $35 billion of which was reinvested in U.S. operations abroad to help strengthen the competitive position of U.S. owned firms; and $55 billion was remitted to the United States, where it was used to finance expansion, undertake R&D and reward shareholders. This return flow also makes a substantial contribution to the nation's balance of payments.

The United States economy also benefits to the extent that exports follow from outward direct investment. Trade between U.S. parent firms and their subsidiaries is an important part of overall U.S. merchandise trade. In 1994, just over $100 billion (or nearly 25 percent) of U.S. merchandise exports were generated between U.S. parents and their affiliates.

Finally, it is important to recognize that the MAI will advance inward foreign direct investment. Foreign-owned companies make important contributions to our nation's economic strength and enhance the economic base of state and local entities. Foreign investors also add to our technology capabilities by investing substantially in research and development in their U.S. facilities. The weight of evidence found in this book points to the advantages for workers' wages and firm productivity. Both foreign-based and U.S. MNCs outperform purely domestic enterprises as they extend across national boundaries.

CONCLUSION

If a country, or more precisely a company based within a nation-state, expects to compete effectively in the next century, it must have a physical presence in global markets. In the late twentieth century, and no doubt in the future, a presence means an investment. To facilitate direct investment, countries should move to liberalize investment early in the next century as they have liberalized trade in the 1990s; that means negotiating to reduce restrictions and establishing a framework for international investors—a multilateral agreement on direct investment. If and when it is concluded, whether by the OECD or another organization, the agreement should be open to accession by all countries and serve as a standard for integrating investment issues into the WTO, where it will ultimately become part of WTO disciplines at this time. A high standards agreement offers the best opportunity to achieve these objectives. It would provide a basis to move beyond "us versus them" disputes and set the stage for unfettered investment flows to and from the United States in the years ahead.

NOTES

This chapter is an elaboration of the personal view of the author presented at the University of South Carolina conference, "Beyond Us and Them: Foreign Ownership and U.S. Competitiveness," Georgetown University, September 22-23, 1995. The section on "Investment in the Uruguay Round" draws heavily on Daniel Price and Konstantinos Adamantopoulos, "Towards a Multilateral Investment Regime: Results in the Uruguay Round and Prospects in the OECD," *International Banking and Financial Law*, March 1995 (London).

1. These requirements serve to protect domestic companies and reflect a strong element of economic nationalism.

2. A company that is not accorded full national treatment when it enters a market is put at a competitive disadvantage in that market.

REFERENCES

Davis, Lester A. 1995. *U.S. Jobs Supported by Goods and Services Exports 1983-1992*, May. Washington, D.C.: GPO.

Department of Commerce. 1995. *Survey of Current Business*, Bureau of Economic Analysis, June. Washington, D.C.: GPO.

McKinsey and Company. 1987. *Winning in the World Market*, a report for The American Business Conference, November.

United Nations Conference on Trade and Development (UNCTAD). 1994. *World Investment Report 1994: Transnational Corporations, Employment and the Workplace*, Division on Transnational Corporations and Investment. New York: United Nations.

U.S. Council for International Business. 1995. *Statement on the Multilateral Agreement on Investment*. New York, March.

Acronyms and Abbreviations

ABB — Asea Brown Boveri
ANOVA — analysis of variance
AT&T — American Telephone and Telegraph
ATP — Advanced Technology Program
BEA — Bureau of Economic Analysis
BIT — Bilateral Investment Treaties
BLS — Bureau of Labor Statistics
BT — British Telecommunications
CA — Central Auxiliary
CAFE — corporate average fuel economy
CEA — Council of Economic Advisors
CEO — chief executive officer
CFIUS — Committee on Foreign Investment in the United States
CIA — Central Intelligence Agency
CIBER — Center of International Business Education and Research
CM — Census of Manufacturers
CNT — conditional national treatment
CRADA — Cooperative Research and Development Agreements
CSP — corporate social performance
CSR — corporate social responsibility
CTO — Chief Technical Officer
DARPA — Defense Advanced Research Project Agency
DOC-3 — Department of Commerce classification for high technology goods-producing industries
DOE — Department of Energy
EC — European Community
ECO — effective competitive opportunities
EPA — Environmental Protection Agency
ES9100 — 1987 Large Company Survey
EU — European Union
FCC — Federal Communications Commission
FCNs — Friendship, Commerce, and Navigation Treaties
FDI — foreign direct investment
FDIUS — foreign direct investment in the United States
FTC — Federal Trade Commission
GAO — General Accounting Office
GATS — General Agreement on Trade in Services
GATT — General Agreement on Tariffs and Trade
GDP — Gross Domestic Product
GII — Global Information Infrastructure
GM — General Motors
GNP — Gross National Product
HDTV — high definition television
H-H — Herfindahl-Hirschman index of concentration
IBGR — International business-government relations
IFT — intrafirm trade
LDCs — less-developed countries
M&A — merger and acquisition
MAI — Multilateral Agreement on Investment
MCI — Microwave Communications Incorporated

MFN — Most-favored nation

MITI — Ministry of International Trade and Industry

MNC — multinational corporation

MNE — multinational enterprise

NAFTA — North American Free Trade Agreement

NAP — North American Philips

NBER — National Bureau of Economic Research

NIST — National Institute of Standards and Technology

NSF — National Science Foundation

NTB — nontariff barriers to trade

NUMMI — New United Motor Manufacturing, Inc.

Oa — ownership-specific competitive advantages of parent companies which arise from possession of a specific asset or group of assets (see Dunning)

OECD — Organisation for Economic Co-operation and Development

Ot — ownership-specific competitive advantages of parent companies which arise from the method by which the parent company coordinates its advantages with others (see Dunning)

OTA — Office of Technology Assessment

R&D — research and development

REIO — Regional Economic Integration Organization

SIC — Standard Industrial Classification

SME — small- and medium-sized enterprise

SMT — Survey of Manufacturing Technology

SSA — Special Security Arrangement

TFP — Total Factor Productivity

TNE — transnational enterprises

Triad — countries of Japan, North America, and Western Europe (Reich)

TRIM — trade related investment measure

UNCTAD — United Nations Conference on Trade and Development

UK — United Kingdom

USAF — US Air Force

USDIA — US direct investment abroad

WTO — World Trade Organization

Index

About the Editors and Contributors

EDITORS

Douglas P. Woodward is director of the Division of Research and associate professor of economics in The Darla Moore School of Business at the University of South Carolina. His primary research interests are foreign direct investments. He has published articles on these and other topics. He has testified before Congress on many occasions. Dr. Woodward is co-author of a book on foreign direct investment in the United States, *The New Competitors* (1989). The book was ranked as one of the top ten business and economics books of 1989 by *Business Week*. In 1990, *The New Competitors* was listed by *Fortune* as one of the books CEOs are reading. Dr. Woodward has been quoted frequently in the local and national press, including *The New York Times*, *The Washington Post*, *The Wall Street Journal*, *Business Week*, *The Economist*, and *U.S. News and World Report*. National television and radio appearances include CNN, C-SPAN, and National Public Radio. He has spoken at many forums around the country on U.S. competitiveness and economic development.

Douglas Nigh is associate professor of international business at the University of South Carolina (USC) and research director of USC's Center for International Business Education and Research. He received his Ph.D. in international management from the UCLA and his MBA and BA in economics from Indiana University. He was recently elected program chair of the International Management Division of the Academy of Management. Also a co-founder of the International Association for Business and Society, he is a past-president of this association. His latest book is *International Business: An Emerging Vision*, co-edited with Brian Toyne.

CONTRIBUTORS

Cynthia A. Beltz is a research fellow at the American Enterprise Institute for Public Policy Research, Washington, D.C. She has testified before the House Budget and Science committees on technology and trade issues. She is editor of *The Foreign Investment Debate* (1995) and *Financing Entrepreneurs* (1994), and author of *High Tech Maneuvers: The Industrial Policies of HDTV* (1992) and *The Global Communications Revolution: The WTO and the Internet* (1997).

Davis B. Bobrow is professor of public and international affairs and political science, University of Pittsburgh. He has written extensively on international political economy and security and on treatment of the multinational corporation. He has served as a staff member of the Advanced Research Projects Agency and a consultant to the Office of the Secretary of Defense and to the Internal Revenue Service (Office of Foreign Business Study).

Stephen J. Canner is Vice President for Investment and Financial Policy at the U.S. Council for International Business. Prior to joining the council, Canner was director of the Office of International Investment at the U.S. Treasury, where he directed Treasury work on many important international investment and related issues.

Cletus C. Coughlin is a vice president and associate director of research at the Federal Reserve Bank of St. Louis. He is also employed as an adjunct professor at Washington University. His principal research interests are the formation and effects of U.S. trade policy and how international trade and investment relate to regional economies.

Donald H. Dalton is a research economist in the Office of Business and Industrial Analysis, Economics and Statistics Administration of the U.S. Department of Commerce. He specializes in the area of foreign direct investment in the United States and international technology transfer. He currently serves on the Inter-Agency Enforcement Group to monitor the U.S.-Japan Agreement on Autos and Auto Parts. Most of his recent work has been on the globalization of industrial research and development.

Mark E. Doms is an economist in the industrial output section of the Board of Governors of the Federal Reserve System. Before working for the Federal Reserve, Doms worked for the U.S. Bureau of the Census and the Organisation for Economic Co-operation and Development. His research has focused on technological change, productivity, and energy use in manufacturing.

John H. Dunning holds a dual appointment as emeritus professor in international business studies at the University of Reading, U.K., and State of New Jersey Professor of International Business at Rutgers University, New Jersey. He is also senior economic advisor to the Transnational Corporations and Investment Division of UNCTAD and chair of the London-based Economics Advisory Group. He has authored or edited thirty-two books on the economics of international direct investment and the multinational enterprise and on industrial and regional economics.

Kathleen A. Getz is an assistant professor of management and international business at the Kogod College of Business Administration of the American University. Her research focus is corporate political activity and multilateral regulation. She is an active member of the International Association for Business and Society and the Social Issues in Management division of the Academy of Management, as well as consultant to several professional societies in the Washington, D.C., area.

Edward M. Graham is Senior Fellow at the Institute for International Economics in Washington, D.C. Previously he has served on the faculties of MIT and the University of North Carolina and as an international economist at the U.S. Treasury in Washington, D.C. Graham has written extensively on international direct investment and multinational enterprises. His books include *Global Corporations and National Governments* (1996), *Foreign Direct Investment in the United States* (1995), coauthored with Professor Paul Krugman of MIT, and *Competition Policy for the Global Economy* (1997), co-edited with

J. David Richardson. Other works include over fifty published articles in scholarly journals or academic conference volumes and over thirty articles in non-scholarly publications.

J. Bradford Jensen, prior to joining the Heinz School of Public Policy and Management at Carnegie Mellon University, was an economist at the Center for Economic Studies at the U.S. Bureau of the Census. Jensen conducts research on firm productivity and competitiveness, with a focus on the role of international trade in the manufacturing sector. Jensen (with coauthors) has published in academic journals, including the *Brookings Paper on Economic Activity: Microeconomics* and the *Journal of International Economics*.

John M. Kline is a professor and director of the Landegger Program in International Business Diplomacy at the Georgetown University School of Foreign Service. His research interests are foreign direct investment, international business diplomacy, and business-government relations. Kline is the author of *International Codes and Multinational Business* (1985) and *Foreign Investment Strategies in Restructuring Economies* (Quorum Books 1992) and numerous scholarly articles. He serves as a consultant to several international corporations and intergovernmental organizations and has conducted studies for the United Nations Centre on Transnational Corporations.

Jeffrey A. Krug is assistant professor of management at the University of Memphis. His research interests include cross-border mergers and acquisitions, top management teams, and foreign direct investment theory. He teaches international management and business strategy and in the Faculty Development in International Business (FDIB) program.

Robert T. Kudrle is professor of public affairs and director of the Orville and Jane Freeman Center for International Economic Policy, Hubert H. Humphrey Institute of Public Affairs, University of Minnesota, where he has also served as associate dean for research. Professor Kudrle is past coeditor of *International Studies Quarterly* and has published widely on industrial organization, public policy toward business, international economic policy, and the political economy of social services. Much of his recent research concerns economic relations among the industrial countries. He has consulted on many national and international agencies.

Sumiye Okubo is Director, Office of International Macroeconomic Analysis in the Office of the Chief Economist, Economics and Statistics Administration, Department of Commerce. Her research interests include international trade and foreign investment, international fiscal and financial policies, technological innovation, and the economy of Japan. She is also an adjunct professor at George Washington University in Washington, D.C.

Lois S. Peters is associate professor and director, Doctoral Program, Lally School of Management and Technology. For more than a decade, she has focused on partnering and cooperation among and between multinational firms, entrepreneurial small firms, and universities. Recently, she has expanded her work to include study of management of innovation and the internal research and development activities of multinational firms. In 1992, she was a visiting professor at the Max-Planck-Institut für Gessellschaftsforschung, contributing to their studies on technological innovation and learning their approaches to network analysis.

Tammie S. Pinkston is a change management consultant based in the Atlanta office of Andersen Consulting. Her research focus is the telecommunications industry, with a special emphasis on organization design and development as well as change navigation. She is a member of the Academy of Management and the International Association for Business and Society.

Edward J. Ray is a professor of economics, Senior Vice Provost for Academic Affairs, and Chief Information Officer at Ohio State University. His research interests include the history of protectionism in the United States, the determinants of U.S. foreign direct investment and foreign direct investment in the United States, and the structure of tariff and non-tariff trade barriers in the United States and abroad. He has published in leading economics journals, including *The American Economic Review, The Journal of Political Economy*, and *The Quarterly Journal of Economics*. His book entitled *U.S. Protectionism and the World Debt Crisis* was published by Quorum Books in 1989.

Simon Reich is a professor in the Graduate School of Public and International Affairs at the University of Pittsburgh. His research interests concern foreign direct investment. Reich is the author of several books and articles in the field of international political economy. Reich also works on a variety of subjects regarding Germany, including a recent book coauthored with Andrei S. Markovits entitled *The German Predicament: Memory and Power in the New Europe*. Reich spent three years working at the U.S. Congressional Office of Technology Assessment.

Manuel G. Serapio, Jr., is an associate professor of international business and management at the Graduate School of Business and Administration at the University of Colorado at Denver. He has published widely on the subject of the internationalization of research and development. His most recent papers have appeared in *Management International Review* and *Research Technology Management*.

ISBN 1-56720-113-X

9 781567 201130

90000>

EAN

HARDCOVER BAR CODE